Services Marketing

Integrating Customer Focus Across the Firm

Sixth Edition

Valarie A. Zeithaml
University of North Carolina at Chapel Hill

Mary Jo Bitner
Arizona State University

Dwayne D. Gremler
Bowling Green State University

McGraw-Hill Irwin

SERVICES MARKETING: INTEGRATING CUSTOMER FOCUS ACROSS THE FIRM, SIXTH EDITION

Published by McGraw-Hill, a business unit of The McGraw-Hill Companies, Inc., 1221 Avenue of the Americas, New York, NY 10020. Copyright © 2013 by The McGraw-Hill Companies, Inc. All rights reserved. Printed in the United States of America. Previous Editions © 2009, 2006, and 2003. No part of this publication may be reproduced or distributed in any form or by any means, or stored in a database or retrieval system, without the prior written consent of The McGraw-Hill Companies, Inc., including, but not limited to, in any network or other electronic storage or transmission, or broadcast for distance learning.

Some ancillaries, including electronic and print components, may not be available to customers outside the United States.

2 3 4 5 6 7 8 9 0 QVR/LEH1 0 9 8 7 6 5 4 3 2

ISBN 978-0-07-811205-8
MHID 0-07-811205-2

Vice President & Editor-in-Chief: *Brent Gordon*
Vice President & Director of Specialized Publishing: *Janice M. Roerig-Blong*
Publisher: *Paul Ducham*
Sponsoring Editor: *Daryl Bruflodt*
Marketing Coordinator: *Colleen P. Havens*
Development Editor: *Lorraine Buczek*
Senior Project Manager: *Joyce Watters*
Design Coordinator: *Brenda A. Rolwes*
Cover Designer: *Studio Montage, St. Louis, Missouri*
Cover Images: *Woman Using Self check-in Terminal:* © *Thinkstock/Getty Images RF; Male Doctor smiling at Female Patient:* © *Purestock/ Getty Images RF; Businessmen Shaking Hands:* © *Cutcaster RF*
Buyer: *Kara Kudronowicz*
Media Project Manager: *Prashanthi Nadipalli*
Compositor: *Laserwords Private Limited*
Typeface: *10.5/12 Times New Roman PS Std*
Printer: *Quad/Graphics*

All credits appearing on page or at the end of the book are considered to be an extension of the copyright page.

Library of Congress Cataloging-in-Publication Data

Zeithaml, Valarie A.
  Services marketing: integrating customer focus across the firm/Valarie A. Zeithaml, Mary Jo Bitner, Dwayne D. Gremler.—6th ed.
    p. cm.
  ISBN-978-0-07-811205-8 (alk. paper)
  ISBN-0-07-811205-2
  1. Service industries—Marketing. 2. Customer services. 3. Marketing. I. Bitner, Mary Jo. II. Gremler, Dwayne D. III. Title.
HD9980.5.Z45 2013
658.8—dc23
                                                    2011051073

Aan mijn alleriefste, Jan Benedict Steenkamp—soul mate, inspiration, and biggest supporter. And to Jaiman Nair Zeithaml, the new light in my life.

—V.A.Z.

To my husband, Rich, for his unending love and support.

—M.J.B.

To my wife, Candy, and daughters, Samantha and Mallory, for their many years of love, support, and encouragement.

—D.D.G.

About the Authors

Mary Jo Bitner (left), Dwayne Gremler,
and Valarie Zeithaml

Valarie A. Zeithaml   *University of North Carolina–Chapel Hill*

VALARIE ZEITHAML is the David S. Van Pelt Professor of Marketing at the Kenan-Flagler Business School of the University of North Carolina at Chapel Hill. Since receiving her MBA and PhD in marketing from the Robert H. Smith School of Business at the University of Maryland, Dr. Zeithaml has devoted her career to researching and teaching the topics of service quality and services management. She is the co-author of *Delivering Quality Service: Balancing Customer Perceptions and Expectations* (The Free Press, 1990), now in its 20th printing, and *Driving Customer Equity: How Customer Lifetime Value Is Reshaping Corporate Strategy* (The Free Press, 2000). In 2002, Driving Customer Equity won the first Berry–American Marketing Association Book Prize for the best marketing book of the past three years.

In 2008, Dr. Zeithaml won the Paul D. Converse Award from the American Marketing Association. The Converse Award, granted every four years to one or more persons, acknowledges enduring contributions to marketing through one or more journal articles, books, or a body of work. She was recognized for her work with colleagues on service quality, specifically for two articles: "A Conceptual Model of Service Quality and Its Implications for Future Research," published in the *Journal of Marketing*, and "SERVQUAL: A Multiple-Item Scale for Measuring Service Quality," in the *Journal of Retailing*. The former paper created the Gaps Model of Service Quality on which this textbook is based. In 2009, she received the American Marketing Association/Irwin/McGraw-Hill Distinguished Marketing Educator Award for lifetime leadership in marketing education and extensive contributions to the field of marketing.

With colleagues, she also won the 2009 Sheth Foundation/*Journal of Marketing* Award for the article, "Return on Marketing: Using Customer Equity to Focus Marketing Strategy," which appeared in 2004. The award recognizes scholarship based on the benefits of time and hindsight and acknowledges contributions and outcomes made to marketing theory and practice. In 2004, Dr. Zeithaml received both the Innovative Contributor to Marketing Award given by the Marketing Management Association and the Outstanding Marketing Educator Award given by the Academy of Marketing Science. In 2001, she received the American Marketing Association's Career Contributions to the Services Discipline Award.

Dr. Zeithaml has won five teaching awards, including the Gerald Barrett Faculty Award from the University of North Carolina and the Fuqua School Outstanding MBA Teaching Award from Duke University. She is also the recipient of numerous research awards, including the Robert Ferber Consumer Research Award from the *Journal of Consumer Research;* the Harold H. Maynard Award from the *Journal of Marketing;* the MSI Paul Root Award from the *Journal of Marketing;* the Jagdish Sheth Award from the *Journal of the Academy of Marketing Science;* and the William F. O'Dell Award from the *Journal of Marketing Research.* She has consulted with more than 60 service and product companies. Dr. Zeithaml served on the Board of Directors of the American Marketing Association from 2000 to 2003 and was an Aacademic Ttrustee of the Marketing Science Institute between 2000 and 2006.

Mary Jo Bitner   *Arizona State University*

MARY JO BITNER is the executive director of the Center for Services Leadership, PetSmart Chair in Services Leadership, and professor of marketing at the W. P. Carey School of Business, Arizona State University (ASU). In her career as a professor and researcher, Dr. Bitner has been recognized as one of the founders and pioneers in the field of service marketing and management worldwide. At ASU she was a founding faculty member of the Center for Services Leadership and has been a leader in its emergence as the premier university-based center for the study of services marketing and management.

In the middle 1990s, Dr. Bitner led the development of the W. P. Carey MBA marketing and service leadership specialization, a unique full-year focus within the nationally ranked W. P. Carey MBA. The degree specialization has existed for over 15 years, and alumni now work in companies worldwide, leading the implementation of service and customer-focused strategies. Dr. Bitner has also taught service courses many times in China through ASU's China Executive MBA program and served as a Distinguished Faculty member at Fudan University, Shanghai, China.

Dr. Bitner has received several teaching awards and research recognition for her contributions to the discipline. In 2003, she was awarded the Career Contributions to the Service Discipline Award presented by the Services Marketing group of the American Marketing Association. She was also named an IBM Faculty Fellow for her leadership and pioneering work in service science. At ASU, Dr. Bitner has received the W. P. Carey School of Business Graduate Teaching Excellence Award and the award for Outstanding Professor, PhD Programs.

Dr. Bitner has taught and consulted with numerous service and manufacturing businesses who seek to excel and compete through service. Her current research is concerned with service infusion strategies in goods-dominant companies and the strategic roles of technology and contact employees in determining customer satisfaction with services. She has published articles relevant to services marketing and management in the *Journal of Marketing, Journal of Service Research, Journal of Business Research, Journal of Retailing, Journal of Service Management, Journal of the Academy of Marketing Science,* and the *Academy of Management Executive.*

Dwayne D. Gremler   *Bowling Green State University*

DWAYNE D. GREMLER is professor of Marketing at Bowling Green State University (BGSU). He received his MBA and PhD degrees from the W. P. Carey School of Business at Arizona State University. Throughout his academic career, Dr. Gremler has been a passionate advocate for the research and instruction of services marketing issues. He has served as chair of the American Marketing Association's Services Marketing Special Interest Group and has helped organize services marketing conferences in Australia, The Netherlands, France, Portugal, Finland, and the United States. Dr. Gremler has been invited to conduct seminars and present research on services marketing issues in several countries. Dr. Gremler's research addresses customer loyalty in service businesses, customer–employee interactions in service delivery, service guarantees, and word-of-mouth communication. He has published articles in the *Journal of Marketing, Journal of the Academy of Marketing Science, Journal of Service Research, Journal of Retailing, Journal of Business Research, International Journal of Service Industry Management,* and *Journal of Marketing Education.* In 2006 Dr. Gremler was a Fulbright Scholar at the University of Maastricht, The Netherlands. He has also been the recipient of several research awards at BGSU, including the College of Business Administration Outstanding Scholar Award and the Robert A. Patton Scholarly Achievement Award. Dr. Gremler has also received several teaching awards, including the *Academy of Marketing Science* Outstanding Marketing Teacher Award (2009), the Alumni Undergraduate Teaching Award from the College of Business at Bowling Green State University (2010), and the Hormel Teaching Excellence Award from the Marketing Management Association (2011).

Preface

This text is for students and businesspeople who recognize the vital role that services play in the economy and its future. The advanced economies of the world are now dominated by services, and virtually all companies view service as critical to retaining their customers today and in the future. Manufacturing and product-dominant companies that, in the past, have depended on their physical products for their livelihood now recognize that service provides one of their few sustainable competitive advantages.

We wrote this book in recognition of the ever-growing importance of services and the unique challenges faced by service managers.

WHY A SERVICES MARKETING TEXT?

Since the beginning of our academic careers in marketing, we have devoted our research and teaching efforts to topics in services marketing. We strongly believe that services marketing is different from goods marketing in significant ways and that it requires strategies and tactics that traditional marketing texts do not fully reflect. This text is unique in both content and structure, and we hope that you will learn as much from it as we have in writing and revising it now for almost 20 years. Over this time period we have incorporated major changes and developments in the field, keeping the book up to date with new knowledge, changes in management practice, and the global economic trend toward services.

Content Overview

The foundation of the text is the recognition that services present special challenges that must be identified and addressed. Issues commonly encountered in service organizations—the inability to inventory, difficulty in synchronizing demand and supply, challenges in controlling the performance quality of human interactions, and customer participation as cocreators of value—need to be articulated and tackled by managers. Many of the strategies include information and approaches that are new to managers across industries. We wrote the text to help students and managers understand and address these special challenges of services marketing.

The development of strong customer relationships through quality service (and services) are at the heart of the book's content. The topics covered are equally applicable to organizations whose core product is service (such as banks, transportation companies, hotels, hospitals, educational institutions, professional services, telecommunication) and to organizations that depend on service excellence for competitive advantage (high-technology manufacturers, automotive and industrial products, and so on). Rarely do we repeat material from marketing principles or marketing strategy texts. Instead, we adjust, when necessary, standard content on topics such as distribution, pricing, and promotion to account for service characteristics.

The book's content focuses on knowledge needed to implement service strategies for competitive advantage across industries. Included are frameworks for customer-focused management and strategies for increasing customer satisfaction and retention through service. In addition to standard marketing topics (such as pricing), this text introduces students to entirely new topics that include management and measurement of service quality, service recovery, the linking of customer measurement to performance measurement, service blueprinting, customer cocreation, and cross-functional treatment of issues through integration of marketing with disciplines such as operations and human resources. Each of these topics represents pivotal content for tomorrow's businesses as they structure around process rather than task, engage in one-to-one marketing, mass customize their offerings, cocreate value with their customers, and attempt to build strong relationships with their customers.

New Features

This edition contains the following new features:

1. Streamlined coverage of key topics to eliminate redundancies.
2. Elimination of two chapters—"Consumer Behavior in Services" and "Delivering Service through Intermediaries"—based on feedback from reviewers. These chapters will still be available in the Instructor's Manual for those professors who wish to continue to teach the material.
3. Four New cases: Zappos.com; United Breaks Guitars; Michelin Fleet Solutions; and ISS Iceland.
4. New research references and examples in every chapter.
5. Updated data for key charts and examples.
6. A new model of service recovery strategies and a significantly revised organization of the chapter, which includes strategies for "fixing the customer" and "fixing the problem."
7. Significant new material and revised framework in the chapter on service innovation and design.
8. Increased coverage throughout of business-to-business (B2B) services and the trends toward service infusion in goods-dominant companies.
9. Updated focus on globalization, technology, and strategic service issues through new or improved features in every chapter.
10. Focus on digital and social marketing in the chapter "Integrated Service Marketing Communication," as well as examples on these topics throughout the book.

Distinguishing Content Features

The distinguishing features of our text include the following:

1. The only services marketing textbook based on the Gaps Model of Service Quality framework, which departs significantly from other marketing and services marketing textbooks.
2. Greater emphasis on the topic of service quality than existing marketing and service marketing texts.
3. Introduction of three service Ps to the traditional marketing mix and increased focus on customer relationships and relationship marketing strategies.
4. Significant focus on customer expectations and perceptions and what they imply for marketers.
5. A feature called "Strategy Insight" in each chapter—a feature that focuses on emerging or existing strategic initiatives involving services.
6. Increased coverage of business-to-business service applications.
7. Two original cases written specifically for this textbook, one on JetBlue's service disaster in 2007 and one on Caterpillar's decision to become an integrated solution provider.
8. Increased technology and Internet coverage, including updated "Technology Spotlight" boxes in each chapter.

9. A chapter on service recovery that includes a conceptual framework for understanding the topic.

10. A chapter on the financial and economic impact of service quality.

11. A chapter on customer-defined service standards.

12. Cross-functional treatment of issues through integration of marketing with other disciplines such as operations and human resource management.

13. Consumer-based pricing and value pricing strategies.

14. Description of a set of tools that must be added to basic marketing techniques when dealing with services rather than goods.

15. An entire chapter that recognizes human resource challenges and human resource strategies for delivering customer-focused services.

16. Coverage of service innovation with a detailed and complete introduction to service blueprinting—a technique for describing, designing, and positioning services.

17. Coverage of the customer's role in service delivery and strategies for making customers productive partners in service and value creation.

18. A chapter on the role of physical evidence, particularly the physical environment, or "servicescape."

19. "Global Feature" boxes in each chapter and expanded examples of global services marketing.

Conceptual and Research Foundations

We synthesized research and conceptual material from many talented academics and practitioners to create this text. We rely on the work of researchers and businesspeople from diverse disciplines such as marketing, human resources, operations, and management. Because the field of services marketing is international in its roots, we also have drawn from work originating around the globe. We have continued this strong conceptual grounding in the sixth edition by integrating new research into every chapter. The framework of the book is managerially focused, with every chapter presenting company examples and strategies for addressing issues in the chapter.

Conceptual Frameworks in Chapters

We developed integrating frameworks in most chapters. For example, we created new frameworks for understanding service recovery strategies, service pricing, integrated marketing communications, customer relationships, customer roles, and internal marketing.

Unique Structure

The text features a structure completely different from the standard 4P (marketing mix) structure of most marketing texts. The text is organized around the gaps model of service quality, which is described fully in Chapter 2. Beginning with Chapter 3, the text is organized into parts around the gaps model. For example, Chapters 3 and 4 each deal with an aspect of the customer gap—customer expectations and perceptions, respectively—to form the focus for services marketing strategies. The managerial content in the rest of the chapters is framed by the gaps model using part openers that build the model gap by gap. Each part of the book includes multiple chapters with strategies for understanding and closing these critical gaps.

WHAT COURSES AND STUDENTS CAN USE THE TEXT?

In our years of experience teaching services marketing, we have found that a broad cross section of students is drawn to learning about services marketing. Students with career interests in service industries as well as goods industries with high service components (such as industrial products, high-tech products, and durable products) want and need to understand these topics. Students who wish to become consultants and entrepreneurs want to learn the strategic view of marketing, which involves not just physical goods but also the myriad services that envelop and add value to these goods. Virtually all students—even those who will work for packaged goods firms—will face employers needing to understand the basics of services marketing and management.

Although services marketing courses are usually designated as marketing electives, a large number of enrollees in our classes have been finance students seeking to broaden their knowledge and career opportunities. Business students with human resource, information technology, accounting, and operations majors also enroll, as do nonbusiness students from such diverse disciplines as health administration, recreation and parks, public and nonprofit administration, law, sports management, and library science.

Students need only a basic marketing course as a prerequisite for a services marketing course and this text. The primary target audience for the text is services marketing classes at the undergraduate (junior or senior elective courses), graduate (both masters and doctoral courses), and executive student levels. Other target audiences are (1) service management classes at both the undergraduate and graduate levels and (2) marketing management classes at the graduate level in which a professor wishes to provide more comprehensive teaching of services than is possible with a standard marketing management text. A subset of chapters would also provide a more concise text for use in a quarter-length or mini-semester course. A further reduced set of chapters may be used to supplement undergraduate and graduate basic marketing courses to enhance the treatment of services.

WHAT CAN WE PROVIDE EDUCATORS TO TEACH SERVICES MARKETING?

As a team, we have accumulated more than 65 years of experience teaching the subject of services marketing. We set out to create a text that represents the approaches we have found most effective. We incorporated all that we have learned in our many years of teaching services marketing—teaching materials, student exercises, case analyses, research, and PowerPoint slides, which you can find online at www.mhhe.com/Zeithaml6e, along with a comprehensive instructor's manual and test bank.

HOW MANY PARTS AND CHAPTERS ARE INCLUDED, AND WHAT DO THEY COVER?

The text material includes 16 chapters divided into seven parts. Part 1 includes an introduction in Chapter 1 and an overview of the gaps model in Chapter 2. Part 2 considers the customer gap by examining customer expectations and perceptions. Part 3 focuses on listening to customer requirements, including chapters covering marketing research for services, building customer relationships, and service recovery. Part 4 involves aligning service strategy through design and standards and includes chapters on service innovation and design, customer-defined service standards, and physical evidence and the servicescape. Part 5 concerns the delivery and performance of service and has chapters on employees' and customers' roles in service delivery, as well as managing demand and capacity. Part 6 focuses on managing services promises and includes chapters on integrated services marketing communications and pricing of services. Finally, Part 7 examines the financial and economic effect of service quality.

THE SUPPLEMENTARY MATERIALS

Instructor's Manual

The *Instructor's Manual* includes sample syllabi, suggestions for in-class exercises and projects, teaching notes for each of the cases included in the text, and answers to end-of-chapter discussion questions and exercises. The *Instructor's Manual* uses the "active learning" educational paradigm, which involves students in constructing their own learning experiences and exposes them to the collegial patterns present in work situations. Active learning offers an educational underpinning for the pivotal work-force skills required in business, among them oral and written communication skills, listening skills, and critical thinking and problem solving.

PowerPoint

We have provided PowerPoint slides online for each chapter and case, including figures and tables from the text that are useful for instructors in class. The full-color PowerPoint slides were created to present a coordinated look for course presentation.

Test Bank

We have also provided test bank files and a computerized test bank, which are available on this text's website. Instructors can easily formulate quizzes and tests from this trusted source.

ACKNOWLEDGMENTS

We owe a great deal to the pioneering service researchers and scholars who developed the field of services marketing. They include John Bateson, Leonard Berry, Bernard Booms, David Bowen, Steve Brown, Larry Crosby, John Czepiel, Ray Fisk, William George, Christian Gronroos, Steve Grove, Evert Gummesson, Chuck Lamb, the late Christopher Lovelock, Parsu Parasuraman, Ben Schneider, Lynn Shostack, and Carol Surprenant. We also owe gratitude to the second generation of service researchers who broadened and enriched the services marketing field. When we attempted to compile a list of those researchers, we realized that it was too extensive to include here. The length of that list is testament to the influence of the early pioneers and to the importance that services marketing has achieved both in academia and in practice.

We remain indebted to Parsu Parasuraman and Len Berry, who have been research partners of Dr. Zeithaml's since 1982. The gaps model around which the text is structured was developed in collaboration with them, as was the model of customer expectations used in Chapter 3. Much of the research and measurement content in this text was shaped by what the team found in a 15-year program of research on service quality.

Dr. Zeithaml is particularly indebted to her long-time colleague A. "Parsu" Parasuraman, who has been her continuing collaborator over the 30 years she has been in academia. An inspiring and creative talent, Parsu has always been willing to work with her—and many other colleagues—as a mentor and partner. He is also her treasured friend. She also thanks the W. P. Carey School of Business at Arizona State University and the Center for Services Leadership. For three decades, ASU has been her second academic home, and she has grown through her continued and intensified involvement with the faculty and the center in recent years. She is grateful to Holger "HoPi" Pietzsch of the Latin American Division of Caterpillar Inc. Working with Caterpillar Inc. to provide integrated solutions with products and services led to one of the original cases in this textbook. She also thanks her colleagues and MBA students at the University of North Carolina. The students' interest in the topic of services marketing, their creativity in approaching the papers and assignments, and their continuing contact are appreciated. As always, she credits the Marketing Science Institute (MSI), of which she was a researcher and an academic trustee, for the support and ongoing inspiration from its many executive members, conferences, and working papers. She is especially indebted to David Reibstein and Leigh McAllister, both of whom served as MSI academic directors, for their leadership and talent in bridging the gap between academia and practice.

Dr. Bitner expresses special thanks to the W. P. Carey School of Business at Arizona State University, in particular to Stephen W. Brown and the Center for Services Leadership staff. Their support and encouragement have been invaluable throughout the multiple editions of this book. Dr. Bitner also acknowledges the many ideas and examples provided by the 50 member companies of the Center for Services Leadership that are committed to service excellence and from which she has the opportunity to continually learn. For this edition, Dr. Bitner wants to again acknowledge the continued leadership of the IBM Corporation through its research divisions, in particular James Spohrer, for inspiring academics, government employees, and businesspeople around the world to begin focusing on the science of service. She is also grateful to Buck Pei, Associate Dean for Asia Programs at the W. P. Carey School, for providing the opportunity to teach a course on service excellence in ASU's China EMBA. The experience has enriched this book and provided tremendous learning. She also acknowledges and thanks her colleague Amy Ostrom for her support and invaluable assistance in sharing examples, new research, and creative teaching innovations. Finally, Dr. Bitner is grateful to the fine group of Arizona State services doctoral students she has worked with, who have shaped her thinking and supported the text: Lois Mohr, Bill Faranda, Amy Rodie, Kevin Gwinner, Matt Meuter, Steve Tax, Dwayne Gremler, Lance Bettencourt, Susan Cadwallader, Felicia Morgan, Thomas Hollmann, Andrew Gallan, Martin Mende, Mei Li, Shruti Saxena, and Nancy Sirianni.

Dr. Gremler expresses thanks to several people, beginning with his mentor, Steve Brown, for his advice and encouragement. He thanks other Arizona State University faculty who served as role models and encouragers, including John Schlacter, Michael Mokwa, and David Altheide. Dr. Gremler acknowledges the support of fellow doctoral student colleagues from Arizona State University who have gone on to successful careers and who continue to serve as role models and encouragers, including Kevin Gwinner, Mark Houston, John Eaton, and Lance Bettencourt. Dr. Gremler also expresses thanks to colleagues at various universities who have invited him to speak in their countries in recent years and who have provided insight into services marketing issues internationally, including Jos Lemmink, Ko de Ruyter, Hans Kasper, Chiara Orsingher, Stefan Michel, Thorsten Hennig-Thurau, Silke Michalski, Brigitte Auriacombe, David Martin Ruiz, Caroline Wiertz, Vince Mitchell, Sina Fichtel, Nina Specht, Kathy Tyler, Bo Edvardsson, Patrik Larsson, Tor Andreassen, Jens Hogreve, Andreas Eggert, Andreas Bausch, Javier Reynoso, Thorsten Gruber, Lia Patrício, Lisa Brüggen, Jeroen Bleijerveld, Marcel van Birgelen, Josée Bloemer, and Cécile Delcourt. Finally, a special thanks to Candy Gremler for her unending willingness to serve as copy editor, encourager, wife, and friend.

The panel of academics who helped us by completing a survey include Dan Gossett, The University of Texas–Arlington; William Edward Steiger, University of Central Florida; Julie Anna Guidry, Louisiana State University; Mark Rosenbaum, Northern Illinois University; and Troy A. Festervand, Middle Tennessee State University.

Finally, we would like to acknowledge the professional efforts of the McGraw-Hill Higher Education staff. Our sincere thanks to Brent Gordon, Paul Ducham, Daryl Bruflodt, Lorraine Buczek, Joyce Watters, Brenda Rolwes, and Colleen Havens.

Valarie A. Zeithaml

Mary Jo Bitner

Dwayne D. Gremler

Brief Contents

Detailed Contents

List of Boxes

Part One

Foundations for Services Marketing

Chapter 1 Introduction to Services

Chapter 2 Conceptual Framework of the Book: The Gaps Model of Service Quality

This first part of the text provides you with the foundations needed to begin your study of services marketing. The first chapter identifies up-to-date trends, issues, and opportunities in services as a backdrop for the strategies addressed in remaining chapters. The second chapter introduces the gaps model of service quality, the framework that provides the structure for the text. The remaining parts of the book include information and strategies to address specific gaps, giving you the tools and knowledge to become a services marketing leader.

Chapter One

Introduction to Services

This chapter's objectives are to

1. Explain what services are and identify important trends in services.
2. Explain the need for special services marketing concepts and practices and why the need has developed and is accelerating.
3. Explore the profound impact of technology on service.
4. Outline the basic differences between goods and services and the resulting challenges and opportunities for service businesses.
5. Introduce the expanded marketing mix for services and the philosophy of customer focus as powerful frameworks and themes that are fundamental to the rest of the text.

"Services are going to move in this decade to being the front edge of the industry."

This quote from IBM's former CEO, Louis V. Gerstner, illustrates the changes sweeping across industry in the 21st century. Many businesses that were once viewed as manufacturing giants are shifting their focus to services. And, in many ways, IBM has led the pack. Actions of Sam Palmisano, IBM's CEO following Gerstner, have reinforced this focus on service. In his tenure, Mr. Palmisano led IBM in the expansion of its outsourcing businesses and accentuated its focus on client solutions. He also led IBM in its purchase of PricewaterhouseCoopers to gain broader strategic service consulting expertise and in its focus in service "products" and solutions.

In a company brochure IBM states that it is the largest *service* business in the world. It is the global leader in information technology (IT) services and consulting with approximately 200,000 service professionals around the world. Through its Global Services division, IBM offers product support services, professional consulting services, and network computing services. Many businesses have outsourced entire service functions to IBM, counting on the company to provide the services better than anyone else. The service side of IBM, including technology and business services, brings in nearly $60 billion, significantly more than half the company's total revenue. The service strategy has been very successful for IBM to date and promises to be the engine of growth into the future.

No one in IBM would suggest that these positive results have been easily achieved. Switching from a manufacturing to a service and customer focus is indeed a challenge.

It requires changes in management mind-set, changes in culture, changes in the ways people work and are rewarded, and new ways of implementing customer solutions. At IBM this change has evolved over decades and continues today. This switch to service has carried over into IBM's research division as well, where hundreds of researchers worldwide currently focus on service science and service innovation.

Many large manufacturing and IT companies have viewed IBM's success and are pushing to make the same transition to services. It is not as easy as it looks. In moving into services, companies discover what service businesses such as hospitality, consulting, health care, financial services, and telecommunications have known for years: services marketing and management are different—not totally unique, but different from marketing and management for consumer goods and manufactured products. Selling and delivering a computer is not the same as selling and delivering a service that solves a customer's problem.[1]

As the opening vignette suggests, services are not limited to service industries, services can be very profitable, and services are challenging to manage and market. Services represent a huge and growing percentage of the world economy, yet in many countries, including the United States, customer perceptions of service are not good.[2] In fact, the University of Michigan's American Customer Satisfaction Index has shown consistently lower scores for services when compared to other products.[3] Others have noted that productivity for many service industries also lags the manufacturing sector. Given the economic growth in services, their profit and competitive advantage potential, and the overall lower levels of customer satisfaction and productivity for services, it seems that the potential and opportunities for companies that can excel in service marketing, management, and delivery have never been greater.

This text will give you a lens with which to approach the marketing and management of services. What you learn can be applied in a company like IBM with a traditional manufacturing history or in pure service businesses. You will learn tools, strategies, and approaches for developing and delivering profitable services that can provide competitive advantage to firms. At the base of services marketing and management you will find a strong customer focus that extends across all functions of the firm—thus the subtitle of this book, "integrating customer focus across the firm."

WHAT ARE SERVICES?

Put in the most simple terms, *services are deeds, processes, and performances* provided or coproduced by one entity or person for another entity or person. Our opening vignette illustrates what is meant by this definition. The services offered by IBM are not tangible things that can be touched, seen, and felt, but rather are intangible deeds and performances provided and/or coproduced for its customers. To be concrete, IBM offers repair and maintenance service for its equipment, consulting services for IT and e-commerce applications, training services, web design and hosting, and other services. These services may include a final, tangible report, a website, or in the case of training, tangible instructional materials. But for the most part, the entire service is represented to the client through problem analysis activities, meetings with the client, follow-up calls, and reporting—a series of deeds, processes, and performances. Similarly, the core offerings of hospitals, hotels, banks, and utilities are primarily deeds and actions performed for customers, or coproduced with them.

Although we will rely on the simple, broad definition of *services,* you should be aware that over time *services* and the *service sector of the economy* have been defined in subtly different ways. The variety of definitions can often explain the confusion or disagreements people have when discussing services and when describing industries that constitute the service sector of the economy. Compatible with our simple, broad definition is one that defines services to include "all economic activities whose output is not a physical product or construction, is generally consumed at the time it is produced, and provides added value in forms (such as convenience, amusement, timeliness, comfort, or health) that are essentially intangible concerns of its first purchaser."[4] The breadth of industries making up the service sector of the U.S. economy is illustrated in Figure 1.1.

Service Industries, Service as a Product, Customer Service, and Derived Service

As we begin our discussion of services marketing and management, it is important to draw distinctions between *service industries and companies, service as a product, customer service,* and *derived service.* The tools and strategies you will learn in this text can be applied to any of these categories.

Service industries and companies include those industries and companies typically classified within the service sector where the core product is a service. All of the following companies can be considered pure service companies: Marriott International (lodging), American Airlines (transportation), Charles Schwab (financial services), and Mayo Clinic (health care). The total services sector comprises a wide range of service industries, as suggested by Figure 1.1. Companies in these industries sell services as their core offering.

FIGURE 1.1
Contributions of Service Industries to U.S. Gross Domestic Product, 2009

Source: *Survey of Current Business,* Online, March 2011.

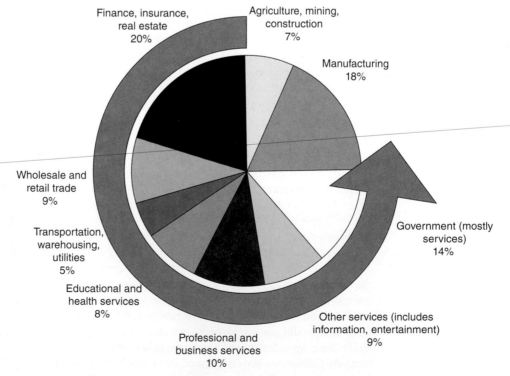

Service as a product represents a wide range of intangible product offerings that customers value and pay for in the marketplace. Service products are sold by service companies and by nonservice companies such as manufacturers and technology companies. For example, IBM and Hewlett-Packard offer information technology consulting services to the marketplace, competing with firms such as Accenture, a traditional pure service firm. Other industry examples include department stores like Macy's that sell services such as gift wrapping and shipping, and pet stores like PetSmart that sell pet grooming and training services.

Customer service is also a critical aspect of what we mean by "service." Customer service is the service provided in support of a company's core products. Companies typically do not charge for customer service. Customer service can occur on-site (as when a retail employee helps a customer find a desired item or answers a question), or it can occur over the phone or via the Internet through chat in real time. Many companies operate customer service call centers, often staffed around the clock. Quality customer service is essential to building customer relationships. It should not, however, be confused with the services provided for sale by the company.

Derived service is yet another way to look at what service means. In an award-winning article in the *Journal of Marketing,* Steve Vargo and Bob Lusch argue for a new logic for marketing that suggests that all products and physical goods are valued for the services they provide.[5] Drawing on the work of respected economists, marketers, and philosophers, they suggest that the value derived from physical goods is really the service provided by the good, not the good itself. For example, they suggest that a pharmaceutical drug provides medical service, a razor provides barbering service, and computers provide information and data manipulation service. Although this view is somewhat abstract, it suggests an even broader, more inclusive, view of the meaning of *service.*

Tangibility Spectrum

The broad definition of service implies that intangibility is a key determinant of whether an offering is a service. Although this is true, it is also true that very few products are purely intangible or totally tangible. Instead, services tend to be *more intangible* than manufactured products, and manufactured products tend to be *more tangible* than services. For example, the fast-food industry, while classified as a service, also has many tangible components such as the food, the packaging, and so on. Automobiles, while classified within the manufacturing sector, also supply many intangibles, such as transportation and navigation services. The tangibility spectrum shown in Figure 1.2 captures this idea. Throughout this text, when we refer to services we will be assuming the broad definition of services and acknowledging that there are very few "pure services" or "pure goods." The issues and approaches we discuss are directed toward those offerings that lie on the right side, the intangible side, of the spectrum shown in Figure 1.2.

Trends in the Service Sector

Although you often hear and read that many modern economies are dominated by services, the United States and other countries did not become service economies overnight. As early as 1929, 55 percent of the working population was employed in the service sector in the United States, and approximately 54 percent of the gross national product was generated by services in 1948. The data in Figures 1.3 and 1.4 show that the trend toward services has continued, until in 2009 services represented 75 percent of the gross domestic product (GDP) and 83 percent of employment. Note also that these data do not include services provided by manufacturing companies. The number of employees and value of the services they produce would be classified as manufacturing sector data.

FIGURE 1.2 Tangibility Spectrum

Source: G. Lynn Shostack, "Breaking Free from Product Marketing," *Journal of Marketing* 41 (April 1977), pp. 73–80. Reprinted with permission of the American Marketing Association.

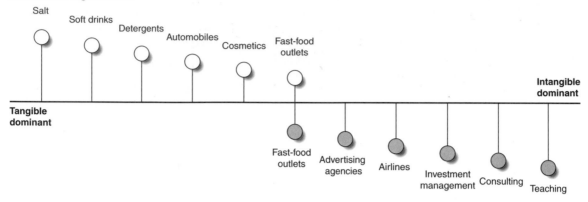

WHY SERVICE MARKETING?

Why is it important to learn about service marketing, service quality, and service management? What are the differences in services versus manufactured-goods marketing that have led to the demand for books and courses on services? Many forces have led to the growth of services marketing, and many industries, companies, and individuals have defined the scope of the concepts, frameworks, and strategies that define the field.

Service-Based Economies

First, services marketing concepts and strategies have developed in response to the tremendous growth of service industries, resulting in their increased importance to the U.S. and world economies. As was noted, in 2009 the service sector represented more than 80 percent of total employment and 75 percent of gross domestic product of the United

FIGURE 1.3
Percentage of U.S. Labor Force by Industry

Sources: *Survey of Current Business,* Online, March 2011; *Survey of Current Business,* February 2001, Table B.8, July 1988, Table 6.6B, and July 1992, Table 6.4C; E. Ginzberg and G. J. Vojta, "The Service Sector of the U.S. Economy," *Scientific American* 244, no. 3 (1981), pp. 31–39.

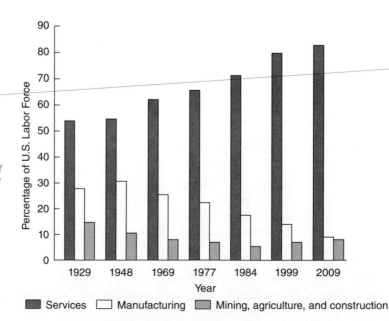

FIGURE 1.4
Percentage of U.S. Gross Domestic Product by Industry

Sources: *Survey of Current Business,* Online, March 2011; *Survey of Current Business,* February 2001, Table B.3, and August 1996, Table 11; E. Ginzberg and G. J. Vojta, "The Service Sector of the U.S. Economy," *Scientific American* 244, no. 3 (1981), pp. 31–39.

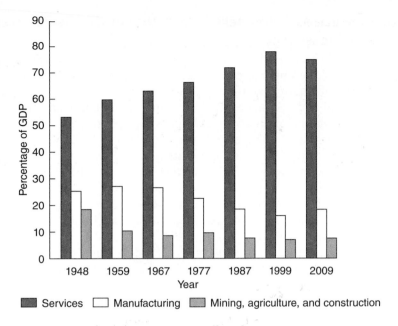

States. Almost all the absolute growth in numbers of jobs and the fastest growth rates in job formation are in service industries, particularly health care and IT professional services.

Another indicator of the economic importance of services is that trade in services is growing worldwide. In fact, while the U.S. balance of trade in goods remains in the red, exports of services have jumped 84 percent since 2000 and there was a $144 billion trade surplus in services in 2008. In fact, the U.S. ranks number one in the world in sales of services abroad.[6]

There is a growing market for services and increasing dominance of services in economies worldwide (see the accompanying table). This growth is apparent in established economies as well as emerging economies such as China, where the central government has placed a priority on service sector growth. The growth of the service sector has drawn increasing attention to the challenges of service sector industries worldwide.

Country	Percent of GDP Attributed to Services
Hong Kong	92
United States	77
Singapore	76
Japan	76
United Kingdom	75
Netherlands	75
Australia	75
France	72
Sweden	72
Germany	72
New Zealand	72
Canada	71
Brazil	67
Mexico	63
India	55
China	43

Source: *The CIA World Fact Book,* 2010.

Service as a Business Imperative in Goods-Focused Businesses

Early in the development of the field of services marketing and management, most of the impetus came from service industries such as banking, transportation, hospitality, and health care. As these traditional service industries have evolved and become even more competitive, the need for effective service management and marketing strategies has continued. Now, however, companies across industries have discovered the value of service innovation and service growth strategies.[7] Manufacturers (e.g., GE, Caterpillar), technology companies (e.g., Avnet, Xerox, IBM), retailers (e.g., PetSmart), and even packaged goods companies (e.g., Procter & Gamble) have begun to discover the potential for service-led growth. (See Chapter 8 and the Strategy Insight in that chapter.) All of these companies have realized that an excellent product is not a guarantee for long-term success.

For example Xerox now provides a document management service, whereby it can take over the management of all documents (digital and paper) within an organization. This type of service lies far beyond its typical printer repair and maintenance service business. In a different industry, PetSmart, a very large pet retailer, attributes nearly all of its growth in recent years to its services, including pet hotels, grooming, and training. Very recently, Procter & Gamble began a push into services tied to a few of its renowned brands. It is experimenting with Mr. Clean Car Wash and a franchise model for Tide Dry Cleaners. Knowing the tremendous value of these brands, Procter & Gamble has been very meticulous and careful in its extension of these brands into services. To expand their service business expertise, many technology companies have partnered with or purchased service businesses. IBM purchased PricewaterhouseCoopers, Hewlett-Packard purchased EDS, and Dell acquired Perot Systems.

Why are all these companies choosing to focus on services? There are a number of reasons. First, the commoditization of products in many industries has resulted in price and margin pressures on many physical goods. Services can help firms to customize their offerings, adding value for customers. Second, customers are demanding services and solutions, especially in business-to-business markets. In many situations, customers demand a solution to their problem or challenge that involves multiple products and services. They look to their providers to create and deliver these product-service solutions. Third, services often have higher profit margins than products and can thus provide platforms for firm profitability. As you will learn in later chapters, customer loyalty and customer satisfaction are driven in large part by service quality and service offerings. Again, this knowledge provides firms with another reason to develop services and cement customer loyalty through high-quality service. Finally, many industries are highly competitive today and service can be a differentiator in a crowded market.

As firms transition into services, they often encounter serious challenges in terms of culture change, sales and channel issues, and a need for expertise in designing and delivering services. These companies are typically engineering, technology, science, or operations driven. Their expertise is anchored in what they produce. As these companies transition and seek to grow through service, they find they need a new service logic, and the special concepts and approaches for managing and marketing services become increasingly apparent.[8]

Services are driving IBM's growth in the 21st century.

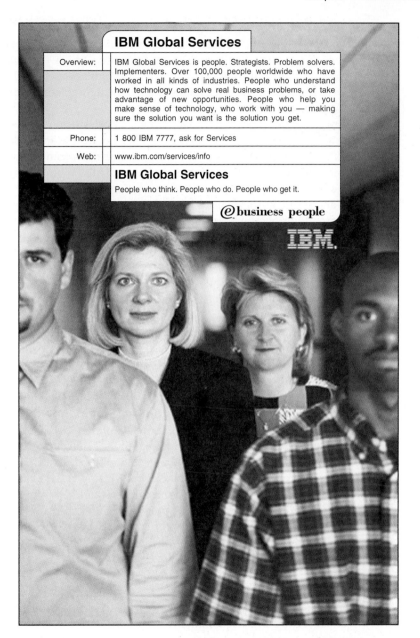

IBM Global Services

Overview:	IBM Global Services is people. Strategists. Problem solvers. Implementers. Over 100,000 people worldwide who have worked in all kinds of industries. People who understand how technology can solve real business problems, or take advantage of new opportunities. People who help you make sense of technology, who work with you — making sure the solution you want is the solution you get.
Phone:	1 800 IBM 7777, ask for Services
Web:	www.ibm.com/services/info

IBM Global Services

People who think. People who do. People who get it.

e business people

IBM.

Deregulated Industries and Professional Service Needs

Specific demand for service marketing concepts has come from deregulated industries and professional services as both these groups have gone through rapid changes in the ways they do business. In the past several decades many very large service industries, including airlines, banking, telecommunications, and trucking, have been deregulated by the U.S. government. Similar deregulatory moves have taken place in many other countries as well. As a result, marketing decisions that used to be tightly controlled by the government are now partially, and in some cases totally, within the control of individual firms.[9] For example, until 1978 all airline fares, routes, and commissions paid to travel agents were determined and monitored by the government. Since that time airlines have been free to set their own pricing structures and determine which routes they will fly. Deregulation created turmoil in the airline industry, accelerating the need for more sophisticated, customer-based, and competition-sensitive marketing.

Providers of professional services (such as physicians, lawyers, accountants, engineers, and architects) have also demanded new concepts and approaches for their businesses as these industries have become increasingly competitive and as professional standards have been modified to allow advertising. Whereas traditionally the professions avoided even using the word *marketing,* they now seek better ways to understand and segment their customers, to ensure the delivery of quality services, and to strengthen their positions amid a growing number of competitors.

Service Marketing Is Different

As the previously mentioned forces coincided and evolved, businesspeople realized that marketing and managing services presented issues and challenges not faced in manufacturing and packaged goods companies. These differences and challenges were captured in a series of interviews by management consultant Gary Knisely in 1979 (see Exhibit 1.1). For example, when a firm's core offering is a deed performed by an employee (such as engineering consulting), how can the firm ensure consistent product quality to the marketplace? As service businesses began to turn to marketing and decided to hire marketing people, they naturally recruited from the best marketers in the world—Procter & Gamble, General Foods, Kodak. People who moved from marketing in packaged goods industries to marketing in health care, banking, and other service industries found that their skills and experiences were not directly transferable. They faced issues and dilemmas in marketing services that their experiences in packaged goods and manufacturing had not prepared them for. These people realized the need for new concepts and approaches for marketing and managing service businesses.

Service marketers responded to these forces and began to work across disciplines and with academics and business practitioners from around the world to develop and document marketing practices for services. As the field evolved, it expanded to address the concerns and needs of *any* business in which service is an integral part of the offering.

Service Equals Profits

In the final decades of the 20th century, many firms jumped on the service bandwagon, investing in service initiatives and promoting service quality as ways to differentiate themselves and create competitive advantage. Many of these investments were based on faith and intuition by managers who believed in serving customers well and who believed in their hearts that quality service made good business sense. Indeed, a dedication to quality service has been the foundation for success for many firms, across industries. In his book *Discovering the Soul of Service,* Leonard Berry describes in detail 14 such companies.[10] The companies featured in his book had been in business an average of 31 years when the book was written. These companies had been profitable in all but 5 of their combined 407 years of existence. Berry discovered through his research that these successful businesses share devotion to nine common service themes, among them values-driven leadership, commitment to investments in employee success, and trust-based relationships with customers and other partners at the foundation of the organization.

Exhibit 1.1 Is the Marketing of Services Different? A Historical Perspective

In 1979 Gary Knisely, a principal of the consulting firm Johnson Smith & Knisely, asked the title question to practicing service marketers. Specifically, Knisely interviewed several high-ranking marketing executives who had all gone to work in consumer services after extensive experience in the consumer packaged goods industry (known for its marketing prowess).

These executives found differences, all right. Their discoveries came from attempts to apply (with mixed success, it turned out) consumer goods marketing practices directly to services. James L. Schorr of Holiday Inns Inc., formerly with Procter & Gamble, found that he could not overlay a consumer goods firm's marketing system onto a service firm. He, and the other executives interviewed, expressed certain recurring themes. First, more variables exist in the marketing mix for services than for consumer goods. Schorr claimed that in a service business, marketing and operations are more closely linked than in a manufacturing business; thus, the service production process is part of the marketing process. Second, customer interface is a major difference between goods marketing and services marketing. Executives from packaged goods companies never had to think in terms of a direct dialogue with their customers. For Schorr, the marketing of hotel rooms boiled down to a "people-on-people" sale. Robert L. Catlin, in relating his experience in the airline industry, stated, "Your people are as much of your product in the consumer's mind as any other attribute of the service." People buy products because they believe they work. But with services, people deal with people they like and they tend to buy services because they believe they will like them. This thought process makes the customer–employee interface a critical component of marketing.

The executives also commented on how the marketing mix variables common to both goods and services have vastly different implications for marketing strategy in the two contexts. In the distribution and selling of services, the firm cannot rely on well-stocked shelves past which the consumer can push a cart and make selections. Consumers' exposure to the full range of need-fulfilling service products may be limited by the salesperson's "mental inventory" of services and how he or she prioritizes them. You could say that the service product manager is competing for the "mental shelf space" of the firm's sales personnel. For Rodney Woods, group marketing officer at United States Trust Co., pricing was the most critical factor in the marketing of services versus products. For Woods, determining the costs associated with service production and delivery proved very difficult, much more of a challenge than he had faced in his earlier career working with such large packaged goods companies as Pillsbury, Procter & Gamble, and Bristol-Myers. Also, the benefits of using price as a promotional weapon were not as apparent. Promotional price cuts tended to erode hard-fought positioning and image.

While scholars debated early on the issue of whether marketing management differs for goods versus services, for top managers with experience in both areas the differences were pronounced in 1979. They still are today. The differences that these early service marketers noted were the impetus for many of the ideas, concepts, and strategies practiced today.

Source: This discussion is based on interviews conducted by Gary Knisely that appeared in *Advertising Age* on January 15, 1979; February 19, 1979; March 19, 1979; and May 14, 1979.

Since the mid-1990s firms have demanded hard evidence of the bottom-line effectiveness of service strategies. And researchers are building a convincing case that service strategies, implemented appropriately, can be very profitable. Work sponsored by the Marketing Science Institute suggests that corporate strategies focused on customer satisfaction, revenue generation, and service quality may actually be more profitable than strategies focused on cost cutting or strategies that attempt to do both simultaneously.[11] Research out of the Harvard Business School built a case for the "service–profit chain," linking internal service and employee satisfaction to customer value and ultimately to profits.[12] And considerable research shows linkages from customer satisfaction (often driven by service outcomes) to profits.[13] From the University of Michigan American Customer Satisfaction Index (ACSI) come data suggesting that customer satisfaction is directly linked to shareholder value. Firms in the top 25 percent of the ACSI rankings show significantly higher shareholder value than do firms in the bottom 25 percent. Research based on ACSI data also shows that the top 20 percent of ACSI firms significantly outperform the Standard & Poor's (S&P) 500, NASDAQ, and Dow Jones Industrial Average.[14]

An important key to these successes is that the right strategies are chosen and that these strategies are implemented appropriately and well. Much of what you learn from this text will guide you in making such correct choices and in providing superior implementation. Throughout the text we will point out the profit implications and tradeoffs to be made with service strategies. See this chapter's Strategy Insight for four ways that firms successfully and profitably compete through service. In Chapter 16 we will come back to this issue by providing integrated coverage of the financial and profit impact of service.

But "Service Stinks"

Despite the importance of service and the bottom-line profit potential for service, consumers perceive that overall the quality of service is declining.[15] We see *BusinessWeek* magazine blatantly condemning service in its cover story "Why Service Stinks" and a *Wall Street Journal* editorial questioning service quality and value that is entitled "We Pay Them to Be Rude to Us."[16] And although there are exceptions in every industry, American Customer Satisfaction Index scores for service industries are generally lower than the average for all industries. Particularly low are ACSI scores in the transportation, communications, and utilities sectors.[17]

This condemnation of service is troubling when, at some level, service has never been better. For example, think of just one industry—health care. The ability to prevent and treat diseases has never been greater, resulting in an ever-increasing life expectancy in the United States and in most other industrialized countries. Or take the communications industries—communicating quickly, effectively, and cheaply with people all over the world has never been easier. Access to vast quantities of information, entertainment, and music is unbelievable compared to what people had just 10 years ago. So clearly, in some ways and in many industries, service is better than ever.

Despite these obvious improvements, there is hard evidence that consumers perceive a lower quality of service overall and are less satisfied. There are many explanations as to why this decline in customer satisfaction with services has occurred, but it is difficult to point precisely to the reason. Plausible explanations include these:

- With more companies offering tiered service based on the calculated profitability of different market segments, many customers are, in fact, getting less service than they have in the past.
- Increasing use by companies of self-service and technology-based service is perceived as less service because no human interaction or human personalization is provided.
- Technology-based services (automated voice systems, Internet-based services, technology kiosks) are hard to implement by companies and difficult to use by customers, with many failures and with poorly designed systems in place.
- Customer expectations are higher in all industries because of the excellent service they receive from some companies. Thus, they expect the same from all and are frequently disappointed.
- Organizations have cut costs to the extent that they are too lean and too understaffed to provide quality service.

Strategy Insight Competing Strategically through Service

Firms can compete profitably through services in a variety of ways. Through our work with companies across industries and through benchmarking other companies, we see four strategic themes emerge as the primary ways that firms can compete through service. Although firms tend to emphasize one or two of these strategic choices at a given time, it may be possible to do more.

EXEMPLARY OUT-OF-THE-BOX CUSTOMER SERVICE

There are some organizations whose competitive advantage is their reputation for out-of-the-box customer service. Southwest Airlines, Mayo Clinic, Gallery Furniture (a hugely successful furniture store in Texas), and Zanes Cycles (a small bicycle shop in Connecticut) are just a few examples. These organizations focus on going out of their way for customers and providing customer service in unique ways. Special services that these companies provide include

- At Southwest Airlines, a distinctive sense of humor among employees as well as in-flight games and jokes.
- At Mayo Clinic, a grand piano in the lobby and doctors who sit physically close to patients, look them in the eye, and truly believe that "the best interest of the patient is the only interest to be considered."
- At Gallery Furniture, free food and day care for children.
- At Zanes Cycles, a "flat tire club."

INNOVATIVE, CUTTING-EDGE SERVICES

Other organizations compete through providing innovative and cutting-edge services—being the first and/or best in their industry or being on the forefront of new inventions, technology, or science. Examples here include Amazon.com, the first company to introduce really effective and innovative online retailing. Mayo Clinic falls into this category as well. It is on the leading edge of medicine in the United States and typically sees only patients who have hard-to-diagnose or complex problems. The clinic's research-based, team-oriented, consultative model of medicine keeps it on the forefront.

Being innovative does not necessarily mean that the organization invents something totally new; perhaps its service approach is simply new to that industry. Yellow Transportation (part of YRC Worldwide), an old-line trucking company, reinvented itself as a transportation company by successfully introducing guarantees, express services, and time-definite delivery into this somewhat stodgy industry.

VALUE-ADDED, REVENUE-PRODUCING SERVICES

A major trend in manufacturing, information technology, and other nonservice industries in recent years is the introduction of value-added, revenue-producing services. Firms in these industries have recognized that they cannot compete on the sales and margins produced by their manufactured products alone. Many firms, such as IBM, Hewlett-Packard, Siemens, and General Electric, have integrated services into their mix of offerings. In some cases, as with IBM (see the opening vignette in this chapter), services have actually taken over as the growth engine for the company.

This focus on revenue-producing services also extends to retailers. For example, PetSmart, the largest pet retailer in the United States, has introduced a host of new services in recent years as a way to compete effectively in this relatively low-margin industry. The company targets "pet parents" in its advertising, and its special services include pet training, grooming, and overnight care.

A SERVICE CULTURE THAT DIFFERENTIATES

Finally, a firm can compete by nurturing a service culture that attracts the very best workers in the industry. In attracting the best workers, the company has an advantage over the competition in terms of providing the very best services and thus becoming both the "employer of choice" and the "provider of choice" in its industry. This approach is used, for example, by Southwest Airlines, Mayo Clinic, Disney, and Marriott Hotels. At Marriott, the underlying company philosophy is "take care of your employees and they will take care of your guests." This philosophy permeates all the Marriott brands, from Fairfield Inns to the Ritz Carlton, giving Marriott a worldwide competitive advantage in its industry.

Source: Center for Services Leadership, W. P. Carey School of Business, Arizona State University (www.wpcarey.asu. edu/csl). See also M. J. Bitner and S. Brown, "The Service Imperative," *Business Horizons,* 50th Anniversary Issue, 51 (January–February 2008), pp. 39–46.

- The competitive job market results in less-skilled people working in frontline service jobs; talented workers soon get promoted or leave for better opportunities.
- Many companies give lip service to customer focus and service quality, but they fail to provide the training, compensation, and support of employees needed to actually deliver quality service.

These explanations of the causes of declining customer satisfaction can be debated. But for managers, students, and teachers of service marketing and management, the message is clear: there is plenty of work to be done. In this text we will provide many examples of best practices—companies that understand how to get it right and are succeeding with service. We will also delineate many tools, concepts, and strategies that can help to reverse the "service stinks" mind-set.

SERVICE AND TECHNOLOGY

The preceding sections examined the roots of services marketing and the reasons the field exists. Another major trend—technology, specifically information technology—is shaping the field and profoundly influencing the practice of service marketing. In this section we explore trends in technology (positive *and* negative) to set the stage for topics that will be discussed throughout this text. In each chapter you will find a Technology Spotlight box that highlights the influence of technology on issues related to the particular chapter. Together with globalization, the influence of technology is the most profound trend affecting services marketing today.

New Service Offerings

Looking to the past, it is apparent how technology was the basic force behind service innovations now taken for granted. Automated voice mail, interactive voice response systems, fax machines, automated teller machines (ATMs), and other common services were possible only because of new technologies. Just think how dramatically different your world would be without these basic technology services.

More recently, people have seen the explosion of the Internet, resulting in a host of new services. Internet-based companies like Amazon and eBay offer services previously unheard of and smart phones now offer innumerable service applications that were not even imaginable in the recent past. Even established companies find that the Internet provides a way to offer new services as well.[18] For example, *The Wall Street Journal* offers an interactive edition that allows customers to organize the newspaper's content to suit their individual preferences and needs.

Many new technology services are on the horizon. For example, the "connected car" allows people to access all kinds of existing and new services while on the road. In-car systems provide recommendations for shopping by informing drivers when they are within a certain number of miles of their preferred retailer. On a road trip, the system may provide weather forecasts and warnings, and when it is time to stop for the night, the car's system can book a room at a nearby hotel, recommend a restaurant, and make dinner reservations. Other technological advances are making it possible for medical professionals to monitor patients' conditions remotely and even to provide medical diagnoses, treatment, and surgery guidance via technology interfaces. Similarly, large equipment manufacturers like John Deere, Caterpillar, and General Electric can now remotely monitor and service equipment, as well as provide sophisticated information and data to their clients via the Internet.

New Ways to Deliver Service

In addition to providing opportunities for new service offerings, technology is providing approaches for delivering existing services in more accessible, convenient, productive ways. Technology facilitates basic customer service functions (bill paying, questions, checking account records, order tracking), transactions (both retail and business-to-business), and learning or information seeking. Our Technology Spotlight traces how, through history, evolving technologies have changed one aspect of service, namely, customer service, forever. Companies have moved from face-to-face service to telephone-based service to widespread use of interactive voice response systems to Internet-based customer service and now to wireless service. Interestingly, many companies are coming full circle and now offer human contact as the ultimate form of customer service!

Technology also facilitates transactions by offering a direct vehicle for making purchases and conducting business. In the financial services field, Charles Schwab transformed itself from a traditional broker to an online financial services company that currently conducts more than 70 percent of its customer transactions online. Internet banking is also growing worldwide with the Dutch bank, ING Direct, leading the way in the United States. ING regularly attracts deposits away from its much larger competitors.[19] Technology has also transformed service delivery and transactions for many business-to business firms. For example, technology giant Cisco Systems offers virtually all its customer service and ordering functions to its business customers via technology.

Finally, technology, specifically the Internet, provides an easy way for customers to learn, do research, and collaborate with each other. Access to information has never been easier. For example, more than 20,000 websites currently offer health-related information. Many provide answers to specific disease, drug, and treatment questions. In a study of online health care information usage, the Pew organization found that, among Americans with Internet access, 80 percent had looked for health or medical information on the Web.[20]

Enabling Both Customers and Employees

Technology enables both customers and employees to be more effective in getting and providing service.[21] Through self-service technologies, customers can serve themselves more effectively. Via online banking, customers can access their accounts, check balances, apply for loans, shift money among accounts, and take care of just about any banking need they might have—all without the assistance of the bank's employees. Online shopping and hundreds of service applications available via the Internet and smart phones have transformed the lives of consumers forever. Through social media, individuals and companies can communicate and collaborate with each other as well.

For employees, technology can provide tremendous support in making them more effective and efficient in delivering service. Customer relationship management and sales support software are broad categories of technology that can aid frontline employees in providing better service. By having immediate access to information about their product and service offerings as well as about particular customers, employees are better able to serve them. This type of information allows employees to customize services to fit the customer's needs. They can also be much more efficient and timely than in the old days when most customer and product information was in paper files or in the heads of sales and customer service representatives.

Technology Spotlight The Changing Face of Customer Service

Excellent customer service—the daily, ongoing support of a company's offerings—is critical in creating brand identity and ultimate success. It includes answering questions, taking orders, dealing with billing issues, handling complaints, scheduling appointments, and similar activities. These essential functions can make or break an organization's relationships with its customers. The quality of customer care can significantly impact brand identity for service, manufacturing, and consumer products companies. Because of its importance in creating impressions and sustaining customer relationships, customer service has sometimes been called the "front door" of the organization or its "face."

So how has the "face" of customer service changed with the influx of technology? Long ago all customer service was provided face-to-face through direct personal interaction between employees and customers. To get service you had to visit stores or service providers in person. The telephone changed this, allowing customers to call companies and speak directly with employees, typically Monday–Friday, 8 a.m.–5 p.m. Customer service became less personal,

but without a doubt more efficient, through use of the telephone. With the evolution of computer technology, customer service representatives (CSRs) became even more efficient. Through computer information systems and customer data files, CSRs are able to call up customer records at their workstations to answer questions on the spot.

Over time, because communication and computer technologies allowed it, large organizations began to centralize their customer service functions, consolidating into a few large call centers that could be located anywhere in the country or the world. For example, a large percentage of IBM's customer service calls in North America are handled out of its sales and service center in Toronto, Canada, and calls can be handled 24 hours per day. But still, in these types of call centers, customer service is, for the most part, an interpersonal event, with customers talking directly, one-on-one with an employee.

The advent and rapid proliferation of the efficient, but much maligned, automated voice response systems changed personal customer service in many organizations into menu-driven, automated

Extending the Global Reach of Services

Technology infusion results in the potential for reaching out to customers around the globe in ways not possible before. The Internet itself knows no boundaries, and therefore information, customer service, and transactions can move across countries and across continents, reaching any customer who has access to the Web. Technology also allows employees of international companies to stay in touch easily—to share information, to ask questions, to serve on virtual teams together. All this technology facilitates the global reach as well as the effectiveness of service businesses. Our Global Feature focuses on the migration of service jobs and the ability to produce services almost anywhere.

The Internet *Is* a Service

An interesting way to look at the influence of technology is to realize that the Internet is just "one big service." All businesses and organizations that operate on the Internet are essentially providing services—whether they are giving information, performing basic customer service functions, facilitating transactions, or promoting social interactions among individuals. Thus, all the tools, concepts, and strategies you learn in studying service marketing and management have direct application in an Internet or e-business world. Although technology and the Internet have profoundly changed how people do business and what offerings are possible, it is clear exchanges. In almost every industry and any business context, consumers encounter these types of systems, and many are quite frustrating—for example, when a system has a long, confusing set of menu options or when no menu option seems to fit the purpose of the call. Similarly, customers become angered when they cannot get out of the automated system easily or when there is no option to speak to a live person.

Beyond automated telecom systems, the explosion of the Internet has also dramatically changed customer service for many companies. Service can now be provided on the Internet via e-mails, website robots, FAQs, and online chats. In these cases there is no direct human interaction, and customers actually perform their own service.

With the relentless proliferation of technology solutions, firms are finding that expectations for customer service have changed. Customers are demanding choices in how they get customer service, whether it be via phone, automated voice system, fax, e-mail, or Internet self-service. Although customers often enjoy technology-based service and even demand it in many cases, they dislike it when it does not work

reliably (a common problem), when it does not seem to have any advantages over the interpersonal service alternatives, and when there are no systems in place to recover from failures. Interestingly, when things do not work as they are supposed to on an Internet site or through an automated response system, customers are quick to look for more traditional interpersonal (in person or via telephone) options, coming full circle to where they started. Somewhat ironically, the leading *Internet* bank in Europe and the United States, ING Direct, prides itself on staffing its toll-free customer service phone lines with real *people,* not automated menu systems!

Sources: J. A. Nickell, "To Voice Mail Hell and Back," *Business 2.0,* July 10, 2001, pp. 49–53; M. L. Meuter, A. L. Ostrom, R. I. Roundtree, and M. J. Bitner, "Self-Service Technologies: Understanding Customer Satisfaction with Technology-Based Service Encounters," *Journal of Marketing* 64 (July 2000), pp. 50–64; S. Ali, "If you want to Scream, Press . . . ," *The Wall Street Journal,* October 30, 2006, p. R4; B. Kiviat, "How a Man on a Mission (and a Harley) Reinvented Banking," *Time,* June 25, 2007, pp. 45–46; J. Light, "With Customer Service, Real Person Trumps Text," *The Wall Street Journal,* April 25, 2011, p. B7.

that customers still want basic service. They want what they have always wanted: dependable outcomes, easy access, responsive systems, flexibility, apologies, and compensation when things go wrong. But now they expect these outcomes from technology-based businesses and from e-commerce solutions.[22] With hindsight it is obvious that many dot-com start-ups suffered and even failed because of lack of basic customer knowledge and failure of implementation, logistics, and service follow-up.[23]

The Paradoxes and Dark Side of Technology and Service

Although there is clearly great potential for technology to support and enhance services, there are potential negative outcomes as well. David Mick and Susan Fournier, well-regarded consumer researchers, have pointed out the many paradoxes of technology products and services for consumers, as shown in Table 1.1.[24] This section highlights some of the general concerns.

Customer concerns about privacy and confidentiality raise major issues for firms as they seek to learn about and interact directly with customers through the Internet. These types of concerns are what have stymied and precluded many efforts to advance technology applications in the health care industry, for example. Nor are all customers equally interested in using technology as a means of interacting with companies. Research exploring "customer technology readiness" suggests that some customers

With the ever-growing sophistication of information technology, the global reach of organizations is increasing at a spectacular rate. Activities that used to require close proximity and personal contact can now often be accomplished via the Internet, video, and telecommunication technologies. This advancement means that the jobs that produce and support these activities can be done almost anywhere in the world. The result has been referred to as a "migration of service jobs" out of countries such as the United States and the United Kingdom to countries such as India, Pakistan, the Philippines, Eastern European countries, and, more recently, Columbia and Brazil.

This globalization of services is in many ways inevitable, but it comes with considerable controversy. One clear concern is that some of the highest-paying service jobs are being "lost" to lower-wage countries, and this concern is very real for the individuals whose jobs are lost. However, the numbers are not as large as perhaps imagined. Forrester Research in Cambridge, Massachusetts, estimates that, by the year 2015, 3.3 million high-tech and service jobs will have moved overseas from the United States. Others estimate the number to be much higher. On the other side of this concern are arguments that offshore jobs will spur innovation, job creation in other areas, and increases in productivity that will benefit the consumer and keep companies competitive in the global marketplace. In fact, the Bureau of Labor Statistics estimated that, between 2000 and 2010, 22 million new U.S. jobs (mostly in business services, health care, social services, transportation, and communications) would be created. Although the specific outcomes of service job migration are not totally known, it is safe to say that the globalization of services will continue, resulting in further shrinking of the boundaries among people and countries.

Service job migration involves not just call centers and IT help lines but also services that span industries and levels of skills. Software development, IT consulting, chip design, financial analysis, industrial engineering, analytics, and drug research are just a few examples of services performed in India for global firms. Even medical diagnoses and reading of medical records can be done remotely via video, Internet, and scanning technologies.

Why is service job migration happening now? The root of the acceleration is the rapid development and accessibility of sophisticated information technologies. Services are information intensive, and information can now be shared readily without direct personal contact. For example, at the John F. Welch Technology Center in Bangalore, close to 3,000 Indian researchers and engineers engage in research for General Electric's divisions. Projects span such diverse areas as developing materials

Call center in India.

for use in DVDs, boosting the productivity of GE plants, and tweaking the designs of turbine engine blades. The design work can be done in India (perhaps even teaming with engineers elsewhere), and the results can be sent instantaneously wherever they are needed. Other examples: more than 20,000 U.S. tax returns annually are prepared and filed by certified public accountants (CPAs) working in India; Indian financial analysts digest the latest disclosures of U.S. companies and file reports the next day; and other workers in India sort through mounds of consumer data provided by non-Indian company clients to determine behavior patterns and develop ideas for marketing. In each of these cases, *where* the work is done is not important or meaningful to the client as long as it is done well and on time.

A major reason that this movement of jobs is possible is that countries outside the developed world are now producing highly skilled, well-educated workforces, particularly in China and India. These workers typically work for far less compensation than their U.S. or U.K. counterparts, allowing global companies to reduce labor costs on the one hand and increase overall productivity on the other. The quality of the work can be very high as well. However, as the growth in offshoring continues and competition for talent increases, firms are zeroing in on cultural and language gaps that can limit quality with some firms, bringing services—particularly call centers—back to their home base.

U. Karmarkar, "Will You Survive the Services Revolution?" *Harvard Business Review,* 82 (June 2004), pp. 100–107; M. Kripalani and P. Engardio, "The Rise of India," *Business Week,* December 8, 2003; S. A. Teicher, "A Not So Simple Path," *Christian Science Monitor,* February 23, 2004; M. N. Baily and D. Farrell, "Exploding the Myths of Offshoring," *The McKinsey Quarterly,* online at www.mckinseyquarterly.com, July 2004; S. Ali, "If You Want to Scream, Press . . . ," *The Wall Street Journal,* October 30, 2006, R4; A. Vashistha and A. Vashistha, *The Offshore Nation* (New York: McGraw-Hill, 2006); S. Lohr, "At IBM, a Smarter Way to Outsource," *The New York Times,* July 5, 2007.

TABLE 1.1 **Eight Central Paradoxes of Technological Products**

Source: D. G. Mick and S. Fournier, "Paradoxes of Technology: Consumer Cognizance, Emotions, and Coping Strategies," *Journal of Consumer Research* 25 (September 1998), pp. 123–147. Copyright © 1998 University of Chicago Press. Reprinted by permission.

Paradox	Description
Control/chaos	Technology can facilitate regulation or order, and technology can lead to upheaval or disorder.
Freedom/enslavement	Technology can facilitate independence or fewer restrictions, and technology can lead to dependence or more restrictions.
New/obsolete	New technologies provide the user with the most recently developed benefits of scientific knowledge, and new technologies are already or soon to be outmoded as they reach the marketplace.
Competence/incompetence	Technology can facilitate feelings of intelligence or efficacy, and technology can lead to feelings of ignorance or ineptitude.
Efficiency/inefficiency	Technology can facilitate less effort or time spent in certain activities, and technology can lead to more effort or time in certain activities.
Fulfills/creates needs	Technology can facilitate the fulfillment of needs or desires, and technology can lead to the development or awareness of needs or desires previously unrealized.
Assimilation/isolation	Technology can facilitate human togetherness, and technology can lead to human separation.
Engaging/disengaging	Technology can facilitate involvement, flow, or activity, and technology can lead to disconnection, disruption, or passivity.

are simply not interested in using or ready to use technology.[25] Employees can also be reluctant to accept and integrate technology into their work lives—especially when they perceive, rightly or wrongly, that the technology will substitute for human labor and perhaps eliminate their jobs.

With technology infusion comes a loss of human contact, which many people believe is detrimental purely from a quality of life and human relationships perspective. Parents may lament that their children spend hours in front of computer screens, interacting with games, seeking information, and relating to their friends only through instant messaging and Facebook without any face-to-face human contact. And workers in organizations become more and more reliant on communicating through technology—even communicating via e-mail or online chat sessions with the person in the next office!

Finally, the payback in technology investments is often uncertain. It may take a long time for an investment to result in productivity or customer satisfaction gains. Sometimes it never happens. For example, McKinsey & Company reports that a firm projected a $40 million savings from moving its billing and service calls to the Web. Instead, it suffered a $16 million loss as a result of lower usage by customers than projected, unanticipated follow-up calls and e-mails to the call center from those who had used the Web application initially, and loss of revenue from lack of cross-selling opportunities.[26]

CHARACTERISTICS OF SERVICES

There is general agreement that differences between goods and services exist and that the distinctive characteristics discussed in this section result in challenges (as well as advantages) for managers of services.[27] It is also important to realize that each of these characteristics could be arranged on a continuum similar to the tangibility spectrum shown in Figure 1.1. That is, services tend to be more heterogeneous, more intangible, and more difficult to evaluate than goods, but the differences between goods and services are not black and white by any means.[28]

Table 1.2 summarizes the differences between goods and services and the implications of these characteristics. Many of the strategies, tools, and frameworks in this text were developed to address these characteristics, which, until the 1980s, had been largely ignored by marketers. Recently it has been suggested that these distinctive characteristics should not be viewed as unique to services but that they are also relevant to goods, that "all products are services," and that "economic exchange is fundamentally about service provision."[29] This view suggests that all types of organizations may be able to gain valuable insights from service marketing frameworks, tools, and strategies.

Intangibility

The most basic distinguishing characteristic of services is intangibility. Because services are performances or actions rather than objects, they cannot be seen, felt, tasted, or touched in the same manner that you can sense tangible goods. For example, health care services are actions (such as surgery, diagnosis, examination, and treatment) performed by providers and directed toward patients and their families. These services cannot be seen or touched by the patient, although the patient may be able to see and touch certain tangible components of the service (like the equipment or hospital room). In fact, many services such as health care are difficult to grasp even mentally. Even after a diagnosis or surgery has been completed the patient may not fully comprehend the service performed, although tangible evidence of the service (e.g., incision, bandaging, pain) may be apparent.

TABLE 1.2 Comparing Goods and Services

Source: A. Parasuraman, V. A. Zeithaml, and L. L. Berry, "A Conceptual Model of Service Quality and Its Implications for Future Research." *Journal of Marketing* 49 (Fall 1985) pp. 41–50. Reprinted by permission of the American Marketing Association.

Goods	Services	Resulting Implications
Tangible	Intangible	Services cannot be inventoried. Services cannot be easily patented. Services cannot be readily displayed or communicated. Pricing is difficult.
Standardized	Heterogeneous	Service delivery and customer satisfaction depend on employee and customer actions. Service quality depends on many uncontrollable factors. There is no sure knowledge that the service delivered matches what was planned and promoted.
Production separate from consumption	Simultaneous production and consumption	Customers participate in and affect the transaction. Customers affect each other. Employees affect the service outcome. Decentralization may be essential. Mass production is difficult.
Nonperishable	Perishable	It is difficult to synchronize supply and demand with services. Services cannot be returned or resold.

Resulting Marketing Implications Intangibility presents several marketing challenges. Services cannot be inventoried, and therefore fluctuations in demand are often difficult to manage. For example, there is tremendous demand for resort accommodations in Phoenix in February but little demand in July. Yet resort owners have the same number of rooms to sell year-round. Services cannot be easily patented, and new service concepts can therefore easily be copied by competitors. Services cannot be readily displayed or easily communicated to customers, so quality may be difficult for consumers to assess. Decisions about what to include in advertising and other promotional materials are challenging, as is pricing. The actual costs of a "unit of service" are hard to determine, and the price–quality relationship is complex.

Heterogeneity

Because services are performances, frequently produced by humans, no two services will be precisely alike. The employees delivering the service frequently are the service in the customer's eyes, and people may differ in their performance from day to day or even hour to hour. Heterogeneity also results because no two customers are precisely alike; each will have unique demands or experience the service in a unique way. Because services are often coproduced and cocreated with customers, customer behaviors will also introduce variability and uncertainties, resulting in heterogeneity of outcomes. Thus, the heterogeneity connected with services is largely the result of human interaction (between and among employees and customers) and human behaviors, as well as all of the vagaries that accompany them. For example, a tax accountant may provide a different service experience to two different customers on the same day depending on their individual needs and personalities and on whether the accountant is interviewing them when he or she is fresh in the morning or tired at the end of a long day of meetings.

Resulting Marketing Implications Because services are heterogeneous across time, organizations, and people, ensuring consistent service quality is challenging. Quality actually depends on many factors that cannot be fully controlled by the service supplier, such as the ability of the customer to articulate his or her needs, the ability and willingness of personnel to satisfy those needs, the presence (or absence) of other customers, and the level of demand for the service. Because of these complicating factors, the service manager cannot always know for sure that the service is being delivered in a manner consistent with what was originally planned and promoted. Sometimes services are provided by a third party, further increasing the potential heterogeneity of the offering.

Simultaneous Production and Consumption

Whereas most goods are produced first, then sold and consumed, many services are sold first and then produced and consumed simultaneously. For example, an automobile can be manufactured in Detroit, shipped to San Francisco, sold two months later, and consumed over a period of years. But restaurant services cannot be provided until they have been sold, and the dining experience is essentially produced and consumed at the same time. Frequently in service situations like the restaurant this also means that customers are present while the service is being produced and thus view and may even take part in the production process as coproducers or cocreators of the service. Simultaneity also means that customers will frequently interact with each other during the service production process and thus may affect each others' experiences. For example, strangers seated next to each other in an airplane may well affect the nature of the service experience for each other. That passengers understand this fact is clearly

Students in a university class cocreate the service experience with each other and the professor.

apparent in the way business travelers will often go to great lengths to be sure they are not seated next to families with small children. Another outcome of simultaneous production and consumption is that service producers find themselves playing a role as part of the product itself and as an essential ingredient in the service experience for the consumer. The accompanying photo illustrates a common and complex example of simultaneous cocreation of a service—a university classroom. Interestingly, with the advent of technology, many services can now be produced and consumed at different points in time, resulting in fewer challenges related to this characteristic for some providers.[30]

Resulting Marketing Implications   Because services often (although not always) are produced and consumed at the same time, mass production is difficult. The quality of service and customer satisfaction will be highly dependent on what happens in "real time," including actions of employees, the interactions between employees and customers, and interactions among customers themselves. Clearly the real-time nature of services also results in advantages in terms of opportunities to customize offerings for individual consumers. Simultaneous production and consumption also means that it is not usually possible to gain significant economies of scale through centralization. Often, operations need to be relatively decentralized, so that the service can be delivered directly to the customer in convenient locations, although the growth of technology-delivered services is changing this requirement for many services. Also because of simultaneous production and consumption, the customer is involved in and observes the production process and thus may affect (positively or negatively) the outcome of the service transaction.

Perishability

Perishability refers to the fact that services cannot be saved, stored, resold, or returned. A seat on an airplane or in a restaurant, an hour of a lawyer's time, or space in a shipping container not used or purchased cannot be reclaimed and used or resold at a later time. Perishability is in contrast to goods that can be stored in inventory or resold another day, or even returned if the consumer is unhappy. Would it not be nice if a bad haircut could be returned or resold to another customer? Perishability makes this action an unlikely possibility for most services.

Resulting Marketing Implications   A primary issue that marketers face in relation to service perishability is the inability to inventory. Demand forecasting and creative planning for capacity utilization are therefore important and challenging decision areas. The fact that services cannot typically be returned or resold also implies a need for strong recovery strategies when things do go wrong. For example, although a bad haircut cannot be returned, the hairdresser can and should have strategies for recovering the customer's goodwill if and when such a problem occurs.

Search, Experience, and Credence Qualities

One framework for isolating differences in evaluation processes between goods and services is a classification of properties of offerings proposed by economists.[31] Economists first distinguished between two categories of properties of products: *search qualities,* attributes that a customer can determine before purchasing a product, and *experience qualities,* attributes that can be discerned only after purchase or during consumption. Search qualities include color, style, price, fit, feel, hardness, and smell; experience qualities include taste, wearability, and comfort. Products such as automobiles, clothing, furniture, and jewelry are high in search qualities because their attributes can be almost completely determined and evaluated before purchase. Products such as vacations and restaurant meals are high in experience qualities because their attributes cannot be fully known or assessed until they have been purchased and are being consumed. A third category, *credence qualities,* includes characteristics that the consumer may find impossible to evaluate even after purchase and consumption.[32] Examples of offerings high in credence qualities are appendix operations, brake relinings on a car, and computer software updates. Few consumers possess medical, mechanical, or technical skills sufficient to evaluate whether these services are necessary or are performed properly, even after they have been prescribed and produced by the provider.

Figure 1.5 arrays products that are high in search, experience, or credence qualities along a continuum of evaluation ranging from easy to evaluate to difficult to evaluate. Products high in search qualities are the easiest to evaluate (left end of the continuum). Products high in experience qualities are more difficult to evaluate because they must be purchased and consumed before assessment is possible (center of the continuum).

FIGURE 1.5
Continuum of Evaluation for Different Types of Products

Evaluation Qualities of Goods and Services

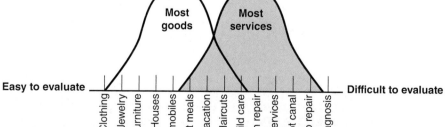

Products high in credence qualities are the most difficult to evaluate because the customer may be unaware of or may lack sufficient knowledge to appraise whether the offerings satisfy given wants or needs even after usage and/or consumption (right end of the continuum). Most goods fall to the left of the continuum, whereas most services fall to the right because of the characteristics of services just described. These characteristics make services more difficult to evaluate than goods, particularly in advance of purchase. Difficulty in evaluation, in turn, forces consumers to rely on different cues and processes when deciding upon and assessing services.

Challenges and Questions for Service Marketers

Because of the basic characteristics of services, marketers of services face some very distinctive challenges. Answers to questions such as the ones listed here still elude managers of services:

How can service quality be defined and improved when the product is intangible and nonstandardized?

How can new services be designed and tested effectively when the service is essentially an intangible process?

How can the firm be certain it is communicating a consistent and relevant image when so many elements of the marketing mix communicate to customers and some of these elements are the service providers themselves?

How does the firm accommodate fluctuating demand when capacity is fixed and the service itself is perishable?

How can the firm best motivate and select service employees who, because the service is delivered in real time, become a critical part of the product itself?

How should prices be set when it is difficult to determine actual costs of production and price may be inextricably intertwined with perceptions of quality?

How should the firm be organized so that good strategic and tactical decisions are made when a decision in any of the functional areas of marketing, operations, and human resources may have significant impact on the other two areas?

How can the balance between standardization and personalization be determined to maximize both the efficiency of the organization and the satisfaction of its customers?

How can the organization protect new service concepts from competitors when service processes cannot be readily patented?

How does the firm communicate quality and value to customers when the offering is intangible and cannot be readily tried or displayed prior to the purchase decision?

How can the organization ensure the delivery of consistent quality service when both the organization's employees and the customers themselves can affect the service outcome?

SERVICE MARKETING MIX

The preceding questions are some of the many raised by managers and marketers of services that will be addressed throughout the text through a variety of tools and strategies. Sometimes these tools are adaptations of traditional marketing tools, as with the service marketing mix presented here. Other times they are new, as in the case of service blueprinting presented in Chapter 8.

Traditional Marketing Mix

One of the most basic concepts in marketing is the *marketing mix,* defined as the elements an organization controls that can be used to satisfy or communicate with customers. The traditional marketing mix is composed of the four Ps: *product, place* (distribution), *promotion,* and *price.* These elements appear as core decision variables in any marketing text or marketing plan. The notion of a mix implies that all the variables are interrelated and depend on each other to some extent. Further, the marketing mix philosophy implies an optimal mix of the four factors for a given market segment at a given point in time.

Key strategy decision areas for each of the four Ps are captured in the top four groups in Table 1.3. Careful management of product, place, promotion, and price will clearly also be essential to the successful marketing of services. However, the strategies for the four Ps require some modifications when applied to services. For example, traditionally promotion is thought of as involving decisions related to sales, advertising, sales promotions, and publicity. In services these factors are also important, but because many services are produced and consumed simultaneously, service delivery people (such as clerks, ticket takers, nurses, and phone personnel) are involved in real-time promotion of the service even if their jobs are typically defined in terms of the operational functions they perform.

TABLE 1.3
Expanded Marketing Mix for Services

Product	Place	Promotion	Price
Physical good features	Channel type	Promotion blend	Flexibility
Quality level	Exposure	Salespeople	Price level
Accessories	Intermediaries	Selection	Terms
Packaging	Outlet locations	Training	Differentiation
Warranties	Transportation	Incentives	Discounts
Product lines	Storage	Advertising	Allowances
Branding	Managing channels	Media types	
		Types of ads	
		Sales promotion	
		Publicity	
		Internet/Web strategy	

People	Physical Evidence	Process
Employees	Facility design	Flow of activities
Recruiting	Equipment	Standardized
Training	Signage	Customized
Motivation	Employee dress	Number of steps
Rewards	Web pages	Simple
Teamwork	Other tangibles	Complex
Customers	Reports	Customer involvement
Education	Business cards	
Training	Statements	
	Guarantees	

Expanded Mix for Services

Because services are usually produced and consumed simultaneously, customers are often present in the firm's factory, interact directly with the firm's personnel, and are actually part of the service production process. Also, because services are intangible, customers will often be looking for any tangible cue to help them understand the nature of the service experience. For example, in the hotel industry the design and decor of the hotel as well as the appearance and attitudes of its employees will influence customer perceptions and experiences.

Acknowledgment of the importance of these additional variables has led service marketers to adopt the concept of an *expanded marketing mix* for services shown in the three remaining groups in Table 1.3.[33] In addition to the traditional four Ps, the services marketing mix includes *people, physical evidence,* and *process.*

> **People** All human actors who play a part in service delivery and thus influence the buyer's perceptions: namely, the firm's personnel, the customer, and other customers in the service environment.

All the human actors participating in the delivery of a service provide cues to the customer regarding the nature of the service itself. Their attitudes and behaviors, how these people are dressed, and their personal appearance all influence the customer's perceptions of the service. In fact, for some services, such as consulting, counseling, teaching, and other professional relationship–based services, the provider *is* the service. In other cases the contact person may play what appears to be a relatively small part in service delivery—for instance, a cable service installer, an airline baggage handler, or an equipment delivery dispatcher. Yet research suggests that even these providers may be the focal point of service encounters that can prove critical for the organization.

In many service situations, customers themselves can also influence service delivery, thus affecting service quality and their own satisfaction. For example, a client of a consulting company can influence the quality of service received by providing needed and timely information and by implementing recommendations provided by the consultant. Similarly, health care patients greatly affect the quality of service they receive when they either comply or do not comply with health regimens prescribed by the provider.

Customers not only influence their own service outcomes, but they can influence other customers as well. In a theater, at a ballgame, in a classroom, or online, customers can influence the quality of service received by others—either enhancing or detracting from other customers' experiences.

> **Physical evidence** The environment in which the service is delivered and where the firm and customer interact, as well as any tangible components that facilitate performance or communication of the service.

The physical evidence of service includes all the tangible representations of the service such as brochures, letterhead, business cards, reports, signage, equipment, and web pages. In some cases it includes the physical facility where the service is offered—the "servicescape"—for example, a retail bank branch facility. In other cases, such as telecommunication services, the physical facility is irrelevant. In this case other tangibles such as billing statements and appearance of the service vehicle and installer may be important indicators of quality. Especially when consumers have little on which to judge the actual quality of service, they will rely on these cues, just as they rely on the cues provided by the people and the service process. Physical evidence cues provide excellent opportunities for the firm to send consistent and strong messages regarding the organization's purpose, the intended market segments, and the nature of the service.

Process   The procedures, mechanisms, and flow of activities by which the service is delivered—the service delivery and operating systems.

The delivery steps that the customer experiences, or the operational flow of the service, also give customers evidence on which to judge the service. Some services are very complex, requiring the customer to follow a complicated and extensive series of actions to complete the process. Highly bureaucratized services frequently follow this pattern, and the logic of the steps involved often escapes the customer. Another distinguishing characteristic of the process that can provide evidence to the customer is whether the service follows a production-line/standardized approach or whether the process is an empowered/customized one. None of these characteristics of the service is inherently better or worse than another. Rather, the point is that these process characteristics are another form of evidence used by the customer to judge service. For example, two successful airline companies, Southwest and Singapore Airlines, follow extremely different process models. Southwest is a no-frills (no food, no assigned seats), low-priced airline that offers frequent, relatively short domestic flights. All the evidence it provides is consistent with its vision and market position, as illustrated in Exhibit 1.2. Singapore Airlines, on the other hand, focuses on the business traveler and is concerned with meeting individual traveler needs. Thus, its process is highly customized to the individual, and employees are empowered to provide nonstandard service when needed. Both airlines have been very successful.

The three new marketing mix elements (people, physical evidence, and process) are included in the marketing mix as separate elements because they are particularly salient for services, they are within the control of the firm and any or all of them may influence the customer's initial decision to purchase a service as well as the customer's level of satisfaction and repurchase decisions. The traditional elements as well as the new marketing mix elements will be explored in depth in future chapters.

STAYING FOCUSED ON THE CUSTOMER

A critical theme running throughout the text is *customer focus*. In fact, the subtitle of the book is "integrating customer focus across the firm." From the firm's point of view, this means that all strategies are developed with an eye on the customer, and all implementations are carried out with an understanding of their impact on the customer. From a practical perspective, decisions regarding new services and communication plans will integrate the customer's point of view; operations and human resource decisions will be considered in terms of their impact on customers. All the tools, strategies, and frameworks included in this text have customers at their foundation. The service marketing mix just described is clearly an important tool that addresses the uniqueness of services, keeping the customer at the center.

In this text, we also view customers as assets to be valued, developed, and retained. The strategies and tools we offer thus focus on customer relationship building and loyalty as opposed to a more transactional focus in which customers are viewed as one-time revenue producers. This text looks at customer relationship management not as a software program but as an entire architecture or business philosophy. Every chapter in the text can be considered a component needed to build a complete customer relationship management approach.

Southwest Airlines occupies a solid position in the minds of U.S. air travelers as a reliable, convenient, fun, low-fare, no-frills airline. Translated, this position means high value—a position reinforced by all elements of Southwest's service marketing mix. It has maintained this position consistently for more than 40 years while making money every year; no other U.S. airline comes close to this record.

Success has come for a number of reasons. One is the airline's low cost structure. It flies only one type of plane (Boeing 737s), which lowers costs because of the fuel efficiency of the aircraft itself combined with the ability to standardize maintenance and operational procedures. The airline also keeps its costs down by not serving meals, having no preassigned seats, and keeping employee turnover very low. Herb Kelleher (president of Southwest from its inception until 2001, and subsequently serving as chairman) was famous for his belief that employees come first, not customers. The Dallas-based carrier has managed to be the low-cost provider and a preferred employer while enjoying high levels of customer satisfaction and strong customer loyalty. Southwest Airlines has the best customer service record in the airline industry and has won the industry's "Triple Crown" for best baggage handling, best on-time performance, and best customer complaint statistics many times.

Observing Southwest Airlines' success, it is clear that all of its marketing mix elements are aligned around its highly successful market position. The three traditional service marketing mix elements all strongly reinforce the value image of the airline:

- **People** Southwest uses its people and customers very effectively to communicate its position. Employees are unionized, yet they are trained to have fun, are allowed to define what "fun" means, and are given authority to do what it takes to make flights lighthearted and enjoyable. People are hired at Southwest for their attitudes; technical skills can be and are trained. And they are the most productive workforce in the U.S. airline industry. Customers also are included in the atmosphere of fun, and many get into the act by joking with the crew and each other and by flooding the airline with letters expressing their satisfaction.
- **Process** The service delivery process at Southwest also reinforces its position. There are no assigned

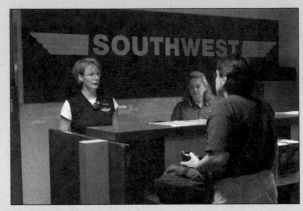

Southwest Airlines employee serving a customer.

seats on the aircraft, so passengers line up and are "herded" by assigned groups and numbers onto the plane, where they jockey for seats. With very few exceptions, the airline does not transfer baggage to connecting flights on other airlines. Food is not served in flight. In all, the process is very efficient, standardized, and low-cost, allowing for quick turnaround and low fares. Customers are very much part of the service process, taking on their roles willingly.

- **Physical evidence** All the tangibles associated with Southwest further reinforce the market position. Employees dress casually, wearing shorts in the summer to reinforce the "fun" and further emphasize the airline's commitment to its employees' comfort. No in-flight meal service confirms the low-price image through the absence of tangibles—no food. Because many people joke about airline food, its absence for many is not viewed as a value detractor. Southwest's simple, easy-to-use website is yet another form of consistent, tangible evidence that supports the airline's strong positioning and reinforces its image.

The consistent positioning using the service marketing mix reinforces the unique image in the customer's mind, giving Southwest Airlines its high-value position.

Source: K. Freiberg and J. Freiberg, *Nuts! Southwest Airlines' Crazy Recipe for Business and Personal Success* (Austin, TX: Bard Press, 1996); K. Labich, "Is Herb Kelleher America's Best CEO?" *Fortune,* May 2, 1994; H. Kelleher and K. Brooker, "The Chairman of the Board Looks Back," *Fortune,* May 28, 2001, pp. 62–76; J. H. Gitell, *The Southwest Airlines Way* (New York: McGraw-Hill, 2003).

Summary

This chapter has set the stage for further learning about services marketing by presenting information on changes in the world economy and business practice that have driven the focus on service: the fact that services dominate the modern economies of the world; the focus on service as a competitive business imperative; specific needs of the deregulated and professional service industries; the role of new service concepts growing from technological advances; and the realization that the characteristics of services result in unique challenges and opportunities. The chapter presented a broad definition of services as deeds, processes, and performances, and it drew distinctions among pure service, value-added service, customer service, and derived service.

Building on this fundamental understanding of the service economy, the chapter presents the key characteristics of services that underlie the need for distinct strategies and concepts for managing service businesses. These basic characteristics are that services are intangible, heterogeneous, produced and consumed simultaneously, and perishable. Because of these characteristics, service managers face a number of challenges in marketing, including the complex problem of how to deliver quality services consistently.

The chapter ended by describing two themes that provide the foundation for future chapters: the expanded marketing mix for services and customer focus as a unifying theme. The remainder of the text focuses on exploring the unique opportunities and challenges faced by organizations that sell and deliver services and on developing solutions that will help you become an effective service champion and manager.

Discussion Questions

1. What distinguishes service offerings from customer service? Provide specific examples.
2. How is technology changing the nature of customer service and service offerings?
3. What are the basic characteristics of services compared with goods? What are the implications of these characteristics for IBM Global Service, for Southwest Airlines, or for the company you work for?
4. One of the underlying frameworks for the text is the expanded marketing mix for services. Discuss why each of the three new mix elements (process, people, and physical evidence) is included. How might each of these communicate with or help to satisfy an organization's customers?
5. Think of a service job you have had or currently have. How effective, in your opinion, was or is the organization in managing the elements of the service marketing mix?
6. Again, think of a service job you have had or currently have. How did or does the organization handle relevant challenges listed in Table 1.2?
7. How can quality service be used in a manufacturing context for competitive advantage? Think of your answer to this question in the context of automobiles, computers, or some other manufactured product you have purchased.

Exercises

1. Roughly calculate your budget for an average month. What percentage of your budget goes for services versus goods? Do the services you purchase have value? In what sense? If you had to cut back on your expenses, what would you cut out?

2. Visit two local retail service providers that you believe are positioned very differently (such as Kmart and Nordstrom, or Burger King and a fine restaurant). From your own observations, compare their strategies on the elements of the services marketing mix.

3. Try a service you have never tried before on the Internet or on your smart phone. Analyze the benefits of this service. Was enough information provided to make the service easy to use? How would you compare this service to other methods of obtaining the same benefits?

Notes

1. "Hiding in Plain Sight: Service Innovation, a New Priority for Chief Executives," IBM Corporation, IBM Institute for Business Value, 2006, www.ibm.com/iibv; D. Kirkpatrick, "Inside Sam's $100 Billion Growth Machine," *Fortune,* June 14, 2004, pp. 80–98; W. M. Bulkeley, "These Days, Big Blue Is About Big Services Not Just Big Boxes," *The Wall Street Journal,* June 11, 2001, p. A1; A. Radding, "How IBM Is Applying Science to the World of Service," *Consulting Magazine,*" May 2006; J. Bramante, R. Frank, and J. Dolan, "IBM 2000–2010: Continuously Transforming the Corporation While Delivering Performance," *Strategy and Leadership* 38, no. 3 (2010), pp. 35–43.

2. D. Brady, "Why Service Stinks," *BusinessWeek,* October 23, 2000, pp. 118–128.

3. www.theacsi.org.

4. J. B. Quinn, J. J. Baruch, and P. C. Paquette, "Technology in Services," *Scientific American* 257, no. 6 (December 1987), pp. 50–58.

5. S. L. Vargo and R. F. Lusch, "Evolving to a New Dominant Logic for Marketing," *Journal of Marketing* 68 (January 2004), pp. 1–17; R. F. Lusch and S. L. Vargo (eds.), *The Service-Dominant Logic of Marketing: Dialog, Debate, and Directions* (New York: M. E. Sharpe, 2006); *Journal of the Academy of Marketing Science,* Special Issue or the Service-Dominant Logic, Winter 2008.

6. W. M. Cox, "An Order of Prosperity to Go," *The New York Times,* February 17, 2010.

7. M. Sawhney, S. Balasubramanian, and V. V. Krishnan, "Creating Growth with Services," *Sloan Management Review,* 45 (Winter 2004), pp. 34–43.

8. For research on the topic of goods firms transitioning to services, see: R. Oliva and R. Kallenberg, "Managing the Transition from Products to Services," *International Journal of Service Industry Management* 14, no. 2 (2003), pp. 160–172; W. A. Neu and S. W. Brown, "Forming Successful Business-to-Business Services in Goods-Dominant Firms," *Journal of Service Research,* 8 (August 2005), pp. 3–17; W. Reinartz and W. Ulaga, "How to Sell Services More Profitably," *Harvard Business Review,* 86 (May 2008), pp. 90–96; A. Gustafsson, S. Brax, and L. Witell (eds), "Service Infusion in Manufacturing Industries," special issue of the *Journal of Service Management* 21, no. 5 (2010). S. W. Brown, A. Gustafsson, and L. Witell, "Service Logic: Transforming Product-Focused Businesses," Center for Services Leadership, white paper 2011, www.wpcarey.asu.edu/csl. V. A. Zeithaml, S. W. Brown, and M. J. Bitner, "The Service Continuum: Delineating a Conceptual Domain for Researchers and Managers," working paper, Center for Services Leadership, Arizona State University, 2011.

9. R. H. K. Vietor, *Contrived Competition* (Cambridge, MA: Harvard University Press, 1994).

10. L. Berry, *Discovering the Soul of Service* (New York: The Free Press, 1999).

11. R. T. Rust, C. Moorman, and P. R. Dickson, "Getting Return on Quality: Revenue Expansion, Cost Reduction, or Both?" *Journal of Marketing* 66 (October 2002), pp. 7–24.

12. J. L. Heskett, T. O. Jones, G. W. Loveman, W. E. Sasser Jr., and L. A. Schlesinger, "Putting the Service–Profit Chain to Work," *Harvard Business Review,* 72 (March–April 1994), pp. 164–174.

13. E. W. Anderson and V. Mittal, "Strengthening the Satisfaction–Profit Chain," *Journal of Service Research* 3 (November 2000), pp. 107–120; S. Gupta, and V. A. Zeithaml, "Customer Metrics and Their Impact on Financial Performance," *Marketing Science* (December 2006), pp. 718–739.

14. C. Fornell, S. Mithias, F. V. Morgeson III, and M. S. Krishnan, "Customer Satisfaction and Stock Prices; High Returns, Low Risk," *Journal of Marketing,* 70 (January 2006), pp. 3–14; "Economic Indicator," www.theacsi.org, accessed January 10, 2011.

15. C. Fishman, "But Wait, You Promised . . . ," *Fast Company,* April 2001, pp. 116–127.

16. D. Brady, "Why Service Stinks," *BusinessWeek,* October 23, 2000, pp. 116–128; P. Noonan, "We Pay Them to Be Rude to Us," *The Wall Street Journal,* August 14–15, 2010, p. A11.

17. www.theacsi.org, accessed January 10, 2011.

18. L. P. Willcocks and R. Plant, "Getting from Bricks to Clicks," *Sloan Management Review,* 42 (Spring 2001), pp. 50–59.

19. B. Kiviat, "How a Man on a Mission (and a Harley) Reinvented Banking," *Time,* June 25, 2007, pp. 45–46.

20. "The Social Life of Health Information, 2011," Pew Internet and American Life Project, www.pewinternet.org, accessed, July 7, 2011.

21. M. J. Bitner, S. W. Brown, and M. L. Meuter, "Technology Infusion in Service Encounters," *Journal of the Academy of Marketing Science* 28 (Winter 2000), pp. 138–149.

22. M. J. Bitner, "Self-Service Technologies: What Do Customers Expect?" *Marketing Management,* 10 (Spring 2001), pp. 10–11.

23. R. Hallowell, "Service in E-Commerce: Findings from Exploratory Research," Harvard Business School, Module Note, N9-800-418, May 31, 2000.

24. D. G. Mick and S. Fournier, "Paradoxes of Technology: Consumer Cognizance, Emotions, and Coping Strategies," *Journal of Consumer Research* 25 (September 1998), pp. 123–147.

25. A. Parasuraman and C. L. Colby, *Techno-Ready Marketing: How and Why Your Customers Adopt Technology* (New York: The Free Press, 2001).

26. "Customer Care in a New World," McKinsey & Company, 2001.

27. Discussion of these issues is found in many services marketing publications. The discussion here is based on V. A. Zeithaml, A. Parasuraman, and L. L. Berry, "Problems and Strategies in Services Marketing," *Journal of Marketing* 49 (Spring 1985), pp. 33–46. For another viewpoint on the subject of goods vs. services, see: C. Lovelock and E. Gummesson, "Whither Services Marketing? In Search of a New Paradigm and Fresh Perspectives," *Journal of Service Research,* 7 (August 2004), pp. 20–41.

28. For research supporting the idea of goods–services continua, see D. Iacobucci, "An Empirical Examination of Some Basic Tenets in Services: Goods–Services

Continua," in *Advances in Services Marketing and Management,* T. A. Swartz, D. E. Bowen, and S. W. Brown eds. (Greenwich, CT: JAI Press, 1992), vol. 1, pp. 23–52.

29. S. L. Vargo and R. F. Lusch, "The Four Service Marketing Myths," *Journal of Service Research* 6 (May 2004), pp. 324–335.

30. H. T. Keh and J. Pang, "Customer Reactions to Service Separation," *Journal of Marketing,* 74 (March 2010), pp. 55–70.

31. P. Nelson, "Information and Consumer Behavior," *Journal of Political Economy,* 78, no. 20 (1970), pp. 311–329.

32. M. R. Darby and E. Karni, "Free Competition and the Optimal Amount of Fraud," *Journal of Law and Economics,* 16 (April 1973), pp. 67–86.

33. B. H. Booms and M. J. Bitner, "Marketing Strategies and Organizational Structures for Service Firms," in *Marketing of Services,* J. H. Donnelly and W. R. George eds. (Chicago: American Marketing Association, 1981), pp. 47–51.

Chapter Two

Conceptual Framework of the Book: The Gaps Model of Service Quality

This chapter's objectives are to

1. Introduce the framework, called the gaps model of service quality, used to organize this textbook.
2. Demonstrate that the gaps model is a useful framework for understanding service quality in an organization.
3. Demonstrate that the most critical service quality gap to close is the customer gap, the difference between customer expectations and perceptions.
4. Show that four gaps that occur in companies, which we call provider gaps, are collectively responsible for the customer gap.
5. Identify the factors responsible for each of the four provider gaps.

Service Quality at The Oaks at Ojai

Nestled in the sunny Ojai Valley about 90 minutes north of Los Angeles is an award-winning family-owned fitness spa that contradicts the spa stereotype. It is not a fat farm where overweight guests starve to lose weight. It is not a spot to spend endless hours getting beauty treatments, although the standard ones are available. Instead, The Oaks at Ojai is an understated and unpretentious—yet exceedingly charming—health and fitness destination that commands a 67 percent guest return rate. *Travel and Leisure Magazine* named it one of the 10 best destination spas in the world. *Spa Finder Magazine* heralded it as the 2009 Reader's Choice. *Spa Magazine* readers voted it in the top five for favorite affordable spa, favorite spa for cuisine, favorite spa for traveling solo, and favorite destination spa in the United States. In sum, The Oaks at Ojai is America's Best Spa Value. A full two-thirds of the spa's guests are repeat

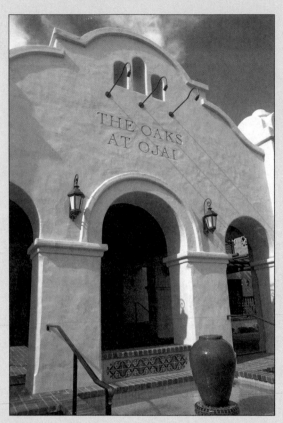

The Oaks at Ojai Spa.

visitors, and they claim that their experience is unsurpassed by all other spas. Remarkably, employee turnover is also less than half of the rest of the industry.

What makes The Oaks at Ojai excel among competitors—keeping customers and retaining employees? It is not just the healthy food, although the low-fat, 1,000–1,200-per-day menus are both filling and delicious. It is not just the 12 exercise classes per day (including Zumba dancing, weight training, hula hooping, belly dancing, and muscle conditioning), the biking, the swimming, or the vigorous mountain hikes in the foothill terrain of the Ojai Valley. Instead, The Oaks excels at creating a well-managed service experience that puts guests at ease, educates them in healthy living, and challenges them to simultaneously have fun and get fit.

The inspiration for The Oaks experience is its founder, 75-year-old Sheila Cluff, formerly a competitive ice skater and a woman so fit that she can do 50 full push-ups at a time. Sheila opened The Oaks in the 1970s and still teaches classes and leads mountain hikes. Meeting Sheila, in fact, is a major attraction of The Oaks, and she makes a point of greeting and personally motivating each guest. Her staff members, many of whom have worked for her for 30 years, are committed to delivering the best service possible. That begins with check-in, where the friendly staffers greet guests as if they were old friends, typically remembering their names. Following check-in, guests are given schedules, oriented to the spa's activities and features, and encouraged to complete their own schedules for their stay.

Every event happens on time and with precision. The exercise room door closes exactly on the hour, and the lights in the dining rooms turn on exactly at the scheduled beginning of meals. Each meal is delivered quickly and at the right temperature for guests, and special requests are honored accurately. A 3 p.m. snack of vegetables and dip appears right at 3, as does the 20-calorie fruit smoothie at 5 p.m. If at any point a guest has an issue, responsive staffers correct it quickly and willingly.

Each employee has been selected and trained with care. The exercise leaders are the best in southern California, each an expert in her specialty. Guest dancers from Texas are brought in to teach country line dancing, and novel artistic dancers educate guests in yoga dancing and dance movement. Experts on healthy living and cooking speak at special seminars in the evenings. Massage therapists, needed to smooth out sore muscles, represent a wide array of techniques. Even the cleaning staff and bus boys are well trained and skilled in their jobs.

Just before leaving, each guest is asked to complete a questionnaire to provide his or her individual feedback. Questions are specific, and management meets weekly to review each one, taking care to make improvements suggested by guests. On returning home, each guest who completed a questionnaire receives a letter of thanks and a promise to work on any issues mentioned.

Because of its loyal following, The Oaks does not need to spend money on advertising. Instead, it depends on word of mouth and publicity, both of which bring many new and former guests to fill the spa year-round.

Effective service marketing is a complex undertaking that involves many different strategies, skills, and tasks. Executives of service organizations have long been confused about how to approach this complicated topic in an organized manner. This textbook is designed around one approach: viewing services in a structured, integrated way called the *gaps model of service quality.*[1] This model positions the key concepts, strategies, and decisions in services marketing and will be used to guide the structure of the rest of this book; sections of the book are tied to each of the gaps described in this chapter.

THE CUSTOMER GAP

The *customer gap* is the difference between customer expectations and perceptions (see Figure 2.1). Customer expectations are standards or reference points that customers bring into the service experience, whereas customer perceptions are subjective assessments of actual service experiences. Customer expectations often consist of what a customer believes should or will happen. For example, when you visit an expensive restaurant, you expect a high level of service, one that is considerably superior to the level you would expect in a fast-food restaurant. Closing the gap between what customers expect and what they perceive is critical to delivering quality service; it forms the basis for the gaps model.

Because customer satisfaction and customer focus are so critical to the competitiveness of firms, any company interested in delivering quality service must begin with a clear understanding of its customers. This understanding is relatively easy for an organization as small as The Oaks at Ojai but very difficult for a large organization in which managers are not in direct contact with customers. For this reason, we will devote the first part of the textbook to describing the relevant customer concepts, so that the focus of everything can relate back to these concepts. Considerable evidence exists that consumer evaluation processes differ for goods and services and that these differences affect the way service providers market their organizations. Unfortunately, much of what is known and written about consumer evaluation processes pertains specifically to goods.

The sources of customer expectations are marketer-controlled factors (such as pricing, advertising, and sales promises) as well as factors that the marketer has limited ability to affect (innate personal needs, word-of-mouth communications, and competitive offerings). In a perfect world, expectations and perceptions would be identical: customers would perceive that they have received what they thought they would and should. In practice these concepts are often, separated by some distance. Broadly, it is the goal of services marketing

FIGURE 2.1
The Customer Gap

to bridge this distance, and we will devote virtually the entire textbook to describing strategies and practices designed to close this customer gap. We will describe customer expectations in detail in Chapter 3 and customer perceptions in Chapter 4.

THE PROVIDER GAPS

To close the all-important customer gap, the gaps model suggests that four other gaps—the *provider gaps*—need to be closed. These gaps occur within the organization providing the service (hence the term *provider gaps*) and include

Gap 1: The listening gap
Gap 2: The service design and standards gap
Gap 3: The service performance gap
Gap 4: The communication gap

The rest of this chapter is devoted to a description of the full gaps model.

Provider Gap 1: the Listening Gap

Provider gap 1, the *listening gap,* is the difference between customer expectations of service and company understanding of those expectations. The primary reason that many firms do not meet customers' expectations is that the firms lack an accurate understanding of exactly what those expectations are. Many reasons exist for managers not being aware of what customers expect: they may not interact directly with customers, they may be unwilling to ask about expectations, or they may be unprepared to address them. When people with the authority to set priorities and the responsibility to do so do not fully understand customers' service expectations, they may trigger a chain of bad decisions and suboptimal resource allocations that result in perceptions of poor service quality. In this text, we broaden the responsibility for the first provider gap from managers alone to any employee in the organization with the authority to change or influence service policies and procedures. In today's changing organizations, the authority to make adjustments in service delivery is often delegated to empowered teams and frontline people. In business-to-business situations, in particular, account teams make their own decisions about how to address their clients' unique expectations.

Figure 2.2 shows the key factors responsible for provider gap 1, the listening gap. An inadequate *customer research orientation* is one of the critical factors. When management or empowered employees do not acquire accurate information about customers' expectations, this gap is large. Formal and informal methods to capture information about customer expectations must be developed through customer research. Techniques involving a variety of traditional research approaches—among them customer interviews, survey research, complaint systems, and customer panels—must be used to stay close to the customer. More innovative techniques, such as structured brainstorming and service quality gap analysis, are often needed. This chapter's Global Feature discusses one of these innovative techniques, which IKEA and other companies have used to identify customer expectations.

Another key factor that is related to the listening gap is lack of *upward communication.* Frontline employees often know a great deal about customers; if management is not in contact with frontline employees and does not understand what they know, the gap widens.

Also related to the listening gap is a lack of company strategies to retain customers and strengthen relationships with them, an approach called *relationship marketing.* When organizations have strong relationships with existing customers, provider gap 1 is less likely to occur. Relationship marketing is distinct from transactional marketing,

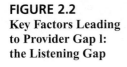

FIGURE 2.2
Key Factors Leading to Provider Gap l: the Listening Gap

which is a more conventional emphasis on acquiring new customers rather than on retaining them. Relationship marketing has always been a practice of wise business-to-business firms (such as IBM and General Electric) that recognize that clients have the potential to spend more with them if they provide excellent service. Other business-to-business firms, and many companies that sell to end-customers, often take a short-term view and see each sale as a transaction. When companies focus too much on attracting new customers, they may fail to understand the changing needs and expectations of their current customers. Technology affords companies the ability to acquire and integrate vast quantities of customer data, which can be used to build relationships. Frequent flyer travel programs conducted by airlines, car rental companies, and hotels are among the most familiar programs of this type.

The final key factor associated with provider gap 1 is lack of *service recovery.* Even the strongest companies, with the best of intentions and clear understanding of their customers' expectations, sometimes fail. It is critical for an organization to understand the importance of service recovery—why people complain, what they expect when they complain, and how to develop effective service recovery strategies for dealing with inevitable service failures. Such strategies might involve a well-defined complaint-handling procedure and an emphasis on empowering employees to react on the spot, in real time, to fix the failure; other times it involves a service guarantee or ways to compensate the customer for the unfulfilled promise.

To address the factors in the listening gap, this text will cover topics that include how to understand customers through multiple research strategies (Chapter 5), how to build strong relationships and understand customer needs over time (Chapter 6), and how to implement recovery strategies when things go wrong (Chapter 7). Through these strategies, this first gap can be minimized.

Provider Gap 2: the Service Design and Standards Gap

Accurate perceptions of customers' expectations are necessary, but not sufficient, for delivering superior service. Another prerequisite is the presence of service designs and performance standards that reflect those accurate perceptions. A recurring theme in service companies is the difficulty experienced in translating customer expectations into

Finding out what customers expect is the first step in closing all the gaps in an organization to provide service excellence. In Chapter 5 we will talk about many ways that companies determine customer perceptions, including customer surveys and complaints, but understanding what customers expect can often be more challenging. Putting customers in the "wish mode" is an innovative approach to closing gap 1 that proved successful for IKEA, the world's largest furniture retailer, when it opened its Chicago retail outlet. In this approach, nine groups of a dozen customers each were asked to dream up their ideal IKEA shopping experience. They were told to pretend that all IKEA stores had been destroyed and that new ones had to be designed from scratch. How would the store look? What would the shopping experience be like? Jason Magidson, who helped IKEA create the process, reported that customers responded with statements like the following:

> "I never feel disoriented because I always know exactly where I am in relation to every department."

> "If I am buying one item, all of the other items that go with it are nearby."

> "Shopping is a pleasant, relaxing experience."

Even though they were not technical experts, customers were asked to actually draw up a design for a store that would satisfy their needs.

What is significant about IKEA's approach is not just that the company asked customers what they expected but that it subsequently incorporated these expectations into the service design for the store. Designers created a multistory octagonal building with an atrium in the center that formed a home base for shoppers, addressing their concern about being able to find items easily. In keeping with another customer expectation, items were grouped together with related products. When shoppers were tired or hungry, they could go to the cafeteria-style restaurant on the upper floor that served Swedish food. IKEA's customers were so satisfied with the store (85 percent rated it as "excellent" or "very good") that they returned more and spent about an hour longer than they did in other IKEA stores. These actions close gap 2 because service design was based on customer expectations.

IKEA has done an excellent job of closing all four provider gaps. The company's supplier network is carefully chosen and managed to ensure quality and consistency. Despite the fact that the company has stores in more than 30 countries, it keeps standards, designs, and approaches very consistent everywhere, thereby reducing the service design and standards gap. The company also makes important changes to standards when necessary. In 2006, the company took a major step to address a customer need to reduce long wait times. When company managers realized that wait times were so long that customers were leaving the stores without paying for their items because of congestion at checkout, they implemented a "line busting" initiative using handheld technology. In peak times, extra retail associates now roam the checkout area and invite credit card customers to step out of line and pay with a handheld unit and get a receipt from a mobile printer.

Servicescapes—the indoor and outdoor physical environments—are unique and customer focused, further closing gap 2. IKEA is also well known for its strong employee culture and careful hiring and training—factors that help reduce gap 3. In Chapter 12, we will tell you about another way the company closes gap 3: its innovative service concept that involves customers in the delivery, assembly, and creation of its products. To accomplish this service, the company educates its customers thoroughly with its scriptlike catalogs, thereby helping to close gap 4.

Sources: Jason Magidson and Gregg Brandyberry, "Putting Customers in the 'Wish Mode,'" *Harvard Business Review,* September 2001, pp. 26–27; "Who You Gonna Call?" *Chain Store Age,* January 2006, p. 8.

service quality specifications that employees can understand and execute. These problems are reflected in provider gap 2, the difference between company understanding of customer expectations and the development of customer-driven service designs and standards. Customer-driven standards are different from the conventional performance standards that companies establish for service in that they are based on pivotal customer requirements that are visible to and measured by customers. They are operations standards set to correspond to customer expectations and priorities rather than to company concerns such as productivity or efficiency.

As shown in Figure 2.3, provider gap 2—which we call the *service design and standards gap*—exists in service organizations for a variety of reasons. Those people responsible for setting standards, typically management, sometimes believe that customer expectations are unreasonable or unrealistic. They may also believe that the degree of variability inherent in service defies standardization and therefore that setting standards will not achieve the desired goal. Although some of these assumptions are valid in some situations, they are often only rationalizations of management's reluctance to tackle head-on the difficult challenges of creating service standards to deliver excellent service. Technology changes and improvements are particularly helpful in closing this gap, as the Technology Spotlight in this chapter describes.

Because services are intangible, they are difficult to describe and communicate. This difficulty becomes especially evident when new services are being developed. It is critical that all people involved (managers, frontline employees, and behind-the-scenes support staff) work with the same concepts of the new service, based on customer needs and expectations. For a service that already exists, any attempt to improve it will also suffer unless everyone has the same vision of the service and associated issues. One of the most important ways to avoid provider gap 2 is to clearly design services without oversimplification, incompleteness, subjectivity, and bias. To do so, tools are needed to ensure that new and existing services are developed and improved in as careful a manner as possible. Chapter 8 describes the tools that are most effective in *service development and design,* including service blueprinting, a unique tool for services.

The quality of service delivered by customer contact personnel is critically influenced by the standards against which they are evaluated and compensated. Standards signal to contact personnel what management priorities are and which types of performance really count. When service standards are absent or when the standards in place do not reflect

FIGURE 2.3
Key Factors Leading to Provider Gap 2: the Service Design and Standards Gap

customers' expectations, quality of service as perceived by customers is likely to suffer. When standards do reflect what customers expect, perceptions of the quality of service they receive are likely to be enhanced. Chapter 9 discusses the topic of *customer-defined service standards* and shows that if they are developed appropriately they can have a powerful positive impact on closing both provider gap 2 and the customer gap.

In Chapter 10 we focus on the roles of physical evidence in service design and in meeting customer expectations. By *physical evidence,* we mean everything from business cards to reports, signage, Internet presence, equipment, and facilities used to deliver the service. The *servicescape,* the physical setting where the service is delivered, is a particular focus of Chapter 10. Think of a restaurant, a hotel, a theme park, a health club, a hospital, or a school. The servicescape—the physical facility—is critical in these industries in terms of communicating about the service and making the entire experience pleasurable. In these cases the servicescape plays a variety of roles, from serving as a visual metaphor of what the company stands for to actually facilitating the activities of both consumers and employees. In Chapter 10 we explore the importance of physical evidence, the variety of roles it plays, and strategies for effectively designing physical evidence and the servicescape to meet customer expectations.

Provider Gap 3: the Service Performance Gap

Once service designs and standards are in place, it would seem that the firm is well on its way to delivering high-quality service. This assumption is true but is still not enough to deliver excellent service. The firm must have systems, processes, and people in place to ensure that service delivery actually matches (or is even better than) the designs and standards in place.

Provider gap 3—the *service performance gap*—is the discrepancy between the development of customer-driven service standards and actual service performance by company employees. Even when guidelines exist for performing services well and treating customers correctly, high-quality service performance is not a certainty. Standards must be backed by appropriate resources (people, systems, and technology) and must be enforced to be effective—that is, employees must be measured and compensated on the basis of performance along those standards. Thus, even when standards accurately reflect customers' expectations, if the company fails to provide support for those standards—if it does not facilitate, encourage, and require their achievement—standards do no good. When the level of service delivery falls short of the standards, it falls short of what customers expect as well. Narrowing the performance gap—by ensuring that all the resources needed to achieve the standards are in place—reduces the customer gap.

Research has identified many of the critical inhibitors to closing the service performance gap (see Figure 2.4). These factors include *employees* who do not clearly understand the roles they are to play in the company, employees who experience conflict between customers and company management, poor employee selection, inadequate technology, inappropriate compensation and recognition, and lack of empowerment and teamwork. These factors all relate to the company's human resource function and involve internal practices such as recruitment, training, feedback, job design, motivation, and organizational structure. To deliver better service performance, these issues must be addressed across functions (such as marketing and human resources).

Another important variable in provider gap 3 is the *customer.* Even if contact employees and intermediaries are 100 percent consistent in their service delivery, the uncontrollable variables of the customer can introduce variability in service delivery. If customers do not perform their roles appropriately—if, for example, they fail to provide all the information necessary to the provider or neglect to read and follow

FIGURE 2.4
**Key Factors Leading
to Provider Gap
3: the Service
Performance Gap**

Customer-driven service designs and standards

Gap 3

• *Deficiencies in human resource policies*
　Ineffective recruitment
　Role ambiguity and role conflict
　Poor employee–technology job fit
　Inappropriate evaluation and compensation systems
　Lack of empowerment, perceived control, and teamwork
• *Failure to match supply and demand*
　Failure to smooth peaks and valleys of demand
　Inappropriate customer mix
　Overreliance on price to smooth demand
• *Customers not fulfilling roles*
　Customers lack knowledge of their roles and responsibilities
　Customers negatively impact each other
• *Problems with service intermediaries*
　Channel conflict over objectives and performance
　Channel conflict over costs and rewards
　Difficulty controlling quality and consistency
　Tension between empowerment and control

Service delivery

instructions—service quality is jeopardized. Customers can also negatively influence the quality of service received by others if they are disruptive or take more than their share of a service provider's time. Understanding customer roles and how customers themselves can influence service delivery and outcomes is critical.

A third difficulty associated with provider gap 3 involves the challenge in delivering service through such *intermediaries* as retailers, franchisees, agents, and brokers. Because quality in service occurs in the human interaction between customers and service providers, company control over the service encounter is crucial, yet it rarely is fully possible. Most service (and many manufacturing) companies face an even more formidable task: attaining service excellence and consistency in the presence of intermediaries who represent them and interact with their customers yet are not under their direct control. Franchisers of services depend on their franchisees to execute service delivery as they have specified it. And it is that execution by the franchisee which the customer uses to evaluate the service quality of the company. With franchises and other types of intermediaries, someone other than the producer is responsible for the fulfillment of quality service. For this reason, a firm must develop ways to either control these intermediaries or motivate them to meet company goals.

Another issue in the service performance gap is the need in service firms to *synchronize demand and capacity*. Because services are perishable and cannot be inventoried, service companies frequently face situations of over- or underdemand. Lacking inventories to handle overdemand, companies lose sales when capacity is inadequate to handle customer needs. On the other hand, capacity is frequently underutilized in slow periods. Most service companies rely on operations strategies such as cross-training employees or varying the size of the employee pool to synchronize supply and demand. Marketing .strategies for managing demand—such as price changes, advertising, promotion, and alternative service offerings—can supplement approaches for managing supply.

Technology Spotlight Technology's Critical Impact on the Gaps Model of Service Quality

An early hallmark of services was the fact that they could not be provided remotely, that service was a local function provided in the intimate setting of a provider-customer relationship. Technology has relaxed this fundamental interpersonal, real-time requirement, resulting in increasing accessibility and globalization of services, which can now be delivered and consumed anytime, anywhere. Many of these changes were not anticipated or reflected in the initial development of the gaps model.

Technology—in particular, information technology—has dramatically influenced the nature of services themselves, how they are delivered, and the practice of service innovation and service management. Technology has had an impact on each of the gaps in the gaps model, as we will demonstrate.

TECHNOLOGY'S INFLUENCE ON THE CUSTOMER GAP

Technological advances have significantly influenced the customer gap. First, the nature of services themselves has changed. Now, many services are delivered by technology rather than in person by employees. Consider the personal photography industry. Not long ago, personal photos were taken by individuals, the film was processed by a service provider, and additional prints could be ordered and shared among friends and family. Putting together albums of photos and sharing photos with others was a labor-intensive process, often involving significant time, expense, and linking together of many different service providers. Now, individuals use digital cameras to take as many photos as they wish, and they can print, manage, and share their photos online. This is just one small example of the proliferation of self-service technologies that have changed consumers' lives.

Technology has also dramatically changed how customers learn about services. The ability to search the Web and view photos of service locations, compare prices, and even experience services through virtual tours has dramatically changed the amount and type of information customers have prior to purchasing services. The availability of this information has influenced their expectations and ability to compare and judge services. In earlier days, customers found it difficult to gather this type of information and lacked the ability to compare services as easily as they could for tangible goods that were displayed side-by-side in a retail store. To some extent, the Internet now provides this type of comparability for services.

TECHNOLOGY'S INFLUENCE ON PROVIDER GAP 1

The primary way technology has influenced provider gap 1 is in allowing firms to know their customers in ways not imagined in the past. Among the most powerful facilitators of these influences are marketing research conducted on the Internet (improving ways to listen to customers) and technology-powered customer relationship management, or CRM (facilitating relationship-building with thousands, even millions, of customers through database marketing).

One of the most intriguing technological innovations is online customer research, replacing traditional comment cards and intrusive telephone calls with cyber surveys that are challenging and even fun for consumers. The application is growing rapidly, and the reasons are obvious—Internet research has many benefits to marketers, including more willing respondents, the speed of collecting and analyzing data, equivalent or better data quality, the ability to target hard-to-reach populations such as high-income consumers, and the opportunity to use multimedia to present video and audio to give respondents a true sense of a service being researched. Internet research is also less expensive than traditional research—10 to 80 percent less expensive than other approaches. The Internet eliminates the postage, phone, labor, and printing costs that are typical with other survey approaches. Respondents also seem to complete Web-based surveys in half the time it would take an interviewer to conduct the survey, perhaps contributing to the lack of need for incentives.

TECHNOLOGY'S IMPACT ON PROVIDER GAP 2

The focus of the design and standards gap was on designing interpersonal services and real-time operational processes to meet customer expectations. The variability inherent in interpersonal services made designing and standardizing them quite difficult. There is now increasing focus on technology-enabled services and processes to close provider gap 2. Increasingly, customer expectations can be met through technology-enabled, highly standardized services provided on the Web. One example is book sales and services (just one of its many product lines) provided online by Amazon. Through its highly sophisticated technology infrastructure, the company is able to provide standardized ordering, payment, tracking, and recommendation services at the individual consumer level. Attempting to provide this level of service in a traditional book sales context to masses of people would be very idiosyncratic, inconsistent, and costly if it were done at the level Amazon performs online. Furthermore, technology has made Amazon's Kindle book downloading possible, allowing customers to read books as soon as they decide they want to purchase them.

Technology has been the basic force behind service innovations now taken for granted such as Internet-based information and transaction services and various smart services—for example the "connected car," smart meters for monitoring energy consumption, and remote health monitoring services. Internet-based companies like e-Bay and Facebook have sprung up, offering services previously unheard of or even imagined. And established companies have developed new services based on information technology. Advances in information technology are also making it possible for whole suites of services, including phone, Internet, video, photography, and e-mail, to be available through one device such as the iPhone and similar products.

Technology has also facilitated the development of new services to meet needs and expectations that weren't even conceived of in prior decades. In health care, the ability to monitor patient conditions remotely and to train physicians in simulated surgical techniques via video technology are just two additional examples of technology-based services that meet customer expectations in innovative ways.

TECHNOLOGY'S IMPACT ON PROVIDER GAP 3

Technological advances have allowed customer-contact employees to become more efficient and effective in serving customers. For example, today's technology allows Symantec customer service representatives to have several online "chats" with many customers simultaneously. In attempting to resolve customer problems or answer their questions regarding the company's software products (e.g., Norton Internet Security), technological tools allow an employee to remotely connect to a customer's computer to fix a problem. Such capability allows employees to resolve problems much faster (increasing employee efficiency) and generally creates a more satisfying customer experience. Thus, many firms explore ways that technology can be used to empower employees and close the service performance gap.

Technology has also empowered customers. Through technology, customers can be more involved in cocreating and even adding value to their service experience. 1Self-service technologies—services produced entirely by the customer without any direct involvement or interaction with the firm's employees—have also changed the way companies think about closing provider gap 3. These technologies are proliferating as companies see the potential cost savings and efficiencies that can be achieved, as well as potential sales growth, increased customer satisfaction, and competitive advantage. Medical websites allow patients access to information about particular diseases, drugs and drug interactions, and specific doctors and hospitals; in this case, technology enables patients to make more informed health care decisions. As these examples illustrate, such technological advances have facilitated customer participation in service delivery—changing the way that gap 3 is conceptualized and ultimately closed.

TECHNOLOGY'S IMPACT ON PROVIDER GAP 4

Traditional communication channels have been affected by technology infusion. There are a number of new channels through which service firms can communicate with their customers, including blogs, targeted e-mails, customer communities, and employee chat. The number of channels and modes of communication that must be integrated effectively have exploded, exacerbating the challenge of providing consistent messages across all of them. These new channels are not simply options that service firms can consider—more and more, they are becoming *expected* by customers as means of communication.

Online brand communities and easy/quick mass communication via the Internet are new channels that, whether provider or customer controlled, can influence customer expectations for service firms. While it is well known that word-of-mouth communication has always been especially important for services, these new avenues of peer-to-peer and customer-to-customer communication make word of mouth communication an even more important influence in setting expectations for services.

Technology also results in the potential for reaching out to customers around the globe in ways that were not possible in the not-so-distant past, when services were limited to local provision. The Internet itself knows no boundaries, and therefore information, customer service, and transactions can move across countries and continents, reaching any customer who has access to the Web.

Source: Mary Jo Bitner, Valarie A. Zeithaml, and Dwayne D. Gremler, "Technology's Critical Impact on the Gaps Model of Service Quality," in *The Handbook of Service Science,* Paul Maglio, Jim Spohrer and Cheryl Kieliszewski (eds.),: Springer, New York, NY, 2009.

We will discuss strategies to deal with the roles of employees in Chapter 11, customers in Chapter 12, and demand and capacity in Chapter 13.

Provider Gap 4: the Communication Gap

Provider gap 4, the *communication gap,* illustrates the difference between service delivery and the service provider's external communications. Promises made by a service company through its media advertising, sales force, and other communications may raise customer expectations, the standards against which customers assess service quality. The discrepancy between actual and promised services, therefore, can widen the customer gap. Broken promises can occur for many reasons: overpromising in advertising or personal selling, inadequate coordination between operations and marketing, and differences in policies and procedures across service outlets. Figure 2.5 shows the key factors that lead to the communication gap.

In addition to unduly elevating expectations through exaggerated claims, there are other, less obvious ways in which external communications influence customers' service quality assessments. Service companies frequently fail to capitalize on opportunities to educate customers to use services appropriately. They also neglect to manage customer expectations of what will be delivered in service transactions and relationships.

One of the major difficulties associated with provider gap 4 is that communications to consumers involve issues that cross organizational boundaries. Because service advertising promises what people do, and because what people do cannot be controlled the way machines that produce physical goods can be controlled, this type of communication involves functions other than the marketing department. This type of marketing is what we call *interactive marketing*—the marketing between contact people and customers—and it must be coordinated with the conventional types of *external marketing* used in product and service firms. When employees who promote the service do not fully understand the reality of service delivery, they are likely to make exaggerated promises or fail to communicate to

FIGURE 2.5
Key Factors Leading to Provider Gap 4: the Communication Gap

- *Lack of integrated services marketing communications*
  Tendency to view each external communication as independent
  Not including interactive marketing in communications plan
  Absence of strong internal marketing program
- *Ineffective management of customer expectations*
  Not managing customer expectation through all forms of communication
  Not adequately educating customers
- *Overpromising*
  Overpromising in advertising
  Overpromising in personal selling
  Overpromising through physical evidence cues
- *Inadequate horizontal communications*
  Insufficient communication between sales and operations
  Insufficient communication between advertising and operations
  Differences in policies and procedures across branches or units
- *Inappropriate pricing*
  High prices that raise customer expectations
  Prices that are not tied to customer perceptions of value

customers aspects of the service intended to serve them well. The result is poor service quality perceptions. Effectively coordinating actual service delivery with external communications, therefore, narrows the communications gap and favorably affects the customer gap.

Another issue in provider gap 4 is associated with the pricing of services. In packaged goods (and even in durable goods), customers possess enough price knowledge before purchase to be able to judge whether a price is fair or in line with competition. With services, customers often have no internal reference points for prices before purchase and consumption. Pricing strategies such as discounting, "everyday prices," and couponing obviously need to be different in service situations in which the customer has no initial sense of prices. Techniques for developing prices for services are more complicated than those for pricing tangible goods.

In summary, external communications—whether from marketing communications or pricing—can create a larger customer gap by raising expectations about service delivery. In addition to improving service delivery, companies must also manage all communications to customers, so that inflated promises do not lead to higher expectations. Chapter 16 will discuss integrated services marketing communications, and Chapter 15 will cover pricing to accomplish these objectives.

PUTTING IT ALL TOGETHER: CLOSING THE GAPS

The full conceptual model, shown in Figure 2.6, conveys a clear message to managers wishing to improve their quality of service: the key to closing the customer gap is to close provider gaps 1 through 4 and keep them closed. To the extent that one or more of provider gaps 1 through 4 exist, customers perceive service quality shortfalls. The gaps model of service quality serves as a framework for service organizations attempting to improve quality service and services marketing. The Strategy Insight provides a *service quality gaps audit* based on the model.

The model begins where the process of improving service quality begins: with an understanding of the nature and extent of the customer gap. Given the service organization's need to focus on the customer and to use knowledge about the customer to drive business strategy, this foundation of emphasis is warranted.

FIGURE 2.6
Gaps Model of Service Quality

Strategy Insight Using the Gaps Model to Assess an Organization's Service Strategy

The gaps model featured in this chapter and used as a framework for this textbook is a useful way to audit the service performance and capabilities of an organization. The model has been used by many companies as an assessment or service audit tool because it is comprehensive and offers a way for companies to examine all the factors that influence service quality. To use the tool, a company documents what it knows about each gap and the factors that affect the size of the gap. Although you will learn much more about each of these gaps throughout the book, we provide here a basic gaps audit. In Exercise 1 at the end of the chapter, we propose that you use this audit with a company to determine its service quality gaps. As practice, you could evaluate the Oaks at Ojai, the inn featured in the opening vignette, to see how its approaches work to close each of the gaps.

Service Quality Gaps Model Audit

For each of the following factors in the gaps, indicate the effectiveness of the organization on that factor. Use a 1 to 10 scale where 1 is "poor" and 10 is "excellent."

	1 = Poor 10 = Excellent
Customer Gap	
1. How well does the company understand customer expectations of service quality?	
2. How well does the company understand customer perceptions of service?	
Provider Gap I, the Listening Gap	
1. Market Research Orientation	
• Are the amount and type of market research adequate to understand customer expectations of service?	
• Does the company use this information in decisions about service provision?	
2. Upward Communication	
• Do managers and customers interact enough for management to know what customers expect?	
• Do contact people tell management what customers expect?	
3. Relationship Focus	
• To what extent does the company understand the expectations of different customer segments?	
• To what extent does the company focus on relationships with customers rather than transactions?	
4. Service Recovery	
• How effective are the service recovery efforts of the organization?	
• How well does the organization plan for service failures?	
Score for Provider Gap 1	
Provider Gap 2, the Service Design and Standards Gap	
5. Systematic Service Design	
• How effective is the company's service development process?	
• How well are new services defined for customers and employees?	
6. Presence of Customer-Defined Standards	
• How effective are the company's service standards?	
• Are they defined to correspond to customer expectations?	
• How effective is the process for setting and tracking service quality goals?	

	1 = Poor **10 = Excellent**

7. Appropriate Physical Evidence and Servicescape
- Are the company's physical facilities, equipment, and other tangibles appropriate to the service offering?
- Are the company's physical facilities, equipment, and other tangibles attractive and effective?

Score for Provider Gap 2

Provider Gap 3, the Service Performance Gap

8. Effective Human Resource Policies
- How effectively does the company recruit, hire, train, compensate, and empower employees?
- Is service quality delivery consistent across employees, teams, units, and branches?

9. Effective Role Fulfillment by Customers
- Do customers understand their roles and responsibilities?
- Does the company manage customers to fulfill their roles, especially customers that are incompatible?

10. Effective Alignment with Service Intermediaries
- How well are service intermediaries aligned with the company?
- Is there conflict over objectives and performance, costs and rewards?
- Is service quality delivery consistent across the outlets?

11. Alignment of Demand and Capacity
- How well is the company able to match supply with demand fluctuations?

Score for Provider Gap 3

Provider Gap 4, the Communication Gap

12. Integrated Services Marketing Communications
- How well do all company communications—including the interactions between company employees and customers—express the same message and level of service quality?
- How well does the company communicate to customers about what will be provided to them?
- Does the company avoid overpromising and overselling?
- How well do different parts of the organization communicate with each other, so that service quality equals what is promised?

13. Pricing
- Is the company careful not to price so high that customer expectations are raised?
- Does the company price in line with customer perceptions of value?

Score for Provider Gap 4

The score for each gap should be compared to the maximum score possible. Are particular gaps weaker than others? Which areas in each gap need attention? As you go through the rest of the book, we will provide more detail about how to improve the factors in each of the gaps.

Summary

This chapter presented the integrated gaps model of service quality (shown in Figure 2.6), a framework for understanding and improving service delivery. The entire text will be organized around this model of service quality, which focuses on five pivotal gaps in delivering and marketing service:

> *The customer gap:* Difference between customer expectations and perceptions
> *Provider gap 1:* the listening gap
> *Provider gap 2:* the service design and standards gap
> *Provider gap 3:* the service performance gap
> *Provider gap 4:* the communication gap

The gaps model positions the key concepts, strategies, and decisions in service marketing in a manner that begins with the customer and builds the organization's tasks around what is needed to close the gap between customer expectations and perceptions. The final chapter in the book, Chapter 16, discusses the financial implications of service quality, reviewing the research and company data that indicates linkages between service quality and financial performance.

Discussion Questions

1. Think about a service you receive. Is there a gap between your expectations and perceptions of that service? What do you expect that you do not receive?
2. Consider the "wish mode" discussion about IKEA. Think about a service that you receive regularly and put yourself in the wish mode. How would you change the service and the way it is provided?
3. If you were the manager of a service organization and wanted to apply the gaps model to improve service, which gap would you start with? Why? In what order would you proceed to close the gaps?
4. Can provider gap 4, the communication gap, be closed prior to closing any of the other three provider gaps? How?
5. Which of the four provider gaps do you believe is hardest to close? Why?

Exercises

1. Choose an organization to interview, and use the integrated gaps model of service quality as a framework. Ask the manager whether the organization suffers from any of the factors listed in the figures in this chapter. Which factor in each of Figures 2.2 through 2.5 does the manager consider the most troublesome? What does the company do to try to address the problems?
2. Use the Internet to locate the website of Disney, Marriott, Ritz-Carlton, or any other well-known, high-quality service organization. Which provider gaps has the company closed? How can you tell?
3. Interview a nonprofit or public sector organization in your area (it could be some part of your school if it is a state school). Find out if the integrated gaps model of service quality framework makes sense in the context of its organization.

Notes

1. The gaps model of service quality that provides the structure for this text was developed by and is fully presented in Valarie A. Zeithaml, A. Parasuraman, and Leonard L. Berry, *Delivering Quality Service: Balancing Customer Perceptions and Expectations* (New York: The Free Press, 1990).

Part Two

Focus on the Customer

THE CUSTOMER GAP

The figure shows a pair of boxes from the gaps model of service quality that correspond to two concepts—*customer expectations* and *customer perceptions*—that play a major role in services marketing. Customer expectations are the standards of performance or reference points for performance against which service experiences are compared, and they are often formulated in terms of what a customer believes should or will happen. Customer perceptions are subjective assessments of actual service experiences.

The Customer Gap

We devote the second part of the textbook to describing this gap and other relevant customer concepts because excellent services marketing requires a focus on the customer. We detail what is known about, customer expectations in Chapter 3, and customer perceptions in Chapter 4. Knowing what customers want and how they assess what they receive is the foundation for designing effective services.

Chapter Three

Customer Expectations of Service

This chapter's objectives are to

1. Recognize that customers hold different types of expectations for service performance.
2. Discuss several sources of customer expectations of service.
3. Acknowledge that the types and sources of expectations are similar for end consumers and business customers, for pure service and product-related service, for experienced customers and inexperienced customers.
4. Delineate some important issues surrounding customer expectations.

Undoubtedly, the greatest gap between customer expectations and service delivery exists when customers travel from one country to another. For example, in Japan the customer is supreme. At the morning opening of large department stores in Tokyo, sales personnel line up to welcome patrons and bow as they enter! When one of us—who could speak no Japanese—visited Tokyo a few years ago, as many as eight salespeople willingly tried to help find a calligraphy pen. Although the pen was a very low-priced item, several attendants rushed from counter to counter to find someone to translate, several others spread out to find pens that might serve as the perfect gift, and still others searched for maps to other stores where the perfect pen could be found.

Because of the wonderful treatment Japanese customers are used to in their home country, they often have service expectations that exceed service delivery even when shopping in "civilized" countries such as Great Britain: "Hideo Majima, 57, a Japanese tourist, looked puzzled and annoyed. He was standing in a London department store while two shop assistants conversed instead of serving him. He left without buying

Tokyo sales personnel provide excellent customer service.

anything."[1] His annoyance is understandable when you realize the standard of service treatment in Japan.

Expectations of hotel service may also differ from one country to another. In the United States, a "two-star" designation for a hotel is generally interpreted to mean customers can expect guest rooms to be clean; beds to be comfortable; rooms to be sparsely decorated and equipped with some modern conveniences such as a microwave oven, refrigerator, color television, sofa bed, telephone, and coffee maker; and the hotel to provide daily maid service. For such hotels the customer is not expecting (and does not want to pay for) luxury, extra service, beautiful, spacious lobbies, or room service availability but still wants to have a fairly decent, clean, and safe place to stay. The hotel might also include a work desk, voicemail, and high-speed Internet access in the room. However, experienced travelers to Great Britain would be very surprised to find this level of service at a two-star hotel in London.

In fact, another one of us had firsthand experience with differing customer expectations with hotel service in London. In particular, a four-night hotel stay was booked for a family of four (including two children) at what was promised by a travel agent to be a two-star hotel. However, this London hotel did not meet expectations of a two-star hotel. Instead, the hotel had rooms for a maximum of two people, slanting floors (and, therefore, beds), 24-inch-wide showers stalls, room entry doors that did not fully latch, hallways with no lights, and a huge hole in the wall behind one toilet with insects coming and going as they pleased. In addition, the daily "maid service" consisted of simply emptying the trash cans in the rooms and leaving the door to one of the rooms unlatched. No new towels or sheets were provided, and no cleaning of any kind was done in the room. Clearly the level of service did not match expectations, although seasoned European travelers were not surprised when we told of our service experience. Obviously, not all two-star London hotels have such "features." However, we were surprised to find that many of our European friends did not find our service experience to be extremely unusual for a two-star hotel in a large, expensive city like London. Their expectations of service are quite different from ours. Imagine how our friend Majima-san would have felt about this service experience!

Customer expectations are beliefs about service delivery that serve as standards or reference points against which performance is judged. Because customers compare their perceptions of performance with these reference points when evaluating service quality, thorough knowledge about customer expectations is critical to service marketers. Knowing what the customer expects is the first and possibly most critical step in delivering quality service. Being wrong about what customers want can mean losing a customer's business when another company hits the target exactly. Being wrong can also mean expending money, time, and other resources on things that do not count to the customer. Being wrong can even mean not surviving in a fiercely competitive market.

Among the aspects of expectations that need to be explored and understood for successful services marketing are the following: What types of expectations do customers hold about services? What factors most influence the formation of these expectations? What role do these factors play in changing expectations? How can a service company meet or exceed customer expectations?

In this chapter we provide a framework for thinking about customer expectations.[2] The chapter is divided into three main sections: (1) the meaning and types of expected service, (2) factors that influence customer expectations of service, and (3) issues involving customers' service expectations.

SERVICE EXPECTATIONS

To say that expectations are reference points against which service delivery is compared is only a beginning. The level of expectation can vary widely depending on the reference point the customer holds. Although most everyone has an intuitive sense of what expectations are, service marketers need a far more thorough and clear definition of expectations to comprehend, measure, and manage them.

Imagine that you are planning to go to a restaurant. Figure 3.1 displays a continuum of possible service expectations. On the left of the continuum are different types or levels of expectations, ranging from high (top) to low (bottom). At each point we give a name to the type of expectation and illustrate on the right side of the figure what it might mean in terms of a restaurant you are considering. Note how important the expectation you hold will be to your eventual assessment of the restaurant's performance. Suppose you went into a restaurant for which you hold the minimum tolerable expectation, paid very little money, and were served immediately with good food. Alternatively, suppose that you went to a restaurant for which you had the highest (ideal) expectations, paid a lot of money, and were served good (but not fantastic) food. Which restaurant experience would you judge to be best? The answer is likely to depend on the reference point that you brought to the experience.

Because the idea of customer expectations is so critical to evaluation of service, we start this chapter by talking about the types of expectations.

FIGURE 3.1
Possible Levels of Customer Expectations

Source: R. K. Teas, "Expectations, Performance Evaluation, and Consumers' Perceptions of Quality," *Journal of Marketing,* October 1993, pp. 18–34. Reprinted by permission of the American Marketing Association.

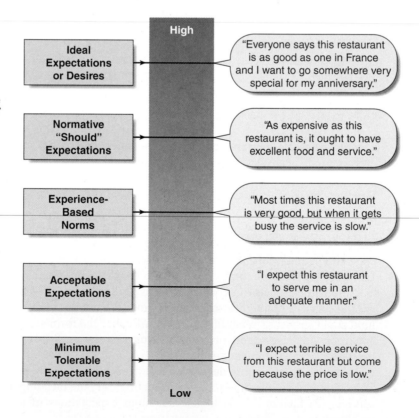

Types of Expectations

As we show in Figure 3.1, customers hold different types of expectations about service. For purposes of our discussion in the rest of this chapter, we focus on two types. The highest can be termed *desired service:* the level of service the customer hopes to receive—the "wished for" level of performance. Desired service is a blend of what the customer believes "can be" and "should be."[3] For example, consumers who sign up for an online dating service expect to find compatible, attractive, interesting people to date and perhaps even someone to marry. This expectation reflects the hopes and wishes of these consumers. In a similar way, you are likely to engage the services of your college's placement office when you are ready to graduate. What are your expectations of the service? In all likelihood you want the office to find you a job—the right job in the right place for the right salary—because that is what you hope and wish for.

However, you probably also see that the economy may constrain the availability of ideal job openings in companies. And not all companies you may be interested in have a relationship with your university's placement office. In this situation and in general, customers hope to achieve their service desires but recognize this is not always possible. We call the threshold level of acceptable service *adequate service—* the minimum level of service the customer will accept.[4] In the economic slowdown that began in 2008, many college graduates who were trained for high-skilled jobs accepted entry-level positions at fast-food restaurants or internships for no pay. Their hopes and desires were still high, but they recognized that they could not attain those desires in the market that existed at the time. Their standard of adequate service from the placement office was much lower than their desired service. Some graduates accepted any job for which they could earn a salary, and others agreed to nonpaying, short-term positions as interns to gain experience. Adequate service represents the "minimum tolerable expectation,"[5] the bottom level of performance acceptable to the customer.

Figure 3.2 shows these two expectation standards as the upper and lower boundaries for customer expectations. This figure portrays the idea that customers assess service performance on the basis of two standard boundaries: what they desire and what they deem acceptable. This chapter's Global Feature illustrates some of the challenges firms face in understanding what customers' expectations are, particularly when delivering service to customers in another country.

FIGURE 3.2
**Dual Customer
Expectation Levels**

The characteristics of services often make it difficult for customers to know what to expect from a service provider. Imagine the difficulty of knowing what to expect if you were to "outsource" many of the day-to-day tasks you perform to someone whom you never meet in person and who lives in a foreign country. Many families face this situation when they select a service provider located overseas.

OFFSHORING OF PERSONAL CONSUMER SERVICES

As indicated in Chapter 1, many U.S. companies are involved in offshore outsourcing of services. More than $20 billion is spent annually on services provided outside of the United States. A growing percentage of U.S. families are now using service providers in foreign countries to complete personal tasks for them. Thanks to the technology available to many households today, including instant messaging, computer scanners, and e-mail attachments, services that can be completed without requiring face-to-face interaction have the potential to be done overseas. Some of the services that can be outsourced to foreign countries include interior design, word processing, legal services, mural painting, wedding planning, personal website design, and landscape design. To illustrate,

- One customer wanted to create a short, but professional-looking, video to show at his sister's wedding. He found a graphic artist in Romania, who created a two-minute video with a space theme set to the music of *Star Wars* that was a hit at the wedding. The cost for everything? Only $59.
- A man was looking for a graphic artist to illustrate a children's book his mother had written for her grandchildren about her early childhood experiences in New York City. Rather than search for a graphic artist through a local telephone directory, he described his project on the guru.com website. Within a week he received 80 bids from artists in countries like Malaysia, Ukraine, and Lebanon. He ended up hiring a woman from the Philippines who offered to do 25 drawings for $300.
- One family hired an online tutor for their daughter. After obtaining quotes around $40/hour for local tutoring services, they found an online tutor from India who charged $99/month for two-hour, five-day-per-week sessions. The lessons simply required the family to have a digital tablet, instant messaging, and a headset for communication.

EXPECTATIONS OF SERVICE

Outsourcing services at the consumer level raises some issues. As discussed in this chapter, desired service expectations are influenced by explicit service promises, implicit service promises, word-of-mouth communication, and past experience. However, when outsourcing personal services in the manner listed earlier, many of these factors may not be present. For example, in many cases communication with such service providers be conducted via e-mail—providing a limited amount of cues upon which promises are based, word-of-mouth recommendations may be restricted to Internet sources, and customers may have no experience with such services. To further complicate the matter for customers, many have limited exposure to having *any* previous work done for them through the Internet, and most are likely to have never hired a foreign service provider.

In such settings, customers may attempt to communicate their expectations of service, but face obstacles in doing so. If the service provider's native language is not English, there is a good chance for misunderstanding.

The Zone of Tolerance

As we discussed in Chapter 1, services are heterogeneous in that performance may vary across providers, across employees from the same provider, and even with the same service employee. The extent to which customers recognize and are willing to accept this variation is called the *zone of tolerance* and is shown in Figure 3.3. If service drops below adequate service—the minimum level considered acceptable—customers will be frustrated and most likely dissatisfied with the company. If service performance is above the zone of tolerance at the top end—where performance

For example, one customer had a language issue with an outsourcer based in Egypt. The outsourcer put together a personal website for the customer—but drafts included several misspelled words. Not surprisingly, e-mails with instructions and explanations were labored because of the language gap. Thus, customers looking to outsource services to foreign providers may anticipate having to put significant energy and effort into communicating expectations.

Wall Street Journal reporter Ellen Gamerman asked an India-based outsourcer to design a change-of-address card for someone who was moving from New York to Arizona. Although he did a good job with the design, there were a couple of communication miscues: (1) he initially put evergreens in the desert background and (2) he had the car in the card driving west to east initially, not east to west. When the instructions were initially given, she did not spell out exactly what she wanted—she gave him a general idea of the theme of the card, then asked him to be creative. Although he was happy to make changes to correct these issues, the price went up to cover the changes.

Using a foreign service provider may require customers to reset their expectations. One customer decided to use outsourcing for his personal income taxes. After he e-mailed his earnings and scanned receipts, his tax return was completed in two days at a cost of $50—about one-third of what a U.S. firm like H&R Block charges. However, he had to file his return as "self-prepared," since it was not prepared by a U.S. accountant.

Another issue customers may face is one of trust: how willing are customers to entrust a worker thousands of miles away—and in a foreign country—with projects of a personal nature? To provide some information about the quality of service a customer might expect from a service provider, services on auction sites like guru.com provide a ratings system similar to that provided on eBay. Some vendors post short videos of themselves and their offices on the Internet to help shape customers' expectations and gain their trust.

Some U.S. customers receive tutoring service from providers in India.

Sources: Ellen Gamerman, "Outsourcing Your Life," *The Wall Street Journal*, June 2, 2007, pp. P1, P4; Alan Blinder, "Offshoring: The Next Industrial Revolution?" *Foreign Affairs* 85 (March/April 2006), pp. 113–118; Ellen Gamerman, e-mail communication, July 30, 2007.

exceeds desired service—customers will be very pleased and probably quite surprised as well. You might consider the zone of tolerance as the range in which customers do not particularly notice service performance. When it falls outside the range (either very low or very high), the service gets the customer's attention in either a positive or negative way. As an example, consider the service at a checkout line in a grocery store. Most customers hold a range of acceptable times for this service encounter—probably somewhere between 5 and 10 minutes. If service consumes that period of time, customers probably do not pay much attention to the wait. If a customer enters the line and finds a sufficient number of checkout personnel to serve her in the first 2 or 3 minutes, she may notice the service and judge it as excellent. On the other

FIGURE 3.3
The Zone of
Tolerance

hand, if a customer has to wait in line for 15 minutes, he may begin to grumble and look at his watch. The more the wait falls below the zone of tolerance (10 minutes in this example), the more frustrated he becomes.

Customers' service expectations are characterized by a range of levels (like those shown in Figure 3.3), bounded by desired and adequate service, rather than a single level. This tolerance zone, representing the difference between desired service and the level of service considered adequate, can expand and contract for a given customer. An airline customer's zone of tolerance will narrow when she is running late and is concerned about making her plane. A minute's delay for anything that occurs prior to boarding the plane seems much longer, and her adequate service level increases. On the other hand, a customer who arrives at the airport early may have a larger tolerance zone, making the wait in line far less noticeable than when he is pressed for time. This example shows that the marketer must understand not just the size and boundary levels for the zone of tolerance but also when and how the tolerance zone fluctuates for a given customer.

Different Customers Possess Different Zones of Tolerance

Another aspect of variability in the range of reasonable services is that different customers possess different tolerance zones. Some customers have narrow zones of tolerance (often because what they consider to be minimally acceptable is greater), requiring a tighter range of service from providers, whereas other customers have a greater range of expectations of service. For example, very busy customers would likely always be pressed for time, desire short wait times in general, and hold a constrained range for the length of acceptable wait times. When it comes to meeting plumbers or appliance repair personnel at their homes, customers who work outside the home have a more restricted window of acceptable time duration for that appointment than do customers who work in their homes or do not work at all.

A customer's zone of tolerance increases or decreases depending on a number of factors, including company-controlled factors such as price. When prices increase, customers tend to be less tolerant of poor service. In this case, the zone of tolerance decreases because the adequate service level shifts upward. Later in this chapter we will describe many different factors, some company controlled and others customer controlled, that lead to the narrowing or widening of the tolerance zone.

The fluctuation in a customer's zone of tolerance is more a function of changes in the adequate service level, which moves readily up and down because of situational circumstances, than in the desired service level, which tends to move upward incrementally because of accumulated experiences. Desired service is relatively idiosyncratic and stable compared with adequate service, which moves up and down

FIGURE 3.4
**Differing Zones
of Tolerance for
Different Service
Dimensions**

Adapted from L. L. Berry,
A. Parasuraman, and
V. A. Zeithaml, "Ten Lessons
for Improving Service
Quality," *Marketing Science
Institute,* Report No. 93–104
(May 1993).

and in response to competition and other factors. Fluctuation in the zone of tolerance can be likened to an accordion's movement, but with most of the gyration coming from one side (the adequate service level) rather than the other (the desired service level).

Zones of Tolerance Vary for Service Dimensions

Customers' tolerance zones also vary with different service attributes or dimensions. The more important the factor, the narrower the zone of tolerance is likely to be. In general, customers are likely to be less tolerant about unreliable service (broken promises or service errors) than other service deficiencies, which means that they have higher expectations for this factor. In addition to higher expectations for the most important service dimensions and attributes, customers may relax their expectations for the less important factors, making the zone of tolerance for the most important service dimension smaller and the desired and adequate service levels higher.[6] Figure 3.4 portrays the likely difference in tolerance zones for the most important and the least important factors.[7]

FACTORS THAT INFLUENCE CUSTOMER EXPECTATIONS OF SERVICE

Because expectations play such a critical role in customer evaluation of services, marketers need to understand the factors that shape them. In this section of the chapter we describe some of the key influences on customer expectations.

Sources of Desired Service Expectations

Personal Needs

As shown in Figure 3.5, there are three major influences on desired service level. The first, *personal needs,* are those states or conditions essential to the physical or psychological well-being of the customer and are pivotal factors that shape what customers desire in service. Personal needs can fall into many categories, including physical, social, psychological, and functional. A fan who regularly goes to baseball games right from work, and is therefore thirsty and hungry, hopes and desires that the food and drink vendors will pass by his section frequently, whereas a fan who regularly has dinner elsewhere has a lower level of desired service from the vendors. A customer with high social and dependency needs may have relatively high expectations for a hotel's ancillary services, hoping, for example, that the hotel has a bar with live music and

FIGURE 3.5
Factors that
Influence Desired
Service

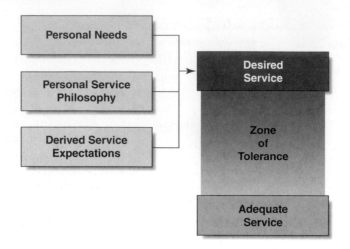

dancing. The effect of personal needs on desired service is illustrated by the different expectations held by two business insurance customers:

> I expect [an insurance] broker to do a great deal of my work because I don't have the staff . . . I expect the broker to know a great deal about my business and communicate that knowledge to the underwriter.

> My expectations are different . . . I do have a staff to do our certificates, etc., and use the broker minimally.[8]

Personal Service Philosophy

A second influence on desired service expectations is *personal service philosophy*—the customer's underlying generic attitude about the meaning of service and the proper conduct of service providers. If you have ever been employed as a waitperson in a restaurant, you are likely to have standards for restaurant service that have been shaped by your training and experience in that role. You might, for example, believe that waiters should not keep customers waiting longer than 15 minutes to take their orders. Knowing the way a kitchen operates, you may be less tolerant of lukewarm food or errors in the order than customers who have not held the role of waitperson. In general, customers who are themselves in service businesses or have worked for them in the past seem to have especially strong service philosophies.

Derived Service Expectations

Another influence on desired service expectations is called *derived service expectations,* which occur when customer expectations are driven by another person or group of people. A niece from a big family who is planning a 90th birthday party for a favorite aunt is representing the entire family in selecting a restaurant for a successful celebration. Her needs are driven in part by expectations derived from the other family members. A parent choosing a vacation for the family, a spouse selecting a home-cleaning service, an employee choosing an office for the firm—all these customers' individual expectations are intensified because they represent and must answer to other parties who will receive the service. In the context of business-to-business service, customer expectations are driven by the expectations of their own customers. The head of an information technology department in an insurance company, who is the business customer of a large computer vendor, has expectations based on those of the insurance customers she serves: when the computer equipment is down, her customers complain. Her need to keep the system up and running is not just her own desire but is derived from the pressure of her firm's customers.

Sources of Adequate Service Expectations

A different set of determinants affects adequate service, the level of service the customer finds acceptable. In general, these influences are short-term and tend to fluctuate more than the factors that influence desired service. In this section we discuss three factors shown in Figure 3.6, which influence adequate service: perceived service alternatives, situational factors, and predicted service.

Problems with the initial service can also lead to heightened expectations. Performing a service right the first time is very important because customers value service reliability above all other dimensions. If the service fails in the recovery phase, fixing it right the second time (i.e., being reliable in service recovery) is even more critical than it was the first time. Automobile repair service provides a case in point. If a problem with your automobile's brakes sends you to a car repair provider, you expect the company to fix the brakes. If you experience further problems with the brakes after the repair, the level of service you consider to be adequate will increase. In these and other situations where temporary service intensifiers are present, the level of adequate service will increase and the zone of tolerance will narrow.

Perceived Service Alternatives

Perceived service alternatives are other providers from whom the customer can obtain service. If customers believe they have multiple service providers to choose from, or if they can provide the service for themselves (such as lawn care or personal grooming), their levels of adequate service are higher than those of customers who believe it is not possible to get better service elsewhere. An airline customer who lives in a small town with a tiny airport, for example, has a reduced set of options in airline travel. This customer will be more tolerant of the service performance of the carriers in the town because few alternatives exist. She will accept the limited schedule of flights and lower levels of service more than the customer in a big city who has myriad flights and airlines from which to choose. The customer's perception that service alternatives exist raises the level of adequate service and narrows the zone of tolerance.

It is important that service marketers fully understand the complete set of options that customers view as perceived alternatives. In the small town–small airport example just discussed, the set of alternatives from the customer's point of view is likely to include more than just other airlines: limousine service to a nearby large city, rail service, or driving. In general, service marketers must discover the alternatives that

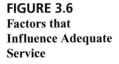

FIGURE 3.6
Factors that Influence Adequate Service

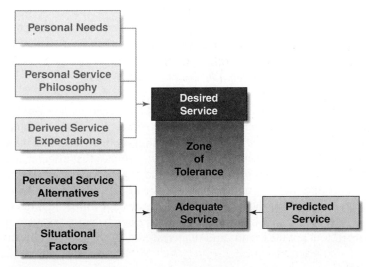

Technology Spotlight Customer Expectations of Airport Services Using Technology

One of the most difficult tasks that marketers face is understanding what customers expect from services, and nowhere is this problem more evident than when these services involve technology. Customers almost always resist technology initially—perhaps because they do not understand it, perhaps because they fear change—even when the technology leads to improved service. Technology that makes obtaining service easier and faster is springing up all over, even in airports around the country. Customers are accepting some new service technologies and resisting others. Here we discuss two innovations that are meeting different fates.

One service technology that has been accepted by customers is automatic airline check-in: customers walk up to computer screens, slide credit cards, and use touch pads to retrieve their boarding passes and receipts. Unless the flight is international, customers can check luggage automatically as well, and an attendant takes their luggage from them before they go to their gates. Customers can also check their seat assignments and change them if there are open seats available. The service generally takes less time than working with an attendant, and most airlines now have more computers than they previously had lines for attendants, saving customers considerable time. When these computer screens were first installed, customers were not sure what to expect and did not know how to use them. Airlines that supplied extra employees to stand and help customers use the computers found success in converting customers from the human handling to the technology. Today, most customers prefer the computers because of their speed and ease.

Another airport technology that has been accepted more slowly by customers is called Exit Express and is a technology substitute for toll booths as customers leave airport parking areas. It works like this: before customers exit the airport, they use a machine (similar to a subway token machine) to pay their parking fees in advance. They insert their parking ticket, then their credit card or cash, and receive back their stamped parking ticket. When they exit the parking lot, they use one of the many Exit Express lanes, insert their paid ticket, and leave. Airports typically still retain a small number of lanes that use live employees and operate in the traditional way. Surprisingly, many airports are finding that customers do not use Exit Express technology as much as expected.

Why are many customers resisting the Exit Express technology that clearly meets or exceeds their expectations of getting out of the airport quickly? One possible reason is that they do not understand how the system works, even though a loudspeaker in the parking lots trumpets the new system continuously. They also may not clearly see the benefits being provided, possibly because the airport does not communicate them well enough, leading customers to believe that the old system with toll booths is quick enough. Another reason is that most airports have

the customer views as comparable rather than those in the company's competitive set. For example, airline companies must fully understand customer views of new service technologies (see Technology Spotlight).

Situational Factors

Levels of adequate service are also influenced by *situational factors* that are generally considered contemporary in nature. One type is *uncontrollable situational factors,* which include service performance conditions that customers view as beyond the control of the service provider. For example, catastrophes that affect a large number of people at one time (tornadoes or earthquakes) may lower service expectations for insurance customers in other geographic locations because they recognize that insurers are inundated with demands for their services. During the days following the Hurricane Katrina disaster, telephone and Internet service was poor because so many people were trying to get in touch with friends and relatives. Similarly, guests at the Ritz-Carlton, Omni, and

Some airlines allow customers to check in by using a mobile phone.

not stationed employees near the technology (i.e., check-out kiosk) to familiarize customers with it and to deal with service failures, as the airlines did with automatic check-in. Customers may also fear that, if something were to go wrong, they would be embarrassed and not know how to resolve the situation. A final compelling reason is that many customers distrust the technology the way they used to distrust automated teller machine (ATM) technology when it was first introduced.

Over the years customers have adapted to changes in various aspects of airline travel brought on by technology. Less than 15 years ago most travelers carried tickets issued by the airlines, which allowed them

to get boarding passes. When "advanced check-in" became available on most domestic U.S. flights, customers grew accustomed to checking in before arriving at the airport (as much as 24 hours in advance of departure) and printing their boarding passes themselves. In more recent years, many airlines have begun to send electronic boarding passes (complete with a bar code) directly to customers' mobile phones—thus removing the requirement for customers to carry a physical (printed) boarding pass altogether. As with Exit Express, some customers have been slow to embrace the use of electronic boarding passes—and for similar reasons: they do not understand how the technology works, they do not understand how to retrieve their electronic boarding pass, they get anxious when having to retrieve it quickly on their phone when other passengers are waiting in line behind them, and they are not sure what to do if the technology fails them during their travels.

If services enhanced by technology are to meet the expectations of customers, they must be trusted, understood, and introduced as valuable to customers. Otherwise, the promise of meeting or exceeding customer expectations will not be realized despite large investments.

Source: M. L. Meuter, M. J. Bitner, A. L. Ostrom, and S. W. Brown, "Choosing among Alternative Service Delivery Modes: An Investigation of Customer Trial of Self-Service Technologies," *Journal of Marketing* 69 (April 2005), pp. 61–83.

Marriott hotels in New Orleans quickly realized that they should not expect the level of service to which they had become accustomed. Customers of all these services were quite forgiving during these days because they understood the source of the problem. Customers who recognize that situational factors are not the fault of the service company may accept lower levels of adequate service, given the context. Situational factors often temporarily lower the level of adequate service, widening the zone of tolerance.

Personal situational factors, consist of short-term, individual factors that make a customer more aware of the need for service. Personal emergency situations in which service is urgently needed (such as an accident and the need for automobile insurance or a breakdown in office equipment during a busy period) raise the level of adequate service expectations, particularly in terms of the level of responsiveness required and considered acceptable. A mail-order company that depends on toll-free phone lines for receiving all customer orders will tend to be more demanding of its telephone service provider during peak demand periods. Any system breakdown will be tolerated less

FIGURE 3.7
Factors that
Influence Desired
and Predicted
Service

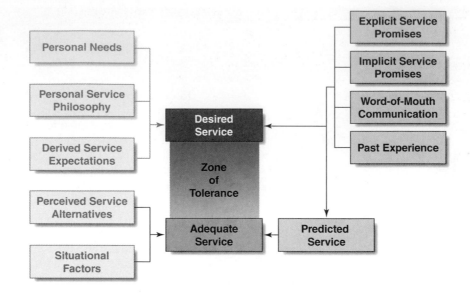

during these intense periods than at other times. The impact of personal situational factors is evident in these comments by two participants in a research study:

> An automobile insurance customer: The nature of my problem influences my expectations, for example, a broken window versus a DWI accident requiring brain surgery.

> A business equipment repair customer: I had calibration problems with the X-ray equipment. They should have come out and fixed it in a matter of hours because of the urgency.[9]

Predicted Service

The final factor that influences adequate service is *predicted service* (Figure 3.7), the level of service that customers believe they are likely to get. This type of service expectation can be viewed as predictions made by customers about what is likely to happen during an impending transaction or exchange. Predicted service performance implies some objective calculation of the probability of performance or estimate of anticipated service performance level. If customers predict good service, their levels of adequate service are likely to be higher than if they predict poor service. For example, full-time residents in a college town usually predict faster restaurant service during the summer months when students are not on campus. This prediction will probably lead them to have higher standards for adequate service in restaurants during the summer than during school months. On the other hand, customers of telephone companies, cable service providers, and utilities in a college town know that installation service from these firms will be difficult to obtain during the first few weeks of school when myriad students are setting up their apartments for the year. In this case, levels of adequate service decrease and zones of tolerance widen.

Predicted service is typically an estimate or a calculation of the service that a customer will receive in an individual transaction rather than in the overall relationship with a service provider. Whereas desired and adequate service expectations are global assessments comprising many individual service transactions, predicted service is almost always an estimate of what will happen in the next service encounter or transaction that the customer experiences. For this reason, predicted service is viewed in this model as an influencer of adequate service.

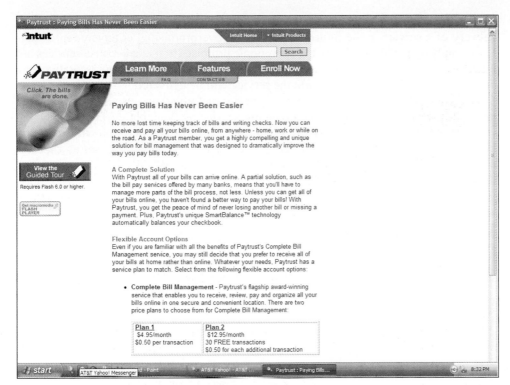

Paytrust's explicit service promises that influence desired service.

Sources of Both Desired and Predicted Service Expectations

When consumers are interested in purchasing services, they are likely to seek or take in information from several different sources. For example, they may call a store, ask a friend, or deliberately track newspaper advertisements to find the needed service at the lowest price. They may also receive service information by watching television, surfing the Internet, or hearing an unsolicited comment from a colleague about a service that was performed well. In addition to these active and passive types of external search for information, consumers may conduct an internal search by reviewing the information held in memory about the service. This section discusses four factors that influence both desired service and predicted service expectations: explicit service promises, implicit service promises, word-of-mouth communication, and past experience.

Explicit Service Promises

Explicit service promises are personal and nonpersonal statements about the service made by the organization to customers. The statements are personal when they are communicated by the firm's salespeople or service personnel; they are nonpersonal when they come from the company's web pages, advertising, brochures, and other written publications. The web page depicted above displays the promises made on the Internet by Paytrust, an online bill-paying service offered by the Intuit Corporation. On this web page Paytrust influences customers' expectations by indicating that *all* bills can be received and paid online and that checkbooks can automatically be balanced. Explicit service promises are one of the few influences on expectations that are completely within the control of the service provider.

Promising exactly what will ultimately be delivered would seem a logical and appropriate way to manage customer expectations and ensure that reality fits the promises. However, companies and the personnel who represent them often deliberately overpromise to obtain business or inadvertently overpromise by stating their best estimates about delivery of a service in the future. In addition to overpromising, company representatives simply do not always know the appropriate promises to make because services are often customized and therefore not easily defined and repeated; the representative may not know when or in what final form the service will be delivered.

All types of explicit service promises have a direct effect on desired service expectation. If a bank manager portrays a banking service as available 24 hours a day, the customer's desires for that service (as well as the service of competitors) will be shaped by this promise. A hotel customer describes the impact of explicit promises on expectations: "They get you real pumped up with the beautiful ad. When you go in you expect the bells and whistles to go off. Usually they don't." A business equipment repair customer states, "When you buy a piece of equipment you expect to get a competitive advantage from it. Service is promised with the sale of the equipment." A particularly dangerous promise that many companies today make to their business customers is to provide a "total solution" to their business needs. This promise is very difficult to deliver.

Explicit service promises influence the levels of both desired service and predicted service. They shape what customers desire in general as well as what they predict will happen in the next service encounter from a particular service provider or in a certain service encounter.

A service firm with a "posh" interior is likely to lead to greater customer expectations.

Implicit Service Promises

Implicit service promises are service-related cues, other than explicit promises, that lead to inferences about what the service should and will be like. These quality cues are dominated by price and the tangibles associated with the service. In general, the higher the price and the more impressive the tangibles, the more a customer will expect from the service. Consider a customer who shops for insurance, finding two firms charging radically different prices. She may infer that the firm with the higher price should and will provide higher-quality service and better coverage. Similarly, a customer who stays at a posh hotel with a luxurious lobby is likely to desire and predict a higher standard of service than from a hotel with less impressive facilities.

Word-of-Mouth Communication

The importance of *word-of-mouth communication* in shaping expectations of service is well documented.[10] These statements made by parties other than the organization—such as those found on social networking websites—convey to customers what the service will be like and influence both predicted and desired service.[11] Word-of-mouth communication carries particular weight as an information source because it is perceived as unbiased. Word-of-mouth communication tends to be very important in services that are difficult for customers to evaluate before purchase and before having direct experience of them. Experts (including *Consumer Reports,* friends, and family) and Internet forums are also word-of-mouth sources that can affect the levels of desired and predicted service.

Past Experience

Past experience, the customer's previous exposure to service that is relevant to the focal service, is another force in shaping predictions and desires. For example, you probably compare each stay in a particular hotel with all previous stays in that hotel.

Strategy Insight   How Service Marketers Can Influence Customers' Expectations

How might a manager of a service organization use the information we have developed in this chapter to create, improve, or market services? First, managers need to know the pertinent expectation sources and their relative importance for a customer population, a customer segment, and perhaps even a particular customer. They need to know, for instance, the relative weight of word-of-mouth communication, explicit service promises, implicit service promises, and past experience in shaping desired service and predicted service. Some of these sources are more stable and permanent in their influence (such as personal service philosophy and personal needs) than the others, which fluctuate considerably over time (like perceived service alternatives and situational factors). We provide here some ways that customer expectations might be influenced.

Factor	Possible Influence Strategies
Personal needs	• Educate customers on ways the service addresses their needs.
Personal service philosophy	• Use market research to profile personal service philosophies of customers and use this information in designing and delivering services.
Derived service expectations	• Use market research to determine sources of derived service expectations and their requirements. Then, focus advertising and marketing strategy on ways the service allows the focal customer to satisfy the requirements of the influencing customer(s).
Perceived service alternatives	• Be fully aware of competitive offerings and, where possible and appropriate, match them.
Situational factors	• Increase service delivery capacity during peak periods or in emergencies. • Use service guarantees to assure customers about service recovery regardless of the situational factors that occur.
Predicted service	• Tell customers when service provision is higher than what can normally be expected, so that predictions of future service encounters will not be inflated.
Explicit service promises	• Make realistic and accurate promises that reflect the service actually delivered rather than an idealized version of the service. • Ask contact people for feedback on the accuracy of promises made in advertising and personal selling. • Avoid engaging in price or advertising wars with competitors because they take the focus off customers and escalate promises beyond the level at which they can be met. • Formalize service promises through a service guarantee that focuses company employees on the promise and that provides feedback on the number of times promises are not fulfilled.
Implicit service promises	• Ensure that service tangibles are consistent with and accurately reflect the type and level of service provided. • Ensure that price premiums can be justified by higher levels of performance by the company on important service attributes.
Word-of-mouth communications	• Simulate word of mouth in advertising by using testimonials and opinion leaders. • Identify influencers and opinion leaders for the service and concentrate marketing efforts on them. • Use incentives with existing customers to encourage them to say positive things about the service.
Past experience	• Use marketing research to profile customers' previous experience with similar services.

But past experience with the focal hotel is likely to be a very limited view of your past experience. You may also compare each stay with your experiences in other hotels and hotel chains. Customers also compare across industries: hospital patients, for example, compare hospital stays against the standard of hotel visits. Cable service customers tend to compare cable service with the standards set by telephone service, one reason cable service is often judged to be poor. Past experience may incorporate previous experience with the focal service provider, typical performance of similar service offerings, and experience with the last service purchased.[12]

The different sources vary in terms of their credibility as well as their potential to be influenced by the marketer. The Strategy Insight shows the breakdown of various factors and how service marketers can influence them. Chapter 14 will detail these and other strategies that services marketers can use to match delivery to promises and thereby manage expectations.

ISSUES INVOLVING CUSTOMERS' SERVICE EXPECTATIONS

The following issues represent topics of particular interest to service marketers about customer expectations. In this section we discuss frequently asked questions about customer expectations:

- What does a service marketer do if customer expectations are "unrealistic"?
- Should a company try to delight the customer?
- How does a company exceed customers' service expectations?
- Do customers' service expectations continually escalate?
- How does a service company stay ahead of competition in meeting customer expectations?

What Does a Service Marketer Do if Customer Expectations Are "Unrealistic"?

One inhibitor to learning about customer expectations is management's and employees' fear of asking. This apprehension often stems from the belief that customer expectations will be extravagant and unrealistic and that by asking about them a company will set itself up for even loftier expectation levels (that is, "unrealistic" levels). However, compelling evidence, shown in Exhibit 3.1, suggests that customers' main expectations of service are quite simple and basic: "Simply put, customers expect service companies to do what they are supposed to do. They expect fundamentals, not fanciness; performance, not empty promises."[13] Customers want service to be delivered as promised. They want planes to take off on time, hotel rooms to be clean, food to be hot, and service providers to show up when scheduled. Unfortunately, many service customers are disappointed and let down when companies fail to meet these basic service expectations.

A simple way to learn if customers' expectations are realistic is to ask them. Asking customers about their expectations does not so much raise the levels of the expectations themselves but rather heightens the belief that the company will do something with the information that surfaces. Arguably the worst thing a company can do is show a strong interest in understanding what customers expect and then never act on the information. At a minimum, a company should acknowledge to customers that it has received and heard their input and that it will expend effort trying to address their issues. The company may not be able to—and indeed does not always have to—deliver to expressed expectations. An alternative and appropriate response would be to let customers know

Exhibit 3.1   Service Customers Want the Basics

Type of Service	Type of Customer	Principal Expectations
Automobile repair	Consumers	• Be competent. ("Fix it right the first time.") • Explain things. ("Explain why I need the suggested repairs—provide an itemized list.") • Be respectful. ("Don't treat me like a dumb female.")
Automobile insurance	Consumers	• Keep me informed. ("I shouldn't have to learn about insurance law changes from the newspaper.") • Be on my side. ("I don't want them to treat me like a criminal just because I have a claim.") • Play fair. ("Don't drop me when something goes wrong.") • Protect me from catastrophe. ("Make sure my estate is covered in the event of a major accident.") • Provide prompt service. ("I want fast settlement of claims.")
Hotel	Consumers	• Provide a clean room. ("Don't have a deep-pile carpet that can't be completely cleaned . . . you can literally see germs down there.") • Provide a secure room. ("Good bolts and peephole on door.") • Treat me like a guest. ("It is almost like they're looking you over to decide whether they're going to let you have a room.") • Keep your promise. ("They said the room would be ready, but it wasn't at the promised time.")
Property and casualty insurance	Business customers	• Fulfill obligations. ("Pay up.") • Learn my business and work with me. ("I expect them to know me and my company.") • Protect me from catastrophe. ("They should cover my risk exposure so there is no single big loss.") • Provide prompt service. ("Fast claim service.")
Equipment repair	Business customers	• Share my sense of urgency. ("Speed of response. One time I had to buy a second piece of equipment because of the huge downtime with the first piece.") • Be competent. ("Sometimes you are quoting stuff from their instruction manuals to their own people and they don't even know what it means.") • Be prepared. ("Have all the parts ready.")
Truck and tractor rental/leasing	Business customers	• Keep the equipment running. ("Need to have equipment working all of the time—that is the key.") • Be flexible. ("The leasing company should have the flexibility to rent us equipment when we need it.") • Provide full service. ("Get rid of all the paperwork and headaches.")

Source: Reprinted from "Understanding Customer Expectations of Service" by A. Parasuraman, L. L. Berry, and V. A. Zeithaml, *Sloan Management Review* 32 (Spring 1991), pp. 39–48, by permission of publisher. From MIT Sloan Management Review. Copyright © 1991 by Massachusetts Institute of Technology. All rights reserved. Distributed by Tribune Media Services.

the reasons that desired service is not being provided at the present time or describe the efforts planned to deliver such service in the future. Another approach could be a campaign to educate customers about ways to use and improve the service they currently receive. Giving customers progress updates as service is improved to address their needs and desires is sensible because it allows the company to get credit for incremental efforts to improve service.

Should a Company Try to Delight the Customer?

Some management consultants urge service companies to "delight" customers to gain a competitive edge. The *delight* that they refer to is a profoundly positive emotional state that results from having one's expectations exceeded to a surprising degree.[14] One author describes the type of service that results in delight as "positively outrageous service"—that which is unexpected, random, extraordinary, and disproportionately positive.[15]

A way that managers can conceive of delight, as depicted in Figure 3.8, is to consider product and service features in terms of concentric rings.[16] The innermost bull's-eye refers to attributes central to the basic function of the product or service, called *musts.* Their provision is not particularly noticeable, but their absence would be. Around the musts is a ring called *satisfiers:* features that have the potential to further satisfaction beyond the basic function of the product. At the next and final outer level are *delights,* or product features that are unexpected and surprisingly enjoyable. These features are things that consumers would not expect to find and are therefore highly surprised and sometimes excited when they receive them. For example, in your classes the musts consist of professors, rooms, syllabi, and class meetings. Satisfiers might include interesting course lectures, professors who are entertaining or friendly, and good audiovisual aids provided in the classroom. Delights might include a free textbook for students signing up for the course or punch and cookies provided for the first day of class.

Delighting customers may seem like a good idea, and can lead to repeat purchasing and customer loyalty,[17] but this level of service provision comes with extra effort and cost to the firm. Therefore, the benefits of providing delight must be weighed. Among the considerations are the staying power and competitive implications of delight.

FIGURE 3.8
Musts, Satisfiers, and Delights

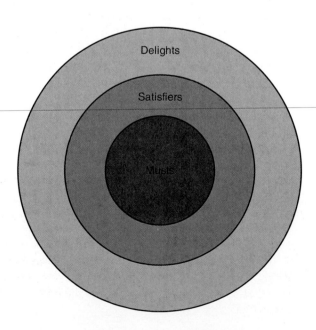

Staying power involves the question of how long a company can expect an experience of delight to maintain the consumer's attention. If it is fleeting and the customer forgets it immediately, it may not be worth the cost. Alternatively, if the customer remembers the delight and adjusts her level of expectation upward accordingly, it will cost the company more just to satisfy, effectively raising the bar for the future. Research indicates that delighting customers does, in fact, raise expectations and make it more difficult for a company to satisfy customers in the future.[18]

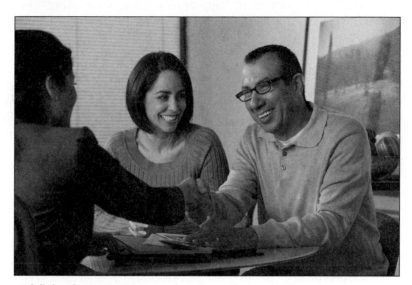

A delighted customer.

The competitive implication of delight relates to its impact on expectations of other firms in the same industry. If a competitor in the same industry is unable to copy the delight strategy, it will be disadvantaged by the consumer's increased expectations. If you were offered that free textbook in one of your classes, you might then expect to receive one in each of your classes. Those classes not offering the free textbook might not have high enrollment levels compared to the delighting class. If a competitor can easily copy the delight strategy, however, neither firm benefits (although the consumer does!), and all firms may be hurt because their costs increase and profits erode. The implication is that, if companies choose to delight, they should do so in areas that cannot be copied by other firms.

How Does a Company Exceed Customer Service Expectations?

Many companies talk about exceeding customer expectations—delighting and surprising them by giving more than they expect. One such example is Pebble Beach Resort, located along the Pacific coast of northern California. The golf resort not only talks about exceeding customer expectations, it actually prints the following phrase on the back side of employee business cards: "Exceed the expectations of every guest, by providing a once in a lifetime experience, every time." This philosophy raises the question, Should a service provider try simply to meet customer expectations or to exceed them?

First, it is essential to recognize that exceeding customer expectations of the basics is virtually impossible. Honoring promises—having the reserved room available, meeting deadlines, showing up for meetings, delivering the core service—is what the company is supposed to do. Companies are *supposed* to be accurate and dependable and provide the service they promised to provide.[19] As you examine the examples of basic expectations of customers in Exhibit 3.1, ask yourself if a provider's doing any of these things would delight you. The conclusion you should reach is that it is very difficult to surprise or delight customers consistently by delivering reliable service.

How, then, does a company delight its customers and exceed their expectations? In virtually any service, developing a customer relationship is one approach for exceeding service expectations. The United Services Automobile Association (USAA), a provider of insurance to military personnel and their dependents, illustrates how a large company that seldom has face-to-face interactions with its customers can surprise and delight them with its personalization of service and knowledge of the customer. Using a state-of-the-art imaging system, all USAA employees can access any customer's entire information file in seconds, giving them full knowledge of the customer's history and requirements and the status of the customer's recent interactions with the company. Expecting a lower level of personalization from an insurance company and from most any service interaction on the telephone, USAA's customers are surprised and impressed with the care and concern that employees demonstrate.

Using a similar type of information technology, Ritz-Carlton Hotels, a two-time recipient of the Malcolm Baldrige Quality Award, provides highly personalized attention to its customers. The company trains each of its employees to note guest likes and dislikes and to record these into a computerized guest history profile. The company has information on the preferences of several hundred thousand repeat Ritz-Carlton guests, resulting in more personalized service. The aim is not simply to meet expectations of guests but to provide them with a "memorable visit." The company uses the guest history information to exceed customers' expectations of the way they will be treated. When a repeat customer calls the hotel's central reservations number to book accommodations, the reservation agent can call up the individual's preference information. The agent then sends this information electronically to the particular hotel at which the reservation is made. The hotel puts the data in a daily guest recognition and preference report circulated to employees. Employees then greet the repeat guest personally at check-in and ensure that the guest's needs/preferences are anticipated and met.[20]

How well does this approach work? Quite well. According to an independent survey of luxury hotels conducted annually by J. D. Power and Associates, the Ritz-Carlton was the top-rated hotel in terms of customer satisfaction four times between 2007 and 2011.[21]

Another way to exceed expectations is to deliberately underpromise the service to increase the likelihood of exceeding customer expectations.[22] The strategy is to underpromise and overdeliver. If every service promise is less than what will eventually happen, customers can be delighted frequently. Although this reasoning sounds logical, a firm should weigh two potential problems before using this strategy. First, customers with whom a company interacts regularly are likely to notice the underpromising and adjust their expectations accordingly, negating the desired benefit of delight. Customers will recognize the pattern of underpromising when time after time a firm promises one delivery time ("we cannot get that to you before 5 p.m. tomorrow") yet constantly exceeds it (by delivering at noon). Second, underpromising in a sales situation potentially reduces the competitive appeal of an offering and must be tempered by what the competition is offering. When competitive pressures are high, presenting a cohesive and honest portrayal of the service both explicitly (through advertising and personal selling) and implicitly (such as through the appearance of service facilities and the price of the service) may be wiser. Controlling the firm's promises, making them consistent with the deliverable service, may be a better approach.

A final way to exceed expectations without raising them in the future is to position unusual service as unique rather than the standard. On a flight between Raleigh-Durham and Charlotte, North Carolina, one of us experienced an example of this strategy. The flight is extremely short, less than half an hour, and typically too brief for beverage service. On that flight, however, a crew member announced over the intercom that an unusually ambitious crew wanted to try to serve beverages, anyway. He warned passengers that the crew may not get to all of us and positioned the service as unique by imploring passengers not to expect beverage service on other flights. In this scenario, passengers seemed delighted but their expectations for regular service were not heightened by the action. (To this day, we have never received beverage service on that route, but are really not expecting it!)

Do Customers' Service Expectations Continually Escalate?

As we illustrated in the beginning of this chapter, customers' service expectations are dynamic. In both the credit card and mobile telephone industries, as in many competitive service industries, battling companies seek to best each other and thereby raise the level of service above that of competing companies. Service expectations—in this case, adequate service expectations—rise as quickly as service delivery or promises rise. In a highly competitive and rapidly changing industry, expectations can thus rise quickly. For this reason companies need to monitor adequate service expectations continually—the more turbulent the industry, the more frequent is the monitoring needed.

Desired service expectations, on the other hand, are far more stable. Because they are driven by more enduring factors, such as personal needs or personal service philosophy, they tend to be high to begin with and remain high.

How Does a Service Company Stay Ahead of Competition in Meeting Customer Expectations?

All else being equal, a company's goal is to meet customer expectations better than its competitors. Given the fact that adequate service expectations change rapidly in a turbulent environment, how can a company ensure that it stays ahead of competition?

The adequate service level reflects the minimum performance level expected by customers after they consider a variety of personal and external factors (Figure 3.7), including the availability of service options from other providers. Companies whose service performance falls short of this level are clearly at a competitive disadvantage, with the disadvantage escalating as the gap widens. These companies' customers may well be "reluctant" customers, ready to take their business elsewhere the moment they perceive an acceptable alternative exists.

If they are to use service quality for competitive advantage, companies must perform above the adequate service level. This level, however, may signal only a temporary advantage. Customers' adequate service levels, which are less stable than desired service levels, will rise rapidly when competitors promise and deliver a higher level of service. If a company's level of service is barely above the adequate service level to begin with, a competitor can quickly erode that advantage. To develop a true customer franchise—immutable customer loyalty—companies must not only consistently exceed the adequate service level but also reach the desired service level. Exceptional service can intensify customers' loyalty to a point at which they are impervious to competitive options.

Firms might also consider how they present their promises to customers relative to the competition. In Chapter 14 we describe various techniques for communicating a firm's promises, but for now consider two options. First, if the salesperson knows that no competitor can meet an inflated sales promise in an industry, he could point that fact out to the customer, thereby refuting the promise made by competitive sales-people. The second option is for the provider to follow a sale with a "reality check" about service delivery. One of us bought a new house from a builder. Typical sales promises were made about the quality of the home, some less than accurate, to make the sale. Before closing on the house, the builder conducted a final check on the house. At the front door, the builder pointed out that each new home has between 3,000 and 5,000 individual elements and that in his experience the typical new home has 100 to 150 defects. Armed with this reality check, the 32 defects found in the house then seemed to be a relatively small amount.

Summary

Using a conceptual framework of the nature and determinants of customer expectations of service, we showed in this chapter that customers hold two types of service expectations: desired service, which reflects what customers want, and adequate service, or the minimum level of service customers are willing to accept. The desired service level is less subject to change than the adequate service level. A zone of tolerance separates these two levels of expectations. This zone of tolerance varies across customers and can expand or contract for the same customer.

Customer expectations are influenced by a variety of factors. Desired service expectations are influenced by personal needs, personal service philosophy, derived service expectations, explicit service promises, implicit service promises, word-of-mouth communication, and the customer's past experience. Adequate service expectations are influenced by perceived service alternatives and situational factors. These sources of expectations are the same for end consumers and business customers, for pure service and product-related service, and for experienced customers and inexperienced customers.

Discussion Questions

1. What is the difference between desired service and adequate service? Why would a service marketer need to understand both types of service expectations?
2. Consider a recent service purchase that you have made. Which of the factors influencing expectations were the most important in your decision? Why?
3. Why are desired service expectations more stable than adequate service expectations?
4. How do the technology changes discussed in the Technology Spotlight in this chapter influence customer expectations?
5. Describe several instances in which a service company's explicit service promises were inflated and led you to be disappointed with the service outcome.

6. Consider a small business preparing to buy a computer system. Which of the influences on customer expectations do you believe will be pivotal? Which factors will have the most influence? Which factors will have the least importance in this decision?

7. What strategies can you add to the Strategy Insight in this chapter for influencing the factors?

8. Do you believe that any of your service expectations are unrealistic? Which ones? Should a service marketer try to address unrealistic customer expectations?

9. In your opinion, what service companies have effectively built customer franchises (immutable customer loyalty)?

10. Intuitively, it would seem that managers want their customers to have wide tolerance zones for service. But if customers do have these wide zones of tolerance for service, is it more difficult for firms with superior service to earn customer loyalty? Would superior service firms be better off to attempt to narrow customers' tolerance zones to reduce the competitive appeal of mediocre providers?

11. Should service marketers delight their customers?

Exercises

1. What factors influenced your expectations of this course? Which were the most important factors? How would your expectations change if this were a required course? (Alternatively, if this course *is* required, would your expectations change if this were an optional course?)

2. Keep a service journal for a day and document your use of services. Ask yourself before each service encounter to indicate your predicted service of that encounter. After the encounter, note whether your expectations were met or exceeded. How does the answer to this question relate to your desire to do business with that service firm again?

3. List five incidents in which a service company has exceeded your expectations. How did you react to the service? Did these incidents change the way you viewed subsequent interactions with each of the companies? In what way?

Notes

1. "Japanese Put Tourism on a Higher Plane," *International Herald Tribune,* February 3, 1992, p. 8.

2. The model on which this chapter is based is taken from V. A. Zeithaml, L. L. Berry, and A. Parasuraman, "The Nature and Determinants of Customer Expectations of Service," *Journal of the Academy of Marketing Science* 21 (Winter 1993), pp. 1–12.

3. See sources such as C. Gronroos, *Strategic Management and Marketing in the Service Sector* (Helsingfors, Sweden: Swedish School of Economics and Business Administration, 1982); R. K. Teas and T. E. DeCarlo, "An Examination and Extension of the Zone-of-Tolerance Model: A Comparison to Performance-Based Models of Perceived Quality," *Journal of Service Research* 6 (February 2004), pp. 272–286; K. B. Yap and J. C. Sweeney, "Zone-of-Tolerance Moderates the Service Quality-Outcome Relationship," *Journal of Services Marketing* 21, no. 2 (2007), pp. 137–148.

4. R. B. Woodruff, E. R. Cadotte, and R. L. Jenkins, "Expectations and Norms in Models of Consumer Satisfaction," *Journal of Marketing Research* 24 (August 1987), pp. 305–314.

5. J. A. Miller, "Studying Satisfaction, Modifying Models, Eliciting Expectations, Posing Problems, and Making Meaningful Measurements," in *Conceptualization and Measurement of Consumer Satisfaction and Dissatisfaction,* ed. H. K. Hunt (Bloomington: Indiana University School of Business, 1977), pp. 72–91.

6. A. Parasuraman, L. L. Berry, and V. A. Zeithaml, "Understanding Customer Expectations of Service," *Sloan Management Review* 32 (Spring 1991), p. 42.

7. L. L. Berry, A. Parasuraman, and V. A. Zeithaml, "Ten Lessons for Improving Service Quality," *Marketing Science Institute,* Report No. 93–104 (May 1993).

8. Zeithaml, Berry, and Parasuraman, "Customer Expectations of Service," p. 7.

9. Ibid., p. 8.

10. D. L. Davis, J. G. Guiltinan, and W. H. Jones, "Service Characteristics, Consumer Research, and the Classification of Retail Services," *Journal of Retailing* 55 (Fall 1979), pp. 3–21; W. R. George and L. L. Berry, "Guidelines for the Advertising of Services," *Business Horizons* 24 (May–June 1981), pp. 52–56; F. v. Wangenheim and T. Bayón, "The Effect of Word-of-Mouth on Services Switching: Measurement and Moderating Variables," *European Journal of Marketing* 38 no. 9–10 (2004), pp. 1173–85; T. J. Brown, T. E. Barry, P. A. Dacin, and R. F. Gunst, "Spreading the Word: Investigating Antecedents of Consumers' Positive Word-of-Mouth Intentions and Behaviors in a Retailing Context," *Journal of the Academy of Marketing Science* 33 (Spring 2005), pp. 123–138.

11. M. Trusov, R. E. Bucklin, and K. Pauwels, "Effects of Word-of-Mouth versus Traditional Marketing: Findings from an Internet Social Networking Site," *Journal of Marketing* 73 (September 2009), pp. 90–102.

12. Discussions of the role of past experience in shaping customer expectations of service are included in L. L. Berry, "Cultivating Service Brand Equity," *Journal of the Academy of Marketing Science* 28 (Winter 2000), pp. 128–137; and R. L. Hess Jr., S. Ganesan, and N. M. Klein, "Interactional Service Failures in a Psuedorelationship: The Role of Organizational Attributions," *Journal of Retailing* 83 (January 2007), pp. 79–95.

13. Parasuraman, Berry, and Zeithaml, "Understanding Customer Expectations," p. 40.

14. R. T. Rust and R. L. Oliver, "Should We Delight the Customer?" *Journal of the Academy of Marketing Science* 28 (Winter 2000), pp. 86–94.

15. T. S. Gross, *Positively Outrageous Service* (New York: Warner Books, 1994).

16. J. Clemmer, "The Three Rings of Perceived Value," *Canadian Manager* 15 (Summer 1990), pp. 12–15.

17. T. Keiningham and T. Vavra, *The Customer Delight Principle: Exceeding Customers' Expectations for Bottom-Line Success* (New York: Mcgraw-Hill, 2001); R. Chitturi, R. Raghunathan, and V. Mahajan, "Delight by Design: The Role of Hedonic versus Utilitarian Benefits," *Journal of Marketing* 72 (May 2008), pp. 48-63; D. C. Barnes, M. B. Beauchamp, and C. Webster, "To Delight, or Not to Delight? This Is the Question Service Firms Must Address," *Journal of Marketing Theory and Practice* 18 (Summer 2010), pp. 275-283.

18. Rust and Oliver, "Should We Delight the Customer?"

19. Parasuraman, Berry, and Zeithaml, "Understanding Customer Expectations," p. 41.

20. "How the Ritz-Carlton Hotel Company Delivers 'Memorable' Service to Customers," *Executive Report on Customer Satisfaction* 6, no. 5 (March 15, 1993), pp. 1–4.

21. J. D. Power and Associates, *http://businesscenter.jdpower.com/,* accessed December 20, 2011.

22. W. H. Davidow and B. Uttal, "Service Companies: Focus or Falter," *Harvard Business* Review 67 (July–August), pp. 77–85.

Chapter **Four**

Customer Perceptions of Service

This chapter's objectives are to

1. Provide a solid basis for understanding what influences customer perceptions of service and the relationships among customer satisfaction, service quality, and individual service encounters.
2. Demonstrate the importance of customer satisfaction—what it is, the factors that influence it, and the significant outcomes resulting from it.
3. Develop critical knowledge of service quality and its five key dimensions: reliability, responsiveness, empathy, assurance, and tangibles.
4. Show that service encounters, or the "moments of truth," are the essential building blocks from which customers form their perceptions.

Zane's Cycles: Service as a Strategic Differentiator

For Zane's Cycles in Branford, Connecticut, service has been the company's key to success and what truly differentiates it from competing bike stores.[1] Chris Zane, its forty-something chief executive officer (CEO), has owned the business since he was 16 years old, when he convinced his grandfather to loan him $20,000 to buy the store from its original owner. As a young man he built the business on basic principles such as "unparalleled service," "one-to-one marketing," "customer relationships," and "employee respect and empowerment." Since then, the business has grown to more than $10 million in annual sales (including retail and corporate sales), and Zane's has eliminated all but a small handful of the original 16 competitors. Moreover, the company has developed highly successful ways to compete with the likes of Walmart and has built a whole new business providing bicycles to corporations for incentive gifts to their employees. So how does Zane's compete? What are some of the things that Chris Zane has done to provide exemplary, out-of-the-box service—service that has driven his competitors out of business? Here are a few examples of the company's exemplary service strategies:

- *Lifetime free service.* Zane's provides "lifetime free service" on the bikes it sells, because it is in the service business, not just the bike business. Of course, lifetime free service (free service for as long as the customer owns the bike) is also a good way to get customers to return to the shop, providing an opportunity to build a lasting relationship.

- *Lifetime parts warranty.* Following the lifetime free service strategy, Zane's soon realized that it should also offer a lifetime warranty on parts as well. He is able to do this by having a small number of vendor partners and holding them accountable for their products.

- *90-day price protection.* To quell possible rumors and beliefs that Zane's is high priced (to cover the lifetime guarantees), the company instituted a 90-day price protection guarantee, so that customers can go back within 90 days to receive a cash rebate, plus 10 percent, if they find the same bike elsewhere for less money. Because Zane's is truly in the relationship business, few customers shop the competitors or meticulously compare prices, so the plan results in very few refunds. And, when they do give a refund, the customer frequently spends the cash right on the spot, in the store!

- *Flat insurance.* For those first-time bike purchasers or less experienced bikers, the idea of a flat tire seems daunting. So Zane's offers "flat insurance" for a nominal annual fee. Although few tires are ever fixed under the policy, those bikers that do go back to the store to use their flat insurance are treated like royalty. Everything stops, the bike is taken to the back, where the tire is changed and the bike is cleaned up—all in record time with much fanfare. Again, the customer (and anyone else in the store) is treated to an unexpected, delightful experience, and relationships are strengthened, all at little cost to Zane's—especially given the amount of the flat insurance that is sold and never used!

- *Less than $1 giveaways.* Another way that Zane's delights customers is by giving away small but essential parts that cost less than $1. He figures these giveaways result in additional purchases (at the same time or on another visit) far beyond the few cents it costs to provide them.

- *Kids' play area.* The kids' play area in Zane's is a popular place for youngsters to play and remain entertained while their parents shop. Some are even able to purchase the infamous "Christmas Bike" right under the noses of their preoccupied children!

- *Coffee and Snapple bar, with free coffee.* To provide a social context and a place for folks to wait when the store is busy, Chris Zane built a mahogany coffee bar, modeled after a similar cozy coffee bar he had seen in a bike shop on a trip to Switzerland. Here, coffee and other drinks are offered, and customers can watch bike repairs going on through a huge glass window. And, because the cost of a cup of coffee is less than $1, of course, there is no charge!

- *Kids bike upgrades.* One of the most innovative service strategies at Zane's is one that helps them compete head on with Walmart. This is the trade-in policy that allows parents to buy a child's bike and then trade it in for full price, credited toward a larger bike. Like many of their service plans, this one is retroactive. When they first started it, Zane's sent postcards to everyone who had bought a small bicycle within the past few years, letting them know about the upgrade plan.

You might wonder how all of these seemingly "too good to be true" service offers can be provided without draining profits. The fact is that Zane's is very profitable and financially successful. There is nothing "soft" about this strategy, and Chris Zane is as focused on hard-nosed, quantitative financial analytics as any other excellent CEO. What Zane has figured out, much to the chagrin of his competitors, is that great service can be the key to cementing customer loyalty and that customer loyalty, in the end, is what drives growth and profits. No wonder Zane's was one of *Fast Company* magazine's "Local Heroes" in its Customer First Awards.

Zane's Cycles in Branford, Connecticut, USA

Quality bikes, excellent service quality, lots of little extras, and the unexpected attention of Zane's team members all add up to customer satisfaction for customers of Zane's Cycles. The same is true for other landmark service companies such as Lands' End, IBM Global Services, Amazon.com, and Ritz-Carlton Hotels. In all of these companies, the quality of the core product and exemplary customer service result in high customer satisfaction ratings.

CUSTOMER PERCEPTIONS

How customers perceive services, how they assess whether they have experienced quality service and whether they are satisfied are the subjects of this chapter. We will be focusing on the *perceived service* box in the gaps model. As we move through this chapter, keep in mind that perceptions are always considered relative to expectations. Because expectations are dynamic, evaluations may also shift over time—from person to person and from culture to culture. What is considered quality service or the things that satisfy customers today may be different tomorrow. Also keep in mind that the entire discussion of quality and satisfaction is based on *customers' perceptions of the service*—not some predetermined objective criteria of what service is or should be.

FIGURE 4.1
Customer Perceptions of Quality and Customer Satisfaction

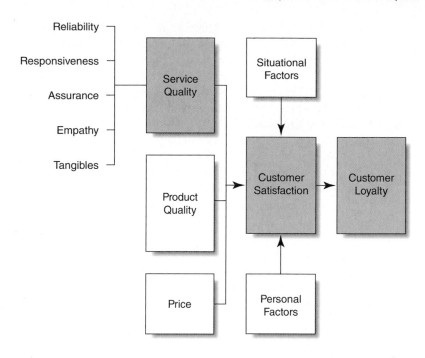

Satisfaction versus Service Quality

Practitioners and writers in the popular press tend to use the terms *satisfaction* and *quality* interchangeably, but researchers have attempted to be more precise about the meanings and measurement of the two concepts, resulting in considerable debate.[2] Consensus is that the two concepts are fundamentally different in terms of their underlying causes and outcomes.[3] Although they have certain things in common, *satisfaction* is generally viewed as a broader concept, whereas *service quality* focuses specifically on dimensions of service. Based on this view, *perceived service quality* is a component of customer satisfaction. Figure 4.1 graphically illustrates the relationships between the two concepts.

As shown in Figure 4.1, service quality is a focused evaluation that reflects the customer's perception of reliability, assurance, responsiveness, empathy, and tangibles.[4] Satisfaction, on the other hand, is more inclusive: it is influenced by perceptions of service quality, product quality, and price, as well as situational factors and personal factors. For example, service quality of a health club is judged on attributes such as whether equipment is available and in working order when needed, how responsive the staff are to customer needs, how skilled the trainers are, and whether the facility is well maintained. Customer satisfaction with the health club is a broader concept that will certainly be influenced by perceptions of service quality but that will also include perceptions of product quality (such as the quality of products sold in the pro shop), the price of membership,[5] personal factors such as the consumer's emotional state, and even uncontrollable situational factors such as weather conditions and experiences driving to and from the health club.[6]

Transaction versus Cumulative Perceptions

In considering perceptions, it is also important to recognize that customers will have perceptions of single, transaction-specific encounters as well as overall perceptions of a company based on all their experiences.[7] For example, a bank customer will have a perception of how he was treated in a particular encounter with an employee at a branch and will form a perception of that transaction based on elements of the service experienced during that transaction. That perception is at a very micro, transaction-specific level. The same bank customer will also have overall perceptions of the bank based on all his encounters over a period of time. The experiences might include multiple in-person encounters at the bank branch, online banking experiences, and experiences using the bank's ATMs across many cities. At an even more general level, the customer may have perceptions of banking services or the whole banking industry as a result of all his experiences with banks and everything he knows about banking.

Research suggests that it is important to understand all these types of perceptions for different reasons and that the viewpoints are complementary rather than competing.[8] Understanding perceptions at the transaction-specific level is critical for diagnosing service issues and making immediate changes. These isolated encounters are also the building blocks for overall, cumulative experience evaluations, as you will learn later in this chapter. On the other hand, cumulative experience evaluations are likely to be better predictors of overall loyalty to a company. That is, customer loyalty most often results from the customer's assessment of all her experiences, not just one encounter. (For an exception to this rule, look ahead to Exhibit 4.2).

CUSTOMER SATISFACTION

What Is Customer Satisfaction?

"Everyone knows what satisfaction is until asked to give a definition. Then, it seems, nobody knows."[9] This quote from Richard Oliver, respected expert and long-time writer and researcher on the topic of customer satisfaction, expresses the challenge of defining this most basic of customer concepts. Building from previous definitions, Oliver offers his own formal definition (p. 13):

> Satisfaction is the consumer's fulfillment response. It is a judgment that a product or service feature, or the product or service itself, provides a pleasurable level of consumption-related fulfillment.

In less technical terms, we interpret this definition to mean that *satisfaction* is the customer's evaluation of a product or service in terms of whether that product or service has met the customer's needs and expectations. Failure to meet needs and expectations is assumed to result in *dissatisfaction* with the product or service.

In addition to a sense of *fulfillment* in the knowledge that one's needs have been met, satisfaction can also be related to other types of feelings, depending on the context or type of service.[10] For example, satisfaction can be viewed as *contentment*—more of a passive response that customers may associate with services they do not think a lot about or services that they receive routinely over time. Satisfaction may also be associated with feelings of *pleasure* for services that make the customer feel good or are associated with a sense of happiness. For those services that really surprise the customer in a positive way, satisfaction may mean *delight*. In some situations, where the removal of a negative leads to satisfaction, the customer may associate a sense of *relief* with satisfaction. Finally, satisfaction may be associated with feelings of *ambivalence* when there is a mix of positive and negative experiences associated with the product or service.

Although customer satisfaction tends to be measured at a particular point in time as if it were static, satisfaction is a dynamic, target that may evolve over time, influenced by a variety of factors.[11] Particularly when product usage or the service experience takes place over time, satisfaction may be highly variable, depending on which point in the usage or experience cycle one is focusing on. Similarly, in the case of very new services or a service not previously experienced, customer expectations may be barely forming at the point of initial purchase; these expectations will solidify as the process unfolds and the customer begins to form his or her perceptions. Through the service cycle the customer may have a variety of experiences—some good, some not good—and each will ultimately impact satisfaction.

What Determines Customer Satisfaction?

As shown in Figure 4.1, customer satisfaction is influenced by specific product or service features, perceptions of product and service quality, and price. In addition, personal factors such as the customer's mood or emotional state and situational factors such as family member opinions influence satisfaction.

Product and Service Features

Customer satisfaction with a product or service is influenced significantly by the customer's evaluation of product or service features.[12] For a service such as a resort hotel, important features might include the pool area, access to golf facilities, restaurants, room comfort and privacy, the helpfulness and courtesy of staff, room price, and so forth. In conducting satisfaction studies, most firms determine through some means (often focus groups) what the important features and attributes are for their service and then measure perceptions of those features as well as overall service satisfaction. Research has shown that customers of services make trade-offs among different service features (e.g., price level versus quality versus friendliness of personnel versus level of customization), depending on the type of service being evaluated and the criticality of the service.[13]

Customer Emotions

Customers' emotions can also affect their perceptions of satisfaction with products and services.[14] These emotions can be stable, preexisting emotions—for example, mood state or life satisfaction. Think of times when you are at a very happy stage in your life (such as when you are on vacation), and your good, happy mood and positive frame of mind have influenced how you feel about the services you experience. Alternatively, when you are in a bad mood, your negative feelings may carry over into how you respond to services, causing you to overreact or respond negatively to any little problem.

Specific emotions may also be induced by the consumption experience itself, influencing a customer's satisfaction with the service. Research done in a river-rafting context showed that the river guides had a strong effect on their customers' emotional responses to the trip and that those feelings (both positive and negative) were linked to overall trip satisfaction.[15] Positive emotions such as happiness, pleasure, elation, and a sense of warm-heartedness enhanced customers' satisfaction with the rafting trip. In turn, negative emotions such as sadness, sorrow, regret, and anger led to diminished customer satisfaction. Overall, in the rafting context, positive emotions had a stronger effect than negative ones. (These positive emotions are apparent in the photo shown on page 82.) In a different context, drawing on emotional contagion theory, researchers found that the authenticity of employees' emotional display directly affected customers' emotions in a video retail and consulting service.[16] Similar emotional contagion effects were found in a sequence of multiple emotional displays by employees in the context of restaurant service recovery in China. In this research employees' positive and negative emotions both affected the customer's emotional state and ultimate satisfaction.[17]

River rafters experience many positive emotions, increasing their satisfaction with the service.

Attributions for Service Success or Failure

Attributions—the perceived causes of events—influence perceptions of satisfaction as well.[18] When customers have been surprised by an outcome (the service is either much better or much worse than expected), they tend to look for the reasons, and their assessments of the reasons can influence their satisfaction. For example, if a customer of a weight-loss organization fails to lose weight as hoped for, she will likely search for the causes—was it something she did, was the diet plan ineffective, or did circumstances simply not allow her to follow the diet regimen—before determining her level of satisfaction or dissatisfaction with the weight-loss company.[19] For many services, customers take at least partial responsibility for how things turn out.

Even when customers do not take responsibility for the outcome, customer satisfaction may be influenced by other kinds of attributions. For example, research done in a travel agency context found that customers were less dissatisfied with a pricing error made by the agent if they felt that the reason was outside the agent's control or if they felt that it was a rare mistake, unlikely to occur again.[20]

Perceptions of Equity or Fairness

Customer satisfaction is also influenced by perceptions of equity and fairness.[21] Customers ask themselves: Have I been treated fairly compared with other customers? Did other customers get better treatment, better prices, or better-quality service? Did I pay a fair price for the service? Was I treated well in exchange for what I paid and the effort I expended? Notions of fairness are central to customers' perceptions of satisfaction with products and services, particularly in service recovery situations. As you will learn in Chapter 7, satisfaction with a service provider following a service failure is largely determined by perceptions of fair treatment. The example of Sears Auto Centers division illustrates consumers' strong reactions to unfair treatment.[22] Over a decade ago the division was charged with defrauding customers in 44 states by performing unnecessary repairs. Sears employee rewards had been based on the quantity of repairs sold, resulting in substantial unnecessary charges to customers. The $27 million that Sears paid to settle complaints and the additional loss of business all resulted from extreme dissatisfaction of its customers over the unfair treatment.

Other Customers, Family Members, and Coworkers

In addition to product and service features and one's own feelings and beliefs, customer satisfaction is often influenced by other people.[23] For example, family decisions about a vacation destination and satisfaction with the trip are dynamic phenomena, influenced by the reactions and emotions of individual family members.[24] Later, what family members express in terms of satisfaction or dissatisfaction with the trip will be influenced by stories retold among the family and selective memories of the events. Similarly, the satisfaction of the rafters in the photo is certainly influenced by individual perceptions, but it is also influenced greatly by the experiences, behavior, and views of the other rafters. In a business setting, satisfaction with a new service or technology—for example, a new customer relationship management software service—will be influenced not only by individuals' personal experiences with the software itself but also by what others say about it in the company, how others use it and feel about it, and how widely it is adopted in the organization.

National Customer Satisfaction Indexes

Because of the importance of customer satisfaction to firms and overall quality of life, many countries have a national index that measures and tracks customer satisfaction at a macro level.[25] Many public policymakers believe that these measures could and should be used as tools for evaluating the health of the nation's economy, along with traditional measures of productivity and price. Customer satisfaction indexes begin to get at the *quality* of economic output, whereas more traditional economic indicators tend to focus only on *quantity*. The first such measure was the Swedish Customer Satisfaction Barometer introduced in 1989.[26] Later, similar indexes were introduced in Germany (Deutsche Kundenbarometer, or DK, in 1992), the United States (American Customer Satisfaction Index, ACSI, in 1994), and Switzerland (Swiss Index of Customer Satisfaction, SWICS, in 1998).[27] More recently, other countries, including the United Kingdom, Indonesia, the Dominican Republic, Turkey, Mexico, Colombia, and Singapore, have adopted the ACSI methodology in creating national customer satisfaction indices.[28]

The American Customer Satisfaction Index

The American Customer Satisfaction Index (ACSI),[29] developed by researchers at the National Quality Research Center at the University of Michigan, is a measure of satisfaction with goods and services. The measure tracks, on a quarterly basis, customer perceptions across 200 firms representing all major economic sectors, including government agencies. Within each industry group, major industry segments are included, and within each industry, the largest companies in that industry are selected to participate. For each company approximately 250 interviews are conducted with current customers. Each company receives an ACSI score computed from its customers' perceptions of quality, value, satisfaction, expectations, complaints, and future loyalty.[30]

   The 2010 ACSI results by industry are shown in Table 4.1.[31] The table shows that, overall, customers tend to be most satisfied with nondurables (like soft drinks and personal care products), a bit less satisfied with durables (such as cars, household appliances, and electronics), and the least satisfied with services (like airlines and telephone wireless and cable services). With the exception of Internet retailers, which

TABLE 4.1
American Customer Satisfaction Index— Ratings by Industry

Source: "American Customer Satisfaction Index—Ratings by Industry," ACSI website, www.theacsi.org. Reprinted by permission of American Customer Satisfaction Index, www.theascsi.org.

Industry	2010 ACSI Score	Percent Change in ACSI Score from Previous Year
Electronics	85	2.4
Soft drinks	84	−1.2
Express delivery	84	1.2
Personal care and cleaning products	83	−2.4
Apparel	83	1.2
Pet food	83	−1.2
Breweries	82	−2.4
Automobiles and light vehicles	82	−2.4
Major appliances	82	1.2
Food manufacturing	81	−2.4
Internet retail	80	−3.6
Life insurance	80	1.3
Property and casualty insurance	80	0.0
Athletic shoes	80	0.0
Limited service restaurants	79	5.3
Internet brokerage	78	0.0
Personal computers	78	4.0
Internet travel	78	1.3
Specialty retail stores	78	1.3
Computer software	78	2.6
Health and personal care stores	77	−1.3
Hotels	77	2.7
Hospitals	77	5.5
Internet portals and search engines	77	−7.2
Network and cable TV news	77	4.1
Banks	76	1.3
Cigarettes	76	5.6
Department and discount stores	76	1.3
Supermarkets	75	−1.3
Cellular phones	75	−1.3
Internet news and information	74	0.0
U.S. Postal Service	74	4.2
Investor-owned utilities	74	NA
Motion pictures	73	−3.9
Municipal utilities	73	NA
Health insurance	73	−2.7
Fixed line telephone service	73	−2.7
Wireless telephone service	71	−1.4
Gasoline stations	70	−7.9
Internet social media	70	NA
Newspapers	65	−1.5
Airlines	65	0.0

rank near the top, other online services rank near the middle. The observation that services tend to rank lower in the ACSI rankings than do durable and nondurable products is a trend observed across the ACSI's history. It is important to point out, however, that these rankings are industry averages. Almost every industry has some strong performers in terms of customer satisfaction. For example, in 2010 scores for airlines ranged from 56 (Delta) to 81 (Southwest Airlines).

We can only conjecture about the reasons for lower satisfaction with services in general. Perhaps it is because downsizing and right-sizing in service businesses have resulted in stressed and overworked frontline service providers who are unable to provide the level of service demanded. Perhaps it is due to the inherent heterogeneity of services discussed in Chapter 1; in other words, because services are difficult to standardize, and each customer has his or her own unique expectations, the result may be greater variability and potentially lower overall satisfaction. Perhaps it is due to difficulty finding qualified frontline service providers for consumer service businesses. Perhaps it is due to rising customer expectations rather than any real or absolute decline in actual service. Whatever the reason, there is much room for improvement in customer satisfaction ratings across service industries.

Outcomes of Customer Satisfaction

Why all this attention to customer satisfaction? As mentioned in the previous section, some public policymakers believe that customer satisfaction is an important indicator of national economic health. They believe that it is not enough to track economic efficiency and pricing statistics. Satisfaction, they believe, is also an important indicator of well-being. Further, many believe that customer satisfaction is correlated with other measures of economic health such as corporate earnings and stock value. Through the ACSI data, researchers at the University of Michigan have been able to document a clear relationship between ACSI scores and market value added (MVA), which measures the firm's success in creating wealth for shareholders. This relationship is depicted in Figure 4.2, which shows MVA averages for the top 25 percent of ACSI firms and the bottom 25 percent.[32]

FIGURE 4.2 **ACSI and Market Value Added**

Source: ACSI website, www.theacsi.org, About ACSI, "Economic Indicator," accessed July 11, 2011. Reprinted by permission of American Customer Satisfaction Index, www.theacsi.org.

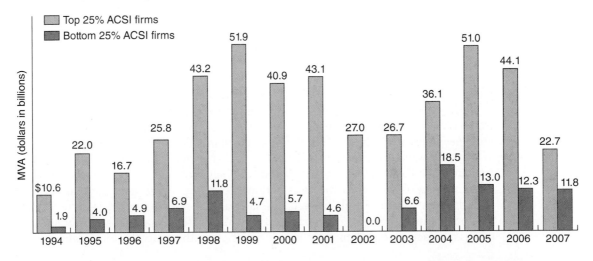

FIGURE 4.3
Relationship between Customer Satisfaction and Loyalty in Competitive Industries

Source: J. L. Heskett, W. E. Sasser Jr., and L. A. Schlesinger, *The Service Profit Chain: How Leading Companies Link Profit and Growth to Loyalty, Satisfaction, and Value* (New York: The Free Press, 1997), p. 83. Copyright © 1997 by J. L. Heskett, W. E. Sasser, Jr., and L. A. Schlesinger. Reprinted with the permission of The Free Press, a Division of Simon & Schuster, Inc.

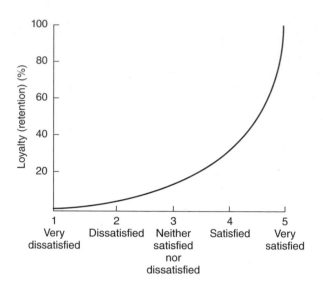

Beyond these macroeconomic implications, however, individual firms have discovered that increasing levels of customer satisfaction can be linked to customer loyalty and profits.[33] Research also shows that firms that invest in service and excel in customer satisfaction offer excess returns to their shareholders. One study found that firms that did better than their competition in terms of satisfying customers (as measured by the ACSI) generated superior returns at a lower systematic risk.[34] Another study found that retailer announcements of customer service strategies resulted in a significant abnormal return for these firms and increased market value of 1.09 percent on average.[35] Research has also shown that portfolios of stocks consisting of firms with high levels and positive changes in customer satisfaction outperform other portfolio combinations.[36]

As shown in Figure 4.3, there is an important relationship between customer satisfaction and customer loyalty. This relationship is particularly strong when customers are very satisfied. Thus, firms that simply aim to satisfy customers may not be doing enough to engender loyalty—they must instead aim to more than satisfy or even delight their customers. Xerox Corporation was one of the first, if not the first, companies to pinpoint this relationship. Xerox discovered through its extensive customer research that customers giving Xerox a 5 (very satisfied) on a satisfaction scale were six times more likely to repurchase Xerox equipment than were those giving the company a 4 (somewhat satisfied).[37] Enterprise Rent-A-Car has also learned through its research that customers who give the highest rating to their rental experience are three times more likely to rent again than are those who give the company the second-highest rating.[38] Information provided by TARP Worldwide Inc.—based on data from 10 studies, including 8,000 customers worldwide from across industries—drew similar conclusions. TARP found that 96 percent of those customers who are "very satisfied" say they will "definitely repurchase" from the same company. The number drops precipitously to only 52 percent for those customers who are "somewhat satisfied." Only 7 percent of customers who are "neutral or very dissatisfied" say they will definitely repurchase.[39]

At the opposite end of the satisfaction spectrum, researchers have also found that there is a strong link between dissatisfaction and disloyalty—or defection. Customer loyalty can fall off precipitously when customers reach a particular level of dissatisfaction or when they are dissatisfied with critically important service attributes.[40] We discuss these relationships and the implications for relationship and loyalty marketing in Chapter 6, but suffice it to say here that clear linkages have been drawn between customer satisfaction, loyalty, and firm profitability. Thus, many companies are spending significant time and money understanding the underpinnings of customer satisfaction and ways that they can improve.

SERVICE QUALITY

We now turn to *service quality,* a critical element of customer perceptions. In the case of pure services (e.g., health care, financial services, education), service quality will be the dominant element in customers' evaluations. In cases in which customer service or services are offered in combination with a physical product (e.g., IT services, auto services), service quality may also be critical in determining customer satisfaction. Figure 4.1 highlighted these relationships. We will focus here on the left side of Figure 4.1, examining the underlying factors that form perceptions of service quality. First we discuss *what* customers evaluate; then we look specifically at the five dimensions of service that customers rely on in forming their judgments.

Outcome, Interaction, and Physical Environment Quality

What is it that consumers evaluate when judging service quality? Over the years, service researchers have suggested that consumers judge the quality of services based on their perceptions of the technical outcome provided, the process by which that outcome was delivered, and the quality of the physical surroundings where the service is delivered.[41] For example, in the case of a lawsuit, a legal services client will judge the quality of the technical outcome, or how the court case was resolved, as well as the quality of the interaction. Interaction quality includes such factors as the lawyer's timeliness in returning phone calls, his empathy for the client, and his courtesy and listening skills. Similarly, a restaurant customer will judge the service on her perceptions of the meal (technical outcome quality) and on how the meal was served and how the employees interacted with her (interaction quality). The decor and surroundings (physical environment quality) of both the law firm and the restaurant will also affect the customer's perceptions of overall service quality.

Service Quality Dimensions

Research suggests that customers do not perceive quality in a unidimensional way but rather judge quality based on multiple factors relevant to the context. The dimensions of service quality have been identified through the pioneering research of Parsu Parasuraman, Valarie Zeithaml, and Leonard Berry. Their research has identified five dimensions of service quality that apply across a variety of service contexts.[42] The five dimensions defined here are shown in Figure 4.1 as drivers of service quality. These five dimensions appear again in Chapter 5, along with the scale developed to measure them, SERVQUAL.

- *Reliability:* ability to perform the promised service dependably and accurately.
- *Responsiveness:* willingness to help customers and provide prompt service.
- *Assurance:* employees' knowledge and courtesy and their ability to inspire trust and confidence.
- *Empathy:* caring, individualized attention given to customers.
- *Tangibles:* appearance of physical facilities, equipment, personnel, and communication materials.

The development of the service quality dimensions of reliability, responsiveness, assurance, empathy, and tangibles was based on research conducted across multiple contexts within the United States. As a general rule, reliability comes through as the most important dimension of service quality in the United States, with responsiveness also being relatively important when compared with the remaining three dimensions. But what happens when we look across cultures? Are the service quality dimensions still important? Which ones are most important? Answers to these questions can be extremely valuable for companies delivering services across cultures or in multicultural environments.

Researchers have used Geert Hofstede's well-established cultural dimensions to assess whether service quality importance would vary across different cultural orientations. For example, *power distance* refers to the extent to which status differences are expected and accepted within a culture. Research has suggested that most Asian countries are characterized by high power distance, whereas many Western countries score lower on power distance measures. Broadly speaking, *individualism* reflects a self-orientation that is characteristic of Western culture, whereas its opposite, *collectivism,* is more typical of the East. Similar comparisons across cultures have been made for the other dimensions: *masculinity, uncertainty avoidance,* and *long-term orientation.* The question is whether these types of cultural differences affect the importance consumers place on the service quality dimensions.

The figure shown here suggests strong differences in the importance of service quality dimensions across clusters of customers defined by different cultural dimensions. The cultural profile of the clusters is described as

Followers: Large power distance, high collectivism, high masculinity, neutral uncertainty avoidance, and short-term orientation.

Balance seekers: Small power distance, high collectivism, neutral masculinity, high uncertainty avoidance, and medium-term orientation.

Self-confidents: Small power distance, high individualism, medium femininity, low uncertainty avoidance, and long-term orientation.

Sensory seekers: Large power distance, medium individualism, high masculinity, low uncertainty avoidance, and short-term orientation.

Functional analyzers: Small power distance, medium individualism, high femininity, high uncertainty avoidance, and long-term orientation.

From this figure it is clear that the service quality dimensions are relevant across cultures, but their relative importance varies depending on cultural value orientation. For example, small power distance cultures with high to medium individualism and long-term

These dimensions represent how consumers organize information about service quality in their minds. On the basis of exploratory and quantitative research, these five dimensions were found relevant for banking, insurance, appliance repair and maintenance, securities brokerage, long-distance telephone service, automobile repair service, and others. The dimensions are also applicable to retail and business services, and logic suggests they would be relevant for internal services as well. Sometimes customers use all the dimensions to determine service quality perceptions, at other times not. For example, for an ATM, empathy is not likely to be a relevant dimension. And in a phone encounter to schedule a repair, tangibles will not be relevant.

Research suggests that cultural differences also affect the relative importance placed on the five dimensions, as discussed in our Global Feature. Interesting differences in service quality dimensions themselves also emerge in country-specific studies. For example, research in Pakistan that builds upon the original service quality dimensions revealed the following dimensions of service quality: tangibles, reliability, assurance, sincerity, personalization, and formality.[43] This study also illustrated that cultural differences may cause the original dimensions to be interpreted slightly differently as well. In Pakistan, "reliability" was not as absolute in its meaning, but rate these dimensions as less important. The tangibles dimension shows the widest variation, with sensory seekers rating it most important and functional analyzers rating it least important.

The researchers in this study suggest a number of implications for companies serving multiple cultures. For example, if the target market has a follower cultural profile, service providers may want to emphasize training their employees to have professional knowledge and be trustworthy to gain the trust of these customers, combined with tangibles and empathy to convey service quality. On the other hand, to serve self-confidents, providers should emphasize equipping and empowering the employees so they are capable of providing reliable, responsive service.

orientation (self-confidents and functional analyzers) rate reliability and responsiveness as most important. On the other hand, cultures with large power distance and high masculinity (followers and sensory seekers)

Sources: G. Hofstede, *Cultures and Organizations: Software of the Mind* (New York, McGraw-Hill, 1991); O. Furrer, B. Shaw-Ching Liu, and D. Sudharshan, "The Relationships between Culture and Service Quality Perceptions," *Journal of Service Research* 2 (May 2000), pp. 355–371; www.geert-hofstede.com.

rather was interpreted as "promises are mostly kept," "minimum errors are made on reports or statements," and "service is usually available when needed."

In the following pages we expand on each of the five original SERVQUAL dimensions and provide illustrations of how customers judge them.

Reliability: Delivering on Promises

Of the five dimensions, reliability has been consistently shown to be the most important determinant of perceptions of service quality among U.S. customers.[44] *Reliability* is defined as the ability to perform the promised service dependably and accurately. In its broadest sense, reliability means that the company delivers on its promises—promises about delivery, service provision, problem resolution, and pricing. Customers want to do business with companies that keep their promises, particularly their promises about the service outcomes and core service attributes.

One company that effectively communicates and delivers on the reliability dimension is Federal Express (FedEx). The reliability message of FedEx—when it "absolutely, positively has to get there"—reflects the company's service positioning. But even when firms do not choose to position themselves explicitly on

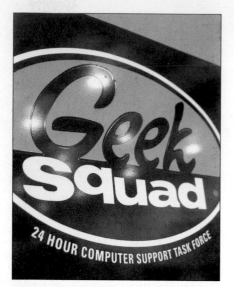

The Geek Squad emphasize the service quality dimension of *responsiveness* in its service positioning.

reliability, as FedEx has, this dimension is extremely important to consumers. All firms need to be aware of customer expectations of reliability. Firms that do not provide the core service that customers think they are buying fail their customers in the most direct way.

Responsiveness: Being Willing to Help

Responsiveness is the willingness to help customers and to provide prompt service. This dimension emphasizes attentiveness and promptness in dealing with customer requests, questions, complaints, and problems. Responsiveness is communicated to customers by the length of time they have to wait for assistance, answers to questions, or attention to problems.

To excel on the dimension of responsiveness, a company must view the process of service delivery and the handling of requests from the customer's point of view rather than from the company's point of view. Standards for speed and promptness that reflect the company's view of internal process requirements may be very different from the customer's requirements for speed and promptness. To truly distinguish themselves on responsiveness, companies need well-staffed customer service departments as well as responsive frontline people in all contact positions. The Geek Squad's 24-hour computer assistance service built its reputation on responsive, quick service "because viruses aren't known for keeping business hours," as their ads state (see photo). Responsiveness perceptions are diminished when customers must wait to get through by telephone, are put through to a complex voice mail system, or have trouble accessing the firm's website.

Assurance: Inspiring Trust and Confidence

Assurance is defined as employees' knowledge and courtesy and the ability of the firm and its employees to inspire customer trust and confidence. This dimension is likely to be particularly important for services that customers perceive as high risk or for services of which they feel uncertain about their ability to evaluate outcomes—for example, banking, insurance, brokerage, medical, and legal services.

Trust and confidence may be embodied in the person who links the customer to the company, such as securities brokers, insurance agents, lawyers, or counselors. In such service contexts the company seeks to build trust and loyalty between key contact people and individual customers. The "personal banker" concept captures this idea: customers are assigned to a banker who will get to know them individually and who will coordinate all their banking services.

In other situations, trust and confidence are embodied in the organization itself. Insurance companies such as Allstate ("You're in good hands with Allstate") and Prudential ("Own a piece of the rock") illustrate efforts to create trusting relationships between customers and the company as a whole. An ad campaign by FedEx uses the tag line "Relax, it's FedEx," going beyond its traditional reliability message to focus on assurance and trust.

Empathy: Treating Customers as Individuals

Empathy is defined as the caring, individualized attention that the firm provides its customers. The essence of empathy is conveying, through personalized service, that customers are unique and special and that their needs are understood. Customers want to feel understood by and important to firms that provide service to them. Personnel at small service firms often know customers by name and build relationships that reflect their personal knowledge of customer requirements and preferences. When such a small firm competes with larger firms, the ability to be empathetic may give the small firm a clear advantage.

In business-to-business services, customers want supplier firms to understand their industries and issues. Many small computer consulting firms successfully compete with large vendors by positioning themselves as specialists in particular industries. Even though larger firms have superior resources, the small firms are perceived as more knowledgeable about customers' specific issues and needs and are able to offer more customized services.

Tangibles: Representing the Service Physically

Tangibles are defined as the appearance of physical facilities, equipment, personnel, and communication materials. Tangibles provide physical representations or images of the service that customers, particularly new customers, will use to evaluate quality. Service industries that emphasize tangibles in their strategies include services in which the customer visits the establishment to receive the service, such as restaurants and hotels, retail stores, and entertainment companies.

Although tangibles are often used by service companies to enhance their image, provide continuity, and signal quality to customers, most companies combine tangibles with another dimension to create a service quality strategy for the firm. For example, Jiffy Lube emphasizes both responsiveness and tangibles—providing fast, efficient service and a comfortable, clean waiting area. In contrast, firms that do not pay attention to the tangibles dimension of the service strategy can confuse and even destroy an otherwise good strategy.

Table 4.2 provides examples of how customers judge each of the five dimensions of service quality across a variety of service contexts, including both consumer and business services.

E-Service Quality

The growth of e-tailing and e-services has led many companies to wonder how consumers evaluate service quality on the Web and whether the criteria are different from those used to judge the quality of non-Internet services.[45] A study sponsored by the Marketing Science Institute, was conducted to understand how consumers judge e-service quality.[46] In that study, *E-S-QUAL* is defined as the extent to which a website facilitates efficient and effective shopping, purchasing, and delivery. Through exploratory focus groups and two phases of empirical data collection and analysis, this research identified seven dimensions that are critical for core service evaluation (four dimensions) and service recovery evaluation (three dimensions).

The four core dimensions that customers use to judge websites at which they experience no questions or problems are as follows:[47]

Efficiency: The ease and speed of accessing and using the site.

Fulfillment: The extent to which the site's promises about order delivery and item availability are fulfilled.

System availability: The correct technical functioning of the site.

Privacy: The degree to which the site is safe and protects customer information.

TABLE 4.2 **Examples of How Customers Judge the Five Dimensions of Service Quality**

Industry	Reliability	Responsiveness	Assurance	Empathy	Tangibles
Car repair (consumer)	Problem fixed the first time and ready when promised	Accessible; no waiting; responds to requests	Knowledgeable mechanics	Acknowledges customer by name; remembers previous problems and preferences	Repair facility; waiting area; uniforms; equipment
Airline (consumer)	Flights to promised destinations depart and arrive on schedule	Prompt and speedy system for ticketing, in-flight baggage handling	Trusted name; good safety record; competent employees	Understands special individual needs; anticipates customer needs	Aircraft; ticketing counters; baggage area; uniforms
Medical care (consumer)	Appointments are kept on schedule; diagnoses prove accurate	Accessible; no waiting; willingness to listen	Knowledge; skills; credentials; reputation	Acknowledges patient as a person; remembers previous problems; listens well; has patience	Waiting room; exam room; equipment; written materials
Architecture (business)	Delivers plans when promised and within budget	Returns phone calls; adapts to changes	Credentials; reputation; name in the community; knowledge and skills	Understands client's industry; acknowledges and adapts to specific client needs; gets to know the client	Office area; reports; plans themselves; billing statements; dress of employees
Information processing (internal)	Provides needed information when requested	Prompt response to requests; not "bureaucratic"; deals with problems promptly	Knowledgeable staff; well trained; credentials	Knows internal customers as individuals; understands individual and departmental needs	Internal reports; office area; dress of employees
Internet brokerage (consumer and business)	Provides correct information and executes customer requests accurately	Quick website with easy access and no down time	Credible information sources on the site; brand recognition; credentials apparent on site	Responds with human interaction as needed	Appearance of the website as well as flyers, brochures, and other print materials

The study also revealed three dimensions that customers use to judge recovery service when they have problems or questions:

Responsiveness: The effective handling of problems and returns through the site.

Compensation: The degree to which the site compensates customers for problems.

Contact: The availability of assistance through telephone or online representatives.

L.L.Bean's Internet website, shown in the photo on page 93, exhibits all of the qualities of an excellent e-tailer. The company excels on the core dimensions of e-service quality, and they also offer excellent and easy to understand recovery through their service guarantee.

L.L.Bean excels on E-S-QUAL.

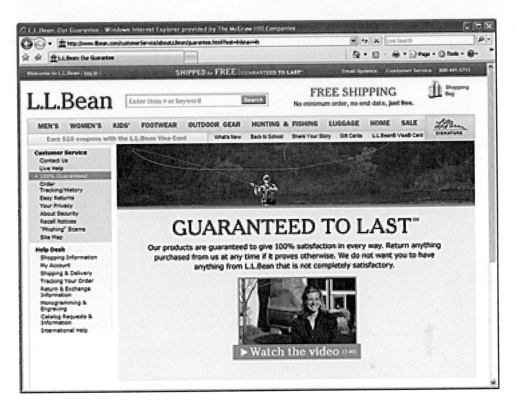

SERVICE ENCOUNTERS: THE BUILDING BLOCKS FOR CUSTOMER PERCEPTIONS

We have just finished a discussion of customer perceptions, specifically customer satisfaction and service quality. As discussed in our Strategy Insight, companies today recognize that they can compete more effectively by distinguishing themselves with respect to service quality, satisfaction, and loyalty. Next we turn to what have been termed the building blocks for customer perceptions—service encounters, or "moments of truth." Service encounters are where promises are kept or broken and where the proverbial rubber meets the road—sometimes called "real-time marketing." It is from these service encounters that customers build their perceptions.

Service Encounters or Moments of Truth

From the customer's point of view, the most vivid impression of service occurs in the *service encounter,* or *moment of truth,* when the customer interacts with the service firm. For example, among the service encounters that a hotel customer experiences are checking into the hotel, being taken to a room by a bellperson, eating a restaurant meal, requesting a wake-up call, and checking out. You could think of the linking of these moments of truth as a service encounter cascade (see Figure 4.4). It is in these encounters that customers receive a snapshot of the organization's service quality, and each encounter contributes to the customer's overall satisfaction and willingness to do business with the organization again. From the organization's point of view, each encounter thus presents an opportunity to prove its potential as a quality service provider and to increase customer loyalty, as suggested by the ad for Doubletree Hotels shown on page 96.

Strategy Insight   Customer Satisfaction, Loyalty, and Service as Corporate Strategies

CEOs of many highly successful, growth-oriented companies are preoccupied with customer satisfaction, loyalty, and service. They see these corporate objectives as critical challenges but also as the keys to their companies' continued profitable growth. Since the economic downturn following 2008, many organizations have reinvigorated their corporate focus on service in order to build customer loyalty.

Measures of improvement in satisfaction and loyalty often are a basis for managers' and employees' incentive compensation, stock performance, growth predictions, and service improvement strategies. Take these specific examples:

- At Enterprise Rent-A-Car, branch managers must meet or exceed corporate customer satisfaction and loyalty averages based on the ESQi (Enterprise Service Quality index) to be eligible for promotion. Clearly this requirement motivates them to develop cross-functional approaches and strategies that will improve satisfaction in their branches.
- Harrah's Entertainment developed a strategy to link frontline employee rewards directly to customer satisfaction. Every employee—from slot attendants to chefs—was told: "If your service can persuade one customer to make one more visit a year with us, you've had a good shift. If

you can persuade three, you've had a great shift." The company also implemented a bonus plan to reward hourly workers with extra cash for achieving improved customer satisfaction scores.
- General Electric, recognized every year as one of the world's top 10 largest businesses, uses customer satisfaction and loyalty to guide corporate strategy in its business units. For example, at GE Healthcare Financial Services, key findings from its loyalty scores, net promoter scores, and related surveys have allowed the company to develop programs designed to improve customer relationships and efficiency.
- During the economic recovery, post-2008, many executives have increased their focus on customer service in order to gain market share. For example, drugstore chain Walgreens has trained its pharmacists to spend more time helping customers by answering their questions about illnesses; Comcast has put all of its call-center agents through new customer service training; and American Express is expanding its program to enhance customer service among its agents.

As these examples show, customer satisfaction, loyalty, and service quality are used to predict growth and reward performance; thus, measuring them appropriately and using the measures wisely

FIGURE 4.4
A Service Encounter Cascade for a Hotel Visit

Enterprise focuses strategically on customer satisfaction in all its branches.

One measurement approach, "Net Promoter," was developed by loyalty expert Frederick Reichheld based on business case studies conducted by his firm. Net Promoter has gained tremendous popularity across industries. The research advocates *one* customer loyalty question as the best for most industries in terms of predicting repeat customer purchases, growth, or referrals. The question is "How likely is it that you would recommend [company X] to a friend or colleague?" Based on this question many firms now use Reichheld's "Net Promoter" metric (the proportional difference between a firm's "promoters" and "detractors" based on this one question) to predict growth and loyalty.

Sources: T. Keiningham, B. Cooil, T. W. Andreassen, and L. Aksoy, "A Longitudinal Examination of Net Promoter and Firm Revenue Growth," *Journal of Marketing,* 71 (July 2007), pp. 39–51; F. F. Reichheld, *The Ultimate Question: Driving Good Profits and True Growth* (Boston: Harvard Business School Press, 2006); F. Reichheld and R. Markay, *The Ultimate Question 2.0* (Boston: Harvard Business School Press, 2011); G. Loveman, "Diamonds in the Data Mine," *Harvard Business Review,* May 2003, pp. 109–113; C. J. Loomis, "The Big Surprise Is Enterprise," *Fortune,* July 24, 2006, pp. 141–150; J. McGregor, "Will You Recommend Us?" *BusinessWeek,* January 30, 2006, pp. 94–95; GE 2007 Customer Citizenship Report, GE website; M. Sanserino and C. Tuna, "Companies Strive Harder to Please Customers," *The Wall Street Journal,* July 27, 2009, p. B4; D. Mattioli, "Customer Service as a Growth Engine," *The Wall Street Journal,* June 7, 2010, p. B6.

are critical. A multitude of ways to measure customer satisfaction, loyalty, and quality exist, but all are not equally useful. Some are better for predicting outcomes such as growth and performance, while other types of satisfaction and quality measures are needed for diagnosing underlying problems and making improvements.

Some services have few service encounters, and others have many. The Disney Corporation estimates that each of its amusement park customers experiences about 74 service encounters and that a negative experience in any one of them can lead to a negative overall evaluation. Mistakes or problems that occur in the early stages of the service cascade may be particularly critical. Marriott Hotels learned this through its extensive customer research to determine what service elements contribute most to customer loyalty. It found that four of the top five factors come into play in the first 10 minutes of the guest's stay.[48]

The Importance of Encounters

Although early events in the encounter cascade are likely to be especially important, *any* encounter can be critical in determining customer satisfaction and loyalty. If a customer is interacting with a firm for the first time, that initial encounter will create a first impression of the organization. In these first encounter situations, the customer frequently has no other basis for judging the organization, and the initial phone contact or face-to-face experience with a representative of the firm can take on significant importance in the customer's perceptions of quality. A customer calling for repair service on a household appliance may well hang up and call a different company if he is treated rudely by a customer service representative, put on hold for a lengthy period, or told that two weeks is the soonest someone can be sent out to make the repair. Even if the technical quality of the firm's repair service is superior, the firm may not get the chance to demonstrate it if the initial telephone encounter drives the customer away.

Even when the customer has had multiple interactions with a firm, each individual encounter is important in creating a composite image of the firm in the customer's memory. In today's technology-mediated world, these encounters can occur online through websites and other Internet-based channels as well as in person or over the phone. Many positive experiences add up to a composite image of high quality, whereas

Every service encounter is an opportunity to build satisfaction and quality.

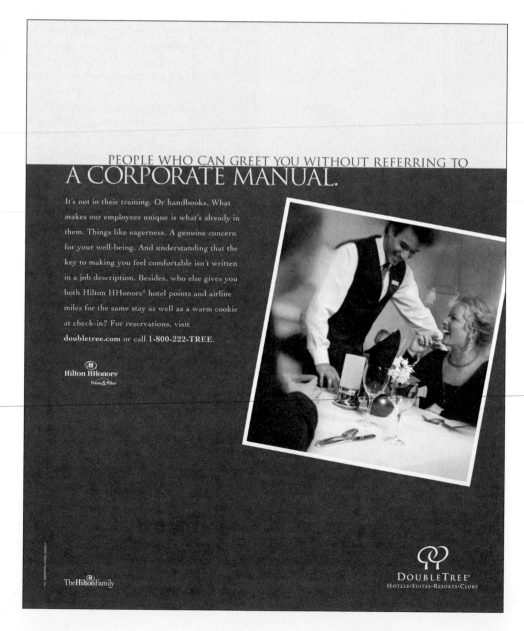

Exhibit 4.1   One Critical Encounter Destroys 30-Year Relationship

"If you have $1 in a bank or $1 million, I think they owe you the courtesy of stamping your parking ticket," said John Barrier. One day Mr. Barrier paid a visit to his bank in Spokane, Washington. He was wearing his usual shabby clothes and pulled up in his pickup truck, parking in the lot next to the bank. After cashing a check, he went outside to drive away and was stopped by a parking attendant who told him there was a 60-cent fee but that he could get his parking slip validated in the bank and park for free. No problem, Barrier thought and he went back into the bank (where, by the way, he had been banking for 30 years). The teller looked him up and down and refused to stamp his slip, telling him that the bank validated parking only for people who have transactions with the bank and that cashing a check wasn't a transaction. Mr. Barrier then asked to see the bank manager, who also looked him up and down, stood back, and "gave me one of those kinds of looks," also refusing to validate the parking bill. Mr. Barrier then said, "Fine. You don't need me, and I don't need you." He withdrew all his money and took it down the street to a competing bank, where the first check he deposited was for $1,000,000.

Source: "Shabby Millionaire Closes Account, Gives Bank Lesson about Snobbery." Reprinted with permission of United Press International from *The Arizona Republic* issue of February 21, 1989, p. A3.

many negative interactions have the opposite effect. On the other hand, a combination of positive and negative interactions leave the customer feeling unsure of the firm's quality, doubtful of its consistency in service delivery, and vulnerable to the appeals of competitors. For example, a large corporate customer of an institutional food provider that provides food service in all its company dining rooms and cafeterias could have a series of positive encounters with the account manager or salesperson who handles the account. These encounters may occur through multiple channels, including online, through the corporate website, via e-mail, over the phone, or in person. These experiences could be followed by positive encounters with the operations staff who actually set up the food service facilities. However, even with these positive encounters, later negative experiences with the staff who serve the food or the accounting department that administers the billing procedures can result in a mixture of overall quality impressions. This variation in experiences could result in the corporate customer wondering about the quality of the organization and unsure of what to expect in the future. Each encounter with different people and departments representing the food service provider adds to or detracts from the potential for a continuing relationship.

Logic suggests that not all encounters are equally important in building relationships. For every organization, certain encounters are probably key to customer satisfaction. For Marriott Hotels, as noted, the early encounters are most important. In a hospital context, a study of patients revealed that encounters with nursing staff were more important in predicting satisfaction than were encounters with meal service or patient discharge personnel.[49]

In addition to these key encounters, there are some momentous encounters that, like the proverbial "one bad apple," simply ruin the rest and drive the customer away no matter how many or what type of encounters have occurred in the past. These momentous encounters can occur in connection with very important events (such as the failure to deliver an essential piece of equipment before a critical deadline), or they may seem inconsequential, as in the story of the bank customer described in Exhibit 4.1. Similarly, momentous positive encounters can sometimes bind a customer to an organization for life. Research in a call center context concludes that, although the average quality of the individual events in a service encounter sequence are important, satisfaction can be enhanced by providing a positive peak experience within the sequence.[50]

This and other research suggest that "not all events in an experience sequence are created equal" and that, in fact, there are benefits to be gained by creating truly delightful (or "peak") experiences at predetermined points in the sequence.

Types of Service Encounters

A service encounter occurs every time a customer interacts with the service organization. There are three general types of service encounters: *remote encounters, technology-mediated encounters,* and *face-to-face encounters.*[51] A customer may experience any of these types of encounters, or a combination of all three, in his or her interactions with a service firm.

First, encounters can occur without any direct human contact (*remote encounters*), such as when a customer interacts with a bank through the ATM system, with a retailer through its website, or with a mail-order service through automated touch-tone phone ordering. Remote encounters also occur when the firm sends its billing statements or communicates other types of information to customers by regular mail or e-mail. Although there is no direct human contact in these remote encounters, each represents an opportunity for the firm to reinforce or establish quality perceptions in the customer. In remote encounters the tangible evidence of the service and the quality of the technical processes and systems become the primary bases for judging quality. More and more services are being delivered through technology, particularly with the advent of Internet applications. Retail purchases, airline ticketing, repair and maintenance troubleshooting, and package and shipment tracking are just a few examples of services available via the Internet. All these types of service encounters can be considered remote encounters (see our Technology Spotlight).

In many organizations (such as insurance companies, utilities, and telecommunications), the most frequent type of encounter between an end-customer and the firm occurs over the telephone or via simultaneous texting, live chats or other platforms that allow technology-based communication with a real person in real time (*technology-mediated encounters*). Almost all firms (whether goods manufacturers or service businesses) rely on basic telephone encounters to some extent for customer service, general inquiry, or order-taking functions. The judgment of quality in phone encounters is different than in remote encounters because there is greater potential variability in the interaction.[52] Tone of voice, employee knowledge, and effectiveness/efficiency in handling customer issues become important criteria for judging quality in these encounters. For real time e-mail or text exchanges or live chat encounters, where there is no human voice to rely on for cues, the actual words chosen and tone of the communication will determine perceptions of quality.

A third type of encounter is the one that occurs between an employee and a customer in direct personal contact (*face-to-face encounters*). At Mayo Clinic, face-to-face encounters occur between patients and reception staff, nurses, doctors, lab technicians, food service workers, pharmacy staff, and others. For a company such as IBM, in a business-to-business setting, direct encounters occur between the business customer and salespeople, delivery personnel, maintenance representatives, and professional consultants. Determining and understanding service quality issues in face-to-face contexts is the most complex of all. Both verbal and nonverbal behaviors are important determinants of quality, as are tangible cues such as employee dress and other symbols of service (equipment, informational brochures, physical setting). In face-to-face encounters the customer also plays a role in creating quality service for herself through her own behavior during the interaction.

Sources of Pleasure and Displeawsure in Service Encounters

Because of the importance of service encounters in building perceptions, researchers have extensively analyzed service encounters in many contexts to determine the sources of customers' favorable and unfavorable impressions. The research uses the critical incident technique to get customers and employees to provide verbatim stories about satisfying and dissatisfying service encounters they have experienced (see Chapter 5 for a detailed description and references for this research technique.)

On the basis of research that documents thousands of service encounter stories, four common themes—recovery (after failure), adaptability, spontaneity, and coping—have been identified as the sources of customer satisfaction/dissatisfaction in memorable service encounters.[53] Each of the themes is discussed here, and sample stories from the research of both satisfying and dissatisfying incidents for each theme are given in Exhibit 4.2. The themes encompass service behaviors in encounters spanning a wide variety of industries.

Recovery—Employee Response to Service Delivery System Failures

The first theme includes all incidents in which there has been a failure of the service delivery system and an employee is required to respond in some way to consumer complaints and disappointments. The failure may be, for example, a hotel room that is not available, an airplane flight that is delayed six hours, an incorrect item sent from a mail-order company, or a critical error on an internal document. The content or form of the employee's response is what causes the customer to remember the event either favorably or unfavorably.

Adaptability—Employee Response to Customer Needs and Requests

A second theme underlying satisfaction/dissatisfaction in service encounters is how adaptable the service delivery system is when the customer has special needs or requests that place demands on the process. In these cases, customers judge service encounter quality in terms of the flexibility of the employees and the system. Incidents categorized within this theme all contain an implicit or explicit request for customization of the service to meet a need. Much of what customers see as special needs or requests may actually be rather routine from the employee's point of view; what is important is that the customer perceives that something special is being done for her based on her own individual needs. External customers and internal customers alike are pleased when the service provider puts forth the effort to accommodate and adjust the system to meet their requirements. On the flip side, they are angered and frustrated by an unwillingness to try to accommodate and by promises that are never followed through. Contact employees also see their abilities to adapt the system as being a prominent source of customer satisfaction, and often they are equally frustrated by constraints that keep them from being flexible.

Spontaneity—Unprompted and Unsolicited Employee Actions

Even when there is no system failure and no special request or need, customers can still remember service encounters as being very satisfying or very dissatisfying. Employee spontaneity in delivering memorably good or poor service is the third theme. Satisfying incidents in this group represent very pleasant surprises for the customer (special attention, being treated like royalty, receiving something nice but not requested), whereas

Technology Spotlight   Customers Love Amazon

Amazon.com's website states that the company "seeks to be Earth's most customer-centric company, where customers can find and discover anything they might want to buy online." Jeff Bezos, CEO of Amazon, whose company name has become a household word worldwide, has always believed that his customers come first, and in his 2011 letter to shareowners he states that "the long-term interests of shareowners are perfectly aligned with the interests of customers." Building on this clear focus on customers, relationships, and value, net sales were up 40 percent in 2010, reaching $34.2 billion for the year. The 2010 American Customer Satisfaction Index reflected a rating of 87 for Amazon—one of the highest ratings of any company in any industry, and certainly much higher than the 80 average rating for all Internet retailers, the average of 70 for Internet social media, and the 65–75 ratings for many other service businesses. According to Bezos, "Customers come first. If you focus on what customers want and build a relationship, they will allow you to make money."

Few would deny that Amazon is a master of technology and technology-based services for consumers. In fact, other companies, such as Target and Office Depot, have sought a technology partnership with Amazon to benefit from the company's experience and success with customers. Amazon provides Internet retail services for both these companies, and it provides Web services, fulfillment, and technology infrastructure services to many other companies.For example, in 2009 Amazon acquired renowned Internet retailer Zappos.com, bringing its customer-zealot CEO, Tony Hsieh, into the Amazon family.

In its core business, online book sales, Amazon has taken a historically interpersonally dominated transaction and successfully transformed it to a Web-based service experience. Let's take a closer look at what the company is doing in this space and why customers love it so much. Since its inception in July 1995, Amazon has grown to the point where it offers more book titles than any bricks-and-mortar bookstore could ever hope to stock, so selection and availability of titles are one key to its popularity with customers. But that is just the beginning. In addition to a wide selection, Amazon has invested significant effort to simulate the feel of a neighborhood bookstore, where a patron can mingle with other customers, discuss books, and get recommendations from bookstore employees. Over the years, Amazon has incorporated user feedback into product pages and added the "look inside" feature, so that readers can sample books easily. It offers a personalized shopping experience for each customer, along with convenient checkout through its "1-Click®Shopping" and a very popular "free shipping" service for one annual fee. Amazon allows customers to find related books on virtually any topic by simply typing key words and initiating a search of its massive database. Its one-to-one marketing system allows the company to track what individual customers buy and let them know of additional titles that might interest them. This marketing is done while the customer is shopping, as well as through periodic direct e-mail that identifies books specifically related to the customer's past purchase patterns and interests.

In 2007, Amazon introduced the Kindle, a technology device that allows customers to read books and other print materials on a personal electronic reader. But the Kindle is more than a reading device—it also allows owners to shop for books, read reviews, and purchase and download books in seconds via a wireless connection that operates 24 hours per day. Its trademarked Whispersinc technology ensures that customers have their reading library with them wherever they go and that they have all of their highlights, notes, and most recently read pages immediately accessible. In only a few years, sales of books on Kindle overtook those of paper books as the most popular format for Amazon book sales. In early 2011, the company was selling 115 Kindle books for every 100 paperbacks—a trend that is expected to continue. As with its other innovations and services, Amazon has designed the Kindle from the customer's perspective, enhancing the design and changing features to ensure the loyalty of serious readers, rather than to keep up with the latest available bells and whistles of technology. The technology that powers the Kindle is invisible to the customer, and the enhancements are made to improve the experience. As Bezos has said, "For the vast majority of books, adding video and animation is not going to be helpful. It is distracting rather than

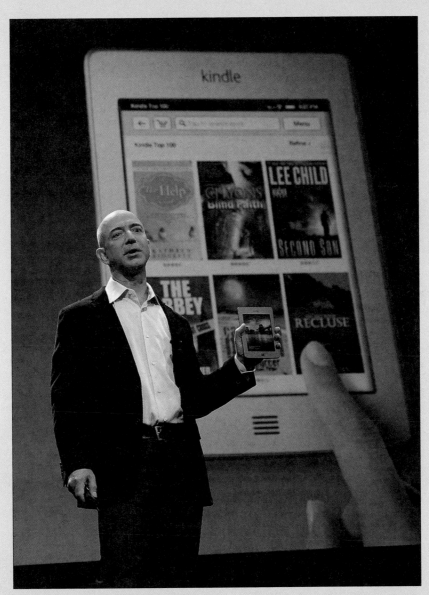

Jeff Bezos, CEO, and the Amazon Kindle.

enhancing. You are not going to improve Hemingway by adding video snippets."

As Amazon stays on the forefront of technology-delivered retail and reading services, few doubters of its long-term success remain. By all acounts, the philosophy of keeping the customer central to the firm's strategy seems to have paid off.

Sources: Amazon.com, www.amazon.com, accessed July 18, 2011; ACSI results at www.theacsi.org, 2011; A. Penenberg, "The Evolution of Amazon," *Fast Company*, July–August 2009,pp. 66–72, 74;J. Authors, "An Amazing 10-year Amazonian Adventure LONG VIEW," *Financial Times*, April 28, 2007, p. 24; G. Fowler, "Kindle to Go 'Mass Market,'" *The Wall Street Journal*, July 29, 2010, p. 6; S. Woo, "Amazon Grows—at a High Price," *The Wall Street Journal*, January 28, 2011, p. B1.

Exhibit 4.2 Service Encounter Themes

THEME 1: RECOVERY

Satisfactory	Dissatisfactory
They lost my room reservation but the manager gave me the V.P. suite for the same price.	We had made advance reservations at the hotel. When we arrived we found we had no room—no explanation, no apologies, and no assistance in finding another hotel.
Even though I did not make any complaint about the hour-and-a-half wait, the waitress kept apologizing and said the bill was on the house.	One of my suitcases was all dented up and looked like it had been dropped from 30,000 feet. When I tried to make a claim for my damaged luggage, the employee insinuated that I was lying and trying to cheat them.

THEME 2: ADAPTABILITY

Satisfactory	Dissatisfactory
I did not have an appointment to see a doctor; however, my allergy nurse spoke to a practitioner's assistant and worked me into the schedule. I received treatment after a 10-minute wait. I was very satisfied with the special treatment I received, the short wait, and the quality of the service.	My young son, flying alone, was to be assisted by the flight attendant from start to finish. At the Albany airport she left him alone in the airport with no one to escort him to his connecting flight.
It was snowing outside—my car broke down. I checked 10 hotels and there were no rooms. Finally, one understood my situation and offered to rent me a bed and set it up in a small banquet room.	Despite our repeated requests, the hotel staff would not deal with the noisy people partying in the hall at 3 a.m.

THEME 3: SPONTANEITY

Satisfactory	Dissatisfactory
We always travel with our teddy bears. When we got back to our room at the hotel we saw that the cleaning person had arranged our bears very comfortably in a chair. The bears were holding hands.	The lady at the front desk acted as if we were bothering her. She was watching TV and paying more attention to the TV than to the hotel guests.
The anesthesiologist took extra time to explain exactly what I would be aware of and promised to take special care in making sure I did not wake up during surgery. It impressed me that the anesthesiologist came to settle my nerves and explain the medicine I was getting because of my cold.	I needed a few more minutes to decide on a dinner. The waitress said, "If you would read the menu and not the road map, you would know what you want to order."

THEME 4: COPING

Satisfactory	Dissatisfactory
A person who became intoxicated on a flight started speaking loudly, annoying the other passengers. The flight attendant asked the passenger if he would be driving when the plane landed and offered him coffee. He accepted the coffee and became quieter and friendlier.	An intoxicated man began pinching the female flight attendants. One attendant told him to stop, but he continued and then hit another passenger. The copilot was called and asked the man to sit down and leave the others alone, but the passenger refused. The copilot then "decked" the man, knocking him into his seat.

dissatisfying incidents in this group represent negative and unacceptable employee behaviors (rudeness, stealing, discrimination, ignoring the customer).

Coping—Employee Response to Problem Customers

The incidents categorized in this group came to light when employees were asked to describe service encounter incidents in which customers were either very satisfied or dissatisfied. In addition to describing incidents of the types outlined under the first three themes, employees described many incidents in which customers were the cause of their own dissatisfaction. Such customers were basically uncooperative—that is, unwilling to cooperate with the service provider, other customers, industry regulations, and/or laws. In these cases nothing the employee could do would result in the customer feeling pleased about the encounter. The term *coping* is used to describe these incidents because coping is the behavior generally required of employees to handle problem customer encounters. Rarely are such encounters satisfying from the customer's point of view.[54] Also of interest is that customers themselves did not relate any "problem customer" incidents. That is, customers either do not see, or choose not to remember or retell, stories of the times when they themselves were unreasonable to the point of causing their own dissatisfactory service encounter.

Table 4.3 summarizes the specific employee behaviors that cause satisfaction and dissatisfaction in service encounters according to the four themes just presented: recovery, adaptability, spontaneity, and coping. The left side of the table suggests what employees do that results in positive encounters, whereas the right side summarizes negative behaviors within each theme.

Technology-Based Service Encounters

All the research on service encounters described thus far and the resulting themes underlying service encounter evaluations are based on interpersonal services—that is, face-to-face encounters between customers and employees of service organizations. Researchers have also examined the sources of pleasure and displeasure in technology-based service encounters.[55] These types of encounters involve customers interacting with Internet-based services, automated phone services, kiosk services, and services delivered via DVD or video technology. Often these systems are referred to as *self-service technologies* (*SSTs*) because the customer essentially provides his or her own service.

The research on SSTs reveals some different themes in terms of what drives customer satisfaction and dissatisfaction. The following themes were identified from analysis of hundreds of critical incident stories across a wide range of contexts, including Internet retailing, Internet-based services, ATMs, automated phone systems, and others:

For Satisfying SSTs

Solved an intensified need. Customers in this category were thrilled that the technology could bail them out of a difficult situation—for example, a cash machine that came to the rescue, allowing the customer to get cash to pay a cab driver and get to work on time when a car had broken down.

Better than the alternative. Many SST stories related to how the technology-based service was in some way better than the alternative—easy to use, saved time, available when and where the customer needed it, saved money.

Did its job. Because there are so many failures of technology, many customers are simply thrilled when the SST works as it should!

TABLE 4.3 General Service Behaviors Based on Service Encounter Themes—Dos and Don'ts

Theme	Do	Don't
Recovery	Acknowledge problem Explain causes Apologize Compensate/upgrade Lay out options Take responsibility	Ignore customer Blame customer Leave customer to fend for himself or herself Downgrade Act as if nothing is wrong "Pass the buck"
Adaptability	Recognize the seriousness of the need Acknowledge Anticipate Attempt to accommodate Adjust the system Explain rules/policies Take responsibility	Ignore Promise but fail to follow through Show unwillingness to try Embarrass the customer Laugh at the customer Avoid responsibility "Pass the buck"
Spontaneity	Take time Be attentive Anticipate needs Listen Provide information Show empathy	Exhibit impatience Ignore Yell/laugh/swear Steal from customers Discriminate
Coping	Listen Try to accommodate Explain Let go of the customer	Take customer's dissatisfaction personally Let customer's dissatisfaction affect others

For Dissatisfying SSTs

Technology failure. Many dissatisfying SST stories relate to the technology simply not working as promised—it is not available when needed, PIN numbers do not work, or systems are offline.

Process failure. Often the technology seems to work, but later the customer discovers that a back-office or follow-up process, which the customer assumed was connected, does not work. For example, a product order seems to be placed successfully, but it never arrives or the wrong product is delivered.

Poor design. Many stories relate to the customer's dissatisfaction with how the technology is designed, in terms of either the technical process (technology is confusing, menu options are unclear) or the actual service design (delivery takes too long, service is inflexible).

Customer-driven failure. In some cases, the customers told stories of their own inabilities or failures to use the technology properly. These types of stories are (of course) much less common than stories blaming the technology or the company.

For all of the dissatisfying SST stories, there is clearly an element of service failure. Interestingly, the research revealed little attempt in these technology-based encounters to recover from the failure—unlike the interpersonal service encounters described earlier, where excellent service recovery can be a foundation for retaining and even producing very satisfied customers. As companies progress with SSTs and become better at delivering service this way, we expect that growing numbers will be able to deliver superior service via technology. Many are doing it already, as our Technology Spotlight on Amazon.com illustrated. In the future we believe that many firms will be able to deliver highly reliable, responsive, customized services via technology and will offer easy and effective means for service recovery when failure does occur.[56]

Summary	This chapter described customer perceptions of service by first introducing two critical concepts: customer satisfaction and service quality. These critical customer perceptions were defined and discussed in terms of the factors that influence each of them. Customer satisfaction is a broad perception influenced by features and attributes of the product as well as by customers' emotional responses, their attributions, and their perceptions of fairness. Service quality, the customer's perception of the service component of a product, is also a critical determinant of customer satisfaction. Sometimes, as in the case of a pure service, service quality may be the *most* critical determinant of satisfaction. Perceptions of service quality are based on five dimensions: reliability, assurance, empathy, responsiveness, and tangibles.

Another major purpose of the chapter was to introduce the idea of service encounters, or "moments of truth," as the building blocks for both satisfaction and quality. Every service encounter (whether remote, technology-mediated, or in person) is an opportunity to build customer perceptions of quality and satisfaction. The underlying themes of pleasure and displeasure in service encounters were also described. The importance of managing the evidence of service in every encounter was discussed.

Chapters 3 and 4 have provided you with a grounding in customer issues relevant to services. These two chapters are intended to give you a solid understanding of service expectations and perceptions. Through the rest of the book, we illustrate strategies that firms can use to close the gap between customer expectations and perceptions. |

Discussion Questions	1. What is customer satisfaction, and why is it so important? Discuss how customer satisfaction can be influenced by each of the following: product attributes and features, customer emotions, attributions for success or failure, perceptions of fairness, and family members or other customers.
2. What is the ACSI? Do you believe that such national indicators of customer satisfaction should be included as benchmarks of national economic well-being similar to gross domestic product (GDP), price indicators, and productivity measures?
3. Why do service companies generally receive lower satisfaction ratings in the ACSI than nondurable and durable product companies?
4. Discuss the differences between perceptions of service quality and customer satisfaction.
5. List and define the five dimensions of service quality. Describe the services provided by a firm you do business with (e.g., your bank, your doctor, your favorite restaurant) on each of the dimensions. In your mind, has this organization distinguished itself from its competitors on any particular service quality dimension?
6. Describe a remote encounter, a technology-mediated encounter (phone, real-time texting, or live chat), and a face-to-face encounter that you have had recently. How

did you evaluate the encounter, and what were the most important factors determining your satisfaction/dissatisfaction in each case?

7. Describe an "encounter cascade" for an airplane flight. In your opinion, what are the most important encounters in this cascade for determining your overall impression of the quality of the airline?

8. Why did the gentleman described in Exhibit 4.1 leave his bank after 30 years? What were the underlying causes of his dissatisfaction in that instance, and why would that cause him to leave the bank?

9. Assume that you are a manager of a health club. Discuss general strategies you might use to maximize customers' positive perceptions of your club. How would you know if you were successful?

Exercises

1. Keep a journal of your service encounters with different organizations (at least five) during the week. For each journal entry, ask yourself the following questions: What circumstances led up to this encounter? What did the employee say or do? How did you evaluate this encounter? What exactly made you evaluate the encounter that way? What should the organization have done differently (if anything)? Categorize your encounters according to the four themes of service encounter satisfaction/dissatisfaction (recovery, adaptability, spontaneity, coping).

2. Interview someone with a non-U.S. cultural background. Ask the person about service quality, whether the five dimensions of quality are relevant, and which are most important in determining the quality of banking services (or some other type of service) in the person's country.

3. Interview an employee of a local service business. Ask the person to discuss each of the five dimensions of service quality with you as it relates to the person's company. Which dimensions are most important? Are any dimensions *not* relevant in this context? Which dimensions does the company do best? Why? Which dimensions could benefit from improvement? Why?

4. Interview a manager, an owner, or a president of a business. Discuss with this person the strategies he or she uses to ensure customer satisfaction. How does service quality enter into the strategies, or does it? Find out how this person measures customer satisfaction and/or service quality.

5. Visit Amazon.com's website. Visit a traditional bookstore. How would you compare the two experiences? Compare and contrast the factors that most influenced your satisfaction and perceptions of service quality in the two different situations. When would you choose to use one versus the other?

Notes

1. C. Zane, *Reinventing the Wheel,* Dallas, TX: BenBella Books, 2011; "Creating Lifetime Customers," http://www.Christopherzanecom/media/, accessed July 2011; A. Danigelis, "Local Hero: Zane's Cycles," *Fast Company,* September 2006, p. 60; D. Fenn, *Alpha Dogs: How Your Small Business Can Become a Leader of the Pack* (New York: Collins, 2003); Chris Zane presentation at "Compete through Service" Symposium, November 2010, Center for Services Leadership, Arizona State University.

2. For more discussion of the debate on the distinctions between quality and satisfaction, see A. Parasuraman, V. A. Zeithaml, and L. L. Berry, "Reassessment of Expectations as a Comparison Standard in Measuring Service Quality: Implications

for Future Research," *Journal of Marketing* 58 (January 1994), pp. 111–124; R. L. Oliver, "A Conceptual Model of Service Quality and Service Satisfaction: Compatible Goals, Different Concepts," in *Advances in Services Marketing and Management,* vol. 2, ed. T. A. Swartz, D. E. Bowen, and S. W. Brown (Greenwich, CT: JAI Press, 1994), pp. 65–85; M. J. Bitner and A. R. Hubbert, "Encounter Satisfaction vs. Overall Satisfaction vs. Quality: The Customer's Voice," in *Service Quality: New Directions in Theory and Practice,* ed. R. T. Rust and R. L. Oliver (Newbury Park, CA: Sage, 1993), pp. 71–93; D. Iacobucci et al., "The Calculus of Service Quality and Customer Satisfaction: Theory and Empirical Differentiation and Integration," in *Advances in Services Marketing and Management,* vol. 3, ed. T. A. Swartz, D. E. Bowen, and S. W. Brown (Greenwich, CT: JAI Press, 1994), pp. 1–67; P. A. Dabholkar, C. D. Shepherd, and D. I. Thorpe, "A Comprehensive Framework for Service Quality: An Investigation of Critical Conceptual and Measurement Issues through a Longitudinal Study," *Journal of Retailing* 7 (Summer 2000), pp. 139–173; J. J. Cronin Jr., M. K. Brady, and G. T. M. Hult, "Assessing the Effects of Quality, Value, and Customer Satisfaction on Consumer Behavioral Intentions in Service Environments," *Journal of Retailing* 76 (Summer 2000), pp. 193–218.

3. See, in particular, Parasuraman, Zeithaml, and Berry, "Reassessment of Expectations"; Oliver, "A Conceptual Model of Service Quality"; and M. K. Brady and J. J. Cronin Jr., "Some New Thoughts on Conceptualizing Perceived Service Quality: A Hierarchical Approach," *Journal of Marketing* 65 (July 2001), pp. 34–49.

4. A. Parasuraman, V. A. Zeithaml, and L. L. Berry, "SERVQUAL: A Multiple-Item Scale for Measuring Consumer Perceptions of Service Quality," *Journal of Retailing* 64 (Spring 1988), pp. 12–40.

5. Parasuraman, Zeithaml, and Berry, "Reassessment of Expectations."

6. Oliver, "A Conceptual Model of Service Quality."

7. See V. Mittal, P. Kumar, and M. Tsiros, "Attribute-Level Performance, Satisfaction, and Behavioral Intentions over Time," *Journal of Marketing* 63 (April 1999), pp. 88–101; L. L. Olsen and M. D. Johnson, "Service Equity, Satisfaction, and Loyalty: From Transaction-Specific to Cumulative Evaluations," *Journal of Service Research* 5 (February 2003), pp. 184–195; P. C. Verhoef, G. Antonides, and A. N. De Hoog, "Service Encounters as a Sequence of Events: The Importance of Peak Experiences," *Journal of Service Research* 7 (August 2004), pp. 53–64.

8. Olsen and Johnson, "Service Equity, Satisfaction, and Loyalty."

9. R. L. Oliver, *Satisfaction: A Behavioral Perspective on the Consumer* (New York: McGraw-Hill, 1997).

10. For a more detailed discussion of the different types of satisfaction, see E. Arnould, L. Price, and G. Zinkhan, *Consumers,* 2nd ed. (New York: McGraw-Hill, 2004), pp. 754–796.

11. S. Fournier and D. G. Mick, "Rediscovering Satisfaction," *Journal of Marketing* 63 (October 1999), pp. 5–23; Verhoef et al., "Service Encounters as a Sequence of Events."

12. Oliver, *Satisfaction,* chap. 2.

13. A. Ostrom and D. Iacobucci, "Consumer Trade-Offs and the Evaluation of Services," *Journal of Marketing* 59 (January 1995), pp. 17–28.

14. For more on emotions and satisfaction, see Oliver, *Satisfaction,* chap. 11; L. L. Price, E. J. Arnould, and S. L. Deibler, "Consumers' Emotional Responses to

Service Encounters," *International Journal of Service Industry Management* 6, no. 3 (1995), pp. 34–63.

15. L. L. Price, E. J. Arnould, and P. Tierney, "Going to Extremes: Managing Service Encounters and Assessing Provider Performance," *Journal of Marketing* 59 (April 1995), pp. 83–97.

16. T. Hennig-Thurau, M. Groth, M. Paul, and D. D. Gremler, "Are All Smiles Created Equal? How Emotional Contagion and Emotional Labor Affect Service Relationships," *Journal of Marketing* 70 (July 2006), pp. 58–73.

17. J. Du, X. Fan, and T. Feng, "Multiple Emotional Contagions in Service Encounters," *Journal of the Academy of Marketing Science,* 39, no. 3 (June 2011), pp. 449–466.

18. For more on attributions and satisfaction, see V. S. Folkes, "Recent Attribution Research in Consumer Behavior: A Review and New Directions," *Journal of Consumer Research* 14 (March 1988), pp. 548–565; and Oliver, *Satisfaction,* chap. 10.

19. A. R. Hubbert, "Customer Co-Creation of Service Outcomes: Effects of Locus of Causality Attributions," doctoral dissertation, Arizona State University, Tempe, Arizona, 1995.

20. M. J. Bitner, "Evaluating Service Encounters: The Effects of Physical Surroundings and Employee Responses," *Journal of Marketing* 54 (April 1990), pp. 69–82.

21. For more on fairness and satisfaction, see E. C. Clemmer and B. Schneider, "Fair Service," in *Advances in Services Marketing and Management,* vol. 5, ed. T. A. Swartz, D. E. Bowen, and S. W. Brown (Greenwich, CT: JAI Press, 1996), pp. 109–126; Oliver, *Satisfaction,* chap. 7; and Olsen and Johnson, "Service Equity, Satisfaction, and Loyalty."

22. As described in K. Seiders and L. L. Berry, "Service Fairness: What It Is and Why It Matters," *Academy of Management Executive* 12 (May 1998), pp. 8–20.

23. Fournier and Mick, "Rediscovering Satisfaction."

24. A. M. Epp and L. L. Price, "Designing Solutions around Customer Network Identity Goals," *Journal of Marketing,* 75 (March 2011), pp. 36–54.

25. C. Fornell, M. D. Johnson, E. W. Anderson, J. Cha, and B. E. Bryant, "The American Customer Satisfaction Index: Nature, Purpose, and Findings," *Journal of Marketing* 60 (October 1996), pp. 7–18; *ACSI 10-Year Report Analysis (1994–2004),* University of Michigan, National Quality Research Center, 2005; www.theacsi.org.

26. E. W. Anderson, C. Fornell, and D. R. Lehmann, "Customer Satisfaction, Market Share, and Profitability: Findings from Sweden," *Journal of Marketing* 58 (July 1994), pp. 53–66.

27. M. Bruhn and M. A. Grund, "Theory, Development and Implementation of National Customer Satisfaction Indices: The Swiss Index of Customer Satisfaction (SWICS)," *Total Quality Management* 11, no. 7 (2000), pp. S1017–S1028; A. Meyer and F. Dornach, "The German Customer Barometer," http://www.servicebarometer.de.or.

28. See www.theacsi.org and F. V. Morgeson III, S. Mithas, T. L. Keiningham, and L. Aksoy, "An Investigation of the Cross-national Determinants of Customer Satisfaction," *Journal of the Academy of Marketing Science,* 39 (April 2011), pp. 198–215.

29. Fornell et al., "The American Customer Satisfaction Index;" *ACSI 10-Year Report Analysis.*

30. For a listing of companies and their scores, go to the ACSI website at www. theacsi.org.

31. ACSI website, www.theacsi.org.

32. Ibid, "About ACSI," "Economic Indicator," website accessed July 11, 2011.

33. See J. L. Heskett, W. E. Sasser Jr., and L. A. Schlesinger, *The Service Profit Chain* (New York: Free Press, 1997); S. Gupta and V. A. Zeithaml, "Customer Metrics and Their Impact on Financial Performance," *Marketing Science,* 25 (November–December), 2006, pp. 718–739.

34. C. Fornell, S. Mithas, F. V. Morgeson III, and M.S. Krishnan, "Customer Satisfaction and Stock Prices: High Returns, Low Risk," *Journal of Marketing* 70 (January 2006), pp. 3–14.

35. M. A. Wiles, "The Effect of Customer Service on Retailers' Shareholder Wealth: The Role of Availability and Reputation Cues," *Journal of Retailing,* Special Issue on Service Excellence 83 (January 2007), pp. 19–32.

36. L. Aksoy, B. Cooil, C. Groening, T. L. Keiningham, and A. Yalcin, "The Long-Term Stock Market Valuation of Customer Satisfaction," *Journal of Marketing,* 72 (July 2008), pp. 105–122.

37. M. A. J. Menezes and J. Serbin, *Xerox Corporation: The Customer Satisfaction Program,* case no. 591-055 (Boston: Harvard Business School, 1991).

38. F. F. Reichheld, "The One Number You Need to Grow," *Harvard Business Review,* December 2003, pp. 47–54.

39. Information provided by TARP Worldwide, Inc., August 2007.

40. E. W. Anderson and V. Mittal, "Strengthening the Satisfaction–Profit Chain," *Journal of Service Research* 3 (November 2000), pp. 107–120; B. Hindo, "Satisfaction Not Guaranteed," *BusinessWeek,* June 19, 2006, pp. 32–36.

41. Brady and Cronin, "Some New Thoughts on Conceptualizing Perceived Service Quality"; C. Gronroos, "A Service Quality Model and Its Marketing Implications," *European Journal of Marketing* 18, no. 4 (1984), pp. 36–44; R. T. Rust and R. L. Oliver, "Service Quality Insights and Managerial Implications from the Frontier," in *Service Quality: New Directions in Theory and Practice,* ed. R. T. Rust and R. L. Oliver (Thousand Oaks, CA: Sage, 1994), pp. 1–19; M. J. Bitner, "Managing the Evidence of Service," in *The Service Quality Handbook,* ed. E. E. Scheuing and W. F. Christopher (New York, AMACOM, 1993), pp. 358–370.

42. Parasuraman, Zeithaml, and Berry, "SERVQUAL: A Multiple-Item Scale." Details on the SERVQUAL Scale and the actual items used to assess the dimensions are provided in Chapter 5.

43. N. Raajpoot, "Reconceptualizing Service Encounter Quality in a Non-Western Context," *Journal of Service Research* 7 (Novemer 2004), pp. 181–201.

44. Parasuraman, Zeithaml, and Berry, "SERVQUAL: A Multiple-Item Scale."

45. For a review of service quality delivery via the Web See: V. A. Zeithaml, A. Parasuraman, and A. Malhotra, "Service Quality Delivery through Web Sites: A Critical Review of Extant Knowledge," *Journal of the Academy of Marketing Science* 30 (Fall 2002), pp. 362–375. See also: M. Wolfinbarger and M. Gilly, "Etailq: Dimensionalizing, Measuring and Predicting Etail Quality," Journal of Retailing 79, no. 3 (2003), pp. 183–198; B. B. Holloway and S. E. Beatty, "Satisfiers and Dissatisfiers in the Online Environment," *Journal of Service Research,* 10, no. 4 (May 2008), pp. 347–364.

46. A. Parasuraman, V. A. Zeithaml, and A. Malhotra, "E-S-QUAL: A Multiple-Item Scale for Assessing Electronic Service Quality," *Journal of Service Research* 7 (February 2005), pp. 213–233.

47. Ibid.

48. "How Marriott Makes a Great First Impression," *The Service Edge* 6, no. 5 (May 1993), p. 5.

49. A. G. Woodside, L. L. Frey, and R. T. Daly, "Linking Service Quality, Customer Satisfaction, and Behavioral Intention," *Journal of Health Care Marketing* 9 (December 1989), pp. 5–17.

50. Verhoef et al., "Service Encounters as a Sequence of Events."

51. G. L. Shostack, "Planning the Service Encounter," in *The Service Encounter,* ed. J. A. Czepiel, M. R. Solomon, and C. F. Surprenant (Lexington, MA: Lexington Books, 1985), pp. 243–254.

52. Ibid.

53. For a complete discussion of the research on which this section is based, see M. J. Bitner, B. H. Booms, and M. S. Tetreault, "The Service Encounter: Diagnosing Favorable and Unfavorable Incidents," *Journal of Marketing* 54 (January 1990), pp. 71–84; M. J. Bitner, B. H. Booms, and L. A. Mohr, "Critical Service Encounters: The Employee's View," *Journal of Marketing* 58 (October 1994), pp. 95–106; D. Gremler and M. J. Bitner, "Classifying Service Encounter Satisfaction across Industries," in *Marketing Theory and Applications,* ed. C. T. Allen et al. (Chicago: American Marketing Association, 1992), pp. 111–118; D. Gremler, M. J. Bitner, and K. R. Evans, "The Internal Service Encounter," *Journal of Service Industry Management* 5, no. 2 (1994), pp. 34–56.

54. Bitner, Booms, and Mohr, "Critical Service Encounters."

55. This discussion is based on research and results presented in M. L. Meuter, A. L. Ostrom, R. I. Roundtree, and M. J. Bitner, "Self-Service Technologies: Understanding Customer Satisfaction with Technology-Based Service Encounters," *Journal of Marketing* 64 (July 2000), pp. 50–64.

56. M. J. Bitner, S. W. Brown, and M. L. Meuter, "Technology Infusion in Service Encounters," *Journal of the Academy of Marketing Science* 28 (Winter 2000), pp. 138–149; Parasuraman, Zeithaml, and Malhotra, "E-S-QUAL: A Multiple-Item Scale."

Part Three

Understanding Customer Requirements

THE LISTENING GAP

Not knowing what customers expect is one of the root causes of not delivering to customer expectations. Provider gap 1, the listening gap, is the difference between customer expectations of service and company understanding of those expectations. Note that in the accompanying figure we created a link between the customer and the company, showing customer expectations above the line that dissects the model and provider perceptions of those expectations below the line. This alignment signifies that what customers expect is not always the same as what companies believe they expect.

Provider Gap 1: The Listening Gap

Part 3 describes three ways to close provider gap 1. In Chapter 5, we detail ways that companies listen to customers through research. Both formal and informal methods of customer research are described, including surveys, critical incident studies, and complaint solicitation. Upward communication from frontline employees to managers, another key factor in listening to customers, is also discussed.

Chapter 6 covers company strategies to retain customers and strengthen relationships with them, an approach called relationship marketing. Relationship marketing is distinct from transactional marketing, the more conventional approach that tends to focus on acquiring new customers rather than retaining them. When organizations have strong relationships with existing customers, opportunities for in-depth listening increase over time, and the listening gap is less likely to occur. A variety of strategies, including the creation of switching barriers and the development of relationship bonds, are suggested as a means of relationship development and, ultimately, the cultivation of customer loyalty.

Chapter 7 describes service recovery, the other major strategy needed to close provider gap 1. Service recovery involves understanding why customers complain, what they expect when they complain, and how to deal with service failures. Firms engaged in service recovery must, along with other approaches, create a complaint-handling procedure, empower employees to react in real time to fix failures, and guarantee service. Excellent service recovery strategies seek to gain insight from service failures, allowing firms to better understand customers and their expectations.

Chapter **Five**

Listening to Customers through Research

This chapter's objectives are to

1. Present the types of and guidelines for customer research in services.
2. Show how customer research information can and should be used for services.
3. Describe the strategies by which companies can facilitate interaction and communication between management and customers.
4. Present ways that companies can and do facilitate interaction between contact people and management.

Listening to Customers through Social Media

Social media are one of the newest and most helpful tools available to companies wanting to know what their customers think of them. These media provide ways that firms can—by watching, monitoring, and mining information—get a quick pulse on their customers' expectations and frustrations. Online exchanges among customers offer firms the opportunity to hear complaints, deal with them quickly, make adjustments that customers desire, and find out who a company's biggest fans are. Consider just a few examples:

- Comcast, after being criticized in social media for poor service quality with viral videos and unflattering tweets, fought back and is now the exemplar of "social customer service." The company has "digital detectives," who hunt vigorously through social media for consumer comments and complaints. They monitor blogs, Twitter, forums, Facebook—everywhere their customers might be talking about them. When they find a complaint, they immediately send a response from their Twitter account Comcastcares: "Anything I can help with?" Rather than referring the customer to a customer service line to resolve the problem, employees handle the problem right in the social medium in which the complaint was made. This provides rapid response to the problem.
- Dominos Pizza, in response to thousands of direct consumer feedback messages on social channels, completely revamped its pizza to reflect changing tastes

(and to counter a damaging employee-posted video of the employee tampering with the food).

- Hilton Hotels developed a software tool to monitor and aggregate customer comments from websites, blogs, and social media sites such as Twitter. Monitoring is therefore constant and thorough and can even spot and deal with systemic problems.

- Starwood Hotels and Marriott use commercial software called ReviewAnalyst to monitor more than a dozen websites, such as TripAdvisor, Priceline, and YouTube. One special benefit of this software is that it immediately alerts the hotels when pre-identified problem terms, such as *bedbugs, eviction,* and *security* are mentioned.

Not all companies pay attention to social media, and this failure can hurt them. Dave Carroll, a musician whose $3,500 Taylor guitar had its neck broken during baggage handling on a United Airlines flight, complained to United employees about customer service but was told he was ineligible for compensation. He was so frustrated with both the damage to his guitar and the futility of not being heard by the company that he wrote a song about his negative experience. His band, Sons of Maxwell, created a music video and posted it on YouTube in 2009. The unfortunate result for United? The song received 10 million hits on YouTube and was described in media all over the world.

Social media make gathering insights from customers easier than traditional techniques, such as surveys, customer service lines, and comment cards. Reporting problems on social media requires less effort from customers and eliminates the need to pursue customers to obtain feedback. Firms that use social media well can converse and keep open dialogues with customers, making customers feel heard. Social media also allow for better-quality feedback; the type of information firms receive is similar to what they get from focus groups, but costs are much lower and the number of customers who provide input much higher.

How should companies best handle online complaints? A study by Lightspeed Research and the Internet Advertising Bureau indicated that 25 percent of the respondents who complain on Facebook or Twitter expect a reply within 60 minutes, and 6 percent expect a response within 10 minutes. These studies clearly demonstrate that companies must include social media among their listening tools but—most importantly—must develop ways within the organization to handle complaints that arise.

Sources: V. Kumar and Yashoda Bhagwat, "Listen to the Customer," *Marketing Research,* Summer 2010, pp. 14–19; Thomas M. Tripp and Yany Gregoire, "When Unhappy Customers Strick Back on the Internet," *MIT Sloan Management Review,* January 2011, pp. 1–8; Roger Yu, "Hearing Online Critiques: More Hotel Managers Read and Respond to Guests' Remarks," *USA Today,* March 23, 2010, p. 4B; Alison Diana, "Social Media Users Expect Rapid Response to Complaints," *Information Week,* January 12, 2011; Myra Golden, "How Do You Engage Consumers in Social Media? Three Words: 'Can I Help,'" Myra Golden Media Blog, May 2, 2011.

Despite a genuine interest in meeting customer expectations, many companies miss the mark by thinking inside out—they believe they know what customers *should* want and deliver that, rather than finding out what they *do* want. When this happens, companies provide services that do not match customer expectations: important features are left out, and the levels of performance on features that are provided are inadequate. Because services have few clearly defined and tangible cues, this difficulty may be considerably larger than it is in manufacturing firms. A far better approach involves thinking *outside in*—determining customer expectations and then delivering to them. Thinking outside in uses marketing research to understand customers and their requirements fully. Marketing research, the subject of this chapter, involves far more than conventional surveys. It consists of a portfolio of listening strategies that allow companies to deliver service to customer expectations.

USING CUSTOMER RESEARCH TO UNDERSTAND CUSTOMER EXPECTATIONS

Finding out what customers expect is essential to providing service quality, and customer research is a key vehicle for understanding customer expectations and perceptions of services. In services, as with any offering, a firm that does no customer research at all is unlikely to understand its customers. A firm that does customer research, but not on the topic of customer expectations, may also fail to know what is needed to stay in tune with changing customer requirements. Customer research must focus on service issues such as what features are most important to customers, what levels of these features customers expect, and what customers think the company can and should do when problems occur in service delivery. Even when a service firm is small and has limited resources to conduct research, avenues are open to explore what customers expect.

In this section we discuss the elements of service marketing research programs that help companies identify customer expectations and perceptions. In the sections that follow, we will discuss ways in which the tactics of general customer research may need to be adjusted to maximize its effectiveness in services.

Research Objectives for Services

The first step in designing service marketing research is without doubt the most critical: defining the problem and research objectives. This is where the service marketer poses the questions to be answered or problems to be solved with research. Does the company want to know how customers view the service provided by the company, what customer requirements are, how customers will respond to a new service introduction, or what customers will want from the company five years from now? Each of these research questions requires a different research strategy. Thus, it is essential to devote time and resources to define the problem thoroughly and accurately. In spite of the importance of this first stage, many customer research studies are initiated without adequate attention to objectives.

Research objectives translate into action questions. While many different questions are likely to be part of a customer research program, the following are the most common research objectives in services:

- To discover customer requirements or expectations for service
- To monitor and track service performance
- To assess overall company performance compared with that of competition
- To assess gaps between customer expectations and perceptions
- To identify dissatisfied customers, so that service recovery can be attempted
- To gauge the effectiveness of changes in service delivery

- To appraise the service performance of individuals and teams for evaluation, recognition, and rewards
- To determine customer expectations for a new service
- To monitor changing customer expectations in an industry
- To forecast future expectations of customers

These research objectives are similar in many ways to the research conducted for physical products: both aim to assess customer requirements, dissatisfaction, and demand. Service research, however, incorporates additional elements that require specific attention.

First, service research must continually monitor and track service performance because performance is subject to human variability and heterogeneity. Conducting performance research at a single point in time, as might be done for a physical product such as an automobile, would be insufficient in services. A major focus of service research involves capturing human performance—at the level of individual employee, team, branch, organization as a whole, and competition. Another focus of service research involves documenting the process by which service is performed. Even when service employees are performing well, a service provider must continue to track performance because the potential for variation in processes associated with service delivery always exists.

A second distinction in service research is the need to consider and monitor the gap between expectations and perceptions. This gap is dynamic because both perceptions and expectations fluctuate. Does the gap exist because performance is declining, because performance varies with demand and supply level, or because expectations are escalating?

Exhibit 5.1 lists a number of service research objectives. Once objectives such as these have been identified, they will point the way to decisions about the most appropriate type of research, methods of data collection, and ways to use the information. The additional columns in this table are described in sections of this chapter.

Criteria for an Effective Service Research Program

A *service research program* can be defined as the portfolio of research studies and types needed to address research objectives and execute an overall measurement strategy. Many types of research could be considered in a research program. Understanding the criteria for an effective service research program (see Figure 5.1) will help a company evaluate different types of research and choose the ones most appropriate for its research objectives. In this section we discuss these criteria.

Includes Qualitative and Quantitative Research

Marketing research is not limited to surveys and statistics. Some forms of research, called *qualitative research,* are exploratory and preliminary and are conducted to clarify problem definition, prepare for more formal research, or gain insight when more formal research is not necessary. Trader Joe's, the specialty food retailer that sells mostly private-label products, listens closely to customers using informal, qualitative research. This research is not done through focus groups or contact centers, and the company has neither a toll-free number nor a customer care e-mail address. The company finds out what customers want by talking to them—managers ("captains") spend most of the day on the floor, where there are always multiple product samplings taking place, and anyone on the sales staff ("crew members") can directly e-mail a buyer to tell them what people are liking or not.[1] Insights gained through one-on-one conversations like those at Trader Joe's, customer focus groups, critical incidents research (described more

FIGURE 5.1
Criteria for an
Effective Service
Research Program

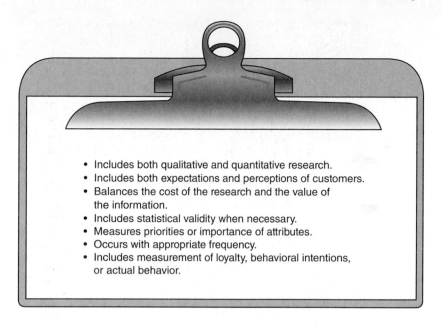

- Includes both qualitative and quantitative research.
- Includes both expectations and perceptions of customers.
- Balances the cost of the research and the value of the information.
- Includes statistical validity when necessary.
- Measures priorities or importance of attributes.
- Occurs with appropriate frequency.
- Includes measurement of loyalty, behavioral intentions, or actual behavior.

fully later in this chapter), and direct observation of service transactions show the marketer the right questions to ask of consumers. Because the results of qualitative research play a major role in designing quantitative research, it is often the first type of research done. Qualitative research can also be conducted after quantitative research to make the numbers in computer printouts meaningful by giving managers the perspective and sensitivity that are critical in interpreting data and initiating improvement efforts.[2]

Quantitative research in marketing is designed to describe the nature, attitudes, or behaviors of customers empirically and to test specific hypotheses that a service marketer wants to examine. These studies are key for quantifying the customers' satisfaction, the importance of service attributes, the extent of service quality gaps, and perceptions of value. Such studies also provide managers with yardsticks for evaluating competitors. Finally, results from quantitative studies can highlight specific service deficiencies that can be more deeply probed through follow-up qualitative research.

Includes Both Perceptions and Expectations of Customers

As we discussed in Chapter 3, expectations serve as standards or reference points for customers. In evaluating service quality, customers compare what they perceive they get in a service encounter with their expectations of that encounter. For this reason, a measurement program that captures only perceptions of service is missing a critical part of the service quality equation. Companies also need to incorporate measures of customer expectations.

Measurement of expectations can be included in a research program in multiple ways. First, basic research that relates to customers' requirements—that identifies the service features or attributes that matter to customers—can be considered expectation research. In this form, the *content* of customer expectations is captured, initially in some form of qualitative research such as focus group interviews. Research on the *levels* of customer expectations also is needed. This type of research quantitatively assesses the levels of customer expectations and compares these with perception levels, usually by calculating the gap between expectations and perceptions.

Type of Research	Primary Research Objectives	Qualitative/ Quantitative	Costs of Information		
			Monetary	Time	Frequency
Complaint solicitation	To identify/attend to dissatisfied customers	Qualitative	Low	Low	Continuous
	To identify common service failure points				
Critical incident studies	To identify "best practices" at transaction level	Qualitative	Low	Moderate	Periodic
	To identify customer requirements as input for quantitative studies				
	To identify common service failure points				
	To identify systemic strengths and weaknesses in customer-contact services				
Requirements research	To identify customer requirements as input for quantitative research	Qualitative	Moderate	Moderate	Periodic
Relationship surveys and SERVQUAL surveys	To monitor and track service performance	Quantitative	Moderate	Moderate	Annual
	To assess overall company performance compared with that of competition				
	To determine links between satisfaction and behavioral intentions				
	To assess gaps between customer expectations and perceptions				
Trailer calls or posttransaction surveys	To obtain immediate feedback on performance of service transactions	Quantitative	Low	Low	Continuous
	To measure effectiveness of changes in service delivery				
	To assess service performance of individuals and teams				
	To use as input for process improvements				
	To identify common service failure points				
Social media	To identify/attend to dissatisfied customers	Qualitative and quantitative	Low	Moderate	Continuous
	To encourage word of mouth				
	To measure the impact of other advertising				

Balances the Cost of the Research and the Value of the Information

An assessment of the cost of research compared with its benefits or value to the company is another key criterion. One cost is monetary, including direct costs to customer research companies, payments to respondents, and internal company costs incurred by employees collecting the information. Time costs are also important, including the

Type of Research	Primary Research Objectives	Qualitative/ Quantitative	Costs of Information		
			Monetary	Time	Frequency
Service expectation meetings and reviews	To create dialogue with important customers	Qualitative	Moderate	Moderate	Annual
	To identify what individual large customers expect and then to ensure that it is delivered				
	To close the loop with important customers				
Process checkpoint evaluations	To determine customer perceptions of long-term professional services during service provision	Quantitative	Moderate	Moderate	Periodic
	To identify service problems and solve them early in the service relationship				
Market-oriented ethnography	To research customers in natural settings	Qualitative	Moderate	High	Periodic
	To study customers from cultures other than America in an unbiased way				
Mystery shopping	To measure individual employee performance for evaluation, recognition, or rewards	Quantitative	Low	Low	Quarterly
		Qualitative			
	To identify systemic strengths and weaknesses in customer-contact services				
Customer panels	To monitor changing customer expectations	Qualitative	Moderate	Moderate	Continuous
	To provide a forum for customers to suggest and evaluate new service ideas				
Lost customer research	To identify reasons for customer defection	Qualitative	Low	Low	Continuous
	To assess gaps between customer expectations and perceptions				
Future expectations research	To forecast future expectations of customers	Qualitative	High	High	Periodic
	To develop and test new service ideas				
Database customer research	To identify the individual requirements of customers using information technology and database information	Quantitative	High	High	Continuous

time commitment needed internally by employees to administer the research and the interval between data collection and availability for use by the firm. These and other costs must be weighed against the gains to the company in improved decision making, retained customers, and successful new product launches.

Includes Statistical Validity When Necessary

We have already seen that research has multiple and diverse objectives. These objectives determine the appropriate type of research and methodology. To illustrate, some companies use research not so much to measure as to build relationships with customers—to allow contact employees to find out what customers desire, to diagnose the strengths and weaknesses of their and the firm's efforts to address the desires, to prepare a plan to meet requirements, and to confirm after a period of time (usually one year) that the company has executed the plan. The underlying objective of this type of research is to allow contact people to identify specific action items that will gain the maximum return in customer satisfaction for individual customers. This type of research does not need sophisticated quantitative analysis, anonymity of customers, careful control of sampling, or strong statistical controls.

On the other hand, research used to track overall service quality that will be used for bonuses and salary increases of salespeople must be carefully controlled for sampling bias and statistical validity. One of us worked with a company that paid salespeople on the basis of customers' satisfaction scores while allowing the salespeople to control the customers sampled. Obviously, the salespeople quickly learned that they could have surveys sent only to satisfied customers, artificially inflating the scores and—of course—undermining the confidence in the measurement system.

Not all forms of research have statistical validity, and not all forms need it. Most forms of qualitative research, for example, do not possess statistical validity.

Measures Priorities or Importance

Customers have many service requirements, but not all are equally important. One of the most common mistakes managers make in trying to improve service is spending resources on the wrong initiatives, only to become discouraged because customer perceptions of the firm's service do not improve! Measuring the relative importance of service dimensions and attributes helps managers to channel resources effectively; therefore, research must document the priorities of the customer.

Occurs with Appropriate Frequency

Because customer expectations and perceptions are dynamic, companies need to institute a service quality research process, not just do isolated studies. A single study of service provides only a "snapshot" view of one moment in time. For full understanding of the marketplace's acceptance of a company's service, customer research must be ongoing. Without a pattern of studies repeated with appropriate frequency, managers cannot tell whether the firm is moving forward or falling back and which of their service improvement initiatives are working. Just what does "ongoing research" mean in terms of frequency? The answer is specific to the type of service and to the purpose and method of each type of service research a company might do. As we discuss the different types in the following section, you will see the frequency with which each type of research could be conducted.

Includes Measures of Loyalty, Behavioral Intentions, or Behavior

An important trend in service research involves measuring the positive and negative consequences of service quality along with overall satisfaction or service quality scores. Among the most frequently used generic *behavioral intentions* are willingness to recommend the service to others and repurchase intent. These behavioral intentions can be viewed as positive and negative consequences of service quality. Positive behavioral intentions include saying positive things about the company, recommending the company to others, remaining loyal, spending more with the company, and paying a price premium. Negative behavioral intentions include saying negative things to others, doing less business with the company, switching to another company, and complaining to outside organizations such as the Better Business Bureau and to other companies using social media outlets. Other, more specific behaviors differ by service; for example, behaviors related to medical care include following instructions from the doctor, taking medications, and returning for follow-up. Tracking these areas can help a company estimate the relative value of service improvements to the company and can identify customers who are in danger of defecting.

ELEMENTS IN AN EFFECTIVE SERVICE MARKETING RESEARCH PROGRAM

A good service marketing research program includes multiple types of research studies. The composite of studies and types of research will differ by company because the range of uses for service quality research—from employee performance assessment to advertising campaign development to strategic planning—requires a rich, multifaceted flow of information. If a company were to engage in virtually all types of service research, the portfolio would look like Exhibit 5.1, but few companies do all types of research. The particular portfolio for any company will match company resources and address the key areas needed to understand the customers of the business. So that it will be easier for you to identify the appropriate type of research for different research objectives, we list the objectives in column 2 of Exhibit 5.1. In the following sections we describe each major type of research and show the way each type addresses the criteria associated with it. The Technology Spotlight discusses research conducted online.

Complaint Solicitation

You may have complained to employees of service organizations, only to find that nothing happens with your complaint. No one rushes to solve it, and the next time you experience the service the same problem is present. How frustrating! Good service organizations take complaints seriously. Not only do they listen to complaints but they also employ *complaint solicitation* as a way of communicating about what can be done to improve their service and their service employees. Vail Resorts, which owns the Vail, Breckenridge, Heavenly, Keystone, and Beaver Creek resorts, has an innovative way to capture complaints and comments of its customers. The resort hires researchers to ride the lifts with skiers and ask and record into handheld computer devices customers' responses to questions about their perceptions of the resorts. Then the researchers ski down the mountain and ride up again with other customers. At the end of the day, the researchers download the results into a computer at the base. The researchers survey 200 skiers per week, looking for patterns of customer comments and complaints. For example, if the researchers receive a number of complaints about certain lift lines or service in one of the restaurants, they will alert managers in those areas so the problems can be resolved quickly. At the end of the week, the data are collected and reported at weekly meetings.

Firms that use complaints as research collect and document them, then use the information to identify dissatisfied customers, correct individual problems where possible, and identify common service failure points. Although this research is used for both goods and services, it has a critical real-time purpose in services—to improve failure points and to improve or correct the performance of contact personnel. Research on complaints is one of the easiest types for firms to conduct, leading many companies to depend solely on complaints to stay in touch with customers. Unfortunately, there is evidence suggesting that customer complaints alone are a woefully inadequate source

Technology Spotlight Conducting Customer Research on the Web

One of the most intriguing applications of the Internet is online research, replacing comment cards and intrusive telephone calls with cyber-surveys that are challenging and fun for consumers. The application is growing rapidly. In 2005, companies spent more than $1.1 billion on online market research, a 16 percent increase over 2004. Annual spending is expected to reach $26 billion by 2010. The reasons are obvious—Internet research has many benefits to marketers besides more willing respondents, including the following:

- *Speed.* Rather than the three to four months required to collect data through mail questionnaires, or the six to eight weeks needed to train interviewers and obtain data from telephone questionnaires, online surveys can be prepared and executed quickly. A sample of 300 to 400, large enough for many studies, can be completed in a weekend and the results made available for viewing by clients on a secure website the following week. One market research firm reportedly completed 1,000 customer satisfaction surveys in only two hours.

- *Equivalent quality.* Deutskens and colleagues found that the quality of the data when using an online method is comparable: "in the context of a large business-to-business service quality assessment, an analysis of the accuracy and completeness of respondent answers to both open and closed questions suggests that online and mail surveys produce equivalent results."[3]

- *Ability to target hard-to-reach populations.* One of the traditional difficulties in research, particularly segmentation research, is to identify and access respondents who fit a particular lifestyle or interest profile. The hard-to-reach, business-to-business market accounts for about a quarter of all customer research studies conducted by U.S. research firms. Doctors, lawyers, other professionals, and working mothers are all valuable but difficult-to-access groups of customers. These people might read special interest magazines (such as professional or hobby publications) that are expensive to advertise in. They could be reached in surveys only by having the service company purchase at great cost the mailing list of that magazine. However, online sites for special interests are quite simple to identify, access, and insert survey banners in.

- *Ability to target customers with money.* Online research allows service companies to reach customers who have higher incomes, higher education levels, and greater willingness to spend. Consumers with computers who use online services regularly tend to be in these demographic target groups, and they can be effectively surveyed with online research. Compared with the sample that would be obtained from traditional research using all telephone subscribers, the sample of online users is often far better in terms of marketing potential.

- *Opportunity to use multimedia to present video and audio.* Telephone surveys are limited to voice alone, whereas mail surveys are constrained to two-dimensional visuals. In the past, to present the full range of audio and video needed to give respondents the true sense of a service being researched, surveys had to be conducted in person and were, therefore, very expensive ($30 to $150 per person, depending on the topic and sample). Online research offers broader stimuli potential

of information. As discussed in Chapter 7, only a small percentage of customers with problems actually complain to the company; the rest stay dissatisfied, telling other people about their dissatisfaction.

To be effective, complaint solicitation requires rigorous recording of numbers and types of complaints through many channels and then working to eliminate the most frequent problems. Complaint channels include employees at the front line, intermediary organizations like retailers who deliver service, managers, and complaints to third parties such as customer advocate groups. Companies must both solve individual customer problems and identify overall patterns to eliminate failure points. More through all multimedia possibilities at a fraction of the cost.

- *No interviewers—and therefore no interviewer errors or interviewer bias.* Bias occurs when the interviewer is in a bad mood, tired, impatient, or not objective. These problems occur with human interviews but not cyber-interviews.

- *Control over data quality, which can eliminate contradictory or nonsensical answers.* With traditional surveys, researchers need a step called "data cleaning and editing," in which all data are checked for such problems; electronic checks can be built into online surveys that take care of this problem as it occurs.

- *Inexpensive research.* Data collection costs can be the most expensive part of a study, and the most expensive part of data collection can be paying subjects to participate. Online customer research, astonishingly, is 10 to 80 percent less expensive than other approaches. The Internet also eliminates the postage, phone, labor, and printing costs that are typical with other survey approaches. Respondents also seem to complete Web-based surveys in half the time it would take an interviewer to conduct the survey, perhaps contributing to the lack of need for incentives.

One additional, but to date undersubstantiated, benefit is higher response rate—reportedly as high as 70 percent—possibly stemming from the fact that the interactive nature of cyber-research can make answering surveys fun for respondents. While it is getting more difficult to get consumers to answer traditional surveys, the entertainment value of cyber-surveys makes it easier to recruit participants. One study shows that consumers are five times more likely to complete an electronic survey than the same survey with written materials and that researchers obtain the following three additional benefits: (1) consumers "play" an e-survey longer, answering more questions than in a traditional survey; (2) people tend to concentrate more fully on their answers; and (3) the entertainment value of an e-survey actually lowers the respondent's perceived time to complete the survey.

The advantages of online research likely far outnumber the disadvantages. However, marketers need to be aware that there are also drawbacks. Perhaps the major problem is the composition of the sample. Unlike the process used with most telephone and mail surveys, the population of responders is not usually selected but is a matter of convenience, consisting of whoever responds to the survey. This is a particular problem when respondents are recruited from other websites and click through to the survey. In these cases, marketers may not even know who the responders are and whether they are, in fact, the right profile for answering the survey. To address this problem, companies are prequalifying respondents by telephone or e-mail, then asking for enough demographic information to ensure that the respondents meet the desired requirements. They can also ask qualifying questions early in the Web survey to screen respondents.

Sources: R. Weible and J. Wallace, "Cyber Research: The Impact of the Internet on Data Collection," *Marketing Research,* Fall 1998, pp. 19–24; R. Nadilo, "On-Line Research Taps Consumers Who Spend," *Marketing News,* June 8, 1998, p. 12; R. Kottler, "Eight Tips Offer Best Practices for Online Market Research, *Marketing News,* April 1, 2005; E. Deutskens, K. Ruyter, and M. Wetzels, "An Assessment of Equivalence Between Online and Mail Surveys in Service Research," *Journal of Service Research,* 8 (May 2006), 346–355.

sophisticated forms of complaint resolution define "complaint" broadly to include all comments—both negative and positive—as well as questions from customers. Firms should build depositories for this information and report results frequently, perhaps weekly or monthly.

Critical Incident Studies

The *critical incident technique (CIT),* is a qualitative interview procedure in which customers are asked to provide verbatim stories about satisfying and dissatisfying service encounters they have experienced. According to a summary of the use of the technique in services, CIT has been used to study satisfaction in hotels, restaurants, airlines,

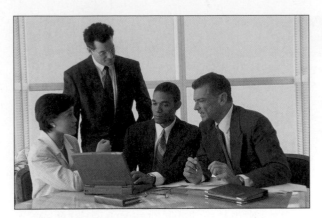

Customers discuss services using the critical incident technique.

amusement parks, automotive repair, retailing, banking, cable television, public transportation, and education.[4] The studies have explored a wide range of service topics: consumer evaluation of services, service failure and recovery, employees, customer participation in service delivery, and service experience.[5] With this technique, customers (either internal or external) are asked the following questions:

Think of a time when, as a customer, you had a particularly *satisfying* (or *dissatisfying*) interaction. When did the incident happen?

What specific circumstances led up to this situation?

Exactly what did the employee (or firm member) say or do?

What resulted that made you feel the interaction was *satisfying* (or *dissatisfying*)?

What could or should have been done differently?

Sometimes contact employees are asked to put themselves in the shoes of a customer and answer the same questions: "Put yourself in the shoes of *customers* of your firm. In other words, try to see your firm through your customers' eyes. Now think of a recent time when a customer of your firm had a particularly *satisfying/unsatisfying* interaction with you or a fellow employee." The stories are then analyzed to determine common themes of satisfaction/dissatisfaction underlying the events. In Chapter 4, we described the four common themes that are sources of pleasure and displeasure in service encounters—recovery (after failure), adaptability, spontaneity, and coping—that have been identified through research. Individual companies conduct these studies to identify sources of satisfaction and dissatisfaction for their firms or industries.

CIT has many benefits. First, data are collected from the respondents' perspective and are usually vivid because they are expressed in consumers' own words and reflect the way they think. Second, the method provides concrete information about the way the company and its employees behave and react, thereby making the research easy to translate into action. Third, like most qualitative methods, the research is particularly useful when the topic or service is new and very little other information exists. Finally, the method is well suited for assessing perceptions of customers from different cultures because it allows respondents to share their perceptions rather than answer researcher-defined questions.[6]

Requirements Research

Requirements research involves identifying the benefits and attributes that customers expect in a service. This type of research is very basic and essential because it determines the type of questions that will be asked in surveys and ultimately the improvements that will be attempted by the firm. Because these studies are so foundational, qualitative techniques are appropriate to begin them. Quantitative techniques may follow, usually during a pretest stage of survey development. Individual companies conduct these studies to identify sources of satisfaction and dissatisfaction for their firms or industries.

An approach to requirements research that has been effective in service industries is to examine existing research about customer requirements in similar service industries. The five dimensions of service quality are generalizable across industries, and sometimes the way these dimensions are manifest is also remarkably similar. Hospital patients and customers of hotels, for example, expect many of the same features when using these two services. Besides expert medical care, patients in hospitals expect comfortable rooms, courteous staff, and food that tastes good—the same features that are salient to hotel customers. In these and other industries that share common customer expectations, managers may find it helpful to seek knowledge from existing research in the related service industry. Because hotels have used marketing and customer research longer than hospitals have, insights into hotel guests' expectations can inform about hospital patients' expectations. Hospital administrators at Albert Einstein Medical Center in Philadelphia, for example, asked a group of nine local hotel executives for advice in understanding and handling patients. Many improvements resulted, including better food, easier-to-read name tags, more prominent information desks, and radios in many rooms.[7]

Relationship and SERVQUAL Surveys

One category of surveys are named *relationship surveys* because they pose questions about all elements in the customer's relationship with the company (including service, product, and price). This comprehensive approach can help a company diagnose its relationship strengths and weaknesses. For example, Federal Express conducts many different customer satisfaction studies to assess satisfaction, identify reasons for dissatisfaction, and monitor satisfaction over time. They conduct 2,400 telephone interviews per quarter, measuring 17 domestic service attributes, 22 export service attributes, 8 drop-box attributes, and 8 service center attributes. They also conduct 10 targeted satisfaction studies on specialized business functions.

Relationship surveys typically monitor and track service performance annually, with an initial survey providing a baseline. Relationship surveys are also effective in comparing company performance with that of competitors, often focusing on the best competitor's performance as a benchmark. When used for this purpose, the sponsor of the survey is not identified, and questions are asked about both the focal company and one or more competitors.

A sound measure of service quality is necessary for identifying the aspects of service needing performance improvement, assessing how much improvement is needed on each aspect, and evaluating the impact of improvement efforts. Unlike goods quality, which can be measured objectively by such indicators as durability and number of defects, service quality is abstract and is best captured by surveys that measure customer evaluations of service. One of the first measures to be developed specifically to measure service quality was the *SERVQUAL survey.*

The SERVQUAL scale involves a survey containing 21 service attributes, grouped into the five service quality dimensions (discussed in Chapter 4) of reliability, responsiveness, assurance, empathy, and tangibles. The survey sometimes asks customers to provide two different ratings on each attribute—one reflecting the level of service they would expect from excellent companies in a sector and the other reflecting their perception of the service delivered by a specific company within that sector. The difference between the expectation and perception ratings constitutes a quantified measure of service quality. Exhibit 5.2 shows the items on the basic SERVQUAL scale as well

The SERVQUAL scale was first published in 1988 and has undergone numerous improvements and revisions since then. The scale contains 21 perception items that are distributed throughout the five service quality dimensions. The scale also contains expectation items.

Although many different formats of the SERVQUAL scale are now in use, we show here the basic 21 perception items as well as a sampling of ways the expectation items have been posed.

PERCEPTIONS

Perceptions Statements in the Reliability Dimension

	Strongly Disagree						Strongly Agree
1. When XYZ Company promises to do something by a certain time, it does so.	1	2	3	4	5	6	7
2. XYZ Company performs the service right the first time.	1	2	3	4	5	6	7
3. XYZ Company provides its services at the time it promises to do so.	1	2	3	4	5	6	7
4. XYZ Company insists on error-free records.	1	2	3	4	5	6	7

Statements in the Responsiveness Dimension

1. XYZ Company keeps customers informed about when services will be performed.	1	2	3	4	5	6	7
2. Employees in XYZ Company give you prompt service.	1	2	3	4	5	6	7
3. Employees in XYZ Company are always willing to help you.	1	2	3	4	5	6	7
4. Employees in XYZ Company are never too busy to respond to your request.	1	2	3	4	5	6	7

Statements in the Assurance Dimension

1. The behavior of employees in XYZ Company instills confidence in you.	1	2	3	4	5	6	7
2. You feel safe in your transactions with XYZ Company.	1	2	3	4	5	6	7
3. Employees in XYZ Company are consistently courteous with you.	1	2	3	4	5	6	7
4. Employees in XYZ Company have the knowledge to answer your questions.	1	2	3	4	5	6	7

Statements in the Empathy Dimension

1. XYZ Company gives you individual attention.	1	2	3	4	5	6	7
2. XYZ Company has employees who give you personal attention.	1	2	3	4	5	6	7
3. XYZ Company has your best interests at heart.	1	2	3	4	5	6	7
4. Employees of XYZ Company understand your specific needs.	1	2	3	4	5	6	7
5. XYZ Company has operating hours that are convenient to all its customers.	1	2	3	4	5	6	7

PERCEPTIONS *(continued)*

Statements in the Tangibles Dimension	Strongly Disagree						Strongly Agree
1. XYZ Company has modern-looking equipment.	1	2	3	4	5	6	7
2. XYZ Company's physical facilities are visually appealing.	1	2	3	4	5	6	7
3. XYZ Company's employees appear neat.	1	2	3	4	5	6	7
4. Materials associated with the service (such as pamphlets or statements) are visually appealing at XYZ Company.	1	2	3	4	5	6	7

EXPECTATIONS: Several Formats for Measuring Customer Expectations Using Versions of SERVQUAL

There are a number of different ways that expectations can be asked in surveys. We present four of these types below: (1) matching expectations statements, (2) referent expectations formats, (3) statements that combine both expectations and perceptions, and (4) statements that cover different types of expectations.

Matching Expectations Statements (Paired with the Previous Perception Statements)

	Strongly Disagree						Strongly Agree
When customers have a problem, excellent firms will show a sincere interest in solving it.	1	2	3	4	5	6	7

Referent Expectations Formats

1. Considering a "world-class" company to be a "7," how would you rate XYZ Company's performance on the following service features?

	Low						High
Sincere, interested employees	1	2	3	4	5	6	7
Service delivered right the first time	1	2	3	4	5	6	7

2. Compared with the level of service you expect from an excellent company, how would you rate XYZ Company's performance on the following?

	Low						High
Sincere, interested employees	1	2	3	4	5	6	7
Service delivered right the first time	1	2	3	4	5	6	7

Combined Expectations/Perceptions Statements

For each of the following statements, circle the number that indicates how XYZ Company's service compares with the level you expect:

	Lower Than My Desired Service Level			The Same as My Desired Service Level			Higher Than My Desired Service Level		
1. Prompt service	1	2	3	4	5	6	7	8	9
2. Courteous employees	1	2	3	4	5	6	7	8	9

(continued)

Exhibit 5.2   (concluded)

Expectations Distinguishing between Desired Service and Adequate Service

For each of the following statements, circle the number that indicates how XYZ Company's performance compares with your *minimum service level* and with your *desired service level*.

When it comes to ...	Compared with my *minimum* service level XYZ's service performance is			Compared with my *desired* service level XYZ's service performance is		
	Lower	Same	Higher	Lower	Same	Higher
1. Prompt service	1 2 3	4 5 6	7 8 9	1 2 3	4 5 6	7 8 9
2. Employees who are consistently courteous	1 2 3	4 5 6	7 8 9	1 2 3	4 5 6	7 8 9

Source: A. Parasuraman, V. A. Zeithaml, and L. L. Berry, "SERVQUAL: A Multiple-Item Scale for Measuring Consumer Perceptions of Service Quality," *Journal of Retailing* 64, no. 1 (Spring 1988). Reprinted by permission of C. Samuel Craig.

as the phrasing of the expectations and perceptions portions of the scale.[8] Data gathered through a SERVQUAL survey can be used for a variety of purposes:

- To determine the average gap score (between customers' perceptions and expectations) for each service attribute.
- To assess a company's service quality along each of the five SERVQUAL dimensions.
- To track customers' expectations and perceptions (on individual service attributes and/or on the SERVQUAL dimensions) over time.
- To compare a company's SERVQUAL scores against those of competitors.
- To identify and examine customer segments that differ significantly in their assessments of a company's service performance.
- To assess internal service quality (that is, the quality of service rendered by one department or division of a company to others within the same company).

This instrument has spawned many studies focusing on service quality assessment and is used all over the world in service industries. Published studies have used SERVQUAL and adaptations of it in a variety of contexts: real estate brokers, physicians in private practice, public recreation programs, dental schools, business school placement centers, tire stores, motor carrier companies, accounting firms, discount and department stores, gas and electric utility companies, hospitals, banking, pest control, dry cleaning, fast food, and higher education.

Trailer Calls or Posttransaction Surveys

Whereas the purpose of SERVQUAL and relationship surveys is usually to gauge the overall relationship with the customer, the purpose of transaction surveys is to capture information about key service encounters with the customer. In this method, customers are asked a short list of questions immediately after a particular transaction (hence the name *trailer calls*) about their satisfaction with the transaction and contact personnel with whom they interacted. Because the surveys are administered continuously to a broad spectrum of customers, they are more effective than complaint solicitation (where the information comes only from dissatisfied customers).

At checkout, immediately after staying at Fairfield Inns, customers are asked to use a computer terminal to answer four or five questions about their stay in the hotel. This approach has obvious benefits over the ubiquitous comment cards left in rooms—the response rate is far higher because the process engages customers and takes only a few minutes. In other companies, transaction surveys are by e-mail (Best Buy, Geek Squad, and Panera Bread). Customers are asked to complete a survey by calling an 800-number or going to a website listed on their receipt. The incentive for completing the survey is a chance to win prizes or coupons from the stores.

A strong benefit of this type of research is that it often appears to customers that the call is following up to ensure that they are satisfied; consequently, the request does double duty as a market research tool and customer service. This type of research is simple and fresh and provides management with continuous information about interactions with customers. Further, the research allows management to associate service quality performance with individual contact personnel, so that high performance can be rewarded and low performance corrected. It also serves as an incentive for employees to provide better service because they understand how and when they are being evaluated. One posttransaction study that you may be familiar with is the BizRate.com study that follows online purchases. When a consumer makes a purchase at one of BizRate's online partners (which include many major companies), a message automatically pops up on the site and invites consumers to fill out a survey. Consumers who agree are asked questions about ease of ordering, product selection, website navigation, and customer support.

Service Expectation Meetings and Reviews

In business-to-business situations when large accounts are involved, a form of customer research that is highly effective involves eliciting the expectations of the client at a specified time of the year and then following up later (usually after a year) to determine whether the expectations were fulfilled. Even when the company produces a physical product, the meetings deal almost completely with the service expected and provided by an account or sales team assigned to the client. Unlike other forms of research we have discussed, these meetings are not conducted by unbiased researchers but are instead initiated and facilitated by senior members of the account team, so that they can listen carefully to the client's expectations. You may be surprised to find that such interaction does not come naturally to sales teams who are used to talking *to* clients rather than listening carefully to their needs. Consequently, teams have to be carefully trained not to defend or explain but instead to comprehend. One company found that the only way it could teach its salespeople not to talk on these interviews was to take a marketing researcher along to gently kick the salesperson under the table whenever he or she strayed from the format!

The format, when appropriate, consists of (1) asking clients what they expect in terms of 8 to 10 basic requirements determined from focus group research, (2) inquiring what particular aspects of these requirements the account team performed well in the past as well as what aspects need improvement, and (3) requesting that the client rank the relative importance of the requirements. After getting the input, senior account members go back to their teams and plan their goals for the year around client requirements. The next step is verifying with the client that the account plan will satisfy requirements or, when it will not, managing expectations to let the client know what cannot be accomplished. After executing the plan for the year, the senior account personnel then return to the client, determine whether the plan has been successfully executed and expectations met, and establish a new set of expectations for the coming year.

Process Checkpoint Evaluations

With professional services such as consulting, construction, and architecture, services are provided over a long period, and there are no obvious ways or times to collect customer information. Waiting until the entire project is complete—which could last years—is undesirable because myriad unresolvable problems could have occurred by then. But discrete service encounters to calibrate customer perceptions are also not usually available. In these situations, the smart service provider defines a process for delivering the services and then structures the feedback around the process, checking in at frequent points to ensure that the client's expectations are being met. For example, a management consulting firm might establish the following process for delivering its services to clients: (1) collect information, (2) diagnose problems, (3) recommend alternative solutions, (4) select alternatives, and (5) implement solutions. Next, it could agree with the client up-front that it will communicate at major *process checkpoints*—after diagnosing the problem, before selecting the alternative, and so on—to make certain that the job is progressing as planned.

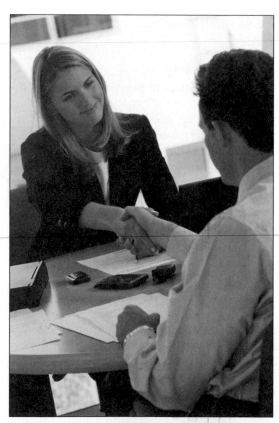

In professional service, evaluations are made at important checkpoints in the process.

Market-Oriented Ethnography

Structured questionnaires, make key assumptions about what people are conscious of or can recall about their behavior and what they are willing to explain to researchers about their opinions. To fully understand how customers assess and use services, it may be necessary and effective to use other approaches, such as *market-oriented ethnography.* The new product/service firm called IDEO is founded on this approach to design research. This set of approaches allows researchers to observe consumption behavior in natural settings. The goal is to enter the consumer's world as much as possible—observing how and when a service is used in an actual home environment or consumption environment, such as watching consumers eat in restaurants or attend concerts. Among the techniques used are observation, interviews, documents, and examination of material possessions such as artifacts. Observation involves entering the experience as a participant observer and watching what occurs rather than asking questions about it. One-on-one interviews, particularly with key informants in the culture rather than consumers themselves, can provide compelling insights into culture-based behavior. Studying existing documents and cultural artifacts can also provide valuable insights, especially about lifestyles and usage patterns.[9]

Best Western International used this technique to better understand its senior market. Rather than bringing participants into focus group facilities and asking them questions, the company paid 25 over-55 couples to videotape themselves on cross-country journeys. The firm was able to listen to how couples actually made decisions rather than the way they reported them. The insights they gained from this research were decidedly different from what they would have learned otherwise. Most noteworthy was the finding that seniors who talked hotel clerks into better deals on rooms did not need the lower price to afford staying at the hotel—they were simply after the thrill of the deal, as illustrated in this description:

> The 60-ish woman caught on the grainy videotape is sitting on her hotel bed, addressing her husband after a long day spent on the road. "Good job!" she exults. "We beat the s—t out of the front desk and got a terrific room."[10]

These customers then spent their discount money on better dinners elsewhere, contributing nothing to Best Western. "The degree of discount clearly isn't what it used to be in importance—and we got that right out of the research," claimed the manager of programs for Best Western. This finding would be highly unlikely using traditional research and asking customers directly, for few customers would admit to being willing to pay a higher price for a service.

Mystery Shopping

In this form of research, which is unique to services, companies hire outside research organizations to send people into service establishments and experience the service as if they were customers. These *mystery shoppers* are trained in the criteria important to customers of the establishment. They deliver objective assessments about service performance by completing questionnaires about service standards or, in other cases, open-ended questions that have a qualitative feel to them. Questionnaires contain items that represent important quality or service issues to customers. Au Bon Pain, for example, sends mystery shoppers to its stores to buy meals and then complete questionnaires about the servers, the restaurant, and the food. Servers are evaluated on standards that include the following:

Acknowledged within three seconds after reaching first place in line.

Acknowledged pleasantly.

Server suggested additional items.

Server requested payment prior to delivering order.

Received receipt.

Received correct change.

Correct order received.

Au Bon Pain motivates workers to perform to service standards by using the mystery shopper program as a key element in its compensation and reward system. Individual workers who receive positive scores have their names posted on the store's bulletin board and receive letters of congratulations as well as bonuses. Managers whose stores earn high scores can receive on-the-spot bonuses of "Club Excellence" dollars that can be traded like green stamps for items in a company catalog. Perhaps more important, the overall scores received by shift and district managers qualify them for monthly profit-sharing cash bonuses. A score lower than 78 percent removes them from consideration for a bonus, whereas high numbers lead to good bonuses.

Mystery shopping keeps workers on their toes because they know they may be evaluated at any time. They know they are being judged on the company's service standards and therefore carry out the standards more consistently than if they were not going to be judged. Mystery shopping can be a very effective way of reinforcing service standards.

Customer Panels

Customer panels are groups of customers assembled to provide attitudes and perceptions about a service over time. They offer the company regular and timely customer information—virtually a pulse on the market. Firms can use customer panels to represent large segments of end-customers.

Customer panels are used in the entertainment industry to screen movies before they are released to the public. After a rough cut of a film has been created, the movie is viewed by a panel of consumers that matches the demographic target. In the most basic of these panels, consumers participate in postscreening interviews or focus groups in which they report on their responses to the movie. They may be asked questions as general as their reactions to the ending of the movie and as specific as whether they understood different aspects of the plot line. Based on these panels, movies are revised and edited to ensure that they are communicating the desired message and that they will succeed in the marketplace. In extreme situations, entire endings of movies have been changed to be more consistent with customer attitudes.

Lost Customer Research

This type of research involves deliberately seeking customers who have dropped the company's service to inquire about their reasons for leaving. Some *lost customer research* is similar to exit interviews with employees in that it asks open-ended, in-depth questions to expose the reasons for defection and the particular events that led to dissatisfaction. It is also possible to use more standard surveys on lost customers. For example, a midwestern manufacturer used a mail survey to ask former customers about its performance during different stages of the customer–vendor relationship. The survey also sought specific reasons for customers' defections and asked customers to describe problems that triggered their decreases in purchases.

One benefit of this type of research is that it identifies failure points and common problems in the service and can help establish an early-warning system for future defectors. Another benefit is that the research can be used to calculate the cost of lost customers.

Future Expectations Research

Customer expectations are dynamic and can change very rapidly in markets that are highly competitive and volatile. As competition increases, as tastes change, and as consumers become more knowledgeable, companies must continue to update their information and strategies. In dynamic market situations, companies want to understand not just current customer expectations but also future expectations—the service features desired in the future. *Future expectations research* includes different types. First, *features research* involves environmental scanning and querying of customers about desirable features of possible services. *Lead user research* brings in customers who are opinion leaders/innovators and asks them what requirements are not currently being met by existing products or services.

The question of customer involvement in expectation studies is often debated. Designers and developers claim that consumers do not know what they might want, especially in industries or services that are new and rapidly changing. Consumers and marketing researchers, on the other hand, counter that services developed independently of customer input are likely to be targeted at needs that do not exist. To study this question, researchers assessed the contributions made by users compared with professional developers for end-user telecom services. Three groups were studied: users alone, developers alone, and users with a design expert present to provide information on feasibility. Findings showed that users created more original but less producible ideas. However, inviting users to test and explore possibilities once a prototype has been created can produce positive results.[11]

ANALYZING AND INTERPRETING CUSTOMER RESEARCH FINDINGS

One of the biggest challenges facing a customer researcher is converting a complex set of data to a form that can be read and understood quickly by executives, managers, and other employees who will make decisions from the research. For example, database management is being adopted as a strategic initiative by many firms (see the Strategy Insight box), but merely having a sophisticated database does not ensure that the findings will be useful to managers. Many of the people who use customer research findings have not been trained in statistics and have neither the time nor the expertise to analyze computer printouts and other technical research information. The goal in this stage of the customer research process is to communicate information clearly to the right people in a timely fashion. Among considerations are the following: Who gets this information? Why do they need it? How will they use it? Does it mean the same thing across cultures? When users feel confident that they understand the data, they are far more likely to apply it appropriately. When managers do not understand how to interpret the data, or when they lack confidence in the research, the investment of time, skill, and effort will be lost.

Depicting marketing research findings graphically is a powerful way to communicate research information. Here are samples of graphic representations of the types of marketing research data we have discussed throughout this chapter.

Zones of Tolerance Charts

When companies collect data on the dual expectation levels described in Chapter 3—desired service and adequate service—along with performance data, they can convey the information concisely on zones of tolerance charts. Figure 5.2 plots customer

FIGURE 5.2
Service Quality Perceptions Relative to Zones of Tolerance by Dimensions

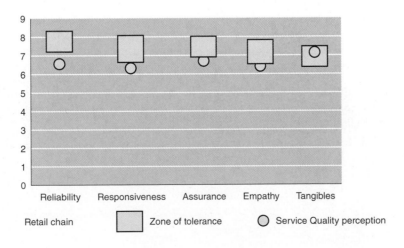

Strategy Insight From Greeting Cards to Gambling, Companies Bet on Database Customer Research

Most of the customer research approaches in this chapter study patterns of customers in groups. Surveys examine the service quality perceptions of the totality of a firm's customers to get a sense of how they feel as a group. Focus groups identify the needs of important service segments, and lost customer research pinpoints the primary reasons why exiting customers are dissatisfied enough to leave the company. However, an important and powerful form of research—called *database marketing* or *customer relationship management (CRM)*—studies customers one by one to develop profiles on their individual needs, behaviors, and responses to marketing. This approach allows a company to get very close to its customers and to tailor services to individuals.

Individual customer research is founded on a database that allows a company to tell customers apart and remember them uniquely. You may be most familiar with this form of data collection in grocery store loyalty cards—like VIC for Harris Teeter or MVP for Food Lion—that capture information about your purchases and offer you tailored coupons and specials based on your buying patterns. One of the most familiar examples of using a technology database to remember customers is Ritz-Carlton's frequent guest registry, which documents the preferences of each frequent guest. (Does he like a smoking or nonsmoking room? Feather pillows? Does she read *USA Today* or *The Wall Street Journal?*) Each time a guest visits, new observations about preferences are entered, so that the institution itself comes to "know" each guest.

The following are two innovative examples of database marketing and how they are applied to understand and market to individual customers.

HALLMARK GOLD CROWN

Hallmark's database, capable of recognizing customers in all 3,000 Hallmark retail stores, tracks purchases, contacts, and communications, so that it learns what each customer values about the relationship with the company. This information includes what core product or benefit has the most value to the customer and what differentiates Hallmark from its competition. The mechanism by which the company tracks this information is a Gold Crown Card, which customers use to accumulate points for purchases. They receive personalized point statements, newsletters, reward certificates, and individualized news of products and events at local stores. The top 10 percent of customers—who buy more cards and ornaments than others—get special amenities such as longer bonus periods and their own priority toll-free number, as well as very targeted communication about the specific products they value.

Hallmark turns the information it collects into one-on-one marketing communications using three key aspects of consumer shopping behavior: types of products purchased, purchase frequency, and time since last purchase. If the customer has not been in the stores for a period of time, the company sends a special offer to bring her back. If she has been in recently, a thank-you message is mailed. When the customers' favorite items are in season—such as ornaments at Christmas—offers and information are mailed to encourage purchase.

Several times a year Hallmark executives sit down with preferred and regular members to hear how they feel about the program, what they would like to see added or changed, and how they react to product offerings. Results of the program have been impressive. The program has more than 17 million permanent cardholders, 12 million who have purchased in the last 6-month period, and over 14 million who have purchased in the last 12 months. Member sales represent 35 percent of total store transactions and 45 percent of total store sales.

HARRAH'S ENTERTAINMENT INC.

The gambling industry has long recognized that certain customers are better than others and that encouraging the "high rollers" to spend time in one's casinos is a worthwhile and profitable strategy. One of the main ways they encourage increased patronage is "comping"—giving free drinks, hotel rooms, limousines, and sometimes chips to top customers. The strategy has been limited in most casinos to customers who could be identified and followed, making the approach spotty and missing many potential repeat patrons. Harrah's Entertainment, which owns and operates 17 gambling casinos in places such as Las Vegas and Atlantic City, found a more systematic way to extend the practice to a wider group of customers. Harrah's developed a customer relationship management system called the Total Rewards program, a loyalty program that tracks the names and addresses of repeat visitors along with what slot machines they play, how long they play, and how much money they gamble. The company's approach uses a Total Rewards Card that any customer can obtain—often with the incentive of covering their slot losses for half an hour up to $100. To earn points toward drinks, rooms, and other benefits, customers allow their cards to be swiped on the casino floor to monitor the sums gambled and time spent at slot machines and card tables. Harrah's is counting on customers wanting the points enough to agree to be tracked.

Although individual players can earn platinum or diamond status based on their gambling levels, the program is designed for mass markets. The average Harrah's customer gambles less than $3,000 annually and goes to Vegas just once or twice a year. This program allows Harrah's to determine how profitable all customers are as individuals and make special offers tailored to their casino behavior to keep them coming back. The company can now turn the program into immediate rewards. For example, Harrah's data can identify when a customer is losing, thereby providing him or her with an immediate credit toward future gambling. Printers placed at the gaming machines issue customers these real-time credits.

When analysis showed that core customers were slot players, the company recognized that it needed an approach to track a much wider group of visitors than it had considered in the past. The Total Rewards Card was an ideal way to allow everyone to participate and to gather data on all customers. Tracking also showed them that customers with the highest lifetime values were those who regularly stopped by to gamble after work—rather than those who went for a few days—demonstrating that the industry's typical inducements of free hotel stays and steak dinners were not the best way to encourage repeat business.

THE VALUE OF DATABASE CUSTOMER RESEARCH

Database marketing has applications in virtually any service in which customers make repeat purchases. Underlying the approach is the necessity for the company to create customer information files that integrate different data sources on individual customers, including demographics, segmentation, usage information, customer satisfaction data, and accounting and financial information. Although the approach raises privacy concerns with some customers, research is enhanced using databases. A company no longer needs to depend on surveys but can instead track actual behavior. It no longer needs to guess which demographics are most related to psychographic segmentation information—the company can run an analysis to provide valid and reliable data on the topic.

Sources: F. Newell, *loyalty.com* (New York: McGraw-Hill, 2000), pp. 232–238; C. T. Heun, "Harrah's Bets on IT to Understand Its Customers," *Informationweek,* December 11, 2000; Gary Loveman, "Diamonds in the Data Mine," *Harvard Business Review,* May 2003, pp. 109–112; www. harrahs.com, 2011; www.hallmark.com, 2007; "Getting to Know You," *Chain Store Age,* November 2005, p. 51.

When conducting customer research in emerging markets—Brazil, Russia, India, and China—U.S.-based marketers need to adapt their practices to be successful. As authors Linda Steinbach and Virginia Weil claim, marketers need important background information before conducting research to be sure they don't make bad decisions based on the wrong information or analysis. These authors, global key account directors from a top international customer research firm called Synovate, offer helpful lists of do's and don'ts for each of the four emerging markets. The following insights are excerpted from the article listed at the end of this Global Feature.

BRAZIL

In doing research in Brazil, a marketer must realize the following:

- Secondary research, including "official" statistics, is not to be fully trusted, in part because of the small number of sources but also because there are discrepancies among the sources.

- Because consumers are concerned about violence, face-to-face interviewers are unlikely to get inside people's homes to interview them. Telephone and Web surveys are better options.

- Personal contacts are very important, so knowing someone who knows someone allows researchers much quicker access. In a similar vein, references are essential. If you have done business with someone a Brazilian knows and respects, that information will be very useful.

- Price is important for both general consumers and business purchasers.

RUSSIA

Steinbach and Weil recommend that, when companies are conducting research in Russia, they should connect with local companies because most Russian managers prefer to speak Russian and deal with Russians. Other facts to know include the following:

- Secondary research is not likely to be accurate due to limited sources and discrepancies among them.

- Face-to-face surveys for B-to-B are greatly preferred over telephone surveys.

- The local postal service takes several weeks to deliver a package or survey, so use another means of distribution.

- While personal contacts are very important, cold calling is also effective.

- Most researchers in Russia have a math background, leading to very specific explanations of solutions when they present findings.

- For each recommendation, companies in Russia must be convinced that it reflects Russian realities, as they strongly believe that Russia is very different from the rest of the world.

service quality perceptions relative to customers' zones of tolerance. Perceptions of company performance are indicated by the circles, and the zones of tolerance boxes are bounded on the top by the desired service score and on the bottom by the adequate service score. When the perception scores are within the boxes, as is the case for the tangibles dimension of service quality in Figure 5.2, the company is delivering service that is above customers' minimum level of expectations. When the perception scores are below the boxes, the company's service performance is lower than the minimum level, and customers are dissatisfied with the company's service.[12]

Importance/Performance Matrices

One of the most useful forms of analysis in customer research is the *importance/performance matrix*. This chart combines information about customer perceptions and importance ratings. An example is shown in Figure 5.3. Attribute importance is represented on the vertical axis from high (top) to low (bottom). Performance is shown on the horizontal axis from low (left) to high (right). There are many variations of these matrices: some companies define the horizontal axis as the gap between expectations and perceptions, or as performance relative to competition. The shading on the chart indicates

- Russia has 11 time zones, and temperatures range from 0 to -40 degrees, so outdoor marketing or research initiatives can be affected.
- To be representative of the nation, a survey should cover at least 53 cities across seven regions of total territory.
- Shared responsibility (collectivism), rather than individualism, is a core value.

INDIA

Only 70 percent of adults are literate, and one-third of Indians live on the equivalent of 70 cents per day. Some of these demographics affect research, as do the following:

- Keep consumer research simple. The quality of interviews on complex concepts is likely to be low.
- English is the language of business, but there are 14 "first languages" among consumers and many dialects. For this reason, telephone interviewing for research must be regionalized for language.
- Many people will not want to do in-home interviews because they are sensitive about the poverty of their homes.
- For B-to-B surveys, e-mail is popular and phone interviews possible, but in-person interviews are difficult.
- Corruption in the public sector is common and cash payments to grease the wheels at any level may be requested.

- Gender relations are important. Many women, or their male partners, will be uncomfortable with male interviewers in informal environments.

CHINA

China has 1.3 billion consumers and is therefore a key market for many products. The following are facts to know about research done there:

- Politics, religion, and sex are considered to be too sensitive as topics and can never be included in surveys.
- Because company personnel are spread across large distances, face-to-face B-to-B interviews are difficult to conduct.
- Mandarin is the official language, but local dialects are still strong.
- Online interviews work if the target audience is educated and younger than 40 years old.
- Because China is big, the behavioral styles and sophistication of marketers and researchers can differ by region.
- Most projects require many meetings and involve many people.
- The Chinese have a deep respect for hierarchy and saving face is critical.
- In business, it is important to capture the sense of "Guanzi": personal rather than corporate relationships.

EXCERPTED WITH PERMISSION FROM L. Steinbach and V. Weil, "From Tactical to Personal: Synovate's Tips for Conducting Market Research in Emerging Markets," *Marketing News*, April 30, 2011.

FIGURE 5.3
Importance/ Performance Matrix

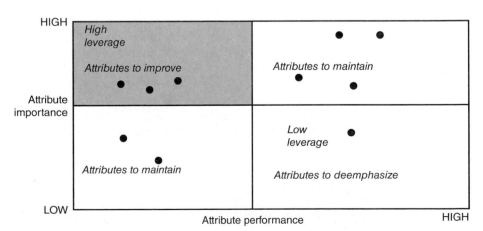

the area of highest leverage for service quality improvements—where importance is high and performance is low. In this quadrant are the attributes that most need to be improved. In the adjacent upper quadrant are attributes to be maintained, ones that a company performs well and that are very important to customers. The lower two quadrants contain attributes that are less important, some of which are performed well and others poorly. Neither of these quadrants merit as much attention in terms of service improvements as the upper quadrants because customers are not as concerned about the attributes that are plotted in them as they are the attributes in the upper quadrants.

USING MARKETING RESEARCH INFORMATION

Conducting research about customer expectations is only the first part of understanding the customer, even if the research is appropriately designed, executed, and presented. A service firm must also use the research findings in a meaningful way—to drive change or improvement in the way service is delivered. The misuse (or even nonuse) of research data can lead to a large gap in *understanding customer expectations.* When managers do not read research reports because they are too busy dealing with the day-to-day challenges of the business, companies fail to use the resources available to them. And when customers participate in research studies but never see changes in the way the company does business, they feel frustrated and annoyed with the company. Understanding how to make the best use of research—to apply what has been learned to the business—is a key way to close the gap between customer expectations and management perceptions of customer expectations. Managers must learn to turn research information and insights into action and to recognize that the purpose of research is to drive improvement and customer satisfaction.

The research plan should specify the mechanism by which customer data will be used. The research should be actionable: timely, specific, and credible. It can also have a mechanism that allows a company to respond to dissatisfied customers immediately.

UPWARD COMMUNICATION

In some service firms, especially small and localized firms, owners or managers may be in constant contact with customers, thereby gaining firsthand knowledge of customer expectations and perceptions. But in large service organizations, managers do not always get the opportunity to experience firsthand what their customers want.

The larger a company is, the more difficult it is for managers to interact directly with the customer and the less firsthand information they have about customer expectations. Even when they read and digest research reports, managers can lose the reality of the customer if they never get the opportunity to experience delivery of the actual service. A theoretical view of how things are supposed to work cannot provide the richness of the service encounter. To truly understand customer needs, management benefits from hands-on knowledge of what really happens in stores, on customer service telephone lines, in service queues, and in face-to-face service encounters. If the listening gap is to be closed, managers in large firms need some form of customer contact.

Objectives for Upward Communication

Exhibit 5.3 shows the major research objectives for improving upward communication in an organization. These objectives include gaining firsthand knowledge about customers, improving internal service quality, gaining firsthand knowledge of employees,

Exhibit 5.3 Elements in an Effective Program of Upward Communication

Type of Interaction or Research	Research Objective	Qualitative/ Quantitative	Cost of Information		
			Money	Time	Frequency
Executive visits to customers	To gain firsthand knowledge about customers	Qualitative	Moderate	Moderate	Continuous
Executive listenings	To gain firsthand knowledge about customers	Qualitative	Low	Low	Continuous
Research on intermediate customers	To gain in-depth information on end-customers	Quantitative	Moderate	Moderate	Annual
Employee internal satisfaction surveys	To improve internal service quality	Quantitative	Moderate	Moderate	Annual
Employee visits or listenings	To gain firsthand knowledge about employees	Qualitative	Moderate	Moderate	Continuous
Employee suggestions	To obtain ideas for service improvements	Qualitative	Low	Low	Continuous

and obtaining ideas for service improvement. These objectives can be met by two types of interactive activities in the organization: one designed to improve the type and effectiveness of communications from customers to management and the other designed to improve communications between employees and management.

Research for Upward Communication

Executive Visits to Customers

This approach is frequently used in business-to-business service marketing. In some visits, executives of the company make sales or service calls with customer contact personnel (salespeople). In other situations, executives of the selling company arrange meetings with executives at a similar level in client companies.

Executive or Management Listening to Customers

Direct interaction with customers adds clarity and depth to managers' understanding of customer expectations and needs. Many companies require executives to perform entry-level jobs to promote understanding of their customers. One vice president from DaVita Inc., the nation's number 2 dialysis-treatment operator, spent three days in spring 2007 helping treat seriously ill patients alongside technicians.[13] A growing number of service companies—including Walt Disney, Continental Airlines, Amazon. com, and Sysco—require that managers spend time on the line, interacting with customers and experiencing service delivery. A formal program for encouraging informal interaction is often the best way to ensure that the contact takes place.

Research on Intermediate Customers

Intermediate customers (such as contact employees, dealers, distributors, agents, and brokers) are people the company serves who serve the end-customer. Researching the needs and expectations of these customers *in serving the end-customer* can be a useful and efficient way to both improve service to and obtain information about end-users. The interaction with intermediate customers provides opportunities for understanding end-customers' expectations and problems. It can also help the company learn about and satisfy the service expectations of intermediate customers, a process critical in their providing quality service to end-customers.

Research on Internal Customers

Employees who perform services are themselves customers of internal services on which they depend heavily to do their jobs well. As discussed in Chapter 11, there is a strong and direct link between the quality of internal service that employees receive and the quality of the service they provide their own customers. For this reason, it is important to conduct employee research that focuses on the service that internal customers give and receive. In many companies this focus requires adapting existing employee opinion research to focus on service satisfaction. Employee research complements customer research when service quality is the issue being investigated. Customer research provides insight into what is occurring, whereas employee research provides insight into why. The two types of research play unique and equally important roles in improving service quality. Companies that focus service quality research exclusively on external customers are missing a rich and vital source of information.

Executive or Management Listening Approaches to Employees

Employees who actually perform the service have the best possible vantage point for observing the service and identifying impediments to its quality. Customer contact personnel are in regular contact with customers and thereby come to understand a great deal about customer expectations and perceptions. If the information they know can be passed on to top management, top managers' understanding of the customer may improve. In fact, it could be said that in many companies top management's understanding of the customer depends largely on the extent and types of communication received from customer contact personnel and from noncompany contact personnel (such as independent insurance agents and retailers) who represent the company and its services. When these channels of communication are closed, management may not get feedback about problems encountered in service delivery and about how customer expectations are changing.

Sam Walton, the late founder of the highly successful discount retailer Walmart, once remarked, "Our best ideas come from delivery and stock boys."[14] To stay in touch with the source of new ideas, Walton spent endless hours in stores, working the floor, helping clerks, or approving personal checks, even showing up at the loading dock with a bag of doughnuts for a surprised crew of workers.[15] He was well known for having his plane drop him next to a wheat field, where he would meet a Walmart truck driver. Giving his pilot instructions to meet him at another landing strip 200 miles down the road, he would make the trip with the Walmart driver, listening to what he had to say about the company.

Employee Suggestions

Most companies have some form of employee suggestion program whereby contact personnel can communicate to management their ideas for improving work. Suggestion systems have come a long way from the traditional suggestion box. Effective suggestion systems are ones in which employees are empowered to see their suggestions

Exhibit 5.4 Employees Provide Upward Communication at Cabela's, "World's Foremost Outfitter"

Unless you fish, hunt, shoot, camp, or cave, you may not know Cabela's, the largest mail order, Internet, and retail outdoor outfitter in the world. Established in 1961 as a specialty cataloger selling fly fishing lures, the company grew rapidly because of its philosophy that the customer was number 1 and that employees were critical to realizing that philosophy. Because the company was a catalog retailer for the first 30 years of its existence, it relied heavily on employees who were knowledgeable about the outdoors to describe products to consumers.

Its incredibly large (245,000 items) and varied (hunting, archery, shooting, optics, camping, boating, fishing) product mix make Cabela's the ultimate source for outdoor-focused customer needs and wants, but its many items make it difficult to match customers with products. From this challenge was born a novel and creative solution, one that made employees as happy as it made customers. The company decided to loan products to employees so they could learn what the products were like by using them. The extensive loaner program allows employees, who are typically outdoor enthusiasts themselves, to borrow the products

for a month and learn to ask the same questions customers would ask. Employees then become experts both on products and on experiences that customers will have using them.

After using the product, the employee returns and teaches everyone else about the product—both by giving a talk to others and by filling out a form about the product's pros and cons. This information becomes part of a giant product database, called "Item notes," that allows easy access to employees, even call center reps, so that customer questions—even the most esoteric ones—can be answered quickly and accurately. The company also invites a small number of knowledgeable customers to borrow products and contribute information as well.

The upward communication extends to the company's cofounder, Jim Cabela, who intercepts and reads all customer comments as they come in before routing them to the appropriate employee. He likes to keep an eye on what customers want to know, so that he can be sure his employees are staying informed.

Source: Michael A. Prospero, "Leading Listener Winner: Cabela's," *Fast Company,* October 2005, p. 47.

through, supervisors can implement proposals immediately, employees participate for continuous improvement in their jobs, supervisors respond quickly to ideas, and coaching is provided in ways to handle suggestions. In today's companies, suggestions from employees are facilitated by self-directed work teams that encourage employees to identify problems and then work to develop solutions to those problems.

Benefits of Upward Communication

Upward communication of this sort provides information to upper-level managers about activities and performances throughout the organization. Specific types of communication that may be relevant are formal (such as reports of problems and exceptions in service delivery) and informal (like discussions between contact personnel and upper-level managers). Managers who stay close to their contact people benefit not only by keeping their employees happy but also by learning more about their customers.[16] These companies encourage, appreciate, and reward upward communication from contact people, as Exhibit 5.4 shows. Through this important channel, management learns about customer expectations from employees in regular contact with customers and can thereby reduce the size of provider gap 1.

Summary

This chapter discussed the role of customer research in understanding customer perceptions and expectations. The chapter began by describing criteria for effective service research that should be incorporated into a service marketing research program. Next, we discussed the elements in an effective service marketing research program and indicated how the approaches satisfied the criteria. In addition to the types and techniques of research (shown in Exhibit 5.1), the boxes in this chapter showed how electronic and other technologies add to the information that managers can collect.

The chapter described key forms of service research, including critical incident studies, mystery shopping, service expectation meetings and reviews, process checkpoint evaluations, and database research. Important topics in researching services—including developing research objectives—were also described. Finally, upward communication, ways in which management obtains and uses information from customers and customer contact personnel, was discussed. These topics combine to help close the listening gap—the gap between customer expectations and company understanding of customer expectations and the first of four provider gaps in the gaps model of service quality.

Discussion Questions

1. Give five reasons research objectives must be established before customer research is conducted.
2. Why are both qualitative and quantitative research methods needed in a service marketing research program?
3. Why does the frequency of research differ across the research methods shown in Exhibit 5.1?
4. Compare and contrast the types of research that help a company identify common failure points (see column 2 in Exhibit 5.1). Which of the types do you think produces better information? Why?
5. In what situations does a service company need requirements research?
6. What reasons can you give for companies' lack of use of research information? How might you motivate managers to use the information to a greater extent? How might you motivate frontline workers to use the information?
7. Given a specific customer research budget, what would be your recommendations for the percentage to be spent on customer research versus upward communication? Why?
8. What kinds of information could be gleaned from research on intermediate customers? What would intermediate customers know that service providers might not?
9. For what types of products and services would research on the Internet be preferable to traditional research?

Exercises

1. Choose a local service organization to interview about customer research. Find out what the firm's objectives are and the types of customer research it currently uses. Using the information in this chapter, think about the effectiveness of its customer research. What are the strengths? Weaknesses?

2. Choose one of the services you consume. If you were in charge of creating a survey for that service, what questions would you ask on the survey? Give several examples. What type of survey (relationship versus transaction based) would be most appropriate for the service? What recommendations would you give to management of the company about making such a survey actionable?

3. If you were the marketing director of your college or university, what types of research (see Exhibit 5.1) would be essential for understanding both external and internal customers? If you could choose only three types of research, which ones would you select? Why?

4. Using the SERVQUAL scale in this chapter, create a questionnaire for a service firm that you use. Give the questionnaire to 10 people, and describe what you learn.

5. To get an idea of the power of the critical incident technique, try it yourself with reference to restaurant service. Think of a time when, as a customer, you had a particularly satisfying interaction with a restaurant. Follow the instructions here, which are identical to the instructions in an actual study, and observe the insights you obtain about your requirements in restaurant service:

   a. When did the incident happen?

   b. What specific circumstances led up to this situation?

   c. Exactly what did the employee (or firm) say or do?

   d. What resulted that made you feel the interaction was satisfying?

   e. What could or should have been done differently?

Notes

1. J. McGregor, "Customers First: 2004 Fast Company Customers First Awards," *Fast Company,* October 2004, pp. 79–88.

2. A. Parasuraman, L. L. Berry, and V. A. Zeithaml, "Guidelines for Conducting Service Quality Research," *Marketing Research: A Magazine of Management and Applications,* December 1990, pp. 34–44.

3. J. Neff, "Chasing the Cheaters Who Undermine Online Research," *Advertising Age*, March 31, 2008, p. 12; B. Johnson, "Forget Phone and Mail: Online's the Best Place to Administer Surveys," *Advertising Age*, July 17, 2006, p. 23.

4. This section is based on a comprehensive assessment of the critical incident technique in D. D. Gremler, "The Critical Incident Technique in Service Research," *Journal of Service Research* 7 (August 2004), pp. 65–89.

5. For detailed discussions of the critical incident technique, see J. C. Flanagan, "The Critical Incident Technique," *Psychological Bulletin* 51 (July 1954), pp. 327–358; M. J. Bitner, J. D. Nyquist, and B. H. Booms, "The Critical Incident as a Technique for Analyzing the Service Encounter," in *Services Marketing in a Changing Environment,* ed. T. M. Bloch, G. D. Upah, and V. A. Zeithaml (Chicago: American Marketing Association, 1985), pp. 48–51; S. Wilson-Pessano, "Defining Professional Competence: The Critical Incident Technique 40 Years Later," presentation to the Annual Meeting of the American Educational Research Association, New Orleans, 1988; I. Roos, "Methods of Investigating Critical Incidents," *Journal of*

Service Research 4 (February 2002), pp. 193–204; Gremler, "The Critical Incident Technique in Service Research."

6. Ibid.

7. J. Carey, J. Buckley, and J. Smith, "Hospital Hospitality," *Newsweek,* February 11, 1985, p. 78.

8. See V. A. Zeithaml and A. Parasuraman, *Service Quality,* MSI Relevant Knowledge Series (Cambridge, MA: Marketing Science Institute, 2004) for a complete review of this research, including the many publications by the original authors of SERVQUAL and the extensions by other authors.

9. E. Day, "Researchers Must Enter Consumer's World," *Marketing News,* August 17, 1998, p. 17.

10. G. Khermouch, "Consumers in the Mist," *BusinessWeek,* February 26, 2001, pp. 92–93.

11. P. R. Magnusson, J. Mathing, and P. Kristensson, "Managing User Involvement in Service Innovation: Experiments with Innovating End Users," *Journal of Service Research* 6 (November 2003), pp. 111–124.

12. A. Parasuraman, V. A. Zeithaml, and L. L. Berry, "Moving Forward in Service Quality Research," *Marketing Science Institute Report No. 94–114,* September 1994.

13. J. S. Lublin, "Top Brass Try Life in the Trenches," *The Wall Street Journal,* June 25, 2007, p. B1.

14. S. Koepp, "Make That Sale, Mr. Sam," *Time,* May 18, 1987.

15. Ibid.

16. Zeithaml, Parasuraman, and Berry, *Delivering Quality Service,* p. 64.

Chapter Six

Building Customer Relationships

This chapter's objectives are to

1. Explain relationship marketing, its goals, and the benefits of long-term relationships for firms and customers.
2. Explain why and how to estimate customer relationship value.
3. Introduce the concept of customer profitability segments as a strategy for focusing relationship marketing efforts.
4. Present relationship development strategies—including quality core service, switching barriers, and relationship bonds.
5. Identify challenges in relationship development, including the somewhat controversial idea that "the customer is not always right."

USAA Focuses on Long-Term Relationships

United Services Automobile Association (USAA) is a preeminent example of an organization focused on building long-term relationships with customers—or what it refers to as members.[1] Member retention has been a core value of USAA since long before customer loyalty became a popular business concept. In business since 1922, USAA provides for the insurance needs of a highly targeted market segment: current and former U.S. military personnel and their families. Headquartered in San Antonio, Texas, USAA owns and manages more than $110 billion in assets. It has been ranked number 1 or 2 every year from 2007–2010 in *BusinessWeek's* annual list of "Customer Service Champs." USAA also consistently appears on *Fortune* magazine's list of the 100 best companies to work for in America. Member retention figures approach 100 percent;[2] in fact, the most likely reason for a member to leave USAA is death.

The goal of USAA is to "think about the events in the life of a career officer and then work out ways to help him get through them." USAA is intent on serving its current member base and growing with them. To do this, USAA relies heavily on extensive research through surveys and a member advisory board that meets regularly with executives. USAA also focuses on retaining the best employees and rewarding them for member-oriented objectives such as percentage of member questions or requests handled on the first call with no need for follow-up. USAA

USAA: a regular at the top of *BusinessWeek's* annual rankings for customer service.

believes so strongly in the importance of member retention that a portion of managers' and executives' bonuses are based on this metric. Such emphasis has been rewarded: independent research firms report that 81 percent of USAA's members believe the organization does what is best for them rather than for the bottom line.[3]

USAA: *Business Week's* customer service champs for 2007

A striking example of how USAA attempts to listen to its members is illustrated in this excerpt from *BusinessWeek:*

> Many companies give lip service to listening to the "voice of the customer." At USAA, that voice is transformed into what it calls "surround sound"—a comprehensive approach to training its employees to empathize with its members' unique needs. "We want to cover the light moments, the heart-wrenching moments, what it's like to be bored in the field," says Elizabeth D. Conklyn, USAA's [former] executive vice-president for people services. "We try to develop empathy, not only for our members but also for the family side."[4]
>
> USAA has developed an enhanced military awareness program that requires member service representatives to engage in tasks that allow them to empathize with their members. For example, employees may have to strap on a military helmet, 65-pound backpack, and flak vest; consume a "meal ready to eat" given to soldiers in the field; and read real letters from troops stationed abroad. It is not uncommon for an employee to read a letter, written by a soldier to his mother, from someone who later died in a war.

USAA provides a strong example of an organization that has focused on keeping its customers and building long-term relationships with them. Unlike the USAA example, however, many companies fail to understand customers accurately because they fail to focus on customer relationships. They tend to fixate on acquiring new customers rather than viewing customers as assets that they need to nurture and retain. By concentrating on new customers, firms can easily fall into the traps of short-term promotions, price discounts, or catchy ads that bring customers in but are not enough to bring them back. By adopting a relationship philosophy, on the other hand, companies begin to understand customers over time and in great depth and are better able to meet their changing needs and expectations.

Marketing strategies for understanding customers over time and building long-term relationships are the subjects of this chapter.

RELATIONSHIP MARKETING

There has been a shift from a transactions to a relationship focus in marketing. Customers become partners and the firm must make long-term commitments to maintaining those relationships with quality, service, and innovation.[5]

A company interested in a committed relationship with its customers will experience long-term benefits.

Relationship marketing essentially represents a paradigm shift within marketing—away from an acquisitions/transaction focus toward a retention/ relationship focus.[6] Relationship marketing (or relationship management) is a philosophy of doing business, a strategic orientation, that focuses on *keeping and improving* relationships with current customers rather than on acquiring new customers. This philosophy assumes that many consumers and business customers prefer to have an ongoing relationship with one organization rather than to switch continually among providers in their search for value. Building on this assumption and another that suggests it is usually less expensive to keep a current customer than to attract a new one, successful marketers develop effective strategies for retaining customers. Our opening example shows how USAA has built its business around a relationship philosophy.

It has been suggested that firms frequently focus on attracting customers (the "first act") but then pay little attention to what they should do to keep them (the "second act").[7] Ideas expressed in an interview with James L. Schorr, then executive vice president of marketing at Holiday Inns, illustrate this point.[8] In the interview he referred to the "bucket theory of marketing." By this he meant that marketing can be thought of as a big bucket: it is what the sales, advertising, and promotion programs do that pours customers into the top of the bucket. As long as these programs are effective, the bucket stays full. However, "There's only one problem," he said, "there's a hole in the bucket." When the business is running well and the hotel is delivering on its promises, any holes are small and few customers are leaving. As indicated in Figure 6.1, when the operation is weak and customers are not satisfied with what they get—and therefore the relationship is weak—people start falling out of the bucket through the holes faster than they can be poured in through the top.

The bucket theory illustrates why a relationship strategy that focuses on plugging the holes in the bucket makes so much sense. Historically, marketers have been more concerned with acquisition of customers, so a shift to a relationship strategy often represents changes in mind-set, organizational culture, and employee reward systems. For example, the sales incentive systems in many organizations are set up to reward bringing in new customers. There are often fewer (or no) rewards for retaining current accounts. Thus, even when people see the logic of customer retention, the existing organizational systems may not support its implementation.

The Evolution of Customer Relationships

Firms' relationships with their customers, like other social relationships, tend to evolve over time. Scholars have suggested that marketing exchange relationships between

FIGURE 6.1
Holes in the Bucket: Why Relationship Development Makes Sense

providers and customers often have the potential to evolve from strangers to acquaintances to friends to partners. Exhibit 6.1 illustrates different issues at each successive level of the relationship.[9]

Customers as Strangers

Strangers are those customers who have not yet had any transactions (interactions) with a firm and may not even be aware of the firm. At the industry level, strangers may be conceptualized as customers who have not yet entered the market; at the firm level, they may include customers of competitors. Clearly the firm has no relationship with the customer at this point. Consequently, the firm's primary goal with these potential customers ("strangers") is to initiate communication with them to *attract* them and *acquire* their business. Thus, the primary marketing efforts directed toward such customers deal with familiarizing those potential customers with the firm's offerings and, subsequently, encouraging them to give the firm a try.

Customers as Acquaintances

Once customer awareness and trial are achieved, familiarity is established and the customer and the firm become *acquaintances,* creating the basis for an exchange relationship. A primary goal for the firm at this stage of the relationship is *satisfying* the customer. In the acquaintance stage, firms are generally concerned about providing a value proposition to customers comparable with that of competitors. For a customer, an acquaintanceship is effective as long as the customer is relatively satisfied and what is being received in the exchange is perceived as fair value. With repetitive interactions, the customer gains experience and becomes more familiar with the firm's offerings. These encounters can help reduce uncertainty about the benefits expected in the exchange and, therefore, increase the attractiveness of the company relative to the competition. Repetitive interactions improve the firm's knowledge of the customer, helping to facilitate marketing, sales, and service efforts. Thus, an acquaintance relationship facilitates transactions primarily through the reduction of the customer's perceived risk and the provider's costs.

Customers as Friends

As a customer continues to make purchases from a firm and to receive value in the exchange relationship, the firm begins to acquire specific knowledge of the customer's needs, allowing it to create an offering that directly addresses the customer's situation. The provision of a unique offering, and thus differential value, transforms the relationship from acquaintance to *friendship.* This transition, particularly in service exchange relationships, requires the development of trust.[10] Because customers may not be able to assess a service outcome prior to purchase and consumption, they may not be able to discern service performance even after experiencing it and, therefore, must trust the provider to do what is promised. As customers become friends they not only become familiar with the company but also come to trust that it provides superior value.

Exhibit 6.1 A Typology of Exchange Relationships

Customers As . . .	Strangers	Acquaintances	Friends	Partners
Product offering	Attractive relative to competitive offerings or alternative purchases.	Parity product as a form of industry standard.	Differentiated product adapted to specific market segments.	Customized product and dedicated resources adapted to an individual customer or organization.
Source of competitive advantage	Attractiveness	Satisfaction	Satisfaction + trust	Satisfaction + trust + commitment
Buying activity	Interest, exploration, and trial.	Satisfaction facilitates and reinforces buying activity and reduces need to search for market information.	Trust in firm is needed to continue the buying activity.	Commitment in the form of information sharing and idiosyncratic investments is needed to achieve customized product and to adjust product continuously to changing needs and situations.
Focus of selling activities	Awareness of firm's offerings (encouraging trial) facilitates initial selling.	Familiarity and general knowledge of customer (identification) facilitates selling.	Specific knowledge of customer's need and situation facilitates selling.	Specific knowledge of customer's need and situation and idiosyncratic investments facilitates selling.
Relationship time horizon	*None:* Buyer may have had no previous interactions with or knowledge of the firm.	*Short:* Generally short because the buyer can often switch firms without much effort or cost.	*Medium:* Generally longer than acquaintance relationships because trust in a differentiated position takes a longer time to build and imitate.	*Long:* Generally long because it takes time to build (or replace) interconnected activities and to develop a detailed knowledge of a customer's needs and the unique resources of a supplier to commit resources to the relationship.
Sustainability of competitive advantage	*Low:* Generally low, as firm must continually find ways to be attractive, in terms of the value offered, to induce trial.	*Low:* Generally low, but competitors can vary in how they build unique value into selling and serving even if the product is a form of industry standard.	*Medium:* Generally medium, but depends on ability of competitors to understand heterogeneity of customer needs and situations and the ability to transform this knowledge into meaningful, differentiated products.	*High:* Generally high, but depends on how unique and effective the interconnected activities between customer and supplier are organized.
Primary relationship marketing goal	*Acquire* the customer's business.	*Satisfy* the customer's needs and wants.	*Retain* the customer's business.	*Enhance* the relationship with the customer.

Source: Adapted from M. D. Johnson and F. Seines, "Customer Portfolio Management: Toward a Dynamic Theory of Exchange Relationships," *Journal of Marketing* 68 (April 2004), p. 5. Reprinted by permission of the American Marketing Association.

Technology Spotlight   Customer Information Systems Help Enhance the Customer Relationship

The potential of today's customer information systems far exceeds any traditional marketing information system that has gone before. The amount of information about individual customers that can now be captured allows the organization to customize to the individual level what previously would have been undifferentiated services.

HILTON'S OnQ SYSTEM

Hilton Hotels has an integrated technology platform called "OnQ" that provides the basis for its customer relationship management (CRM) system. OnQ centralizes all of the personal profile information that guests provide to Hilton—via hotel or central reservations, their websites, or membership in the HHonors loyalty program—to create a "Guest Profile Manager." Profiles are created for any guest who is an HHonors member or simply visits a Hilton hotel at least four times within a year. Such a system requires an extraordinary investment in information technology to capture information from Hilton's over 3,500 hotels and nearly 600,000 rooms in six continents and more than 80 countries worldwide. The information collected via OnQ is combined with the customer's stay history and any prior complaints made during previous visits. The entire packet of information enables many of Hilton's 130,000 employees to recognize and reward guests with appropriate welcome messages, room upgrades, or information related to previous visits.

USING THE INFORMATION TO DEVELOP RELATIONSHIPS WITH CUSTOMERS

OnQ provides a mechanism for Hilton Hotels to learn—and remember—customer interests and preferences. Tim Harvey, chief information officer for Hilton, describes it this way:

> It's like when your grandmother comes to your house. You know exactly who she is. You know

exactly what she eats for breakfast. You know what kind of pillow she likes. You know whether she can climb the stairs or not so you know what room to put her in. We have the same passion about our hotel business. We want to know who our customers are and we want to take care of those customers every time we have an opportunity to touch them. So the value of OnQ is primarily having that information with that in-depth knowledge about customers.

Collecting information on all of its customers is not an easy task, particularly given the many different hotels in the Hilton family of brands: the company owns, manages, or franchises a hotel portfolio of some of the best known and highly regarded brands, including Hilton, Conrad Hotels & Resorts, Doubletree, Embassy Suites, Hampton Inn, Hilton Garden Inn, Homewood Suites, and the Waldorf-Astoria. OnQ provides a method for capturing and managing information on Hilton customers across a diverse set of properties, differing brands, and various countries with local requirements.

PROVIDING GUESTS WITH OPTIONS

Some customers prefer to initiate contact with Hilton via the Internet; about 20 percent of all rooms, representing about $2.3 billion, are sold in this manner. However, in spite of the lack of face-to-face contact, OnQ has allowed Hilton to create a personal relationship with these customers. Once a customer identifies him- or herself when using the Internet, Hilton knows if the customer is an HHonors member, the customer's preferred room type, and the customer's preferred in-room amenities. OnQ also provides the capability for customers to check into their hotel via the Internet prior to arriving—just as customers do for an airline seat. Customers can view the hotel floor plan, see all of the rooms available, and then pick the room they want—perhaps on the

A primary goal for firms at the friendship stage of the relationship is customer *retention*. A firm's potential to develop sustainable competitive advantage through friends should be higher than for acquaintances because the offering is more unique (and more difficult for competition to imitate) and the customer comes to trust that uniqueness.[11]

west side of the building for those who like to sleep in late or one close to the pool.

Hilton also allows organizers of relatively small groups to book their entire group event or meeting from start to finish on the Internet—and receive

The Chicago Hilton.

immediate confirmation of their reservation. Potential customers who represent groups requiring 25 rooms or less—such as family reunions, wedding parties, or those attending a sporting event—can see about room availability across all Hilton brands and locations. Through OnQ amateur event planners, small-business owners, or family representatives can find a hotel that best fits their needs based on price, room types, and proximity to local attractions. Organizers can reserve guest rooms, meeting spaces, food and beverages, audio/visual equipment, and more up to one year in advance without a request for proposal or a waiting period. Additionally, OnQ enables planners to manage their room block, including instant, online access 24/7 to their group reservation details and guest room information. Planners can instantly see who has booked guest rooms for their event or can reserve rooms on behalf of guests, thus keeping track of the total head count at all times.

THE RESULTS

How well has OnQ worked in managing customer relationships? Three of the Hilton brands (Hilton Garden Inn, Embassy Suites, and Homewood Suites) regularly receive the top awards for customer satisfaction in their respective hotel segments by independent research conducted by J. D. Power and Associates. Both Hilton Garden Inn and Embassy Suites have received the number 1 ranking at least six times since 2001, and another brand (Hampton Inn) is generally within the top three. Additionally, Harvey estimated that Hilton's "share of wallet" from its best customers increased from 40 percent to 60 percent once OnQ was fully operational. Hilton's relationship with its many customers has certainly been enhanced through OnQ.

Sources: Tim Harvey, Interview on ZDNet.com, http://video.zdnet.com/CIOSessions/?p=143, accessed July 16, 2010; www.hilton.com, accessed July 16, 2010.

Customers as Partners

As a customer continues to interact with a firm, the level of trust often deepens and the customer may receive more customized product offerings and interactions. The trust developed in the friendship stage is a necessary but not sufficient condition for a customer–firm *partnership* to develop.[12] That is, the creation of trust leads to (ideally) the creation of commitment—and that is the condition necessary for customers to extend the time perspective of a relationship.[13] The deepening of trust and the establishment of commitment reduce the customer's need to solve problems in the traditional sense of "finding a better alternative." Thus, to move the relationship into a partner relationship, a firm must use customer knowledge and information systems to deliver highly personalized and customized offerings.

At the partnership stage, the firm is concerned with *enhancing* the relationship. Customers are more likely to stay in the relationship if they feel that the company understands their changing needs and is willing to invest in the relationship by constantly improving and evolving its product and service mix. By enhancing these relationships, the firm expects such customers to be less likely to be lured away by competitors and more likely to buy additional products and services from the company over time. These loyal customers not only provide a solid base for the organization, they may represent growth potential. This is certainly true for USAA, our opening example in this chapter, whose officer members' needs for insurance increase over their lifetimes as well as the lifetimes of their children. Other examples abound. A bank checking account customer becomes a better customer when she sets up a savings account, takes out a loan, and/or uses the financial advising services of the bank. And a corporate account becomes a better customer when it chooses to do 75 percent of its business with a particular provider rather than splitting the business equally among three providers. In recent years, in fact, many companies have aspired to be the "exclusive provider" of a particular product or service for their customers. Over time these enhanced relationships can increase market share and profits for the organization. Our Technology Spotlight features Hilton Hotels and how the company is successfully using information technology to enhance relationships with their customers.

FIGURE 6.2
The Goal of Relationship Marketing: Moving Customers Up the Ladder

The Goal of Relationship Marketing

The discussion of the evolution of customer relationships demonstrates how a firm's relationship with its customers might be enhanced as customers move further along this relationship continuum. As the relationship value of a customer increases, the provider is more likely to pursue a closer relationship. Thus, the primary goal of relationship marketing is *to build and maintain a base of committed customers who are profitable for the organization.* Figure 6.2 graphically illustrates the goals of relationship marketing. The overriding goal is to move customers up the ladder (i.e., along the relationship continuum) from the point at which they are strangers that need to be attracted through to the point at which they are highly valued, long-term customers whose relationship with the firm has been enhanced. From a customer's problem-solving perspective, the formation of satisfaction, trust, and commitment corresponds to the customer's willingness to more fully engage in an exchange relationship as an acquaintance, friend, and partner, respectively. From a firm's resource-allocation perspective, the delivery of differential, and perhaps customized, value corresponds to the extent of its ability and/or desire to create an acquaintance, friend, or partner relationship with the customer. As customers make the transition from satisfaction-based acquaintanceships to trust-based friendships to commitment-based partnerships, increases are required in both the value received and the level of cooperation.

Benefits for Customers and Firms

Both parties in the customer–firm relationship can benefit from customer retention. That is, it is not only in the best interest of the organization to build and maintain a loyal customer base, but customers themselves also benefit from long-term associations.

Benefits for Customers

Assuming they have a choice, customers will remain loyal to a firm when they receive greater value relative to what they expect from competing firms. *Value* represents a trade-off for the consumer between the "give" and the "get" components. Consumers are more likely to stay in a relationship when the gets (quality, satisfaction, specific benefits) exceed the gives (monetary and nonmonetary costs). When firms can consistently deliver value from the customer's point of view, clearly the customer benefits and has an incentive to stay in the relationship.

Beyond the specific inherent benefits of receiving service value, customers also benefit in other ways from long-term associations with firms. Sometimes these relationship benefits keep customers loyal to a firm more than the attributes of the core service. Research has uncovered specific types of relational benefits that customers experience in long-term service relationships including confidence benefits, social benefits, and special treatment benefits.[14]

Confidence Benefits Confidence benefits comprise feelings of trust or confidence in the provider along with a sense of reduced anxiety and comfort in knowing what to expect. One customer described his confidence that resulted from having developed a relationship with a service provider:

> There is a comfort [in having] a certain level of experience [with the service provider]. In other words, I know that I am going to be treated right because they know me . . . I don't have any anxiety that I will have a less-than-acceptable experience . . . You know it's going to be good in advance, or if something is wrong it will be taken care of.[15]

Across all the services studied in the research cited in the previous section, confidence benefits were the most important to customers.

Human nature is such that most consumers would prefer not to change service providers, particularly when there is a considerable investment in the relationship. The costs of switching are frequently high in terms of dollar costs of transferring business and the associated psychological and time-related costs. Most consumers (whether individuals or businesses) have many competing demands for their time and money and are continually searching for ways to balance and simplify decision making to improve the quality of their lives. When they develop confidence in—and can maintain a relationship with—a service provider, they free up time for other concerns and priorities.

Social Benefits Over time, customers develop a sense of familiarity and even a social relationship with their service providers. These ties make it less likely that they will switch, even if they learn about a competitor that might have better quality or a lower price. This customer's description of her hair stylist in a quote from the research previously cited illustrates the concept of social benefits:

> I like him. . . . He's really funny and always has lots of good jokes. He's kind of like a friend now. . . . It's more fun to deal with somebody that you're used to. You enjoy doing business with them.

In some long-term customer–firm relationships, a service provider may actually become part of the consumer's social support system.[16] Hairdressers, as in the example just cited, often serve as personal confidants. Less common examples include proprietors of local retail stores who become central figures in neighborhood networks, the health club or restaurant manager who knows her customers personally, the private school principal who knows an entire family and its special needs, and the river guide who befriends patrons on a long rafting trip.[17]

These types of personal relationships can develop for business-to-business customers as well as for end-consumers of services. The social support benefits resulting from these relationships are important to the consumer's quality of life (personal and/or work life) above and beyond the technical benefits of the service provided. Many times the close personal and professional relationships that develop between service providers and clients are the basis for the customer's loyalty. The flip side of this customer benefit is the risk to the firm of losing customers when a valued employee leaves the firm and takes customers with him or her.[18]

Special Treatment Benefits Special treatment includes getting the benefit of the doubt, being given a special deal or price, and getting preferential treatment as exemplified by the following quotes from the research:

> I think you get special treatment [when you have established a relationship]. My pediatrician allowed me to use the back door to the office so my daughter could avoid contact with other sick children. Other times I have been in a hurry and they take me right back.

> You should get the benefit of the doubt in many situations. For example, I always pay my VISA bill on time, before a service charge is assessed. One time my payment didn't quite arrive on time. When I called them, by looking at my past history, they realized that I always make an early payment. Therefore, they waived the service charge.

Interestingly, in some service industries special treatment benefits, while important, are found to be less important than the other types of benefits received.[19] Although special treatment benefits can clearly be critical for customer loyalty in some industries (think of frequent flyer benefits in the airline industry), they seem to be less important to customers in other industries (such as medical services or legal services).

Benefits for Firms

The benefits to organizations of maintaining and developing a loyal customer base are numerous. In addition to the economic benefits that a firm receives from cultivating close relationships with its customers, a variety of customer behavior benefits and human resource management benefits are also often received.

Economic Benefits One of the most commonly cited economic benefits of customer retention is *increased purchases* over time, as illustrated in Figure 6.3. The figure summarizes results of studies showing that across industries customers generally spent more each year with a particular relationship partner than they did in the preceding period.[20] As customers get to know a firm and are satisfied with the quality of its services relative to that of its competitors, they tend to give more of their business to the firm. Research also suggests that highly satisfied customers are *willing to pay more* for a provider's services.[21]

Another economic benefit for the firm is *lower costs*. Some estimates suggest that repeat purchases by established customers require as much as 90 percent less marketing expenditure.[22] Many start-up costs are associated with attracting new customers, including advertising and other promotion costs, the operating costs of setting up new accounts, and time costs of getting to know the customers. Sometimes these initial costs outweigh the revenue expected from the new customers in the short term, so it is to the firm's advantage to cultivate long-term relationships. In Chapter 16 we provide more specifics on the financial impact of customer retention.

FIGURE 6.3
Profit Generated by a Customer over Time

Source: Adapted and reprinted by permission of *Harvard Business Review.* An exhibit from "Zero Defection: Quality Comes to Services," by F. F. Reichheld and W. E. Sasser, Jr., *Harvard Business Review* 68 (September–October 1990). Copyright © 1990 by the Harvard Business School Publishing Corporation; all rights reserved.

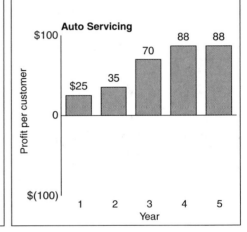

Customer Behavior Benefits The contribution that loyal customers make to a service business can go well beyond their direct financial impact on the firm.[23] Maybe the most easily recognized customer behavior benefit that a firm receives from long-term customers is the free advertising provided through *word-of-mouth communication.* When a product is complex and difficult to evaluate and when risk is involved in the decision to buy it—as is the case with many services—consumers often look to others for advice on which providers to consider. Satisfied, loyal customers are likely to provide a firm with strong word-of-mouth endorsements. This form of advertising can be more effective than any paid advertising that the firm might use, and it has the added benefit of reducing the costs of attracting new customers.

In addition to word-of-mouth communication, a second customer behavior benefit can be *social support* provided to other customers in the form of friendships or encouragement.[24] At a physical therapy clinic, for example, a patient who is recovering from knee surgery is likely to think more highly of the clinic when fellow patients provide encouragement and emotional

Satisfied, loyal customers are likely to provide a service provider with strong word-of-mouth endorsements.

support to the patient during the rehabilitation process. Loyal customers may also serve as *mentors* and, because of their experience with the provider, help other customers understand the explicitly or implicitly stated rules of conduct.[25]

Human Resource Management Benefits Loyal customers may also provide a firm with human resource management benefits. First, loyal customers may, because of their experience with and knowledge of the provider, be able to contribute to the coproduction of the service by *assisting in service delivery*; often the more experienced customers can make the service employees' job easier. For example, a regular patient of a medical service provider is likely to know how the system works; she would know to bring her medication with her on a visit, to plan on paying by debit card (having previously learned that the office cannot process personal checks), and to schedule an annual mammogram without waiting for her doctor to prompt her. A second benefit is that customers who are loyal and thus familiar with a firm's processes and procedures are likely to have more realistic expectations of what the firm can achieve for them.[26] A third benefit of customer retention is *employee retention.* It is easier for a firm to retain employees when it has a stable base of satisfied customers. People like to work for companies whose customers are happy and loyal. Their jobs are more satisfying, and they are able to spend more of their time fostering relationships than scrambling for new customers. In turn, customers are more satisfied and become even better customers—a positive upward spiral. Because employees stay with the firm longer, service quality improves and costs of turnover are reduced, adding further to profits.

RELATIONSHIP VALUE OF CUSTOMERS

Relationship value of a customer is a concept or calculation that looks at customers from the point of view of their lifetime revenue and/or profitability contributions to a company. This type of calculation is needed when companies start thinking of building long-term relationships with their customers. Just what is the potential financial value of those long-term relationships? Or, to put it another way, what are the financial implications of *losing* a customer? In the next paragraphs we consider some of the factors that influence a customer's relationship value and show some ways it can be estimated. In Chapter 16 we provide more detail on lifetime value financial calculations.

The lifetime or relationship value of a customer is influenced by the length of an average "lifetime," the average revenues generated per relevant time period over the lifetime, sales of additional products and services over time, referrals generated by the customer over time, and costs associated with serving the customer. *Lifetime value* sometimes refers to lifetime revenue stream only; when costs are considered, the more appropriate term to use is *lifetime profitability.* Exhibit 6.2 provides an example of some factors that could be considered when calculating the potential relationship value of a Quicken (personal finance) software customer.

If companies knew how much it really costs to lose a customer, they would be able to accurately evaluate investments designed to retain customers. One way of documenting the dollar value of loyal customers is to estimate the increased value or profits that accrue for each additional customer who remains loyal to the company rather than defecting to the competition. Bain & Co. has found that when the retention or loyalty rate rises by 5 percentage points the total firm profits can increase from 35 percent to 95 percent.[27]

With sophisticated accounting systems to document actual costs and revenue streams over time, a firm can be quite precise in documenting the dollar value and

Exhibit 6.2 Calculating the Relationship Value of a Quicken Customer

Intuit Corporation's Quicken Software for personal finance can be purchased for about $60.* However, the relationship value of a Quicken customer to Intuit is potentially much more. How can this be?

First, consider the additional products available to Quicken customers. Once a customer gets hooked on using the software, there are several other Quicken products she might find appealing. For example, Quicken provides a bill-paying service for $10 per month. Quicken customers can print their own checks and send them in matching envelopes for about $70 (for a box of 250). For about $60, Quicken customers can purchase Turbo Tax, a software product that can automatically use previously created Quicken data to prepare federal and state income tax returns. Quicken also offers a Home Inventory Manager for $30 and software for creating wills for $60. If a customer uses all these services, the revenue generated in just one year would be $400. (Intuit provides several other services, such as small-business accounting software and home mortgages, which might be of interest to Quicken customers. Quicken also offers its customers a credit card; there is no annual fee, but the card has the potential to generate revenues from interest payments on outstanding balances.)

After the first year, a satisfied Quicken customer is likely to continue to purchase annual software updates to acquire the latest product features and tax information. Over the course of five years, the revenue generated from this single customer would be more than $2,000.

Finally, Quicken's satisfied customers are likely to refer new customers to Intuit, thus further enhancing the value of the initial customer relationship. Even one new customer referral per year can increase the relationship value potential of the first customer to several thousand dollars in just a few years!

*Figures in this example are based on 2011 prices as listed on http://www.intuit.com.

costs of retaining customers. These systems attempt to estimate the dollar value of *all* the benefits and costs associated with a loyal customer, not just the long-term revenue stream. The value of word-of-mouth advertising, employee retention, and declining account maintenance costs can also enter into the calculation.[28]

For example, Table 6.1 shows how First Data Corporation estimates the lifetime value of an average business customer at its TeleCheck International subsidiary. TeleCheck is a large check acceptance company that provides a range of financial services for business customers related to check guarantees, verifications, and collection services. By including estimates over a five-year lifetime of increased revenues from its core product (QuickResponse), declining per-unit service costs, increasing revenues from a new product (FastTrack), and profit from referrals, the company estimated that an annual increase in revenue of 20 percent on its base product would result in a 33 percent annual increase in operating profit over a five-year customer life.[29]

CUSTOMER PROFITABILITY SEGMENTS

Companies may want to treat all customers with excellent service, but they generally find that customers differ in their relationship value and that it may be neither practical nor profitable to meet (or to exceed) *all* customers' expectations.[30] FedEx Corporation,

TABLE 6.1 Lifetime Value of an Average Business Customer at Telecheck International

Source: Reprinted with permission of The Free Press, a Division of Simon & Schuster, Inc., adapted from J. L. Heskett, W. E. Sasser, Jr., and L. A. Schlesinger, *The Service Profit Chain: How Leading Companies Link Profit and Growth to Loyalty* (New York: The Free Press, 1997), p. 201. Copyright © 1997 by J. L. Heskett, W. E. Sasser, and L. A. Schlesinger.

	Year 0	Year 1	Year 2	Year 3	Year 4	Year 5
Revenue: [a]						
QuickResponse	—	$33,000	$39,600	$47,520	$57,024	$68,429
FastTrack	—	—	5,500	6,600	7,920	9,504
Costs:						
QuickResponse	$6,600	$24,090	$28,908	$34,690	$41,627	$49,953
FastTrack	—	—	4,152	4,983	5,980	7,175
Lifetime customer value:						
QuickResponse profit	($6,600)	$ 8,910	$10,692	$12,830	$15,397	$18,476
FastTrack profit	—	—	1,348	1,617	1,940	2,329
Reduced overhead allocation [b]	—	—	1,155	1,486	1,663	1,995
Profit from referrals [c]	—	—	1,100	1,650	3,300	6,600
Total profit	($6,600)	$ 8,910	$14,295	$17,583	$22,300	$29,400

Note: Product names and data have been disguised. As a result, profit on these products is overstated.
[a]Assuming revenue increases on both products of 20 percent per year.
[b]Declining at the rate of 15 percent per year in relation to revenue, to reflect lower costs of customer relationship associated with both customer and supplier learning curve effects.
[c]Estimated, based on assumptions concerning (1) the importance of referrals to new customers from old customers, (2) the frequency with which satisfied customers refer new customers, (3) the size of customers referred, and (4) the lifetime value calculations for new customers.

for example, once categorized its customers internally as "the good, the bad, and the ugly"—based on their profitability. Rather than treating all its customers the same, the company paid particular attention to enhancing their relationships with the good, moving the bad to the good, and discouraging the ugly.[31] Other companies also try to identify segments—or, more appropriately, tiers of customers—that differ in current and/or future profitability to a firm.[32] This approach goes beyond usage or volume segmentation because it tracks costs and revenues for segments of customers, thereby capturing their financial worth to companies. After identifying profitability bands, the firm offers services and service levels in line with the identified segments. Building a high-loyalty customer base of the right customers increases profits. Research suggests that it is not uncommon for a service firm to see profits increase by more than 60 percent when the retention of the right customers increases by 5 percent.[33]

Profitability Tiers—the Customer Pyramid

Although some people may view the FedEx grouping of customers into "the good, the bad, and the ugly" as negative, descriptive labels of the tiers can be very useful internally. Labels are especially valuable if they help the company keep track of which customers are profitable. Virtually all firms are aware at some level that their customers differ in profitability and that a minority of their customers account for the highest proportion of sales or profit.

One useful approach for thinking of how customers differ in terms of profitability is the four-tier system, shown in Figure 6.4, which includes the following:

1. The *platinum tier* describes the company's most profitable customers, typically those who are heavy users of the product, are not overly price sensitive, are willing to invest in and try new offerings, and are committed customers of the firm.

FIGURE 6.4
The Customer
Pyramid

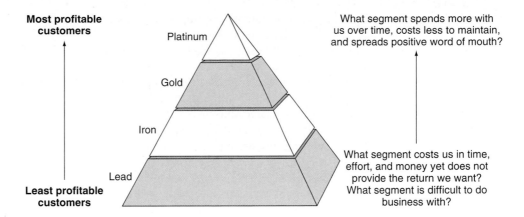

Most profitable customers

Least profitable customers

Platinum

Gold

Iron

Lead

What segment spends more with us over time, costs less to maintain, and spreads positive word of mouth?

What segment costs us in time, effort, and money yet does not provide the return we want? What segment is difficult to do business with?

2. The *gold tier* differs from the platinum tier in that profitability levels are not as high, perhaps because these customers are not as loyal or they want price discounts that limit margins. They may be heavy users who minimize risk by working with multiple providers rather than just the focal company.

3. The *iron tier* contains essential customers who provide the volume needed to utilize the firm's capacity, but their spending levels, loyalty, and profitability are not substantial enough for special treatment.

4. The *lead tier* consists of customers who are costing the company money. They demand more attention than they are due given their spending and profitability and are sometimes problem customers—complaining about the firm to others and tying up the firm's resources.

Note that this classification is superficially reminiscent of, but very different from, traditional usage segmentation performed by airlines such as American Airlines. Two differences are obvious. First, in the customer pyramid, profitability rather than usage defines all levels. Second, the lower levels actually articulate classes of customers who require a different sort of attention. The firm must work either to change the customers' behavior—to make them more profitable through increases in revenue—or to change the firm's cost structure to make them more profitable through decreases in costs.

Once a system has been established for categorizing customers, the multiple levels can be identified, motivated, served, and expected to deliver differential levels of profit. Companies improve their opportunities for profit when they increase shares of purchases by customers who either have the greatest need for the services or show the greatest loyalty to a single provider. By strengthening relationships with the loyal customers, increasing sales with existing customers, and increasing the profitability on each sale opportunity, companies thereby increase the potential of each customer.

The Customer's View of Profitability Tiers

Whereas profitability tiers make sense from the company's point of view, customers are not always understanding, nor do they appreciate being categorized into a less desirable segment.[34] For example, at some companies (e.g., eTrade), the top clients have their own individual account representative, whom they can contact personally. The next tier of clients may be handled by representatives who each have a limited number (e.g., 100) of clients. Meanwhile, most clients are served by a website, an 800-number, or an automated voice response system. Customers are often aware of this unequal treatment, and many resist and resent it. It makes perfect sense from a business perspective, but customers are often disappointed in the level of service they receive and give firms poor marks for quality as a result. Therefore, it is important that firms communicate with customers so they understand the level of service they can expect and what they would need to do or pay to receive faster or more personalized service.

The ability to segment customers narrowly based on profitability implications also raises questions of privacy for customers. To know who is profitable and who is not, companies must collect large amounts of individualized behavioral and personal data on consumers. Many consumers today resent what they perceive as an intrusion into their lives in this way, especially when it results in differential treatment that they perceive is unfair.

Making Business Decisions Using Profitability Tiers

Prudent business managers are well aware that past customer purchase behavior, although useful in making predictions, can be misleading.[35] What a customer spends today, or has spent in the past, may not necessarily be reflective of what he or she will do (or be worth) in the future. Banks serving college students know this well—a typical college student generally has minimal financial service needs (i.e., a checking account and a debit card) and tends to not have a high level of deposits. However, within a few years that student may embark on a professional career, start a family, and/or purchase a house, and thus require several financial services and become a potentially very profitable customer to the bank. Generally speaking, a firm would like to keep its consistent big spenders and lose the erratic small spenders. But all too often a firm also has two other groups they must consider: erratic big spenders and consistent small spenders. So, in some situations where consistent cash flow is a concern, it may be helpful to a firm to have a portfolio of customers that includes steady customers, even if they have a history of being less profitable.[36]

Some service providers have actually been quite successful in targeting customers who were previously considered to be unworthy of another firm's marketing efforts.[37] Paychex, a payroll processing company, became very successful in serving small businesses that the major companies in this industry did not think were large enough to serve profitably. Similarly, Progressive Insurance became very successful in selling automobile insurance to undesirable customers—young drivers and those with poor driving records—that most of the competition did not feel had a sufficient relationship value. As these examples suggest, firms should think carefully and strategically when applying customer value calculations.

RELATIONSHIP DEVELOPMENT STRATEGIES

To this point in the chapter, we have focused on the rationale for relationship marketing, the benefits (to both firms and customers) of the development of strong exchange relationships, and an understanding of the relationship value of a customer. In this section we examine a variety of factors that influence the development of strong customer relationships, including the customer's overall evaluation of a firm's offering, bonds created with customers by the firm, and barriers that the customer faces in leaving a relationship. These factors, illustrated in Figure 6.5, provide the rationale for specific strategies that firms often use to keep their current customers.

Core Service Provision

Retention strategies will have little long-term success unless the firm has a solid base of service quality and customer satisfaction on which to build. All the retention strategies that we describe in this section are built on the assumption of competitive quality

FIGURE 6.5
Relationship
Development Model

Source: Adapted from
D. D. Gremler and
S. W. Brown, "Service
Loyalty: Antecedents,
Components, and Outcomes,"
in *1998 AMA Winter
Educators' Conference:
Marketing Theory and
Applications,* Vol. 9, D.
Grewal and C. Pechmann,
eds. Chicago, IL: American
Marketing Association,
pp. 165–166.

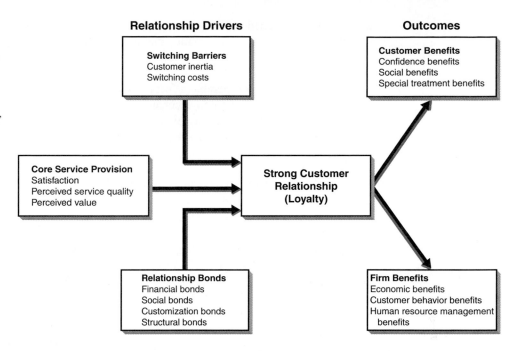

and value being offered. Clearly, a firm needs to begin the relationship development process by providing a good core service delivery that, at a minimum, meets customer expectations and provides customers with perceived value;[38] it does no good to design relationship strategies for inferior services. Two earlier examples, Intuit and USAA, provide convincing support for the argument that excellence in the core service or product offered is essential to a successful relationship strategy. Both of these companies have benefited tremendously from their loyal customer base; both offer excellent quality; both use relationship strategies to enhance their success.

Switching Barriers

When considering a switch in service providers, a customer may face a number of barriers that make it difficult to leave one service provider and begin a relationship with another. Literature suggests that these *switching barriers* influence consumers' decisions to exit from relationships with firms and, therefore, help to facilitate customer retention.[39]

Customer Inertia

One reason that customers commit to developing relationships with firms is that a certain amount of effort may be required to change firms. Sometimes consumers simplistically state that "it's just not worth it" to switch providers. *Inertia* may even explain why some dissatisfied customers stay with a provider. In discussing why people remain in relationships (in general) that they no longer find satisfying, scholars suggest that people may stay because breaking the relationship would require them to restructure their life—to develop new habits of living, to refashion old friendships, and to find new ones.[40] All would require effort and a change in behavior—and people do not like to change their behavior.

To retain customers, firms might consider increasing the *perceived effort* required on the part of the customer to switch service providers.[41] If a customer believes that a great deal of effort is needed to change companies, the customer is more likely to stay put. For example, automobile repair facilities might keep a complete and detailed maintenance history of a customer's vehicle. These records remove from the customer the burden of having to remember all the services performed on the vehicle and would force the customer to expend considerable effort in providing a complete maintenance history if the vehicle were taken to a new mechanic. Conversely, if a firm is looking to attract a competitor's customers, it might automate the process for switching providers as much as possible to overcome customer inertia.

Switching Costs

In many instances, customers develop loyalty to an organization in part because of costs involved in changing to and purchasing from a different firm. These costs, both real and perceived, monetary and nonmonetary, are termed *switching costs.* Switching costs include investments of time, money, or effort—such as setup costs, learning costs, and contractual costs—that make it challenging for the customer to move to another provider.[42] To illustrate, a patient may incur *setup costs* such as paying for a complete physical when changing doctors or for new X-rays when switching dentists. *Learning costs* are those costs associated with learning the idiosyncrasies of how to use a product or service; in many situations, a customer who wishes to switch firms may need to accumulate new user skills or customer know-how. *Contractual costs* arise when the customer is required to pay a penalty to switch providers (e.g., prepayment charges for customer-initiated switching of mortgage companies or mobile telephone services), making it financially difficult, if not impossible, for the customer to initiate an early termination of the relationship.

To retain customers, firms might consider increasing their switching costs to make it difficult for customers to exit the relationship (or at least create the perception of difficulty). Indeed, many firms explicitly specify such costs in the contracts that they require their customers to sign (e.g., mobile telephone services, health clubs). To attract new customers, a service provider might consider implementing strategies designed to *lower* the switching costs of customers not currently using the provider. To reduce the setup costs involved when switching, providers could complete the paperwork required from the customer. Some banks, for example, employ "switch kits" that automatically move a customer's online billing information from a competitor's bank; such kits remove the switching costs surrounding one of the biggest barriers preventing customers from changing banks—transferring online bill payments.[43]

Relationship Bonds

Switching barriers tend to serve as constraints that keep customers in relationships with firms because they "have to."[44] However, firms can engage in activities that encourage customers to remain in the relationship because they "want to"—thus creating relationship bonds. In this section we present a framework which suggests that relationship marketing can occur at different levels and that each successive level of strategy results in ties that bind the customer a little closer to the firm—and thus increase the potential for sustained competitive advantage.[45] Building on the levels of the retention strategy idea, Figure 6.6 illustrates four types of retention strategies. Recall, however, that the most successful retention strategies are built on foundations of core service excellence.

Level 1—Financial Bonds

At level 1, the customer is tied to the firm primarily through financial incentives— lower prices for greater volume purchases or lower prices for customers who have been with the firm a long time. For example, think about the airline industry and

FIGURE 6.6
Levels of
Relationship
Strategies

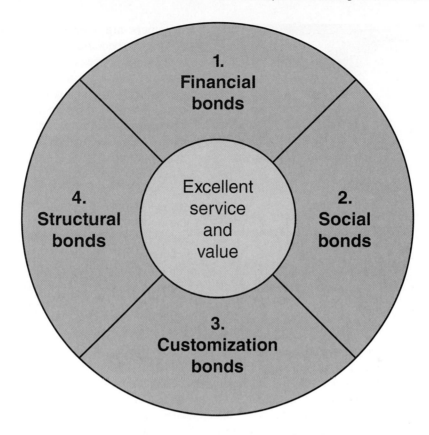

related travel service industries like hotels and car rental companies. Frequent-flyer programs provide financial incentives and rewards for travelers who bring more of their business to a particular airline. Hotels and car rental companies do the same. One reason these financial incentive programs flourish is that they are not difficult to initiate and frequently result in at least short-term profit gains. Unfortunately, financial incentives do not generally provide long-term advantages to a firm because, unless combined with another relationship strategy, they do not differentiate the firm in the long run because they are generally not difficult for competitors to imitate.

Other types of retention strategies that depend primarily on financial rewards are focused on bundling and cross-selling of services. Frequent-flyer programs provide a common example. Many airlines link their reward programs with hotel chains, auto rental, and in some cases credit card usage. By linking airline mileage points earned to usage of other firms' services, customers can enjoy even greater financial benefits in exchange for their loyalty.

Although widely and increasingly used as retention tactics, loyalty programs based on financial rewards merit caution.[46] As mentioned earlier, these programs are often easily imitated. Thus, any increased usage or loyalty from customers may be short-lived. And, these strategies are not likely to be successful unless they are structured to truly lead to repeat or increased usage rather than serving as means to attract new customers and potentially causing endless switching among competitors.

Level 2—Social Bonds

Level 2 strategies bind customers to the firm through more than financial incentives. Although price is still assumed to be important, level 2 strategies seek to build long-term relationships through social and interpersonal as well as financial bonds.[47]

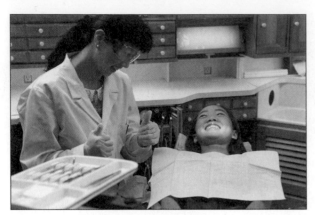

Level 2 strategies create positive social bonds between the client and service provider employees.

Customers are viewed as "clients," not nameless faces, and become individuals whose needs and wants the firm seeks to understand.

Social, interpersonal bonds are common among professional service providers (lawyers, accountants, teachers) and their clients as well as among personal care providers (hairdressers, counselors, health care providers) and their clients.[48] A dentist who takes a few minutes to review her patient's file before going into the exam room is able to jog her memory on personal facts about the patient (occupation, family details, interests, dental health history). By bringing these personal details into the conversation, the dentist reveals her genuine interest in the patient as an individual and builds social bonds.

Interpersonal bonds are also common in business-to-business relationships in which customers develop relationships with salespeople and/or relationship managers working with their firms.[49] Recognizing the value of continuous relationships in building loyalty, Caterpillar Corporation credits its success to its extensive, stable distribution organization worldwide. Caterpillar is the world's largest manufacturer of mining, construction, and agricultural heavy equipment. Although its engineering and product quality are superior, the company attributes much of its success to its strong dealer network and product support services offered throughout the world. Knowledge of the local market and the close relationships with customers that Caterpillar's dealers provide is invaluable. Caterpillar's dealers tend to be prominent business leaders in their service territories who are deeply involved in community activities; the social bonds formed from these long-term relationships with customers are an important ingredient in the company's success.

Sometimes relationships are formed with the organization because of the social bonds that develop *among customers* rather than between customers and the provider of the service.[50] Such bonds are often formed in health clubs, country clubs, educational settings, and other service environments where customers interact with each other. Over time the social relationships they have with other customers are important factors that keep them from switching to another organization. One company that has built a significant strategy around customer-to-customer bonds is Harley Davidson, with its local Harley Owners Groups, or HOGs. HOGs are involved in local rallies, tours, and parties as well as in national HOG events organized by the company. Through the HOGs, Harley customers come to know each other and develop a sense of community around their common interest—motorcycle riding—as illustrated in the photo on page 165.

Social bonds alone may not tie the customer permanently to the firm, but they are much more difficult for competitors to imitate than are price incentives.[51] In the absence of strong reasons to shift to another provider, interpersonal bonds can encourage customers to stay in a relationship.[52] In combination with financial incentives, social bonding strategies may be very effective.

Level 3—Customization Bonds

Level 3 strategies involve more than social ties and financial incentives, although there are common elements of level 1 and 2 strategies encompassed within a customization strategy and vice versa. A customization approach suggests customer loyalty can be

Harley Davidson riders develop customer-to-customer bonds through Harley Owners Group (HOG) activities.

encouraged through intimate knowledge of individual customers—often referred to as *customer intimacy*—and through the development of one-to-one solutions that fit the individual customer's needs.

To illustrate customization bonds, consider Pandora—an Internet-based music discovery service that helps its customers find and enjoy music that they like. Based on a huge database that has categorized songs of more than 10,000 different artists based on unique attributes, it customizes its service offering to play music for customers that has the same characteristics of songs or artists they like. A customer can create up to 100 unique "stations" by identifying favorite songs or artists, and then Pandora's expert system analyzes what they like and provides suggestions based on this analysis. To do this Pandora analyzes each song using up to 400 distinct musical characteristics, or "genes," by a trained music analyst. Taken together these genes capture the unique and musical identity of a song—everything from melody, harmony, and rhythm to instrumentation, orchestration, arrangement, lyrics, singing, and vocal harmony—and use this information to customize music to each customer's unique tastes and interests. The earlier Technology Spotlight illustrates how Hilton Hotels uses technology to customize services to a large number of individual customers. Our Global Feature illustrates how Alliance Boots in the United Kingdom has used technology to understand its customers and build one of the world's largest smart card loyalty programs.

Level 4—Structural Bonds

Level 4 strategies are the most difficult to imitate; they involve structural as well as financial, social, and customization bonds between the customer and the firm. Structural bonds are created by providing services to the client that are designed right into the service delivery system. Often, structural bonds are created by providing customized services to the client that are technology based and make the customer more productive.

An example of structural bonds can be seen in a business-to-business health care context with Cardinal Health. By working closely with its hospital customers, Cardinal Health has established ways to improve hospital supply ordering, delivery, and

Cardinal Health's ValueLink creates structural bonds with its hospital customers.

billing that have greatly enhanced its value as a supplier. Many of Cardinal Health's hospital customers use their ValueLink® service, a "just-in-time" distribution program that eliminates their need to maintain and manage large amounts of inventory. Using sophisticated technology and tracking systems to monitor inventory, ValueLink allows Cardinal Health to deliver ready-to-use quantities of supplies as needed—often several times a day—directly to the floors and departments where they are being used. By linking the hospital through its ValueLink service into a database ordering system and by providing enhanced value in the actual delivery, Cardinal Health has structurally tied itself to its more than 200 acute care hospitals in the United States. In addition to the enhanced service that ValueLink provides, Cardinal

Alliance Boots is a trusted brand in Europe.

Alliance Boots, affectionately referred to by its customers simply as "Boots," is one of the best-known and trusted brands in Europe and is considered to be the leading health and beauty retailer in the United Kingdom, Ireland, Norway, The Netherlands, Italy, and Russia. The company, founded in 1887, offers its products through more than 3,200 retail stores.

A foundation for the company's success in recent years is its increased focus on the customer and a desire to develop customer loyalty through a number of retention and relationship strategies. At the heart of the company's loyalty strategy is its Advantage Card, started in 1997. After Boots the Chemists merged with Alliance in 2006, the Advantage Card became one of the world's largest smart card loyalty programs and now has nearly 17 million members. Over 70 percent of Boots's current sales are now linked to the card. The card offers a number of benefits to customers and has helped the company increase sales, but more than that, it has been the foundation for building greater loyalty among Boots's best customers.

Using the card for purchases, Boots's customers receive four points for every pound spent. These points can be redeemed for selected products, aimed to treat customers to something special rather than simply to offer discounts off purchases. In fact, the card is *not* about discounts; rather, it is about treating oneself. Customers can use their points to treat themselves to a simple lunch or to a full day of pampering at a spa. From a financial perspective, the company has seen increasing average transaction values among higher-spending customers. Boots managers say that they have increased

Health estimates that the system reduces the average customer's inventory by 20 percent and saves its customers an average of $600,000 or more each year.[53]

RELATIONSHIP CHALLENGES

Given the many benefits of long-term customer relationships, it would seem that a company would not want to refuse to serve or terminate a relationship with any customer. Yet situations arise in which either the firm, the customer, or both want to end (or have to end) their relationship. This final section of the chapter discusses situations in which the *firm* might actually consider ending the relationship and how that might occur; in the next chapter we discuss situations in which the *customer* might decide to terminate the relationship and switch providers.

The Customer Is *Not* Always Right

The assumption that *all* customers are good customers is very compatible with the belief that "the customer is always right," an almost sacrosanct tenet of business. Yet any service worker can tell you that this statement is *not* always true, and in some

The Boots Advantage Card helps build customer loyalty.

discounts using interactive kiosks in more than 500 stores. The card can be used for purchases at the Boots online store; many products offered on the site are not available in Boots stores. In addition, the site provides access to an online magazine, answers to questions, a chat room, and other features and services. A credit card version of the Advantage Card was launched in 2001, and Boots joined with the Department of Health to enable card holders to register with the National Health Service Organ Donor program.

From the company's perspective as well, the card is much more than a reward program. Data generated through the card are used to understand customers and to anticipate and identify individual needs in health and beauty care products. The Advantage Card program has allowed Boots to gain customer insight, build a database that allows the company to tailor offerings to individual customers' needs, develop incremental sales by building customer loyalty, and use the customer knowledge to develop and introduce new products and services.

Through the program, Boots has learned that the more broadly customers buy, in more categories over time, the more they visit Boots stores. The result has been customization of product and service offerings and more sales and greater loyalty from its best customers.

Sources: Frederick Newell, *Loyalty.com* (New York: McGraw-Hill, 2000), chap. 24, pp. 239–245; www.boots-uk.com, 2011.

loyalty and spending from people who were already good and profitable customers—a clear win for the company.

A number of initiatives are tied to the Advantage Card, taking it beyond a pure points reward program from the customer's perspective. For example, Boots mails a first-class health and beauty magazine to the top-spending 3 million Advantage Card holders. The magazine is Britain's biggest health and beauty magazine; it is not viewed as a "Boots" magazine but rather as a health and beauty magazine sent by Boots. Cardholders also have access to additional benefits and

cases it may be preferable for the firm to not continue its relationship with a customer. The following discussion presents a view of customer relationships that suggests that all relationships may not be beneficial and that every customer is not right all the time.

The Wrong Segment

A company cannot target its services to all customers; some segments are more appropriate than others. It would not be beneficial to either the company or the customer for a company to establish a relationship with a customer whose needs the company cannot meet. For example, a school offering a lock-step, daytime MBA program would not encourage full-time working people to apply for its program, nor would a law firm specializing in government issues want to establish a relationship with individuals seeking advice on trusts and estates. In both cases, the organization most likely would struggle to deliver services that meet the expectations of these people. Often firms give in to the temptation to make a sale by agreeing to serve a customer who would be better served by someone else.

Similarly, it would not be wise to forge relationships simultaneously with incompatible market segments. In many service businesses (such as restaurants, hotels, tour package operators, entertainment, and education), customers experience the service together and can influence each other's perceptions about value received. Thus, to maximize service to core segments, an organization may choose to turn away marginally profitable segments that would be incompatible. For example, a conference hotel may find that mixing executives in town for a serious educational program with students in town for a regional track meet is not wise. If the executives are deemed to be key long-term customers, the hotel may choose to pass up the sports group in the interest of retaining the executives.

Not Profitable in the Long Term

In the absence of ethical or legal mandates, organizations will prefer *not* to have long-term relationships with unprofitable customers. Some segments of customers will not be profitable for the company even if their needs can be met by the services offered. Some examples of this situation are when there are not enough customers in the segment to make it profitable to serve, when the segment cannot afford to pay the cost of the service, and when the projected revenue flows from the segment would not cover the costs incurred to originate and maintain their business.

At the individual customer level, it may not be profitable for a firm to engage in a relationship with a customer who has bad credit or who is a poor risk for some other reason. Retailers, banks, mortgage companies, and credit card companies routinely refuse to do business with individuals whose credit histories are unreliable. Although the short-term sale may be beneficial, the long-term risk of nonpayment makes the relationship unwise from the company's point of view. Similarly, some car rental companies check into the driving records of customers and reject bad-risk drivers.[54] This practice, while controversial, is logical from the car rental companies' point of view because they can cut back on insurance costs and accident claims (thus reducing rental costs for good drivers) by not doing business with accident-prone drivers.

Beyond the monetary costs associated with serving the wrong customers, there can be substantial time investments in some customers that, if actually computed, would make them unprofitable for the organization. Everyone has had the experience of waiting in a bank, a retail store, or even an educational setting while a particularly demanding customer seems to use more than his share of the service provider's time. The dollar value of the time spent with a specific customer is typically not computed or calculated into the price of the service.

In a business-to-business relationship, the variability in time commitment to customers is even more apparent. Some customers may use considerable resources of a service provider through inordinate numbers of phone calls, excessive requests for information, and other time-consuming activities. In the legal profession, clients are billed for every hour of the firm's time that they use because time is essentially the only resource the firm has. Yet in other service businesses, all clients essentially pay the same regardless of the time demands they place on the organization.

Some customers may be difficult, if not impossible, to serve.

Difficult Customers

Managers have repeated the phrase "the customer is always right" so often that you would expect it to be accepted by every employee in every service organization. So why isn't it? Perhaps because it simply is not true. The customer is not always right. No matter how frequently it is said, repeating that mantra does not make it become reality, and service employees know it.

In many situations, firms have service encounters that fail because of *dysfunctional customers.* Dysfunctional customer behavior consists of the actions by customers who intentionally, or perhaps unintentionally, act in a manner that in some way disrupts otherwise functional service encounters.[55] Such customers have been described as "customers from hell," "problem customers," or "jay customers." One of us was awakened during a hotel stay at 4:00 a.m. by drunk customers who were arguing with each other in a room above; management eventually called the police and asked them to escort the customers off the property. An Enterprise Rent-A-Car customer demanded that she not be charged for any of the two weeks that she had a car because, near the end of the rental period, she found a small stain in the back seat.[56] Such behavior is considered dysfunctional from the perspective of the service provider and perhaps fellow customers.

Dysfunctional customer behavior can affect employees, other customers, and the organization. Research suggests that exposure to dysfunctional customer behavior can have psychological, emotional, behavioral, and physical effects on employees.[57] For example, customer-contact employees who are exposed to rude, threatening, obstructive, aggressive, or disruptive behavior by customers often have their mood, motivation, or morale negatively affected. Such customers are difficult to work with and often create stress for employees.[58] (See photo on page 168 for one example.) Dysfunctional customers can also have an impact on other customers: such behavior can spoil the service experience for other customers, and the dysfunctional customer behavior may become contagious for other customers witnessing it. Finally, dysfunctional customer behavior can create both direct costs and indirect costs for the organization. Direct costs of such behavior can include the expense of restoring damaged property, increased insurance premiums, property loss by theft, costs incurred in compensating customers affected by the dysfunctional behavior of others, and costs incurred through illegitimate claims by dysfunctional customers. Additionally, indirect costs might include increased workloads for staff required to deal with dysfunctional behavior as well as increased costs for attracting and retaining appropriate personnel and, perhaps, for absenteeism payments.

Ending Business Relationships

As suggested in the previous section, firms may identify some customers who are not in their targeted segment, who are not profitable in the long run, or who are difficult to work with or dysfunctional. A company may *not* want to continue in a relationship with every customer. For the effective management of service relationships, managers should not only know how to establish a relationship but also how to end one. However, gracefully exiting a relationship may not be easy. Customers may end up feeling disappointed, confused, or hurt if a firm attempts to terminate the relationship. Our Strategy Insight illustrates how three firms chose to end relationships with their customers.

Relationship Endings

Relationships end in different ways—depending on the type of relationship in place.[59] In some situations, a relationship is established for a certain purpose and/or time period and then dissolves when it has served its purpose or the time frame has elapsed. For example, a house painting service may be engaged with the customer for four days while painting the house exterior, but both parties understand that the end of the relationship is predetermined—the end occurs when the house has been painted and the customer has paid for the service. Sometimes a relationship has a natural ending.[60]

Strategy Insight "The Customer Is Always Right": Rethinking an Old Tenet

The old tenet "the customer is always right" has operated as the basic rule in business for so long that for many firms it has become entrenched as an "absolute truth." The practical reality, however, is that sometimes the customer is wrong. When taken to the extreme, the issue for the firm becomes what to do about it. Service managers understand that there are situations when employees should be fired. In some situations, this strategy may need to be applied to customers, too.

SPRINT/NEXTEL FIRES 1,000 CUSTOMERS

On June 29, 2007, Sprint/Nextel sent a letter to about 1,000 of its 53 million customers telling them, in effect, they had been fired from the company. In doing so Sprint was attempting to rid itself of customers who frequented its customer service lines by informing them that it was canceling their service at the end of the next month. In these letters the company stated: "While we have worked to resolve your issues and questions to the best of our ability, the number of inquiries you have made to us during this time has led us to determine that we are unable to meet your current wireless needs."

The customers were told their service agreements were being terminated, they would not owe anything on their final bill, and the company would waive its standard early termination fees. They also were told to switch to another wireless provider by July 30 if they wanted to keep their phone number.

These 1,000 customers had been calling Sprint's customer service an average of 25 times a month, which is 40 times more frequently than a typical customer. Sprint determined these customers were not generating enough revenue to make up for the high cost of serving them. The company conducted an internal review, lasting more than six months, to determine what types of problems these customers had and what information they were seeking when they contacted the customer service department. The review found that the these customers often were calling about the same problems over and over after Sprint officials felt they had resolved the issue. Additionally, some callers were repeatedly asking for information about other customers' accounts, which customer service representatives are not allowed to divulge. Sprint indicated that the amount of time being spent to resolve the same issues again and again was affecting their ability to serve other customers.

The Results

Initially Sprint's move made headlines in the business press, stimulated negative word of mouth from some portion of these 1,000 customers, and may have cost them some new customers in the short run. But it also improved the customer experience for other customers calling customer service. Indeed, customer service improved to the point that just three years later Sprint was named one of the top 40 Customer Service Champions by J. D. Power and Associates.

ZANE'S CYCLES TELLS CUSTOMER: "GET OUT . . . AND TELL ALL YOUR FRIENDS"

A *Business Horizons* article tells the following story of a bicycle store well known for its dedication to customer service—Zane's Cycles in Branford, Connecticut (for more insights into Zane's Cycles, see our Chapter 4 opener):

> A father was picking up a repaired bicycle for his daughter, who, without telling him, had approved the recommended replacement of both tires (a $40 service). Although the employee patiently and repeatedly explained that the purchase was

A disgruntled Spint/Nextel customer.

approved and offered to further verify it, the customer made accusatory remarks and yelled at her angrily, saying at one point, "Either you think I'm stupid or you're stupid. You're trying to rip me off." At that point, Chris Zane, the store's owner, walked up to the customer and said, "I'm Chris Zane, get out of my store, and tell all your friends!" After the customer wordlessly slapped $40 on the counter and stormed out, the besieged employee looked at Zane and asked "'. . . and tell all your friends'?"

Zane explained to her and other employees who had gravitated to the front of the store that he wanted it to be clear that he valued his employee infinitely more than a rude, belligerent customer. "I also explained that this was the first time I had ever thrown a customer out of the store and that I would not tolerate my employees being mistreated by anyone . . . I believe that my employees need to know that I respect them and expect them to respect our customers. Simply, if I am willing to fire an employee for mistreating a customer (and I have) then I must also be willing to fire a customer for mistreating an employee."

The Results
After returning home and thinking about the service encounter, the fired customer phoned the owner to apologize three hours later. He explained that he had argued with his wife prior to visiting the store and was therefore already in a poor mood. Once the customer returned home and verified the accuracy of the store employee's explanation, he realized he had been unreasonable. The customer asked if he could be allowed to shop in the store again. He also commented that he respected the owner for supporting his employee even if it might mean losing a customer. Mr. Zane thanked him for the call, welcomed him back to the store, and indicated that the apology would be conveyed to the employee.

EVENTS PLANNER TELLS MAJOR CLIENT: "NEVER AGAIN"
Capitol Services Inc. (CSI)—an event planning company in Washington, DC—spent considerable time and money attempting to secure a major automobile company's potentially very lucrative business. In the midst of the first-ever event for the client at a museum in Washington, DC, the person overseeing the event (who was not an employee of the company but working for a third party) became very demanding, degrading, and disrespectful to the CSI staff. Nearly everything the firm did was, in her opinion, not good enough. The entire team, who was in the midst of delivering an event exactly as promised, was being micromanaged. CSI employees felt they were being abused, and for no good reason. David Hainline, company president, approached the client representative and said that CSI would finish the event but would never conduct business again with her—knowing full well this decision might result in the loss of a client with a very high potential relationship value.

The Results
The event was delivered as promised, but the belligerent staff member was not happy. After the event was completed, she demanded that CSI reduce the amount owed for their services—so CSI reduced the amount by $60,000. Months later Hainline had a meeting with the automobile company and began the meeting with an explanation of the situation that had occurred at the Smithsonian. The company understood, and agreed to use CSI to organize future events for them in Washington, DC. And CSI employees felt valued and supported by the management team.

ENDING A CUSTOMER RELATIONSHIP MAY BE THE RIGHT STRATEGIC DECISION
Service providers are not obligated to serve any and all customers, no matter how much revenue they might generate. Although service marketing strategies intended to develop relationships with customers receive much attention—and rightly so—from managers, occasionally selecting a strategy that results in ending a relationship with a customer may be the most prudent approach to take.

Sources: S. Srivastava, "Sprint Drops Clients over Excessive Inquiries," *The Wall Street Journal,* July 7, 2007, p. A3; L. L. Berry and K. Seiders, "Serving Unfair Customers," *Business Horizons* 51 (January/February 2008), pp. 29–37; D. Hainline, President, Capitol Services Inc., Washington, DC, personal interview, August 15, 2007.

Piano lessons for children, for example, often cease as the child gets older and develops interests in other musical areas (such as singing or playing the saxophone); in such situations, the need for the relationship has diminished or become obsolete. In other situations, an event may occur that forces the relationship to end; a provider who relocates to the other side of town may force some customers to select a different company. Or an ending may occur because the customer is not fulfilling his obligations. For example, a bank may choose to end the relationship with a customer who regularly has insufficient funds in her checking account. Whatever the reason for ending the relationship, firms should clearly communicate their reasons for wanting (or needing) to terminate it, so that customers understand what is occurring and why.[61]

Should Firms Fire Their Customers?

A logical conclusion to be drawn from the discussion of the challenges firms face in customer relationships is that perhaps firms should seek to get rid of those customers who are not right for the company. Many companies make these types of decisions based on the belief that troublesome customers are usually less profitable and less loyal and that it may be counterproductive to retain their business. Another reason for "firing" a customer is the negative effect that these customers can have on employee quality of life and morale.

One company took reducing its customer base to the extreme. Nypro, a global company specializing in molded plastics applications and packaging services for such clients as Gillette, Abbott Laboratories, Hewlett-Packard, and other large organizations,[62] reduced its customer base in the 1980s from 800 to approximately 30 clients on the belief that it could better serve those clients and grow more effectively if it focused on fewer relationships. Nypro adopted a customer intimacy strategy and tied itself closely to this much smaller number of clients. Some of these clients have now been with Nypro for more than 40 years and have become quite valuable; in 2009, 5 of these clients generated greater than $50 million in revenue and 21 other clients more than $10 million.

Although it may sound like a good idea, firing customers is not that simple and needs to be done in a way that avoids negative publicity or negative word of mouth. Sometimes raising prices or charging for services that previously had been given away for free can move unprofitable customers out of the company. Helping a client find a new provider who can better meet its needs is another way to gracefully exit a nonproductive relationship. If the customer has become too demanding, the relationship may be salvaged by negotiating expectations or finding more efficient ways to serve the client. If not, both parties may need to find an agreeable way to end the relationship.

Summary

In this chapter we focused on the rationale for, benefits of, and strategies for developing long-term relationships with customers. It should be obvious by now that organizations that focus only on acquiring new customers may well fail to understand their current customers; thus, while a company may be bringing customers in through the front door, equal or greater numbers may be exiting. Estimates of lifetime relationship value accentuate the importance of retaining current customers.

The particular strategy that an organization uses to retain its current customers can and should be customized to fit the industry, the culture, and the customer needs of the organization. However, in general, customer relationships are driven by a variety of factors that influence the development of strong customer relationships, including (1) the customer's overall evaluation of the quality of a firm's core service offering, (2) the switching barriers that the customer faces in leaving a relationship, and (3) the relationship bonds the firm has developed with that customer. By developing strong relationships with customers and by focusing on factors that influence customer relationships, the organization will accurately understand customer expectations over time and consequently will narrow service quality gap 1.

The chapter concluded with a discussion of the challenges that firms face in developing relationships with customers. Although long-term customer relationships are critical and can be very profitable, firms should not attempt to build relationships with just any customer. In other words, "the customer is not always right." Indeed, in some situations it may be best for firms to discontinue relationships with some customers—for the sake of the customer, the firm, or both.

Discussion Questions

1. Discuss how relationship marketing or retention marketing is different from the traditional emphasis in marketing.
2. Describe how a firm's relationships with customers may evolve over time. For each level of relationship discussed in the chapter, identify a firm with which you have that level of relationship, and discuss how its marketing efforts differ from those of other firms.
3. Think about a service organization that retains you as a loyal customer. Why are you loyal to this provider? What are the benefits to you of staying loyal and not switching to another provider? What would it take for you to switch?
4. With regard to the same service organization, what are the benefits to the organization of keeping you as a customer? Calculate your "lifetime value" to the organization.
5. Describe the logic behind "customer profitability segmentation" from the company's point of view. Also discuss what customers may think of the practice.
6. Describe the various switching barriers discussed in the text. What switching barriers might you face in switching banks? Cellphone service providers? Universities?
7. Describe the four levels of retention strategies, and give examples of each type. Again, think of a service organization to which you are loyal. Can you describe the reason(s) you are loyal in terms of the different levels? In other words, what ties you to the organization?
8. Have you ever worked as a frontline service employee? Can you remember having to deal with difficult or "problem" customers? Discuss how you handled such situations. As a manager of frontline employees, how would you help your employees deal with difficult customers?

Exercises

1. Interview the manager of a local service organization. Discuss with the manager the target market(s) for the service. Estimate the lifetime value of a customer in one or more of the target segments. To do this estimate, you will need to get as much information from the manager as you can. If the manager cannot answer all of your questions, make some assumptions.
2. In small groups in class, debate the question "Is the customer always right?" In other words, are there times when the customer may be the wrong customer for the organization?
3. Choose a specific company context (your class project company, the company you work for, or a company in an industry you are familiar with). Calculate the lifetime

value of a customer for this company. You will need to make assumptions to do this calculation, so make your assumptions clear. Using ideas and concepts from this chapter, describe a relationship marketing strategy to increase the number of life-time customers for this firm.

Notes

1. USAA is featured in the following two books, and material in this section is drawn from them: L. L. Berry, *Discovering the Soul of Service* (New York: The Free Press, 1999); F. F. Reichheld, *Loyalty Rules!* (Boston: Harvard Business School Press, 2001).

2. D. Shah, R. T. Rust, A. Parasuraman, R. Staelin, and G. S. Day, "The Path to Customer Centricity," *Journal of Service Research* 9 (November 2006), pp. 113–124.

3. J. McGregor, "Employee Innovator: USAA," *Fast Company,* October 1999, p. 57.

4. J. McGregor, "Customer Service Champs," *BusinessWeek,* March 5, 2007, pp. 52–64.

5. F. E. Webster Jr., "The Changing Role of Marketing in the Corporation," *Journal of Marketing* 56 (October 1992), pp. 1–17.

6. For discussions of relationship marketing and its influence on the marketing of services, consumer goods, strategic alliances, distribution channels, and buyer–seller interactions, see *Journal of the Academy of Marketing Science,* Special Issue on Relationship Marketing (vol. 23, Fall 1995). Some of the early roots of this paradigm shift can be found in C. Gronroos, *Service Management and Marketing* (New York: Lexington Books, 1990); E. Gummesson, "The New Marketing—Developing Long-Term Interactive Relationships," *Long Range Planning* 20 (1987), pp. 10–20. For excellent reviews of relationship marketing across a spectrum of topics, see J. N. Sheth, *Handbook of Relationship Marketing* (Thousand Oaks, CA: Sage, 2000).

7. L. L. Berry and A. Parasuraman, *Marketing Services* (New York: Free Press, 1991), chap. 8.

8. G. Knisely, "Comparing Marketing Management in Package Goods and Service Organizations," a series of interviews appearing in *Advertising Age,* January 15, February 19, March 19, and May 14, 1979.

9. This discussion is based on M. D. Johnson and F. Selnes, "Customer Portfolio Management: Toward a Dynamic Theory of Exchange Relationships," *Journal of Marketing* 68 (April 2004), pp. 1–17.

10. R. M. Morgan and S. D. Hunt, "The Commitment-Trust Theory of Relationship Marketing," *Journal of Marketing* 58 (July 1994), pp. 20–38; N. Bendapudi and L. L. Berry, "Customers' Motivations for Maintaining Relationships with Service Providers," *Journal of Retailing* 73 (Spring 1997), pp. 15–37.

11. Johnson and Selnes, "Customer Portfolio Management."

12. Ibid.

13. See also D. Siredeshmukh, J. Singh, and B. Sabol, "Customer Trust, Value, and Loyalty in Relational Exchanges," *Journal of Marketing* 66 (January 2002), pp. 15–37.

14. The three types of relational benefits discussed in this section are drawn from K. P. Gwinner, D. D. Gremler, and M. J. Bitner, "Relational Benefits in Service Industries: The Customer's Perspective," *Journal of the Academy of Marketing*

Science 26 (Spring 1998), pp. 101–114. For a recent review of research on relational benefits, see D. D. Gremler and K. P. Gwinner, "Relational Benefits Research: A Synthesis," in *Handbook on Research in Relationship Marketing,* ed. R. Morgan, G. Deitz, and J. Parish (*forthcoming*).

15. Gwinner, Gremler, and Bitner, "Relational Benefits in Service Industries: The Customer's Perspective," p. 104.

16. See M. B. Adelman, A. Ahuvia, and C. Goodwin, "Beyond Smiling: Social Support and Service Quality," in *Service Quality: New Directions in Theory and Practice,* ed. R. T. Rust and R. L. Oliver (Thousand Oaks, CA: Sage Publications, 1994), pp. 139–172; C. Goodwin, "Communality as a Dimension of Service Relationships," *Journal of Consumer Psychology* 5, no. 4 (1996), pp. 387–415.

17. E. J. Arnould and L. L. Price, "River Magic: Extraordinary Experience and the Extended Service Encounter," *Journal of Consumer Research* 20 (June 1993), pp. 24–45.

18. N. Bendapudi and R. P. Leone, "How to Lose Your Star Performer without Losing Customers, Too," *Harvard Business Review 79* (November 2001), pp. 104–115.

19. Compare Gwinner, Gremler, and Bitner, "Relational Benefits in Service Industries" and T. Hennig-Thurau, K. P. Gwinner, and D. D. Gremler, "Understanding Relationship Marketing Outcomes: An Integration of Relational Benefits and Relationship Quality," *Journal of Service Research* 4 (February 2002), pp. 230–247 with R. Lacey, J. Suh, and R. M. Morgan, "Differential Effects of Preferential Treatment Levels on Relational Outcomes," *Journal of Service Research* 9 (February 2007), pp. 241–256.

20. F. F. Reichheld and W. E. Sasser Jr., "Zero Defections: Quality Comes to Services," *Harvard Business Review* 68 (September–October 1990), pp. 105–111; F. F. Reichheld, *The Loyalty Effect* (Boston: Harvard Business School Press, 1996); S. Gupta and V. Zeithaml, "Customer Metrics and Their Impact on Financial Performance," *Marketing Science* 25 (November–December 2006), pp. 718–739.

21. C. Homburg, N. Koschate, and W. D. Hoyer, "Do Satisfied Customers Really Pay More? A Study of the Relationship between Customer Satisfaction and Willingness to Pay," *Journal of Marketing* 69 (April 2005), pp. 84–96.

22. R. Dhar and R. Glazer, "Hedging Customers," *Harvard Business Review* 81 (May 2003), pp. 86–92.

23. D. D. Gremler and S. W. Brown, "The Loyalty Ripple Effect: Appreciating the Full Value of Customers," *International Journal of Service Industry Management* 10, no. 3 (1999), pp. 271–291.

24. M. S. Rosenbaum and C. A. Massiah, "When Customers Receive Support from Other Customers: Exploring the Influence of Intercustomer Social Support on Customer Voluntary Performance," *Journal of Service Research* 9 (February 2007), pp. 257–270.

25. S. J. Grove and R. P. Fisk, "The Impact of Other Customers on Service Experiences: A Critical Incident Examination of 'Getting Along,'" *Journal of Retailing* 73 (Spring 1997), pp. 63–85.

26. P. J. Danaher, D. M. Conroy, J. R. McColl-Kennedy, "Who Wants a Relationship? Conditions When Consumers Expect a Relationship with Their Service Provider," *Journal of Service Research* 11 (August 2008), pp. 43–62.

27. Reichheld and Sasser, "Zero Defections."

28. Additional frameworks for calculating lifetime customer value that include a variety of other variables can be found in W. J. Reinartz and V. Kumar, "The Impact of

Customer Relationship Characteristics on Profitable Lifetime Duration," *Journal of Marketing* 67 (January 2003), pp. 77–99; Dhar and Glazer, "Hedging Customers"; H. K. Stahl, K. Matzler, and H. H. Hinterhuber, "Linking Customer Lifetime Value with Shareholder Value," *Industrial Marketing Management* 32, no. 4 (2003), pp. 267–279.

29. This example is cited in J. L. Heskett, W. E. Sasser Jr., and L. A. Schlesinger, *The Service Profit Chain* (New York: The Free Press, 1997), pp. 200–201.

30. For more on customer profitability segments and related strategies, see V. A. Zeithaml, R. T. Rust, and K. N. Lemon, "The Customer Pyramid: Creating and Serving Profitable Customers," *California Management Review* 43 (Summer 2001), pp. 118–142.

31. R. Brooks, "Alienating Customers Isn't Always a Bad Idea, Many Firms Discover," *The Wall Street Journal,* January 7, 1999, p. A1.

32. C. Homburg, M. Droll, and D. Totzek, "Customer Prioritization: Does It Pay Off, and How Should It Be Implemented?" *Journal of Marketing* 72 (September 2008), pp. 110–130.

33. F. Reichheld, "Loyalty-Based Management," *Harvard Business Review* 71 (March–April 1993), pp. 64–74.

34. D. Brady, "Why Service Stinks," *BusinessWeek,* October 23, 2000, pp. 118–128.

35. Dhar and Glazer, "Hedging Customers."

36. C. O. Tarsi, R. N. Bolton, M. D. Hutt, and B. A. Walker, "Balancing Risk and Return in a Customer Portfolio," *Journal of Marketing* 75 (May 2011), pp. 1-17.

37. D. Rosenblum, D. Tomlinson, and L. Scott, "Bottom-Feeding for Blockbuster Businesses," *Harvard Business Review* 81 (March 2003), pp. 52–59.

38. M. D. Johnson, A. Herrman, and F. Huber, "The Evolution of Loyalty Intentions," *Journal of Marketing* 70 (April 2006), pp. 122–132.

39. See T. A. Burnham, J. K. Frels, and V. Mahajan, "Consumer Switching Costs: A Typology, Antecedents, and Consequences," *Journal of the Academy of Marketing Science* 32 (Spring 2003), pp. 109–126; F. Selnes, "An Examination of the Effect of Product Performance on Brand Reputation, Satisfaction, and Loyalty," *European Journal of Marketing* 27, no. 9 (2003), 19–35; M. Colgate, V. T.-U. Tong, C. K.-C. Lee, and J. U. Farley, "Back from the Brink: Why Customers Stay," *Journal of Service Research* 9 (February 2007), pp. 211–228.

40. L. White and V. Yanamandram, "Why Customers Stay: Reasons and Consequences of Inertia in Financial Services," *Managing Service Quality* 14, nos. 2/3 (2004), pp. 183–194.

41. Colgate et al., "Back from the Brink."

42. See J. P. Guiltinan, "A Classification of Switching Costs with Implications for Relationship Marketing," in *Marketing Theory and Practice,* ed. Terry L. Childers et al. (Chicago: American Marketing Association, 1989), pp. 216–220; P. G. Patterson and T. Smith, "A Cross-Cultural Study of Switching Barriers and Propensity to Stay with Service Providers," *Journal of Retailing* 79 (Summer 2003), pp. 107–120; M. A. Jones, K. E. Reynolds, D. L. Mothersbaugh, and S. E. Beatty, "The Positive and Negative Effects of Switching Costs on Relational Outcomes," *Journal of Service Research* 9 (May 2007), pp. 335–355.

43. J. J. Kim, "Banks Push Harder to Get You to Switch—Services Aim to Ease Hassle of Moving Your Accounts," *The Wall Street Journal,* October 12, 2006, p. D1.

44. See Bendapudi and Berry, "Customers' Motivations for Maintaining Relationships with Service Providers"; H. S. Bansal, P. G. Irving, and S. F. Taylor, "A Three-Component Model of Customer Commitment to Service Providers,"*Journal of the Academy of Marketing Science* 32 (Summer 2004), pp. 234–250.

45. Figure 6.6 and the discussion of the four levels of relationship strategies is based on Berry and Parasuraman, *Marketing Services,* pp. 136–142.

46. For more information on cautions to be considered in implementing rewards strategies, see H. T. Keh and Y. H. Lee, "Do Reward Programs Build Loyalty for Services? The Moderating Effect of Satisfaction on Type and Timing of Rewards," *Journal of Retailing* 82 (June 2006), pp. 127–136; L. Meyer-Waarden and C. Benavent, "Rewards That Reward," *The Wall Street Journal, September* 17, 2008, p. R5; J. D. Hansen, G. D. Deitz, and R. M. Morgan, "Taxonomy of Service-based Loyalty Program Members," *Journal of Services Marketing* 24, no. 4 (2010), pp. 271–282.

47. C. K. Yim, D. K. Tse, and K. W. Chan, "Strengthening Customer Loyalty through Intimacy and Passion: Roles of Customer-Firm Affection and Customer-Staff Relationships in Services," *Journal of Marketing Research* 45 (December 2008), pp. 741–756.

48. Colgate et al., "Back from the Brink:"

49. Bendapudi and Leone, "How to Lose Your Star Performer without Losing Customers"; E. Anderson and S. D. Jap, "The Dark Side of Close Relationships," *Sloan Management Review* 46 (Spring 2005), pp. 75–82; R. W. Palmatier, R. P. Dant, D. Grewal, and K. R. Evans, "Factors Influencing the Effectiveness of Relationship Marketing: A Meta-Analysis," *Journal of Marketing* 70 (October 2006), pp. 136–153.

50. Rosenbaum and Massiah, "When Customers Receive Support from Other Customers."

51. W. Ulaga and A. Eggert, "Value-Based DIfferentiation in Business Relationships: Gaining and Sustaining Key Supplier Status," *Journal of Marketing* 70 (January 2006), pp. 119–136.

52. D. D. Gremler and S. W. Brown, "Service Loyalty: Its Nature, Importance, and Implications," in *Advancing Service Quality: A Global Perspective,* ed. Bo Edvardsson et al. (Jamaica, NY: International Service Quality Association, 1996), pp. 171–180; H. Hansen, K. Sandvik, and F. Selnes, "Direct and Indirect Effects of Commitment to a Service Employee on the Intention to Stay," *Journal of Service Research* 5 (May 2003), pp. 356–368.

53. Arthur Andersen, *Best Practices: Building Your Business with Customer-Focused Solutions* (New York: Simon & Schuster, 1998), pp. 125–127; http://www.cardinal.com/, accessed on July 14, 2010.

54. S. Stellin, "Avoiding Surprises at the Car Rental Counter," *The New York Times*, June 4, 2006, p. TR6.

55. See L. C. Harris and K. L. Reynolds, "The Consequences of Dysfunctional Customer Behavior," *Journal of Service Research* 6 (November 2003), p. 145, for cites; see also, A. A. Grandey, D. N. Dickter, and H. P. Sin, "The Customer Is *Not* Always Right: Customer Aggression and Emotion Regulation of Service Employees," *Journal of Organizational Behavior* 25 (2004), pp. 397–418. Also see R. Fisk, S. Grove, L. C. Harris, D. A. Keeffe, K. L. Daunt, R. Russell-Bennett,

and J. Wirtz, "Customers Behaving Badly: A State of the Art Review, Research Agenda, and Implications for Practitioners," *Journal of Services Marketing* 24, no. 6 (2010), pp. 417–429.

56. K. Ohnezeit, recruiting supervisor for Enterprise Rent-A-Car, personal communication, February 12, 2004.

57. See Harris and Reynolds, "The Consequences of Dysfunctional Customer Behavior."

58. L. L. Berry and K. Seiders, "Serving Unfair Customers," *Business Horizons* 51 (January/February 2008), pp. 29–37.

59. For a detailed discussion on relationship ending, see A. Halinen and J. Tähtinen, "A Process Theory of Relationship Ending," *International Journal of Service Industry Management* 13, no. 2 (2002), pp. 163–180.

60. H. Åkerlund, "Fading Customer Relationships in Professional Services," *Managing Service Quality* 15, no. 2 (2005), pp. 156–71.

61. M. Haenlein and A. M. Kaplan, "Unprofitable Customers and Their Management," *Business Horizons* 52 (2009), pp. 89-97; M. Haenlein, A. M. Kaplan, and D. Schoder, "Valuing the Real Option of Abandoning Unprofitable Customers When Calculating Customer Lifetime Value," *Journal of Marketing* 70 (July 2006), pp. 5–20.

62. http://www.nypro.com, accessed July 16, 2010. For similar examples, see R. Flandez, "It Just Isn't Working? Some File for Customer Divorce," *The Wall Street Journal,* November 10, 2009, p. B7.

Chapter Seven

Service Recovery

This chapter's objectives are to

1. Illustrate the importance of recovery from service failures in keeping customers and building loyalty.
2. Discuss the nature of customer complaints and why people do and do not complain.
3. Provide evidence of what customers expect and the kind of responses they want when they do complain.
4. Present strategies for effective service recovery, including ways to "fix the customer" after a service failure and to "fix the problem."
5. Discuss service guarantees—what they are, the benefits of guarantees, and when to use them—as a type of service recovery strategy.

JetBlue and the Valentine's Day Ice Storm at JFK

When JetBlue Airways began flying daily in 2000 from New York City to Fort Lauderdale, Florida, and Buffalo, New York, it promised fares that would be as much as 65 percent lower than competitors. At that time JetBlue had 300 employees and provided its customers with comforts like assigned seating, leather upholstery, and satellite TV on individual screens in every seat. The low fares were an immediate hit with passengers, as they found friendly, snappily dressed flight attendants who served animal crackers, Oreo cookies, and blue potato chips on flights very appealing. Indeed, by early 2007 JetBlue had 9,300 employees and 125 jetliners, operating about 575 daily flights to 52 destinations in the United States and the Caribbean. Customers had come to love the airline. It had won many awards for its service and had regularly been ranked near the top of airline satisfaction ratings by J.D. Power and Associates, among others.

JetBlue's reputation for excellent service was challenged on Valentine's Day, February 14, 2007, when a severe storm dumped 2 inches of ice at New York's JFK Airport. Although the weather created headaches for just about all air carriers in the eastern United States that Wednesday, it was JetBlue who received the most attention. Why? The airline that had developed a reputation for its customer-friendly approach had suffered a startling breakdown. More than 1,000 flights were canceled over the next six days. Passengers were stuck on planes for up to 10 hours. Delays averaged nearly 4 hours. It took nearly a week for JetBlue to return operations to normal.

What actually happened? As discussed in the JetBlue Case in the back of this book, bad weather and poor management decisions led to full gates and a substantial queue

Some JetBlue customers spent as much as nine hours stuck on planes and in terminals.

of planes waiting for gates. JetBlue's initial responses to the weather disruptions on Valentine's Day were not good. While the storm was occurring, and even immediately afterward, JetBlue failed to cancel flights, leaving some passengers stranded on the tarmac for as long as 10 hours. The policy of initially postponing, but not canceling, flights resulted in snowballing cancellations for nearly a week, with long lines at the airport as customers attempted to get on flights.

Unfortunately for JetBlue, this happened in the media capital of the world—thus, its service failures received major attention in the press. Perhaps the most devastating blow of all was delivered by *BusinessWeek;* the magazine described the situation as "one extraordinary stumble" on its March 5 cover touting its first-ever rating of the best firms in customer service. Why did JetBlue receive such attention when airlines such as Delta and American had had similar problems? Customers had come to expect more from JetBlue than from other airlines.

Clearly this service failure received more attention in the press than most failures that customers experience. Customers obviously would prefer to not have experienced such a failure, but even more important in many situations is how a firm responds to such a situation. So how did JetBlue ultimately respond to this service failure? We explore this situation further in the JetBlue case included in the back of the textbook.

The preceding two chapters have given you a foundation for understanding customers' service expectations through research as well as through knowing them as individuals and developing strong relationships with them. These strategies, matched with effective service design, delivery, and communication—treated in other parts of the text—form the foundations for service success. But in all service contexts—whether customer service, consumer services, or business-to-business services—service failure is inevitable. Failure is inevitable even for the best of firms with the best of intentions, even for those with world-class service systems.

To fully understand and retain their customers, firms must know what customers expect when service failures occur and must implement effective strategies for service recovery. Our chapter-opening vignette illustrates the problems a firm can face when it has a service failure.

THE IMPACT OF SERVICE FAILURE AND RECOVERY

A *service failure* is generally described as service performance that falls below a customer's expectations in such a way that leads to customer dissatisfaction. *Service recovery* refers to the actions taken by an organization in response to a service failure. Failures occur for all kinds of reasons—the service may be unavailable when promised, it may be delivered late or too slowly, the outcome may be incorrect or poorly executed,

FIGURE 7.1
Complaining Customers: The Tip of the Iceberg

Source: Data from TARP Worldwide Inc., 2007.

1%–5% complain to management or company headquarters

45% complain to a frontline employee

50% encounter a problem but do not complain

or employees may be rude or uncaring.[1] Although these types of failures bring about negative feelings from customers, research suggests that only a portion (45 percent) of customers who experience a problem with service delivery actually complain to the employees serving them, and a very small number (1 to 5 percent) complain to management or the company headquarters.[2] This phenomenon, commonly referred to as the "tip of the iceberg" and demonstrated in Figure 7.1, suggests every complaint that management actually receives represents 20 to 100 other customers who experienced the problem and did not complain. Service failures left unfixed can result in customers leaving, telling other customers about their negative experiences, and even challenging the organization through consumer rights organizations or legal channels.

Service Recovery Effects

Research has shown that resolving customer problems effectively has a strong impact on customer satisfaction, loyalty, word-of-mouth communication, and bottom-line performance.[3] That is, customers who experience service failures, but who are ultimately satisfied based on recovery efforts by the firm, will be more loyal than those whose problems are not resolved. That loyalty translates into profitability, as you learned in Chapter 6. Data from TARP Worldwide verify this relationship, as shown in Figure 7.2.[4] Among customers from service businesses who complain

FIGURE 7.2
Unhappy Customers' Repurchase Intentions

Source: TARP Worldwide Inc. Service Industry Data, 2007.

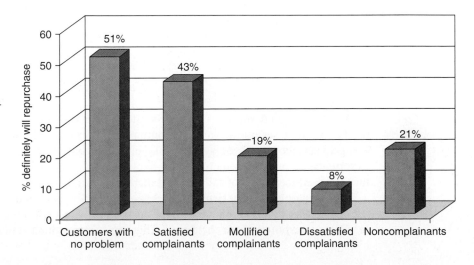

% definitely will repurchase

- Customers with no problem: 51%
- Satisfied complainants: 43%
- Mollified complainants: 19%
- Dissatisfied complainants: 8%
- Noncomplainants: 21%

Yours is a Very Bad Hotel

A graphic complaint prepared for:

J___ C___

General Manager

L___ R___

Front Desk Manager

DoubleTree Club Hotel

2828 Southwest Freeway

Business travelers Tom F. and Shane A. experienced poor service from a hotel in the southwestern United States and decided to create a PowerPoint slide show as a way to vent their frustrations. Their intent was to chronicle the "shabby treatment" they received at a Doubletree Inn while on a business trip. The men sent the PowerPoint presentation to two managers at the hotel, two clients from the city where it is located, and Shane's mother-in-law. Within a month this presentation, entitled "Yours is a Very Bad Hotel," had been circulated around the globe. As a result, the Seattle-based Web consultants received more than 9,000 e-mail

and have their problems satisfactorily resolved, 43 percent indicate they would definitely purchase again from the same provider—illustrating the power of good service recovery. However, this study and other research have found that customers who are dissatisfied with the recovery process after making a complaint are less likely to repurchase than those who do not complain—suggesting the power of poor service recovery![5]

A well-designed service recovery strategy also provides information that can be used to improve service as part of a continuous improvement effort. By making adjustments to service processes, systems, and outcomes based on previous service recovery experiences, companies increase the likelihood of "doing it right the first time." In turn, this reduces costs of failures and increases initial customer satisfaction.

Unfortunately, many firms do not employ effective recovery strategies. Studies suggest as much as 60 percent of customers who experience a serious problem receive no response from the firm.[6] There are tremendous downsides to having no messages from six continents, and their experience was written up in *USA Today.*

The trouble began one early morning that November when the two businessmen, delayed in their arrival at Doubletree (owned by Hilton Hotels) because of a late-arriving plane, stepped up to the front desk at about 2:00 a.m. with a confirmation and credit card guarantee for late arrival. Unfortunately, the hotel was overbooked and their rooms had been given away hours earlier. Although disappointed, they understood. "These things happen, and we didn't expect miracles," recalled Tom. However, as a "card-carrying Hilton HHonors Gold VIP" who had logged 100,000 miles of business travel the previous year, Tom and his traveling companion, Shane, did expect an apology and a prompt resolution from the employee they would later dub "Night Clerk Mike." Instead, as they noted in the slide show, they received "insolence plus insults" and, eventually, two smokers' rooms in a "dump" of a hotel several miles away (and 15 minutes farther) from the downtown area where they were to have a meeting later that morning.

Once the disappointed travelers returned to Seattle, they detailed their frustrations via bar charts, graphs, and statistical analyses. ("Lifetime chances of dying in a bathtub: 1 in 10,455. Chances of winning the U.K. Lottery: 1 in 13,983,816. Chance of us returning to the Doubletree: Worse than any of those.") After the two had created and e-mailed the PowerPoint file to the hotel managers, they encouraged the three extra people to whom they sent the file to "share it with a few of your friends," anticipating that no more than a few dozen fellow travelers would ever see the PowerPoint slide show. Instead, the response "percolated beyond our wildest dreams," said Tom. At various points in time *The Wall Street Journal, Forbes, MSNBC,* and *Travel Weekly* ran short stories—without any direct input from the travelers—based on a Frequently Asked Questions web page the two businessmen had created in response to inquiries they had received about their experience.

Tom and Shane received hundreds of requests from business schools and hospitality companies to use the slide show as an example of "customer service gone horribly wrong." And in addition to the response from supportive well-wishers, the presentation generated an offer of a free two-night stay at any Hilton hotel. The two men declined the offer in lieu of a $1,000 charitable donation to a local charity, Toys for Tots, and encouraged their "fans" to do the same. Hotel management also provided the men with a list of actions taken to improve employee training and overbooking policies. All these changes occurred simply because two men documented their frustrations and made it available to a couple of friends via the Internet!

service recovery or ineffective service recovery strategies. Poor recovery following a bad service experience creates, in effect, two poor experiences and can lead to customers who are so dissatisfied that they actively pursue opportunities to openly criticize the company.[7] When customers experience a service failure, they talk about it to others, no matter what the outcome. Research has found that customers who are satisfied with a firm's recovery efforts talk to an average of 8 people, whereas those customers who are dissatisfied with the response talk to an average of 18.5 people.[8] With the ability to share such stories on the Internet, the potential reach of such dissatisfied customers is even greater. (See Exhibit 7.1 about the two Doubletree Inn customers who were not happy with the company's service recovery efforts.) Further, repeated service failures without an effective recovery strategy in place can aggravate even the best employees. The reduction in employee morale and even the loss of employees can be huge but often overlooked costs of not having an effective service recovery strategy.

The Service Recovery Paradox

Occasionally some businesses have customers who are initially dissatisfied with a service experience and then experience a high level of excellent service recovery, seemingly leading them to be even more satisfied and more likely to repurchase than if no problem had occurred at all; that is, they appear to be more satisfied after they experience a service failure than they otherwise would have been![9] To illustrate, consider a rental car customer who arrives to check in and finds that no automobile is available of the size reserved and the price quoted. In an effort to recover, the car rental agent immediately upgrades this customer to a much better vehicle at the original price. The customer, thrilled with this compensation, reports that she is extremely satisfied with this experience, is even more impressed with the firm than she was before, and vows to be loyal into the future. Although such extreme instances are relatively rare, this idea—that an initially disappointed customer who has experienced good service recovery might be even more satisfied and loyal as a result—has been labeled the *recovery paradox.*

So should a firm "screw up" just a little, so that it can "fix the problem" superbly? If doing so would actually lead to more satisfied customers, is this strategy worth pursuing? The logical, but not very rational, conclusion is that companies should *plan to disappoint customers*, so they can recover well and (hopefully) gain even greater loyalty from them!

What are the problems with such an approach?

- As we indicated earlier in this chapter, a vast majority of customers do not complain when they experience a problem. The possibility of a recovery exists only in situations in which the firm is aware of a problem and is able to recover well; if customers do not make the firm aware of the failure—and most do not—dissatisfaction is most likely to be the result.
- It is expensive to fix mistakes; re-creating or reworking a service may be quite costly to a firm.
- It would appear somewhat ludicrous to encourage service failures—after all, reliability ("doing it right the first time") is the most critical determinant of service quality across industries.
- Research suggests that, even if a customer's satisfaction with the firm increases as a result of the great service recovery, repurchase intentions and image perceptions of the firm do not increase—that is, customers do not necessarily think more highly of the firm in the long run.[10]
- Although the recovery paradox suggests that a customer *may* end up more satisfied after experiencing excellent recovery, there is certainly no guarantee that the customer actually *will* end up more satisfied.

The recovery paradox is highly dependent on the context and situation; although one customer may find it easy to forgive a restaurant that provides him with a gift certificate for a later date for having lost his dinner reservation, another customer who had planned to propose marriage to his date over dinner may not be all that happy with the same recovery scenario.

The intrigue stimulated by the recovery paradox has led to empirical research specifically on this issue. Although anecdotal evidence provides some support for the recovery paradox, research seems to indicate that this phenomenon is not pervasive. In one study, researchers found that only the very highest levels of customers' service recovery ratings resulted in increased satisfaction and loyalty.[11] This research suggests that customers weigh their most recent experiences heavily in their determination of whether to buy again. If the most recent experience is negative, overall feelings about the company will decrease, and repurchase intentions will diminish significantly. Unless the recovery effort is absolutely superlative, it cannot overcome the negative impression of the initial experience enough to build repurchase intentions beyond the point at which they would be if the service had been provided correctly in the first place. Other studies suggest the conditions under which a service recovery paradox is most likely to occur is when the failure is not considered by the customer to be severe, the customer has not experienced prior failures with the firm, the cause of the failure is viewed as unstable by the customer, or the customer perceives that the company had little control over the cause of the failure.[12] Apparently, conditions must be just right in order for the recovery paradox to be present.

Given the mixed opinions on the extent to which the recovery paradox exists, "doing it right the first time" is still the best and safest strategy in the long run. However, when a failure does occur, then every effort at a superior recovery should be made to mitigate its negative effects. If the failure can be fully overcome, if the failure is less critical, or if the recovery effort is clearly superlative, it may be possible to observe evidence of the recovery paradox.[13]

HOW CUSTOMERS RESPOND TO SERVICE FAILURES

Customers who experience service failures can respond in a variety of ways, as illustrated in Figure 7.3.[14] It is assumed that, following a failure, dissatisfaction at some level will occur for the customer. In fact, research suggests that a variety of negative emotions can occur following a service failure, including such feelings as anger, discontent, disappointment, self-pity, anxiety, and regret.[15] These initial negative responses will affect how customers evaluate the service recovery effort and presumably their ultimate decision to return to the provider or not.

Many customers are very passive about their dissatisfaction, simply saying or doing nothing. Whether they take action or not, at some point the customers will decide whether to stay with that provider or switch to a competitor. As we already have pointed out, customers who do not complain are not very likely to return. For companies, customer passivity in the face of dissatisfaction is a threat to future success.

Why People Do (and Do Not) Complain

Customers who are unlikely to take any action—the majority of customers in most situations, as indicated in Figure 7.1—have many reasons for not doing anything. They often see complaining as a waste of their time and effort.[16] They do not believe anything positive will occur for them or others based on their actions. Sometimes they do not know how to complain—they do not understand the process or may not realize that avenues are open to them to voice their complaints. In some cases non-complainers may engage in "emotion-focused coping" to deal with their negative experiences. This type of coping involves self-blame, denial, and possibly seeking social support.[17] They may feel that the failure was somehow their fault and that they do not deserve redress.

FIGURE 7.3   **Customer Complaint Actions Following Service Failure**

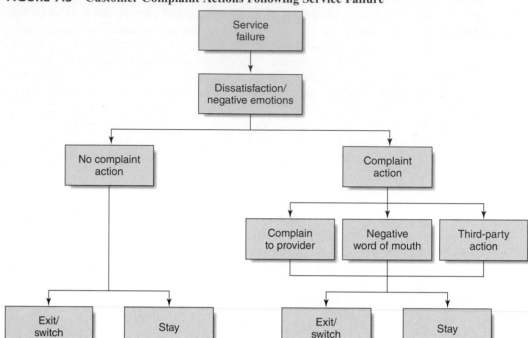

Some customers are more likely to complain than others for a variety of reasons. These customers believe that positive consequences may occur and that there are social benefits of complaining, and their personal norms support their complaining behavior. They believe they should and will be provided compensation for the service failure in some form. They believe that fair treatment and good service are their due and that, in cases of service failure, someone should make good. In some cases they feel a social obligation to complain—to help others avoid similar situations or to punish the service provider. A very small number of customers have "complaining" personalities—they just like to complain or cause trouble.

Personal relevance of the failure can also influence whether people complain.[18] If the service failure is really important, if the failure has critical consequences for the customer, or if the customer has much ego involvement in the service experience, then he or she is more likely to complain. The situation at Doubletree Inn, which was described in Exhibit 7.1, illustrates a failure for a service that was considered especially important to two customers. In such situations, when customer emotions are high, customer rage may result.[19]

Customers are more likely to complain about expensive, high risk, and ego involving services (like vacation packages, airline travel, and medical services) than they are about less expensive, frequently purchased services (fast-food drive-through service, a cab ride, a call to a customer service help line). These latter services are simply not important enough to warrant the time to complain. Unfortunately, even though the experience may not be important to the customer at the moment, a dissatisfying encounter can still drive him or her to a competitor the next time the service is needed.

Types of Customer Complaint Actions

If customers initiate actions following service failure, the action can be of various types. A dissatisfied customer can choose to complain on the spot to the service provider, giving the company the opportunity to respond immediately. This reaction is often the best-case scenario for the company because it has a second chance right at that moment to satisfy the customer, keep his or her business in the future, and potentially avoid any negative word of mouth. Customers who do not complain immediately may choose to complain later to the provider by phone, in writing, or via the Internet. Again, the company has a chance to recover. Researchers refer to these proactive types of complaining behavior as *voice* responses or *seeking redress*.

Some customers choose not to complain directly to the provider but rather spread negative word of mouth about the company to friends, relatives, and coworkers. This negative word-of-mouth communication can be extremely detrimental because it can reinforce the customer's feelings of negativism and spread that negative impression to others. Further, the company has no chance to recover unless the negative word of mouth is accompanied by a complaint directly to the company. In recent years, customers have taken to complaining via the Internet. A variety of websites, including web-based consumer opinion platforms, blogs, and a variety of social media (including Twitter and Facebook),[20] have been created to facilitate customer complaints, and in doing so, provide customers with the possibility of spreading negative word-of-mouth communication to a much broader audience. Some customers become so dissatisfied with a product or service failure that they construct websites targeting the firm's current and prospective customers. On these sites,[21] angry customers convey their grievances against the firm in ways designed to convince other customers of the firm's incompetence and evil.[22]

Finally, customers may choose to complain to third parties such as the Better Business Bureau, to consumer affairs arms of the government, to a licensing authority, to a professional association, or to a private attorney. No matter the action (or inaction), ultimately the customers determine whether to patronize the service provider again or to switch to another provider.

Types of Complainers

Research suggests that people can be grouped into four categories based on how they respond to failures: *passives, voicers, irates,* and *activists.*[23] Although the proportion of the types of complainers is likely to vary across industries and contexts, it is likely that these four types of complainers will be relatively consistent and that each type can be found in all companies and industries.

Passives

This group of customers is least likely to take any action. They are unlikely to say anything to the provider, less likely than others to spread negative word of mouth, and unlikely to complain to a third party. They often doubt the effectiveness of complaining, thinking that the consequences will not merit the time and effort they will expend. Sometimes their personal values or norms argue against complaining.

Voicers

These customers actively complain to the service provider, but they are less likely to spread negative word of mouth, switch patronage, or go to third parties with their complaints. *These customers should be viewed as the service provider's best friends.* They actively complain and thus give the company a second chance. They tend to believe complaining

Irate customers are likely to share their frustrations with others.

has social benefits and therefore do not hesitate to voice their opinions. They believe that the consequences of complaining to the provider can be very positive, and they believe less in other types of complaining such as spreading negative word of mouth or talking to third parties. Their personal norms are consistent with complaining.

Irates

These customers are more likely than others to engage in negative word-of-mouth communication with friends and relatives and to switch providers. They are about average in their propensity to complain to the provider and are unlikely to complain to third parties. As their label suggests, they are more angry with the provider, although they do believe that complaining to the provider can have social benefits. They are less likely to give the service provider a second chance and instead will switch to a competitor, spreading the word to friends and relatives along the way. Such customers are more likely than the other types to go to the trouble of creating blogs on the Internet to share their frustrations with others.

Activists

These customers are characterized by above-average propensity to complain on all dimensions: they will complain to the provider, they will tell others, and they are more likely than any other group to complain to third parties. Complaining fits with their personal norms. They have a very optimistic sense of the potential positive consequences of all types of complaining.

SERVICE RECOVERY STRATEGIES: FIXING THE CUSTOMER

Many companies have learned the importance of providing excellent recovery for disappointed customers. In the next two sections we examine their strategies and share examples of benchmark companies and what they are doing. It will become clear that excellent service recovery is really a combination of a variety of strategies, illustrated in Figure 7.4. Generally speaking, service recovery strategies fall into two general types. One type includes the actions taken by the firm to restore the relationship with the customer—that is, to "fix the customer." The second type is the actions taken to correct the problem and, ideally, to prevent it from recurring—that is, to "fix the problem." Clearly both types of actions are important, but in many situations fixing the customer needs to be done before fixing the problem. Thus, we begin by examining strategies that involve fixing the customer.

When they take the time and effort to complain, customers generally have high expectations. They not only expect a response, but also expect the firm to be accountable. They expect to be helped quickly. They expect to be compensated for their grief and for the hassle of being inconvenienced. And they expect to be treated nicely in the process. Exhibit 7.2 epitomizes this kind of service recovery.

FIGURE 7.4
Service Recovery Strategies

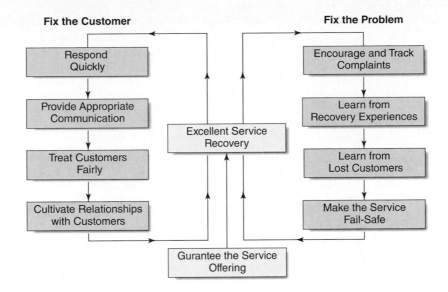

Respond Quickly

Complaining customers want quick responses.[24] Thus, when the company has service failures or receives complaints from customers, it must be prepared to act on them quickly. As indicated in Figure 7.5, research conducted on service customers has found that more than half of all customers who have problems resolved immediately or within 24 hours are "completely satisfied" with the action taken by the company.[25] Unfortunately, many companies require customers to contact multiple employees (a practice often referred to as "ping-ponging") before getting a problem resolved; one study found that an average of 4.7 contacts is typically needed to resolve a complaint.[26] Other research suggests that, if a problem can be handled by the first contact, customers are satisfied with the firm's response 46 percent of the time; however, once 3 or more contacts are needed the percentage of customers who are satisfied with the response drops to 21 percent.[27] The lesson here? A quick response to a service failure can go a long way in appeasing a dissatisfied customer.

The ability to provide immediate responses requires not only systems and procedures that allow quick action but also empowered employees. That is, to enable them to respond quickly, employees should be trained and empowered to solve problems as they occur. A problem not solved can quickly escalate. As we indicated earlier, customers often experience ping-ponging from employee to employee when service failures occur. Empowerment of employees, a practice discussed in more detail in Chapter 11, can often allow for quick responses and help placate dissatisfied customers. The Ritz-Carlton, for example, insists that the first person to hear a complaint from a customer "owns" that complaint until the employee is sure it is resolved. If a maintenance employee hears a complaint from a customer while the employee is in the middle of fixing a light in the hotel corridor, he owns that complaint and is charged with making sure that the problem is handled appropriately before returning to his work.

Another way that problems or complaints can be handled quickly is by building systems that allow customers to actually solve their own service needs and fix their own problems. Typically, this approach is done through technology. Customers directly interact with the company's technology to perform their own customer service, which provides

Exhibit 7.2 Story of a Service Hero

A good recovery can turn angry, frustrated customers into loyal ones. It can, in fact, create more goodwill than if things had gone smoothly in the first place. A classic story of excellent service recovery comes from Club Med–Cancun, part of the Paris-based Club Mediterranèe; its response to a service nightmare won the loyalty of one group of vacationers and is still being retold two decades later.

The vacationers had nothing but trouble getting from New York to their Mexican destination. The flight took off 6 hours late, made two unexpected stops, and circled 30 minutes before it could land. Because of all the delays and mishaps, the plane was en route for 10 hours more than planned and ran out of food and drinks. It finally arrived at two o'clock in the morning, with a landing so rough that oxygen masks and luggage dropped from overhead. By the time the plane pulled up to the gate, the soured passengers were faint with hunger and convinced that their vacation was ruined before it had even started. One lawyer on board was already collecting names and addresses for a class-action lawsuit.

Silvio de Bortoli, the general manager of the Cancun resort and a legend throughout the organization for his ability to satisfy customers, got word of the horrendous flight and immediately created an antidote. He took half the staff to the airport, where they laid out a table of snacks and drinks and set up a stereo system to play lively music. As the guests filed through the gate, they received personal greetings, help with their bags, a sympathetic ear, and a chauffeured ride to the resort. Waiting for them at Club Med was a lavish banquet, complete with mariachi band and champagne. Moreover, the staff had rallied other guests to wake up and greet the newcomers, and the partying continued until sunrise. Many guests said it was the most fun they'd had since college.

In the end, the vacationers had a better experience than if their flight from New York had gone like clockwork. Although the company probably couldn't measure it, Club Mediterranèe won market share that night. After all, the battle for market share is won not by analyzing demographic trends, ratings points, and other global measures but by pleasing customers one at a time.

Source: Reprinted by permission of *Harvard Business Review*. An excerpt from C. W. L. Hart, J. L. Heskett, and W. E. Sasser Jr., "The Profitable Art of Service Recovery," *Harvard Business Review* 68 (July–August 1990), pp. 148, 149. Copyright © 1990 by the Harvard Business School Publishing Corporation. All rights reserved.

FIGURE 7.5
Customer Satisfaction with Timeliness of Firm Responses to Service Failures

Source: TARP Worldwide Inc., Service Industry Data, 2007.

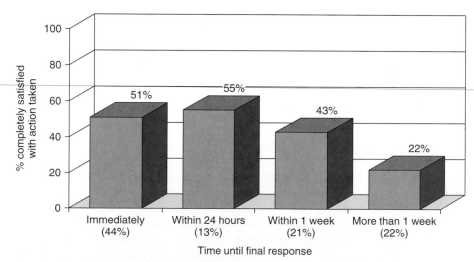

The numbers across the bottom are the percentage of the total sample whose response (by the firm) was received in that time frame. So, for example, 44 percent of the sample received an immediate response. Of that group, 51 percent were completely satisfied with the response.

them with instant answers. FedEx uses this strategy for its package tracking service, for example, as does Symantec for its Internet security software products. Our Technology Spotlight features a company that is a master at online customer service—Cisco Systems.

Provide Appropriate Communication

Display Understanding Accountability

In many service failure situations, customers are not looking for extreme actions from the firm; however, they are looking to understand what happened and for firms to be accountable for their actions (or inactions).[28] Research by the Customer Care Alliance has identified the eight most common "remedies" that customers seek when they experience a serious problem;[29] three of these remedies are to have the product repaired or service fixed, to be reimbursed for the hassle of having experienced a problem, and to receive a free product or service in the future. Interestingly, however, the other five remedies—including an explanation by the firm as to what happened, assurance that the problem will not be repeated, a thank you for the customer's business, an apology from the firm, and an opportunity for the customer to vent his or her frustrations to the firm—cost the firm very little to provide.

Customers who experience a service failure often want an explanation by the firm as to what happened.

These five nonmonetary remedies consist primarily of providing employees the opportunity to communicate with customers. Understanding and accountability are very important to many customers after a service failure because, if they perceive an injustice has occurred, someone is to blame. Customers expect an apology when things go wrong, and a company that provides one demonstrates courtesy and respect; customers also want to know what the company is going to do to ensure that the problem does not recur.[30] As the figures in Table 7.1 suggest, customer discontent can be moderated if firms simply communicate well with customers. Customers clearly value such communication, because these nonmonetary remedies are positively related to satisfaction with the complaint process, continued loyalty, and positive word-of-mouth communication.[31]

TABLE 7.1
Customer Dissatisfaction from Firm Responses to Service Failures

Firm Response	Percentage of Customers Dissatisfied with Action Taken
Do nothing	79%
Explain what happened	20
Provide customer an opportunity to vent frustrations	17
Apologize to customer	10
Thank customer for business	10
Assure customer problem will not recur	6

Source: 2007 National Customer Rage Study conducted by Customer Care Alliance.

Technology Spotlight   Cisco Systems—Customers Recover for Themselves

One of the challenges of high growth and increasingly diversified product lines is learning how to handle customers' service needs quickly. This is a challenge continually faced by Cisco, a worldwide leader in enabling people to make powerful connections—whether in business, education, philanthropy, or creativity. Cisco hardware, software, and service offerings are used to create the Internet solutions that make networks possible and provide Cisco clients (and their customers) with easy access to information anywhere, at any time. As networks become mission-critical to Cisco's customers and their business, failures in this environment become extremely costly very quickly. Customers want to know that their problems can be solved immediately, and they want control over the situation and its solution.

To address these issues—high growth coupled with the critical and increasingly complex nature of the business—Cisco has turned to the Internet to build upon its already world-class suite of customer service offerings. The resulting Cisco support website and online communities provide documentation, suggestions, and tools to help troubleshoot and resolve technical issues with Cisco products and technologies. This online offering has set Cisco apart in its industry and helped the company build customer loyalty in a highly competitive environment.

CUSTOMERS USING TECHNOLOGY TO SOLVE PROBLEMS THEMSELVES

Essentially, Cisco has enabled customers to be in charge of much of their own service and support through the company's corporate self-support website and online communities. In most cases, customers can solve their own service problems, with no intervention from Cisco personnel—allowing Cisco staff to focus on complex issues that require hands-on support. Through the Cisco self-support website, access to information is immediate. This is

important because speed and immediacy are frequently key concerns for customers in these mission-critical situations. The Cisco Support Community includes (1) community forums, which provide customers with the ability to ask questions and acquire information on problems they have encountered from fellow Cisco customers from other companies, (2) opportunities to acquire the latest support-related knowledge through a variety of programs and blogs led by Cisco experts, and (3) technical support documents and tutorials published by Cisco experts and partners on such issues as local area networks, network management, security, and data storage.

Over the past few years Cisco has evolved to provide to a unified customer experience that is channel and location agnostic by bringing together all of the previously mentioned modalities of support. Customers can now contact Cisco for support through any modality (i.e., communities, self-support, agents) and get all of the right support without having to jump back and forth between various channels. Cisco refers to this approach as Smart Interactions—which it sees as having three components.

The first component is a *unified customer experience*. Smart Interactions provides Cisco with the ability to offer a unified support experience for its customers and partners across all the modalities it provides. With Smart Interactions, all of Cisco's support channels have been coordinated to provide a seamless and consistent experience for its customers.

Although customers can use the telephone to speak to a call center agent, more than ever they are demanding real-time access to information and expertise when they encounter problems and expect to resolve them through a variety of channels. Smart Interactions provides Cisco customers support at a time that is convenient to them, whether they are "on the road," helping their clients, or troubleshooting

Supply Adequate Explanations

In many service failures, customers try to understand why the failure occurred. Explanations can help to diffuse negative reactions and convey respect for the customer.[32] Research suggests that when the firm's ability to provide an adequate outcome is not successful, further dissatisfaction can be reduced if an adequate explanation is on site. One such channel is the Cisco Support Community. The community is continually available and is up-to-date in its understanding of issues and resolutions—even call center agents frequently look to the community to help them diagnose problems. Those in the community who are particularly frequent contributors to helping others are given the title of "Cisco VIP." These people have a "badge" placed next to their user name on the communities; the badge indicates their VIP status and displays the category in which they earned their status. ("Cisco Designated VIPs" are the top contributors and are often invited to advise the communities on community direction, features, and other items.)

The second component of Smart Interactions is *anytime, anywhere support*. Recognizing customer needs for anytime/anywhere engagement with Cisco expertise and tools, Cisco has expanded its customer support experience into social media and mobile devices. Indeed, customers are increasingly using these tools when troubleshooting problems they encounter while using Cisco products. Often these issues arise when they are away from the office, making it difficult to access Cisco resources from a more traditional personal computer or laptop. In early 2011, Cisco launched applications (apps) for technical support on both the iPhone and, more recently, the iPad. The ease of use offered by the iPad app has been a hit—particularly among younger customers and those in emerging markets. When they encounter problems, Cisco customers can also participate in discussion forums, get real-time access to Cisco experts, and access technical support resources directly from Facebook, Twitter, LinkedIn, and YouTube. As of 2011, over 100,000 Cisco customers were regular users of at least one of these four sources.

The third component is *proactive support*. Cisco leverages the communities to equip its customers and partners with Cisco's latest intellectual capital before issues occur. Cisco also wants community members to turn around and help others more proactively. To do so, Cisco experts from a wide array of organizations are sharing their latest knowledge through interactive "Ask the Expert" sessions, live Web casts, video tutorials, and the Cisco Support Community Blog. The intent is for customers to be thinking about and exposed to issues they may face, so that than can resolve problems before they occur—the ultimate service recovery!

THE RESULTS

The goal of the Smart Interactions approach is to make Cisco support seamless to all of its customers and allow them to assemble a wealth of knowledge, participate in a stream of forum discussions, and learn from technical experts in the community to resolve whatever problems they face. Through its continual innovation in providing service to its customers on the Internet, Cisco has recognized tremendous benefits. Currently, 80 percent of customer support problems are handled via the Cisco.com self-support site and communities, using intellectual property provided by Cisco experts and self-help tools that allow customers to diagnose and solve their own problems. Customer satisfaction and loyalty have increased with the introduction of Internet-based customer service and support communities, productivity has increased as Cisco Support Community has helped resolve customer issues, and the company saves approximately $300 million per year through case deflection to its communities and self-support site. This is truly a win–win situation for Cisco's bottom line, its employees, and its business customers.

Sources: www.cisco.com/support, accessed August 2011; e-mail communications from Jason Cassee, Executive Communications, Cisco Services, August 2011.

provided to the customer.[33] In order for an explanation to be perceived as adequate, it must possess two primary characteristics. First, the *content* of the explanation must be appropriate; relevant facts and pertinent information are important in helping the customer understand what occurred. Second, the *style* of the delivery of the explanation, or how the explanation is delivered, can also reduce customer dissatisfaction.

Style includes the personal characteristics of the explanation givers, including their credibility and sincerity. Explanations perceived by customers as honest, sincere, and not manipulative are generally the most effective. Part of the frustration of the Doubletree Inn customers mentioned in Exhibit 7.1 was the result of not receiving an adequate explanation from the hotel; they never received an explanation as to why their confirmed, guaranteed reservations were not held, and the night clerk apparently interacted with them in a very apathetic manner.

Treat Customers Fairly

Customers also want justice and fairness in handling their complaints. Service recovery experts Steve Brown and Steve Tax have documented three specific types of justice that customers are looking for following their complaints: *outcome fairness, procedural fairness,* and *interactional fairness.*[34] Outcome fairness concerns the results that customers receive from their complaints; *procedural fairness* refers to the policies, rules, and timeliness of the complaint process; and interactional fairness focuses on the interpersonal treatment received during the complaint process.[35] Exhibit 7.3 shows examples of each type of fairness taken from Brown and Tax's study of customers who reported on their experiences with complaint resolution. Our Global Feature discusses how customers across cultures view fair service recovery.

Outcome Fairness

In their service recovery efforts firms should provide customers with outcomes, or compensation, that match the level of their dissatisfaction. This compensation can take the form of actual monetary compensation, an apology, future free service, reduced charges, repairs, and/or replacements. Customers expect equity in the exchange—that is, they want to feel that the company has "paid" for its mistakes in a manner at least equal to what the customer has suffered. The company's "punishment should fit the crime." Customers expect equality—that is, they want to be compensated in a manner similar to other customers who have experienced the same type of service failure. They also appreciate it when a company gives them choices in terms of compensation. For example, a student whose senior portraits taken by a professional studio are not properly printed could be offered the choice of a refund or a free sitting and package of portraits as compensation for the original portraits not arriving as promised. Outcome fairness is especially important in settings in which customers have particularly negative emotional responses to the service failure; in such situations recovery efforts should focus on improving the outcome from the customer's point of view.[36]

In the Club Med example in Exhibit 7.2, customers were compensated by being met at the airport with snacks and drinks, being chauffeured to the resort, being served a lavish buffet, and being treated to an all-night party that was not part of the package initially. These guests had suffered a lot through the delay of their long-awaited vacation, and the compensation definitely was more than adequate, given the service failure was not even Club Med's fault.

On the other hand, customers can be uncomfortable if they are overly compensated. Early in its experience with service guarantees, Domino's Pizza offered not to charge for a pizza if the driver arrived after the 30-minute guaranteed delivery time. Many customers were not comfortable asking for this level of compensation, especially if the driver was only a few minutes late. In this case "the punishment was greater than the crime." For a while Domino's changed the compensation to a more reasonable $3 off for late deliveries. Later the time guarantee was dropped altogether because of problems it caused with employees who were driving too fast to make their deliveries.

Exhibit 7.3 Fairness Themes in Service Recovery

	Fair	Unfair
Outcome fairness: the results that customers receive from complaints	*"The waitress agreed that there was a problem. She took the sandwiches back to the kitchen and had them replaced. We were also given a free drink."* *"They were very thorough with my complaint. One week later I received a coupon for a free oil change and an apology from the shop owner."*	*"Their refusal to refund our money or make up for the inconvenience and cold food was inexcusable."* *"If I wanted a refund, I had to go back to the store the next day. It's a 20-minute drive; the refund was barely worth the trouble."* *"All I wanted was for the ticket agent to apologize for doubting my story. I never got the apology."*
Procedural fairness: the policies, rules, and timeliness of the complaint process	*"The hotel manager said that it didn't matter to her who was at fault, she would take responsibility for the problem immediately."* *"The sales manager called me back one week after my complaint to check if the problem was taken care of to my satisfaction."*	*"They should have assisted me with the problem instead of giving me a phone number to call. No one returned my calls, and I never had a chance to speak to a real person."* *"I had to tell my problem to too many people. I had to become irate in order to talk with the manager, who was apparently the only one who could provide a solution."*
Interactional fairness: the interpersonal treatment received during the complaint process	*"The loan officer was very courteous, knowledgeable, and considerate—he kept me informed about the progress of the complaint."* *"The teller explained that they had a power outage that morning so things were delayed. He went through a lot of files [effort] so that I would not have to come back the next day."*	*"The person who handled my complaint about the faulty air conditioner repair wasn't going to do anything about it and didn't seem to care."* *"The receptionist was very rude; she made it seem like the doctor's time was important but mine was not."*

Procedural Fairness

In addition to fair compensation, firms should treat customers fairly in terms of policies, rules, and timeliness of the complaint process. Customers want easy access to the complaint process, and they want things handled quickly, preferably by the first person they contact. They appreciate companies that can be adaptable in their procedures,

Service failure is inevitable, no matter what the context, country, or culture. Appropriate service recovery procedures, therefore, are needed by all firms. Service firms operating in several countries, as well as those operating in multi-ethnic countries like the United States, United Kingdom, or Australia, need to be sensitive to the cultural diversity and subsequently differing expectations of service and of service recovery.

ATTRIBUTION EXPECTATIONS

When service failures occur, customers spontaneously infer or attribute blame for the unexpected event. Researchers Anna Mattila and Paul Patterson have explored service recovery across cultures and found in Western countries, when the failure is caused by some external factor beyond the control of the service firm, customers will attribute the problem to the context or situation surrounding the service failure—particularly if an explanation is offered by the firm as to what happened. Such action can diminish the blame customers attribute to the firm and its staff, and thus not detract from their perceptions of overall perceived quality. For customers from Eastern cultures, however, a causal explanation has relatively little impact on where the blame for the failure is attributed. These customers prefer other remedies, such as a speedy resolution to the problem and a genuine apology from a manager (rather than a frontline employee) to regain "face" in the eyes of their family and friends. Eastern customers also have a lower tolerance to uncertain and ambiguous situations. Thus, when a failure is being remedied, these customers would prefer having a sense of control—the firm can provide this by keeping them informed of exactly what is being done to rectify the situation.

FAIRNESS EXPECTATIONS

Outcome Fairness

Mattila and Patterson also investigated service recovery fairness issues. In their studies they found Western (i.e., American) customers are more interested in and expect to receive tangible compensation (i.e., a discount) when a service failure occurs than are Eastern (i.e., Thai or Malaysian) customers. Offering compensation is particularly effective in restoring a sense of fairness among American customers; apparently, American consumers are particularly concerned with outcome fairness. Indeed, American customers are generally more assertive and more used to asking for reparation than consumers from Eastern cultures. Previous research on service recovery in Western contexts consistently showed that compensation has a positive

effect on postrecovery satisfaction and loyalty. Eastern customers, who typically tend to be high on uncertainty avoidance, prefer other types of remedies when service failure occurs. In Eastern cultures there is a tendency to focus on avoidance of losses rather than on individual gains. East Asian customers emphasize the need to fit in with others and to avoid conflict and confrontation.

Interactional Fairness

Mattila and Patterson's research suggests that, in Western cultures, offering an explanation for service failure might shift the customer's focus away from thinking that the service provider is incompetent, uncaring, or lazy. Such an explanation tends to cause Western customers to pay more attention to the situation as a cause of the failure. Eastern customers, however, are more likely to be aware of situational constraints, seek to maintain social harmony, and avoid causing a loss of face. For them, interactional fairness appears to be particularly salient. Thus, providing an explanation and treating the offended Eastern customers in a courteous, formal, and empathetic manner is more important than the compensation offered.

Procedural Fairness

For service firms operating in the United States, hassle-free and fast recovery procedures that lead to compensation for any losses or inconveniences triggered by a service failure are preferred by customers. Although compensation is generally the primary driver of American customers' fairness perceptions, speed and convenience in the recovery process also appear to be valued. In Eastern cultures, a genuine apology from a manager (rather than a customer-contact employee) is particularly desirable; such a procedure allows customers to regain "face" in the eyes of their family and friends. Eastern customers would also prefer to have a sense of control, so having management constantly inform them of what is being done to rectify the situation is also appealing to them.

In service recovery, as in any service situation, companies need to be sensitive to the fact that culture and other factors play a role. As these studies suggest, customers in all cultures expect strong service recovery but preferences for the type of recovery or which fairness dimension to emphasize may vary.

Sources: A. S. Mattila and P. G. Patterson, "Service Recovery and Fairness Perceptions in Collectivist and Individualist Contexts," *Journal of Service Research* 6 (May 2004), pp. 336–346; A. S. Mattila and P. G. Patterson, "The Impact of Culture on Consumers' Perceptions of Service Recovery Efforts," *Journal of Retailing* 80 (Fall 2004), pp. 196–206.

so that the recovery effort can match their individual circumstances. In some cases, particularly in business-to-business services, companies actually ask the customer, "What can we do to compensate you for our failure?" Many times what the customer asks for is actually less than the company might have expected.

Fair procedures are characterized by clarity, speed, and absence of hassles. Unfair procedures are those that customers perceive as slow, prolonged, illogical, and inconvenient. Customers also feel it is unfair if they have to prove their case—when the company's assumption seems to be they are wrong or lying until they can prove otherwise.

In the Club Med case in Exhibit 7.2, the recovery happened as quickly as possible when the passengers landed in Mexico. Even though the problems were not Club Med's fault, the company went out of its way to compensate the delayed guests immediately on arrival. The vacationers had no more hassles once they were on the ground.

Interactional Fairness

Above and beyond providing fair compensation and hassle-free, quick procedures, firms need to treat customers politely, with care and honesty, during the service recovery process. This form of fairness can dominate the others if customers feel the company and its employees have uncaring attitudes and have done little to try to resolve the problem. This type of behavior on the part of employees may seem strange—why would they treat customers rudely or in an uncaring manner under these circumstances? Often it is due to lack of training and empowerment—a frustrated frontline employee who has no authority to compensate the customer may easily respond in an aloof or uncaring manner, especially if the customer is angry and/or rude.

In the Club Med case in Exhibit 7.2, Silvio de Bortoli and his staff were gracious, caring, and upbeat when they greeted the long-delayed passengers. They personally met them at the airport, even though it was late at night. They even involved other guests already staying at the resort to greet the new arrivals and party with them, making them feel welcome and helping to give their vacation a jump start.

Cultivate Relationships with Customers

In Chapter 6 we discussed the importance of developing long-term relationships with customers. One additional benefit of relationship marketing is that if the firm fails in service delivery, those customers who have a strong relationship with the firm are often more forgiving of service failures and more open to the firm's service recovery efforts. That is, it may be easier to "fix the customer" if the firm has established a strong relationship with that customer; indeed, research suggests that strong customer–firm relationships can help shield the firm from the negative effects of failures on customer satisfaction.[37] To illustrate, one study demonstrated that the presence of rapport between customers and employees provided several service recovery benefits, including increased postfailure satisfaction, increased loyalty intentions, and decreased negative word-of-mouth communication.[38] Another study found that customers who expect the relationship to continue also tend to have lower service recovery expectations and may demand less immediate compensation for a failure because they consider the balance of equity across a longer time horizon.[39] Thus, cultivation of strong customer relationships can provide an important buffer to service firms when failures occur.[40]

Strategy Insight   Eliciting Complaints and Reports of Service Failure

Service failures can occur in a variety of ways and at numerous times throughout the service delivery process. However, in many cases it is difficult, if not impossible, for the firm to know that a service failure has occurred unless the customer informs the firm accordingly. Unfortunately, a relatively low percentage of customers will actually complain to the firm. Thus, a major challenge facing management is how to get customers to complain when they experience a service failure and/or they are not satisfied with service delivery. What can a firm do to elicit complaints? Here are some issues to consider.

- *Develop the mind-set that complaints are good.* Too often the complaining customer is looked on by employees in the organization as the *enemy*— someone to be conquered and subdued. The more prudent approach is to develop the mind-set that the complaining customer is the firm's *friend.* Complaints provide valuable feedback to the firm, giving it the opportunity not only to address the service failure for the complaining customer but also to identify problems that other (less vocal) customers may also be experiencing (the "tip of the iceberg" phenomenon). One scholar suggests that "complainers ought to be treated with the dignity and respect afforded to

the highest-priced analysts and consultants." One company puts all customers who have complained on a VIP list. Accepting complaints is truly reflective of firms who are close to their customers.

- *Make complaining easy.* If the firm truly wants to hear from customers who experience poor service, it needs to make it easy for them to share their experiences with the firm. Sometimes customers have no idea whom to speak to if they have a complaint, what the process is, or what will be involved. Complaining should be easy—the last thing customers want when they are dissatisfied is to face a complex, difficult-to-access process for complaining. Customers should know where to go and/or whom to talk to when they encounter problems, and they should be made to feel confident that something positive will result from their efforts. Technological advances have made it possible to provide customers with multiple avenues to complain, including toll-free customer call centers, company e-mail addresses, and website feedback forms. The firm should regularly communicate to customers that complaining is easy and that it welcomes and appreciates such feedback.

- *Be an active listener.* Employees should be encouraged and trained to actively listen to customers,

SERVICE RECOVERY STRATEGIES: FIXING THE PROBLEM

Often the most pressing and immediate need in service recovery is to "fix the customer." However, in many situations the actual problem created by the poor service delivery also needs to be fixed. This may require reworking, redoing, or redelivering the service, if possible, to provide what the customer initially expected. And, if the problem is likely to recur for this or other customers, then the service delivery process may need to be fixed, too. This section highlights strategies that can be used to help the firm "fix the problem" both in the short term and in the long term.

Encourage and Track Complaints

Even if an organization aims for 100 percent service quality, failures occur. A critical component of a service recovery strategy is thus to encourage and track complaints. Our Strategy Insight describes several ways in which customer complaints can be encouraged.

Firms can utilize a number of ways to encourage and track complaints. Customer research can be designed specifically for this purpose through satisfaction surveys, critical incident studies, and lost customer research, as discussed in Chapter 5. Toll-free call centers, e-mail, and a variety of social media are now used to facilitate, encourage, and track complaints. Software applications in a number of companies also allow complaints to be analyzed, sorted, responded to, and tracked automatically.[41]

particularly to see if they can pick up on any cues to suggest less-than-ideal service. A restaurant customer might respond "fine" to the waiter's question "How is your meal?" However, the customer's body language and tone of voice, or the amount of food not eaten, might indicate that all is not fine. Some customers may not be assertive in voicing their displeasure, but they may drop clues to suggest that something is amiss. Employees as well as managers should be consistently listening not only to the customer's actual words but also to what he or she may really be trying or wanting to communicate.

- *Ask customers about specific service issues.* A very simple, informal way to find out about any service failure is simply to ask. Managers at one hotel with a high percentage of business travelers make it a point to be at the front desk between 7:45 and 8:45 a.m. every day, because approximately 80 percent of their business travelers check out at that time. During the checkout process, managers avoid questions that can be answered with a simple "yes," "OK," or "fine" (e.g., "How was your stay?") and instead ask questions that force customers to provide specific feedback (e.g., "How could we have improved the technology accommodations in your room?" or "What needs to be done to improve our recreation center?"). Asking customers very specific questions that cannot be answered with a simple "yes" or "no" may provide customers with an easy way to point out expectations that were not fulfilled.

- *Conduct short, trailer surveys.* A follow-up telephone call to a customer still in the midst of the service experience can help to identify problems in real time and thus enable real-time recovery. Enterprise Rent-A-Car Company, for example, regularly calls customers a day after they have picked up a rental car and asks the customer if everything is okay with the car. Customers who report problems, such as a broken window or a car that smells of smoke, are brought a replacement vehicle that day without any additional questions or hassle. Trailer surveys work especially well in business-to-business services in addressing problems early, before they become major issues.

Sources: S. S. Tax and S. W. Brown, "Recovering and Learning from Service Failure," *Sloan Management Review* 40 (Fall 1998), pp. 75–88; O. Harari, "Thank Heaven for Complainers," *Management Review* 81 (January 1992), p. 59.

In some cases technology can anticipate problems and complaints before they happen, allowing service employees to diagnose problems before the customer recognizes they exist. At companies such as IBM, John Deere, and Caterpillar, information systems have been implemented to anticipate equipment failures and to send out an electronic alert to the local field technician with the nature of the problem as well as which parts and tools will be needed to make the repair—a repair the customer does not yet know is needed.[42]

Learn from Recovery Experiences

"Problem-resolution situations are more than just opportunities to fix flawed services and strengthen ties with customers. They are also a valuable—but frequently ignored or underutilized—source of diagnostic, prescriptive information for improving customer service."[43] By tracking service recovery efforts and solutions, managers can often learn about systematic problems in the delivery system that need fixing. By conducting root-cause analysis, firms can identify the sources of the problems and modify processes, sometimes almost eliminating the need for recovery. At Ritz-Carlton Hotels, all employees carry service recovery forms called "instant action forms" with them at all times, so that they can immediately record service failures and suggest actions to address them. Each employee "owns" any complaint that he or she receives and is responsible for seeing that service recovery occurs. In turn, the

FIGURE 7.6
The 100 Percent
Hampton Inn®
Hotels Guarantee

employees report to management these sources of service failure and the remedies. At Hampton Inn® Hotels, whenever the service guarantee (see Figure 7.6) is invoked, the reason for the customer's dissatisfaction is recorded as part of the process and the information forwarded to management. Such information is then entered into a database and analyzed to identify patterns and systemic service issues that need to be fixed. If common themes are observed across a number of failure situations, changes are made to service processes or attributes. In addition, at the Ritz-Carlton the information is entered into the customer's personal data file, so when that customer stays at any Ritz-Carlton again (no matter what hotel), employees can be aware of the previous experience, ensuring that it does not happen again for that customer.

Learn from Lost Customers

Another key component of an effective service recovery strategy is to learn from the customers who defect or decide to leave. Formal marketing research to discover the reasons customers have left can assist in preventing failures in the future. This type of research is difficult, even painful for companies, however. No one really likes to examine their failures. Yet such examination is essential for preventing the same mistakes and losing more customers in the future.[44]

As presented in Chapter 5, lost customer research typically involves in-depth probing of customers to determine their true reasons for leaving. This information is most effectively obtained by depth interviews, administered by skilled interviewers who truly understand the business. It may be best to have this type of research done by senior people in the company, particularly in business-to-business contexts in which customers are large and the impact of even one lost customer is great. The type of depth analysis often requires a series of "why" questions or "tell me more about that" questions to get at the actual, core reason for the customer's defection.[45]

In conducting this kind of research, a firm must focus on important or profitable customers who have left—not just everyone who has left the company. An insurance company in Australia once began this type of research to learn about their lost customers, only to find that the customers they were losing tended to be their least profitable customers, anyway. They quickly determined that depth research on how to keep these unprofitable customers would not be a good investment!

Make the Service Fail-Safe—Do It Right the First Time!

The first rule of service quality, and arguably the best service recovery strategy, is to do it right the first time. In this way recovery is unnecessary, customers get what they expect, and the costs of redoing the service and compensating for errors can be avoided. As you have already learned, reliability, or doing it right the first time, is the most important dimension of service quality across industry contexts.[46] Indeed, research suggests that many customers stay in a relationship because they have not experienced a (negative) critical incident.[47]

Dick Chase, noted service operations expert, suggests that services adopt the quality notion of *poka yokes* to improve service reliability.[48] Poka yokes are automatic warnings or controls in place to ensure that mistakes are not made; essentially, they are quality control mechanisms, typically used on assembly lines. Chase suggests that poka yokes can be devised in service settings to "mistakeproof" the service, ensure that essential procedures are followed, and ensure that service steps are carried out in the proper order and in a timely manner. In a hospital setting, numerous poka yokes ensure that procedures are followed to avoid potentially life-threatening mistakes. For example, trays for surgical instruments have indentations for specific instruments, and each instrument is nested in its appropriate spot. In this way surgeons and their staff know that all instruments are in their places prior to closing the patient's incision.[49]

Similarly, poka yokes can be devised to ensure that the tangibles associated with the service are clean and well maintained and that documents are accurate and up-to-date. Poka yokes can also be implemented for employee behaviors (checklists, role-playing and practice, reminder signs) and even for ensuring that customers perform effectively. Many of the strategies we discuss in Parts 4 and 5 of the text ("Aligning Service Design and Standards" and "Delivering and Performing Service") are aimed at ensuring service reliability and can be viewed as applications of the basic fail-safe notion of poka yokes.

Even more fundamentally, it is important for a firm to create a culture of zero defections to ensure doing it right the first time.[50] Within a zero defections culture, everyone understands the importance of reliability. Employees and managers aim to satisfy every customer and look for ways to improve service. Employees in a zero defections culture fully understand and appreciate the "relationship value of a customer" concept that was presented in Chapter 6. Thus, they are motivated to provide quality service *every time* and to *every customer.*

SERVICE GUARANTEES

A guarantee is a particular type of recovery tool that can be used to both "fix the customer" and "fix the problem." In a business context, a *guarantee* is a pledge or assurance that a product offered by a firm will perform as promised, and if not then some form of reparation will be undertaken by the firm. Although guarantees are relatively common for manufactured products, they have only recently been used for services. Traditionally, many people believed that a service simply could not be guaranteed, given its intangible and variable nature. What would be guaranteed? With a tangible product, the customer is guaranteed that it will perform as promised and, if not, that it can be returned. With a service, it is generally not possible to receive a return or to "undo" what has been performed. The skepticism about service guarantees is being dispelled, however, as more and more companies find they can guarantee their service and that there are tremendous benefits for doing so.

Companies are finding that effective service guarantees can complement the company's service recovery strategy—serving as one tool to help support the service recovery strategies depicted in Figure 7.4. The Hampton Inn® Hotels guarantee shown in Figure 7.6 is an example of such an effective guarantee.

Characteristics of Effective Guarantees

Certain characteristics tend to make some guarantees more effective than others. Christopher Hart has argued that the most effective guarantees tend to have similar characteristics, including being unconditional, meaningful, easy to understand, and easy to invoke.[51]

Unconditional

Hart contends that effective guarantees should be *unconditional*—no strings attached. The Hampton Inn® Hotels guarantee does not impose any conditions. Some guarantees can appear as if they were written by the legal department (and often are), with all kinds of restrictions, proof required, and limitations. Guarantees with such restrictions are generally not effective.

Meaningful

An effective guarantee should be *meaningful*. Guaranteeing what is obvious or expected is not meaningful to customers. For example, a water delivery company offered a guarantee to deliver water on the day promised or a free jug of water would be provided next time. In that industry, delivery on the day scheduled was an expectation nearly always met by every competitor—thus, the guarantee was not meaningful to the customer. It was a bit like guaranteeing four wheels on an automobile! The payout, if a problem occurs, should also be meaningful. Customers expect to be reimbursed in a manner that fully compensates them for their dissatisfaction, their time, and even for the hassle involved. One of us has offered university students a guarantee in our Services Markeing classes; compensation for poor service, which includes reimbursement for the cost of the three-credit course, is generally perceived by students as quite meaningful.[52]

Easy to Understand

A firm's guarantee should also be *easy to understand* and communicate to both customers and employees. Sometimes the wording is confusing, the guarantee language is verbose, or the guarantee contains so many restrictions and conditions that neither customers nor employees are certain what is being guaranteed. Bennigan's restaurants guarantees that lunch will be served quickly—within 15 minutes with its Lunch Crunch guarantee. The promise "It's Fast or It's Free" makes it clear to customers that they will not have to spend a lot of time waiting for lunch; the guarantee also makes it clear to employees that lunches should take no longer than 15 minutes to get to customers.

Easy to Invoke

Similarly, an effective guarantee should be *easy to invoke*. British Airways offered a guarantee, presented on page 203, to exceed the expectations of its business class customers. To invoke the guarantee, customers merely had to complete an online form and explain why the service at British Airways did not meet or exceed their expectations. Requiring customers to write a detailed letter and/or provide documented proof of service failure are common pitfalls that make invoking a guarantee time-consuming and not worth it to the customer, particularly if the dollar value of the service is relatively low.

Types of Service Guarantees

Service guarantees can be *unconditional satisfaction guarantees* or *service attribute guarantees*. For unconditional satisfaction guarantees, any aspect of the service, whether related to the outcome or the delivery process, should be to the customer's liking—there are no limits or conditions. The Hampton Inn® Hotels guarantee is an

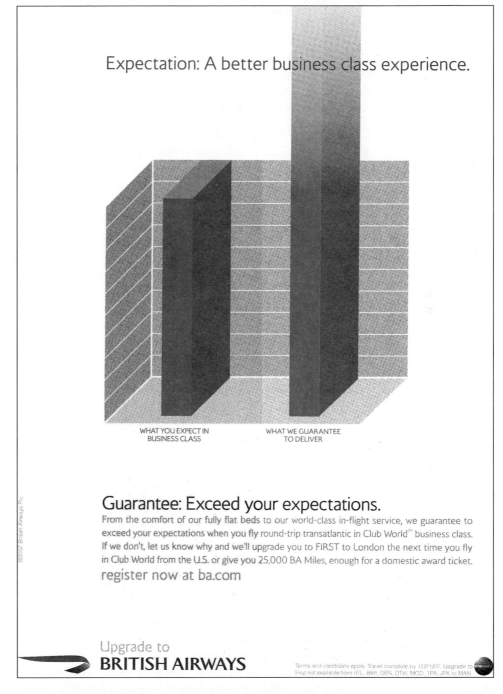

unconditional satisfaction guarantee. In another context, Bain & Company, a management consulting firm, has offered some clients an unconditional guarantee for its services.[53] If clients are unhappy, they do not pay for the service. Pro Staff offers an unconditional guarantee to any client using its staffing service; if the client organization is unhappy with the person assigned to the client, the client is not billed. Lands' End, a catalog retailer, has abbreviated its guarantee to "Guaranteed. Period."

In other cases, firms offer guarantees of particular attributes of the service that are important to customers. FedEx guarantees package delivery by a certain time. In introducing a new seat design in first class, British Airways advertised "Comfort guaranteed or you get 25,000 miles." McDonald's advertised a guarantee that stated "Hot Food; Fast, Friendly Delivery; Double-Check Drive-Thru Accuracy. . . We'll make it right, or your next meal is on us." The Bennigan's guarantee mentioned earlier ensured customers would not have to wait longer than 15 minutes to receive their lunch. In all these cases, the companies have guaranteed specific elements of the service that they know are important to customers.

Benefits of Service Guarantees

Service organizations are now recognizing that guarantees can serve not only as a marketing tool but also as a means for defining, cultivating, and maintaining quality throughout an organization. The benefits to the company of an effective service guarantee are numerous:[54]

- *A good guarantee forces the company to focus on its customers.* To develop a meaningful guarantee, the company must know what is important to its customers—what they expect and value. In many cases "satisfaction" is guaranteed, but for the guarantee to work effectively, the company must clearly understand what satisfaction means for its customers (what they value and expect).

- *An effective guarantee sets clear standards for the organization.* It prompts the company to clearly define what it expects of its employees and to communicate that expectation to them. The guarantee gives employees service-oriented goals that can quickly align employee behaviors with customer strategies. For example, Pizza Hut's guarantee "If you're not satisfied with your pizza, let our restaurant know. We'll make it right or give you your money back" lets employees know exactly what they should do if a customer complains. It is also clear to employees that making it right for the customer is an important company goal.

- *A good guarantee generates immediate and relevant feedback from customers.* Having a guarantee can provide an incentive for customers to complain and thereby provides more representative feedback to the company than simply relying on a relatively small number of customers to voice their concerns. The guarantee communicates to customers that they have the right to complain.

- *When the guarantee is invoked there is an instant opportunity to recover.* Dissatisfaction can perhaps be controlled, or at least not allowed to grow, if the customer is exposed to instant recovery. A quick recovery can go a long way toward satisfying the customer and helping retain loyalty.

- *Information generated through the guarantee can be tracked and integrated into continuous improvement efforts.* Guarantees can provide a somewhat structured mechanism for listening to the cusomter, thus helping to close the listening gap. A feedback link between customers and service operations decisions can be strengthened through the guarantee.

- *For customers, the guarantee reduces their sense of risk and builds confidence in the organization.* Because services are intangible and often highly personal or ego-involving, customers seek information and cues that will help reduce their sense of uncertainty. Guarantees have been shown to reduce risk and increase positive evaluation of the service prior to purchase.[55]

The bottom line for the company is that an effective guarantee can affect profitability through building customer awareness and loyalty, through positive word-of-mouth communication, and through reduction in costs as service improvements are made and

Exhibit 7.4 Questions to Consider in Implementing a Service Guarantee

DECIDING WHO DECIDES

- Is there a guarantee champion in the company?
- Is senior management committed to a guarantee?
- Is the guarantee design a team effort?
- Are customers providing input?

WHEN DOES A GUARANTEE MAKE SENSE?

- How high are quality standards?
- Can we afford a guarantee?
- How high is customer risk?
- Are competitors offering a guarantee?
- Is the company's culture compatible with a guarantee?

WHAT TYPE OF GUARANTEE SHOULD WE OFFER?

- Should we offer an unconditional guarantee or a specific-outcome one?
- Is our service measurable?
- What should our specific guarantee be about?
- What are the uncontrollables?
- Is the company particularly susceptible to unreasonable triggerings?
- What should the payout be?
- Will a refund send the wrong message?
- Could a full refund make customers feel guilty?
- Is the guarantee easy to invoke?

Source: A. L. Ostrom and C. W. L. Hart, "Service Guarantees: Research and Practice," in *Handbook of Services Marketing and Management,* ed. D. Iacobucci and T. Swartz (Thousand Oaks, CA: Sage Publications, 2000). © 2000 by Sage Publications. Reprinted by permission of Sage Publications.

service recovery expenses are reduced. Indirectly, the guarantee can reduce costs of employee turnover through creating a more positive service culture.

When to Use (or Not Use) a Guarantee

Service guarantees are not appropriate for every company and certainly not in every service situation. Before putting a guarantee strategy in place, a firm needs to address a number of important questions (see Exhibit 7.4). A guarantee is probably *not* the right strategy when:

- *Existing service quality in the company is poor.* Before instituting a guarantee, the company should fix any significant quality problems. A guarantee will certainly draw attention to failures and to poor service quality, so the costs of implementing the guarantee could easily outweigh any benefits. These costs include actual monetary payouts to customers for poor service as well as costs associated with customer goodwill.

- *A guarantee does not fit the company's image.* If the company already has a reputation for very high quality, and in fact implicitly guarantees its service, then a formal guarantee is most likely unnecessary. For example, if the Four Seasons Hotel were to offer an explicit guarantee, it could confuse customers who already expect the highest of quality, implicitly guaranteed, from this high-end hotel chain. Research suggests that the benefits of offering a guarantee for a high-end hotel like the Four Seasons or the Ritz-Carlton may be significantly less than the benefits that a hotel of lesser quality would offer, and the benefits might not be justified by the costs.[56]

- *Service quality is truly uncontrollable.* Service providers can encounter situations in which service quality is truly uncontrollable. To illustrate, it would not be a good practice for a university to guarantee that all MBA students will get the job they want immediately upon graduation—it cannot control what jobs are available in the marketplace. Similarly, an airline flying out of Chicago in the winter would probably not guarantee on-time departure because of the unpredictability and uncontrollability of the weather.

- *Potential exists for customer abuse of the guarantee.* Fear of opportunistic customer behavior, including customer cheating or fraudulent invocation of service guarantees, is a common reason that firms hesitate to offer guarantees.[57] One study found that guarantees are more likely to be abused when offered in situations in which a large percentage of customers are not regular (repeat) customers.[58] However, customer abuse of service guarantees is fairly minimal and not at all widespread.[59] For example, each year Hampton Inn® Hotels refunds less than 0.5 percent of its total room revenue to dissatisfied customers.

- *Costs of the guarantee outweigh the benefits.* As it would with any quality investment, the company will want to carefully calculate expected costs (payouts for failures and costs of making improvements) against anticipated benefits (customer loyalty, quality improvements, attraction of new customers, word-of-mouth advertising).

- *Customers perceive little risk in the service.* Guarantees are usually most effective when customers are uncertain about the company and/or the quality of its services. The guarantee can allay uncertainties and help reduce risk.[60] If customers perceive little risk, if the service is relatively inexpensive with many potential alternative providers, and if quality is relatively invariable, then a guarantee will likely produce little effectiveness for the company other than perhaps some promotional value.

SWITCHING VERSUS STAYING FOLLOWING SERVICE RECOVERY

Ultimately, how a service failure is handled and the customer's reaction to the recovery effort can influence future decisions to remain loyal to the service provider or to switch to another provider. In a study of 720 HMO members, researchers found that those who were not satisfied with service recovery were much more likely to switch to a different health care provider than were those who were happy with how their problems were addressed.[61] Whether customers switch to a new provider following service failure will depend, in addition, on a number of other factors. The magnitude and criticality of the failure will clearly be a factor in future repurchase decisions. The more serious the failure, the more likely the customer is to switch, no matter what the recovery effort.[62]

The nature of the customer's relationship with the firm may also influence whether the customer stays or switches providers. Research suggests that customers who have "true relationships" with their service providers are more forgiving of poorly handled service failures and are less likely to switch than are those who have a "pseudo-relationship" or a "first-time encounter" type of relationship.[63] A true relationship is one in which the customer has had repeated contact over time with the same service provider. A first-time encounter relationship is one in which the customer has had only one contact, on a transaction basis, with the provider. And a pseudo-relationship is one in which the customer has interacted many times with the same company, but with different service providers each time.

Other research reveals that a customer's attitude toward switching strongly influences whether he or she ultimately stays with the provider and that this attitude will be even more influential than basic satisfaction with the service.[64] This research suggests that certain customers will have a greater propensity to switch service providers no matter how their service failure situations are handled. Research in an online service context, for example, shows that demographic factors such as age and income as well as individual factors such as risk aversion influence whether a customer continues to use an online service or switches to another provider.[65] The profile of an "online service switcher" emerged in the research as a person who was influenced to subscribe to the service through positive word-of-mouth communication, who used the service less, who was less satisfied and less involved with the service, who had a lower income and education level, and who had a lower propensity for taking risks.

Finally, the decision to switch to a different service provider may not occur immediately following service failure or poor service recovery but may follow an accumulation of events. That is, service switching can be viewed as a process resulting from a series of decisions and critical service encounters over time rather than one specific moment in time when a decision is made.[66] This process orientation suggests that companies could track customer interactions and predict the likelihood of defection based on a series of events, intervening earlier in the process to head off the customer's decision to switch.

Although customers decide to switch service providers for a variety of reasons, service failure and poor service recovery are often a cause of such behavior. A study of approximately 500 service-switching incidents identified eight broad themes underlying the decision to defect.[67] These themes (pricing, inconvenience, core service failure, service encounter failure, response to service failure, competition, ethical problems, and involuntary switching) are shown in Figure 7.7. In about 200 of the incidents, a single theme was identified as the cause for switching service providers, and the two largest categories were related to service failure. Core service failure was the cause of switching for 25 percent of the respondents, and service encounter failure was the reason for switching services for an additional 20 percent of the sample. In incidents that listed two themes, 29 percent listed core service failure and 18 percent service encounter failure as contributing to their desire to switch providers; poor response to failure was mentioned by an additional 11 percent of the respondents as the cause for switching. As these findings suggest, service failure can cause customers to switch companies. To minimize the impact of service failure, excellent service recovery is needed.

FIGURE 7.7
Causes of Service Switching

Source: Reprinted with permission of the American Marketing Association. From S. Keaveney, "Customer Switching Behavior in Service Industries: An Exploratory Study," *Journal of Marketing* 59 (April 1995), pp. 71–82.

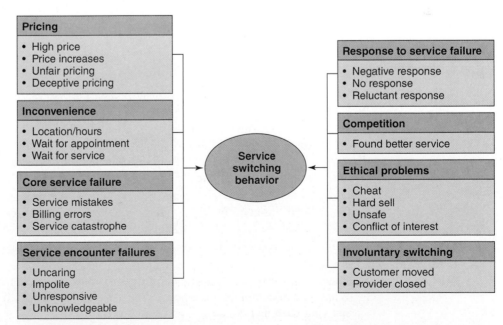

Summary

Part 3 of this text (Chapters 5, 6, and 7) focuses on the critical importance of understanding customer expectations as well as many of the strategies firms use to accomplish this goal. Part of understanding customer expectations is being prepared for and knowing what to do when things go wrong or when the service fails. In this chapter we focused on service recovery, the actions taken by an organization in response to a service failure.

You learned in this chapter the importance of an effective service recovery strategy for retaining customers and increasing positive word-of-mouth communication. Another major benefit of an effective service recovery strategy is that the information it provides can be useful for service improvement. The potential downsides of poor service recovery are tremendous—negative word of mouth, lost customers, and declining business when quality issues are not addressed.

In this chapter you learned how customers respond to service failures and why some complain, while others do not. You learned that customers expect to be treated fairly when they complain—not just in terms of the actual outcome or compensation they receive but also in terms of the procedures used and how they are treated interpersonally. We pointed out in this chapter that there is tremendous room for improvement in service recovery effectiveness across firms and industries.

The second half of the chapter focused on two types of strategies that firms are using for service recovery. To "fix the customer" after a service failure, firms should (1) respond quickly; (2) provide appropriate communication with customers after the service has failed; (3) treat customers fairly throughout the service recovery process; and (4) cultivate relationships with customers to perhaps create a buffer when failures do occur. To "fix the problem" and prevent future recurrences of a service failure, firms should (1) encourage and track complaints; (2) learn from recovery experiences; (3) learn from lost customers; and, ideally, (4) make the service fail-safe by doing it right the first time. The chapter ended with a discussion of service guarantees as a tool used by many firms to facilitate service recovery and to listen to customers—thereby helping to close the listening gap. You learned the elements of a good guarantee, the benefits of service guarantees, and the pros and cons of using guarantees under various circumstances.

Discussion Questions

1. Why is it important for a service firm to have a strong recovery strategy? Think of a time when you received less-than-desired service from a particular service organization. Was any effort made to recover? What did the firm do to "fix the customer"? What was done to "fix the problem"? What should/could have been done differently? Do you still buy service from the organization? Why or why not? Did you tell others about your experience?

2. Discuss the benefits to a company of having an effective service recovery strategy. Describe an instance in which you experienced (or delivered as an employee) an effective service recovery. In what ways did the company benefit in this situation?

3. Explain the recovery paradox, and discuss its implications for a service firm manager.

4. Discuss the types of actions that customers can take in response to a service failure. What type of complainer are you? Why? As a manager, would you want to encourage your customers to be voicers? If so, how?

5. Review Exhibit 7.1. What would you have done if you were on the management team at Doubletree Inn?

6. Explain the logic behind these two quotes: "a complaint is a gift" and "the customer who complains is your friend."

7. Choose a firm you are familiar with. Describe how you would design an ideal service recovery strategy for that organization.

8. What are the benefits to the company of an effective service guarantee? Should every service organization have one?

9. Describe three service guarantees that are currently offered by companies or organizations in addition to the ones already described in the chapter. (Examples are readily available on the Internet.) Are your examples good guarantees or poor guarantees based on the criteria presented in this chapter?

Exercises

1. Write a letter of complaint (or voice your complaint in person) to a service organization from which you have experienced less-than-desired service. What do you expect the organization to do to recover? (Later, report to the class the results of your complaint, whether you were satisfied with the recovery, what could/should have been done differently, and whether you will continue using the service.)

2. Interview five people about their service recovery experiences. What happened, and what did they expect the firm to do? Were they treated fairly based on the definition of recovery fairness presented in the chapter? Will they return to the company in the future?

3. Interview a manager about service recovery strategies used in his or her firm. Use the strategies shown in Figure 7.4 to frame your questions.

4. Reread the Technology Spotlight in this chapter, featuring Cisco Systems. Visit Cisco System's support website (www.cisco.com/support). Review what the company is doing to help its customers solve their own problems. Compare what Cisco is doing with the self-service efforts of another service provider of your choice.

5. Choose a service you are familiar with. Explain the service offered and develop a good service guarantee for it. Discuss why your guarantee is a good one, and list the benefits to the company of implementing it.

Notes

1. For research that shows different types of service failures, see M. J. Bitner, B. H. Booms, and M. S. Tetreault, "The Service Encounter: Diagnosing Favorable and Unfavorable Incidents," *Journal of Marketing* 54 (January 1990), pp. 71–84; S. M. Keaveney, "Customer Switching Behavior in Service Industries: An Exploratory Study," *Journal of Marketing* 59 (April 1995), pp. 71–82.

2. Information provided by TARP Worldwide Inc., based on data from 10 studies (representing responses from more than 8,000 customers) conducted in 2006 and 2007. Companies from the following industries were included: retail (stores, catalog and online), auto financing, and insurance (property/casualty).

3. For research on important outcomes associated with service recovery, see S. S. Tax, S. W. Brown, and M. Chandrashekaran, "Customer Evaluations of Service Complaint Experiences: Implications for Relationship Marketing," *Journal of Marketing* 62 (April 1998), pp. 60–76; S. S. Tax and S. W. Brown, "Recovering and Learning from Service Failure," *Sloan Management Review* 40 (Fall 1998), pp. 75–88;

A. K. Smith and R. N. Bolton, "An Experimental Investigation of Customer Reactions to Service Failure and Recovery Encounters," *Journal of Service Research* 1 (August 1998), pp. 65–81; R. N. Bolton, "A Dynamic Model of the Customer's Relationship with a Continuous Service Provider: The Role of Satisfaction," *Marketing Science* 17, no. 1 (1998), pp. 45–65; A. K. Smith and R. N. Bolton, "The Effect of Customers' Emotional Responses to Service Failures on Their Recovery Effort Evaluations and Satisfaction Judgments," *Journal of the Academy of Marketing Science* 30 (Winter 2002), pp. 5–23; C. M. Voorhees, M. K. Brady, and D. M. Horowitz, "A Voice from the Silent Masses: An Exploratory and Comparative Analysis of Noncomplainers," *Journal of the Academy of Marketing Science* 34 (Fall 2006), pp. 514–527; C. Orsingher, S. Valentini, and M. de Angelis, "A Meta-analysis of Satisfaction with Complaint Handling in Services," *Journal of the Academy of Marketing Science* 38 (2010), pp. 169–186.

4. Information included in Figure 7.2 is based on data from 10 studies conducted in 2006 and 2007, TARP Worldwide Inc.

5. Ibid; Voorhees, Brady, and Horowitz, "A Voice from the Silent Masses."

6. 2007, 2005, and 2004 National Customer Rage Studies conducted by Customer Care Alliance in collaboration with the Center for Services Leadership at Arizona State University's W. P. Carey School of Business.

7. Tax and Brown, "Recovering and Learning from Service Failure."

8. Aggregated results of 2003–2007 National Customer Rage surveys conducted by Customer Care Alliance.

9. See C. W. Hart, J. L. Heskett, and W. E. Sasser Jr., "The Profitable Art of Service Recovery," *Harvard Business Review* 68 (July–August 1990), pp. 148–156; M. A. McCollough and S. G. Bharadwaj, "The Recovery Paradox: An Examination of Consumer Satisfaction in Relation to Disconfirmation, Service Quality, and Attribution Based Theories," in *Marketing Theory and Applications,* ed. C. T. Allen et al. (Chicago: American Marketing Association, 1992), p. 119.

10. C. A. de Matos, J. L. Henrique, and C. A. V. Rossi, "Service Recovery Paradox: A Meta-analysis," *Journal of Service Research* 10 (August 2007), pp. 60–77.

11. Smith and Bolton, "An Experimental Investigation of Customer Reactions to Service Failure and Recovery Encounters."

12. V. P. Magnini, J. B. Ford, E. P. Markowski, and E. D. Honeycutt Jr., "The Service Recovery Paradox: Justifiable Theory or Smoldering Myth?" *Journal of Services Marketing* 21, no. 3 (2007), pp. 213–225; J. G. Maxham III and R. G. Netemeyer, "A Longitudinal Study of Complaining Customers' Evaluations of Multiple Service Failures and Recovery Efforts," *Journal of Marketing* 66 (October 2002), pp. 57–71; M. A. McCullough, L. L. Berry, and M. S. Yadav, "An Empirical Investigation of Customer Satisfaction after Service Failure and Recovery," *Journal of Service Research* 3 (November 2000), pp. 121–137.

13. S. Michel and M. L. Meuter, "The Service Recovery Paradox: True but Overrated?" *International Journal of Service Industry Management* 19, no. 4 (2008), pp. 441–457; R. Priluck and V. Lala, "The Impact of the Recovery Paradox on Retailer-Customer Relationships," Managing Service Quality 19, no. 1 (2009), pp. 42-59.

14. For research foundations on typologies of customer responses to failures, see R. L. Day and E. L. Landon Jr., "Towards a Theory of Consumer Complaining Behavior," in *Consumer and Industrial Buying Behavior,* ed. A. Woodside, J. Sheth, and P. Bennett (Amsterdam: North-Holland, 1977); J. Singh, "Consumer

Complaint Intentions and Behavior: Definitional and Taxonomical Issues," *Journal of Marketing* 52 (January 1988), pp. 93–107; J. Singh, "Voice, Exit, and Negative Word-of-Mouth Behaviors: An Investigation across Three Service Categories," *Journal of the Academy of Marketing Science* 18 (Winter 1990), pp. 1–15.

15. Smith and Bolton, "The Effect of Customers' Emotional Responses to Service Failures." M. Zeelenberg and R. Pieters, "Beyond Valence in Customer Dissatisfaction: A Review and New Findings on Behavioral Responses to Regret and Disappointment in Failed Services," *Journal of Business Research* 57 (2004), pp. 445–455.

16. Voorhees, Brady, and Horowitz, "A Voice from the Silent Masses."

17. N. Stephens and K. P. Gwinner, "Why Don't Some People Complain? A Cognitive–Emotive Process Model of Consumer Complaining Behavior," *Journal of the Academy of Marketing Science* 26 (Spring 1998), pp. 172–189.

18. Ibid.

19. For additional reading on customer rage, see J. R. McColl-Kennedy, P. G. Patterson, A. K. Smith, and M. K. Brady, "Customer Rage Episodes: Emotions, Expressions, and Behaviors," *Journal of Retailing* 85, no. 2 (2009), pp. 222–237 and P. G. Patterson, J. R. McColl-Kennedy, A. K. Smith, and Z. Lu, "Customer Rage: Triggers, Tipping Points, and Take-Outs," *California Management Review* 52 (Fall 2009), pp. 6–28.

20. T. Hennig-Thurau, K. P. Gwinner, G. Walsh, and D. D. Gremler, "Electronic Word-of-Mouth via Consumer-Opinion Platforms: What Motivates Consumers to Articulate Themselves on the Internet?" *Journal of Interactive Marketing* 18 (Winter 2004), pp. 38–52.

21. Many such websites exist; examples include www.untied.com (for United Airlines experiences), www.starbucked.com (for Starbucks), and www.homedepotsucks.com (for The Home Depot).

22. J. C. Ward and A. L. Ostrom, "Complaining to the Masses: The Role of Protest Framing in Customer-Created Complaint Web Sites," *Journal of Consumer Research* 33 (September 2006), pp. 220–230.

23. J. Singh, "A Typology of Consumer Dissatisfaction Response Styles," *Journal of Retailing* 66 (Spring 1990), pp. 57–99.

24. Davidow, "Organizational Responses to Customer Complaints."

25. 2007 study conducted by TARP Worldwide Inc.

26. 2007 National Customer Rage Study conducted by Customer Care Alliance.

27. 2007 study conducted by TARP Worldwide Inc.

28. J. R. McColl-Kennedy and B. A. Sparks, "Application of Fairness Theory to Service Failures and Service Recovery," *Journal of Service Research* 5 (February 2003), pp. 251–266; M. Davidow, "Organizational Responses to Customer Complaints: What Works and What Doesn't," *Journal of Service Research* 5 (February 2003), pp. 225–250.

29. 2007 National Customer Rage Study conducted by Customer Care Alliance.

30. Davidow, "Organizational Responses to Customer Complaints." Also see T. Gruber, " I Want to Believe They Really Care: How Complaining Customers Want to Be Treated by Frontline Employees," *Journal of Service Management* 22, no. 1 (2011), pp. 85–110.

31. 2007 National Customer Rage Study conducted by Customer Care Alliance.

32. L. L. Berry and K. Seiders, "Serving Unfair Customers," *Business Horizons* 51 (January/February 2008), pp. 29–37.

33. J. Dunning, A. Pecotich, and A. O'Cass, "What Happens When Things Go Wrong? Retail Sales Explanations and Their Effects," *Psychology and Marketing* 21, no. 7 (2004), pp. 553–572; McColl-Kennedy and Sparks, "Application of Fairness Theory to Service Failures and Service Recovery"; Davidow, "Organizational Responses to Customer Complaints"; Berry and Seiders, "Serving Unfair Customers."

34. See Tax, Brown, and Chandrashekaran, "Customer Evaluations of Service Complaint Experiences"; Tax and Brown, "Recovering and Learning from Service Failure."

35. Tax and Brown, "Recovering and Learning from Service Failure."

36. Smith and Bolton, "The Effect of Customers' Emotional Responses to Service Failures."

37. Hess, Ganesan, and Klein, "Service Failure and Recovery"; Priluck, "Relationship Marketing Can Mitigate Product and Service Failures."

38. T. DeWitt and M. K. Brady, "Rethinking Service Recovery Strategies: The Effect of Rapport on Consumer Responses to Service Failure," *Journal of Service Research* 6 (November 2003), pp. 193–207.

39. Hess, Ganesan, and Klein, "Service Failure and Recovery."

40. Y. Gregoire, T. M. Tripp, and R. Legoux, "When Customer Love Turns into Lasting Hate: The Effects of Relationship Strength and Time on Customer Revenge and Avoidance," *Journal of Marketing* 73 (November 2009), pp. 18–32. However, recent research suggests an opposite effect; that is, customers with strong relationships to a firm may actually "raise the bar" in terms of their service recovery expectations and feel betrayed if the firm fails them. See B. B. Holloway, S. Wang, and S. E. Beatty, "Betrayal? Relationship Quality Implications in Service Recovery," *Journal of Services Marketing* 23, no. 6 (2009), pp. 385–396.

41. L. M. Fisher, "Here Comes Front-Office Automation," *Strategy and Business* 13 (Fourth Quarter, 1999), pp. 53–65; R. A. Shaffer, "Handling Customer Service on the Web," *Fortune,* March 1, 1999, pp. 204, 208.

42. S. W. Brown, "Service Recovery through IT," *Marketing Management* 6, (Fall 1997), pp. 25–27.

43. L. L. Berry and A. Parasuraman, *Marketing Services* (New York: Free Press, 1991), p. 52.

44. F. F. Reichheld, "Learning from Customer Defections," *Harvard Business Review* 74 (March–April 1996), pp. 56–69.

45. Ibid.

46. A. Parasuraman, V. A. Zeithaml, and L. L. Berry, "SERVQUAL: A Multiple-Item Scale for Measuring Consumer Perceptions of Service Quality," *Journal of Retailing* 64 (Spring 1988), pp. 64–79.

47. M. Colgate, V. T.-U. Tong, C. K.-C. Lee, and J. U. Farley, "Back from the Brink: Why Customers Stay," *Journal of Service Research* 9 (February 2007), pp. 211–228.

48. R. B. Chase and D. M. Stewart, "Make Your Service Fail-Safe," *Sloan Management Review* 35 (Spring 1994), pp. 35–44.

49. Ibid.

50. F. R. Reichheld and W. E. Sasser Jr., "Zero Defections: Quality Comes to Services," *Harvard Business Review* 68 (September–October 1990), pp. 105–107.

51. These characteristics are proposed and discussed in C. W. L. Hart, "The Power of Unconditional Guarantees," *Harvard Business Review* 66 (July–August 1988), pp. 54–62; C. W. L. Hart, *Extraordinary Guarantees* (New York: AMACOM, 1993).

52. For more information, see M. A. McCollough and D. D. Gremler, "Guaranteeing Student Satisfaction: An Exercise in Treating Students as Customers," *Journal of Marketing Education* 21 (August 1999), pp. 118–130; D. D. Gremler and M. A. McCollough, "Student Satisfaction Guarantees: An Empirical Examination of Attitudes, Antecedents, and Consequences," *Journal of Marketing Education* 24 (August 2002), pp. 150–160.

53. A. L. Ostrom and C. W. L. Hart, "Service Guarantees: Research and Practice," in *Handbook of Services Marketing and Management,* ed. D. Iacobucci and T. Swartz (Thousand Oaks, CA: Sage, 2000), pp. 299–316.

54. See Ibid.; Hart, "The Power of Unconditional Guarantees," Hart, *Extraordinary Guarantees.*

55. A. L. Ostrom and D. Iacobucci, "The Effect of Guarantees on Consumers' Evaluation of Services," *Journal of Services Marketing* 12, no. 5 (1998), pp. 362–378; S. B. Lidén and P. Skålén, "The Effect of Service Guarantees on Service Recovery," *International Journal of Service Industry Management* 14, no. 1 (2003), pp. 36–58.

56. J. Wirtz, D. Kum, and K. S. Lee, "Should a Firm with a Reputation for Outstanding Service Quality Offer a Service Guarantee?" *Journal of Services Marketing* 14, no. 6 (2000), pp. 502–512.

57. J. Wirtz, "Development of a Service Guarantee Model," *Asia Pacific Journal of Management* 15 (April 1998), pp. 51–75.

58. J. Wirtz and D. Kum, "Consumer Cheating on Service Guarantees," *Journal of the Academy of Marketing Science* 32 (Spring 2004), pp. 159–175.

59. Wirtz, "Development of a Service Guarantee Model."

60. Ostrom and Iacobucci, "The Effect of Guarantees."

61. D. Sarel and H. Marmorstein, "The Role of Service Recovery in HMO Satisfaction," *Marketing Healthcare Services* 19 (Spring 1999), pp. 6–12.

62. McCullough, Berry, and Yadav, "An Empirical Investigation of Customer Satisfaction after Service Failure and Recovery."

63. A. S. Mattila, "The Impact of Relationship Type on Customer Loyalty in a Context of Service Failures," *Journal of Service Research* 4 (November 2001), pp. 91–101; see also R. L. Hess Jr., S. Ganesan, and N. M. Klein, "Service Failure and Recovery: The Impact of Relationship Factors on Customer Satisfaction," *Journal of the Academy of Marketing Science* 31 (Spring 2003), pp. 127–145; R. Priluck, "Relationship Marketing Can Mitigate Product and Service Failures," *Journal of Services Marketing* 17, no. 1 (2003), pp. 37–52.

64. H. S. Bansal and S. F. Taylor, "The Service Provider Switching Model (SPSM)," *Journal of Service Research* 2 (November 1999), pp. 200–218.

65. S. M. Keaveney and M. Parthasarathy, "Customer Switching Behavior in Online Services: An Exploratory Study of the Role of Selected Attitudinal, Behavioral,

and Demographic Factors," *Journal of the Academy of Marketing Science* 29 (Fall 2001), pp. 374–390.

66. I. Roos, "Switching Processes in Customer Relationships," *Journal of Service Research* 2 (August 1999), pp. 68–85; I. Roos and A. Gustafsson, "Understanding Frequent Switching Patterns: A Crucial Element in Managing Customer Relationships," *Journal of Service Research* 10 (August 2007), pp. 93–108.

67. Keaveney, "Customer Switching Behavior in Service Industries."

Part Four

Aligning Service Design and Standards

Meeting customer expectations of service requires not only understanding what the expectations are but also taking action on that knowledge. Action takes several forms: designing innovative services and service improvements based on customer requirements, setting service standards to ensure that services are performed as customers expect, and providing physical evidence that creates the appropriate cues and ambience for service. When action does not take place, there is a gap—service design and standards gap—as shown in the accompanying figure. In this section you will learn to identify the causes of gap 2 as well as effective strategies for closing this gap.

Provider Gap 2 : The Listening Gap

Chapter 8 describes the concepts and tools that are effective for service innovation and design, especially a tool called service blueprinting. Chapter 9 helps you differentiate between company-defined standards and customer-defined standards and to recognize how they can be developed. Chapter 10 explores the strategic importance of physical evidence, the variety of roles it plays, and strategies for effectively designing physical evidence and the servicescape to meet customer expectations.

Chapter Eight

Service Innovation and Design

This chapter's objectives are to

1. Describe the challenges inherent in service innovation and design.
2. Present an array of different types of service innovations, including service offering innovation, innovating around customer roles, and innovation through service solutions.
3. Discuss the importance of engaging customers and employees and employing service design thinking in service innovation.
4. Present the stages and unique elements of the service innovation and development process.
5. Demonstrate the value of service blueprinting as a technique for service innovation and design and how to develop and read service blueprints.

Innovative Services Are the Growth and Profit Engines for PetSmart[1]

Despite the global economic downturn, innovative services continue their strong growth trajectory for the leading U.S. pet retailer, PetSmart. With more than 1,100 pet stores in the United States, Canada, and Puerto Rico and an annual revenue in 2010 of $5.7 billion, PetSmart's vision is to serve "pet parents" through "total lifetime care" of their pets. Pet parents are those people whose furry friends are more like children than pets and who are often willing to sacrifice their own needs before they will sacrifice products or services for their pets. Although down from well over 20 percent average annual revenue growth in the years 2001–2007, PetSmart's services still grew at a rate of 7.5 percent in 2010.

PetSmart views total lifetime care as the provision of products and services to support pets from cradle to grave. Although sales of pet food, toys, and pet accessories are part of this vision, total lifetime care means much more. The company also promotes comprehensive pet training, grooming, day care, and overnight care through its pet hotels. PetSmart PetsHotels not only ensure onsite pet safety and health 24 hours a day but also promote professional care and a total "pet experience." The experience includes group play time, during which pets can socialize with each other; eat special snacks and treats; and a "bone booth," where pet parents can call in and speak

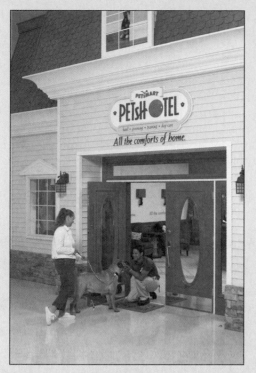

PetSmart's pet hotel concept.

to their pet. Pet parents are offered a choice of accommodations for their pet, ranging from a glassed-in "atrium room" to a suite including a television tuned to animal channels. Other add-on services include personal training camps for dogs during their stay at the hotel, special snacks, and an exit bath. Through its grooming services, PetSmart offers a variety of grooming packages, including bathing, fur trimming and brushing, nail and teeth care, and other specialty services. All of its grooming services carry the "Looks Great Guarantee," that offers money back if pet parents are not pleased with how their pet looks following its appointment.

Innovative services were not always part of PetSmart's offerings to the market. In fact, in the late 1990s, PetSmart was known as PetsMart—emphasis on "Mart"—and was a "big box," warehouse-style retail chain that focused almost exclusively on selling food, toys, and other traditional pet products. The margins on its products were very slim, Walmart was invading its traditional product categories, and a brief experiment with online retail offerings did not solve the dilemma of shrinking profitability. In the early 2000s the move to services, coupled with a focus on operational efficiencies in its traditional retail arena, saved the company. Services have been PetSmart's significant growth and profit engines ever since, and the transition to these innovative services is very consistent with the company's long-term vision and commitment to pets and animals. This commitment is reflected in PetSmart Charities, an independent non-profit organization devoted to animal welfare and pet adoptions. The commitment is also very visible on the website, where every executive is pictured with his or her pet, and every Friday in the corporate offices, when employees are allowed, even encouraged, to bring their pets to work!

For PetSmart, the move to services was bold and required investments in store redesign to accommodate the grooming and hotel areas. These areas needed more space, different layouts, and distinct styles compared to traditional store designs. The move into services also required investments in hiring and training of different types of employees who could interact effectively with pets and pet parents in intimate service settings. For example, when the company moved into grooming in a big way, it realized there were not enough high-quality, trained groomers available to support the new strategy. So the company developed its own 12-week, 400-hour training and certification program for its groomers. The store redesign and groomer training initiatives are indicative of the types of design, human resource, and integration challenges many firms face when they move into the world of service. For PetSmart the move to services was clearly one of the best things it has ever done!

Why has PetSmart, in our chapter opener, been so successful with its service innovations? Why have other companies failed when introducing new services to the market? If you decide to start your own business, or if your company wants to introduce a new service innovation, what can be done to increase the likelihood of success? An analysis of more than 60 studies on new product and service success showed that the dominant and most reliable predictors of success for new introductions relate to *product/service characteristics* (product meeting customer needs, product advantage over competing products, technological sophistication), *strategy characteristics* (dedicated human resources to support the initiative, dedicated research and development [R&D] focused on the new product initiative), *process characteristics* (marketing, predevelopment, technological, and launch proficiencies), and *marketplace characteristics* (market potential).[2] Failures, on the other hand, can be traced to a number of causes: no unique benefits offered, insufficient demand, unrealistic goals for the new product/service, poor fit between the new service and others within the organization's portfolio, poor location, insufficient financial backing, or failure to take the necessary time to develop and introduce the product.[3] Frequently a good service idea fails because of development, design, and specification flaws, topics emphasized in this chapter. As more firms, across industries, move into services as a growth strategy, the challenges of and opportunities for developing and delivering service offerings become even more apparent.

CHALLENGES OF SERVICE INNOVATION AND DESIGN

Because services are largely intangible and process oriented (such as a hospital stay, a golf lesson, an NBA basketball game, or a sophisticated information technology consulting service), they are difficult to describe and communicate. When services are delivered or cocreated with the customer over a long period—a week's resort vacation, a six-month consulting engagement, a multi-year business process outsourcing contract, or 10 weeks on a Weight Watchers program—their complexity increases, and they become even more difficult to define and describe. Further, because services are delivered by employees to customers, they are variable. Rarely are two services alike or experienced in the same way. These fundamental characteristics of service offerings, which we explored in the first chapter of this book, are the heart of the challenge involved in innovating and designing services. Global companies and governments around the world are awakening to these challenges and the recognition that, despite the dominance of services in the world's economies, there is relatively little formal focus on service research and innovation.[4] As the importance of service innovation becomes more and more apparent, significant initiatives are beginning to emerge in countries around the world, as described in our Global Feature.

Because service offerings typically cannot be touched, examined, or easily tried out, people have historically resorted to words in their efforts to describe them. Yet, there are a number of risks inherent in attempting to describe services in words alone.[5] The first risk is *oversimplification.* "To say that 'portfolio management' means 'buying and selling stocks' is like describing the space shuttle as 'something that flies.' Some people will picture a bird, some a helicopter, and some an angel."[6] Words are simply inadequate to describe a complex service system such as financial portfolio management. In our modern global economy, service systems have significantly increased in complexity, often involving networks of service firms, customers, and evolution of offerings over time. Within these complex systems, the risks of oversimplification are even more apparent.

The second risk of using words alone is *incompleteness.* In describing services, people (employees, managers, customers) tend to omit details or elements of the service with which they are not familiar. A person might do a fairly credible job of describing how a discount stock brokerage service takes orders from customers. But would that person be able to describe fully how the monthly statements are created, how the interactive computer system works, and how these two elements of the service are integrated into the order-taking process?

The third risk is *subjectivity.* Any one person describing a service in words will be biased by personal experiences and degree of exposure to the service. There is a natural (and mistaken) tendency to assume that, because all people have gone to a fast-food restaurant, they all understand what that service is. Persons working in different functional areas of the same service organization (a marketing person, an operations person, a finance person) are likely to describe the service very differently as well, biased by their own functional blinders.

A final risk of describing services using words alone is *biased interpretation.* No two people will define "responsive," "quick," or "flexible" in exactly the same way. For example, a supervisor or manager may suggest to a frontline service employee that the employee should try to be more flexible or responsive in providing service to the customer. Unless the term "flexibility" is further defined, the employee is likely to interpret the word differently than the manager.

All these risks and challenges become very apparent in the innovation and service development process, when organizations attempt to design complex services never before experienced by customers or when they attempt to change existing services.[7]

IMPORTANT CONSIDERATIONS FOR SERVICE INNOVATION

In this section we highlight some important considerations when innovating or developing new services. Because of the inherent characteristics of services described in detail in Chapter 1, and the challenges of service development and innovation just described, it has become clear to many service managers that service innovation is different from tangible product innovation. Because services are intangible and process based, and because they frequently involve interactions among and between customers and employees, it is important to involve both customers *and* employees at various points in the innovation process. It is also important to use a systems or design mindset, sometimes referred to as "design thinking," to be sure all elements are considered and integrated. Here we overview these considerations as a backdrop for the tools, techniques, and approaches described in the rest of the chapter.

Involve Customers and Employees

Because services are produced, consumed, and cocreated in real time and often involve interaction between and among employees and customers, it is critical that innovation and new service development processes involve both employees and customers. Employees frequently *are* the service, or at least they perform or deliver the service, and thus their involvement in choosing which new services to develop and how these services should be designed and implemented can be very beneficial. Contact employees are psychologically and physically close to customers and research has shown they can be very helpful in identifying customer needs for innovative new services.[8] Involving employees in service innovation and design also increases the likelihood of new service success because employees can identify the organizational issues that need to be addressed to support the delivery of the service to customers.[9]

*"Boosting innovation in services is central to improving performance of the service sector. . . .
The sector has traditionally been seen as less innovative than manufacturing
and as playing only a supportive role in the innovation system."*

The above quote from the Organization for Economic Cooperation and Development's report titled "Promoting Innovation in Services" is sobering. It is even more sobering when the sheer size and growth of the service sector is factored in. For example, in the United States, services represent nearly 80 percent of the GDP and labor force, and, although the United States is the highest, similar percentages are found in most advanced economies. Further, it is apparent that services are increasing as an economic force in countries such as China, India, and other fast-growing nations. Yet despite the economic domination and growth of services, there is relatively little formal focus within companies and governments on service research and innovation compared with the focus on tangible products and technologies. In recent years, companies and countries have begun to awaken to the need for service innovation. Companies are becoming aware that to grow and profit in the future they need to be globally competitive in services—whether they are a pure service business or a manufacturing or high-tech business. Many national governments are also recognizing the need to invest in service innovation, education, and research, given the realities of the global service economy.

Here we provide some highlights of service innovation initiatives around the globe.

UNITED STATES

Much of the impetus behind the growing awareness of the need for service innovation can be attributed to the leadership of IBM. The company's foresight is catalyzing a global movement to shape the future of service innovation and a potential new discipline IBM calls "service science, management and engineering" (SSME) to develop skilled professionals for the service economy. IBM's research divisions employ 500 service innovation researchers (up from just 50 in 2004), and their message is being heard by other U.S. global companies such as Oracle, Microsoft, and Xerox. Although the primary thrust for service innovation in the United States comes through the private sector, government agencies are beginning to respond as well. In 2007, the America COMPETES Act was passed by Congress, and a section of the act authorizes a study to determine how the federal government should support service research and education. Also in 2007 the Service Research and Innovation Initiative was launched to foster partnerships for service innovation research among business and academics (www.thesrii.org).

CHINA

The Chinese government has emphasized service growth and service innovation as important goals in its five-year plans. In fact, the GDP of the country grew from 34 percent services to 43 percent services in a few years'

Because customers often actively participate in service delivery and/or cocreation, they, too, should be involved in the new service development process. Beyond just providing input on their own needs, customers can help design the service concept and the delivery process, particularly in situations in which the customer personally carries out part of the service process. For example, Bank of America was successful with developing new service innovations in branch banking by relying on results of a series of experiments in its Atlanta branches.[10] The experiments were designed to more rigorously test new service innovations, in real time and with real customers, before launching them more broadly throughout the branch system. Similarly, the Mayo Clinic has established its Center for Innovation in Rochester to experiment with new service innovations by testing them with actual patients and doctors in a prototype setting prior to introducing them (see Exhibit 8.1 later in the chapter).

Employ Service Design Thinking and Techniques

One of the challenges of service innovation and design is that services are processes and they are experiential, taking place over time. In some cases, the time required to deliver time with a goal of significantly more growth in the near term. The need for service innovation is clear in China and stems from a number of different social and economic developments. First, there is the need for infrastructure services (education, health care, transportation) to serve the masses of people moving from the rural areas into the cities in pursuit of jobs and increased economic well-being. A growing manufacturing sector also demands services to transport, ship, finance, and market the goods produced. There is also recognition that the country cannot become a truly global competitor based solely on manufacturing. These factors have led the government and companies to focus strategically on service innovation and growth.

GERMANY

Germany is a country known for its engineering and manufacturing prowess. But, for many years, beginning in the early 1990s, the German government has recognized the need to focus on service and has funded projects and research aimed at service innovation. Through its Federal Ministry of Education and Research, it has begun funding service innovation through the "Innovation with Services" program. To quote from the program's brochure, "Germany's overall innovative strength depends on its largest value-added sector [the service sector] becoming a driver in an increasingly globalized market." One of its primary partners in this work is the Fraunhofer Institute (www.fraunhofer.de), an applied research organization funded in large part by industry and government project grants. The Institute employs more than 18,000 staff, the majority of whom are scientists, researchers, and engineers. Through its Industrial Engineering arm, Faunhofer is currently conducting more than 200 studies on service development and management. In recent years it has established "service labs" to experimentally test service innovations.

FINLAND

The Scandinavian countries boast some of the highest ratings in the world for quality of life and progressive economies. Finland is often very high on such lists. With its service sector currently representing about 68 percent of the economy, Finland also recognizes the need to be innovative in services. Through Tekes (www.tekes.fi), the Finnish Funding Agency for Technology and Innovation, Finland funds research to increase and broaden the services development of Finnish industry and to promote academic research in services related primarily to technology-enabled service innovations. Tekes also has active partnerships for service innovation in the United States, China, Europe, and Japan.

Sources: M. J. Bitner and S. W. Brown, "The Service Imperative," *Business Horizons 50th Anniversary Issue* 51 (January–February 2008), pp. 39–46; "Succeeding through Service Innovation," University of Cambridge Institute for Manufacturing and IBM, October 2007; and Organization for Economic Cooperation and Development, "Promoting Innovation in Services," 2005; www.fraunhofer.de, August 2011; www.tekes.fi, August 2011.

the service may translate into just a few minutes, but other times the service experience can encompass hours, days, weeks, and even years, as in the case of a university degree program or a service outsourcing contract. Services often occur as a sequence of interrelated steps and activities and engage a number of people, processes, and tangible elements. For example, employees, customers, subcontractors, technology, equipment, and physical spaces are often involved in service and therefore need to be considered in its design. As a result, designing a service offering or service system requires interdisciplinary collaboration as well as coordination and input across functions.

Recognizing the complexities and requirements of service innovation, the field of "service design" has emerged and is gaining increasing attention from business practitioners, design consultants, service marketers, and a variety of academic disciplines. In a global study to identify the research priorities for the science of service, service design came to the forefront as one of the top 10 research priorities for the future.[11] There are a number of global consultancy firms that focus their efforts on service design. For example design firm IDEO, based in the United States; Engine Service Design in the U.K; and Live/Work in the U.K. all have practices devoted to service design.

Technology spotlight Facebook: A Radical Service Innovation

When Facebook was launched in Mark Zuckerberg's dormitory room at Harvard University in 2004, it was not much more than a communication vehicle for Harvard students. According to David Kirkpatrick's authoritative book on the company, Facebook's beginnings can be traced to other Zuckerberg projects during the same year at Harvard—first to Course Match (a way to learn about who was registered for a particular class and what classes your friends were taking) and then to Facemash, whose purpose was to figure out who was the hottest person on campus. In the winter of 2004 Zuckerberg launched Thefacebook.com, borrowing from his previous projects and adding elements that invited individuals to create personal profiles of themselves. The original Facebook concept was limited and innocent enough. Similar to most social networks up to that time, its primary purpose was to help people connect socially, often for dating, and its audience was limited initially to Harvard students. Quickly, other schools asked to join Thefacebook and set up sites for their students. By the end of the 2004 academic year, 34 schools had joined and Thefacebook had about 100,000 users. That was the beginning, but it was only the very beginning.

In a few years, Facebook (the name was changed in 2005) grew to be the powerhouse of social media. In 2010, approximately 143 million Americans were active on Facebook, representing 46.8 percent of the entire population! The countries with the most users on Facebook after the United States were, in order, Indonesia, the United Kingdom, Turkey, France, the Philippines, Italy, Canada, Mexico, India, and Germany (see *The Facebook Effect,* p. 16). According to July 2011 Facebook statistics on its website, there are approximately 750 million registered users *worldwide,* and an average user is connected to 80 community pages, groups, and events. The average user also creates 90 pieces of content each month, and more than 30 billion pieces of content are shared each month via blogs, web links, photo albums, and so on. Facebook is a private company that does not share its financials, but it was estimated that the company took in at least $1.5 billion in revenue in 2010.

Clearly, Facebook is a radical service innovation that has shown extraordinary growth and is extremely popular. Nothing like it existed before, and its limits and bounds are unknown. From the original basic social site for Harvard students, the company has evolved to a complex social networking giant. Some claim that entire industries—such as the photo-sharing industry and games—have been transformed through Facebook. Going far beyond its original focus on facilitating individual social connections, Facebook has introduced many new features and mobile phone applications such as

So what is meant by service design and service design thinking? And what do these service design consultancy firms do to help their clients produce great service innovations? While there is not one shared definition, here are two from noted companies and experts:

> "Service design aims to ensure service interfaces are useful, usable, and desirable from the client's point of view and efficient and distinctive from the supplier's point of view." Birgit Mager, professor of service design, University of Cologne, Germany[12]

> "Service design is focused on bringing service strategy and innovative service ideas to life by aligning various internal and external stakeholders around the creation of holistic service experiences for customers, clients, employees, business partners, and/or citizens." Center for Services Leadership, Arizona State University[13]

Given the interdisciplinary and interactional nature of service design and its focus on customer experiences, a set of five principles has been proposed as central to service design thinking:[14]

User-centered: Services should be experienced and designed through the customer's eyes.

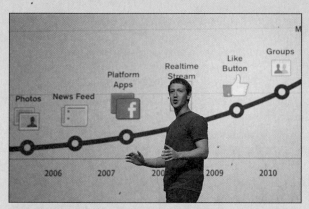

Facebook CEO, Mark Zuckerberg, describes the company's rapid growth.

"Facebook Deals," which allows smartphone users to "check in" at a specific physical location (a restaurant, coffee shop, etc.) and get a small real-time reward for stopping by.

It is easy to imagine that the future of Facebook will be bright, given its history and trajectory. It is highly innovative and far-reaching, and it seems to anticipate and understand the ways that people want to interact through technology. Still, the company has its challenges. The issue of user privacy comes up frequently and was addressed recently by Facebook through the creation of even more stringent options for users to control access to their personal information. Competition is always a challenge, and Google, Facebook's most formidable and direct competitor, is also developing its own social network, which some analysts have dubbed a "Facebook Killer." Google+ is intended to mimic normal social habits in the non-online world, allowing users to divide their friends into discrete groups (e.g., work friends separated from college buddies and family), unlike Facebook, where all friends are lumped into one group.

Time will tell who succeeds and who fails in the online social networking world. No matter how it turns out, it is certain that Mark Zuckerberg and Facebook have launched a revolution and service innovation in networking that will affect individuals, companies, governments, and industries well into the future.

Sources: D. Gelles, "Every Industry Is Going to Be Rethought in a Social Way," *Financial Times,* December 4, 2010, p. 14; D. Kirkpatrick, *The Facebook Effect,* New York: Simon & Schuster Paperbacks, 2010; C. Nuttall and D. Gelles, "Facebook Becomes Bigger Hit Than Google," *Financial Times,* FT.com, published March 16, 2010; www.facebook.com, accessed August 2011; J. Lehrer, "Social Networks Can't Replace Socializing," *The Wall Street Journal,* August 6–7, 2011.

Cocreative: All stakeholders should be included in the service design process.
Sequencing: A service should be visualized as a sequence of interrelated actions.
Evidencing: Intangible services should be visualized in terms of physical artifacts.
Holistic: The entire environment of a service should be considered.

Service designers who adhere to these principles are "engaged visualizing, formulating, and choreographing solutions that are not yet available. They watch and interpret needs and behaviors and transform them into potential future services."[15] Designing, innovating, and improving service experiences based on these principles has resulted in a number of new terms, techniques, and methods being developed and applied, specifically for service innovation.[16] For example, terms such as *customer journey, touchpoints, personas, cocreation,* and *service prototypes* are common among service designers. Methodologies include storytelling, service safaris, shadowing, storyboard, service role-play, and others. One of the primary techniques for service design is service blueprinting, presented in detail later in this chapter. Exhibit 8.1 (later in the chapter), describing Mayo Clinic's Center for Innovation, provides an example of design thinking in action.

TYPES OF SERVICE INNOVATION

[handwritten margin notes: "Get used to tech / to Automation / in self service"]

[handwritten margin notes: "Consulting / stress to / 1st Derivative"]

Service innovation has been defined in various ways. Sometimes when people talk about service innovation they are referring to innovation and improvement related to service offerings themselves. For example, McDonald Corporation's significant restaurant redesign and menu changes in recent years are examples of offering innovations. In other cases service innovation is associated with new internal service processes that will make an organization more productive and efficient. The introduction of new technology support systems for frontline employees represents this type of service innovation. In other cases service innovation is associated with enhancements in the customer experience or significant changes in the role of the customer. For example, the proliferation of self-service innovations has significantly altered the role of the customer in many industries. Our Technology Spotlight on the preceding two pages, featuring Facebook, provides an example of this type of radical service innovation. The term *service innovation* is also tied to major change initiatives within organizations, such as when a traditional manufacturing or operations-driven company decides to transform its entire go-to-market strategy around service and solutions rather than its products. At an even more macro level, service innovation can be tied to entire industries and service systems. For example, many of IBM's current Smarter Planet initiatives are aimed at transforming entire service systems, including health care, education, transportation, and government, through service innovations.

In this section, we cover several meanings and types of service innovations, including service offering innovation, innovating around customer roles, and innovation through service solutions.

Service Offering Innovation

[handwritten margin note: "New services / for New markets?"]

Not all service innovations are "new" to the same degree. New services run the gamut from major or radical introductions to minor style changes, described below.

• *Major or radical innovations* are new services for markets as yet undefined. Past examples include the first broadcast television services and Federal Express's introduction of nationwide, overnight small-package delivery. Many innovations now and in the future will evolve from information, computer, and Internet-based technologies. Often these major innovations create brand-new markets.[17]

• *Start-up businesses* consist of new services for a market already served by existing products that meet the same generic needs. Service examples include the creation of health maintenance organizations to provide an alternative form of health care delivery, online banking for financial transactions, and door-to-door airport shuttle services that compete with traditional taxi and limousine services. Many new mobile phone applications fit in this category.

• *New services for the currently served market* represent attempts to offer existing customers of the organization a service not previously available from the company (although it may be available from other companies). Examples include retailers adding a coffee bar or children's play area, a health club offering nutrition classes, and airlines offering phone and Internet services during flights. Sometimes they represent only modest enhancement services, as in these examples. Other times the offering may represent a radically new stand-alone service such as PetSmart's PetsHotels, described in the chapter opener.

• *Service-line extensions* represent augmentations of the existing service line, such as a restaurant adding new menu items, an airline offering new routes, a law firm offering additional legal services, and a university adding new courses or degrees.

- *Service improvements* represent perhaps the most common type of service innovation. Changes in features of services already offered might involve faster execution of an existing service process, extended hours of service, or augmentations such as added amenities in a hotel room (e.g., the addition of wireless Internet connections).

- *Style changes* represent the most modest service innovations, although they are often highly visible and can have significant effects on customer perceptions, emotions, and attitudes. Changing the color scheme of a restaurant, revising the logo for an organization, redesigning a website, or painting aircraft a different color all represent style changes. These innovations do not fundamentally change the service, only its appearance, similar to how packaging changes are used for consumer products.

Innovating around Customer Roles

The types of service innovations described in the preceding section are tied to the offerings themselves, suggesting that innovation occurs when a service offering is altered or expanded in some way—either radically on one extreme or stylistically at the other extreme. It is also possible that service innovations may come about when the customer's usage or cocreation role is redefined. For example, assuming the customer plays the role of user, buyer, or payer in a service context, new services can result when the previous role is redefined.[18] Many radical innovations effectively redefine the customer's role in these ways. For example, Netflix totally redefined the customer's role for movie rentals. While customers used to visit their local Blockbuster store to rent one or more movies for a predetermined period of time and pay for them on a per-movie basis, Netflix's initial innovation was to allow customers to receive movies through the mail, pay for them on a service contract, and return them whenever they were ready to do so. While it is still possible to receive movies via mail, customers can also stream movies and TV episodes via the Internet to their TVs through Xbox 360, PS3, Wii, or any other device that allows streaming from the Internet, avoiding mail delivery altogether. Thus, while movie watching in the home has not changed, the entire service process for acquiring, receiving, paying for, and returning the movies is radically different.

Innovation through Service Solutions

Many organizations realize that customers are not looking for one stand-alone product or service but, rather, innovative solutions to their problems. Traditional thinking has viewed solutions as "bundles of goods and services" that companies offer to customers. However, research by Kapil Tuli, Ajay Kohli, and Sundar Bharadwaj shows that solutions, as defined by customers, are not bundles of products and services at all, but rather they are sets of customer-facing processes. These relational processes comprise (1) customer requirements definition, (2) customization and integration of goods and/or services, (3) deployment of these integrated solutions, and (4) postdeployment customer support.[19] Another researcher, Lance Bettencourt, suggests that service innovation is the result of understanding customers' problems and the jobs they are trying to get done, then developing solutions to help them reach those goals.[20] In Bettencourt's experience, the keys are to figure out what customers are trying to do and to develop services and solutions around that understanding. Yet other researchers focus on "customer activity chains" and the development of services and solutions to enhance these activities.[21] For example, Kodak Gallery offers all kinds of services online to enhance customers' sharing of memories through photography.

When companies begin to think in terms of solutions for customers, they start to spend more time with customers, listening to and observing their problems and identifying pain points that can be addressed through innovative solutions. In business-to-business contexts this often translates into companies' moving away from their traditional product offerings into activities such as business process outsourcing, consulting around areas of expertise, and managed services.[22] For example, Xerox provides a document management service, whereby it can take over the management of all documents (digital and paper) within an organization. To expand their service and solution expertise, many technology companies have partnered with or purchased service businesses: IBM purchased PricewaterhouseCoopers, Hewlett-Packard acquired Electronic Data Systems (EDS), and Dell acquired Perot Systems.

Solutions are relevant not only in business-to-business contexts. Our chapter opener illustrates PetSmart's move into "cradle-to-grave" solutions for pets and their parents, and Kodak Gallery's solutions are clearly consumer focused. Recent research points out the relevance of designing travel and vacation solutions for customers that take into account the collective and relational goals of family members.[23] The typical approach in the travel industry is to focus on the features and attributes of destinations rather than the sometimes conflicting goals that family members want to achieve through their vacation. In a sense, Facebook (see the Technology Spotlight) is an example of a consumer solution, too—it is a comprehensive, and radically innovative, social solution for consumers, offered online.

STAGES IN SERVICE INNOVATION AND DEVELOPMENT

In this section we focus on the actual steps followed in service innovation and development. The steps can be applied to any type of new service. Much of what is presented in this section has direct parallels in the new product development process for manufactured goods. Because of the inherent characteristics of services, however, the development process for new services requires adaptations.[24] Figure 8.1 shows the basic principles and steps in new service development.[25] Although these steps are similar to those for manufactured goods, their implementation is different for services. The challenges typically lie in defining the concept in the early stages of the development process and again at the prototype development stage. Other challenges come about in the design and implementation of the new service because these steps often involve coordinating human resources, technology, internal processes, and facilities within already-existing systems. Partially because of these challenges, service firms are generally less likely to carry out a structured development process for new innovations than are their manufacturing and consumer-goods counterparts.[26]

An underlying assumption of new product development process models is that new product ideas can be dropped at any stage of the process if they do not satisfy the criteria for success at that stage.[27] Figure 8.1 shows the checkpoints (represented by stop signs) that separate the critical stages of the development process. The checkpoints specify requirements that a new service must meet before it can proceed to the next stage of development.

Despite what Figure 8.1 suggests, however, new service or product development is not always a linear process. Many companies find that some steps can be worked on simultaneously and in some instances a step may even be skipped, particularly for simple products and services. The overlapping of steps and simultaneous development of various pieces of the new service/product development process has been referred to as *flexible product development*. This type of flexible, speedy process is particularly important in technology industries, in which products and services evolve extremely quickly. In these environments, computer technology lets companies monitor customer

FIGURE 8.1
Service Innovation and Development Process

- **Business strategy development or review**

- **New service strategy development**

Front-end planning

- **Idea generation**
  | Screen ideas against new service strategy | STOP |

- **Concept development and evaluation**
  | Test concept with customers and employees | STOP |

- **Business analysis**
  | Test for profitability and feasibility | STOP |

- **Service development and testing**
  | Conduct service prototype test | STOP |

- **Market testing**
  | Test service and other marketing mix elements | STOP |

Implementation

- **Commercialization**

- **Postintroduction evaluation**

opinions and needs during development and change the final offering right up until it is launched. Often, the next version of the service is in planning stages at the same time that the current version is being launched. Even if the stages are handled simultaneously, however, the important checkpoints noted in Figure 8.1 should be assessed to maximize chances of success.

The process shown in Figure 8.1 is divided into two sections: front-end planning and implementation. The front end determines what service concepts will be developed, whereas the back end implements the service concept. When asked where the greatest weaknesses in product and service innovation occur, managers typically report problems with the *fuzzy front end*.[28] The front end is called "fuzzy" because of its relative abstractness, which is even more apparent with intangible, complex, and variable services than with manufactured products.

Front-End Planning

Business Strategy Development or Review

One of the first steps in new service development is to review the organization's mission and vision. The new service strategy and specific new service ideas must fit within the larger strategic mission and vision of the organization. For example, Wells Fargo Bank's mission and vision are to be the industry leader in alternative delivery channels for financial services and to offer customized services to its clientele when and where they need them. Its vast array of ATMs, supermarket branches, and Internet banking services support this strategy. PetSmart, the company featured in this chapter's opening vignette, has as its mission to serve "pet parents" through the "lifetime care of pets." This mission has led to the development of a host of new services, such as training, grooming, overnight care, and day care, in addition to traditional food, toys, and accessories offered in its stores. For both Wells Fargo Bank and PetSmart, the company's new services strategy clearly fits the mission of the company.

New Service Strategy Development

Research suggests that a product portfolio strategy and a defined organizational structure for new product or service development are critical—and are the foundations—for success. The types of new services that will be appropriate depend on the organization's goals, vision, capabilities, and growth plans. By defining a new service innovation strategy (possibly in terms of markets, types of services, time horizon for development, profit criteria, or other relevant factors), the organization will be in a better position to begin generating specific ideas. For example, it may focus its growth on new services at a particular level of the described continuum from major innovations to style changes. Or the organization may define its new service strategy even more specifically in terms of particular markets or market segments or in terms of specific profit generation goals.

One way to begin formulating a new service strategy is to use the framework shown in Figure 8.2 for identifying growth opportunities. The framework allows an organization to identify possible directions for growth and can be helpful as a catalyst for creative ideas. The framework may also later serve as an initial idea screen if, for example, the organization chooses to focus its growth efforts on one or two of the four cells in the matrix. The matrix suggests that companies can develop a growth strategy around current customers or new customers and can focus on current offerings or new service offerings. For example, for quite some time Kentucky Fried Chicken (KFC) has grown through providing its service outside the United States, a form of market development (existing service, new customers). After over two decades of expansion in China, the company has now set its sights on Africa as its new market, expecting to double its number of outlets and revenues in Africa by 2014.[29] The PetSmart services in our opening vignette, on the other hand, are examples of service development (new services, current customers). Procter & Gamble's venture into services through its Tide Dry Cleaners and Mr. Clean Car Washes are examples of yet another type of growth strategy through diversification (new services, new customers). Like Procter & Gamble and PetSmart, many companies are looking to grow strategically through service innovation (see the Strategy Insight).

Idea Generation

The next step in the process is the generation of new ideas that can be passed through the new service strategy screen described in the preceding step. Formal brainstorming, solicitation of ideas from employees and customers, lead user research, and learning about competitors' offerings are some of the most common approaches. Some companies are even collaborating with outsiders (e.g., competitors, vendors, alliance partners) or developing licensing agreements and joint ventures in an effort to exploit all possible sources of new ideas.[30]

FIGURE 8.2
New Service Strategy Matrix for Identifying Growth Opportunities

Source: Adapted from H. I. Ansoff, *Corporate Strategy* (New York: McGraw-Hill, 1965).

Offerings	Markets	
	Current customers	New customers
Existing services	Share building	Market development
New services	Service development	Diversification

Observing customers and how they use the firm's products and services can also generate creative ideas for new innovations. Sometimes referred to as *empathic design,* observation is particularly effective in situations in which customers may not be able to recognize or verbalize their needs.[31] In service businesses, contact personnel, who actually deliver the services and interact directly with consumers, can be particularly good sources of ideas for complementary services and ways to improve current offerings.[32] Some organizations have found that internal networks of employees, across functions and disciplines, can be great sources of innovative ideas; thus, organizational practices that encourage networking and make collaboration easy are also ways to enourage new ideas.[33]

Whether the source of a new idea is inside or outside the organization, some established mechanism should exist for ensuring an ongoing stream of new service possibilities. This mechanism might include a formal service innovation or service R&D department or function with responsibility for generating new ideas, suggestion boxes for employees and customers, new service development teams that meet regularly, surveys and focus groups with customers and employees, or formal competitive analysis to identify new services.

Service Concept Development and Evaluation

Once an idea surfaces that is regarded as a good fit with both the business and the new service strategies, it is ready for initial development. The inherent characteristics of services place complex demands on this phase of the process. Drawing pictures and describing an intangible service in concrete terms are difficult, particularly when the service is not standardized and may be cocreated in real time with customers. It is therefore important that agreement be reached at this stage on exactly what the concept is and what customer need it is filling. By involving multiple parties in sharpening the concept definition, it often becomes apparent that individual views of the concept are not the same. For example, in one documented case, the design and development of a new discount brokerage service was initially described by the bank as a way "to buy and sell stocks for customers at low prices."[34] Through the initial concept development phase it became clear that not everyone in the organization had the same idea about how this description would translate into an actual service and that there were a variety of ways the concept could be developed. Only through multiple iterations of the service—and the raising of hundreds of issues, large and small—was an agreement finally reached on the discount brokerage concept.

After clear definition of the concept, it is important to produce a description of the service that represents its specific characteristics and then determine initial customer and employee responses to the concept. The service design document should describe the problem addressed by the service, discuss the reasons for offering the new service, explain the service process and its benefits, and provide a rationale for purchasing the service.[35] The roles of customers and employees in the delivery process are also described. It may also be very useful to create a concept-level blueprint at this point in the service innovation process. The service concept is then evaluated by asking employees and customers whether they understand the idea of the proposed service, whether they are favorable to the concept, and whether they feel it satisfies an unmet need.

Business Analysis

Assuming that the service concept is favorably evaluated by customers and employees at the concept development stage, the next step is to estimate its economic feasibility and potential profit implications. Demand analysis, revenue projections, cost analyses,

Strategy Insight Strategic Growth through Services

Firms in many industries are discovering the value of strategically focusing on service innovations to provide value for their customers as well as profits and growth for the firm. By adding services to their traditional offerings, firms can differentiate themselves from their competitors and frequently earn higher profit margins on the new services compared with traditional manufactured or retail product offerings. IBM Global Services is perhaps the best known example of this type of solutions strategy (see opening vignette in Chapter 1). Like IBM, many companies are poised to "grow through services" in business-to-consumer as well as business-to-business markets. As they move in this direction, they quickly recognize the great opportunities as well as the complex challenges of introducing new services. Here we highlight three firms from very diverse industries and their growth-through-services strategies.

PROCTER & GAMBLE

Procter & Gamble is one of the world's largest and most admired consumer products companies. So it may come as a surprise that some of their latest ventures are taking the company into innovative services. Through its FutureWorks unit, P&G is extending well-established and respected brands into the realm of service. Tide Dry Cleaners and Mr. Clean Car Wash are two examples. In both cases, P&G looked for fragmented industries in which customer expectations are not particularly high and where P&G brand names could enhance value through proprietary technologies and an improved customer experience. For example, Tide Dry Cleaners feature bright, cheerful, bold-colored signage and interiors, drive-through lanes, and lockers acces-

Tide Dry Cleaners—a new service strategy for Procter and Gamble.

sible for after-hours pickup. The experience and the cleaning quality itself are intended to contrast sharply with consumers' experiences with typical dingy, dark, and sometimes inconvenient dry cleaners. However, P&G's expansion into services must be very deliberate and done with great care so as not to risk harming the parent brand, as both the Mr. Clean and Tide brands are extremely valuable to P&G.

ERICSSON

Headquartered in Sweden, Ericsson is a leading global provider of telecommunications equipment and related services and solutions. Since the mid-1990s, it has pursued a growth strategy focused on customers, services, and solutions that add value to its sophisticated technology products. Ericsson employs about 50,000 service professionals and operates in over 180 countries. Ericsson Global Services focuses on providing services for telecommunication operators around the world, so that these companies can

and operational feasibility are assessed at this stage. Because the development of service concepts is so closely tied to the operational system of the organization, this stage will involve preliminary assumptions about the costs of personnel hiring and training, delivery system enhancements, facility changes, and any other projected operations costs. The organization will pass the results of the business analysis through its profitability and feasibility screen to determine whether the new service idea meets the minimum requirements.

focus on their core business of supporting customers and building revenues. Behind the scenes, through its "managed services" contracts, Ericsson works with operators to upgrade their systems and consults with them on network planning, design, and deployment. In addition to operators, Ericsson works directly with government and private business entities.

For example, since the 1980s, Ericsson has worked in a partnership with the New Zealand police force to support its telecommunication needs through products and services. In 2007 Ericsson signed a 21-year exclusive agreement with them to supply and support a flexible and scalable point-to-point microwave radio network system. The goal for the system is to provide community safety through a customized and secure telecommunications network for New Zealand. As Ericsson continues to move away from its traditional base in manufacturing, the company is reorienting its entire organization toward providing integrated solutions for customers.

PHILIPS ELECTRONICS
Companies such as Philips Electronics, the European electronics giant, are faced with the realities of price competition from cheaper products produced primarily in Asia. The results for many companies are declining sales and growing losses from their products. Part of the solution for these companies is a venture into services. For Philips this has meant branching out into health care by marrying its expertise in consumer marketing and the knowledge in its professional medical division with an unmet demand for personal health care monitoring. The result is Philips Lifeline service, a medical-alert system that gives elderly patients immediate connection to a call center, where personal response associates, with access to their health profiles, can help them. The immediate access is gained by pushing a button on an electronic bracelet or pendant that the person wears. Other related services that Philips offers are ones that allow doctors to monitor patients' vital signs via the Internet and an intelligent pill box that can detect when a person has not taken his or her medication. A box with excess pills automatically calls a designated friend or family member, who can then remind the person to take the medication.

For each of these companies, the move to services represented a significant strategic choice that initially took them into uncharted waters. For P&G it meant learning how to run a service business, including designing the customer experience and hiring and training employees to deliver service on the front line. For Ericsson it meant moving away from a manufacturing and technology mind-set to one that focuses on customers and solutions. For Philips the move was even more dramatic as it began to understand a whole new industry in health care delivery. Yet the potential rewards are great and customer demands for services and solutions are real. These rewards and demands are what compel more and more firms to pursue the strategic service path.

Sources: M. Sawhney, S. Balasubramanian, and V. V. Krishnan, "Creating Growth with Services," *Sloan Management Review* 45 (Winter 2004), pp. 34–43; www.ericsson.com, August 2011; L. Abboud, "Electronics Giant Seeks a Cure in Health Care," *The Wall Street Journal*, July 11, 2007, p. A1; www.healthcare.philips.com, 2011; L. Coleman-Lochner and M. Clothier, "P&G Looks to Franchise Tide Dry Cleaning," *Bloomberg Business Week*, September 2, 2010; B. Brown and S. D. Anthony, "How P&G Tripled Its Innovation Success Rate," *Harvard Business Review* 89 (June 2011), pp. 64–72; L. A. Bettencourt, *Service Innovation* (New York: McGraw-Hill, 2010).

Implementation
Once the new service concept has passed all the front-end planning hurdles, it is ready for the implementation stages of the process.

Service Prototype Development and Testing
In the development of new tangible products, the development and testing stage involves the construction of product prototypes and testing for consumer acceptance.

Exhibit 8.1 Service Innovation at the Mayo Clinic

The Mayo Clinic in the United States is more than 100 years old and one of the most respected names in health care globally. It is consistently listed among the top hospitals in the United States and is known for its collaborative health care model, high levels of service, and position in the forefront of medicine. Following its innovative traditions, Mayo established its Center for Innovation (formerly the SPARC Innovation Lab) to focus on testing and evaluating new practices in health care delivery. While medical and technological advances have changed the face of health care dramatically over the past 50 years, the same is not necessarily true of the way health care is delivered to patients. Everything from patient exam rooms to the patient's waiting experience has changed relatively little in comparison to scientific advances in medicine. Mayo recognized this and determined it should again be in the forefront of innovation—this time in the processes and practices of health care delivery.

The Center for Innovation has become a testing ground for all types of service and delivery innovations at Mayo—innovations that are intended to enhance the patient's experience and that have potential health benefits. Working with the design firm IDEO Mayo designed an experimental lab at its Rochester, Minnesota, facility, where service innovations can be tested with real patients and real Mayo doctors and staff before they are introduced into the clinics. The lab is set up as an actual clinic within the Mayo facility, and experiments are conducted with doctors and patients (of course, with their prior knowledge and consent). The glass walls in the lab reveal inner offices and show support staff working and doctors and patients interacting, thus allowing direct observation of experimental services. The space is highly flexible, so that exam rooms, common spaces, walls, furniture, and computers can be moved around to test different configurations and services.

Center for Innovaton Lab (formerly SPARC) at Mayo Clinic, Rochester.

Again, because services are intangible and simultaneously produced, consumed, and frequently cocreated, this step presents unique challenges. To address these challenges, this stage of service development should involve all who have a stake in the new service: customers and contact employees as well as functional representatives from marketing, operations, and human resources. During this phase, the concept is refined to the point at which a detailed service blueprint illustrating the customer experience and the implementation plan for the service can be produced. The blueprint is likely to evolve over a series of iterations on the basis of input from all involved parties.

In its service innovation practice, the internationally known design firm IDEO makes extensive use of full-scale prototypes and mock-ups to experiment with service concepts, testing both customer reactions and operational aspects of the service. In its work with Marriott's extended stay hotel chain, TownePlace suites, IDEO's Smart Space researchers first spent several weeks living in and talking with

Within the Center for Innovation, researchers focus on complex and important issues for the health care industry in general, with the overarching principle of "patient-centered design." For example, here are some of the topics they have explored and "re-imagined"—the term they use for service improvement and futuristic innovation:

- What would integrated health care look like from the patient's perspective?
- What is the relationship among communication, understanding, and satisfaction for the patient?
- How could exam rooms be reconfigured for a better patient experience and to improve patient–doctor communication?
- How can the on-site check-in process for appointments be improved?
- How can space within the health care facility be optimized to serve patients and staff?
- What are the unmet educational needs of patients, and how can a service be designed to meet those needs?

While innovation in health care delivery practices such as those listed is rare, Mayo's practices within the Center for Innovation are unique—combining principles from service, design, and health care. For example, the patient check-in process at Mayo Rochester was viewed as particularly problematic for patients, with long lines and frustration at having to stand and wait when all they wanted to do was sit down. The multidisciplinary team began by observing and listening to both patients and staff to start the process of identifying innovative solutions to this challenge. Through this human-centered, participatory approach, they developed ideas by conveying narratives that morphed into innovations, which were tested with prototypes in the lab. In the case of the patient check-in process, the basic innovation idea was to develop an automated self-check-in process. Initial prototypes of the self-service check-in kiosk were quite unsophisticated. For example, the first version was a piece of paper representing a computer screen. Later versions of the prototype evolved to inactive computer screens to actual touch screens displayed on a kiosk. At each version of the prototype, the team collected feedback from both patients and staff. The results of this experiment led Mayo to invest resources in investigating a roll-out of this innovative solution.

In another case, an innovation studied in the lab lead to innovative ways to communicate treatment options to diabetic patients who were considering taking statin drugs. A number of patient–doctor communication prototypes were tested to help patients understand their options by conveying information on medical evidence, risk factors, and treatment options via different formats. The prototypes ranged from online information to a one-page decision aid, and each was tested to determine what was most effective for patient participation, preferences, and adherence to the treatment choice. In this case, not only did the innovation improve the patient's experience in the interaction with the physician, but it also resulted in increased likelihood of the patient following through on the treatment plan—ultimately affecting the health outcome itself.

Mayo's commitment to innovation in health care is also seen in its annual "Transform" conferences, which bring together speakers and the latest in thinking related to design and innovation in health care.

Sources: http://centerforinnovation.mayo.edu, 2011; C. Salter, "A Prescription for Innovation," *Fast Company* (April 2006), p. 83.

TownePlace guests to observe and learn how they used the space and what their unmet needs were.[36] The result was a completely redesigned lobby area, including a map wall with notations about local shopping, restaurants, parks, and recreation areas that can be annotated by guests. Another change was a redesigned bedroom that provides the flexibility to be turned into a workspace. To test the design concepts, IDEO built a life-sized lobby and suite out of white foam core and invited Marriott executives, hotel managers, and guests to provide feedback on the prototype. Exhibit 8.1 illustrates how Mayo Clinic's Center for Innovation tests new services and delivery models in its unique experimental setting.

The last step is for each area involved in rendering the service to translate the final blueprint and prototypes into specific implementation plans for its part of the service delivery process. Because service development, design, and delivery, and sometimes cocreation activities, are so intricately intertwined, all parties involved in any aspect of the new service must work together at this stage to delineate the details of the new service. If not, seemingly minor operational details can cause an otherwise good new service idea to fail.

Market Testing

At the market testing stage of the development process, a tangible product might be test marketed in a limited number of trading areas to determine marketplace acceptance of the product as well as other marketing mix variables such as promotion, pricing, and distribution systems. Because new service offerings are often intertwined with the delivery system for existing services, it is difficult to test new services in isolation. And in some cases, it may not be possible to introduce the service to an isolated market area because the organization has only one point of delivery. There are alternative ways of testing the response to marketing mix variables, however. The new service might be offered to employees of the organization and their families for a time to assess their responses to variations in the marketing mix.

It is also extremely important at this stage in the development process to do a pilot run of the service to be sure that the operational details are functioning smoothly. Frequently this step is overlooked, and the actual market introduction may be the first test of whether the service system functions as planned. By this point, mistakes in design are harder to correct. As one noted service expert says, "There is simply no substitute for a proper rehearsal" when introducing a new service.[37]

Commercialization

During the commercialization stage, the service goes live and is introduced to the marketplace. This stage has two primary objectives. The first is to build and maintain acceptance of the new service among large numbers of the service delivery personnel who will be responsible day-to-day for service quality. This task is made easier if acceptance has been built by involving service delivery personnel as one of the key groups in the design and development process all along. The second objective is to monitor all aspects of the service during introduction and through the complete service cycle. If the customer needs six months to experience the entire service, then careful monitoring must be maintained through at least six months. Every detail of the service should be assessed—phone calls, face-to-face transactions, billing, complaints, and delivery problems. Operating efficiency and costs should also be tracked.

Postintroduction Evaluation

At this point, the information gathered during commercialization of the service can be reviewed and changes made to the delivery process, staffing, or marketing mix variables on the basis of actual market response to the offering. No service will ever stay the same. Whether deliberate or unplanned, changes will always occur. Therefore, formalizing the review process to make those changes that enhance service quality from the customer's point of view is critical.

SERVICE BLUEPRINTING: A TECHNIQUE FOR SERVICE INNOVATION AND DESIGN

A stumbling block in service innovation, design, and development is the difficulty of describing and depicting the service at the concept development, service development, and market test stages. One of the keys to matching service specifications to customer expectations is the ability to describe critical service process characteristics objectively and to depict them so that employees, customers, and managers alike know what the

FIGURE 8.3   Service Blueprinting

Service blueprinting
A technique for simultaneously depicting the service process, the points of customer contact, and the evidence of service from the customer's point of view.

service is, can see their roles, and can understand all the steps and flows involved in the service process. In this section, we look in depth at service blueprinting, a useful technique for designing and specifying intangible service processes.[38]

What Is a Service Blueprint?

A *service blueprint* is a picture or map that portrays the customer experience and the service system, so that the different people involved in providing the service can understand it objectively, regardless of their roles or their individual points of view. Blueprints are particularly useful at the design stage of service development. A service blueprint visually displays the service by simultaneously depicting the process of service delivery, the points of customer contact, the roles of customers and employees, and the visible elements of the service (see Figure 8.3). It provides a way to break a service down into its logical components and to depict the steps or tasks in the process, the means by which the tasks are executed, and the evidence of service as the customer experiences it. Blueprinting has its origins in a variety of fields and techniques, including logistics, industrial engineering, decision theory, computer systems analysis, and software engineering—all of which deal with the definition and explanation of processes.[39] Because services are "experiences" rather than objects or technologies, blueprinting is a particularly useful technique for describing them.

Blueprint Components

The key components of service blueprints are shown in Figure 8.4.[40] They are customer actions, onstage/visible contact employee actions, backstage/invisible contact employee actions, and support processes. The conventions for drawing service blueprints are not rigidly defined, and thus the particular symbols used, the number of horizontal lines in the blueprint, and the labels for each part of the blueprint may vary somewhat depending on the complexity of the blueprint being described. These variations are not a problem, as long as you keep in mind the purpose of the blueprint and view it as a useful technique rather than as a set of rigid rules for designing services. In fact, its flexibility—when compared with other process mapping approaches—is one of service blueprinting's major strengths.

The *customer actions* area encompasses the steps, choices, activities, and interactions that the customer performs in the process of purchasing, experiencing, and evaluating the service. The total customer experience is apparent in this area of the blueprint. In a legal services example, the customer actions might include a decision to contact an attorney, phone calls to the attorney, face-to-face meetings, receipt of documents, and receipt of a bill.

Paralleling the customer actions are two areas of contact employee actions. The activities that the contact employee performs that are visible to the customer are the *onstage/visible contact employee actions.* In the legal services setting, the actions of the attorney (the contact employee) visible to the client are, for example, the initial interview, intermediate meetings, and final face-to-face delivery of legal documents.

Those contact employee actions that occur behind the scenes to support the onstage activities are the *backstage/invisible contact employee actions.* In the example, anything the attorney does behind the scenes to prepare for the meetings or to prepare the final documents will appear in this section of the blueprint, together with phone call contacts the customer has with the attorney or other frontline staff in the firm. All *nonvisible* contact employee actions are shown in this area of the blueprint.

The *support processes* section of the blueprint covers the internal services, steps, and interactions that take place to support the contact employees in delivering the service. Again, in our legal example, any service support activities such as legal research by staff, preparation of documents, and secretarial support to set up meetings will be shown in the support processes area of the blueprint.

At the very top of the blueprint you see the *physical evidence* of the service. Typically, above each point of contact the actual physical evidence of the service is listed. In the legal example, the physical evidence of the face-to-face meeting with the attorney would be such items as office decor, written documents, lawyer's clothing, and so forth.

The four key action areas are separated by three horizontal lines. First is the *line of interaction,* representing direct interactions between the customer and the organization. Anytime a vertical line crosses the horizontal line of interaction, a direct contact between the customer and the organization, or a service encounter, has occurred. The next horizontal line is the critically important *line of visibility.* This line separates all service activities visible to the customer from those not visible. In reading blueprints, it is immediately obvious whether the consumer is provided with much visible evidence of the service simply by analyzing how much of the service occurs above the line of visibility versus the activities carried out below the line. This line also separates what the contact employees do onstage from what they do backstage. For example, in a medical examination situation, the doctor would perform the actual exam and answer the patient's questions above the line of visibility, or onstage, whereas she might read

FIGURE 8.4
Service Blueprint Components

the patient's chart in advance and dictate notes following the exam below the line of visibility, or backstage. The third line is the *line of internal interaction,* which separates customer-contact employee activities from those of other service support activities and people. Vertical lines cutting across the line of internal interaction represent internal service encounters.

One of the most significant differences between service blueprints and other process flow diagrams is the primary focus on customers and their experience with the service process. In fact, in designing effective service blueprints it is recommended that the diagramming start with the customer's experience and then work into the delivery system. The boxes shown within each action area depict steps performed or experienced by the actors at that level.

Service Blueprint Examples

Figures 8.5 and 8.6 show service blueprints for two interpersonal services: express mail delivery and an overnight hotel stay.[41] These blueprints are deliberately kept very simple, showing only the most basic steps in the services. Complex diagrams could be developed for each step, and the internal processes could be much more fully developed. In addition to the four action areas separated by the three horizontal lines, these blueprints also show the physical evidence of the service from the customer's point of view at each step of the process.

Examine the express mail delivery blueprint in Figure 8.5. It is clear that from the customer's point of view there are only three steps in the service process: the phone call,

FIGURE 8.5 **Blueprint for Express Mail Delivery Service**

Source: *Service Quality Handbook* by E. E. Scheuing and W. F. Christopher (eds). Copyright 1993 by AM MGMT ASSN / AMACOM (B). Reproduced with permission of AM MGMT ASSN / AMACOM (B) in the format Textbook via Copyright Clearance Center.

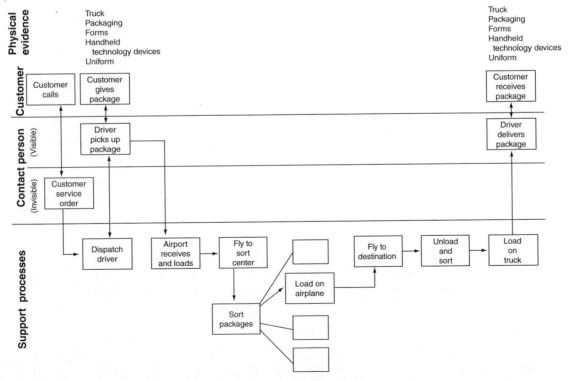

the package pickup, and the package delivery. The process is relatively standardized; the people who perform the service are the phone order-taker and the delivery person; and the physical evidence includes the document package, the transmittal forms, the truck, and the handheld technology device. In some cases the customer may also engage the online or phone-based package tracking system, although it is not depicted here. Although critical for the firm's success, the complex process that occurs behind the line of visibility is of little interest or concern to the customer. However, for the three visible-to-the-customer steps to proceed effectively, invisible internal services are needed. What these steps are and the fact that they support the delivery of the service to the external customer are apparent from the blueprint. Any of the steps in the blueprint could be exploded into a detailed blueprint, if needed for a particular purpose. For example, if the delivery company learned that the "unload and sort" step was taking too long and causing unacceptable delays in delivery, that step could be blueprinted in much greater detail to isolate the problems.

In the case of the overnight hotel stay depicted in Figure 8.6, the customer obviously is more actively involved in the service than he or she is in the express mail service. The guest first checks in, then goes to the hotel room, where a variety of steps take place (receiving bags, sleeping, showering, eating breakfast, and so on), and finally checks out. Imagine how much more complex this process could be and how many more interactions could occur if the service blueprint depicted a week-long vacation at the hotel, or even a three-day business conference. The service blueprint also makes clear (by reading across the line of interaction) those employees who directly interact with the customer. Each step in the customer action area is also associated with various forms of physical evidence, from the hotel parking area and hotel exterior and interior

FIGURE 8.6
Blueprint for Overnight Hotel Stay Service

Source: *Service Quality Handbook* by E. E. Scheuing and W. F. Christopher (eds). Copyright 1993 by AM MGMT ASSN / AMACOM (B). Reproduced with permission of AM MGMT ASSN / AMACOM (B) in the format Textbook via Copyright Clearance Center.

to the forms used at guest registration, the lobby, the room, and the food. In the hotel case, the process is relatively complex (although again somewhat standardized), the people providing the service are a variety of frontline employees, and the physical evidence includes everything from the guest registration form to the lobby and room decor, to the uniforms worn by frontline employees.

Blueprints for Technology-Delivered Self-Service

To this point our discussion of service blueprints has related to services delivered in person, that is services in which employees interact directly with customers at some point in the process. But what about technology-delivered services including self-service websites and interactive kiosks? Can service blueprinting be used effectively to design these types of services? Certainly it can, but the lines of demarcation will change, and some blueprint labels may need to be adapted.

If no employees are involved in the service (except when there is a problem or the service does not function as planned), the contact person areas of the blueprint are not needed. Instead, the area above the line of visibility can be used to illustrate the interface between the customer and the website or the physical interaction with the kiosk. This area can be relabeled *onstage/visible technology.* The backstage contact person actions area are irrelevant in this case.

Many services have both interpersonal and technology-delivered elements. Consider the airline check-in process. The actual check-in may be done through an electronic kiosk, while baggage, security screening, and handling of tickets while boarding are all done by people. In such a case, the blueprint would include all three contact rows: one for technology, one for the onstage contact person (visible), and one for the backstage contact person (invisible). Figure 8.7 is a blueprint for a DVD rental kiosk, showing the technology

FIGURE 8.7
Blueprint for DVD Rental Kiosk

Source: Reprinted with permission of Amy L. Ostrom and Center for Services Leadership, Arizona State University, 2011.

interactions in the added "onstage technology" area of the blueprint. This blueprint also illustrates what the customer experiences if the DVD is scratched. When that happens, the customer calls customer service, a "backstage contact person (invisible)" activity.

Reading and Using Service Blueprints

A service blueprint can be read in a variety of ways, depending on the purpose. If the purpose is to understand the customer's view of the process or the customer experience, the blueprint can be read from left to right, tracking the events in the customer action area. Questions that might be asked include these: How is the service initiated by the customer? What choices does the customer make? Is the customer highly involved in creating the service, or are few actions required of the customer? What is the physical evidence of the service from the customer's point of view? Is the evidence consistent with the organization's strategy and positioning?

If the purpose is to understand contact employees' roles or the integration of onstage technology with contact employee activities, the blueprint can also be read horizontally but this time focusing on the activities directly above and below the line of visibility. Questions that might be asked include these: How rational, efficient, and effective is the process? Who interacts with customers, when, and how often? Is one person responsible for the customer, or is the customer passed off from one contact employee to another? Are interactions and handoffs between people and technology integrated and seamless from the customer's point of view?

If the purpose is to understand the integration of the various elements of the service process, or to identify where particular employees fit into the bigger picture, the blueprint can be analyzed vertically. In this analysis, it becomes clear what tasks and which employees are essential in the delivery of service to the customer. The linkages from internal actions deep within the organization to frontline effects on the customer can also be seen in the blueprint. Questions that might be asked include these: What actions are being performed backstage to support critical customer interaction points? What are the associated support actions? How are handoffs from one employee to another taking place?

If the purpose is service redesign, the blueprint can be looked at as a whole to assess the complexity of the process, how it might be changed, and how changes from the customer's point of view would affect the contact employee and other internal processes, and vice versa. Blueprints can also be used to assess the overall efficiency and productivity of the service system and to evaluate how potential changes will affect the system.[42] The blueprint can also be analyzed to determine likely failure points or bottlenecks in the process, as well as customer pain points. When such points are discovered, a firm can introduce measures to track failures, or that part of the blueprint can be exploded, so that the firm can focus in much greater detail on that piece of the system.

Blueprinting applications in a variety of contexts have demonstrated benefits and uses, including the following:[43]

- Providing a platform for innovation.
- Recognizing roles and interdependencies among functions, people, and organizations.
- Facilitating both strategic and tactical innovations.
- Transferring and storing innovation and service knowledge.
- Designing moments of truth from the customer's point of view.
- Suggesting critical points for measurement and feedback in the service process.
- Clarifying competitive positioning.
- Understanding the ideal customer experience.

Building a Blueprint

Recall that many of the benefits and purposes of building a blueprint evolve from the process of doing it. The development of the blueprint needs to involve a variety of functional representatives as well as information from customers. Drawing or building a blueprint is not a task that should be assigned to one person or one functional area. Figure 8.8 identifies the basic steps in building a blueprint.

Step 1: Identify the Service Process to Be Blueprinted

Blueprints can be developed at a variety of levels, and there needs to be agreement on the starting point. For example, the express mail delivery blueprint shown in Figure 8.5 is at the basic service concept level. Little detail is shown, and variations based on market segment or specific services are not shown. Specific blueprints could be developed for two-day express mail, large accounts, Internet-facilitated services, and/or storefront drop-off centers. Each of these blueprints would share some features with the concept blueprint but would also include unique features. Or if the "sort packages" and "loading" elements of the process were found to be problem areas or bottlenecks, a detailed blueprint of the subprocesses at work in those two steps could be developed.

Step 2: Identify the Customer or Customer Segment Experiencing the Service

A common rationale for market segmentation is that each segment's needs are different and therefore will require variations in the service or product features. Thus, blueprints are most useful when developed for a particular customer or customer segment, assuming that the service process varies across segments. At a very abstract or conceptual level it may be possible to combine customer segments on one blueprint. However, once almost any level of detail is reached, separate blueprints should be developed to avoid confusion and maximize their usefulness.

Step 3: Map the Service Process from the Customer's Point of View

Step 3 involves charting the choices and actions that the customer performs or experiences in purchasing, consuming, and evaluating the service. Identifying the service from the customer's point of view first will help avoid focusing on processes and steps that have no customer impact. This step forces agreement on who the customer is (sometimes no small task) and may involve considerable research and observation to determine exactly how the customer experiences the service. Sometimes the beginning and ending of the service from the customer's point of view are not obvious. For example, research in a hair-cutting context revealed that customers viewed the process as beginning with the phone call to the salon and setting of the appointment, whereas the hair stylists did not typically view the making of appointments as part of the service process.[44] If the blueprint is being developed for an existing service, it may

FIGURE 8.8
Building a Service Blueprint

Exhibit 8.2 Blueprinting in Action at ARAMARK Parks and Destinations

ARAMARK is a global leader in professional services, operating as an outsourcer for food, hospitality, facility management, and uniform services. ARAMARK's customers include large businesses, universities, health care organizations, parks and resorts, convention centers, and other groups. It was ranked first in its industry among *Fortune*'s Most Admired companies in 2007, 2009, 2010, and 2011. The company has approximately 255,000 employees serving clients in 22 countries. One of its divisions is ARAMARK Parks and Destinations, a group that provides services for 17 major park destinations within the United States, including Denali National Park in Alaska, Shenandoah National Park in Virginia, and Lake Powell Destinations and Marinas in the Glen Canyon National Recreation Area of Arizona. Each of the parks has at least three or four service businesses within it that ARAMARK operates on an outsourcing contract.

GOAL: SERVICE IMPROVEMENT AND CUSTOMER RETENTION

A number of years ago, Renee Ryan, then marketing director for ARAMARK Parks, confronted a challenge. It was clear that repeat business at ARAMARK's parks was declining overall. This was particularly the case at Lake Powell Resorts and Marinas in Arizona, where the company operated houseboat rentals, a resort, campgrounds, boat tours, and food service operations. Research revealed that many people were not returning to Lake Powell because their first experience there did not match what they had expected or were accustomed to based on visits to other resort destinations. Ryan employed both traditional and visual (photos, video) blueprints to help convince the organization that changes were in order and specifically what should be done. The results benefited customers through improvements in service and the company through increased repeat business.

First, Ryan developed a blueprint of a typical, quality hotel/resort experience from a typical customer's point of view. Then she blueprinted the Lake Powell resort experience. The comparison of the two blueprints was revealing in terms of differences in basic services, standards, and processes. This comparison process resulted in the development of new services, facilities upgrades, and modernization of key service elements. Through the visual blueprint in particular, showing all aspects of the service through photos and videos, the need for service upgrades became apparent.

Another revelation also jumped out of the blueprint. By visually tracking the customer's experience, it was clear that customers were being asked to work extremely hard for their vacations! To experience the luxurious and not-inexpensive houseboat experience they had purchased, customers first had to create extensive grocery lists, shop in crowded stores near the resort, carry all of their food and belongings down a steep embankment, and haul them out to the boat. Once the trip started, more hard labor was required. Anchoring a large houseboat each night is not a trivial matter, and cooking onboard can be

be helpful at this point in the process to videotape or photograph the service process, as was done in the ARAMARK case illustrated in Exhibit 8.2. Managers and others who are not on the front lines may be quite surprised when they view the actual service experience through their customers' eyes.

Step 4: Map Contact Employee Actions and/or Technology Actions

First the lines of interaction and visibility are drawn, and then the process from the customer contact person's point of view is mapped, distinguishing visible onstage activities from invisible backstage activities. For existing services, this step involves questioning or observing frontline operation employees to learn what they do and which activities are performed in full view of the customer versus which activities are carried out behind the scenes.

For technology-delivered services or those that combine technology and human delivery, the required actions of the technology interface are mapped above the line of visibility as well. If no employees are involved in the service, the area can be relabeled "onstage technology actions." If both human and technology interactions are

Houseboat Vacation on Lake Powell.

services introduced included various levels of concierge services that started with the basic service of taking guests' things to the boat for them and later transporting guests in a cart to the boat dock. Service packages were extended at the high end to include buying groceries for guests and providing executive chefs, who would travel with the party and cook on board. Trained captains could also be hired to lessen the stress of navigation. A variety of services in between were also available a la carte.

RESULTS FOR ARAMARK

The result for Lake Powell of all of these service quality improvements and innovative new services was 50 percent fewer complaints. Repeat business increased by 12 percent, and customer satisfaction also increased dramatically. The blueprints in this case were extremely valuable in that they allowed managers to see the service in ways they had never seen it before. The blueprints also provided a focal point for conversations, leading to change and ultimately to new service standards and measures. Using the blueprinting technique helped people within the parks division develop a true customer focus.

arduous and time consuming. Navigating the houseboat can also be stressful, especially for inexperienced captains. The run-down resort facilities on land, the arduous work required to get on the water, and the stress of navigation all combined to discourage customers from returning after surviving their first Lake Powell vacation.

The blueprinting exercise made all of this extremely vivid for top management and resulted in a suite of new services, renovations of existing facilities, training of staff to perform to new service standards, and new measurement and reward systems. Some of the new

Sources: M. J. Bitner, A. L. Ostrom, and F. N. Morgan, "Service Blueprinting: A Practical Technique for Service Innovation," *California Management Review 50* (Spring 2008), pp. 66–94.; Interview with Renee Ryan; and www.aramark.com, August 2011.

involved, an additional horizontal line can separate "visible contact employee actions" from "visible technology actions." Using the additional line facilitates reading and interpretation of the service blueprint.

Step 5: Link Contact Activities to Needed Support Functions

The line of internal interaction can then be drawn and linkages from contact activities to internal support functions can be identified. In this process, the direct and indirect impact of internal actions on customers becomes apparent. Internal service processes take on added importance when viewed in connection with their link to the customer. Alternatively, certain steps in the process may be viewed as unnecessary if there is no clear link to the customer's experience or to an essential internal support service.

Step 6: Add Evidence of Service at Each Customer Action Step

Finally, the evidence of service can be added to the blueprint to illustrate what the customer sees and experiences as tangible evidence of the service at each step in the

Exhibit 8.3   Frequently Asked Questions about Service Blueprinting

What process should be blueprinted?

What process to map depends on the team or organization's objectives. If these are not clearly defined, then identifying the process can present a challenge. Questions to ask: Why are we blueprinting the service? What is our objective? Where does the service process begin and end? Are we focusing on the entire service, a component of the service, or a period of time?

Can multiple market segments be included on one blueprint?

Generally the answer to this question is no. Assuming that market segments require different service processes or attributes, the blueprint for one segment may look very different from the blueprint for another. Only at a very high level (sometimes called a *concept blueprint*) might it be relevant to map multiple segments simultaneously.

Who should "draw" the blueprint?

A blueprint is a team effort. It should not be assigned as an individual task, certainly not in the developmental stages. All relevant parties should be involved or represented in the effort. The task might include employees across multiple functions in the organization (marketing, operations, human resources, facilities design), as well as customers in some cases.

Should the actual or desired service process be blueprinted?

If a new service is being designed, then clearly it is important to start with the desired service process. However, in cases of service improvement or service redesign, it is very important to map (at least at a conceptual level) the actual service process first. Once the group knows how the service is actually functioning, then the blueprint can be modified or used as a base for changes and improvements.

Should exceptions or recovery processes be incorporated in the blueprint?

It may be possible to map relatively simple, commonly occurring recovery processes onto a blueprint, assuming there are not a lot of these. However, this process can quickly become complex and cause the blueprint to be confusing or unreadable. Often a better strategy is to indicate common fail points on the blueprint and, if needed, develop separate blueprints for the service recovery processes.

What is the appropriate level of detail?

The answer to this question depends on the purpose for doing the blueprint in the first place. If it is to be used primarily to communicate the general nature of the service, then a concept blueprint with few details is best. If it is being used to focus on diagnosing and improving the service process, then more detail is needed. Because some people are more detail oriented than others, this question will always arise and needs to be resolved in any team blueprinting effort.

What symbols should be used?

There is not a lexicon of blueprinting symbols that is required to be used. What is most important is that the symbols be defined, kept relatively simple, and used consistently by the team and across the organization if blueprints are being shared internally.

Should time or dollar costs be included on the blueprint?

Blueprints are very versatile. If reducing the time taken for various parts of the service process is an objective of the blueprinting effort, then time can be included. The same is true for dollar costs or anything else that is relevant as an objective. However, it is not advisable to put such information on the blueprint unless it is of central concern.

process. A photographic blueprint, including photos, slides, or video of the process, can be very useful at this stage to aid in analyzing the impact of tangible evidence and its consistency with the overall strategy and service positioning.

Exhibit 8.3 provides answers to frequently asked questions about service blueprinting.

Summary

Service providers must effectively match customer expectations to new service innovations and actual service process designs. However, because of the very nature of services—specifically, their intangibility, variability, and cocreation elements—the design and development of service offerings are complex and challenging. Many services are only vaguely defined before their introduction to the marketplace. This chapter outlines some of the challenges involved in innovating and designing services and some strategies for effectively overcoming the challenges. The chapter also describes a variety of types of service innovation, including service offering innovation, innovating around customer roles, and innovation through service solutions.

Through adaptations of the new product development process that is commonplace in goods production and manufacturing companies, service providers can begin to not only make their offerings and service solutions more explicit but also avoid failures. The service development process presented in the chapter includes nine stages, beginning with the development of a business and new service strategy and ending with postintroduction evaluation of the new service. Between these initial and ending stages are a number of steps and checkpoints designed to maximize the likelihood of innovation success. Carrying out the stages requires the inclusion of customers, contact employees, business partners, and anyone else who will affect or be affected by the new service.

Service blueprinting, a particularly useful technique for service innovation and design, is described in detail in this chapter. A blueprint can make a complex service concrete through its visual depiction of all the steps, actors, processes, and physical evidence of the service. The key feature of service blueprints is the focus on the customer—the customer's experience is documented first and is kept fully in view as the other features of the blueprint are developed.

Discussion Questions

1. Why is it challenging to innovate, design, and develop services?
2. Why is service innovation so critical for firms and countries?
3. What are the risks of attempting to describe services in words alone?
4. Find and discuss your own examples of the different types of service innovations presented in the "Types of Service Innovation" section in this chapter.
5. Compare and contrast the blueprints in Figures 8.5, 8.6, and 8.7.
6. How might a service blueprint be used for marketing, human resource, and operations decisions? Focus on one of the blueprint examples shown in the text as a context for your answer.
7. Assume that you are a multiproduct service company that wants to grow through adding new services. Describe a logical process you might use to introduce a new service to the marketplace. What steps in the process might be most difficult and why? How might you incorporate service blueprinting into the process?
8. Discuss Figure 8.2 in terms of the four types of opportunities for growth represented there. Choose a company or service, and explain how it could grow by developing new services in each of the four cells.

Exercises

1. Think of a new service you would like to develop if you were an entrepreneur. How would you go about it? Describe what you would do and where you would get your information.
2. Find a new and interesting service in your local area or a service offered on your campus. Document the service process via a service blueprint. To do this

exercise, you will probably need to interview one of the service employees and experience the service yourself, if possible. After you have documented the existing service, use blueprinting concepts to redesign the service or change it in some way.

3. Choose a service you are familiar with and document the customer action steps through a photographic or video blueprint. What is the "evidence of service" from your point of view as a customer?

4. Develop a service blueprint for a technology-delivered service (such as an Internet-based travel service). Compare and contrast this blueprint to one for the same service delivered via more traditional channels (such as a personal travel agent).

5. Compare two services on the Internet. Discuss the design of each in terms of whether it meets your expectations. How could the design or the service process be changed? Which one is most effective, and why?

Notes

1. www.petsmart.com, 2011; C. Dalton, "A Passion for Pets: An Interview with Philip L. Francis, Chairperson and CEO of PetSmart, Inc.," *Business Horizons* 48 (November–December 2005), pp. 469–475; D. Brady and C. Palmeri, "The Pet Economy," *BusinessWeek,* August 6, 2007, p. 44; M. Jarman, "PetSmart Quarterly Income Up 33%," *Arizona Republic,* May 19, 2011, p. D1.

2. D. H. Henard and D. M. Szymanski, "Why Some New Products Are More Successful Than Others," *Journal of Marketing Research* 38 (August 2001), pp. 362–375.

3. R. G. Cooper, *Winning at New Products,* 3rd ed. (Cambridge, MA: Perseus, 2001); R. G. Cooper and S. J. Edgett, *Product Development for the Service Sector* (Cambridge, MA: Perseus Books, 1999); and C. M. Froehle, A. V. Roth, R. B. Chase, and C. A. Voss, "Antecedents of New Service Development Effectiveness," *Journal of Service Research,* 3 (August 2000), pp. 3–17; R. G. Cooper, "Effective Gating: Make Product Innovation More Productive by Using Gates with Teeth," *Marketing Management* 18 (March–April 2009), pp. 12–17.

4. M. J. Bitner and S. W. Brown, "The Service Imperative," *Business Horizons 50th Anniversary Issue,* 51 (January–February 2008), pp. 39–46.

5. G. L. Shostack, "Understanding Services through Blueprinting," in *Advances in Services Marketing and Management,* vol. 1, ed. T. A. Swartz, D. E. Bowen, and S. W. Brown (Greenwich, CT: JAI Press, 1992), pp. 75–90.

6. Ibid., p. 76.

7. For excellent reviews of research and issues in new services development see *Journal of Operations Management* 20 (2002), Special Issue on New Issues and Opportunities in Service Design Research; A. Johne and C. Story, "New Service Development: A Review of the Literature and Annotated Bibliography," *European Journal of Marketing* 32, no. 3–4 (1998), pp. 184–251; B. Edvardsson, A. Gustafsson, M. D. Johnson, and B. Sanden, *New Service Development and Innovation in the New Economy* (Lund, Sweden: Studentlitteratur AB, 2000); and B. Edvardsson, A. Gustafsson, P. Kristensson, P. Magnusson, and J. Matthing, *Involving Customers in New Service Development* (London: Imperial College Press, 2006).

8. A. Ordanini and A. Parasuraman, "Service Innovation Viewed through a Service-Dominant Logic Lens: A Conceptual Framework and Empirical Analysis," Journal of Service *Research* 14 (February 2011), pp. 3–23.

9. B. Schneider and D. E. Bowen, "New Services Design, Development and Implementation and the Employee," in *Developing New Services,* ed. W. R. George and C. Marshall (Chicago: American Marketing Association, 1984), pp. 82–101.

10. S. Thomke, "R&D Comes to Services: Bank of America's Pathbreaking Experiments," *Harvard Business Review* 81 (April 2003), pp. 70–79.

11. A. L. Ostrom, M. J. Bitner, S. W. Brown, K. A. Burkhard, M. Goul, V. Smith-Daniels, H. Demirkan, and E. Rabinovich, "Moving Forward and Making a Difference: Research Priorities for the Science of Service," *Journal of Service Research* 13 (February 2010), pp. 4–36.

12. B. Mager on Service Design Network, www.service-design-network.org, accessed August 2011.

13. Ostrom et al., "Moving Forward and Making a Difference."

14. M. Stickdorn and J. Schneider, *This Is Service Design Thinking* (Amsterdam:, 2010), pp. 34–35.

15. Mager, www.service-design-network.org.

16. For additional detail and background on service design and service design thinking see: S. Dasu and R. B. Chase, "Designing the Soft Side of Customer Service," *Sloan Management Review*, 52, no. 1 (Fall 2010), pp. 33–39; L. G. Zomerdijk and C. A. Voss, "Service Design for Experience-Centric Services," *Journal of Service Research* 13 (February 2010), pp. 67–82; L. Patricio, R. P. Fisk, J. Falcao e Cunha, and L. Constantine, "Multilevel Service Design: From Customer Value Constellation to Service Experience Blueprinting," *Journal of Service Research* 14 (May 2011), pp. 180–200; Stickdorn and Schneider, *This Is Service Design Thinking*; Service Design Network, www.service-design-network.org.

17. L. L. Berry, V. Shankar, J. T. Parish, S. Cadwallader, and T. Dotzel, "Creating New Markets through Service Innovation," *Sloan Management Review* 47 (Winter 2006), pp. 56–63.

18. S. Michel, S. W. Brown and A. S. Gallan, "An Expanded and Strategic View of Discontinuous Innovations: Deploying a Service Dominant Logic," *Journal of the Academy of Marketing Science* (March 2008), pp. 54–66.

19. K. R. Tuli, A. K Kohli, and S. G. Bharadwaj, "Rethinking Customer Solutions: From Product Bundles to Relational Processes," *Journal of Marketing*, 71 (July), 2007, pp. 1–17.

20. L. A. Bettencourt, *Service Innovation*, New York: McGraw-Hill, 2010; L. A. Bettencourt and A. W. Ulwick, "The Customer-Centered Innovation Map," *Harvard Business Review*, 86 (5), May 2008, pp. 109–114.

21. M. Sawhney, S. Balasubramanian, and V. V. Krishnan, "Creating Growth with Services," *MIT Sloan Management Review*, Winter 2004, pp. 34–43.

22. See: C. Gronroos and P. Helle, "Adopting a Service Logic in Manufacturing," *Journal of Service Management*, 21 (5), 2010, 564–590; H. Gebauer, A. Gustafsson, and L. Witell, "Competitive Advantage Through Service Differentiation by Manufacturing Companies," *Journal of Business Research*, forthcoming, 2011; W. Ulaga and W. J. Reinartz, "Hybrid Offerings: How Manufacturing Firms Combine Goods and Services Successfully," *Journal of Marketing,* forthcoming, 2011;

V. A. Zeithaml, S. W. Brown, and M. J. Bitner, "The Service Continuum: Delineating a Conceptual Domain for Researchers and Managers," working paper, Center for Services Leadership, Arizona State University, 2011.

23. A. M. Epp and L. L. Price, "Designing Solutions Around Customer Network Identity Goals," *Journal of Marketing*, 75 (March), 2011, pp. 36–54.

24. For a discussion of these adaptations and related research issues, see I. Stuart, "Designing and Executing Memorable Service Experiences: Lights, Camera, Experiment, Integrate, Action!" *Business Horizons* 49 (2006), pp. 149–159; M. V. Tatikonda and V. A. Zeithaml, "Managing the New Service Development Process: Synthesis of Multidisciplinary Literature and Directions for Future Research," in *New Directions in Supply Chain Management: Technology, Strategy, and Implementation,* ed. T. Boone and R. Ganeshan (New York: AMACOM, 2002), pp. 200–236; and B. Edvardsson et al., *New Service Development and Innovation in the New Economy.*

25. See M. J. Bowers, "An Exploration into New Service Development: Organization, Process, and Structure," doctoral dissertation, Texas A&M University, 1985; A. Khurana and S. R. Rosenthal, "Integrating the Fuzzy Front End of New Product Development," *Sloan Management Review* 38 (Winter 1997), pp. 103–120; and R. G. Cooper, *Winning at New Products,* 3rd ed. (Cambridge, MA: Perseus Publishing, 2001). J. Hauser, G. J. Tellis, and A. Griffin, "Research on Innovation: A Review and Agenda for Marketing Science," *Marketing Science* 25 (November–December 2006), pp. 687–717.

26. See A. Griffin, "PDMA Research on New Product Development Practices: Updating Trends and Benchmarking Best Practices," *Journal of Product Innovation Management* 14 (1997), pp. 429–458; Thomke, "R&D Comes to Services"; Organization for Economic Cooperation and Development, "Promoting Innovation in Services," 2005.

27. R. G. Cooper, "Stage Gate Systems for New Product Success," *Marketing Management* 1, no. 4 (1992), pp. 20–29; J. Hawser, G. J. Tellis and A. Griffin, "Research on Innovations. A Review and Agenda for Marketing Science," *Marketing Science* 25 (63, 2006) pp. 687–717; Cooper, "Effective Gating."

28. A. Khurana and S. R. Rosenthal, "Integrating the Fuzzy Front End of New Product Development," *Sloan Management Review* 38 (Winter 1997), pp. 103–120.

29. J. Jargon, "KFC Savors Potential in Africa," *The Wall Street Journal*, December 8, 2010, p. B1.

30. D. Rigby and C. Zook, "Open-Market Innovation," *Harvard Business Review* 80 (October 2002), pp. 80–89.

31. D. Leonard and J. F. Rayport, "Spark Innovation through Empathic Design," *Harvard Business Review* 75 (November–December 1997), pp. 103–113; also see P. Underhill, *Why We Buy: The Science of Shopping* (New York: Simon and Schuster, 2007).

32. See Ordanini and Parasuraman, "Service Innovation Viewed through a Service-Dominant Logic Lens"; H. L. Melton and M. D. Hartline, "Customer and Frontline Employee Influence on New Service Development Performance," *Journal of Service Research* 13 (November 2011), pp. 411–425; L. McCreary, "Kaiser Permanente's Innovation on the Front Lines," *Harvard Business Review* 88 (September 2010), pp. 92–97.

33. R. Cross, A. Hargadon, S. Parise, and R. J. Thomas, "Together We Innovate," *The Wall Street Journal,* September 15–16, 2007, p. R6; J. C. Spender and B. Strong, "Who Has Innovative Ideas? Employees." *Wall Street Journal*, August 23, 2010, p. R5.

34. G. L. Shostack, "Service Design in the Operating Environment," in *Developing New Services,* ed. W. R. George and C. Marshall (Chicago: American Marketing Association, 1984), pp. 27–43.

35. E. E. Scheuing and E. M. Johnson, "A Proposed Model for New Service Development," *Journal of Services Marketing* 3, no. 2 (1989), pp. 25–34.

36. L. Chamberlain, "Going Off the Beaten Path for New Design Ideas," *New York Times,* March 12, 2006, Sunday Business Section.

37. Shostack, "Service Design," p. 35; see also I. Stuart, "Designing and Executing Memorable Service Experiences."

38. The service blueprinting section of the chapter draws from pioneering as well as current works in this area: G. L. Shostack, "Designing Services That Deliver," *Harvard Business Review* 62 (January–February 1984), pp. 133–139; G. L. Shostack, "Service Positioning through Structural Change," *Journal of Marketing* 51 (January 1987), pp. 34–43; and J. Kingman-Brundage, "The ABC's of Service System Blueprinting," in *Designing a Winning Service Strategy,* ed. M. J. Bitner and L. A. Crosby (Chicago: American Marketing Association, 1989), pp. 30–33; M. J. Bitner, A. L. Ostrom, and F. N. Morgan, "Service Blueprinting: A Practical Technique for Service Innovation," *California Management Review* 50 (Spring 2008), pp. 66–94.

39. Shostack, "Understanding Services through Blueprinting."

40. These key components are drawn from Kingman-Brundage, "The ABC's."

41. The text explaining Figures 8.5 and 8.6 relies on M. J. Bitner, "Managing the Evidence of Service," in *The Service Quality Handbook,* ed. E. E. Scheuing and W. F. Christopher (New York: American Management Association, 1993), pp. 358–370.

42. S. Fliess and M. Kleinaltenkamp, "Blueprinting the Service Company: Managing Service Processes Efficiently," *Journal of Business Research* 57 (2004), pp. 392–404.

43. For coverage of the practical benefits of blueprinting see E. Gummesson and J. Kingman-Brundage, "Service Design and Quality: Applying Service Blueprinting and Service Mapping to Railroad Services," in *Quality Management in Services,* ed. P. Kunst and J. Lemmink (Assen/Maastricht, Netherlands: Van Gorcum, 1991); and Bitner et al., "Service Blueprinting."

44. A. R. Hubbert, A. Garcia Sehorn, and S. W. Brown, "Service Expectations: The Consumer vs. the Provider," *International Journal of Service Industry Management* 6, no. 1 (1995), pp. 6–21.

Chapter Nine

Customer-Defined Service Standards

This chapter's objectives are to

1. Distinguish between company-defined and customer-defined service standards.
2. Differentiate among "hard" and "soft" customer-defined service standards and one-time fixes.
3. Explain the critical role of the service encounter sequence in developing customer-defined standards.
4. Illustrate how to translate customer expectations into behaviors and actions that are definable, repeatable, and actionable.
5. Explain the process of developing customer-defined service standards.

FedEx Sets Standards through SQI

Marketing research data are not the only numbers that FedEx tracks to run its business. The company drives its operations with the aid of one of the most comprehensive, customer-defined indices of service standards and measures in the world. FedEx's service quality indicator (SQI) was designed as "unforgiving internal performance measurement" to ensure that the company delivered its goal of "100 percent customer satisfaction after every interaction and transaction and 100 percent service performance on every package handled."[1] The development and implementation of SQI led to a Malcolm Baldrige National Quality Award.

What makes this service index different from those of other companies is its foundation in customer feedback. Since the 1980s, FedEx has documented customer complaints and used the information to improve internal processes. The initial composite listing of the 12 most common customer complaints, originally called the "Hierarchy of Horrors," included wrong day deliveries, right day late deliveries, pickups not made, lost packages, customers misinformed by FedEx, billing and paperwork mistakes, employee performance failures, and damaged packages. Although

The entire FedEx organization is driven by customer-defined service standards.

this list was useful, it fell short of giving management the ability to anticipate and eliminate customer complaints before they occurred.

In 1988 the company developed a 12-item statistical SQI to be a more "comprehensive, pro-active, customer-oriented measure of customer satisfaction and service quality."[2] The items included in SQI have changed slightly over time, as have the weights assigned to each of the items. Recent versions of SQI for FedEx Express have included the following components and weighting (based on relative importance of each component to customers):[3]

Indicator	Weight
Lost packages	50
Damaged packages	30
Failed (call-in) pickup	20
Wrong day/late delivery	15
Failed (regularly scheduled) pickup	10
Missing packages	10
Right day/late delivery	5

Another distinguishing feature of the SQI is its reporting in terms of *numbers* of errors rather than percentages. Management of the company strongly believes that percentages distance the company from the consumer: to report 1 percent of packages late diminishes the reality of 70,000 unhappy customers (1 percent of the approximately 7 million packages shipped a day). The SQI report is disseminated weekly to everyone in the company. On receipt of the report, root causes of recurring service failures are investigated. With a senior officer assigned to each component, and with bonuses for everyone in the company tied to performance on the SQI, the company continuously strives to meet its goal of 100 percent satisfaction with every transaction. In addition to FedEx Express using these items in its SQI, similar SQI metrics are used by other divisions of FedEx, including FedEx Ground, FedEx Freight, FedEx Office, and FedEx Services.[4]

As we saw in Chapters 5, 6, and 7, understanding customer requirements is the first step in delivering high service quality. Once managers of service businesses accurately understand what customers expect, they face a second critical challenge: using this knowledge to set service quality standards and goals for the organization. Service companies often experience difficulty in setting standards to match or exceed customer expectations, partly because doing so requires that the marketing and operations departments within a company work together. In most service companies, integrating the work of the marketing function and the operations function (appropriately called *functional integration*) is not a typical approach; more frequently these two functions operate separately—setting and achieving their own internal goals—rather than pursuing a joint goal of developing operations standards that best meet customer expectations.

Creating service standards that address customer expectations is not a common practice in most firms. Doing so often requires altering the very process by which work is accomplished, which is ingrained in tradition in many companies. Often change requires new equipment or technology. Change also necessitates aligning executives from different parts of the firm to understand collectively the comprehensive view of service quality from the customer's perspective. And almost always, change requires a willingness to be open to different ways of structuring, calibrating, and monitoring the way service is provided.

FACTORS NECESSARY FOR APPROPRIATE SERVICE STANDARDS

Standardization of Service Behaviors and Actions

The translation of customer expectations into specific service quality standards depends on the degree to which tasks and behaviors to be performed can be standardized or routinized. *Standardization* usually implies a nonvarying sequential process—similar to the mass production of goods—in which each step is laid out in order and all outcomes are uniform, whereas *customization* usually refers to some level of adaptation or tailoring of the process to the individual customer.[5] The goal of standardization is for the service firm to produce a consistent service product from one transaction to the next. The goal of customization for the service firm is to develop a service that meets each customer's individual needs. Some executives and managers believe that services cannot be standardized—that customization is essential for providing high-quality service. Managers also may feel that standardizing tasks is inconsistent with employee empowerment—that employees will feel controlled by the company if tasks are standardized. Further, they feel that services are too intangible to be measured. This view leads to vague and loose standard setting with little or no measurement or feedback.

In reality, many service tasks are routine (such as those needed for opening checking accounts or spraying lawns for weeds), and for these, specific rules and standards can be fairly easily established and effectively executed. Employees may welcome knowing how to perform actions most efficiently: it frees them to use their ingenuity in the more personal and individual aspects of their jobs.

Standardization of service can take three forms: (1) substitution of technology for personal contact and human effort, (2) improvement in work methods, and (3) combinations of these two methods. Examples of technology substitution include automatic teller machines, automatic car washes, and airport X-ray machines. Improvements in work methods are illustrated by home cleaning methods by maid services such as Molly Maid or The Maids, as well as routinized tax and accounting services developed by firms such as H&R Block.

Technology and work improvement methods facilitate the standardization of service necessary to provide consistent delivery to customers. By breaking tasks down and providing them efficiently, technology also allows the firm to calibrate service standards such as the length of time a transaction takes, the accuracy with which operations are performed, and the number of problems that occur. In developing work improvements, the firm comes to understand completely the process by which the service is delivered. With this understanding, the firm more easily establishes appropriate service standards.

Standardization, whether accomplished by technology or by improvements in work processes, reduces gap 2. Customer-defined standardization ensures that the most critical elements of a service are performed as expected by customers, not just that every action in a service is executed in a uniform manner. Using customer-defined standardization can, in fact, allow for and be compatible with employee empowerment—a topic discussed in more detail in Chapter 11. One example of this compatibility involves the time limits many companies establish for customer service calls. If their customers' highest priorities involve feeling good about the call or resolving problems, then setting a time limit for calls would be company defined and not in customers' best interests. Companies such as American Express, L.L. Bean, and Zappos.com, in using customer priorities rather than company priorities, have no set standard for the amount of time an employee spends on the telephone with a customer. Instead, they have standards that focus on making the customer satisfied and comfortable, allowing telephone representatives to use their own judgment about the time limits. As these companies have found, standardization of service is not appropriate in all situations. See the Strategy Insight for examples of these situations.

Formal Service Targets and Goals

Companies that have been successful in delivering consistently high service quality are noted for establishing formal standards to guide employees in providing service. These companies have an accurate sense of how well they are performing service that is critical to their customers—how long it takes to conduct transactions, how frequently service fails, how quickly they settle customer complaints—and strive to improve by defining goals that lead them to meet or exceed customer expectations.

One type of formal goal setting that is relevant in service businesses involves specific targets for individual behaviors or actions. As an example, consider the behavior "calls the customer back quickly," an action that signals responsiveness in contact employees. If the service goal for employee behavior is stated in such a general term as "call the customer back quickly," the standard provides little direction for service employees. Different employees will interpret this vague objective in their own ways, leading to inconsistent service: some may call the customer back in 10 minutes, whereas others may wait two to four days. And the firm itself will not be able to determine when or if individual employees meet the goal because its expression is not measurable—virtually any amount of time could be justified as "quickly." On the other hand, if the individual employee's service goal is to call each customer back within four hours, employees have a specific, unambiguous guideline about how quickly they should execute the action (four hours). Whether the goal is met is also unequivocal: if the call occurs within four hours, the company meets the goal; otherwise it does not.

Another type of formal goal setting involves the overall department or company target, most frequently expressed as a percentage, across all executions of the behavior or action. A department might set as its overall goal "to call the customer back within four hours 97 percent of the time" and collect data over a month's or year's time to evaluate the extent to which it meets the target. To illustrate, Puget Sound Energy—a utility company that serves customers in Washington State—has as part of its SQI a goal of answering 75 percent of customer calls with a "live" person within 30 seconds.[6]

Service firms that produce consistently excellent service—firms such as Walt Disney, FedEx, and Singapore Airlines—have very specific, quantified, measurable service goals. Disney calibrates employee performance on myriad behaviors and actions that contribute to guest perceptions of high service quality. Whether they are set and monitored using audits (such as timed actions) or customer perceptions (such as opinions about courtesy), service standards provide a means for formal goal setting.

Customer-, Not *Company-*, Defined Standards

Virtually all companies possess service standards and measures that are *company defined*—they are established to reach internal company goals for productivity, efficiency, cost, or technical quality. One company-defined standard that often does not meet customer expectations is the common practice of voice-activated telephone support systems that do not allow customers to speak to humans. Because these systems save companies money (and actually provide faster service to some customers), many organizations have switched from the labor-intensive practice of having customer

Strategy Insight When Is the Strategy of Customization Better Than Standardization?

This chapter focuses on the benefits of customer-defined standards in the context of situations—hotels, retail stores, service outlets—in which it is important to provide the same service to all or most customers. In these situations, standards establish strong guidelines for technology and employees to ensure consistency and reliability. In other services, providing standardization is neither appropriate nor possible, and customization—providing unique types and levels of service to customers—is a deliberate strategy.

In most "expert" services—such as accounting, consulting, engineering, and dentistry—professionals provide customized and individualized service; standardization of the tasks is often perceived as being impersonal, inadequate, and not in the customer's best interests. Because patient and client needs differ, these professionals offer very customized services that address individual requirements. They must adapt their offerings to the needs of each customer because each situation is different. Even within a given medical specialty, few patients have the same illness with precisely the same symptoms and the same medical history. Therefore, standardizing the amount of time a doctor spends with a patient is rarely possible—and is one of the reasons patients usually must wait before receiving medical services even though they have advance appointments. Because professionals such as accountants and lawyers cannot usually standardize what they provide, they often charge by the hour rather than by the job, which allows them to be compensated for the customized periods of time they spend with clients. It is important to recognize, however, that even in highly customized services, some aspects

of service provision can be routinized. Physicians and dentists, for example, can and do standardize recurring and nontechnical aspects such as checking patients in, weighing patients, taking routine measurements—such as blood pressure and heart rate, billing patients, and collecting payment. In delegating these routine tasks to assistants, physicians and dentists can spend more of their time using their expertise in diagnosis or patient care.

Another situation in which customization is the chosen strategy is in business-to-business contexts, particularly with key accounts. When accounts are large and critical to a provider, most aspects of service provision are customized. At a very basic level, this customization takes the form of service contracts—sometimes referred to as service-level agreements—in which the client and the provider agree on issues such as response time when clients have equipment failures or delivery time and fulfillment when retail clients depend on items being in stock in their stores. At a higher level, customization involves creative problem solving and innovative ideas (as in consulting services).

Finally, many consumer services are designed to be (or appear) very customized. These services include spa and upscale hotel visits, rafting trips, exotic vacations such as safaris, and even haircuts from expensive salons. In these situations, the steps taken to ensure the successful delivery of service are often standardized behind the scenes but appear to the customer to be very individualized. Even Disney theme parks use this approach, employing hundreds of standards to ensure the delivery of "magic" to customers in a seemingly unique way across the many service encounters.

representatives to using these "automated" systems. However, to close gap 2, standards set by companies must be based on customer requirements and expectations rather than just on internal company goals. In this chapter we make the case that company-defined standards are not typically successful in driving behaviors that close provider gap 2. Instead, a company must set *customer-defined standards*: operational standards based on pivotal customer requirements identified by customers. These standards are deliberately chosen to match customer expectations and to be calibrated the way the customer views and expresses them. Because these goals are essential to the provision of excellent service, the rest of this chapter focuses on customer-defined standards.

Knowing customer requirements, priorities, and expectation levels can be both effective and efficient. Anchoring service standards on customers can save money by identifying what the customer values, thus eliminating activities and features that the customer either does not notice or will not pay for. One of the key desires of customers visiting a Department of Motor Vehicles (DMV) office is to not have to wait a long time. In California a few years ago, government officials made it a top priority to improve service at the DMV and get wait-times down—and the results were impressive. Across the entire state, average wait-times in DMV offices were reduced from almost an hour to just under 30 minutes. Among the many changes were the addition of touch-screen kiosks to allow customers to enter information from their registration renewal notices; pay their fees using cash, checks, and credit cards; and within seconds complete their transactions. The government identified what was important to its customers and then implemented processes, hired additional staff, and trained employees to deliver service accordingly.[7] Puget Sound Energy (PSE) has used customer-defined standards for several years. Its customers have identified missed appointments, frequency and duration of power outages, and the amount of time it takes the company to field its calls as among the most important issues. Figure 9.1 displays how PSE did in 9 customer-defined standards in three key areas.

Although customer-defined standards need not conflict with productivity and efficiency, they do not originate with these company concerns. Rather, they are anchored in and steered by customer perceptual measures of service quality or satisfaction. The service standards that evolve from a customer perspective are likely to be different from company-defined service standards.

FIGURE 9.1
Customer Service Standards for Puget Sound Energy

Data Source: Puget Sound Energy.

Standards	Benchmark	Performance achieved
CUSTOMER SATISFACTION		
Percent of customers satisfied with Customer Access Center services,	90 percent or higher	96 percent
Percent of customers satisfied with field services, based on survey	90 percent or higher	96 percent
Number of complaints (per 1,000 customers, per year)	Less than 0.40	0.30
CUSTOMER SERVICES		
Percent of calls answered live within 30 seconds	75 percent or higher	78 percent
OPERATIONS SERVICES		
Frequency of non-major-storm power outages, (per year, per customer)	Less than 1.30 outages	0.86 outages
Length of power outages (per year, per customer)	Less than 5 hours, 20 minutes	4 hours, 47 minutes
Time from customer call to arrival of field technicians for electric system emergencies	No more than 55 minutes	52 minutes
Time from customer call to arrival of field technicians for natural gas emergencies	55 minutes or less	31 minutes
Percent of service appointments kept	92 percent	100 percent *

* Represents rounding to the nearest whole percentage.

TYPES OF CUSTOMER-DEFINED SERVICE STANDARDS

The types of standards that close provider gap 2 are *customer-defined standards*: operational goals and measures based on pivotal customer requirements identified by customers rather than on company concerns such as productivity or efficiency. Consider a typical operations standard such as inventory control. Most firms control inventory from the company's point of view. However, the highly successful office supply retailer Office Depot captures every service measurement related to inventory control *from the customer's point of view.* The company began with the question "What does the customer see?" and answered, "The average number of stockouts per week." Office Depot then designed a customer-focused measurement system based on measures such as the number of complaints and compliments it received about inventory as well as a transaction-based survey with the customer about its performance in this area. These and other customer-defined standards allowed for the translation of customer requirements into goals and guidelines for employee performance. Two major types of customer-defined service standards can be distinguished: "hard" and "soft." These standards will be discussed in the following two sections.

Hard Customer-Defined Standards

All the FedEx standards that constitute its SQI (mentioned in the chapter opener) fall into the category of hard standards and measures: *things that can be counted, timed, or observed* through audits. Exhibit 9.1 shows a sampling of the hard standards that have been established by several service companies. This list includes only those companies with hard standards that are customer defined—based on customers' requirements and perspectives. Because FedEx, one of the companies included in this list, has a relatively simple and standard set of services, it can translate most of its customers' requirements into hard standards and measures. Many of FedEx's standards relate to on-time delivery and not making mistakes, and for good reason. As we stressed in Chapter 3, customer expectations of reliability—fulfillment of service promises—are high. Studies across numerous industries have found that the most frequent customer complaints are associated with poor product performance (29 percent of all complaints) and service mistakes or problems (24 percent of all complaints).[8]

To address the need for reliability, companies can institute a "do it right the first time" and an "honor your promises" value system by establishing reliability standards. An example of a generic reliability standard that is relevant to virtually any service company is "right the first time," which means the service performed is done correctly the first time according to the customer's assessment. If the service involves delivery of physical products, "right the first time" to the customer might mean the shipment is accurate—that it contains all that the customer ordered and nothing that the customer did not order. If the service involves installation of equipment, "right the first time" likely means that the equipment was installed correctly and was able to be used immediately by the customer. Another example of a reliability standard is "right on time," which means that the service is performed at the scheduled time. The company representative arrives when promised or the delivery is made at the time the customer expects it. In more complex services, such as disaster recovery or systems integration in computer service, "right on time" would likely mean that the service was completed by the promised date.

Reliability is often the most important concern of service customers. In electronic retailing, on-time and accurate fulfillment of orders is one of the most important aspects of reliability. One of the best examples of customer-defined hard standards

Exhibit 9.1   Examples of Hard Customer-Defined Standards

Company	Customer Priorities	Customer-Defined Standards
FedEx	On-time delivery	• Number of packages right day, late • Number of packages wrong day, late • Number of late or missed pickups
Cardinal Health	On-time delivery	• Deliver 98 percent of all hospital products when promised
Dell Computer	On-time delivery	• Ship to target (percentage of orders delivered to customers on time with complete accuracy)
	Computer works properly	• Initial field incident rate (frequency of problems encountered by customers)
	Problems fixed right first time	• On time first time fix (percentage of problems fixed on the first visit by a service rep who arrives at the time promised)
Social Security Administration	Telephone access	• 95 percent of calls served within five minutes
Southwest Airlines	Reliability	• On-time arrival
	Responsiveness to complaints	• Two-week reply to letters
Lenscrafters	Quick turnaround on eyeglasses	• Glasses ready in one hour
Fotomat	Quick developing of photographs	• Photographs developed within one hour
Honeywell Home and Building Division	Fast delivery	• Orders entered same day received
	On-time delivery	• Orders delivered when promised
	Order accuracy	• Order 100 percent accurate
Puget Sound Energy	Reliability	• Length of non-major-storm power outages, per year, per customer • Frequency of non-major-storm power outages, per year, per customer • Percent of in-home service appointments kept
	Responsiveness	• Percent of calls answered live within 30 seconds by the Customer Access Center • Time from customer call to arrival of field technicians in response to power system emergencies
Zappos.com	Responsiveness	• Respond to 80 percent of all incoming calls within 20 seconds • Respond to all e-mail messages in less than 4 hours • Respond to live (online) chats in less than 10 seconds
Texas Instruments Defense System	Compliance with commitments	• On-time delivery • Product compliance to requirements
	More personal contact	• Increased number of personal visits

in the Internet context is the set of summary metrics used by Dell Computer for fulfillment:[9]

- *Ship to target (STT)*—the percentage of orders delivered on time with complete accuracy.
- *Initial field incident rate (IFIR)*—the frequency of customer problems.
- *On time first time fix (OTFTF)*—the percentage of problems fixed on the first visit by a service representative arriving at the time promised.

Technology Spotlight The Power of Good Responsiveness Standards

95/5 TELEPHONE RESPONSIVENESS AT THE SOCIAL SECURITY ADMINISTRATION

In the 1990s, at the National Performance Review's recommendation, an executive order required all U.S. federal government agencies that dealt directly with the public to survey their customers and establish customer service standards. By 1998 this order had resulted in more than 4,000 customer service standards from 570 agencies. One of the most successful came from the Social Security Administration (SSA) and illustrates a customer-defined hard standard relating to a technology issue that all customers face in dealing with public and private companies alike: telephone responsiveness.

The SSA knew that access—getting through to the agency on its 800 number—was the single biggest driver of customer satisfaction and public perception of the agency's competency. Unfortunately, customers more often than not repeatedly encountered busy signals on the 60 million calls they placed to the SSA's high-volume 800 number. The National Performance Review suggested to the agency that its service standard ought to be that everyone who called its 800 number would get through on the first try: 100 percent access! The SSA balked, recognizing that its telephone technology, limited employee resources, and wide fluctuations in demand would prevent the standard from being met.

The agency ultimately settled on a more reasonable standard: 95 percent of all callers would be served within five minutes. This standard became a very clear and focused goal that "everybody knew and everybody was shooting for," according to an SSA manager. Early measurements indicated less-than-stellar performance; in 1995 only 73.5 percent of callers got through in five minutes.

What followed was an impressive effort of technology, people, and measurement. According to an expert, "SSA endured tremendous expense, dislocation, pain—and even failure—to meet its standard." First, SSA officials developed a new phone system with AT&T that involved a sophisticated call-routing approach. Second, the organization trained virtually all technical people who held jobs other than in teleservices in those skills, so that they could be shifted during peak hours to help with the volume. Third, the agency restricted leave for teleservice representatives at peak times, increased the use of overtime, and worked with employees to change processes and rules to improve performance.

The low point in performance to the standard was during the transition to the new system. In November 1995, only 57.2 percent of callers got through within five minutes. Even worse was that, on the first day

The Social Security Administration's standard of serving 95 percent of all callers within five minutes was customer-defined.

Dell tracks its performance to these standards and rewards employees on the basis of its "met promises" or reliability, which is often greater than 98 percent.

Hard service standards for responsiveness are set to ensure the speed or promptness with which companies deliver products (within two working days), handle complaints (by sundown each day), answer questions (within two hours), answer the telephone (see the Technology Spotlight), and arrive for repair calls (within 30 minutes of the estimated time). In addition to setting standards that specify levels of response, companies must have well-staffed customer service departments. Responsiveness perceptions diminish when customers wait to get through to the company by telephone, are put on hold, or are dumped into a telephone mail system.

back to work in January 1996, the AT&T 800-number system crashed, leading to even more busy signals. By February, after AT&T fixed the system and the organization got used to its changes, performance improved significantly. The five-minute access rate was 92.1 percent in February and 95.9 percent in November, and it has been above 95 percent ever since.

The SSA standard was successful because it was specific, measurable, and meaningful to customers. Because its results were documented and publicized both within and outside the agency, both employees and management were accountable for performance. Unlike many of the vague, meaningless standards that resulted from the National Performance Review's work with government agencies, this one was a winner.

80/20 TELEPHONE RESPONSIVENESS AT ZAPPOS.COM

Zappos.com is an online shoe company that is well known for its excellent customer service. From its early days, Zappos has put an extremely high priority on being responsive to customers who call, e-mail, or initiate a live chat session with the company. Their reasons for calling might be to check on the status of a shoe order, complain about the fit of a pair of shoes, or ask questions about complimentary products. Based on feedback received from customers, Zappos wanted to be quick to address customers' calls and respond to their needs, so that it could create a positive, pleasant experience for them. Three of the service standards it put into place were (1) to respond to 80 percent of all incoming calls within 20 seconds, (2) to respond to all e-mail messages in less than four hours, and (3) to respond to live (online) chats in less than 10 seconds.

Zappos, unlike many companies, does not make it difficult for customers to contact the firm. Its website makes it easy for customers to find a toll-free telephone number to call or to initiate a live chat with a company representative, and it encourages customers to contact the firm. Zappos uses a call management system technology to constantly monitor the number or calls in the queue, the number of customers having conversations with employees, and the number of employees at lunch or on break. This technology also collects information about a variety of other topics, such as the types of issues being discussed in these calls and the resolutions provided to meet customer needs.

To consistently meet its standard of fielding 80 percent of all incoming calls within 20 seconds, Zappos makes sure that it has a sufficient number of employees available to field calls or chat sessions. The firm employs sophisticated forecasting technology to analyze historical trends regarding incoming calls, such as peak times of the day, days of the week, and months of the year. This technology also takes into account other past trends (such as the number of calls initiated when the company begins to carry a new line of shoes or the growth rate of spending of a particular market segment). All of this information is used to forecast likely demand for inbound traffic to its call center and thus the number of staff needed to help ensure that the company can meet its 80/20 service standard. Similar technology enables Zappos to regularly meet its service standards for responsiveness to e-mail messages and chat sessions.

Sources: D. Osborne, "Higher Standards," *Government Executive,* July 2000, pp. 63–71; e-mail communication with Rob Siefker, Senior Manager for Zappos CLT, Inc., August, 2010.

When it comes to providing service across cultures and continents, service providers need to recognize that customer-defined service standards often need to be adapted. Our Global Feature provides examples of companies with worldwide brands that have found ways to achieve universally high service quality while allowing for local differences in service standards.

Soft Customer-Defined Standards

Not all customer priorities can be counted, timed, or observed through audits. As Albert Einstein said, "Not everything that counts can be counted, and not everything that can be counted, counts." For example, "understanding and knowing the customer"

How do companies adjust for cultural or local differences in service standards if they recognize that these geographic differences are related to varying customer expectations? Companies with worldwide brands have much to lose if their service standards vary too much across countries, and therefore they must find ways to achieve universally high quality while still allowing for local differences.

SERVICE STANDARDS AT FOUR SEASONS: GLOBAL AND LOCAL NORMS

As one of the world's leading operators of luxury hotels and resorts, the Four Seasons Hotel successfully manages 82 properties in 35 countries by balancing universal service standards with standards that vary by country. The company, which has received more AAA Five Diamond awards than any other hotel company and is regularly named as the top choice for travelers in the United States in the "Hotels, Resorts, and Spas" category, owes much of its success to its seven "service culture standards" expected of *all* staff *all* over the world at *all* times. The seven standards, which form the acrostic SERVICE, are:

1. **Smile:** employees will actively greet guests, smile, and speak clearly in a friendly manner.
2. **Eye:** employees will make eye contact, even in passing, with an acknowledgment.
3. **Recognition:** all staff will create a sense of recognition by using the guest's name, when known, in a natural and discreet manner.
4. **Voice:** staff will speak to guests in an attentive, natural, and courteous manner, avoiding pretension and in a clear voice.
5. **Informed:** all guest contact staff will be well informed about their hotel, will take ownership of simple requests, and will not refer guests elsewhere.
6. **Clean:** staff will always appear clean, crisp, well groomed, and well-fitted.
7. **Everyone:** everyone, everywhere, all the time, will show care for our guests.

Global service standards at Four Seasons are adapted, when necessary, to local cultures.

In addition to these culture standards that are expected of all staff all over the world, the hotel has 270 core standards that apply to different aspects of service provision (examples include "the staff will be aware of arriving vehicles and will move toward them, opening doors within 30 seconds" and "unanswered guest room phones will be picked up within 5 rings, or 20 seconds"). Exceptions to these 270 standards are allowed if they make local or cultural sense. For example, in the United States, coffee pots are left on tables at breakfast; in many parts of Europe, including France, customers perceive this practice as a lack of service and servers personally refill coffee cups as needed. Standards for uniforms and decor differ across cultures, but minimum expectations must be met everywhere.

SERVICE STANDARDS AT TOYOTA IN JAPAN

In 2005 Toyota began selling its luxury car, Lexus, in Japan. Although Lexus was already the best-selling luxury brand in the United States, in Japan it had very little name recognition. The company wanted a way to set Lexus apart from the Toyota brand and decided to focus on emphasizing customer service. Japan has a long history of unique customs and Toyota thought that perhaps they could bring that to the Lexus brand. So Toyota approached an etiquette school—the Ogasawara

is a customer priority that cannot be adequately captured by a standard that counts, times, or observes employees. In contrast to hard measures, soft measures must be documented using perceptual data. We call the second category of customer-defined standards *soft standards and measures* because they are opinion-based measures and cannot be directly observed. They must be collected by talking to customers,

Ryu Reihou Institute in Tokyo—that specializes in teaching the art of daily behavior, including the correct way to bow, hold chopsticks, and sit on a tatami mat floor, to help develop techniques that they could apply to selling cars.

Although typical clients of the school are well-bred families who want their children to learn good table manners and posture, the institute spent several months studying Lexus and its employees' interactions with customers. The result was the development of new service standards, several patterned after samurai behaviors. For example, salespersons are instructed to:

- Assume the samurai warrior's "waiting position" by leaning 5 to 10 degrees forward when a customer is looking at a car.
- Bow more deeply to a customer who has purchased a car than to a casual window shopper.
- Display the "Lexus Face," a closed-mouth smile intended to put customers at ease.
- Stand with left hand over right, fingers together and thumbs interlocked, as the samurais did to show they were not about to draw their swords.
- Stand about two arms' lengths from customers when they are looking at a car and come in closer when closing a deal.
- Point with all five fingers to a car door's handle, right hand followed by left, then gracefully open the door with both hands.
- When serving coffee or tea, kneel on the floor with both feet together and both knees on the ground.

Toyota understands that these standards would not work well in many of their markets, particularly the United States, but felt the standards were necessary for the Lexus brand to compete with the two luxury car market leaders—BMW and Mercedes Benz—in Japan.

SERVICE STANDARDS IN PAKISTAN

Research on service quality in Western countries generally finds reliability to be the most important dimension. Western customers expect firms to be dependable and accurate and to do what they have promised. Research in Pakistan, however, suggests that customers have different standards of service quality:

- Reliability has been conceptualized as the ability to perform the promised service dependably and accurately. Although Pakistani customers seem to concur with this conceptualization, they do not expect service delivery to be executed in absolute terms. "Promises are mostly kept" is how reliability would be described. They can apparently tolerate service failure with the content or timing of service as long as an acceptable substitute is provided within an appropriate time frame. It is generally important for them to maintain a long-term relationship with the service provider.
- Pakistani customers seem to include accessibility as a part of their evaluation of a service provider's reliability. This is especially important in case of health care and other public services. Availability of a service at the time when it is needed is of extreme importance in Pakistan.
- Physical safety is also an important factor when Pakistani customers evaluate service offerings. In a society that frequently has law-and-order problems, a customer's physical safety becomes important when doing business with a service provider.

Such findings suggest that service firms from Western cultures doing business in Pakistan can probably succeed with service standards that do not call for perfectly reliable service, emphasize service recovery, focus on delivering service when promised and across a wide range of times, or address issues of personal safety.

Sources: R. Hallowell, D. Bowen, and C. Knoop, "Four Seasons Goes to Paris," *Academy of Management Executive* 16, no. 4 (2002), pp. 7–24; A. Chozick, "The Samurai Sell: Lexus Dealers Bow to Move Swank Cars," *The Wall Street Journal,* July 9, 2007, p. A1; and N. Raajpoot, "Reconceptualizing Service Encounter Quality in a Non-Western Context," *Journal of Service Research* 7 (November 2004), pp. 181–201.

employees, or others. Soft standards provide direction, guidance, and feedback to employees in ways to achieve customer satisfaction and can be examined by measuring customer perceptions and beliefs. Soft standards are especially important for person-to-person interactions such as the selling process and the delivery process for professional services. Exhibit 9.2 displays several examples of soft customer-defined

Exhibit 9.2 Examples of Soft Customer-Defined Standards

Company	Customer Priorities	Customer-Defined Standards
General Electric	Interpersonal skills of operators:	• Take ownership of the call • Follow through with promises made • Be courteous and knowledgeable • Understand the customer's question or request
Ritz-Carlton	Being treated with respect	• React quickly to solve any problems immediately • Use proper telephone etiquette • Do not screen calls • Eliminate call transfers when possible
Nationwide Insurance	Responsiveness	• Provide a human voice on the line when customers report problems
L.L.Bean	Calming human voice; minimal customer anxiety	• Use appropriate tone of voice • Do not engage in other tasks (e.g., arranging gift boxes) while on the telephone with customers
Peninsula Regional Medical Center	Respect	• Keep patient information confidential • Never discuss patients and their care in public areas • Listen to patients with empathy • Be courteous and do not use jargon • Keep noise to a minimum • Never "talk over" a patient
American Express	Resolution of problems	• Resolve problem at first contact (no transfers, other calls, or multiple contacts) • Communicate and give adequate instructions • Take all the time necessary
	Treatment	• Listen • Do everything possible to help • Be appropriately reassuring (open and honest)
	Courtesy of representative	• Put card member at ease • Be patient in explaining billing process • Display sincere interest in helping card member • Listen attentively • Address card member by name • Thank card member at end of call

standards. A casino that one of us has worked with has identified five soft service standards to encourage its employees to provide an appropriate level of attention and respect to its guests—two issues that its customers have indicated are important to them. Two of these standards are for employees to "display a demeanor that could be described as friendly, polite, cheerful, or upbeat" and to "offer an appropriate verbal greeting" when interacting with customers. Unlike the hard service standards described earlier, such soft standards are not easily quantifiable, but a firm's performance on these standards can be assessed via surveys and other means that capture customer perceptions of how the firm is doing on the standards.

Many firms have both hard and soft customer-defined standards. The differences between hard and soft standards are illustrated in Exhibit 9.3 using the customer care standards developed at Ford Motor Company.

Exhibit 9.3 Hard and Soft Standards for Service at Ford Motor Company

In this chapter we discuss two types of customer-defined service standards. "Hard" standards and measures are operational measures that can be counted, timed, or observed through audits. The other category, "soft" standards, makes use of opinion-based measures that cannot be obtained by counting or timing but instead must be asked of the customer. Ford Motor Company provides an example that illustrates the difference between hard and soft standards. Several years ago Ford was looking to develop Customer Care standards for service at their many dealerships. Marketing research involving 2,400 customers asked them about specific expectations for automobile sales and service; Ford used this input to help identify the level of service that dealerships would need to provide to receive "Blue Oval Certified" status. The following seven specific service standards were established as most critical to customers in the service department of dealerships.

1. Appointment available within one day of customer's requested service day.
2. Write-up begins within four minutes or less of customer arrival.
3. Service needs are courteously identified, accurately recorded on repair order, and verified with customer.
4. Vehicle serviced right on the first visit.
5. Service status provided within one minute of inquiry.
6. Vehicle ready at agreed-upon time.
7. Thorough explanation given of work done, coverage, and charges.

HARD STANDARDS AND MEASURES

Several of the standards Ford identified fall into the category of hard standards—they can be counted, timed, or observed through audits. Standards 2 and 5, for example, could be timed by an employee in the service establishment. The hard measure could be either the frequency or percentage of times that the standard's time periods are met or the average times themselves (e.g., average time that write-ups begin). Other standards could be counted or audited, such as standards 1, 4, and 6. The service clerk who answers the telephone could record the number of times that appointments were available within one day of the customer's request. The number of repeat visits could be counted to measure standard 4, and the number of vehicles ready at the agreed-upon time could be tallied as customers came in to pick up their cars.

SOFT STANDARDS AND MEASURES

Consider standards 3 and 7 and note how they differ from the ones we have just discussed. These standards represent desired behaviors that are soft and therefore cannot be counted or timed. For example, the courteous behavior included in standard 3 cannot be counted. Likewise, standard 7 requires a different type of measure—the customer's perception or opinion about whether this behavior was performed appropriately. It is not that soft standards cannot be measured; instead, they must be measured in different ways.

Soft standards provide direction, guidance, and feedback to employees in ways to achieve customer satisfaction and can be quantified by measuring customer perceptions and beliefs. Soft standards are especially important for person-to-person interactions such as the selling process and the delivery process for professional services. To be effective, companies must provide feedback to employees about customer perceptions of their performance.

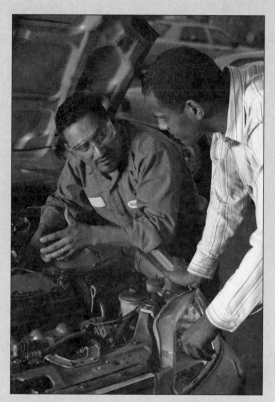

Ford Motor Company Customer Care has a variety of both hard and soft service standards.

One-Time Fixes

When customer research is undertaken to find out what aspects of service need to be changed, requirements can sometimes be met using one-time fixes. *One-time fixes* are technology, policy, or procedure changes that, when instituted, address customer requirements. We further define one-time fixes as company standards that can be met by an outlet (e.g., a franchisee) making a one-time change that does not involve employees and therefore does not require motivation and monitoring to ensure compliance. We include one-time fixes in our discussion of standards because organizations with multiple outlets often must clearly define these standards to ensure consistency. As an example, Hampton Inns' "Make It Hampton" program required that all inns institute 60 new product and service standards, many of which were one-time fixes. The fixes implemented in the first phase of the program included lap desks in rooms, outdoor planter gardens to hide trash containers, red carpet welcome mats, and new lobby artwork and music.[10] The second phase of the program, labeled the "Cloud Nine Bed Experience," included raising all of its 150,000 hotel beds at the time to a standard of 28 to 31 inches off the floor—in line with most home bedrooms today, upgrading pillows to jumbo size, and adding comforters, sheets with a greater thread count, and fitted bottom sheets. Performance standards do not typically need to be developed for such fixes because the one-time change in technology, equipment, furnishings, policies, or procedures accomplishes the desired change.

Two other examples of successful one-time fixes include Hertz's rental car express check-in and Granite Rock's 24-hour express service. In both of these examples, customers expressed a desire to be served in ways different from the past. Hertz's customers had clearly indicated their frustration at waiting in long lines. Granite Rock, a Malcolm Baldrige National Quality Award winner with a "commodity" product, had customers who desired 24-hour availability of ground rock from its quarry.

Whereas most companies in these industries decided for various reasons not to address these customer requirements, Hertz and Granite Rock each responded with one-time fixes that virtually revolutionized the service quality delivered by their companies. Hertz used technology to create Express Checkout, a one-time fix that also resulted in productivity improvements and cost reductions. The company also pioneered a similar one-time fix for hotel Express Check-In, again in response to customers' expressed desires. Granite Rock created an ATM-like system for 24-hour customer access to rock ground to the 14 most popular consistencies. The company created its own Granite Xpress Card that allowed customers to enter, select, and receive their supplies at any time of the day or night.

One-time fixes are often accomplished by technology. Technology can simplify and improve customer service, particularly when it frees company personnel by handling routine, repetitive tasks and transactions. Customer service employees can then spend more time on the personal and possibly more essential portions of the job. In recent years some hospital emergency rooms have added check-in kiosks so that patients who are not experiencing a true "emergency" can enter personal information, thus reducing time spent waiting in line to register and explain symptoms.[11]

DEVELOPMENT OF CUSTOMER-DEFINED SERVICE STANDARDS

Turning Customer Requirements into Specific Behaviors and Actions

How have firms such as FedEx, Puget Sound Energy, and Zappos.com been able to develop commendable customer-defined service standards? Figure 9.2 shows the general process for setting customer-defined service standards.

FIGURE 9.2
Process for Setting Customer-Defined Standards

1. Identify existing or desired service encounter sequence.

2. Translate customer expectations into behaviors/actions.

3. Determine appropriate standards.

| Measure by audits or operating data | ← Hard standards ← | 4. Develop measurements for standards. | → Soft standards → | Measure by transaction-based surveys |

5. Establish target levels for standards.

6. Track measures against standards.

7. Provide feedback about performance to employees.

8. Update target levels and measures.

Step 1: Identify Existing or Desired Service Encounter Sequence

A customer's overall service quality evaluation is the accumulation of evaluations of multiple service experiences. Service encounters are the component pieces needed to establish service standards in a company. In establishing standards firms are concerned with service encounter quality and thus want to understand the specific requirements and priorities of the customer for each service encounter. Therefore, the first step in establishing customer-defined standards is to delineate the *service encounter sequence.* Identifying the sequence can be done by listing the sequential steps and activities that the customer experiences in receiving the service. Alternatively, service blueprints (see Chapter 8) can be used to identify the sequence by noting customer activities across the top of the blueprint. Vertical lines from customer activities into the lower levels of the blueprint signal the points at which service encounters take place. Standards that meet customer expectations for each interaction can then be identified. Ideally, the company would be open to discovering customers' desired service encounter sequences, exploring the ways customers want to do business with the firm.

A firm might also consider which of its service encounters have the greatest impact on customers. Marriott, for example, has found that encounters in the first 10 minutes of a hotel stay

First encounters, such as for a hotel stay, are critical and have a significant impact on customers in most service settings.

are the most critical, leading to a focus on customers' front-desk experiences (such as express check-in). Some research indicates that a strong finish in the final event of the service encounter sequence has a greater impact on overall satisfaction.[12] As a result, other hotels have chosen to focus on the "back end" of the hotel experience—check-out, parking, bellperson services—to leave a strong final impression. To be safe, the Ritz-Carlton assumes both the first and last encounters are important and therefore includes as two of the three "Steps of Service" (part of its famous "Gold Standards") instructions for employees to provide guests with "a warm and sincere greeting" and "a fond farewell [with] a warm good-bye" while using the guests' names.[13]

Step 2: Translate Customer Expectations into Specific Behaviors and Actions

Setting a standard in broad conceptual terms, such as "improve skills in the company," is ineffective because the standard is difficult to interpret, measure, and achieve. When a company collects data, it often captures customer requirements in very abstract terms. In general, contact or field people often find such data are not diagnostic but rather too broad and general. Such research neither tells them specifically what is wrong and right in their customer relationships nor helps them understand what activities can be eliminated, so that the most important actions can be accomplished. In most cases, field people need help translating the data into specific actions to deliver better customer service.

Figure 9.3 shows different levels of abstraction/concreteness for standards in a service firm, arrayed from top (most abstract) to bottom (most concrete and specific). At the very abstract level are customer requirements too general to be useful to employees: customers want satisfaction, value, and relationships. The next level under these very general requirements includes abstract dimensions of service quality already discussed in this text: reliability, responsiveness, empathy, assurance, and tangibles. One level further are attributes which are more specific in describing requirements.[14]

FIGURE 9.3 **What Customers Expect: Getting to Actionable Steps**

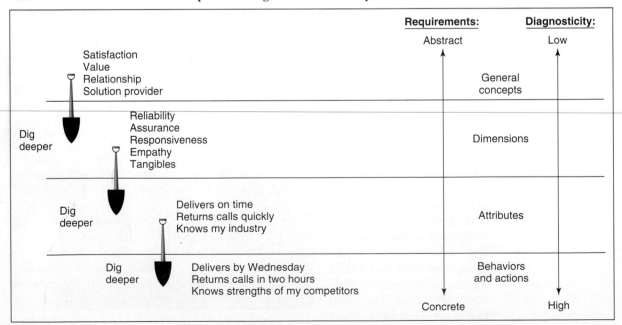

If we dig still deeper beneath the attribute level, we get to specific behaviors and actions at the appropriate level of specificity for setting standards. Thus, in step 2, abstract customer requirements and expectations must be translated into concrete, specific behaviors and actions associated with each service encounter. Abstract requirements (like reliability) can call for a different behavior or action in each service encounter.

Information on behaviors and actions should be gathered and interpreted by an objective source such as a research firm or an inside department with no stake in the ultimate decisions. If the information is filtered through company managers or frontline people with an internal bias, the outcome can easily result in company-defined, rather than customer-defined, standards. Research techniques discussed in Chapter 5 that are relevant for eliciting behaviors and actions include in-depth interviewing of customers, focus group interviews, and other forms of research such as partnering. Using such research, John Robert's Spa, a salon in northeast Ohio, identified seven typical service encounters that the average customer experiences when coming to the spa, including the initial phone call to schedule a visit, arrival at the spa, consultation with an employee prior to receiving any treatment, delivery of the spa service itself, wrap-up of the treatment, paying and exiting the spa, and postexperience contact. For each encounter, specific employee behaviors were identified (see Exhibit 9.4). For example, when the client first enters the spa, the hostess is expected to greet the customer enthusiastically within 10 seconds, confirm the appointment, offer to hang up the customer's coat, offer a tour of the facility (if a new customer), and use the customer's name at least four times during the check-in.

A real-world example of the difference in requirements across the four levels depicted in Figure 9.3 illustrate their practical significance. In a traditional measurement system for a major company's training division, only one aspect of the instructor was included in its class evaluation: ability of instructor. During qualitative research relating to the attributes that satisfy students, three somewhat more specific requirements were elicited: (1) instructor's style, (2) instructor's expertise, and (3) instructor's management of class. Although the articulation of the three attributes was more helpful to instructors than the broad "ability of instructor," management found that the attributes were still too broad to help instructors wanting to improve their course delivery. When the company invested in a customer-defined standards project, the resulting measurement system was far more useful in diagnosing student requirements because the research focused on *specific behaviors and actions* of instructors that met student requirements. Instead of a single broad requirement or three general attributes, the requirements of students were articulated in 14 specific behaviors that related to the instructor and 11 specific actions that related to the course content. These behaviors and actions were clearly more diagnostic for communicating what was good and bad in the courses. An additional benefit of this approach was that feedback on behaviors and actions was perceived as less personal than feedback on traits or personal characteristics. It was also easier for employees of the company to make changes that related to behaviors rather than to personality traits.

Step 3: Determine Appropriate Standards

The next step involves determining whether hard or soft standards should be used to capture a given behavior and action. Recall that hard standards consist of quantifiable measures of employee behaviors and actions; soft standards are often concerned with more abstract requirements or issues, are not as easily quantifiable, and are often much more subjective. One of the biggest mistakes companies make in this step is to hastily choose a hard standard. Companies are accustomed to operational (and often

John Robert's Spa has developed a reputation for extraordinary service as a hair salon. Part of its success stems from its understanding and careful management of the sequence of service encounters customers are subjected to, which it labels the "Customer Experience Cycle." In identifying the seven most typical service encounters that form the basis of its service process, John Robert's has specified precisely what every client should experience when receiving a haircut at John Robert's. The following service standards are expected of employees across these seven encounters.

Preexperience: provided by guest care personnel

- Answer the phone enthusiastically, saying, "Thank you for calling John Robert's Mayfield (salon location). This is Kelly. How can I help you?"
- Allow plenty of time to answer all of the client's questions concerning services, the designers' credentials, availability, and so on.
- Give each client an opportunity to book appointments for additional services.
- Use the client's name at least four times during the call.
- Offer directions to the salon.
- Confirm the service, operator, time, and date.
- As the last thing before hanging up, ask, "Is there anything else I can do for you?"
- Make a confirmation call to the client 24 hours before the appointment.

Start of the experience: provided by hostess

- Greet the client enthusiastically within 8 to 10 seconds.
- Confirm the client's appointment.
- Ask the client to fill out the information card.
- Immediately notify the operator of the client's arrival.
- Offer to hang up the client's coat and to provide a refreshment.
- Inform the client of any delays.
- Offer a tour of the entire facility.

- Show the client where the changing rooms are.
- Monitor the client's wait, and notify the operator again if the client is not taken within 10 minutes of the scheduled appointment.
- Use the client's name at least four times during the check-in.

Preservice: provided by designer

- Provide consultation every time with every client.
- Show portfolio, analyze client's needs, and discuss client's expectations.
- Provide stress-relieving scalp massage.
- For men, provide a minifacial.
- Provide shampoo and conditioner.
- Use a white cape for new clients.

Service: provided by designer

- Give an excellent haircut.
- Massage hands and arms.
- Clean client's jewelry during massage.
- Keep the conversation on a professional level.
- Give lesson on blow-dry styling.
- Explain products used.

Postservice: provided by designer

- Touch-up makeup for all female clients.
- Make client aware of additional services that salon/spa offers.
  - Give complimentary bang trim.
  - Inform client of complimentary blow-dry lesson in the future, to help the client duplicate it on her own.
  - Offer men complimentary neck and sideburn trimmings between visits.
  - Offer referral incentives: $5 gift certificate for every referral and contest with prizes for the clients who refer the most new clients during the year.

easily quantifiable) measures and often have a bias toward them. However, unless the hard standard adequately captures the expected behavior and action, it is not customer defined. The best way to decide whether a hard standard is appropriate is to first establish a soft standard by means of trailer calls and then determine over time which operational aspect most correlates to this soft measure. Figure 9.4 shows the linkage

Conclusion of experience: provided by various staff

- Assistant, operator, and receptionist: give client a friendly and enthusiastic send-off.
- Designer and receptionist: give an opportunity to purchase products used.
- Main operator: give client a business card.
- Receptionist: give client opportunity to schedule next appointment.
- Receptionist: for new clients, give client a new-client package that includes a menu of services, newsletter, business card, magnet, and five-question form. Inform client of 10 percent off next visit if she returns the completed form within six weeks.
- Receptionist: during check-out use client's name at least four times.
- Operator: input personal information (such as name of spouse, children) in computer under client's name for use on future visits.

Postexperience: provided by support staff

- Client receives an enthusiastic phone call within 24 hours.
- Client receives a thank-you postcard within 48 hours.
- Client receives a quarterly newsletter.
- Client receives a birthday card.
- If client has a challenge, handle it immediately on the spot. Make it right. Fill out customer challenge sheet and have management follow up.
- If client is not retained after four months: send out a reminder card that client is due for an appointment.
- If a client is not retained after eight months: send out an incentive to return (such as 25 percent off for next visit).
- If a client is not retained after 12 months: survey with a letter or phone call to find out why.

Source: J. R. DiJulius, *Secret Service: Hidden Systems That Deliver Unforgettable Customer Value* (New York: American Management Association, 2001), pp. 8–11.

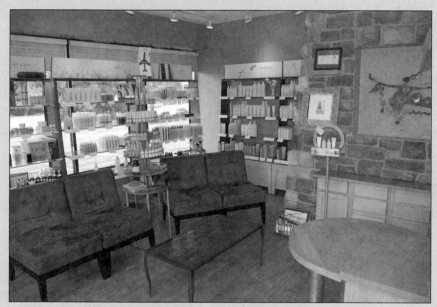

John Robert's Spa has identified service standards expected of employees across the seven most typical service encounters.

between speed of complaint handling (a hard measure) and satisfaction (a soft measure); the figure illustrates that satisfaction strongly depends on the number of hours it takes to resolve a complaint.

Prioritizing the behaviors and actions—of which there will be many—into those for which customer-defined standards will be established is also crucial in determining

FIGURE 9.4
Linkage between
Hard and Soft
Measures for Speed
of Complaint
Handling

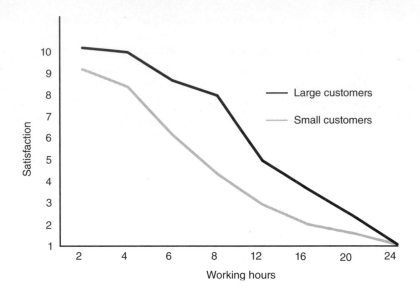

standards. The following are the most important criteria for creation of appropriate service standards.

1. The standards are based on behaviors and actions that are very important to customers.
2. The standards cover performance that needs to be improved or maintained.
3. The standards cover behaviors and actions employees have control over and can improve.
4. The standards are understood and accepted by employees.
5. The standards are predictive rather than reactive—based on current and future customer expectations rather than past complaints.
6. The standards are challenging but realistic.

Step 4: Develop Measurements for Standards

Once companies have determined whether hard or soft standards are appropriate and which specific standards best capture customer requirements, they must develop feedback measures that adequately capture the standards. Two types of measures are hard measurements and soft measurements.

Hard measurements typically involve mechanical counts or technology-enabled measurement of time or errors. What distinguishes these measurements from soft measurements is that they can be measured continuously and operationally without asking the customer's opinion of them. To demonstrate, here are some of the actual measurements of hard standards of the FedEx Express SQI:

- *Missing packages:* the number of packages that do not have a final disposition determined for two consecutive business days.
- *Damaged packages:* the number of claims for cost of contents for packages with visible or concealed damage.
- *Wrong day or late deliveries:* the number of packages delivered after the commitment date.[15]

In these and other hard measurements, assessment involves a count of the number and type of actions or behaviors that are correct or incorrect. Somewhere in the operation system these actions and behaviors are tabulated, frequently through information technology. Other gauges of hard standards include service guarantee lapses (the number of times a service guarantee is invoked because the service did not meet the promise), amounts of time (as in the number of hours or days to respond to a question or complaint or minutes waited in line), and frequencies associated with relevant standards (such as the number of visits made to customers or the number of abandoned telephone inquiries). L.L. Bean earned its reputation for outstanding customer service using continually updated data (i.e., hard measures) on models, colors, and sizes of products in stock. This system allows the company to set and achieve high standards of customer service—and it enables L.L. Bean to fill an incredible 99.4 percent of orders accurately.[16]

The appropriate hard measure to deliver to customer requirements is not always intuitive or obvious, and the potential for counting or tracking an irrelevant aspect of operations is high. For this reason, it is often desirable to link operational performance measures with soft measures (gathered via surveys or trailer calls) to be sure that they are strongly correlated.

Soft measurements are based on customer perceptions that often cannot be directly observed. Two research methods described in Chapter 5 can document customers' opinions about whether performance has met the standards established: relationship surveys and trailer calls. Relationship and SERVQUAL surveys cover all aspects of the customer's relationship with the company, are typically expressed in attributes, and are usually completed once per year. Trailer calls are associated with specific service encounters, are short (approximately six or seven questions), and are administered as close in time to a specific service encounter as possible. For requirements that are longer term and at a higher level of abstraction (such as at the attribute level), annual relationship surveys can document customer perceptions on a periodic basis. Trailer calls can be administered continuously, whenever customers experience a service encounter of the type being considered, to provide data on a continuous basis.

Step 5: Establish Target Levels for the Standards

The next step requires that companies establish target levels for the standards. Without this step the company lacks a way to quantify whether the standards are being met. Figure 9.4 provides a good example of an approach that can be used to set standards for timeliness in responding to complaints in a service company. In this illustration, each time a complaint is made to the company, and each time one is resolved, employees can record the times. They can also ask each customer his or her satisfaction with the performance in resolving the complaint. The company can then plot the information from each complaint to determine how well the company is performing and where the company would like to be in the future. This technique is but one of several for determining the target level for service standards.

Another technique is a simple perception–action correlation study. When the service consists of repetitive processes, companies can relate levels of customer satisfaction with actual performance of a behavior or task. Consider, for example, a study to determine the standard for customers' wait-time in a line. The information gathered should include both customer perceptions of their wait in line (soft perceptual measure) and the amount of time they actually stand in line (hard operations measure). The joint collection of these data over many transactions provides evidence of the sensitivity of customers to different wait-times.

One airline conducted precisely such a study by having a flight attendant intercept customers as they approached the ticket counter. As each customer entered the line, the attendant stamped the entry time on a ticket (using a machine like those in parking lots) and handed the customer the stamped ticket. As the customer exited the line at the end of the transaction, the flight attendant restamped the ticket with the exit time and asked the customer three or four questions about perceptions of the wait in line and satisfaction with the transaction. Aggregating the individual customer data provided a graph that allowed the company to evaluate the impact on perceptions of various levels of line waits.

Step 6: Track Measures against Standards

Roger Milliken, former head of Milliken Industries, is reported to have said, "In God we trust, all others bring data." Successful service businesses, such as FedEx and Disney, have careful and comprehensive fact-based systems that provide information about their operations—allowing them to continually examine how the company is performing in comparison to its service standards. One company that lives and thrives through management by fact is Granite Rock in Watsonville, California, a family-run business that provides concrete, asphalt, and crushed stone products. Granite Rock, which won a Baldrige Award in the small business category, has systems in place to gather, analyze, and act on information. Statistical process control and other types of charts are everywhere, tracking a wide range of issues—from characteristics of its concrete and crushed stone to processes such as the time it takes customers to fill their trucks. Customer complaints are also tracked through what the company calls "product-service discrepancy reports" and root-cause analysis, and updates are distributed to all plants. The reports show how long it takes to resolve complaints and provide detailed quarterly analyses of trends. Plants can track their trends for four years running. When it comes to product quality and customer service, Granite Rock leaves nothing to chance.

Step 7: Provide Feedback about Performance to Employees

Once companies have determined appropriate standards, developed specific measures that best capture customer requirements, and set appropriate target levels for the standards, they must develop mechanisms to provide feedback on employee actions and behaviors. One example of such feedback is employee monitoring—in firms with customer service departments, this involves the practice of supervisors listening in on employee telephone interactions with customers. You may have experienced this practice when you have called customer service numbers for many organizations and noticed that the voice prompts tell you that calls may be monitored for quality purposes. The purpose of such monitoring is often to provide feedback on employee performance to the service standards set by the organization. One critical aspect of developing feedback mechanisms is ensuring that performance captures the process from the customer's view rather than the company's perspective. A supervisor monitoring an employee's handling of a customer service call, for example, should focus not so much on how quickly the employee gets the customer off the telephone but on how adequately she handles the customer's request.

FedEx communicates the performance on its service quality indicator (SQI) weekly, so that everyone in the company knows how the company is performing. When problems occur, they can be identified and corrected. The SQI measurement gives everyone in the company immediate feedback on activity that is strongly related to customer perceptions. In a general sense, data and facts need to be analyzed and distributed to support evaluation and decision making at multiple levels within the company. The data also must be deployed quickly enough that the people who need it to make decisions about service or processes can do so. Responsibility for meeting service requirements must also be communicated throughout the organization. All parts of the organization must be measuring their services to internal customers and, ultimately, measuring how that performance relates to external customer requirements.

Step 8: Periodically Update Target Levels and Measures

The final step involves revising the target levels, measures, and even customer requirements regularly enough to keep up with customer expectations. When FedEx originally developed its SQI, it assigned lost packages a weight of 10; over time, FedEx has found that a lost package is much more important to customers than many of the other issues included in the index and now assigns a weight of 50 to such an event. In its "Fit for You" program, Marriott requires its hotels to include three menu items that fit into diets that are currently popular. Although the company has a standard requirement that all hotels offer three items, each hotel is encouraged to be creative in choosing the particular items and to include seasonal and local variations. One hotel in Wisconsin, for example, offers a Cheesehead Omelet using a Wisconsin cheese. As the vice president of lodging, food, and beverage stated, "We have given them guidelines, and we want the chefs to create something interesting."[17] As these examples suggest, some flexibility in changing service standards might be given to management in certain departments or locations once a basic high level of service has been achieved.

Developing Service Performance Indexes

One outcome of following the process for developing customer-defined standards is a service performance index. *Service performance indexes* are comprehensive composites of the most critical performance standards. Development of an index begins by identifying the set of customer-defined standards that the company will use to drive behavior. Not all service performance indexes contain customer-defined standards, but the best ones, like FedEx's SQI, Ritz-Carlton's SQI, and Singapore Airline's SPI, are based on them. Most companies build these indexes by understanding the most important requirements of the customer, linking these requirements to tangible and measurable aspects of service provision, and using the feedback from these indexes to identify and improve service problems. The most progressive companies also use the feedback for reward and recognition systems within the company.

Summary

This chapter discussed the discrepancy between company perceptions of customer expectations and the standards set to deliver to these expectations. Among the major causes of provider gap 2 are inadequate standardization of service behaviors and actions, absence of formal processes for setting service quality goals, and lack of customer-defined standards. These problems were discussed and detailed, along with strategies to close the gap. To close the service design and standards gap, standards set by companies must be based on customer requirements and expectations rather than just on internal company goals. That is, company-defined standards are typically not successful in driving behaviors that close provider gap 2 and a company must set *customer*-defined standards based on key customer requirements visible to and measured by customers.

In this chapter we described two types of service standards: hard standards, those that can be counted, timed, or observed through audits, and soft standards, customer perceptions that cannot be directly observed. Customer-defined standards are at the heart of service delivery that customers expect: they are the link between customers' expressed expectations and company actions to deliver to those expectations. Creating customer-defined service standards is not a common practice in U.S. firms. Doing so requires that companies' marketing and operations departments work together by using the customer research as input for operations. Unless the operations standards are defined by customer priorities, they are not likely to have an impact on customer perceptions of service.

Discussion Questions

1. How does the service measurement described in this chapter differ from the service measurement in Chapter 5? Which of the two types do you think is most important? Why?

2. In what types of service industries are standards most difficult to develop? Why? Recommend three standards that might be developed in one of the firms from the industries you specify. How would employees react to these standards? How could you gain buy-in for them?

3. Given the need for customer-defined service standards, do firms need company-defined standards at all? Could all standards in a company be customer defined? Why or why not? What functional departments in a firm would object to having all standards be customer defined?

4. What is the difference between hard and soft standards? Which do you think would be more readily accepted by employees? By management? Why?

5. Consider the university or school you currently attend. What are examples of hard standards, soft standards, and one-time fixes that would address student requirements? Does the school currently use such standards for delivery of service to students? Why or why not? Do you think your reasons would apply to private-sector companies as well? To public or nonprofit companies?

6. Think about a service that you currently use; then map out the service encounter sequence for that service. What is your most important requirement in each interaction? Document these requirements, and make certain that they are expressed at the concrete level of behaviors and actions.

Exercises

1. Select a local service firm. Visit the firm and ascertain the service measurements that the company tracks. What hard measures does it monitor? Soft measures? On the basis of what you find, develop a service performance index.

2. Choose one of the peripheral services (such as computer, library, placement) provided by your school. What hard standards would be useful to track to meet student expectations? What soft standards would be appropriate? What one-time fixes would improve service?

3. Think about a service company you have worked for or know about. Using Figure 9.3, write in customer requirements at each of the levels. How far down in the chart can you describe requirements? Is that far enough?

4. Look at three websites from which you can order products (such as amazon.com, llbean.com, and zappos.com). What are the companies' delivery promises? What types of standards might they set for these promises? Are these customer- or company-defined standards?

Notes

1. "Taking the Measure of Quality," *Service Savvy,* March 1992, p. 3.

2. Ibid.

3. E-mail communication from David Spear, manager of global service and quality assurance, FedEx Express, September 17, 2010.

4. 2009 FedEx Annual Report, http://ir.fedex.com/annuals.cfm, accessed October 8, 2010.

5. G. L. Shostack, "Breaking Free from Product Marketing," *Journal of Marketing* 41 (April 1977), pp. 73–80.

6. Puget Sound Energy, "2010 Performance Report," http://www.pse.com/accountsandservices/NewToPSE/Documents/2774_SQI_Report_Card_2010.pdf, accessed July 19, 2011.

7. California Department of Motor Vehicles website, http://www.dmv.ca.gov/pubs/newsrel/archive/2004-12.htm, accessed July 24, 2010.

8. 2005 and 2004 National Customer Rage Studies conducted by Customer Care Alliance in collaboration with the Center for Services Leadership at Arizona State University's W. P. Carey School of Business.

9. F. F. Reichheld and P. Schefter, "E-Loyalty: Your Secret Weapon on the Web," *Harvard Business Review* 78 (July–August 2000), pp. 105–113.

10. J. Weinstein, "Redesigning the Box," *Hotels* 38, no. 3 (2004), p. 7.

11. J. Stengle, "ER Kiosks Let Patients Avoid Long Lines," *Associated Press,* September 13, 2007.

12. See D. E. Hansen and P. J. Danaher, "Inconsistent Performance during the Service Encounter: What's a Good Start Worth?" *Journal of Service Research* 1 (February 1999), pp. 227–235; and V. Dalakas, "The Importance of a Good Ending in a Service Encounter," *Services Marketing Quarterly* 28, no. 1 (2006), pp. 35–53.

13. These are two of the "three Steps of Service" included in Ritz-Carlton's Gold Standards, which can be found on the company website at http://corporate.ritzcarlton.com/en/About/GoldStandards.htm, accessed July 19, 2011.

14. For a comprehensive list of service attributes found to be important across a variety of services, see M. Paul, T. Hennig-Thurau, D. D. Gremler, K. P. Gwinner, and C. Wiertz, "Toward a Theory of Repeated Purchase Drivers for Consumer Services," *Journal of the Academy of Marketing Science* 37 (Summer 2009), pp. 215–237.

15. Based on e-mail communication with David Spear, manager of global service and quality assurance, FedEx Express, September 17, 2010.

16. Statistic was provided by Innovative Systems, Inc., on http://www.innovativesystems.com/success/ll_bean.php, accessed September 20, 2007.

17. R. Oliva, "Out with the Old Breakfast," *Hotels* 38 (April 2004), p. 45.

Chapter **Ten**

Physical Evidence and the Servicescape

This chapter's objectives are to

1. Explain the impact of physical evidence, particularly the servicescape, on customer perceptions and experiences.
2. Illustrate differences in types of servicescapes, the roles played by the servicescape, and the implications for strategy.
3. Explain *why* the servicescape affects customer and employee behavior, using a framework based in marketing, organizational behavior, and environmental psychology.
4. Present elements of an effective physical evidence strategy.

Building a Service Brand Using Physical Evidence[1]

Marriott International Inc., the world's largest hotel company, has a brand for every price point, every occasion, and every type of customer. The company is ranked as the most admired company in the hotel industry and one of the best places to work by *Fortune* magazine. Operating in 71 countries and territories, Marriott employs approximately 130,000 people. From its high-end Ritz-Carlton and J. W. Marriott Hotels to its more budget-oriented Fairfield Inns, the company has been successful at clearly positioning its many brands, distinguishing them from each other, and attracting well-defined market segments for each. According to branding and strategy executives at Marriott, building these distinctive hotel brands involves a complex strategy that meshes hotel design, employee training and selection to match the brand strategy, careful customer segmentation, and specific operational brand standards.

From the customer's perspective, the most visible aspect of Marriott's distinctive brand strategies is the "servicescape," or the physical environment where the service is delivered—the hotel design itself. The luxury design of the Ritz-Carlton brand fits well with its position as the hotel where "ladies and gentlemen serve ladies and gentlemen." On the other hand, the physical presence of a Marriott Courtyard, while still expressing personal comfort and style, is much more efficient and businesslike in its design.

Marriott's most recent hotel brand introduction is a boutique hotel that marries unique, destination-inspired hotel design with sophisticated service. For this concept,

**This Marriott Court-
yard "great room"
design promotes
working and social-
izing among guests.**

a partnership with Ian Schrager, a well-known pioneer in the modern boutique-hotel industry, provided the foundation for Marriott to enter an entirely new market for the company. These types of hotels are generally smaller, upscale properties that emphasize exclusive and unique styles for each location. Starwood's W Hotels epitomize this segment of the market. The specific design elements of this new boutique hotel called "Edition" are critical to the positioning of the concept. The first two uniquely designed Edition hotels opened in Waikiki and Istanbul, and another five are planned in the coming years.

As Marriott looks into its future, branding, along with consistent quality service, will remain an important strategic focus across all of its hotels. The company's vision is "to go from being a logical choice to a brand that's loved," according to company executives. To do that, they aim to connect emotionally with customers across all brands by engaging all of their senses and creating memorable, highly differentiated experiences that are up-to-date and innovative. For example, Marriott has been working with the design firm IDEO and teams of sociologists and anthropologists to identify trends and new innovations for travelers. One series of changes is the introduction of high-tech conveniences for laptops, iPods, and other plug-ins and the latest in TV technology. By introducing the latest technological innovations into the rooms, guests are allowed to experience things they may not even have at home. Another change is the transformation of Courtyard lobbies into "great rooms" for those who prefer social, public places for work rather than their rooms (see accompanying photo).

In this chapter we explore the importance of physical evidence for communicating service quality attributes, setting customer expectations, and creating the service experience. In Chapter 1, when we introduced the expanded marketing mix for services, we defined physical evidence as *the environment in which the service is delivered and in which the firm and the customer interact, and any tangible commodities that facilitate performance or communication of the service.* The first part of this definition encompasses the actual physical facility in which the service is performed, delivered, and consumed; throughout this chapter the physical facility is referred to as the *servicescape.*[2] Physical evidence is particularly important for communicating about credence services (such as auto repair and health care), and it is important for services such as hotels, hospitals, and theme parks that are dominated by experience attributes, as described in our opening vignette on Marriott International.

PHYSICAL EVIDENCE

What Is Physical Evidence?

Customers often rely on tangible cues, or physical evidence, to evaluate the service before its purchase and to assess their satisfaction with the service during and after consumption. Effective design of physical, tangible evidence is important for closing provider gap 2. General elements of physical evidence are shown in Table 10.1. They include all aspects of the organization's physical facility (the servicescape) as well as other forms of tangible communication. Elements of the physical servicescape that affect customers include both exterior attributes (such as signage, parking, and the landscape) and interior attributes (such as design, layout, equipment, and decor). Note that web pages and virtual servicescapes conveyed over the Internet are more recent forms of physical evidence that companies can use to communicate about the service experience, making services more tangible for customers both before and after purchase (see the Technology Spotlight).

Physical evidence examples from different service contexts are given in Table 10.2. It is apparent that some services (such as hospitals, resorts, and child care) rely heavily on physical evidence to communicate and create customer experiences. Others (insurance, express mail) provide limited physical evidence for customers. All the elements

TABLE 10.1
Elements of Physical Evidence

Servicescape	Other Tangibles
Facility exterior	Business cards
Exterior design	Stationery
Signage	Billing statements
Parking	Reports
Landscape	Employee dress
Surrounding environment	Uniforms
Facility interior	Brochures
Interior design	Web pages
Equipment	Virtual servicescape
Signage	
Layout	
Air quality/temperature	
Sound/music/scent/lighting	

TABLE 10.2
Examples of Physical Evidence from the Customer's Point of View

	Physical Evidence	
Service	**Servicescape**	**Other Tangibles**
Insurance	Not applicable	Policy itself Billing statements Periodic updates Company brochure Letters/cards Claims forms Website
Hospital	Building exterior Parking Signs Waiting areas Admissions office Patient care room Medical equipment Recovery room	Uniforms Reports/stationery Billing statements Website
Airline	Airline gate area Airplane exterior Airplane interior (decor, seats, air quality) Check-in kiosks Security screening area Baggage return area	Tickets Food Uniforms Website Packaging
Express mail	Free-standing stores Package drop boxes	Trucks Uniforms Handheld devices Website
Sporting event	Parking Stadium exterior Ticketing area Entrance Seating Restrooms Concession areas Playing field Scoreboard	Tickets Employee uniforms Programs Team mascot Website

of evidence listed for each service communicate something about the service, facilitate performance of the service, and/or add to the customer's total experience. Although we focus in this chapter primarily on the servicescape and its effects, keep in mind that what is said applies to the other forms of evidence as well.

How Does Physical Evidence Affect the Customer Experience?

Physical evidence, particularly the servicescape, can have a profound effect on the customer experience. This is true whether the experience is mundane (e.g., a bus or subway ride), personally meaningful (e.g., a destination wedding experience, or a birthing

Technology Spotlight Virtual Servicescapes: Experiencing Services through the Internet

Web pages and virtual service tours allow customers to preview service experiences through the Internet and see tangible evidence of the service without actually being there. This medium offers firms tremendous potential to communicate experiential aspects of their services in ways that were previously very difficult, if not impossible. Here we present several examples, across different industries.

TRAVEL

Travelers can now preview destinations, view hotels and their rooms, tour natural environments, and "experience" entertainment venues before booking their trips or even deciding where to travel. Before booking a trip to Great Britain, travelers can preview websites that show hotels, bed and breakfast inns, and other lodging all over the country. The exterior of the facilities as well as actual rooms can be examined in selecting accommodations. In planning a trip to visit the national parks of the United States, travelers can view full-length videos of the parks and various tours within the parks. For example, at the Yellowstone site (www.yellowstone.net/onlinetours/) video tours are available of driving loops within the park, complete with the sounds of the park's famous geysers. Detailed maps are also included, allowing a traveler to plan a route and choose among the many possible sights prior to even arriving at the park.

SPORTS AND LEISURE

Through sports and leisure websites and live feeds to technology devices, fans can now view much of the action and preview upcoming sports experiences online. A great example is NASCAR, whose race enthusiasts are among the most loyal sports fans anywhere. And there are a lot of these fans 75 million currently! For those fans who experience a race first-hand, the atmosphere is charged with excitement, the food is plentiful, and a kaleidoscope of paraphernalia is available for sale. And, the race itself is highly involving, with its thundering noise, blurring visuals of cars, and edge-of-the chair anticipation for the eventual winners. As if this live experience were not enough, NASCAR provides many opportunities for fans to experience the servicescape and more through technology. Live video feeds from inside several of the vehicles allow spectators to listen to radio chatter among drivers and drews via smart phones, laptops, or tablets; to see the view from the cockpit of these cars; and even to observe mishaps and accidents close up via video. In addition, NASCAR has an online service, with more than 300,000 subscribers, that provides real-time race information online and a cable service that lets fans watch the race from the perspective of an individual driver.

UNIQUE RETAIL EXPERIENCES

Many of today's unique retail experiences can be conveyed effectively via the Internet to give customers a preview of what they can expect. A great example is Build-A-Bear Workshop®, where children "from 3 to 103" can create their own teddy bears and other furry friends during their visit to the store. Build-A-Bear Workshop operates more than 400 stores worldwide, including company-owned stores in the United States, Puerto Rico, Canada, the United Kingdom, Ireland, and France, and franchise stores in Europe, Asia, Australia, Africa, and the Middle East. The interactive retail entertainment experience itself is memorable and fun, and the highly visual teddy-bear-themed environment throughout the stores is

room at a hospital), or spectacular (e.g., a week-long travel adventure). In all cases, the physical evidence of the service will influence the flow of the experience, the meaning customers attach to it, their satisfaction, their emotional connections with the company delivering the experience, and their social and personal interactions with others experiencing the service.

As marketers and corporate strategists pay more attention to customer experiences, they have recognized the impact of physical space and tangibles in creating those experiences. Lewis Carbone, a leading consultant on experience management, a big part of the fantasy of this special place. For a preview of how it works and what the stores look like, the website of Build-A-Bear Workshop (www. buildabear.com) includes a step-by-step "virtual visit" that shows the various stations in the store and what happens at each one. In creating a furry friend, customers go through the following steps: Choose Me; Hear Me; Stuff Me; Stitch Me; Fluff Me; Name Me; Take Me Home®. The virtual visit on the website shows each stage sequentially, detailing the activities at each step and providing a colorful photo that gives a sense of the store environment and the emotions of its patrons.

HIGHER EDUCATION

One of the most significant decisions that young people and their families make is what university to attend. For students fortunate enough to have the means and abilities, the choices can be endless. The physical environment of the university—the campus itself as well as specific facilities—can play a major role in students' choices as well as their actual experiences. Many universities offer virtual tours of their campuses online allowing students to preview the physical environment in advance. The University of Oregon in the United States has a particularly effective tour on its site that allows students to enter a virtual tour http://admissions.uoregon.edu/ virtualtour and travel down a variety of paths to explore different aspects of the university, including academics, housing, student life, athletics, campus, and community. In following each path on the tour, the prospective student and family members can view additional photos and videos, as well as read information related to that path. In exploring university environments this way, students who are unable to visit, or who wish to narrow their visit choices, are much better informed.

Internet technology clearly provides tremendous opportunities for firms to communicate about their services. Images on the Internet create expectations for customers that set standards for service delivery, and it is critical that the actual services live up to these expectations. Images and virtual service tours presented on the Internet also need to support the positioning of the service brand and be consistent with other marketing messages.

has developed an entire lexicon and management process around the basic idea of "experience engineering" through "clue management."[3] *Clue management* refers to the process of clearly identifying and managing *all* the various clues that customers use to form their impressions and feelings about the company. Included in this set of clues are what Carbone refers to as *mechanics clues,* or the physical and tangible clues that we focus on in this chapter. Other writers and consultants who focus on managing customer experiences also zero in on the importance of tangible evidence and physical facilities in shaping those experiences.[4] Throughout this chapter are numerous examples of how physical evidence communicates with customers and shapes their experiences.

TYPES OF SERVICESCAPES

This chapter relies heavily on ideas and concepts from environmental psychology, a field that encompasses the study of human beings and their relationships with built (human-made), natural, and social environments.[5] The physical setting may be more or less important in achieving the organization's marketing and other goals, depending on certain factors. Table 10.3 is a framework for categorizing service organizations on two dimensions that capture some of the key differences that will affect the management of the servicescape. Organizations that share a cell in the table tend to face similar issues and decisions regarding their physical spaces.

Servicescape Usage

First, organizations differ in terms of *whom* the servicescape will affect. That is, who actually comes into the service facility and thus is potentially influenced by its design— customers, employees, or both groups? The first column of Table 10.3 suggests three types of service organizations that differ on this dimension. At one extreme is the *self-service* environment, in which the customer performs most of the activities and few if any employees are involved. Examples of self-service environments include ATMs, movie theaters, check-in kiosks at airports, self-service entertainment such as golf and theme parks, and online services. In these primarily self-service environments, the organization can plan the servicescape to focus exclusively on marketing goals such as attracting the right market segment, making the facility pleasing and easy to use, and creating the desired service experience for the customer.

At the other extreme of the use dimension is the *remote service,* which has little or no customer involvement with the servicescape. Telecommunications, utilities, financial consultants, editorial, and mail-order services are examples of services that can be provided without the customer ever seeing the service facility. In fact, the facility may

TABLE 10.3
Typology of Service Organizations Based on Variations in Form and Use of the Servicescape

Source: From M. J. Bitner, "Servicescapes: The Impact of Physical Surroundings on Customers and Employees," *Journal of Marketing* 56 (April 1992), pp. 57–71. Reprinted with permission of the American Marketing Association.

Servicescape Usage	Complexity of the Servicescape	
	Elaborate	**Lean**
Self-service (customer only)	Water park eBay	ATM Car wash Simple Internet services Express mail drop box
Interpersonal services (both customer and employee)	Hotel Restaurant Health clinic Hospital Bank Airline School	Dry cleaner Retail cart Hair salon
Remote service (employee only)	Telecommunications Insurance company Utility Many professional services	Telephone mail-order desk Automated voice-messaging services

be in a different state or a different country (see the Global Feature in Chapter 1). In remote services, the facility can be set up to keep employees motivated and to facilitate productivity, teamwork, operational efficiency, or whatever organizational behavior goal is desired without any consideration of customers because they will never see or visit the servicescape. This is the case with SAS, a 14-year veteran of *Fortune* magazine's Best Places to Work list, where it was ranked number one in 2010 and 2011. The company provides health care and high-quality child care on site, along with car cleaning, a beauty salon, and a 66,000-square-foot gym for its over 11,000 employees. Since most of its customers never visit the SAS campus, the facilities can be designed entirely with employee well being and productivity in mind.[6]

In Table 10.3, *interpersonal services* are placed between the two extremes and represent situations in which both the customer and the employee are present and active in the servicescape. Examples abound, such as hotels, restaurants, hospitals, educational settings, and banks. In these situations, the servicescape must be planned to attract, satisfy, and facilitate the activities of both customers and employees simultaneously. Special attention must also be given to how the servicescape affects the nature and quality of the social interactions between and among customers and employees. A cruise ship provides a good example of a setting in which the servicescape must support customers and the employees who work there, as well as facilitate interactions between and within the two groups.

Servicescape Complexity

Table 10.3 suggests another factor that will influence servicescape management, the complexity of the servicescape. Some service environments are very simple, with few elements, few spaces, and few pieces of equipment. Such environments are termed *lean.* Shopping mall information kiosks and FedEx drop-off kiosks and stores are considered lean environments because both provide service from one simple structure. For lean servicescapes, design decisions are relatively straightforward, especially in self-service or remote service situations in which there is no interaction among employees and customers.

Other servicescapes are very complicated, with many elements and many forms. They are termed *elaborate* environments. An example is a hospital with its many floors and rooms, sophisticated equipment, and complex variability in functions performed within the physical facility. In such an elaborate environment, the full range of marketing and organizational objectives theoretically can be approached through careful management of the servicescape. For example, a patient's hospital room can be designed to enhance patient comfort and satisfaction while facilitating employee productivity. Firms such as hospitals that are located in the elaborate interpersonal service cell face the most complex servicescape decisions. To illustrate, when the Mayo Clinic, probably the best-known name in U.S. health care, opened its hospital in Scottsdale, Arizona, the organization painstakingly considered the interrelated goals, needs, and feelings of its employees, doctors, patients, and visitors in designing its distinctive servicescape (see Exhibit 10.4 later in this chapter).

STRATEGIC ROLES OF THE SERVICESCAPE

Within the cells of the typology, the servicescape can play many strategic roles simultaneously. An examination of the variety of roles and how they interact makes clear how strategically important it is to provide appropriate physical evidence of the service. In

Strategy Insight Strategic Positioning through Architectural Design

BusinessWeek and *Architectural Record,* both McGraw-Hill publications, together sponsor an annual international competition to identify the best use of architecture that solves strategic business challenges. Company winners clearly demonstrate the impact of design on people—customers, employees, the general public, or all three. Here we present award winners from several years to illustrate the ways that architecture and servicescapes execute or reinforce strategic decisions and marketing positioning.

APPLE STORES, NEW YORK

In designing its store in New York's Soho district, Apple Computers brought together architects, graphic designers, product developers, merchandising people, and its late CEO Steve Jobs to create a retail space that would both convey the company's philosophy and sell computers. The result is a clean, open, and spacious store that displays only a few computers to create the ambience of a museum. The company establishes a modern feel using a central glass staircase, white walls, and a large skylight. A second-floor area encourages children to play with software and offers a large conference room for Apple product demonstrations. As one judge put it, "the store, like Apple, is all about information, interaction, and access." Apple's 5th Avenue store in New York City, its highest volume store, was also an award winner in a later competition. This cube-shaped store is free of structural steel and it relies on a taut glass skin and glass beams to create a sense of a free-floating structure that sits above the actual retail space. Similar to the Soho store, the "cube" is highly effective at drawing customers in, and its cleanly designed interior provides an inviting atmosphere to experiment with innovative and futuristic Apple products. The store has very high sales per square

foot and the space is beautiful, functional, and very profitable (award winners in 2003 and 2006).

EVERSHEDS LAW OFFICES, LONDON, ENGLAND

Eversheds is a global law firm that seeks to attract the best young talent to its employee ranks. When it relocated its London headquarters, it recognized an

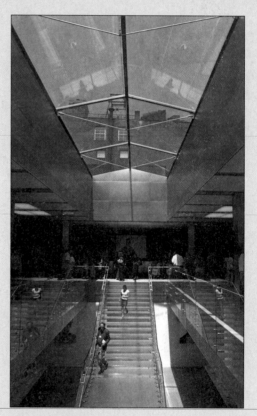

Apple Store, Soho, NY.

fact, the servicescape is frequently one of *the* most important elements used in positioning a service organization (see the Strategy Insight).

Package

Similar to a tangible product's package, the servicescape and other elements of physical evidence essentially "wrap" the service and convey to consumers an external image of what is "inside." Product packages are designed to portray a particular image as well as to evoke a particular sensory or emotional reaction. The physical setting of a service opportunity to attract talent through its workplace design. In seeking to build a law office for the future, the designers conducted extensive research, along with a nine-month prototype trial of the new design at its existing facility. It involved employees in the process from start to finish. The result was a radical shift away from traditional law firm design, including modular furniture that can be moved as needed to foster collaboration and communication among lawyers and staff. There are also added amenities, including lounges, dining venues, showers, bicycle storage, and sleeping accommodations. Sustainability was also at the core of the design. For example, through centralizing much of its information and documents, the firm was able to reduce the number of filed documents by 57 percent and the number of printers by 63 percent. The project had outstanding results as well, with 96 percent of the staff being more motivated to work due to the design of the new workplace (award winner in 2009).

SEKII LADIES CLINIC, JAPAN
To reposition its childbirth clinic in stark contrast to traditional Japanese hospitals, the Sekii Ladies Clinic relied heavily on a novel servicescape design. The new childbirth delivery and recovery rooms are elegant, warm, and simple, and the building itself is modern, open, and light-filled. Combined with interior gardens, the spaces offer mothers a rich, warm experience for childbirth. Delivery rooms and all areas welcome fathers, a departure from the tradition in Japan in which women typically give birth in large public hospitals without family members present. The clinic brings women's health to the forefront rather than hiding it, another Japanese tradition (award winner in 2003).

DARWIN CENTRE MUSEUM, LONDON
The Darwin Centre Museum needed more room to house its huge collection of 22 million zoological specimens and to provide additional laboratory space for its scientists. To meet these objectives, the museum designed a new building that provided both storage and public access to its collections. An atrium in the building allows visitors to view scientists at work, and open shelves display the specimens. Touch-screen terminals provide another means for exploring the collection. The caterpillar-like roof over the building provides a clue to what is inside! Visits to the museum increased sharply when the new building was opened (award winner in 2003).

HUMANE SOCIETY, SAN ANTONIO
Humane societies house lost, neglected, or unwanted animals and provide a community resource for pet adoption. Typically, the facilities are dark, impersonal, and unpleasant for all involved—the animals, employees, volunteers, and potential adoptive families. Such is not the case in San Antonio, Texas, where a new shelter resembling a retail complex was designed to reverse this pattern. Buildings are now organized around a central courtyard, offering a more communal feel, and the interiors of the buildings are comfortable and inviting. Potential adopters meander through aisles of the building as they would in a retail store. The more desirable animals (typically puppies and kittens) are located in the back of the facility so that visitors will pass by the equally deserving adult animals first. Since the opening of the newly designed facility, adoptions have increased by 95 percent, and three times as many adult animals have been adopted (award winner in 2004).

Source: "The *BusinessWeek/Architectural Record* Awards," Special Report, *BusinessWeek*, November 3, 2003, pp. 57–64; and http://archrecord.construction.com/features/bwarAwards/, accessed July 2011.

does the same thing through the interaction of many complex stimuli. The servicescape is the outward appearance of the organization and thus can be critical in forming initial impressions or setting up customer expectations—it is a visual metaphor for the intangible service. This packaging role is particularly important in creating expectations for new customers and for newly established service organizations trying to build a particular image (see Exhibit 10.1). The physical surroundings offer an organization the opportunity to convey an image in a way not unlike the way an individual chooses to "dress for success." The packaging role extends to the appearance of contact personnel through their uniforms or dress and other elements of their outward appearance.[7]

Exhibit 10.1   Using Physical Evidence to Position a New Service

When Speedi-Lube opened its doors in Seattle, Washington, it was one of the first 10-minute oil and lubrication services ever introduced. Now there are thousands of such outlets, but then the concept was totally new. The idea was to offer an alternative to gas stations for basic car lubrication service, quickly (within 10 minutes), with no appointment necessary. Because the concept was unknown to consumers at the time, the owners of Speedi-Lube needed to communicate and position the service clearly so that consumers would form accurate expectations. And because car maintenance is highly intangible and consumers often do not understand what is actually done to their cars, the owners relied heavily on tangible physical evidence to communicate the concept before, during, and after the sale.

To communicate an image of fast, efficient service, Speedi-Lube relied on straightforward, to-the-point advertising using clean, crisp letters. For example, a large billboard read in large blue and white letters: SPEEDI-LUBE, 10-MINUTE OIL CHANGE, NO APPOINTMENT, OPEN 7 DAYS, 9 TO 6. The very buildings in which the service was performed communicated the efficiency theme clearly. In fact, the exteriors of some of the first Speedi-Lube facilities had the look of a fast-food restaurant, consistent with the intended image of speed, efficiency, and predictability. Entrance and exit signs were clearly displayed so that customers going to Speedi-Lube for the first time would know exactly where to drive their cars.

On driving into the service bay, the customer was greeted with additional physical evidence that clearly differentiated Speedi-Lube from its competitors at that time. The service bay was very neat and brightly painted, with a professional-appearing service counter in the bay, where the customer filled out paperwork to get the service. Service personnel in professional uniforms helped with the paperwork, and the customer was invited to wait in a clean and functional waiting area where coffee and magazines were provided. (Alternatively, customers were welcome to stay in the service area to observe the work on their cars.) On one of the waiting room walls was displayed a large schematic, which you see here, showing the underside of an automobile and identifying all the lubrication points and exactly what was being done to the car. This kind of evidence informed customers and gave them confidence in what was being done.

On completion, the customer was given a checklist, itemizing the lubrication services provided. As a finishing touch, the employee lubricated the door locks on the car to indicate that nothing had been overlooked. Three months later Speedi-Lube would send a reminder suggesting that it was time for another oil change.

Schematic of the underside of a car and explanation of the service displayed in Speedi-Lube's customer waiting area.

Interestingly, the same care and resource expenditures given to package design in product marketing are often not provided for services, even though the service package serves a variety of important roles. There are many exceptions to this generality, however. Smart companies like Apple Stores (see the Strategy Insight), Starbucks, FedEx, and Marriott spend a lot of time and money relating their servicescape design to their brand, providing their customers with strong visual metaphors and "service packaging" that conveys the brand positioning. FedEx, for example, embarked on a major overhaul of its image by rethinking and redesigning all its tangibles—everything from its drop boxes to its service centers to the bags carried by its couriers.[8] The idea was to convey a consistent look and feel of "things are simple here," and "here, give us your package; we'll take care of everything."

Facilitator

The servicescape can also serve as a facilitator in aiding the performances of persons in the environment. How the setting is designed can enhance or inhibit the efficient flow of activities in the service setting, making it easier or harder for customers and employees to accomplish their goals. A well-designed, functional facility can make the service a pleasure to experience from the customer's point of view and a pleasure to perform from the employee's. On the other hand, poor and inefficient design may frustrate both customers and employees. For example, an international air traveler who finds himself in a poorly designed airport with few signs, poor ventilation, and few places to sit or eat will find the experience quite dissatisfying, and employees who work there will probably be unmotivated as well.

The same international traveler will appreciate seats on the airplane conducive to work and sleep. The seating itself, part of the physical surroundings of the service, has been improved over the years to better facilitate airline travelers' needs to sleep. In fact, the competition for better seat and aircraft interior design continues as a major point of contention among the international airline carriers, and the results have translated into greater customer satisfaction for business travelers.[9] Some of the new designs include business class seats that recline into "skybeds," leather ottomans in first-class sections, and electronic partition screens between seats in business class. In another context, health care providers have learned through research that many elements of hospital servicescape design can enable or frustrate both patients and providers in accomplishing their goals.[10]

Socializer

The design of the servicescape aids in the socialization of both employees and customers in the sense that it helps convey expected roles, behaviors, and relationships. For example, a new employee in a professional services firm would come to understand her position in the hierarchy partially through noting her office assignment, the quality of her office furnishings, and her location relative to others in the organization.

The design of the facility can also suggest to customers what their role is relative to employees, what parts of the servicescape they are welcome in and which are for employees only, how they should behave while in the environment, and what types of interactions are encouraged. For example, in many Starbucks locations, the company has shifted to more of a traditional coffeehouse environment in which customers spend social time rather than coming in for a quick cup of coffee on the run. To encourage this type of socializing, these Starbucks locations have comfortable lounge chairs, tables, and Wi-Fi set up to encourage customers to interact and to stay longer. The goal is to be the customer's "third place," that is a place where customers think of spending time when not at work or at home (see Exhibit 10.3 later in the chapter for more on third places).

Differentiator

The design of the physical facility can differentiate a firm from its competitors and signal the market segment that the service is intended for. Given its power as a differentiator, changes in the physical environment can be used to reposition a firm and/ or to attract new market segments. In shopping malls the signage, colors used in decor and displays, and type of music wafting from a store signal the intended market segment. In the banking industry, Jyske Bank in Denmark, one of the cases at the end of this book, clearly communicates through its servicescape its differentiation as a bank for consumers and families. The bank has a play area for children, round tables that facilitate discussions between bankers and clients, and a retail store look and feel that distinguish it from traditional banks.

In another context, the servicescape has been used as a major point of differentiation for PetSmart in the introduction of its innovative PetsHotel concept.[11] The hotels, which offer overnight care as well as day care for pets, are designed very differently from typical kennels or veterinary facilities. They feature a lobby area, colorful play areas, comfortable sleeping rooms, television, a "bone booth" for calling in, and other amenities that give the facilities a more residential, homelike appeal than traditional kennels have.

The design of a physical setting can also differentiate one area of a service organization from another. For example, in the hotel industry, one large hotel may have several levels of dining possibilities, each signaled by differences in design. Price differentiation is also often partially achieved through variations in physical setting. Bigger rooms with more physical amenities cost more, just as larger seats with more leg room (generally in first class) are more expensive on an airplane.

FRAMEWORK FOR UNDERSTANDING SERVICESCAPE EFFECTS ON BEHAVIOR

Although it is useful from a strategic point of view to think about the multiple roles of the servicescape and how they interact, making actual decisions about servicescape design requires an understanding of why the effects occur and how to manage them. The next sections of the chapter present a framework or model of environment and behavior relationships in service settings. Beyond influencing behaviors, physical design also affects well-being. Exhibit 10.2 provides an example of research that shows how customers and employees in one industry—health care—are impacted profoundly by servicescape design.

The Underlying Framework

The framework for understanding servicescape effects on behavior follows from basic *stimulus–organism–response* theory. In the framework the multidimensional environment is the *stimulus,* consumers and employees are the *organisms* that respond to the stimuli, and behaviors directed at the environment are the *responses.* The assumptions are that dimensions of the servicescape will affect customers and employees and that they will behave and respond in different ways depending on their internal reactions to the servicescape.

Exhibit 10.2 Servicescapes and Well-being in Health Care

There is solid and growing evidence from the field of "evidence-based design" that the design of health care environments can profoundly influence patient, family, and employee well-being. Notably, researchers have shown that outcomes such as stress reduction, shorter hospital stays, improved health, increased patient satisfaction, and improved safety are all affected by the design of the physical facilities. Here are a few examples of what has been learned.

SOUNDS, MUSIC, AND NOISE REDUCTION
A number of studies have shown that reducing noise and introducing more pleasing sounds such as water falling or music can positively affect patients and staff in hospitals. Minimizing noise, which is a constant challenge in hospitals and other health care settings, can help reduce sleep disturbance and stress and lower blood pressure, among other outcomes. Noise can also distract doctors and nurses, resulting in greater stress, interrupted communication, and errors, so noise reductions have benefits for employees as well.

NATURE AND VISUAL DISTRACTION
Research has shown that positive visual distractions divert patient attention from pain and negative feelings, improving their psychological and emotional well-being. In particular, nature distractions, including such things as gardens, indoor plants, and window views to outdoor nature scenes, have been shown to reduce stress, reduce pain, reduce pain medication usage, and speed recovery. Natural daylight is also very beneficial and has been linked to improved patient outcomes and higher staff productivity.

SINGLE-BED ROOM DESIGN
Many studies have shown the benefits of single-bed rooms for patients instead of multi-bed rooms. The benefits include reduced stress, better sleep, reduction in infection rates, increased patient satisfaction, and shorter hospital stays. A number of these benefits are also experienced by family and other support members who spend time with the patient. Giving the patient control over elements of the room design is also

positive—for example, providing them with the ability to control the lighting and temperature in their rooms.

PATIENT SAFETY
The design of the physical facility can have a huge impact on safety issues that are paramount in health care settings. For example, avoiding patient falls and infections is a major safety issue that can be influenced by physical design. One hospital located all of its patient bathrooms on the side of the room where the head of the bed was located. This simple design feature avoided the patient having to cross the room to use the bathroom, which reduced falls. Flexible room designs that allow equipment to be moved into a patient's room temporarily help avoid transferring patients to different locations during their stay. In other words, the equipment goes to the patient rather than vice versa. Research shows that transferring patients from room to room increases medication errors, patient falls, and the rate of infections.

DESIGN FOR WELL-BEING
Hospital administrators, designers, and architects are paying attention to these and other research results. Many new hospitals are designed with only single-bed rooms, natural lighting where possible, music and gardens, personal technology-based communicators (think *Star Trek* communicators) for staff to avoid audible paging, centralized nursing stations, and adaptable rooms to avoid patient transfers. Family lounges and eating areas and overnight sleeping accommodations for them are also provided to improve patient and family well-being and satisfaction. Exhibit 10.4 later in this chapter describes how the Mayo Clinic Hospital in Scottsdale, Arizona, was designed with many of these evidence-based principles in mind.

Sources: R. S. Ulrich, L. L Berry, X. Quan, and J. T. Parish, "A Conceptual Framework for the Domain of Evidence-Based Design," *Health Environments Research and Design Journal* 4, no. 1 (Fall 2010), pp. 95–114; R. S. Ulrich, C. M. Zimring, X. Zhu, J. DuBose, H. Seo, Y. Choi, and A. Joseph, "A Review of the Research Literature on Evidence-Based Healthcare Design," *Health Environments Research and Design Journal* 1, no. 3 pp. 6–125; "Good Healthcare by Design," The Hastings Center Report 41, no. 1 (January–February 2011),.

A specific example will help illustrate the theory in action. Assume there is a cookie cart parked outside the student union on campus. The cart is colorful and playful in design, and an aroma of baking cookies wafts from it. The design and the aroma are two elements of the servicescape that will affect customers in some way. Now assume you are a hungry student, just out of class, strolling across campus. The fun design of the cart attracts your attention, and simultaneously you smell baking cookies. The fun design and the delicious smell cause you to feel happy, relaxed, and hungry at the same time. You are attracted to the cart and decide to buy a cookie because you have another class to attend before lunch. The movement toward the cart and the purchase of a cookie are behaviors directed at the servicescape. Depending on how much time you have, you may even choose to converse with the vendor or other customers standing around munching cookies, other forms of behavior directed at the servicescape.

The framework shown in Figure 10.1 is detailed in the next sections. It represents a comprehensive stimulus–organism–response model that recognizes complex dimensions of the environment, impacts on multiple parties (customers, employees, and their interactions), multiple types of internal responses (cognitive, emotional, and physiological), and a variety of individual and social behaviors that can result.

Our discussion of the framework will begin on the right side of the model with *behaviors*, since, from a manager's perspective, the desired behaviors and responses are the place to start strategically. Next we will explain and develop the *internal*

FIGURE 10.1   **A Framework for Understanding Physical Environment–User Relationships in Service Organizations**

Source: Adapted from M. J. Bitner, "Servicescapes: The Impact of Physical Surroundings on Customers and Employees," *Journal of Marketing* 56 (April 1992), pp. 57–71.

responses portion of the model. Finally we will turn to the dimensions of the *environment* and the holistic perception of the environment.

Behaviors in the Servicescape

That human behavior is influenced by the physical setting in which it occurs is essentially a truism. Interestingly, however, until the 1960s psychologists largely ignored the effects of physical setting in their attempts to predict and explain behavior. Since that time, a large and steadily growing body of literature within the field of environmental psychology has addressed the relationships between human beings and their built, or physical, environments. Recent focus on the customer experience has also drawn attention to the effects of physical spaces and design on customer behavior.[12] As an example, one recent study explores the effects of a servicescape redesign in a fast-food industry context, looking at both short- and long-term effects on customer perceptions, as well as spending patterns and the store image. The research found that the remodeling positively increased customer perceptions, store image, and the amount of money customers spent in the restaurant, particularly in the short term. After about six months, the effects of the remodeling lost some strength as the remodeled restaurant became the new frame of reference for customers.[13]

Individual Behaviors

Environmental psychologists suggest that individuals react to places with two general, and opposite, forms of behavior: approach and avoidance. *Approach behaviors* include all positive behaviors that might be directed at a particular place, such as a desire to stay, explore, work, and affiliate.[14] *Avoidance behaviors* reflect the opposite—a desire not to stay, to explore, to work, or to affiliate. In a study of consumers in retail environments, researchers found that approach behaviors (including shopping enjoyment, returning, attraction and friendliness toward others, spending money, time spent browsing, and exploration of the store) were influenced by perceptions of the environment.[15] At one 7-Eleven store, the owners played "elevator music" to drive away the youthful market segment that was detracting from the store's image. And our cookie cart example is reminiscent of cinnamon roll bakeries in malls that attract patrons through the power of smell.

In addition to attracting or deterring entry, the servicescape can actually influence the degree of success that consumers and employees experience in executing their plans once inside. Each individual goes to a particular service organization with a goal or purpose that may be aided or hindered by the setting. NBA basketball fans are aided in their enjoyment of the game by adequate, easy-access parking; clear signage directing them to their seats; efficient food service; and clean restrooms. The ability of employees to do their jobs effectively is also influenced by the servicescape. Adequate space, proper equipment, and comfortable temperature and air quality all contribute to an employee's comfort and job satisfaction, causing him or her to be more productive, stay longer, and affiliate positively with coworkers.

Social Interactions

In addition to its effects on their individual behaviors, the servicescape influences the nature and quality of customer and employee interactions, most directly in interpersonal services. It has been stated that "all social interaction is affected by the physical container in which it occurs."[16] The "physical container" can affect the nature of social interaction in terms of the duration of interaction and the actual progression of events. In many service situations, a firm may want to ensure a particular progression

Social interactions are defined partially by the configuration of the servicescape.

of events (a "standard script") and limit the duration of the service. Environmental variables such as physical proximity, seating arrangements, size, and flexibility can define the possibilities and limits of social episodes such as those occurring between customers and employees, or customers and other customers. The Holland America Cruise Line photo shown here illustrates how the design of the servicescape can help define the social rules, conventions, and expectations in force in a given setting, thus defining the nature of social interaction.[17] The close physical proximity of passengers on the sunbathing deck will in and of itself prescribe certain patterns of behavior. This vacation is not designed for a social recluse! Some researchers have implied that recurring social behavior patterns are associated with particular physical settings and that when people encounter typical settings, their social behaviors can be predicted.[18]

Examples of how environments shape social interactions—and how these interactions in turn influence the environment—are abundant.[19] Even casual observation of the retail phenomenon "Nike Town" shows how this form of "entertainment retail" shapes the behaviors of consumers but at the same time allows them to interpret and create their own realities and experiences.[20] In a river-rafting trip, the "wilderness servicescape" profoundly influences the behaviors, interactions, and total experiences of rafting consumers and their guides. In this case the natural, and for the most part uncontrollable, environment is the setting for the service.[21] In some cases, important social bonds and connections are forged within a service place, resulting its becoming a "third place" for the individuals who frequent it (see Exhibit 10.3).[22]

Internal Responses to the Servicescape

Employees and customers respond to dimensions of their physical surroundings cognitively, emotionally, and physiologically, and those responses are what influence their behaviors in the environment (as shown in the middle portion of Figure 10.1). In other words, the perceived servicescape does not directly *cause* people to behave in certain ways. Although the internal responses are discussed independently here, they are clearly interdependent: a person's beliefs about a place, a cognitive response, may well influence the person's emotional response, and vice versa. For example, patients who go into a dentist's office designed to calm and sooth their anxieties (emotional responses) may believe as a result that the dentist is caring and competent (cognitive responses).

Environment and Cognition

The perceived servicescape can have an effect on people's beliefs about a place and their beliefs about the people and products found in that place. In a sense, the servicescape can be viewed as a form of nonverbal communication, imparting meaning through what is called "object language."[23] For example, particular environmental cues such as the type of office furniture and decor and the apparel worn by the lawyer may influence a potential client's beliefs about whether the lawyer is successful, expensive, and trustworthy. In a consumer study, variations in descriptions of store atmospheres were found to alter beliefs about a product (perfume) sold in the store.[24] Another study showed that a travel agent's office decor affected customer attributions and beliefs about the travel agent's behavior.[25] Travel agents whose facilities were more organized and professional were viewed more positively than were those whose facilities were disorganized and unprofessional.

In other cases, perceptions of the servicescape may simply help people distinguish a firm by influencing how it is categorized. The overall perception of the servicescape enables the consumer or employee to categorize the firm mentally. Research shows that in the restaurant industry a particular configuration of environmental cues suggests "fast food," whereas another configuration suggests "elegant sit-down restaurant."[26] In such situations, environmental cues serve as a shortcut device that enables customers to categorize and distinguish among types of restaurants.

Environment and Emotion

In addition to influencing beliefs, the perceived servicescape can directly elicit emotional responses that, in turn, influence behaviors. Just being in a particular place can make a person feel happy, lighthearted, and relaxed, whereas being in another place may make that person feel sad, depressed, and gloomy. The colors, decor, music, and other elements of the atmosphere can have an unexplainable and sometimes very subconsciousness effect on the moods of people in the place. For some people, certain environmental stimuli (noises, smells) common in a dental office can bring on immediate feelings of fear and anxiety. In very different contexts, the marble interior and grandeur of the Supreme Court buildings in Washington, D.C., call up feelings of pride and awe and respect; lively music and bright decor in a local night spot may cause people to feel excited and happy. In all these examples, the response from the consumer probably does not involve thinking but, rather, is just an unexplained emotional feeling.

REI (Recreational Equipment Inc.) provides another example of emotional connection facilitated through architectural design and the servicescape. At its flagship store in Seattle, the company has created an experience for consumers that includes a climbing mountain, a bicycle track, and walking trails. Its store in Minnesota has a cross-country ski trail around it. REI, through its servicescape design, is simulating the experiences and emotions that customers associate with its products, reinforcing a strong approach response to its stores.

Environmental psychologists have researched people's emotional responses to physical settings.[27] They have concluded that any environment, whether natural or engineered, will elicit emotions that can be captured by two basic dimensions: (1) pleasure/displeasure and (2) degree of arousal (amount of stimulation or excitement). Servicescapes that are both pleasant and arousing would be termed *exciting,* whereas those that are pleasant and nonarousing, or sleepy, would be termed *relaxing.* Unpleasant servicescapes that are arousing would be called *distressing,* whereas unpleasant, sleepy servicescapes would be *gloomy.* These basic emotional responses to environments can be used to begin predicting the expected behaviors of consumers and employees who find themselves in a particular type of place.

Environment and Physiology

The perceived servicescape may also affect people in purely physiological ways. Noise that is too loud may cause physical discomfort, the temperature of a room may cause people to shiver or perspire, the air quality may make it difficult to breathe, and the glare of lighting may decrease ability to see and cause physical pain. All these physical

Exhibit 10.3 Social Support in "Third Places"

The social interactions and attachments among customers and between customers and employees in "third places" can provide companionship and emotional support that results in strong attachments and loyalty to the place itself. A third place is a public or commercial place where people gather regularly and voluntarily outside of work (or school) and home, which are viewed as the first two places in people's lives. Often third places are diners, coffee shops, taverns, pubs, or clubs, but a fitness club, a civic center, or other public gathering place could also be a third place. The "Cheers" bar on the popular television show epitomized a third place. Think about what types of places might qualify as a third place for you. Do you have a third place?

A study by Mark Rosenbaum and colleagues showed that people can grow attached to a third place to the point where they depend on it above all other alternatives, they are committed to the place and care about it, they personally identify with it, and they structure their lifestyle around it. This type of attachment happens because of the companionship and emotional support they receive from the other customers and employees in the place, not simply because they like the service or feel comfortable in the physical surroundings. These emotional attachments and interactions are particularly strong for people who are lonely or in need of contact with others. The researchers observed and conducted depth interviews with patrons of Sammy's, a casual dining restaurant in the suburbs of a major U.S. metropolitan area that was clearly a third place for many regulars who frequented the restaurant. Through the interviews, they established that patrons who were lonely or who had lost an established form of social support through death, divorce, or illness, found significant companionship and emotional support at Sammy's. The regular patrons who had lost a spouse through death, divorce, or separation had a full 58 percent of their social supportive relationships with people (customers and employees) at Sammy's. These patrons were also extremely attached and loyal to Sammy's.

The research reinforces the idea that servicescapes, while they are defined by their physical elements, can take on a third place character when they become the source of social interactions, bonds, and support for the people who frequent them. The benefits of this type of support go far beyond the benefits intended by the core service. The regulars at Sammy's receive far more than a good meal in pleasant surroundings. Through their interactions with others, their daily lives are enhanced and they are emotionally better off. As the problems associated with loneliness grow in our modern-day society

(e.g., the population is aging, more and more people are caring for chronically ill family members or friends, divorce is prevalent, and work hours are increasing, resulting in less time for friendships), the importance of third places as a form of social support may grow as well. While consumer support networks do not require a physical presence—for example, online communities can provide social support—physical places are often more accessible and more preferable for nurturing companionship and emotional connections among people.

The Cheers bar epitomized a third place in the well-known television show.

Sources: M. S. Rosenbaum, "Exploring the Social Supportive Role of Third Places in Consumers' Lives," *Journal of Service Research* 9 (August 2006), pp. 59–72; A. Tombs and J. R. McColl-Kennedy, "Social-Servicescape Conceptual Model," *Marketing Theory* 3, no. 4 (2003), pp 447–475; M. S. Rosenbaum, J. Ward, B. A. Walker, and A. L. Ostrom, "A Cup of Coffee with a Dash of Love: An Investigation of Commercial Social Support and Third-Place Attachment," *Journal of Service Research* 10 (August 2007), pp. 43–59; and M. S. Rosenbaum, J. C. Sweeney, and C. Windhorst, "The Restorative Qualities of an Activity-Based, Third Place Cafe for Seniors," *Seniors Housing and Care Journal* 17, no. 1 (2009), pp. 75–90.

responses may, in turn, directly influence whether people stay in and enjoy a particular environment. It is well known that the comfort of seating in a restaurant influences how long people stay. The hard seats historically found in a fast-food restaurant cause most people to leave within a predictable period of time, whereas the soft, cozy chairs in some Starbucks coffee shops have the opposite effect, encouraging people to stay. Similarly, environmental design and related physiological responses affect whether employees can perform their job functions well.

A vast amount of research in engineering and design has addressed human physiological responses to ambient conditions as well as physiological responses to equipment design.[28] Such research fits under the rubric of *human factors design* or *ergonomics*. Human factors research systematically applies relevant information about human capabilities and limitations to the design of items and procedures that people use. For example, Choice Hotels targeted empty-nester couples and senior citizens in the redesign of many of the rooms in its Rodeway and EconoLodge brands. A significant percentage of the rooms in these hotels were converted to senior-friendly suites with brighter lighting, larger-button telephones and TV remotes, and grab bars in the showers.[29] Wall switches have lights so they can be found easily at night. To help people with arthritis, doors have lever handles instead of knobs so that every door and every drawer in the room can be opened with a fist rather than requiring hand and wrist dexterity. In these and other ways, Choice Hotels has uniquely adapted its design to accommodate older guests.

Variations in Individual Responses

In general, people respond to the environment in the ways just described—cognitively, emotionally, physiologically—and their responses influence how they behave in the environment. However, the response will not be the same for every individual, every time. Personality differences as well as temporary conditions such as moods or the purpose for being there can cause variations in how people respond to the servicescape.[30]

One personality trait that has been shown to affect how people respond to environments is *arousal seeking*. Arousal seekers enjoy and look for high levels of stimulation, whereas arousal avoiders prefer lower levels of stimulation. Thus, an arousal avoider in a loud, bright dance club with flashing lights might show strong dislike for the environment, whereas an arousal seeker would be very happy. In a related vein, it has been suggested that some people are better *screeners* of environmental stimuli than others.[31] Screeners of stimuli would be able to experience a high level of stimulation but not be affected by it. Nonscreeners would be highly affected and might exhibit extreme responses even to low levels of stimulation.

The particular purpose for being in a servicescape can also affect a person's response to it. A person who is on an airplane for a 1-hour flight will likely be less affected by the atmosphere on the plane than will the traveler who is embarking on a 14-hour flight from Los Angeles to Shanghai. Similarly, a day-surgery hospital patient will likely be less sensitive and demanding of the hospital environment than would a patient who is spending two weeks in the hospital. And a person who is staying at a resort hotel for a business meeting will respond differently to the environment than will a couple on their honeymoon. Temporary mood states can also cause people to respond differently to environmental stimuli. A person who is feeling frustrated and fatigued after a long day at work is likely to be affected differently by a highly arousing restaurant than the same person would be after a relaxing three-day weekend.

Cultural differences also influence preferences for environmental features and responses to servicescape design. For example, there is a strong cultural preference for the color red in China, whereas Westerners would not share this attraction. And, while Americans and Europeans may prefer to shop in orderly and quiet supermarkets, many Indian shoppers prefer a more jumbled, chaotic environment.[32] This is what India's largest retailer, Pantaloon Retail Ltd, learned when it introduced Western-style supermarkets in India. At first, customers just walked through the wide, pristine aisles and left the store without buying. By studying Indian consumer behavior and focusing on the preferences of Indian shoppers (often the maids, cooks, nannies, and farmers of India, not the elite), Pantaloon redesigned its supermarkets to make them messier, noisier, and more cramped, re-creating in some sense the atmosphere of a public market. This design was appealing to the target market and sales increased far above where they were with the original design.

Environmental Dimensions of the Servicescape

The preceding sections have described customer and employee behaviors in the servicescape and the three primary responses—cognitive, emotional, and physiological—that lead to those behaviors. In this section, we turn to the complex mix of environmental features that influence these responses and behaviors (the left portion of Figure 10.1). Specifically, environmental dimensions of the physical surroundings can include all the objective physical factors that can be controlled by the firm to enhance (or constrain) employee and customer actions. There is an endless list of possibilities: lighting, color, signage, textures, quality of materials, style of furnishings, layout, wall decor, temperature, and so on. In Figure 10.1 and in the discussion that follows, the hundreds of potential elements have been categorized into three composite dimensions: *ambient conditions; spatial layout and functionality;* and *signs, symbols, and artifacts.* Exhibit 10.4 illustrates how the Mayo Clinic took into consideration all these dimensions in designing its hospital to accommodate patients, doctors, employees, and visitors.

Although we discuss the three dimensions separately, environmental psychology explains that people respond to their environments holistically. That is, although individuals perceive discrete stimuli (e.g., they can perceive noise level, color, and decor as distinct elements), it is the total configuration of stimuli that determines their reactions to a place. Hence, although the dimensions of the environment are defined independently in the following sections, it is important to recognize that they are perceived by employees and customers as a holistic pattern of interdependent stimuli. The holistic response is shown in Figure 10.1 as the "perceived servicescape."

Ambient Conditions

Ambient conditions include background characteristics of the environment such as temperature, lighting, noise, music, scent, and color. As a general rule, ambient conditions affect the five senses. Sometimes such dimensions are totally imperceptible (gases, chemicals, infrasound) yet have profound effects, particularly on employees who spend long hours in the environment.

All these factors can affect how people feel, think, and respond to a service establishment. For example, a number of studies have documented the effects of music on consumers' perceptions of products, their perceptions of how long they have waited for service, and the amount of money they spend.[33] When there is music, shoppers tend to perceive that they spend less time shopping and in line than when there is no music. Slower music tempos at lower volumes tend to make people shop more leisurely, and in some cases, they spend more. In the Mayo Hospital lobby, piano music serves to reduce stress (see Exhibit 10.4). Shoppers also spend more time when the music "fits" the product or matches their musical tastes. Other studies have similarly shown the effects of scent on consumer responses.[34] Scent in bakeries, coffee shops, and tobacco shops, for example, can be used to draw people in, and pleasant scents can increase lingering time.

The presence of a scent can reduce perceptions of time spent and improve store evaluations. The effects of ambient conditions are especially noticeable when they are extreme. For example, people attending a symphony in a hall in which the air conditioning has failed and the air is hot and stuffy will be uncomfortable, and their discomfort will be reflected in how they feel about the concert. If the temperature and air quality were within a comfort tolerance zone, these ambient factors would probably go unnoticed.

Spatial Layout and Functionality

Because service environments generally exist to fulfill specific purposes or needs of customers, spatial layout and functionality of the physical surroundings are particularly important. *Spatial layout* refers to the ways in which machinery, equipment, and furnishings are arranged; the size and shape of those items; and the spatial relationships among them. *Functionality* refers to the ability of the same items to facilitate the accomplishment of customer and employee goals. Previous examples in this chapter illustrate the layout and functionality dimensions of the servicescape (e.g., the cruise ship photo earlier and the design of the Mayo Hospital in Exhibit 10.4).

The spatial layout and functionality of the environment are particularly important for customers in self-service environments, where they must perform the service on their own and cannot rely on employees to assist them. Thus, the functionality of an ATM machine and of self-serve restaurants, gasoline pumps, and Internet shopping are critical to success and customer satisfaction.

The importance of facility layout is particularly apparent in retail, hospitality, and leisure settings, where research shows it can influence customer satisfaction, store performance, and consumer search behavior.[35]

Signs, Symbols, and Artifacts

Many items in the physical environment serve as explicit or implicit signals that communicate about the place to its users. *Signs* displayed on the exterior and interior of a structure are examples of explicit communicators. They can be used as labels (name of company, name of department, and so on), for directional purposes (entrances, exits), and to communicate rules of behavior (no smoking, children must be accompanied by an adult). Adequate signs have even been shown to reduce perceived crowding and stress.

Other environmental *symbols* and *artifacts* may communicate less directly than signs, giving implicit cues to users about the meaning of the place and norms and expectations for behavior in the place. Quality construction materials, artwork, certificates and photographs, floor coverings, and personal objects displayed in the environment can all communicate symbolic meaning and create an overall aesthetic impression. The meanings attached to environmental symbols and artifacts are culturally embedded, as illustrated in this chapter's Global Feature on pages 300–301.

Signs, symbols, and artifacts are particularly important in forming first impressions and for communicating service concepts. When customers are unfamiliar with a particular service establishment, they look for environmental cues to help them categorize the place and form their expectations. A study of dentists' offices found that consumers use the environment, in particular its style of decoration and level of quality, as a cue to the competence and manner of the service provider.[36] Another interesting study explored the roles of ethnicity and sexual orientation on consumers' interpretation of symbols within consumption environments. Specifically, the study found that people of Jewish descent observe particular symbols in places that encourage them to feel at home and approach those places.[37] The same study found that homosexuals were also drawn to environments that included particular symbols and artifacts that they identified with. In the presence of other symbols, these groups felt unwelcome or even discriminated against.

Exhibit 10.4 Designing the Mayo Clinic Hospital

Mayo Clinic is the best known health care brand in the United States. More than 100 years old, Mayo operates three clinics across the country. Its original and best-known facility is in Rochester, Minnesota, and the two other clinics are in Jacksonville, Florida, and Scottsdale, Arizona. In 1998 Mayo opened the Mayo Clinic Hospital in Arizona, the first hospital planned, designed, and built by Mayo Clinic. Located on a 210-acre site, the hospital houses 178 hospital rooms on five floors. More than 250 physicians; 950 nursing, technical, and support staff; and 300 volunteers work at the facility. The hospital supports inpatient care for 65 medical and surgical specialties and has a full emergency and urgent care center.

What is unique about this hospital facility is the tremendous care that was taken in its design to serve the needs of patients, doctors, staff, and visitors. The hospital is designed as a "healing environment" focused on patient needs, and focus groups were held with all constituents to determine how the hospital should be designed to facilitate this overall goal. A quotation from the Mayo brothers (founders of the clinic) captures the underlying belief that supported the design of the hospital: "The best interest of the patient is the only interest to be considered." This statement lies at the foundation of all Mayo does, even today, more than 100 years after the Mayo brothers began their practice of medicine. To focus on the best interests of the patient also requires acknowledgment of the needs of the care providers and the patient's family and friend support system. All these interests were clearly considered in the design of the hospital.

A FIVE-STORY ATRIUM LOW-STRESS ENTRY

As patients and others enter the Mayo Hospital, they encounter a five-story enclosed atrium, reminiscent of a luxury hotel lobby. A grand piano sits in the lobby, and volunteers play beautiful, relaxing music throughout the day. An abundance of plants and glass gives the lobby a natural feel and provides a welcoming atmosphere. On entering, visitors see the elevator bank directly in front of them across the atrium, so there is no stress in figuring out where to go.

ALL PATIENT AND VISITOR SERVICES ARE TOGETHER

All services needed by patients and their families (information desk, cafeteria, chapel, patient admissions, gift shop) are located around the atrium, easily visible and accessible. A sense of peace and quiet permeates the lobby—all by deliberate design to reduce stress and promote caring and wellness. There is no confusion here and very little of the atmosphere of a typical hospital entry.

ROOMS ARE DESIGNED AROUND PATIENT NEEDS AND FEELINGS

On disembarking the elevators to go to patient rooms, people again sense relaxation and peace in the environment. As the doors open, patients and guests face a five-story wall of paned glass with views out to the desert and mountains that surround the hospital site. As people progress left or right down well-marked corridors to the patient rooms, the atmosphere becomes even quieter. Rooms (all of them private) are arranged in 12-bed pods surrounding a nursing station. Nurses are within 20 steps of any patient room. Nurses and other attendants use cell phones—there is no paging system with constant announcements, as in many hospitals.

The rooms themselves have interesting features, some designed by patients. For example, rooms contain a multishelf display area on which patients can put cards, flowers, and other personal items. Fold-out, cushioned bedchairs are in each room so family members

GUIDELINES FOR PHYSICAL EVIDENCE STRATEGY

To this point in the chapter we have presented ideas, frameworks, and psychological models for understanding the effects of physical evidence and most specifically the effects of the physical facility or servicescape. In this section, we suggest some general guidelines for an effective physical evidence strategy.[38]

Recognize the Strategic Impact of Physical Evidence

Physical evidence can play a prominent role in determining service quality expectations and perceptions. For some organizations, just acknowledging the impact of physical evidence is a major first step. After this step, they can take advantage of the potential of physical evidence and plan strategically.

can nap or even spend the night with their loved ones. Visitors are never told they must leave. The rooms are arranged with consideration to what patients see from the beds, where they spend the most time. For example, special attention is paid to the ceilings, which patients view while flat on their backs; all rooms have windows; and a white board on the wall at the foot of each bed displays important information that patients want to know (like the name of the nurse on duty, the date, the room phone number, and other information).

DEPARTMENTS THAT WORK TOGETHER ARE ADJACENT

Another interesting design feature in this hospital is that departments that work together are housed very close to each other to facilitate communication and to reduce walking time between areas. This important feature allows caregivers to spend more time with patients and lessens employee fatigue.

MAXIMIZE NURSES' TIME WITH PATIENTS

A critical element in the recovery of patients is the quality of care they are given by nurses. Many of the Mayo Clinic Hospital design features facilitate the quality of nursing care. The pod design puts nurses close to their patients; the white boards in the rooms allow easy communication; the accessible placement of supplies and relevant departments helps maximize the time nurses spend with patients.

It is clear that the design of the Mayo Hospital takes into account the critical importance of the servicescape in facilitating Mayo's primary goal: patient healing. All parties' voices were heard, and the place itself provides an environment that promotes well-being for patients, visitors, doctors, nurses, and other staff.

Mayo Hospital Lobby.

Sources: *Teamwork at Mayo: An Experiment in Cooperative Individualism* (Rochester, MN: Mayo Press, 1998); http://www.mayo.edu; author's personal tour of the Mayo Clinic Hospital in Scottsdale; L. L. Berry and K. D. Seltman, "Building a Strong Services Brand: Lessons from Mayo Clinic," *Business Horizons* 50 (2007), pp. 199–209; and L. L. Berry and K. D. Seltman, *Management Lessons from the Mayo Clinic* (New York: McGraw-Hill, 2008).

For physical evidence strategy to be effective, it must be linked clearly to the organization's overall goals and vision. Thus, planners must know what those goals are and then determine how the physical evidence strategy can support them. At a minimum, the basic service concept must be defined, the target markets (both internal and external) identified, and the firm's broad vision of its future known. Because many evidence decisions are relatively permanent and costly (particularly servicescape decisions), they must be planned and executed deliberately.

Blueprint the Physical Evidence of Service

The next step is to blueprint the service. Everyone in the organization should be able to see the service process and the existing elements of physical evidence. An effective

People's reactions to elements of the physical environment and design are shaped to a large degree by culture and expectations they have formed through their life experiences, dominated by where they live. Just think of one design element—color—and the variety of uses it has across cultures. Other cultural differences—personal space requirements, social distance preferences, sensitivity to crowding—can affect how consumers experience servicescapes around the world.

McDonald's Corporation recognizes these culturally defined expectations in allowing its franchisees around the world tremendous freedom in designing their servicescapes. In most McDonald's franchises, a large percentage of the ownership is retained locally. Employees are nationals, and marketing strategies reflect local consumers' buying and preference patterns. In all cases, the restaurant is a "community institution," involved in social causes as well as local events. McDonald's strategy is to have its restaurants worldwide reflect the cultures and communities in which they are found—to mirror the communities they serve.

Not only are the servicescapes different, but the delivery options are also different around the globe. In the United States, drive-through windows are prevalent, reflecting the country's automobile culture and relative lack of space constraints. In contrast, many people in cities around the world can now have McDonald's food delivered to them via cars, motor scooters, and bicycles. The delivery model works well and is profitable in cities where there is plenty of labor, congested traffic, and little space for stand-alone restaurants, such as Taipei, Taiwan. At the same time that it allows this creative energy to flourish in design, delivery, and marketing strategies, McDonald's is extremely tight on its operating procedures and menu standards.

Although the golden arches are always present, a brief tour around the globe shows the wide variation in McDonald's face to the community:

- Bologna, Italy: In Bologna, known as the "City of Arches" for hundreds of years, McDonald's took on the weathered, crafted look of the neighboring historic arches. Even the floor in the restaurant was done by hand, using old-world techniques. The restaurant used local architects and artists to bring the local architectural feel to the golden arches.
- Paris, France: Near the Sorbonne in Paris, the local McDonald's reflects its studious neighbor. The servicescape there has the look of a leather-bound library with books, statues, and heavy wood furniture.
- Salen, Sweden: On the slopes of Lindvallen Resort in Salen, you can find the world's first "ski-thru" restaurant, named McSki, located next to the main ski lift. The building is different from any other McDonald's restaurant, built in a typical mountain style with wood panels and natural stone from the surroundings. Skiers can simply glide to the counter without taking off their skis, or they can be seated indoors or out.
- McCafés in Europe: A common sight in European McDonald's is the "McCafé" section, where upscale coffees and desserts are sold in a separate area of the restaurant. Upgrades to the McCafé sections in several German McDonald's include wooden floors, leather chairs, a fireplace, and fresh flowers and candles. The comfortable atmosphere and long hours encourage customers to use McCafés as community and business meeting places, not just places to buy a quick meal or a cup of coffee.
- Beijing, China: McDonald's restaurants here have become a "place to hang out," very different from the truly "fast-food" role they have historically played in the United States. They are part of the community, serving young and old, families and couples. Customers can be seen lingering for long periods of time, relaxing, chatting, reading, enjoying the music, or celebrating birthdays. Teenagers and young couples even find the restaurants to be very romantic environments. The emphasis on a Chinese-style family atmosphere is apparent from the interior walls of local restaurants, which are covered by posters emphasizing family values.
- Tokyo, Japan: Although some McDonald's restaurants in Japan are located in prime real-estate districts

way to depict service evidence is through the service blueprint. (Service blueprinting was presented in detail in Chapter 8.) Although service blueprints clearly have multiple purposes, they can be particularly useful in visually capturing physical evidence opportunities. People, processes, and physical evidence can all be seen in the blueprint. The actions involved in service delivery are visible, as are the complexity such as the Ginza in Tokyo, many others are situated near major train stations or other high-traffic locations. The emphasis at these locations is on convenience and speed, not on comfort or socializing. Many of these locations have little frontage space and limited seating. Customers frequently stand while eating, or they may sit on stools at narrow counters. Even the elite Ginza location has few seats. Some locations have a small ordering and service area on the first floor, with limited seating (still primarily stools rather than tables and chairs) on the second floor. Interestingly, while the trend in the United States is to sell healthier menu items, Japanese guests are showing strong preference for big burgers with high calorie counts.

McDonald's has begun an extensive makeover aimed at modernizing the entire chain's overall look. Many existing restaurants have already invested in extensive upgrades that feature a cleaner and simpler overall design; less plastic; warmer, muted colors (terra cotta instead of bright red); Wi-fi access; and different types of seating sections, including bar stools for customers who eat alone and family areas with booths and fabric-covered seating. Of course, the golden arches (being replaced by the "eyebrow" in some current remodels) still play a role in the modernized design.

Sources: *Golden Arches East: McDonald's in East Asia,* ed. J. L. Watson (Stanford, CA: Stanford University Press, 1997); "A Unique Peak," *Franchise Times* 3, no. 4 (1997), p. 46; P. Gogoi, "Mickey D's McMakeover," *BusinessWeek,* May 15, 2006, pp. 42–43; M. Arndt, "Knock Knock, It's Your Big Mac; From Sao Paulo to Shanghai, McDonald's Is Boosting Growth with Speedy Delivery," *BusinessWeek,* July 23, 2007, p. 36; l. Liu, "McDonald's McCafe Takes Aim at Starbucks in Europe," *Business Week,* September 24, 2009; M. Sanchanta and Y. Koh, "McDonald's in Japan Gives New Meaning to Supersize," *The Wall Street Journal,* January 12, 2011, p. 1.

McDonalds restaurant in China.

of the process, the points of human interaction that provide evidence opportunities, and the tangible representations present at each step. To make the blueprint even more useful, photographs or videos of the process can be added to develop a photographic blueprint that provides a vivid picture of physical evidence from the customer's point of view.

Clarify Strategic Roles of the Servicescape

Early in the chapter we discussed the varying roles played by the servicescape and how firms could locate themselves in the typology shown in Table 10.3 to begin to identify their roles. For example, a day care center would locate itself in the "elaborate, interpersonal" cell of the table and quickly see that its servicescape decisions would be relatively complex and that the servicescape strategy may have to consider the needs of both the children and the service providers and could impact marketing, organizational behavior, and consumer satisfaction goals.

Sometimes the servicescape has no role in service delivery or marketing from the customer's point of view, such as in telecommunications services or utilities (although in these cases other forms of physical evidence would still be important). Clarifying the roles played by the servicescape in a particular situation will aid in identifying opportunities and deciding who needs to be consulted in making facility design decisions. Clarifying the strategic role of the servicescape also forces recognition of the importance of the servicescape in creating customer experiences.

Assess and Identify Physical Evidence Opportunities

Once the current forms of evidence and the roles of the servicescape are understood, possible changes and improvements can be identified. One question to ask is, are there missed opportunities to provide service evidence? The service blueprint of an insurance or utility service may show that little if any evidence of service is ever provided to the customer. A strategy might then be developed to provide more evidence of service to show customers exactly what they are paying for. This was the case for a large technology services company that provided a "remote repair service" for its customers. Remote service (sometimes referred to as "smart service") means they were able to anticipate and repair certain technology equipment from afar without the customer actually being aware anything had been done. A blueprint of the service revealed that no physical evidence of the service existed at all. Thus, customers did not appreciate the service they had received nor were they anxious to pay for it. Realizing this, the company developed ways to communicate and provide evidence of the service for customers.

Or it may be discovered that the evidence provided is sending messages that do not enhance the firm's image or goals or that do not match customer expectations. For example, a restaurant might find that its high-price menu cues are not consistent with the design of the restaurant, which suggests "family dining" to its intended market segment. Either the pricing or the facility design would need to be changed, depending on the restaurant's overall strategy.

Another set of questions addresses whether the current physical evidence of service suits the needs and preferences of the target market. To begin answering such questions, the framework for understanding environment–user relationships (Figure 10.1) and the research approaches suggested in this chapter could be employed. And finally, does the evidence strategy take into account the needs (sometimes incompatible) of both customers and employees? This question is particularly relevant in making decisions regarding the servicescape.

Update and Modernize the Evidence

Some aspects of the evidence, particularly the servicescape, require frequent or at least periodic updating and modernizing.[39] Even if the vision, goals, and objectives of the company do not change, time itself takes a toll on physical evidence, necessitating change and modernization. Clearly, an element of fashion is involved, and over time different colors, designs, and styles may come to communicate different messages. Organizations obviously understand this concept when it comes to advertising strategy, but sometimes they overlook the many elements of physical evidence discussed in this chapter.

Work Cross-Functionally

In presenting itself to the consumer, a service firm is concerned with communicating a desired image, with sending consistent and compatible messages through all forms of evidence, and with providing the type of service evidence the target customers want and can understand. Frequently, however, physical evidence decisions are made over time and by various functions within the organization. For example, decisions regarding employee uniforms may be made by the human resources area, servicescape design decisions may be made by the facilities management group, process design decisions are most frequently made by operations managers, and advertising and pricing decisions may be made by the marketing department. Thus, it is not surprising that the physical evidence of service may at times be less than consistent. A multifunction team approach to physical evidence strategy is often necessary, particularly for making decisions about the servicescape.

Summary	In this chapter we explored the roles of physical evidence in forming customer and employee perceptions and shaping customer experiences. Because services are intangible and often produced and consumed at the same time, they can be difficult to comprehend or evaluate before their purchase. The physical evidence of the service thus serves as a primary cue for setting customer expectations before purchase. These tangible cues, particularly the servicescape, also influence customers' responses as they experience the service. Because customers and employees often interact in the servicescape, the physical surroundings also influence employees and the nature of employee–customer interactions.

The chapter focused primarily on the physical servicescape—the physical surroundings or the facility where the service is produced, delivered, and consumed. We presented a typology of servicescapes that illustrated their range of complexity and usage. General strategic roles of the servicescape were also described. We offered a general framework for understanding servicescape effects on employee and customer behaviors. The servicescape can affect the approach and avoidance behaviors of individual customers and employees as well as their social interactions. These behavioral responses come about because the physical environment influences people's beliefs or cognitions about the service organization, their feelings or emotions in response to the place, and their actual physiological reactions while in the physical facility. Three categories of environmental dimensions capture the complex nature of the servicescape: ambient conditions; spatial layout and functionality; and signs, symbols, and artifacts.

Given the importance of physical evidence and its potentially powerful influence on both customers and employees, it is critical for firms to think strategically about the management of the tangible evidence of service. The impact of physical evidence and design decisions needs to be researched and planned as part of the marketing strategy. The chapter concluded with specific guidelines for physical evidence strategy. |

Discussion Questions

1. What is physical evidence, and why have we devoted an entire chapter to it in a services marketing text?

2. Describe and give an example of how servicescapes play each of the following strategic roles: package, facilitator, socializer, and differentiator.

3. Imagine that you own an independent copying and printing shop (similar to FedEx Kinko's). In which cell would you locate your business in the typology of servicescapes shown in Table 10.3? What are the implications for designing your physical facility?

4. How can an effective physical evidence strategy help close provider gap 2? Explain.

5. Why are both customers and employees included in the framework for understanding servicescape effects on behavior (Figure 10.1)? What types of behaviors are influenced by the servicescape according to the framework? Think of examples.

6. Using your own experiences, give examples of times when you have been affected cognitively, emotionally, and physiologically by elements of the servicescape (in any service context).

7. Why is everyone not affected in exactly the same way by the servicescape?

8. Describe the physical environment of your favorite restaurant in terms of the three categories of servicescape dimensions: ambient conditions; spatial layout and functionality; and signs, symbols, and artifacts.

9. Imagine that you are serving as a consultant to a local health club. How would you advise the health club to begin the process of developing an effective physical evidence strategy?

Exercises

1. Choose two very different firms (different market segments or service levels) in the same industry. Observe both establishments. Describe the service "package" in both cases. How does the package help distinguish the two firms? Do you believe that the package sets accurate expectations for what the firm delivers? Is either firm overpromising through the manner in which its servicescape (or other types of physical evidence) communicates with customers?

2. Think of a particular service organization (it can be a class project company, the company you work for, or some other organization) for which you believe physical evidence is particularly important in communicating with and satisfying customers. Prepare the text of a presentation you would give to the manager of that organization to convince him or her of the importance of physical evidence in the organization's marketing strategy.

3. Create a photographic or video blueprint for a service of your choice. Analyze the blueprint from the customer's perspective and suggest changes that could improve the service design.

4. Choose a service organization and collect all forms of physical evidence that the organization uses to communicate with its customers. If customers see the firm's facility, also take a photo of the servicescape. Analyze the evidence in terms of compatibility, consistency, and whether it overpromises or underpromises what the firm can deliver.

5. Visit the websites of several service providers. Does the physical evidence of the website portray an image consistent with other forms of evidence provided by the organizations?

Notes

1. Michael Jannini, "Building a Service Brand," presentation at the 2006 *Compete through Service Symposium,* Arizona State University; C. Yang and D. Brady, "Marriott Hip? Well, It's Trying," *BusinessWeek,* September 26, 2005, pp. 70–72; P. Sanders, "Strange Bedfellows: Marriott, Schrager," *The Wall Street Journal,* June 14, 2007, p. B1; Marriott International website, www.marriott.com, accessed July 2011.

2. The term *servicescape* used throughout this chapter, and much of the content of this chapter, are based, with permission, on M. J. Bitner, "Servicescapes: The Impact of Physical Surroundings on Customers and Employees," *Journal of Marketing* 56 (April 1992), pp. 57–71. For later contributions to this topic, see *Servicescapes: The Concept of Place in Contemporary Markets,* ed. J. F. Sherry Jr. (Chicago: NTC/Contemporary, 1998); and M. J. Bitner, "The Servicescape," in *Handbook of Services Marketing and Management,* ed. T. A. Swartz and D. Iacobucci (Thousand Oaks, CA: Sage, 2000), pp. 37–50.

3. L. P. Carbone, *Clued In: How to Keep Customers Coming Back Again and Again* (Upper Saddle River, NJ: Prentice Hall, 2004). See also L. L. Berry and N. Bendapudi, "Clueing In Customers," *Harvard Business Review,* February 2003, pp. 100–106.

4. J. H. Gilmore and B. J. Pine II, "The Experience Is the Marketing," *Strategic Horizons,* 2002; B. J. Pine II and J. H. Gilmore, *The Experience Economy: Work Is Theater and Every Business Is a Stage* (Boston: Harvard Business School Press, 1999); and B. H. Schmitt, *Experiential Marketing* (New York: The Free Press, 1999).

5. For reviews of environmental psychology, see D. Stokols and I. Altman, *Handbook of Environmental Psychology* (New York: John Wiley, 1987); S. Saegert and G. H. Winkel, "Environmental Psychology," *Annual Review of Psychology* 41 (1990), pp. 441–477; and E. Sundstrom, P. A. Bell, P. L. Busby, and C. Asmus, "Environmental Psychology 1989–1994," *Annual Review of Psychology* 47 (1996), pp. 485–512.

6. http://money.cnn.com/magazines/fortune/bestcompanies/2011/index.html;www.sas.com, accessed July 2011.

7. See M. R. Solomon, "Dressing for the Part: The Role of Costume in the Staging of Servicescape," in Sherry, *Servicescapes;* and A. Rafaeli, "Dress and Behavior of Customer Contact Employees: A Framework for Analysis," in *Advances in Services Marketing and Management,* vol. 2, ed. T. A. Swartz, D. E. Bowen, and S. W. Brown (Greenwich, CT: JAI Press, 1993), pp. 175–212; J. Barlow and P. Stewart, *Branded Customer Service,* San Francisco: Barrett-Koehler Publishers, 2004.

8. S. Casey, "Federal Expressive," www.ecompany.com, May 2001, pp. 45–48.

9. B. Stanley, "Qantas Flaunts Super-Jumbo Perks," *The Wall Street Journal,* July 25, 2007, p. D3; and S. McCartney, "A Bubble Bath and a Glass of Bubbly—at the Airport," *The Wall Street Journal,* July 10, 2007, p. D1.

10. See R. S. Ulrich, L. L. Berry, X. Quan, and J. T. Parish, "A Conceptual Framework for the Domain of Evidence-Based Design," *Health Environments Research and Design Journal* 4, no. 1 (2010), pp. 95–114; J. T. Parish, L. L. Berry, and S. Y. Lam, "The Effect of the Servicescape on Service Workers," *Journal of Service Research* 10 (February 2008), pp. 220–238.

11. www.petsmart.com, 2011; C. M. Dalton, "A Passion for Pets: An Interview with Philip L. Francis, Chairperson and CEO of PetSmart, Inc.," *Business Horizons,*

November–December 2005, pp. 469–475; and D. Brady and C. Palmeri, "The Pet Economy," *BusinessWeek,* August 6, 2007, pp. 45–54.

12. Carbone, *Clued In;* Berry and Bendapudi, "Clueing In Customers"; Gilmore and Pine, "Experience Is the Marketing"; Pine and Gilmore, *The Experience Economy;* Schmitt, *Experiential Marketing;* and L. L. Berry, E. A. Wall, and L. P. Carbone, "Service Clues and Customer Assessment of the Service Experience: Lessons from Marketing," *Academy of Management Perspectives*, 20, no. 2 (2006), pp. 43–57.

13. E. C. Brüggen, B. Foubert, and D. D. Gremler, "Extreme Makeover: Short- and Long- Term Effects of a Remodeled Serviescape," *Journal of Marketing*, 75 (September 2011), pp. 71–87.

14. A. Mehrabian and J. A. Russell, *An Approach to Environmental Psychology* (Cambridge, MA: Massachusetts Institute of Technology, 1974).

15. R. Donovan and J. Rossiter, "Store Atmosphere: An Environmental Psychology Approach," *Journal of Retailing* 58 (Spring 1982), pp. 34–57.

16. D. J. Bennett and J. D. Bennett, "Making the Scene," in *Social Psychology through Symbolic Interactionism,* ed. G. Stone and H. Farberman (Waltham, MA: Ginn-Blaisdell, 1970), pp. 190–196.

17. J. P. Forgas, *Social Episodes* (London: Academic Press, 1979).

18. R. G. Barker, *Ecological Psychology* (Stanford, CA: Stanford University Press, 1968).

19. For a number of excellent papers on this topic spanning a range from toy stores to bridal salons to cybermarketspaces to Japanese retail environments and others, see Sherry, *Servicescapes: The Concept of Place in Contemporary Markets.*

20. J. F. Sherry Jr., "The Soul of the Company Store: Nike Town Chicago and the Emplace Brandscape," in Sherry, *Servicescapes,* pp. 81–108.

21. E. J. Arnould, L. L. Price, and P. Tierney, "The Wilderness Servicescape: An Ironic Commercial Landscape," in Sherry, *Servicescapes,* pp. 403–438.

22. Rosenbaum, "Exploring the Social Supportive Role of Third Places in Consumers' Lives, *Journal of Service Research* 9 (August 2006), pp. 59–72; A. Tombs and J. R. McColl-Kennedy, "Social-Servicescape Conceptual Model," *Marketing Theory* 3, no. 4 (2003), pp. 447–475; and M. S. Rosenbaum, J. Ward, B. A. Walker, and A. L. Ostrom, "A Cup of Coffee with a Dash of Love: An Investigation of Commercial Social Support and Third-Place Attachment," *Journal of Service Research* 10 (August 2007), pp. 43–59.

23. A. Rapoport, *The Meaning of the Built Environment* (Beverly Hills, CA: Sage, 1982); and R. G. Golledge, "Environmental Cognition," in Stokols and Altman, *Handbook of Environmental Psychology,* vol. 1, pp. 131–174.

24. M. P. Gardner and G. Siomkos, "Toward a Methodology for Assessing Effects of In-Store Atmospherics," in *Advances in Consumer Research,* vol. 13, ed. R. J. Lutz (Ann Arbor, MI: Association for Consumer Research, 1986), pp. 27–31.

25. M. J. Bitner, "Evaluating Service Encounters: The Effects of Physical Surroundings and Employee Responses," *Journal of Marketing* 54 (April 1990), pp. 69–82.

26. J. C. Ward, M. J. Bitner, and J. Barnes, "Measuring the Prototypicality and Meaning of Retail Environments," *Journal of Retailing* 68 (Summer 1992) pp. 194–220.

27. See, for example, Mehrabian and Russell, *An Approach to Environmental Psychology;* J. A. Russell and U. F. Lanius, "Adaptation Level and the Affective Appraisal

of Environments," *Journal of Environmental Psychology* 4, no. 2 (1984), pp. 199–235; J. A. Russell and G. Pratt, "A Description of the Affective Quality Attributed to Environments," *Journal of Personality and Social Psychology* 38, no. 2 (1980), pp. 311–322; J. A. Russell and J. Snodgrass, "Emotion and the Environment," in Stokols and Altman, *Handbook of Environmental Psychology,* vol. 1, pp. 245–281; J. A. Russell, L. M. Ward, and G. Pratt, "Affective Quality Attributed to Environments," *Environment and Behavior* 13 (May 1981), pp. 259–288; V. Kaltcheva and B. A. Weitz, "When Should a Retailer Create an Exciting Store Environment," *Journal of Marketing* 70 (January 2006), pp. 107–118.

28. See, for example, M. S. Sanders and E. J. McCormick, *Human Factors in Engineering and Design,* 7th ed. (New York: McGraw-Hill, 1993); and G. Salvendy (ed), *Handbook of Human Factors and Ergonomics* (Hoboken, NJ: Wiley, 2006).

29. "Empty Nests, Full Pockets," *Brandweek,* September 23, 1996, pp. 36ff; and "Lodging Chain to Give Older Guests a Choice," *The Wall Street Journal,* February 19, 1993, p. B1.

30. Mehrabian and Russell, *An Approach to Environmental Psychology;* Russell and Snodgrass, "Emotion and the Environment."

31. A. Mehrabian, "Individual Differences in Stimulus Screening and Arousability," *Journal of Personality* 45, no. 2 (1977), pp. 237–250.

32. E. Bellman, "In India, a Retailer Finds Key to Success Is Clutter," *The Wall Street Journal,* August 8, 2007, p. A1.

33. For research documenting the effects of music on consumers, see J. Baker, D. Grewal, and A. Parasuraman, "The Influence of Store Environment on Quality Inferences and Store Image," *Journal of the Academy of Marketing Science* 22 (Fall 1994), pp. 328–339; J. C. Chebat, C. Gelinas-Chebat, and P. Filliatrault, "Interactive Effects of Musical and Visual Cues on Time Perception: An Application to Waiting Lines in Banks," *Perceptual and Motor Skills* 77 (1993), pp. 995–1020; L. Dube, J. C. Chebat, and S. Morin, "The Effects of Background Music on Consumers' Desire to Affiliate in Buyer–Seller Interactions," *Psychology and Marketing* 12, no. 4 (1995), pp. 305–319; J. D. Herrington and L. M. Capella, "Effects of Music in Service Environments: A Field Study," *Journal of Services Marketing* 10, no. 2 (1996), pp. 26–41; J. D. Herrington and L. M. Capella, "Practical Applications of Music in Service Settings," *Journal of Services Marketing* 8, no. 3 (1994), pp. 50–65; M. K. Hui, L. Dube, and J. C. Chebat, "The Impact of Music on Consumers' Reactions to Waiting for Services," *Journal of Retailing* 73 (Spring 1997), pp. 87–104; A. S. Matila and J. Wirtz, "Congruency of Scent and Music as a Driver of In-Store Evaluations and Behavior," *Journal of Retailing* 77 (Summer 2001), pp. 273–289; L. Dube and S. Morin, "Background Music Pleasure and Store Evaluation: Intensity Effects and Psychological Mechanisms," *Journal of Business Research* 54 (November 2001), pp. 107–113; J. Bakec, A. Parasuraman, D. Grewal, and G. B. Voss, "The Influence of Multiple Store Environment Cues as Perceived Merchandise Value and Patronage Intentions," *Journal of Marketing* 66 (April 2002), pp. 120–141; and S. Morin, L. Dube, and J. Chebat, "The Role of Pleasant Music in Servicescapes: A Test of the Dual Model of Environmental Perception," *Journal of Retailing* 83, no. 1 (2007), pp. 115–130.

34. For research documenting the effects of scent on consumer responses, see D. J. Mitchell, B. E. Kahn, and S. C. Knasko, "There's Something in the Air: Effects of Congruent and Incongruent Ambient Odor on Consumer Decision Making," *Journal of Consumer Research* 22 (September 1995), pp. 229–238; and

E. R. Spangenberg, A. E. Crowley, and P. W. Henderson, "Improving the Store Environment: Do Olfactory Cues Affect Evaluations and Behaviors?" *Journal of Marketing* 60 (April 1996), pp. 67–80.

35. See J. M. Sulek, M. R. Lind, and A. S. Marucheck, "The Impact of a Customer Service Intervention and Facility Design on Firm Performance," *Management Science* 41, no. 11 (1995), pp. 1763–1773; P. A. Titus and P. B. Everett, "Consumer Wayfinding Tasks, Strategies, and Errors: An Exploratory Field Study," *Psychology and Marketing* 13, no. 3 (1996), pp. 265–290; C. Yoo, J. Park, and D. J. MacInnis, "Effects of Store Characteristics and In-Store Emotional Experiences on Store Attitude," *Journal of Business Research* 42 (1998), pp. 253–263; and K. L. Wakefield and J. G. Blodgett, "The Effect of the Servicescape on Customers' Behavioral Intentions in Leisure Service Settings," *Journal of Services Marketing* 10, no. 6 (1996), pp. 45–61; Brüggen, Foubert, and Gremler, "Extreme Makeover: Short- and Long-Term Effects of a Remodeled Servicescape."

36. J. C. Ward and J. P. Eaton, "Service Environments: The Effect of Quality and Decorative Style on Emotions, Expectations, and Attributions," in *Proceedings of the American Marketing Association Summer Educators' Conference,* eds. R. Achrol and A. Mitchell (Chicago: American Marketing Association 1994), pp. 333–334.

37. M. S. Rosenbaum, "The Symbolic Servicescape: Your Kind Is Welcomed Here," *Journal of Consumer Behaviour* 4, no. 4 (2005), pp. 257–267.

38. This section is adapted from M. J. Bitner, "Managing the Evidence of Service," in *The Service Quality Handbook,* ed. E. E. Scheuing and W. F. Christopher (New York: AMACOM, 1993), pp. 358–370.

39. Brüggen, Foubert, and Gremler, "Extreme Makeover: Short- and Long-Term Effects of a Remodeled Servicescape."

Part **Five**

Delivering and Performing Service

Chapter 11 Employees' Roles in Service Delivery

Chapter 12 Customers' Roles in Service Delivery

Chapter 13 Managing Demand and Capacity

In the gaps model of service quality, provider gap 3 (the service performance gap) is the discrepancy between customer-driven service design and standards and actual service delivery (see the accompanying figure). Even when guidelines exist for performing service well and treating customers correctly, high-quality service performance is not a certainty. Part 5 deals with all the ways in which companies ensure that services are performed according to customer-defined designs and standards.

Provider Gap 3: The Service Performance Gap

In Chapter 11, we focus on the key roles that employees play in service delivery and strategies that ensure they are effective in their roles. Issues of particular concern include employees who feel in conflict in their position between customers and company management, having the wrong employees or inadequate technology, inappropriate compensation and recognition, and lack of empowerment and teamwork.

In Chapter 12, we discuss the variability in service performance caused by customers. If customers do not perform appropriately—if they do not follow instructions or if they disturb other customers receiving service at the same time—service quality is jeopardized. Effective service organizations understand the roles of customers in service delivery and cocreation of service experiences and develop strategies to help their customers perform *effectively* in these roles.

Chapter 13 emphasizes the need to synchronize demand and capacity in service organizations to deliver consistent, high-quality service. Service organizations often face situations of over- or underdemand because they lack inventories to smooth demand. Strategies for managing demand, such as price changes, advertising, promotion, and alternative service offerings, as well as strategies for adjusting capacity, such as using part-time employees, outsourcing activities, and renting or sharing facilities and equipment, can help this challenge.

Chapter **Eleven**

Employees' Roles in Service Delivery

This chapter's objectives are to

1. Demonstrate the importance of creating a service culture in which providing excellent service to both internal and external customers is a way of life.
2. Illustrate the pivotal role of service employees in creating customer satisfaction and service quality.
3. Identify the challenges inherent in boundary-spanning roles.
4. Provide examples of strategies for creating customer-oriented service delivery through hiring the right people, developing employees to deliver service quality, providing needed support systems, and retaining the best employees.

Employees Are the Service and the Brand

Noted service expert Leonard Berry has documented that investments in employees are key drivers of sustained business success in companies as diverse as Charles Schwab, Enterprise Rent-A-Car, USAA Insurance, and Chick-fil-A.[1] Why is this true? Why do these companies choose to invest heavily in their employees?

For clues, consider the following true stories:

- On a long overseas Singapore Airlines flight, a restless toddler repeatedly dropped his pacifier. Every time the child would cry, and someone (the mother, another passenger, or a flight attendant) would retrieve the pacifier. Finally, one of the attendants picked up the pacifier, attached it to a ribbon, and sewed it to the child's shirt. The child and mother were happy, and passengers seated nearby gave the attendant a standing ovation.[2]

- A phone associate at Universal Card Services received a call from a customer whose wife, suffering from Alzheimer's disease, had vanished. The man hoped that he could find his wife through tracing her use of her Universal Card. The phone associate placed a hold on the card and arranged to be called personally the moment there was any activity on the card. When it happened, about a week later, the associate contacted the husband, the doctor, and the police, who were then able to assist the missing woman and get her home.[3]

Service employees directly impact customers' satisfaction.

- In a Panera Bread parking lot a couple of years ago one woman attempted to catch another customer (who suffered from multiple sclerosis) as she lost her balance. Both customers ended up falling on the pavement, and the one who caught the other broke her right arm. Before the woman was taken by ambulance to an emergency room for treatment, a Panera employee gave her his card and told her to call him if she needed anything. A couple of hours later she called and asked if she could get a ride back to the restaurant to get her car. Once there, she realized that she could not drive the car—it had a manual transmission and she could not shift gears with a broken arm. While she was attempting to contact family to get a ride home, the Panera employee provided her with a free meal. After not being able to find someone to drive her home, she asked the employee for another favor—to give her a ride home. He did—to a town that was nearly an hour's drive away. The woman was ecstatic and could not believe a "restaurant employee" would do all of this for her.[4]

These stories illustrate the important roles played by service employees in creating satisfied customers and in building customer relationships. The frontline service providers in each example are enormously important to the success of the organizations they represent. They are responsible for understanding customer needs and for interpreting customer requirements in real time (as suggested by the accompanying photo). Leonard Berry has documented that, in case after case, companies that achieve sustained service success all recognize the critical importance of their employees.[5]

In this chapter we focus on service employees and human resource practices that facilitate delivery of quality services. Even when customer expectations are well understood (gap 1) and services have been designed and specified to conform to those expectations (gap 2), there may still be discontinuities in service quality when the service is not delivered as specified. These discontinuities are labeled gap 3—the *service performance gap*—in the service quality framework. Because employees frequently deliver or perform the service, human resource issues are a major cause of this gap. By focusing on the critical role of service employees and by developing strategies that lead to effective customer-oriented service, organizations can begin to close the service performance gap.

SERVICE CULTURE

Before addressing the role of the employee in service delivery, we should look at the bigger picture. The behavior of employees in an organization will be heavily influenced by the culture of that organization or the pervasive norms and values that shape individual and group behavior. *Corporate culture* has been defined as "the pattern of shared values and beliefs that give the members of an organization meaning, and provide them with the rules for behavior in the organization."[6] *Culture* has been defined more informally as "the way we do things around here."

To understand at a personal level what corporate culture is, think of different places you have worked or organizations you have been a member of, such as churches, fraternities, schools, or associations. Your behavior and the behaviors of others were no doubt influenced by the underlying values, norms, and culture of the organization. Even when you first interview for a new job, you can begin to get a sense of the firm's culture through talking to a number of employees and observing behavior. Once you are on the job, your formal training and informal observation of behavior will work together to give you a better picture of the organization's culture.

Experts have suggested that a customer-oriented, service-oriented organization will have at its heart a *service culture,* defined as "a culture where an appreciation for good service exists, and where giving good service to internal as well as ultimate, external customers is considered a natural way of life and one of the most important norms by everyone."[7] This very rich definition has many implications for employee behaviors. First, a service culture exists if there is an "appreciation for good service." This phrase does not mean that the company has an advertising campaign that stresses the importance of service, but people know that good service is appreciated and valued. A second important point in this definition is that good service is given to internal as well as external customers.[8] It is not enough to promise excellent service to final customers; all people within the organization deserve the same kind of service. Finally, in a service culture good service is "a way of life" and it comes naturally because it is an important norm of the organization. Service culture is critical to the creation of a customer-focused organization and has been identified as a source of competitive advantage in companies.[9]

Exhibiting Service Leadership

A strong service culture begins with leaders in the organization who demonstrate a passion for service excellence. Leonard Berry suggests that leaders of successful service firms tend to have similar core values, such as integrity, joy, and respect, and they "infuse those values into the fabric of the organization."[10] Leadership does not consist of bestowing a set of commands from a thick rulebook but, rather, the regular and consistent demonstration of one's values. Employees are more likely to embrace a service culture when they see management living out these values. Espoused values—what managers *say* the values are—tend to have less impact on employees than enacted values—what employees believe the values to be because of what they observe management actually *doing.*[11] That is, culture is driven by what employees perceive that management *really* believes, and employees gain an understanding of what is important in the organization through the daily experiences they have with those people in key roles throughout the organization.

Developing a Service Culture

A service culture cannot be developed overnight, and there is no easy way to sustain a service culture. The human resource and internal marketing practices discussed later in the chapter can help develop a service culture over time. If, however, an organization has a culture rooted in product-, operations-, or government regulation–oriented traditions, no single strategy will change it into a service culture. Hundreds of little (but significant) factors, not just one or two big factors, are required to build and sustain a service culture.[12] Successful companies such as IBM Global Services, Avnet, and General Electric have found that it takes years of consistent, concerted effort to build a service culture and to shift an organization from its old patterns to new ways of doing business. Even for companies such as FedEx, Charles Schwab,

Although international markets offer tremendous opportunities for growth, many companies find significant challenges when they attempt to transport their services to other countries. Services depend on people, are often delivered by people, and involve the interaction between employees and customers. Differences in values, norms of behavior, language, and even the definition of service become evident quickly and have implications for training, hiring, and incentives that can ultimately affect the success of the international expansion. Companies with strong service cultures are faced with the question of whether to try to replicate their culture and values in other countries or to adapt significantly. A few examples illustrate different approaches.

McDONALD'S APPROACH

McDonald's has been very successful in its international expansion. In some ways it has remained very "American" in everything it does—people around the world want an American experience when they go to McDonald's. However, the company is sensitive to cultural differences as well. This subtle blending of the "McDonald's" way with adaptations to cultural nuances has resulted in great success. One way that McDonald's maintains its standards is through its Hamburger University (HU), which is required training for *all* McDonald's employees worldwide before they can become managers. Each year approximately 5,000 employees from more than 100 countries enroll and attend the Advanced

Operations Course at HU, located in Oak Brook, Illinois. The curriculum is 80 percent devoted to communications and human relations skills. Because of the international scope of McDonald's, translators and electronic equipment enable instructors to teach and communicate in 28 languages at one time. The result is that all managers in all countries have the same "ketchup in their veins," and the restaurant's basic human resources and operating philosophies remain fairly stable from operation to operation. Certain adaptations in decor, menu, and other areas of cultural differences are then allowed (see the Global Feature in Chapter 10 for some specific examples).

UPS'S EXPERIENCE

UPS has a strong culture built on employee productivity, highly standardized service delivery processes, and structured training. Its brown trucks and uniforms are instantly recognizable in the United States. In fact, in 2002 UPS launched the largest television and print advertising campaign in its 100-year history around the tag line "What Can Brown Do for You?" As it expanded into countries across Europe, UPS was surprised by some of the challenges of managing a global workforce. Here are some of the surprises: indignation in France, when drivers were told they could not have wine with lunch; protests in Britain, when drivers' dogs were banned from delivery trucks; and dismay in Spain, when it was found that brown UPS trucks resembled the local hearses.

Disney, and the Ritz-Carlton, which started with a strong service and customer focus, sustaining their established service cultures still takes constant attention to hundreds of details.

Transporting a Service Culture

Transporting a service culture through international business expansion is also very challenging. Attempting to "export" a corporate culture to another country creates additional issues. For instance, will the organization's service culture clash with a different *national* culture? If there is a clash, is it over *what* the actual values are or over *how* they are to be enacted? If the issue is over what the values are, and they are core values critical to the firm's competitive advantage, then perhaps the company cannot be successful in that setting. If the issue is over how the values are enacted, then perhaps some service practices can be modified in the new setting. To illustrate, as discussed in Chapter 9, Four Seasons Hotels has created seven globally uniform "SERVICE" standards that it expects of all its employees throughout the world. The company has also identified several core values that it believes transcend national culture. One such value is to anticipate guests' needs. This value has been enacted in the United States by leaving a coffeepot on the table in the hotel restaurant, so that guests can help themselves whenever they like. However, when Four Seasons opened a hotel in Paris, it decided to never leave a coffeepot on restaurant tables; doing so would

DISNEY IN EUROPE

When Disney first expanded into Europe by opening Disneyland Paris, it also faced challenges and surprises. The highly structured, scripted, and customer-oriented approach that Disney used in the United States was not easily duplicated with European employees. In particular, the smiling, friendly, always customer-focused behaviors of Disney's U.S. workforce did not suit the experience and values of young French employees. In attempting to transport the Disney culture and experience to Europe, the company confronted clashing values and norms of behavior in the workplace that made the expansion difficult. Customers also needed to be "trained" in the Disney way—not all cultures are comfortable with waiting in long lines, for example. And not all cultures treat their children the same. For example, in the United States, families will spend lots of money at Disneyland on food, toys, and other things that their children "must" have. Some European cultures view this behavior as highly indulgent, so families will visit the park without buying much beyond the ticket for admission.

A U.S. LAW FIRM GOES TO THE UNITED KINGDOM

Professions such as law and medicine have well-established and quite unique practices across cultures. Pay rates, work styles, and business models can be quite different. So what happens when a law firm seeks to expand its services to another country? Unlike many U.S. law firms that tend to populate their international offices with American lawyers, Weil, Gotshal, and Manges, a New York firm, opened its offices in London by hiring primarily British solicitors who would function as a "firm within a firm." One of the biggest challenges was how to blend the very different American and British legal cultures. First, the U.S. lawyers at Weil, Gotshal, and Manges tend to be workaholics—commonly billing 2,500 hours a year, whereas in London a partner would bill a respectable 1,500 hours. Pay differences were also obvious—$650,000 on average for London partners, $900,000 for Americans. Conflict, rather than synergy, sometimes result from the deeply rooted cultural differences. Despite the challenges, the London office has done quite well; the office now has roughly 100 lawyers, has become the second largest of the firm's worldwide offices, and received the "U.S. Law Firm of the Year in London" award in 2009 and 2010.

Sources: www.mcdonalds.com, accessed December 2010; D. Milbank, "Can Europe Deliver?" *The Wall Street Journal,* September 30, 1994, pp. R15, R23; P. M. Barrett, "Joining the Stampede to Europe, Law Firm Suffers a Few Bruises," *The Wall Street Journal,* April 27, 1999, p. A1; and www.weil.com, accessed December 2010.

not be received favorably by French customers, who generally believe one should not have to pour coffee oneself. Four Seasons did not alter other practices; it continued, for example, its employee-of-the-month program as a way to provide recognition for exceptional service, even though such programs are not generally offered in France.[13] These standards and values reflect Four Seasons's attempt to transport its service culture across national borders, but management is keenly aware that they need to carefully consider how these values are enacted in each hotel.

Although tremendous opportunities exist in the global marketplace, the many legal, cultural, and language barriers become particularly evident for services that depend on human interaction. Our Global Feature highlights some of the issues and experiences of several companies as they attempt to transport their service cultures.

THE CRITICAL ROLE OF SERVICE EMPLOYEES

An often-heard quotation about service organizations goes like this: "In a service organization, if you're not serving the customer, you'd better be serving someone who is."[14] People—frontline employees and those supporting them from behind the scenes—are critical to the success of any service organization. The importance of people in the marketing of services is captured in the *people* element of the service marketing mix, which we described in Chapter 1 as *all the human actors who play a part in service delivery and thus influence the buyer's perceptions: namely, the firm's personnel, the customer, and other customers in the service environment.*

The key focus in this chapter is on customer-contact service employees because:

- They *are* the service.
- They *are* the organization in the customer's eyes.
- They *are* the brand.
- They *are* marketers.

In many cases, the contact employee *is the service*—there is nothing else. For example, in most personal and professional services (like haircutting, personal trainers, child care, limousine services, counseling, and legal services) the contact employee provides the entire service singlehandedly. The offering *is* the employee. Thus, investing in the employee to improve the service parallels making a direct investment in the improvement of a manufactured product.

Even if the contact employee does not perform the service entirely, he or she may still *personify the firm in the customer's eyes.* All the employees of a law firm or health clinic—from the professionals who provide the service to the receptionists and office staff—represent the firm to the client, and everything these individuals do or say can influence perceptions of the organization. Even off-duty employees, such as flight attendants or restaurant employees on a break, reflect the organizations they represent. If they are unprofessional or make rude remarks about or to customers, customers' perceptions of the organization will suffer, even though the employee is not on duty. The Disney Corporation insists that its employees maintain "onstage" attitudes and behaviors whenever they are in front of the public; employees may relax these behaviors only when they are truly behind the scenes or "backstage" in underground tunnels where guests cannot see them in their off-duty times.

Service employees *are the brand.* An Edward Jones financial advisor, a Nordstrom sales associate, a Southwest Airlines flight attendant, an Abercrombie & Fitch retail employee—in each case, the primary image that a customer has of the firm is formed by the interactions the customer has with the employees of that firm. A customer sees Edward Jones as a good provider of financial services if the employees she interacts with are knowledgeable, understanding, and concerned about her financial situation and goals. Similarly, a customer sees Nordstrom as a professional and empathetic company because of interactions he has with its sales associates. Southwest Airlines seeks employees who are outgoing and fun-loving and Abercrombie & Fitch looks to hire people who have a certain "look." Online shoe retailer Zappos makes the hiring process a primary focus of its branding strategy and evaluates potential employees on their ability to serve as brand ambassadors.[15] These companies understand that the brand image is not just built and maintained by the products sold and the advertising: it is a function of the people who work for them. Strategies that recognize the power of employees to create the brand have been referred to as "branded customer service."[16] For firms using such strategies, employees truly "are the brand" and epitomize the company image that each is attempting to create in the minds of its customers.

Because contact employees represent the organization and can directly influence customer satisfaction, they *perform the role of marketers.* They physically embody the product and are walking billboards from a promotional standpoint. Some service employees may also perform more traditional selling roles. For example, bank tellers are often called on to cross-sell bank products, a departure from the traditional teller role of focusing on operational functions only. In this chapter we examine frameworks, tools, and strategies for ensuring that service employees perform their marketing and service functions well.

The Service Triangle

Service marketing is about promises—promises made and promises kept to customers. A strategic framework known as the *service triangle* (illustrated in Figure 11.1) visually reinforces the importance of people in the ability of firms to keep their promises and succeed in building customer relationships.[17] The triangle shows the three interlinked groups that work together to develop, promote, and deliver services. These key players are labeled on the points of the triangle: the *company* (SBU, department, or "management"), the *customers,* and the *providers.* Providers can be the firm's employees, subcontractors, or outsourced entities who actually deliver the company's services. Between these three points on the triangle, three types of marketing must be successfully carried out for a service to succeed: external marketing, interactive marketing, and internal marketing.

On the right side of the triangle are the *external marketing* efforts that the firm engages in to develop its customers' expectations and make promises to customers regarding what is to be delivered. Anyone or anything that communicates to the customer before service delivery can be viewed as part of this external marketing function. But external marketing is just the beginning for service marketers: promises made must be kept. On the bottom of the triangle is what has been termed *interactive marketing* or *real-time marketing.* Here is where promises are kept or broken by the firm's employees, subcontractors, or agents. Those people representing the organization are critical at this juncture. If promises are not kept, customers become dissatisfied and eventually leave. The left side of the triangle suggests the critical role played by *internal marketing.* Management engages in these activities to help the providers deliver on the service promise: recruiting, training, motivating, rewarding, and

FIGURE 11.1
The Service Marketing Triangle

Sources: Adapted from M. J. Bitner, "Building Service Relationships: It's All about Promises," *Journal of the Academy of Marketing Science* 23 (Fall 1995), pp. 246–251; C. Gronroos, *Service Management and Marketing: A Customer Relationship Management Approach,* 2nd ed. (West Sussex, England: John Wiley and Sons, Ltd., 2000), p. 55; and P. Kotler and K. L. Keller, *Marketing Management,* 14th ed. (Upper Saddle River, NJ: Pearson Prentice Hall, 2012), p. 365.

Company (Management)

Internal marketing "Enabling the promise"

External marketing "Making the promise"

Providers

Customers

Interactive marketing "Delivering the promise"

providing equipment and technology. Unless service employees are able and willing to deliver on the promises made, the firm will not be successful.

All three sides of the triangle are essential, and the sides of the triangle should be aligned. That is, what is promised through external marketing should be the same as what is delivered; and the enabling activities inside the organization should be aligned with what is expected of service providers. Strategies for aligning the triangle, particularly the strategies associated with internal marketing, are the subject of this chapter.

Employee Satisfaction, Customer Satisfaction, and Profits

Satisfied employees make for satisfied customers (and satisfied customers can, in turn, reinforce employees' sense of satisfaction in their jobs). Some researchers have even gone so far as to suggest that, unless service employees are happy in their jobs, customer satisfaction will be difficult to achieve.[18]

Through their research with customers and employees in bank branches, Benjamin Schneider and David Bowen have shown that both a *climate for service* and a *climate for employee well-being* are highly correlated with overall customer perceptions of service quality.[19] That is, both service climate and human resource management experiences that *employees* have within their organizations are reflected in how *customers* experience the service. Similar research suggests that employees who feel they are treated fairly by their organizations will treat customers better, resulting in greater customer satisfaction.[20]

The underlying logic connecting employee satisfaction and loyalty to customer satisfaction and loyalty and ultimately profits is illustrated by the *service profit chain* shown in Figure 11.2.[21] In earlier chapters we focused on customer satisfaction and retention; here we focus on employee issues. The service profit chain suggests that there are critical linkages among internal service quality, employee satisfaction/productivity, the value of services provided to the customer, and ultimately customer satisfaction, retention, and profits.

Service profit chain researchers are careful to point out that the model does not suggest causality. That is, employee satisfaction does not *cause* customer satisfaction; rather the two are interrelated and feed off each other.[22] The model does imply that companies that exhibit high levels of success on the elements of the model will be more successful and profitable than those that do not. Studies have found that those

FIGURE 11.2   The Service Profit Chain

Source: Adapted and Reprinted by permission of *Harvard Business Review* an excerpt from J. L. Heskett, T. O. Jones, G. W. Loveman, W. E. Sasser Jr., and L. A. Schlesinger, "Putting the Service-Profit Chain to Work," *Harvard Business Review* 72 (March–April 1994), pp. 164–174. Copyright © 1994 by The Harvard Business School Publishing Corporation; all rights reserved.

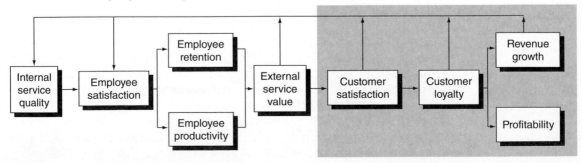

companies included in *Fortune* magazine's list of the "100 Best Companies to Work For in America" deliver higher average annual returns (more than double in the last decade!) to shareholders than do companies making up the Standard and Poor's 500.[23]

The Effect of Employee Behaviors on Service Quality Dimensions

Customers' perceptions of service quality are affected by the customer-oriented behaviors of employees.[24] In fact, all five dimensions of service quality (reliability, responsiveness, assurance, empathy, and tangibles) can be influenced directly by service employees.

Delivering the service as promised—*reliability*—is often totally within the control of frontline employees. Even in the case of automated services (such as ATMs, automated ticketing machines, or self-serve and pay gasoline pumps), behind-the-scenes employees are critical for making sure all the systems are working properly. When services fail or errors are made, employees are essential for setting things right and using their judgment to determine the best course of action for service recovery.

Frontline employees directly influence customer perceptions of *responsiveness* through their personal willingness to help and their promptness in serving customers. Consider the range of responses you receive from different retail store clerks when you need help finding a particular item of clothing. One employee may ignore your presence, whereas another offers to help you search and calls other stores to locate the item. One may help you immediately and efficiently, whereas another may move slowly in accommodating even the simplest request.

The *assurance* dimension of service quality is highly dependent on employees' ability to communicate their credibility and to inspire the customer's trust and confidence in the firm. The reputation of the organization will help, but in the end, individual employees with whom the customer interacts confirm and build trust in the organization or detract from its reputation and ultimately destroy trust. For startup or relatively unknown organizations, credibility, trust, and confidence will be tied totally to employee actions.

It is difficult to imagine how an organization would deliver "caring, individualized attention" to customers independent of its employees. *Empathy* implies that employees will pay attention, listen, adapt, and be flexible in delivering what individual customers need.[25] For example, research documents that when employees are customer oriented, have good rapport with customers, and exhibit perceptive and attentive listening skills, customers will evaluate the service more highly and are more likely to return.[26] Employee appearance and dress are important aspects of the *tangibles* dimension of quality, along with many other factors that are independent of service employees (the service facility, decor, brochures, signage, and so on).

BOUNDARY-SPANNING ROLES

Our focus in this chapter is on frontline service employees who interact directly with customers, although much of what is described and recommended can be applied to internal service employees as well. The frontline service employees are referred to as *boundary spanners* because they operate at the organization's boundary. As indicated in Figure 11.3, boundary spanners provide a link between the external customer and environment and the internal operations of the organization. They serve a critical function in understanding, filtering, and interpreting information and resources to and from the organization and its external constituencies.

FIGURE 11.3
The Critical Roles of
Boundary Spanners

Who are these boundary spanners? What types of people and positions constitute critical boundary-spanning roles? Their skills and experience cover the full spectrum of jobs and careers. In industries such as fast food, hotel, telecommunication, and retail, boundary spanners are generally the least skilled, lowest-paid employees in the organization. They are order-takers, front-desk employees, telephone operators, store clerks, truck drivers, and delivery people. In other industries, boundary spanners are well-paid, highly educated professionals—for example, doctors, lawyers, accountants, consultants, architects, and teachers.

No matter what the level of skill or pay, boundary-spanning positions are often high-stress jobs. In addition to mental and physical skills, these positions require extraordinary levels of emotional labor, frequently demand an ability to handle interpersonal and interorganizational conflict, and they call on the employee to make real-time trade-offs between quality and productivity on the job. These stresses and trade-offs can result in failure to deliver services as specified, which widens the service performance gap.

Emotional Labor

The term *emotional labor* was coined by Arlie Hochschild to refer to the labor that goes beyond the physical or mental skills needed to deliver quality service.[27] In general, boundary-spanning service employees are expected to align their displayed emotions with organizationally desired emotions via their use of emotional labor.[28] Such labor includes delivering smiles, making eye contact, showing sincere interest, and engaging in friendly conversation with people who are essentially strangers and whom they may never see again. Friendliness, courtesy, empathy, and responsiveness directed toward customers all require huge amounts of emotional labor from the frontline employees who shoulder this responsibility for the organization. Emotional labor draws on people's feelings (often requiring them to suppress their true feelings) to be effective in their jobs. A frontline service employee who is having a bad day or is not feeling just right is still expected to put on the face of the organization when dealing with customers. One of the clearest examples of emotional labor is the story (probably apocryphal) of a flight attendant who was approached by a businessman, who said, "Let's have a smile." "Okay," she replied, "I'll tell you what, first you smile and then I'll smile, okay?" He smiled. "Good," she said, "now hold that for 15 hours," and then walked away.[29]

Many of the strategies we will discuss later in the chapter can help organizations and employees deal with the realities of emotional labor on the job. For the organization, such strategies include carefully selecting people who can handle emotional stress, training them in needed skills (like listening and problem solving), and teaching or giving them coping abilities and strategies (via job rotation, scheduled breaks, teamwork, or other techniques).[30] Our Strategy Insight describes additional emotional labor strategies that service firms employ.

Sources of Conflict

Frontline employees often face interpersonal and interorganizational conflicts on the job. Their frustration and confusion can, if left unattended, lead to stress, job dissatisfaction, a diminished ability to serve customers, and burnout.[31] Because they represent the organization to the customer and often need to manage a number of customers simultaneously, frontline employees inevitably have to deal with conflicts, including person/role conflicts, organization/client conflicts, and interclient conflicts, as discussed in the next sections.[32]

Person/Role Conflict

In some situations, boundary spanners feel conflict between what they are asked to do and their own personalities, orientations, or values. In a society such as the United States, where equality and individualism are highly valued, service workers may feel role conflict when they are required to subordinate their feelings or beliefs, as when they are asked to live by the motto "The customer is always right—even when he is wrong." Sometimes there is a conflict between role requirements and the self-image or self-esteem of the employee. An Israeli service expert provides a classic example from that culture:

> In Israel, for instance, most buses are operated by one man, the driver, who is also responsible for selling tickets. No trays are installed in buses for the transferring of bus fare from passenger to driver, and the money is transferred directly. Bus drivers often complain about the humiliating experience of having to stretch out their hands like beggars in order to collect the fare. Another typical case in Israeli buses is when money changes hands and a coin falls down accidentally onto the bus floor. The question, who will bend down to lift the coin, the driver or the passenger, clearly reflects the driver's role conflict.[33]

Whoever stoops to pick up the coin is indicating subservient status.

Person/role conflict also arises when employees are required to wear specific clothing or change some aspect of their appearance to conform to the job requirements. A young lawyer, just out of school, may feel an internal conflict with his new role when his employer requires him to cut his hair and trade his casual clothes for a three-piece suit.

Organization/Client Conflict

A more common type of conflict for frontline service employees is the conflict between their two bosses, the organization and the individual customer. Service employees are typically rewarded for following certain standards, rules, and procedures. Ideally these rules and standards are customer based, as described in Chapter 9. When they are not, or when a customer makes excessive demands, the employee has to decide whether to follow the organization's rules or satisfy the customer's demands. To illustrate, management at an accounting firm may expect an employee to prepare tax returns quickly to maximize revenues during the short tax preparation season. However, the employee's other boss—the customer—may expect personalized attention and a significant amount of her time in preparing the return.[34] The organization/client conflict is greatest when the employee believes the organization is wrong in its policies and

Strategy Insight Strategies for Managing Emotional Labor

Customer contact employees in service positions are often required to display (or, conversely, to withhold display of) a variety of emotions. Such employees are increasingly being required to invest personal identity and expression into their work in many situations. The following description suggests how the experience of the service employee, even in the most routine of occupations, is markedly different from that of the traditional manufacturing worker:

> The assembly-line worker could openly hate his job, despise his supervisor, and even dislike his coworkers, and while this might be an unpleasant state of affairs, if he [completes] his assigned tasks efficiently, his attitude [is] his own problem. For the service worker, inhabiting the job means, at the very least, pretending to like it, and, at most, actually bringing his whole self into the job, liking it, and genuinely caring about the people with whom he interacts.[*]

Emotional labor occurs more often when the job requires frequent contact and long durations of voice contact or face-to-face contact with customers. These employees often need emotional management to deal with such situations. Later in this chapter we suggest many strategies for organizations to create an environment that helps employees deal with the realities of emotional labor on the job. Here we present specific strategies some firms use to more directly support employee efforts to manage their emotions in the face of demanding, obnoxious, or unruly customers.

SCREENING FOR EMOTIONAL LABOR ABILITIES

Many firms look to hire employees who are well suited to meet the emotional labor requirements of the job. Dungarvin, an organization that provides a variety of services to people who have mental and physical disabilities, displays a realistic job preview on its website to indicate to prospective employees the emotional labor requirements. In doing so, Dungarvin's intent is to identify applicants who are

comfortable with the emotional demands required of employees who must regularly interact with clients with special needs. Call centers often provide job candidates with a realistic job preview, in part, to allow a prospective employee to gauge if he or she is well suited to exert the emotional labor required to interact with customers—often frustrated and unhappy ones—on a continual basis. These simulated customer contact exercises also allow the company to assess the level of friendliness and warmth prospective candidates naturally communicate. Such practices help in identifying employees whose values, background, and personality match the job's emotional labor requirements.

TEACHING EMOTIONAL MANAGEMENT SKILLS AND APPROPRIATE BEHAVIORS

Most customer contact employees are taught that they need to be courteous to customers. However, customers have no obligation to return empathy or courtesy. In situations in which customers exercise the privilege of "the customer is always right," employees face challenges in suppressing their true feelings. Seldom do firms provide much training to assist employees in facing these challenges. Arlie Hochschild identifies two forms of emotional labor: *surface acting,* in which employees pretend to feel emotions that are not really present and, in doing so, could involve both suppression of felt emotions and faking of unfelt emotions; and *deep acting,* in which employees attempt to experience the real feelings they are expected (or required) to express to the customer, including the active invocation of thoughts, images, and memories to induce the associated emotion. Retail store clerks and airline flight attendants are often encouraged to engage in deep-acting strategies such as imagining that the client is a friend or that the passenger is a frightened little child flying for the first time. Companies may also train employees in how to avoid absorbing a customer's bad mood, perhaps by having employees spend hours role-playing to suppress their natural

must decide whether to accommodate the client and risk losing a job or to follow the policies. These conflicts are especially severe when service employees depend directly on the customer for income. For example, employees who depend on tips or commissions are likely to face greater levels of organization/client conflict because they have even greater incentives to identify with the customer.

reaction to return negative customer emotions with their own negative emotions.

CAREFULLY FASHIONING THE PHYSICAL WORK ENVIRONMENT

As we discussed in Chapter 10, the environment in which the service is delivered can have an impact on employee behaviors and emotions. MedAire, a company that provides telephone consultation to airlines when medical emergencies arise on flights, regularly has employees in the midst of life-threatening situations. To reduce the stress that MedAire employees face on a daily basis, the company designed its Tempe, Arizona, office with an open floor plan so that all employees are able to look through windows to see trees, grass, and cars driving by. Taking this idea one step further, JetBlue Airways allows its reservation agents to work from home rather than requiring them to sit all day in an office call center.

ALLOWING EMPLOYEES TO VENT

Employees who must exert emotional labor often need to have an outlet to let off steam. Allowing employees to vent lets them get rid of their frustrations. If such venting is done in a group setting, it provides emotional support and encouragement, allows employees to see that others are experiencing the same problems, and delivers a message to employees that the company is aware of and acknowledges the emotional contribution they make. RitzCarlton, Walmart, and other companies regularly set aside time for such venting. In addition to the cathartic benefit this experience can provide, other employees may reveal coping strategies that they have found useful.

GIVING EMPLOYEES A BREAK

In situations in which employees have extended voice or face-to-face contact with customers, a particularly helpful strategy is to allow them a short break to regroup. Many companies with toll-free call centers rotate employees into different positions throughout the day so that they do not spend the entire time on the telephone with customers. Customer contact employees can be reenergized and refreshed after spending a little time away from demanding or difficult situations, even if they take only a few minutes to finish paperwork or complete some other job responsibility. One call center in Australia has a pool table near the employee work area and plays movies while employees work at their desk to reduce the stress of interacting with customers.

HANDING OFF DEMANDING CUSTOMERS TO MANAGERS

Some customers may be too much for an employee to handle. In such situations, to alleviate pressure on the customer contact employee, firms may shift responsibility for the interaction to managers. Wing Zone, a restaurant chain specializing in chicken wings, understands the stress that angry customers can cause employees, many of whom are college students. A majority of the company's orders are taken over the phone, and employees—particularly those with little experience—are trained to simply hand off demanding customers to the nearest manager. And a manager who is unsuccessful in handling the situation is encouraged to direct such customers to the corporate office via a toll-free number.

*Quoted from C. L. Macdonald and C. Sirianni, *Working in the Service Society.* (Philadelphia: Temple University Press, 1996), p. 4.

Sources: A. Hochschild, *The Managed Heart: Commercialization of Human Feeling* (Berkeley: University of California Press, 1983); B. F. Ashforth and R. H. Humphrey, "Emotional Labor in Service Roles: The Influence of Identity," *Academy of Management Review* 18 (1993), pp. 88–115; S. D. Pugh, "Service with a Smile: Emotional Contagion in the Service Encounter," *Academy of Management Journal* 44, no. 5 (2001), pp. 1018–1027; A. A. Grandey, "When 'The Show Must Go On': Surface Acting and Deep Acting as Determinants of Emotional Exhaustion and Peer-Rated Service Delivery," *Academy of Management Journal* 46, no. 1 (2003), pp. 86–96; and T. Hennig-Thurau, M. Groth, M. Paul, and D. D. Gremler, "Are All Smiles Created Equal? How Employee-Customer Emotional Contagion and Emotional Labor Impact Service Relationships," *Journal of Marketing* 70 (July 2006), pp. 58–73.

Interclient Conflict

Sometimes conflict occurs for boundary spanners when incompatible expectations and requirements arise from two or more customers. This situation occurs most often when the service provider is serving customers in turn (a bank teller, a ticketing agent, a doctor) or is serving many customers simultaneously (teachers, entertainers).

When serving customers in turn, the provider may satisfy one customer by spending additional time, customizing the service, and being very flexible in meeting the customer's needs. Meanwhile, waiting customers may become dissatisfied because their needs are not being met in a timely way. Beyond the timing issue, different clients may prefer different modes of service delivery; one client may prefer personal recognition and a degree of familiarity while another client may be "all business" and prefer little interpersonal interaction.

When serving many customers at the same time, employees often find it difficult or impossible to serve the full range of needs of a group of heterogeneous customers. This type of conflict is readily apparent in any college classroom in which the instructor must meet a multitude of student expectations and different preferences for formats and style. It is also apparent in an entertainment venue or any type of group training service.

Quality/Productivity Trade-Offs

Frontline service workers are asked to be both effective and efficient: they are expected to deliver satisfying service to customers and at the same time to be cost-effective and productive in what they do. A physician in an HMO, for example, is expected to deliver caring, quality, individualized service to her patients but at the same time to serve a certain number of patients within a specified time frame. A checker at a grocery store is expected to know his customers and to be polite and courteous, yet also process the groceries accurately and move people through the line quickly.[35] An architectural draftsperson is expected to create quality drawings, yet produce a required quantity of drawings in a given period of time. These essential trade-offs between quality and quantity and between maximum effectiveness and efficiency place real-time demands and pressures on service employees. Technology is being used to an ever-greater degree to balance the quality/quantity trade-off to increase the productivity of service workers and free them to provide higher-quality service for the customer (see the Technology Spotlight).

A vivid example of the quality/productivity trade-off occurred with Verizon employees in Florida. They were frustrated by the firm's requirement that a service call to a customer not go beyond a certain amount of time, regardless of whether the issue was resolved. That is, employees felt the firm's customer service priorities revolved around efficiencies, not solving a customer's problems. They eventually went on strike to get management to reconsider their service processes, and customers subsequently communicated their appreciation.[36]

STRATEGIES FOR DELIVERING SERVICE QUALITY THROUGH PEOPLE

A complex combination of strategies is needed to ensure that service employees are willing and able to deliver quality services and that they stay motivated to perform in customer-oriented, service-minded ways. These strategies for enabling service promises are often referred to as *internal marketing,* as shown on the left side of Figure 11.1.[37] By approaching human resource decisions and strategies with the primary goal to motivate and enable employees to deliver customer-oriented promises successfully, an organization will move toward delivering service quality through its people. The strategies presented here are organized around four basic themes. To build a customer-oriented, service-minded workforce, an organization must (1) hire the right people, (2) develop people to deliver service quality, (3) provide the needed support systems, and (4) retain the best people. Within each

FIGURE 11.4
**Human Resource
Strategies for
Delivering Service
Quality through
People**

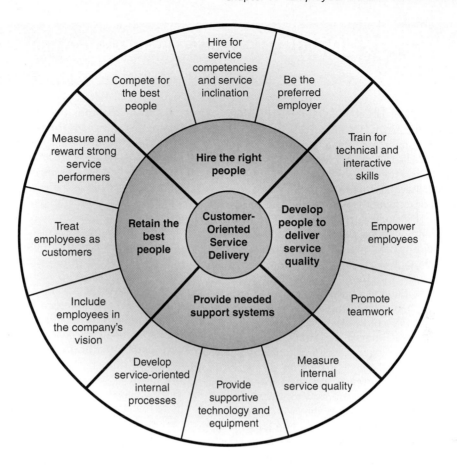

of these basic strategies are a number of specific substrategies for accomplishing the goal, as shown in Figure 11.4.

Hire the Right People

To effectively deliver service quality, considerable attention should be focused on recruiting and hiring service personnel. Such attention is contrary to traditional practices in many service industries, where service personnel are the lowest on the corporate ladder and work for minimum wage. At the other end of the spectrum, in the professional services, the most important recruiting criteria are typically technical training, certifications, and expertise. However, successful service organizations generally look beyond the technical qualifications of applicants to assess their customer and service orientation as well. Figure 11.4 shows a number of ways to go about hiring the right people.

Compete for the Best People

To get the best people, an organization needs to identify them and compete with other organizations to hire them. Leonard Berry and A. Parasuraman refer to this approach as "competing for talent market share."[38] They suggest that firms act as marketers in their pursuit of the best employees, just as they use their marketing expertise to compete for customers. Firms that think of recruiting as a marketing activity will address issues of market (employee) segmentation, product (job) design, and promotion of job availability in ways that attract potentially long-term employees. Intuit, Harrah's, Yahoo!, Marriott, and other firms have changed the title of the head recruiting person

Technology Spotlight   How Technology Is Helping Employees Serve Customers More Effectively and Efficiently

OPTIMIZATION TECHNOLOGY HELPS UPS DRIVERS' RELIABILITY EFFORTS

UPS delivers more than 16 million packages every day. Historically, UPS drivers worked off maps, 3 × 5 note cards, and their own memory to figure out the best way to navigate their routes. However, to more efficiently determine the best routes, UPS has implemented a $600 million route optimization system; each evening, it maps out the next day's schedule for the majority of its more than 88,000 drivers. This software designs each route to minimize the number of left turns, thus reducing the time and gas that drivers waste idling at stoplights. It has also reduced a day or more in transit time in nearly 3 million zip code parings. UPS's technology has allowed it to capture institutional knowledge about its customers. Before, when employees retired or quit, the knowledge of package loading techniques or route tips they had accumulated over the years usually went with them. This knowledge is now captured in a centralized system that shortens the training time for new drivers, lessening the chances of a lapse in customer service. This technology has enabled UPS to run its routes more efficiently, resulting in quicker and more reliable deliveries for its customers.

BLACKBOARD ASSISTS UNIVERSITY INSTRUCTORS

Universities both within and outside the United States use the Internet and other technologies to create a networked learning environment on their campuses. One tool universities use, called Blackboard, provides an infrastructure that increases instructor effectiveness and efficiency. To illustrate, Blackboard helps instructors organize nearly all teaching-related materials. Among the course management capabilities are electronic storage and controlled access of materials (readings, syllabi, assignments, discussion questions), management of class discussion boards, collection of student assignments, administration of online quizzes and exams, administration of group projects, provision of an online gradebook, and many other capabilities. In effect, most course administration tasks required of instructors can be handled by Blackboard. Students also benefit from having one source for accessing course materials, receiving updated course information, and submitting course assignments—without having to bother instructors with such administrative issues.

Blackboard provides instructors with the ability to manage many sections of a course. Instead of having to create material for each section, instructors can create a learning object (e.g., a handout or reading supplement), store it once, and link it to all course sections. Thus, Blackboard makes more effective usage of the instructor's time—providing the instructor with more time to be accessible to students outside of the classroom. Blackboard also provides instructors with an organized way to track and evaluate student learning. For example, Blackboard's e-portfolio option provides an online repository for

---

to "vice president of talent acquisition." Doing so recognizes the importance of the function and helps elevate the role to the strategic importance it deserves.

Hire for Service Competencies and Service Inclination

Once potential employees have been identified, organizations need to be conscientious in interviewing and screening to identify the best people from the pool of candidates. Service employees need two complementary capacities: service competencies and service inclination.[39]

Service competencies are the skills and knowledge necessary to do the job. In many cases, employees demonstrate competencies by achieving particular degrees and certifications, such as attaining a doctor of law (JD) degree and passing the relevant state bar examination for lawyers. Similar rites of passage are required of doctors, airline pilots, university professors, teachers, and many other job seekers before they are ever interviewed for service jobs in their fields. In other cases, service competencies storing student work—making it easy for both faculty *and* students to assess a student's progress in a course.

ELECTRONIC MEDICAL RECORDS SUPPORT MAYO CLINIC STAFF

Mayo Clinic has been described as one of the most powerful services brands in the world and is arguably the leading health care brand in the United States. Although there are many reasons for this (as noted in other places in this text), technology plays a key role in its ability to deliver high-quality care for patients with serious medical needs such as cancer treatment, heart surgery, or neurosurgery. At its Jacksonville, Florida, location Mayo Clinic invested $18 million during the past decade in computer system technology, with a large portion of the emphasis on electronic medical records. Like most hospitals, Mayo's inpatient system is very complex and requires that patient care efforts be coordinated across departments and specialists. The many systems required for patient care, including pharmacy systems, laboratory systems, and monitoring systems, need to be interconnected and to function 24/7 without fail.

Mayo Clinic's order-entry system enables hospital physicians to order tests, treatments, and medications. When an entry is made, it automatically launches a series of activities associated with the patient's care. For example, consider a person being admitted to the oncology department for a cancer treatment. A physician might place an order for the patient to receive an anti-nausea medicine 30 minutes before chemotherapy, then receive three different chemical agents at specific times and in a particular sequence—and it might specify that the treatment be repeated every 12 hours. Mayo's order-entry system automatically notifies physicians, pharmacists, and others in the hospital when a particular treatment needs to be performed and monitors dosage amounts and method of administration (e.g., orally or through a vein).

In addition to a savings of nearly $7 million to its Jacksonville clinic, the automated system makes Mayo medical staff more effective and improves patient care. For example, when new test results are reported in a patient's file, they are highlighted, so that a nurse or doctor sees them immediately. Thus, the medical staff spends less time waiting or looking for patient files. By transitioning to electronic medical records, Mayo has found staff workflow to be better coordinated in the care of patients suffering from chronic diseases. Thus, electronic medical records have enabled Mayo Clinic staff to be even more efficient and effective in delivering quality health care.

Sources: D. Foust, "How Technology Delivers for UPS," *BusinessWeek* (March 5, 2007), p. 60; 2010 UPS Annual Report; L. L. Berry and K. D. Seltman, "Building a Strong Services Brand: Lessons from Mayo Clinic," *Business Horizons* 50 (May–June 2007), pp. 199–209; and A. M. Virzi, "A Complex Operation," *Baseline* (October 2006), pp. 56–59.

may not be degree-related but may instead relate to basic intelligence or physical requirements. A retail clerk, for example, must possess basic math skills and the potential to operate a cash register.

Given the multidimensional nature of service quality, service employees should be screened for more than their service competencies. They should also be screened for *service inclination*—their interest in doing service-related work—which is reflected in their attitudes toward service[40] and orientation toward serving customers and fellow employees. Self-selection suggests that most service jobs will draw applicants with some level of service inclination and that most employees in service organizations are inclined toward service. However, some employees clearly have a greater service inclination than others. Research has shown that service effectiveness is correlated with service-oriented personality characteristics such as helpfulness, thoughtfulness, and sociability[41] and that the best service companies put a greater emphasis on hiring those

Exhibit 11.1   Google Quickly Becomes a Preferred Employer in Its Industry

In 1996 Google's founders, Larry Page and Sergey Brin, developed a new approach to online search that took root in a Stanford University dorm room and quickly spread to information seekers around the globe. They continued to refine their search approaches and in 1998 formed Google—the world's largest search engine—an easy-to-use, free service that usually returns results in a fraction of a second. As of 2011, Google was available in over 180 domains and more than 130 languages.

In its short history Google has become a preferred employer and was ranked number 1 in *Fortune*'s list of the 100 best companies to work for in America in 2007 (its first year of eligibility) and 2008. One study reported that one in four young professionals wants to work at Google. Google has used a variety of approaches to become an employer of choice for over 20,000 employees worldwide, including:

- *The Googleplex*—The Google world headquarters building is located in Mountain View, California, and helps to attract and retain "Googlers" (employees). Some of the essential elements of the facility, which are presented on its company website, include a lobby with piano, lava lamps, and live projection of current search queries from around the world. In the hallways there are bicycles, large rubber exercise balls are on the floors, and press clippings from around

Google employees working together in the company's atrium.

the world are posted on bulletin boards everywhere. A three-dimensional rotating image of the world toggles between displaying points of light representing real-time searches rising from the surface of the

with positive attitudes rather than a specific skill set.[42] An ideal selection process for service employees assesses both service competencies and service inclination, resulting in employee hires who are high on both dimensions.

In addition to traditional employment interviews, many firms use innovative approaches to assessing service inclination and other personal characteristics that fit the organization's needs. Southwest Airlines looks for people who are compassionate and who have common sense, a sense of humor, a "can do" attitude, and an egalitarian sense of themselves (they think in terms of "we" rather than "me"). One way the company assesses these service inclinations is by interviewing potential flight attendants in groups to see how they interact with each other. Pilots are also interviewed in groups to assess their teamwork skills, a critical factor above and beyond the essential technical skills they are required to possess.[43]

Be the Preferred Employer

One way to attract the best people is to be known as the preferred employer in a particular industry or location. UPS regularly conducts a survey among its employees to create an "Employer of Choice Index" and sets annual goals to remain a preferred employer.[44] Google, the online search service provider used daily by customers around the world, also enjoys a reputation as a preferred employer. Google states on its website that it "puts employees first when it comes to daily life" in all of its offices.[45] Exhibit 11.1 provides some insight into why Google has twice been chosen by *Fortune* globe toward space, color-coded by language and viewing traffic patterns for the entire Internet.

- *Recreation facilities*—Google provides a workout room with weights and rowing machines, locker rooms, washers and dryers, a massage room, assorted video games, Foosball, a baby grand piano, a pool table, and Ping-Pong. Twice a week roller hockey is played in the parking lot.

- *Dining facilities*—Google runs 11 free gourmet cafeterias at its headquarters and offers free meals to all its employees. Its food stations include "Charlie's Grill," "Back to Albuquerque," "East Meets West," and "Vegheads." Snack rooms contain bins packed with various cereals, gummy treats, M&Ms, toffee, licorice, cashew nuts, yogurt, carrots, fresh fruit, and other snacks, as well as dozens of different drinks, including fresh juice, soda, and make-your-own cappuccino.

- *Services for employees*—A wide variety of services are provided to Googlers. For example, on-site car washes and oil changes are among the numerous perks Google offers to all its workers. Haircuts are provided on-site. Employees can attend subsidized exercise classes; get a massage; study Mandarin, Japanese, Spanish, or French; and ask a personal concierge to arrange dinner reservations. Other services available to employees include child care, on-site

notaries, and five on-site doctors available for employee checkups, all free of charge. And, when traveling to and from the office, Google operates free, Wi-Fi–enabled shuttle buses from five Bay Area locations for its employees.

- *Other benefits*—Several other benefits are also provided to Google employees. Those who buy a hybrid car receive $5,000. A weekly TGIF party takes place, usually with a live band playing, and a "pajama day" is a frequent occurrence. Lactation rooms, complete with breast pumps (so that nursing mothers do not have to haul equipment to work), are provided. All Google engineers are expected to devote 20 percent of their time to pursuing projects they dream up— Gmail, Google News, and the Google Finance site all resulted from such activity.

It is no surprise that Google receives more than 3,000 resumes per day. However, with such benefits Google almost always wins talent wars against Microsoft and Yahoo!. And if these benefits are not enough to encourage employees to talk up the company, Google provides a $2,000 reward for each person hired as a result of a referral.

Sources: A. Lashinsky, "Search and Enjoy," *Fortune*, January 29, 2007, pp. 70–82; J. Light, "Google Is No. 1 on List of Desired Employers," *The Wall Street Journal*, March 21, 2011, p. B8; and www.google.com, accessed January 2011.

as the "Best Company to Work For" in the past few years and is the preferred employer in its industry.

Other strategies that support a goal of being the preferred employer include extensive training, career and advancement opportunities, excellent internal support, attractive incentives, and quality goods and services with which employees are proud to be associated. SAS Institute, *Fortune's* "Best Company to Work For" in 2010 and 2011, has long been a preferred employer in the statistical software industry. Employees who work for SAS are, for the most part, professional or technical and well paid. A quote from the company's website captures SAS's philosophy about its people: "if you treat employees as if they make a difference to the company, they will make a difference to the company." The company invests heavily in its people: every employee has a private office, a 35-hour schedule is promoted, flexible hours are available, the company provides top-quality day care centers with very reasonable prices on-site, on-site health care, and a free 66,000-square-foot fitness center. For these reasons, the best performers at SAS seldom leave to work for competitors.[46]

In a very different industry, dominated by lower-paid workers, Marriott International has a stated company goal of being the "preferred employer" in its industry. Marriott's philosophy concerning its employees, which sounds very similar to that of SAS, has been stated by Bill Marriott: "if the employees are well taken care of, they'll take care of the customer and the customer will come back . . . that's basically the core value of the company."[47] Marriott uses flexible workplace options (including flex time, telework, compressed work weeks, shift swapping, part-time work, and job sharing), tuition reimbursement, child and elder care discounts, job and life skills training, and companywide health and wellness programs to be the preferred employer in the highly competitive hospitality industry. The company even offers global language learning programs—with 30 languages to choose from. Marriott International, like Google and SAS, is consistently rated among *Fortune*'s list of the top 100 companies to work for.

Develop People to Deliver Service Quality

To grow and maintain a workforce that is customer oriented and focused on delivering quality, an organization must develop its employees to deliver service quality. That is, once it has hired the right employees, the organization must train and work with these individuals to ensure service performance.

Train for Technical and Interactive Skills

To provide quality service, employees need ongoing training in the necessary technical and interactive skills. Examples of *technical skills* are working with accounting systems in hotels, cash machine procedures in a retail store, underwriting procedures in an insurance company, and any operational rules the company has for running its business. Most service organizations are quite conscious of and relatively effective at training employees in technical skills. These skills may be taught through formal education, as is the case at McDonald's Hamburger University, which trains McDonald's managers from all over the world. Additionally, technical skills are often taught through on-the-job training, as when call center service trainees listen in on the conversations of experienced employees. Companies frequently use information technology to train employees in the technical skills and knowledge needed on the job.

Service employees also need training in *interactive skills* that allow them to provide courteous, caring, responsive, and empathetic service. Research suggests firms can teach employees how to develop rapport with customers—one type of interactive skill—by teaching them how to engage in pleasant conversation, ask questions, or use humor as they interact with customers.[48] Employees can be taught conversation prompts to help them identify commonalities with their customers. Several firms, such as Starbucks and the Elysian Hotel in Chicago, are even teaching customer-contact employees improvisation to improve their communication and listening skills, read customers' body language, and establish an immediate rapport with them.[49]

Outback Steakhouse coaches waiters and waitresses to squat next to or even sit at a customer's table and spend a couple of minutes interacting; such action allows them to establish better eye contact with customers and provides opportunities for engaging interactions. Starbucks has created a board game, *Inside Out,* to be used in training sessions to help its baristas to connect with customers.[50] As part of the game, a barista is presented with a specific scenario—say, a sighing customer doing last-minute Christmas shopping has stopped by for a pick-me-up drink—and is challenged to figure out how to cheer up the customer.

Successful companies invest heavily in training and make sure that the training fits their business goals and strategies. For example, at the Ritz-Carlton, all employees go through extensive initial training and are given pocket-sized, laminated credo cards to carry in their wallets. In addition to the credo, the card specifies the three steps of service and Ritz-Carlton's well-known motto "We are Ladies and Gentlemen Serving Ladies and Gentlemen." Further, employees in every hotel attend a brief standing staff meeting each day to review Ritz-Carlton's "Gold Standards" and employee service values, so as to continually reinforce earlier training.

Empower Employees

Many organizations have discovered that, to be truly responsive to customer needs, frontline providers need to be empowered to accommodate customer requests and to recover on the spot when things go wrong. *Empowerment* means giving employees the authority, skills, tools, and desire to serve the customer. Although the key to empowerment is giving employees authority to make decisions on the customer's behalf, authority alone is not enough. Employees need the knowledge and tools to be able to make these decisions, and they need incentives that encourage them to make the right ones. Organizations do not succeed in empowering their employees if they simply tell them, "You now have the authority to do whatever it takes to satisfy the customer." First, employees often do not believe this statement, particularly if the organization has functioned hierarchically or bureaucratically in the past. Second, employees often do not know what it means to "do whatever it takes" if they have not received training, guidelines, and the tools needed to make such decisions. Third, not all employees have a desire to be empowered by the firm.[51]

Research suggests that some of the benefits of empowering frontline service workers include a reduction in job-related stress, improved job satisfaction, greater adaptability, and better outcomes for customers.[52] But such success does not come easily. In fact, some experts have concluded that few organizations have truly taken advantage of, or properly implemented, successful empowerment strategies.[53] Nor is empowerment the answer for all organizations. Exhibit 11.2 enumerates both the costs and the benefits of empowerment.

Promote Teamwork

The nature of many service jobs suggests that customer satisfaction will be enhanced when employees work as teams. Because service jobs are frequently frustrating, demanding, and challenging, a teamwork environment will help alleviate some of the stresses and strains. Employees who feel supported and feel that they have a team backing them up will be better able to maintain their enthusiasm and provide quality service.[54] Such teamwork is the driving force behind the service philosophy at the Mayo Clinic. One of Mayo's core principles encourages all of those in the organization to practice medicine as "an integrated team of compassionate, multidisciplinary physicians, scientists and allied health professionals who are focused on the needs of patients."[55] In addition to being an important ingredient for service quality, "an interactive community of coworkers who help each other, commiserate, and achieve together is a powerful antidote to service burnout."[56] Zappos and Jyske Bank, two of the companies featured in the cases in the back of this book, are both known for developing a team approach to serving clients. By promoting teamwork, an organization can enhance the employees' *abilities* to deliver excellent service, while the camaraderie and support enhance their *inclination* to be excellent service providers.

One way of promoting teamwork is to encourage the attitude that "everyone has a customer." That is, even when employees are not directly responsible for or do not directly interact with the final customer, they need to know whom they serve directly and how the role they play in the total service picture is essential to the final delivery of quality service. If each employee can see how he or she is somehow integral in delivering quality to the final customer and if each employee knows whom to support to make service quality a reality, teamwork will be enhanced. Service blueprints, described in Chapter 8, can serve as useful tools to illustrate for employees their integral roles in delivering service quality to the ultimate customer.

Exhibit 11.2 Potential Benefits and Costs of Empowerment

BENEFITS

- *Quicker responses to customer needs during service delivery.* Employees who are allowed to make decisions on behalf of the customer can make decisions more quickly, bypassing what in the past might have meant a long chain of command or at least a discussion with an immediate supervisor.

- *Quicker responses to dissatisfied customers during service recovery.* When failures occur in the delivery system, customers hope for an immediate recovery effort on the part of the organization. Empowered employees can recover on the spot, and a dissatisfied customer can be turned into a satisfied, even loyal one.

- *Employees feel better about their jobs and themselves.* Giving employees control and authority to make decisions makes them feel responsible and gives them ownership of the customer's satisfaction. Decades of job design research suggest that, when employees have a sense of control and of doing meaningful work, they are more satisfied. The results are lower turnover and less absenteeism.

- *Employees will interact with customers with more warmth and enthusiasm.* Employees feel better about themselves and their work, and these attitudes will spill over into their feelings about customers and will be reflected in their interactions.

- *Empowered employees are a great source of service ideas.* When employees are empowered, they feel responsible for the service outcome and they will be excellent sources of ideas about new services or how to improve current offerings.

- *Great word-of-mouth advertising from customers.* Empowered employees do special and unique things that customers will remember and tell their friends, family, and associates about.

COSTS

- *A potentially greater dollar investment in selection and training.* To find employees who will work well in an empowered environment requires creative, potentially more costly selection procedures. Training will also be more expensive in general because employees need more knowledge about the company, its products, and how to work in flexible ways with customers.

- *Higher labor costs.* The organization may not be able to use as many part-time or seasonal employees, and it may need to pay more for asking employees to assume responsibility.

- *Potentially slower or inconsistent service delivery.* If empowered employees spend more time with all, or even some, customers, then service overall may take longer and may annoy customers who are waiting. Empowerment also means that customers will get what they need or request. When decisions regarding customer satisfaction are left to the discretion of employees, there may be inconsistency in the level of service delivered.

- *May violate customers' perceptions of fair play.* Customers may perceive that sticking to procedures with every customer is fair. Thus, if they see that customers are receiving different levels of service or that employees are cutting special deals with some customers, they may believe that the organization is not fair.

- *Employees may "give away the store" or make bad decisions.* Many people fear that empowered employees will make costly decisions that the organization cannot afford. Although this situation can happen, good training and appropriate guidelines will help.

Source: Reprinted from "The Empowerment of Service Workers: What, Why, How, and When," by D. E. Bowen and E. E. Lawler, *Sloan Management Review* 33 (Spring 1992), pp. 31–39, by permission of the publisher. Copyright 1992 by Massachusetts Institute of Technology. All rights reserved.

Team goals and rewards also promote teamwork. Harrah's Entertainment is one company that provides incentives and compensation focused on teamwork. The casino hotel company's incentive program is weighted toward team results and a relatively small percentage of compensation (often less than 40 percent) is based on individual goals. Everyone in the organization, from meeting planners to blackjack dealers, are rewarded based on customer service scores. When a firm rewards teams of individuals rather than basing all rewards on individual achievements and performance, team efforts and team spirit are encouraged.

Provide Needed Support Systems

To be efficient and effective in their jobs, service workers require internal support systems that are aligned with their need to be customer focused. This point cannot be overemphasized. In fact, without customer-focused internal support and customer-oriented systems, it is nearly impossible for employees to deliver quality service, no matter how much they want to. For example, a bank teller who is rewarded for customer satisfaction as well as for accuracy in bank transactions needs easy access to up-to-date customer records, a well-staffed branch (so that he or she is not constantly facing a long line of impatient customers), and supportive customer-oriented supervisors and back-office staff. In examining customer service outcomes in Australian call centers, researchers found that internal support from supervisors, teammates, and other departments as well as evaluations of technology used on the job were all strongly related to employee satisfaction and ability to serve customers.[57] The following sections suggest strategies for ensuring customer-oriented internal support.

Measure Internal Service Quality

One way to encourage supportive internal service relationships is to measure and reward internal service. By first acknowledging that everyone in the organization has a customer and then measuring customer perceptions of internal service quality, an organization can begin to develop a strong internal quality culture.[58] In its quest to provide the best possible service to patients, the Mayo Clinic formally measures internal service quality between departments annually. An internal customer service audit is one tool that can be used to implement a culture of internal service quality. Through the audit, internal organizations identify their customers, determine their needs, measure how well they are doing, and make improvements. The process parallels market research practices used for external customers.

One risk of measuring and focusing on internal service quality and internal customers is that employees can sometimes get so wrapped up in meeting the needs of internal customers that they forget they are in business to serve the ultimate, external customers.[59] In measuring internal service quality, therefore, it is important to constantly draw the linkages between what is being delivered internally and how it supports the delivery of the final service to customers. Service blueprinting, introduced in Chapter 8, can help illustrate these critical linkages.

Provide Supportive Technology and Equipment

When employees do not have the right equipment or their equipment fails them, they can be easily frustrated in their desire to deliver quality service. To do their jobs effectively and efficiently, service employees need the right equipment and technology. Our Technology Spotlight earlier in this chapter highlights the role of technology in providing support for employees.

Having the right technology and equipment can extend into strategies regarding workplace and workstation design. For example, Zappos provides its customer service representatives with computer systems that provide comprehensive information concerning product inventory in their warehouses—allowing them to provide customers with up-to-date information and options. Hallways in the company's facilities are covered with murals and cartoons, rooms are filled with props, and workspaces are filled with personalized clutter—all designed to create an environment where employees feel like part of a team and are comfortable serving customers. In fact, the atmosphere that Zappos has created in the work environment has become so well known that tours through the cubicles at company headquarters are given almost daily to outsiders.

Develop Service-Oriented Internal Processes

To best support service personnel in their delivery of quality service on the front line, an organization's internal processes should be designed with customer value and customer satisfaction in mind. In other words, internal procedures must support quality service performance. In many companies, internal processes are driven by bureaucratic rules, tradition, cost efficiencies, or the needs of employees. Providing service- and customer-oriented internal processes can therefore imply a need for total redesign of systems. This kind of redesign of systems and processes is known as "process reengineering." Although developing service-oriented internal processes through reengineering sounds sensible, it is probably one of the most difficult strategies to implement, especially in organizations steeped in tradition.

Retain the Best People

An organization that hires the right people, trains and develops them to deliver service quality, and provides the needed support must also work to retain them. Employee turnover, especially when the best service employees are the ones leaving, can be very detrimental to customer satisfaction, employee morale, and overall service quality. And, just as they do with customers, some firms spend a lot of time attracting employees but then tend to take them for granted (or even worse), causing these good employees to search for job alternatives. Although all the strategies depicted earlier in Figure 11.4 will support the retention of the best employees, here we will focus on some strategies that are particularly aimed at this goal.

Include Employees in the Company's Vision

For employees to remain motivated and interested in sticking with the organization and supporting its goals, they need to share an understanding of the organization's vision. People who deliver service day in and day out need to understand how their work fits into the big picture of the organization and its goals. They will be motivated to some extent by their paychecks and other benefits, but the best employees will be attracted away to other opportunities if they are not committed to the vision of the organization. And they cannot be committed to the vision if that vision is kept secret from them. What this strategy means in practice is that the vision is communicated to employees frequently and that it is communicated by top managers, often by the CEO.[60] Respected CEOs such as Howard Schulz of Starbucks, Fred Smith of FedEx, Bill Marriott of Marriott International, Charles Schwab of Schwab, and Tony Hsieh of Zappos are known for communicating their visions clearly and often to employees.

At Sherwin-Williams, management has communicated throughout the organization that its goal is to deliver "Trademark Service." To include all of its customer-contact employees in the company's vision of providing such service, for the past 10 years the company has developed an extensive internal campaign to "treat every customer like a GUEST." The "GUEST" acronym translates as G—Greet every customer, U—Use the customer's name, E—evaluate and fulfill needs, S—Smile with face and voice, and T—Thank and invite them back. These actions are expected of all those in the organization who interact with customers.[61] This approach sends a strong message to employees, reinforcing the company vision. When the vision and direction are clear and motivating, employees are more likely to remain with the company through the inevitable rough spots along the path to the vision.

Treat Employees as Customers

If employees feel valued and their needs are taken care of, they are more likely to stay with the organization. For example, Tom Siebel, founder of Siebel Systems (now part of Oracle), saw the CEO's primary job as cultivating a corporate culture that benefits all employees and customers. "If you build a company and a product or service that delivers high levels of customer satisfaction, and if you spend responsibly and manage your human capital assets well, the other external manifestations of success, like market valuation and revenue growth, will follow."[62]

Many companies have adopted the idea that employees are also customers of the organization and that basic marketing strategies can be directed at them.[63] The products that the organization has to offer its employees are a job (with assorted benefits) and quality of work life. To determine whether the job and work-life needs of employees are being met, organizations conduct periodic internal marketing research to assess employee satisfaction and needs. For example, within American Express Travel Related Services, the Travelers Cheque Group (TCG) had a goal of "Becoming the Best Place to Work" by treating employees as customers.[64] On the basis of the research, TCG launched a number of initiatives to benefit employees: an expanded employee assistance program; a child care resource and referral service; adoption assistance; health care and dependent care reimbursement plans; family leave; family sick days; flexible returns; sabbaticals; improved part-time employee benefits; flexible benefits; and workplace flexibility initiatives, including job-sharing, flexplace, and flextime scheduling. What American Express and many other companies have found is that, to ensure employee satisfaction, productivity, and retention, companies must get involved in the private lives and family support of their workers.[65] Employees appreciate such efforts; American Express is regularly included in *Fortune*'s list of "Top 100 Companies to Work For"—making it all but one year between 2000 and 2011!

Measure and Reward Strong Service Performers

If a company wants the strongest service performers to stay with the organization, it must reward and promote them. This strategy may seem obvious, but often the reward systems in organizations are not set up to reward service excellence. Reward systems may value productivity, sales, or some other dimension that can work *against* providing good service. Even those service workers who are intrinsically motivated to deliver high-quality service will become discouraged at some point and start looking elsewhere if their efforts in providing good service are not recognized and rewarded.

Reward systems need to be linked to the organization's vision and to outcomes that are truly important. For instance, if customer satisfaction and retention are viewed as critical outcomes, service behaviors that increase those outcomes need to be recognized and rewarded. At Harrah's Casinos and Hotels, a portion of employee compensation is linked to customer satisfaction scores as a "Performance Payout," so employees have an investment in achieving excellent service levels. Employees also have a vested interest in the performance of the entire team in serving customers exceptionally well. Beyond monetary incentives, outstanding employees are recognized with special Chairman Awards, and their names are published in Harrah's annual report. Management is also awarded incentives based on the positive improvement in customer service, as 25 percent of a manager's annual bonus is tied to achieving customer service goals.[66] Similarly, Enterprise Rent-a-Car branch managers wishing to move up in the organization can do so only if the customer satisfaction scores from their store are in the upper half of all company stores. Such measures, along with all the analyses and service improvement initiatives behind them, are intended to align employee behavior around satisfying and retaining customers.

In developing new systems and structures to recognize customer focus and customer satisfaction, organizations have turned to a variety of rewards. Traditional approaches such as higher pay, promotions, and one-time monetary awards or prizes can be linked to service performance. In many organizations employees are encouraged to recognize each other by personally giving a "peer award" to an employee they believe has excelled in providing service to the customer. Other types of rewards include special organizational and team celebrations for achieving improved customer satisfaction or for attaining customer retention goals. In most service organizations it is not only the major accomplishments but the daily perseverance and attention to detail that move the organization forward, so recognition of the "small wins" is also important.

In many situations, a customer's relationship is with a specific employee and may be stronger with the *employee* than with the firm. If this employee leaves the firm and is no longer available to the customer, the firm's relationship with the customer may be jeopardized.[67] Clearly a firm should make great efforts to retain such employees; however, in spite of the firm's best efforts, some good employees are going to leave. If the firm is not successful at retaining a key customer-contact employee, what can it do to reduce the impact on the customer? Employees could be rotated occasionally to ensure that the customer has exposure to and is comfortable with more than one employee. Firms might also form teams of employees who are responsible for interacting with each customer. In both cases, the idea is that the customer would have multiple contacts with several employees in the organization, thus reducing the firm's vulnerability to losing the customer, should any one employee leave. Emphasis should also be placed on creating a positive firm image in the minds of its customers and, in so doing, convey that *all* its employees are capable.[68]

CUSTOMER-ORIENTED SERVICE DELIVERY

As indicated by the examples in this chapter, specific approaches for hiring and energizing frontline workers take on a different look and feel across companies, based on the organization's values, culture, history, and vision.[69] For example, "developing people to deliver service quality" is accomplished quite differently at Southwest Airlines than at Disney. At Disney the orientation and training process is highly structured, scripted, and standardized. At Southwest, the emphasis is more on developing needed skills and then empowering employees to be spontaneous and nonscripted in their approach to customers. Although the style and culture of the two organizations are different, both pay special attention to all four basic themes shown in Figure 11.4. Both have made significant investments in their people, recognizing the critical roles they play.

Throughout the book we have advocated a strong customer focus. Firms that have a strong service culture clearly put an emphasis on the customer and the customer's experience. To do so, firms must also create an environment that staunchly supports the customer-contact employee, because this is frequently the person in the organization most responsible for ensuring the customer's experience is delivered as designed. Historically, many firms have viewed senior management as the most important people in the firm, and indeed, organizational charts tend to reflect this view in their

FIGURE 11.5 **Customer-Focused Organizational Chart**

structure. This approach places management at the top of the structure and (implicitly) the customer at the bottom, with customer-contact employees just above them. If the organization's most important people are customers, they should be at the top of the chart, followed by those with whom they have contact. Such a view, illustrated in Figure 11.5, is more consistent with a customer-oriented focus. In effect, the role of top-level management changes from that of commanding to that of facilitating and supporting employees in the organization who are closest to the customer.

The human resource strategies offered in this chapter are a means by which management can support the customer-contact employee. Indeed, a truly customer-oriented management team might actually "flip" the service marketing triangle presented earlier in the chapter, so that the management point is at the bottom of the triangle, with customer and employees equally placed at the top—as illustrated in Figure 11.6. Nordstrom, a company well known for its strong service culture, uses such an "inverted

FIGURE 11.6
Inverted Service
Marketing Triangle

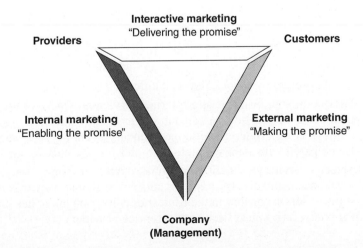

pyramid" in its employee training materials. A statement by Michel Bon, former CEO of France Telecom, succinctly summarizes the philosophy behind such an approach:

> If you sincerely believe that "the customer is king," the second most important person in this kingdom must be the one who has a direct interaction on a daily basis with the one who is king.[70]

By flipping the service marketing triangle, the two groups that are the most important people to the organization—customers and those who interact with customers—are placed in a position of prominence.

Summary

Because many services are delivered by people in real time, closing the service performance gap is heavily dependent on human resource strategies. The successful execution of such strategies begins with the development and nurturing of a true service culture throughout the organization.

Often, service employees *are* the service, and they represent the organization in customers' eyes. They affect service quality perceptions to a large degree through their influence on the five dimensions of service quality: reliability, responsiveness, empathy, assurance, and tangibles. It is essential to match what the customer wants and needs with service employees' abilities to deliver.

In this chapter we focused on service employees to provide you with an understanding of the critical nature of their roles and appreciation of the inherent stresses and conflicts they face. You learned that frontline service jobs demand significant investments of emotional labor and that employees confront a variety of on-the-job conflicts.

Grounded in this understanding of the importance of service employees and the nature of their roles in the organization, you learned strategies for integrating appropriate human resource practices into service firms. The strategies are aimed at allowing employees to effectively satisfy customers as well as be efficient and productive in their jobs. The strategies are organized around four major human resource goals in service organizations: hire the right people, develop people to deliver service quality, provide needed support systems, and retain the best people. A company that works toward implementing these strategies is well on its way to delivering service quality through its people, thereby diminishing gap 3—the service performance gap.

Discussion Questions

1. Define *service culture*. Why is service culture so important? Can a manufacturing firm have a service culture? Why or why not?
2. Why are service employees critical to the success of any service organization? Why do we include an entire chapter on service employees in a marketing course?
3. What is *emotional labor*? How is it different from physical or mental labor?
4. Reflect on your own role as a frontline service provider, whether in a current job or in any full- or part-time service job you have had in the past. Did you experience the kinds of conflicts described in the boundary-spanning roles section of the chapter? Be prepared with some concrete examples for class discussion.
5. Select a service provider (your dentist, doctor, lawyer, hair stylist) with whom you are familiar, and discuss ways this person could positively influence the five dimensions of service quality in the context of delivering his or her services. Do the same for yourself (if you are currently a service provider).

6. Describe the four basic human resource strategy themes and why each plays an important role in building a customer-oriented organization.

7. What is the difference between technical and interactive service skills? Provide examples (preferably from your own work context or from another context with which you are familiar). Why do service employees need training in both?

8. Is empowerment always the best approach for effective service delivery? Why is employee empowerment so controversial?

Exercises

1. Visit the websites of companies with known world-class service cultures (such as Ritz-Carlton, FedEx, Starbucks, or Zappos). How does the information conveyed on the website reinforce the company's service culture?

2. Review the section of the chapter on boundary-spanning roles. Interview at least two frontline service personnel regarding the stresses they experience in their jobs. How do the examples they provide relate to the sources of conflict and trade-offs described in the text?

3. Assume that you are the manager of a crew of frontline customer-service employees in a credit card company. Assume that these employees work over the phone and that they deal primarily with customer requests, questions, and complaints. In this specific context,

   a. Define what is meant by *boundary-spanning roles,* and discuss the basic purposes or functions of participants in these roles.

   b. Discuss two of the potential conflicts that your employees may face on the basis of their roles as boundary spanners.

   c. Discuss how you, as their supervisor, might deal with these conflicts based on what you have learned.

4. Choose one or more of the human resource strategy themes (hire the right people, develop people to deliver service quality, provide needed support systems, retain the best people). Interview a manager in a service organization of your choice regarding his or her current practices within the theme you have chosen. Describe the current practices, and recommend any appropriate changes for improving them.

Notes

1. L. L. Berry, *Discovering the Soul of Service* (New York: The Free Press, 1999).

2. Interview with Singapore Airlines senior vice president of marketing services, included in "How May I Help You?" *Fast Company* (March 2000), pp. 93–126.

3. P. Gallagher, "Getting It Right from the Start," *Journal of Retail Banking* 15 (Spring 1993), pp. 39–41.

4. Chris Shelley, Panera Bread manager, Personal Interview, December 30, 2010.

5. Berry, *Discovering the Soul of Service.*

6. S. M. Davis, *Managing Corporate Culture* (Cambridge, MA: Ballinger, 1985).

7. C. Grönroos, *Service Management and Marketing: Customer Management in Service Competition,* 3rd ed. (West Sussex, UK: John Wiley and Sons, 2007), p. 418.

8. See K. N. Kennedy, F. G. Lassk, and J. R. Goolsby, "Customer Mind-Set of Employees throughout the Organization," *Journal of the Academy of Marketing Science* 30 (Spring 2002), pp. 159–171.

9. R. Hallowell, D. Bowen, and C. Knoop, "Four Seasons Goes to Paris," *Academy of Management Executive* 16, no. 4 (2002), pp. 7–24; J. L. Heskett, L. A. Schlesinger, and E. W. Sasser Jr., *The Service Profit Chain* (New York: The Free Press, 1997); B. Schneider and D. E. Bowen, *Winning the Service Game* (Boston: Harvard Business School Press, 1995); and D. E. Bowen and S. D. Pugh, "Linking Human Resource Management Practices and Customer Outcomes" in *The Routledge Companion to Strategic Human Resource Management,* ed. J. Storey, P. Wright and D. Ulrich (Abingdon, Oxon, UK: Routledge 2008), pp. 509–518.

10. Berry, *Discovering the Soul of Service,* p. 40.

11. Hallowell, Bowen, and Knoop, "Four Seasons Goes to Paris."

12. For an excellent discussion of the complexities involved in creating and sustaining a service culture, see Schneider and Bowen, *Winning the Service Game,* chap. 9. See also Michael D. Hartline, James G. Maxham III, and Daryl O. McKee, "Corridors of Influence in the Dissemination of Customer-Oriented Strategy to Customer-Contact Service Employees," *Journal of Marketing* 64 (April 2000), pp. 35–50.

13. This discussion is based on Hallowell, Bowen, and Knoop, "Four Seasons Goes to Paris."

14. This quote is most frequently attributed to J. Carlzon, former chief executive officer of Scandinavian Airline Systems.

15. P. Andruss, "Your Employees Are Your Brand," *Marketing News*, October 30, 2010, pp. 22-23.

16. J. Barlow and P. Stewart, *Branded Customer Service* (San Francisco: Barett-Koehler, 2004).

17. The conceptualization of the service triangle presented in Figure 11.1 and the related text discussion are based on M. J. Bitner, "Building Service Relationships: It's All about Promises," *Journal of the Academy of Marketing Science* 23 (Fall 1995), pp. 246–251; P. Kotler and K. L. Keller, *Marketing Management,* 14th ed. (Upper Saddle River, NJ: Pearson Prentice Hall, 2012); and Grönroos, *Service Management and Marketing.*

18. See, H. Rosenbluth, "Tales from a Nonconformist Company," *Harvard Business Review* 69 (July–August 1991), pp. 26–36; L. A. Schlesinger and J. L. Heskett, "The Service-Driven Service Company," *Harvard Business Review* 69 (September–October 1991), pp. 71–81; and B. Schneider, M. Ehrhart, D. Mayer, J. Saltz, and K. Niles-Jolley, "Understanding Organization-Customer Links in Service Settings," *Academy of Management Journal* 48 (December 2005), pp. 1017–1032.

19. B. Schneider and D. E. Bowen, "The Service Organization: Human Resources Management Is Crucial," *Organizational Dynamics* 21 (Spring 1993), pp. 39–52.

20. D. E. Bowen, S. W. Gilliland, and R. Folger, "How Being Fair with Employees Spills Over to Customers," *Organizational Dynamics* 27 (Winter 1999), pp. 7–23; S. Masterson, "The Trickle-Down Model of Organizational Justice: Relating Employees' and Customers' Perceptions of and Reactions to Fairness," *Journal of Applied Psychology* 86 (August 2001), pp. 594–604; J. G. Maxham III and R. G. Netemeyer, "Firms Reap What They Sow: The Effects of Shared Values and Perceived Organizational Justice on Customers' Evaluations of Complaint Handling," *Journal of Marketing* 67 (January 2003), pp. 46–62.

21. See J. L. Heskett, T. O. Jones, G. W. Loveman, W. E. Sasser Jr., and L. A. Schlesinger, "Putting the Service–Profit Chain to Work," *Harvard Business Review* 72 (March–April 1994), pp. 164–174; G. W. Loveman, "Employee Satisfaction, Customer

Loyalty, and Financial Performance," *Journal of Service Research* 1 (August 1998), pp. 18–31; A. Rucci, S. P. Kirn, and R. T. Quinn, "The Employee–Customer Profit Chain at Sears," *Harvard Business Review* 76 (January–February 1998), pp. 82–97; and R. Hallowell and L. L. Schlesinger, "The Service–Profit Chain," in *The Handbook for Services Marketing and Management,* ed. T. A. Swartz and D. Iacobucci (Thousand Oaks, CA: Sage, 2000), pp. 203–222.

22. For additional research on the service-profit chain, see J. L. Heskett, W. E. Sasser Jr., and L. A. Schlesinger, *The Value Profit Chain: Treat Employees Like Customers and Customers Like Employees* (New York: The Free Press, 2003); G. A. Geladel and S. Young, "Test of a Service Profit Chain Model in the Retail Banking Sector," *Journal of Occupational and Organizational Psychology* 78 (March 2005), pp. 1–22; R. D. Anderson, R. D. Mackoy, V. B. Thompson, and G. Harrell, "A Bayesian Network Estimation of the Service-Profit Chain for Transport Service Satisfaction," *Decision Sciences* 35 (Fall 2004), pp. 665–689; W. A. Kamakura, V. Mittal, F. de Rosa, and J. A. Mazzon, "Assessing the Service-Profit Chain," *Marketing Science* 21 (Summer 2002), pp. 294–317; R. Silvestro and S. Cross, "Applying the Service Profit Chain in a Retail Environment: Challenging the "Satisfaction Mirror,'" *International Journal of Service Industry Management* 11, no. 3 (2000), pp. 244–268; and Schneider et al., "Understanding Organization-Customer Links in Service Firms."

23. J. Dickler, "Best Employers, Great Returns," *CNNMoney.com,* January 18, 2007, http://money.cnn.com/2007/01/17/magazines/fortune/bestcompanies_performance/, accessed January 2011.

24. M. K. Brady and J. J. Cronin Jr., "Customer Orientation: Effects on Customer Service Perceptions and Outcome Behaviors," *Journal of Service Research* 3 (February 2001), pp. 241–251.

25. L. A. Bettencourt and K. Gwinner, "Customization of the Service Experience: The Role of the Frontline Employee," *International Journal of Service Industry Management* 7, no. 2 (1996), pp. 3–20.

26. For research on the influence of frontline employee behaviors on customers, see D. D. Gremler and K. P. Gwinner, "Customer–Employee Rapport in Service Relationships," *Journal of Service Research* 3 (August 2000), pp. 82–104; and T. J. Brown, J. C. Mowen, D. T. Donavan, and J. W. Licata, "The Customer Orientation of Service Workers: Personality Trait Effects of Self- and Supervisor Performance Ratings," *Journal of Marketing Research* 39 (February 2002), pp. 110–119.

27. A. Hochschild, *The Managed Heart: Commercialization of Human Feeling* (Berkeley: University of California Press, 1983).

28. T. Hennig-Thurau, M. Groth, M. Paul, and D. D. Gremler, "Are All Smiles Created Equal? How Employee-Customer Emotional Contagion and Emotional Labor Impact Service Relationships," *Journal of Marketing* 70 (July 2006), pp. 58–73.

29. A. Hochschild, "Emotional Labor in the Friendly Skies," *Psychology Today* 16 (June 1982), pp. 13–15.

30. For additional discussion on emotional labor strategies, see R. Leidner, "Emotional Labor in Service Work," *Annals of the American Academy of Political and Social Science* 561, no. 1 (1999), pp. 81–95. For discussions of emotional display rules, see A. Grandey, A. Rafaeli, S. Ravid, J. Wirtz, and D. D. Steiner, "Emotional Display Rules at Work: The Special Case of the Customer," *Journal of Service Management* 21, no. 3 (2010), pp. 388–412; J. M. Diefendorff and G. J. Greguras, "Contextualizing Emotional Display Rules: Taking a Closer Look at Targets,

Discrete Emotions, and Behavior Responses," *Journal of Management* 35 (August 2009), pp. 880–98.

31. M. D. Hartline and O. C. Ferrell, "The Management of Customer-Contact Service Employees: An Empirical Investigation," *Journal of Marketing* 60 (October 1996), pp. 52–70; J. Singh, J. R. Goolsby, and G. K. Rhoads, "Burnout and Customer Service Representatives," *Journal of Marketing Research* 31 (November 1994), pp. 558–569; L. A. Bettencourt and S. W. Brown, "Role Stressors and Customer-Oriented Boundary-Spanning Behaviors in Service Organizations," *Journal of the Academy of Marketing Science* 31 (Fall 2003), pp. 394–408.

32. B. Shamir, "Between Service and Servility: Role Conflict in Subordinate Service Roles," *Human Relations* 33, no. 10 (1980), pp. 741–756.

33. Ibid., pp. 744–745.

34. J. Bowen and R. C. Ford, "Managing Service Organizations: Does Having a 'Thing' Make a Difference?" *Journal of Management* 28 (June 2002), pp. 447–469.

35. V. O'Connell, "Stores Count Seconds to Trim Costs," *The Wall Street Journal*, November 13, 2008, p. A1.

36. http://consumerist.com/2008/04/union-hits-picket-line-to-protest-verizons-poor-customer-service.html, accessed January 2011.

37. For discussions of internal marketing, see L. L. Berry and A. Parasuraman, "Marketing to Employees," chap. 9 in *Marketing Services* (New York: The Free Press, 1991); C. Grönroos, "Managing Internal Marketing: A Prerequisite for Successful Customer Management," chap. 14 in *Service Management and Marketing: Customer Management in Service Competition,* 3rd ed. (West Sussex, UK: John Wiley and Sons, 2007).

38. Berry and Parasuraman, "Marketing to Employees," p. 153.

39. This section on hiring for service competencies and service inclination draws from work by B. Schneider and colleagues, specifically B. Schneider and D. Schechter, "Development of a Personnel Selection System for Service Jobs," in *Service Quality: Multidisciplinary and Multinational Perspectives,* ed. S. W. Brown, E. Gummesson, B. Edvardsson, and B. Gustavsson (Lexington, MA: Lexington Books, 1991), pp. 217–236.

40. For an examination of employee interpretations of what "good service" means, see R. Di Mascio, "The Service Models of Frontline Employees," *Journal of Marketing* 74 (July 2010), pp. 63-80.

41. J. Hogan, R. Hogan, and C. M. Busch, "How to Measure Service Orientation," *Journal of Applied Psychology* 69, no. 1 (1984), pp. 167–173. See also Brown et al., "The Customer Orientation of Service Workers"; and D. T. Donavan, T. J. Brown, and J. C. Mowen, "Internal Benefits of Service-Worker Customer Orientation: Job Satisfaction, Commitment, and Organizational Citizenship Behaviors," *Journal of Marketing* 68 (January 2004), pp. 128–146.

42. Bowen and Pugh, "Linking Human Resource Management Practices and Customer Outcomes"; and N. Bendapudi and V. Bendapudi, "Creating the Living Brand," *Harvard Business Review* 83 (May 2005), pp. 124–134.

43. For additional information on Southwest Airlines hiring practices, see C. Mitchell, "Selling the Brand Inside," *Harvard Business Review* 80 (January 2002), pp. 99–105.

44. UPS website, www.responsibility.ups.com/community/Static Files/sustainability/Workplace.pdf, accessed January, 2012.

45. Google website, www.google.com, accessed January 2011.

46. http://money.cnn.com/video/fortune/2010/01/20/f_bctwf_sas.fortune/, accessed January 2011.

47. M. Gunther, "Marriott Family Values," *CNNMoney.com,* May 25, 2007, http://money.cnn.com/2007/05/24/news/companies/pluggedin_gunther_marriott.fortune/index.htm, accessed January 2011.

48. D. Gremler and K. Gwinner, "Rapport-Building Behaviors Used by Retail Employees," *Journal of Retailing* 84 (September 2008), pp. 308–324.

49. J. L. Levere, "Hotel Chains Try Training with Improv and iPods," *The New York Times*, September 7, 2010, p. B4; J. J. Salopek, "Improvisation: Not Just Funny Business," *Training and Development* 58 (May 2004), pp. 116–118.

50. J. Hempel, "Therapy with Your Latte? It's My Job," *BusinessWeek,* October 24, 2005, p. 16.

51. S. A. Bone and J. C. Mowen, "'By-the-Book' Decision Making: How Service Employee Desire for Decision Latitude Influences Customer Selection Decisions," *Journal of Service Research* 13 (May 2010), pp. 184–197.

52. J. C. Chebat and P. Kollias, "The Impact of Empowerment on Customer Contact Employees' Roles in Service Organizations," *Journal of Service Research* 3 (August 2000), pp. 66–81.

53. C. Argyris, "Empowerment: The Emperor's New Clothes," *Harvard Business Review* 76 (May–June 1998), pp. 98–105.

54. J. H. Gittell, "Relationships between Service Providers and Their Impact on Customers," *Journal of Service Research* 4 (May 2002), pp. 299–311.

55. Mayo Clinic website, http://www.mayoclinic.org/tradition-heritage/group-practice.html, accessed January 2011.

56. Berry and Parasuraman, "Marketing to Employees," p. 162.

57. A. Sergeant and S. Frenkel, "When Do Customer-Contact Employees Satisfy Customers?" *Journal of Service Research* 3 (August 2000), pp. 18–34.

58. J. Reynoso and B. Moores, "Operationalising the Quality on Internal Support Operations in Service Organisations," in *Advances in Services Marketing and Management,* Vol. 6, ed. T. A. Swartz, D. E. Bowen, and S. W. Brown (Greenwich, CT: JAI Press, 1997), pp. 147–170.

59. Schneider and Bowen, *Winning the Service Game,* pp. 230–234.

60. O. Gadiesh and J. L. Gilbert, "Transforming Corner-Office Strategy into Frontline Action," *Harvard Business Review* 79 (May 2001), pp. 73–79.

61. Telephone Interview with Guy Papa, Training Manager, The Sherwin-Williams Company, January 6, 2011.

62. B. Fryer, "High Tech the Old Fashioned Way," *Harvard Business Review* 79 (March 2001), pp. 119–125.

63. L. L. Berry, "The Employee as Customer," *Journal of Retail Banking* 3 (March 1981), pp. 33–40; R. L. Cardy, "Employees as Customers?" *Marketing Management* 10, no. 3 (2001), pp. 12–13; M. R. Bowers and C. L. Martin, "Trading Places Redux: Employees as Customers, Customers as Employees," *Journal of Services Marketing* 21, no. 2 (2007), pp. 88–98.

64. C. Hegge-Kleiser, "American Express Travel-Related Services: A Human Resources Approach to Managing Quality," in *Managing Quality in America's Most Admired Companies,* ed. J. W. Spechler (San Francisco: Berrett-Koehler, 1993), pp. 205–212.

65. K. Hammonds, "Balancing Work and Family," *BusinessWeek*, September 16, 1996, pp. 74–84.

66. J. Mackey, "Putting the Service Profit Chain to Work: How to Earn Your Customer's Loyalty," http://www.mufranchisee.com/article/32/, accessed January 2011.

67. N. Bendapudi and R. P. Leone, "Managing Business-to-Business Customer Relationships Following Key Contact Employee Turnover in a Vendor Firm," *Journal of Marketing* 66 (April 2002), pp. 83–101; S. Wang and L. Davis, "Stemming the Tide: Dealing with the Imbalance of Customer Relationship Quality with the Key Contact Employee versus with the Firm," *Journal of Services Marketing* 22, no. 7 (2008), pp. 533–549.

68. Bendapudi and Leone, "Managing Business-to-Business Customer Relationships"; T. Jones, S. F. Taylor, and H. S. Bansal, "Commitment to a Friend, a Service Provider, and a Service Company—Are They Distinctions Worth Making?" *Journal of the Academy of Marketing Science* 36 (Winter 2008), pp. 473–487.

69. J. R. Katzenbach and J. A. Santamaria, "Firing Up the Front Line," *Harvard Business Review* 77 (May–June 1999), pp. 107–117.

70. Quoted in D. Stauffer, "The Art of Delivering Great Customer Service," *Harvard Management Update* 4, no. 9 (September 1999), pp. 1–3.

Chapter **Twelve**

Customers' Roles in Service Delivery

This chapter's objectives are to

1. Illustrate the importance of customers in successful service delivery and cocreation of service experiences.
2. Discuss the variety of roles that service customers play: productive resources for the organization, contributors to quality and satisfaction, competitors.
3. Explain strategies for involving service customers effectively to increase satisfaction, quality, and productivity.

iPrint = Self-Service Printing Online

In the world of Internet-based services, customers play active roles in producing services for themselves with little or no personal interaction with the service provider. As an example, one company, iPrint, was one of the early pioneers in changing the way home-office and small-business customers interact with commercial printers. This change resulted in customers' performing services for themselves that traditionally were provided by brick-and-mortar printing companies. iPrint.com is a privately owned, Web-based custom printing service, describing itself as a "complete, fully automated, self-service online creation, ordering, and commercial printing environment."[1]

iPrint.com launched in 1996 and was one of the very early companies to offer self-service printing services online. Nearly every year since then, iPrint has earned industry awards for e-commerce innovation, website design, and customer service, as well as a number of recognitions by the Stevie Awards for Women in Business. Customers consistently give iPrint high marks for their products, service, ease of use, quality, price, and quick delivery.

Much of the company's success can be attributed to its business model, which gives customers an easy, continually accessible way to independently design, create, and order customized print jobs, sometimes at half the cost of traditional commercial printers. A quote from a satisfied customer is indicative: "Always a good experience to do business with iPrint. Top quality work for a reasonable price delivered in record time—and I don't have to go anywhere to order or pick it up!" Customers of iPrint create their own value through participation in the production of customized printing services. Customers with little or no knowledge of graphic design can easily, quickly, and from the convenience of their own homes or offices create their own designs for a wide range of products. iPrint offers business cards, notepads, stationery, various gift items, stamps, calendars, signs, and promotional products.

Although creating graphic designs can be a complex process with hundreds of variables to consider, iPrint developed a simple step-by-step process to create personalized products. Customers adapt existing designs to meet their specifications and then view the finished products, selecting from a wide range of options such as paper, font, size, and color, as well as art or business logos. Completed designs can be purchased over the Internet and are typically received in a few days. Designs are also automatically saved to allow for easy reordering. Although iPrint notifies customers via e-mail when the order is placed and when it has been printed, customers are also able to actively participate after the order has been placed by tracking it throughout processing, printing, and shipping.

In addition to customer education through detailed, step-by-step instructions, iPrint provides easy access to service providers through e-mail, live chat, or telephone. Customers participating in the design of their own products are rewarded with prices significantly lower than what they would normally pay. iPrint also offers a 100 percent satisfaction guarantee, removing some of the risk customers may feel in ordering customized printed materials online. Through its services iPrint, transformed a people-intensive, manual service business into an electronically automated, self-service function in which its small-business customers are empowered to create their own value and satisfaction. Because they do so much of the work, customers essentially become "coproducers" of the service, enhancing iPrint's productivity, which reduces the company's costs. By effectively coproducing the service, customers are rewarded with quality, personalized results, and reduced prices.

In this chapter we examine the unique and varied roles played by customers in service delivery and cocreation. In some cases, service customers are present in the "factory" (the place the service is produced and/or consumed), interacting with employees and other customers. For example, in a classroom or training situation, students (the customers) are sitting in the factory (the classroom), interacting with the instructor and other students as they consume and cocreate educational services. Because they are present during service production, customers can contribute to or detract from the successful delivery of the service and to their own satisfaction. In a manufacturing context, rarely does the production facility contend with customer presence on the factory floor, nor does it rely on the customer's immediate, real-time input to manufacture the product. As our opening vignette illustrates, service customers can actually produce services themselves and to some extent are responsible for their own satisfaction. Using iPrint's online services, customers cocreate value for themselves and in the process reduce the prices they pay for printing services.

Because customers are participants in service production and delivery, they can contribute to the widening of gap 3, the service performance gap. That is, customers themselves can influence whether the service meets customer-defined specifications. Sometimes customers contribute to gap 3 because they lack understanding of their roles and exactly what they can or should do in a given situation, particularly if the customer is confronting a service concept for the first time.

In other situations customers may understand their roles but be unwilling or unable to perform. In a health club context, members may understand that to get into good physical shape they must follow the workout guidelines set up by the trainers. If work schedule or illness keeps members from living up to their part of the guidelines, the service will not be successful because of customer inaction. In a different service situation, customers may choose not to perform the roles defined for them because they are not rewarded in any way for contributing their effort. For example, many grocery store customers choose not to use the automated self-checkout because they see no benefit in terms of speed or convenience. When service customers are enticed through price reductions, greater convenience, or some other tangible benefit, they are more likely to perform their roles willingly.

Finally, the service performance gap may be widened not through actions or inactions on the part of the customer but because of what *other* customers do. Other customers who are in the service factory either receiving the service simultaneously (passengers on an airplane flight or students in a classroom) or waiting their turn to receive the service sequentially (bank customers waiting in line or Disneyland customers waiting for one of the rides) can influence whether the service is delivered effectively and efficiently.

THE IMPORTANCE OF CUSTOMERS IN SERVICE COCREATION AND DELIVERY

Customer participation at some level is inevitable in all service situations. Services are actions or performances, typically produced and consumed simultaneously. In many situations employees, customers, and even others in the service environment interact to produce the ultimate service outcome. Because they participate, customers are indispensable to the production process of service organizations, and in many situations they can control or contribute significantly to their own dis/satisfaction.[2] This view of participatory customers is consistent with the service-dominant logic of marketing that promotes the idea customers are always cocreators of value.[3] Our Strategy Insight illustrates this broadened view and how it can lead to innovative service strategies and offerings. Recognition of the role of customers is also reflected in the definition of the *people* element of the service marketing mix given in Chapter 1: *all human actors who play a part in service delivery and thus influence the buyer's perceptions; namely, the firm's personnel, the customer, and other customers in the service environment.* Chapter 11 examined the role of the firm's employees in delivering service quality. In this chapter we focus on the customer who is receiving or cocreating the service and on fellow customers in the service environment.

Customer Receiving the Service

Because the customer participates in the delivery process, he or she can contribute to narrowing or widening gap 3 through behaviors that are appropriate or inappropriate, effective or ineffective, productive or unproductive. The level of customer participation—low, medium, or high—varies across services, as shown in Table 12.1. In some cases, all that is required is the customer's physical presence (*low level of participation*), with the employees of the firm doing all the service production work, as in the example of a symphony concert. Symphony-goers must be present to receive the entertainment service, but little else is required once they are seated. In other situations, consumer inputs are required to aid the service organization in creating the service (*moderate level of participation*). Inputs can include *information, effort,* or *physical possessions.* For example, all three of these are required for a certified public accountant (CPA) to prepare a client's tax return effectively: information in the form of tax history, marital status, and number of dependents; effort in putting the information

Strategy Insight Customer Cocreation of Value: The New Strategy Frontier

Consultants, researchers, and strategists are urging companies to think about their customers in new ways. Instead of viewing customers as passive targets and recipients of predesigned goods and services, they encourage a view of customers as *active* cocreators of value. This perspective goes beyond focusing on customer involvement in generating ideas for new products, and it is more than customer participation in service delivery. Instead, this view suggests that the value customers receive is a *cocreated experience* they build for themselves through interactions with service providers and other customers, as well as by choosing and combining elements of the company's offerings to create their own "total experience." Two examples in two very different contexts help make the cocreation idea more concrete and the strategic possibilities apparent.

JOHN DEERE

John Deere is a 175-year-old global firm that serves the knowledge- and capital-intensive farming industry with sophisticated equipment, services, information, and online support for its farm manager customers. The company is geared toward making the farmer's life easier and more productive. The "experience environment" for its innovations is broadly defined to include anything that will help achieve the farmer's professional objectives. For example, new technologies available through

John Deere services connect equipment, owners, operators, and agricultural consultants.

Deere, branded as "FarmSight," can help the farmer monitor equipment remotely to assess the location of the equipment and engine condition, maximize machine operations, and provide agricultural decision support. These remote monitoring and support capabilities are uniquely set up for each farmer and require the farmer's active involvement with the system to fully take advantage of its value. Another service that Deere offers is sensor technologies on its equipment that can precisely map soil conditions and thereby prescribe the application of seeds and fertilizers based on the soil conditions in an area.

together in a useful fashion; and physical possessions such as receipts and past tax returns. In some situations, customers are truly cocreators of the service (*high level of participation*). For these services, customers have important participation roles that affect the nature of the service outcome. For example, in a weight reduction program, the customer, working with a counselor, may actively cocreate a personalized nutritional and exercise program. Then, it is largely up to the customer to carry out the plan and/or enhance it, resulting in value that is unique to that person. Similarly, in a complex or long-term business-to-business consulting engagement, the client can be involved in activities such as identification of issues, shared problem solving, ongoing communication, provision of equipment and work space, and implementation of solutions.[4] Facilitating this type of positive customer participation can help ensure a successful outcome, as described in Exhibit 12.1. Table 12.1 provides several examples of each level of participation for both consumer and business-to-business services. The effectiveness of customer involvement at all the levels will affect organizational productivity and, ultimately, service quality and customer satisfaction.

Depending on the farmer's land conditions and the specific crops he grows, the information provided by the sensors can be customized to the situation and used to better control that farmer's crop yields. Deere also provides educational opportunities for farmers through John Deere University courses and online learning, as well as books and publications. It is up to each farmer to determine how much to participate in the various services, how to use the information provided, and whether to take advantage of other educational opportunities. Deere's strategy and suite of offerings are customer-centric, with the resulting experience being unique to each farmer. Deere has shifted its strategic innovation paradigm to one where value is cocreated through services, solutions, and experiences rather than exclusively through product or technology innovation.

KODAK GALLERY

Kodak Gallery provides a set of services for consumers—all related to photography and experiences associated with photography. Formerly called "Ofoto," the Kodak Gallery is considered one of the best online photo sharing services. It is easy to use, allowing consumers to upload, organize, store, e-mail, and touch up digital photos. But Kodak has gone far beyond simply offering a service for organizing and sharing photos by identifying the entire "photography experience space" and offering options,

merchandise, and services tied to it. For example, through its website, customers can choose to order prints and pick them up at one of thousands of locations. Or customers can choose to create photo albums or use a custom framing option for special photos. They can make cards, calendars, brochures, and other gifts with their photos and order merchandise emblazoned with their photos (everything from coasters to mouse pads to clothing and even blankets for pets). Friends and family can view, purchase, and comment on a customer's photos, thus creating a community around the site. The technology that allows average citizens to easily and economically take hundreds of digital photos was indeed a critical technology innovation. Yet, the services and experiences that Kodak and others provide online are what allow consumers to cocreate a unique photography experience that can be remembered and relived by them and others. Through these experiences, customers dramatically enhance the value of their cameras and photos.

Sources: S. L. Vargo and R. F. Lusch, "Evolving to a New Dominant Logic for Marketing," *Journal of Marketing* 68 (January 2004), pp. 1–17; C. K. Prahalad and V. Ramaswamy, *The Future of Competition: Co-Creating Unique Value with Customers* (Boston, MA: Harvard Business School Press, 2004); M. Sawhney, S. Balasubramanian, and V. V. Krishnan, "Creating Growth with Services," *Sloan Management Review* 45 (Winter 2004), pp. 34–43; www.kodakgallery.com, August 2011; and www.deere.com, August 2011.

Fellow Customers

In many service contexts, customers receive and/or cocreate the service simultaneously with other customers or must wait their turn while other customers are being served. In both cases, "fellow customers" are present in the service environment and can affect the nature of the service outcome or process. Fellow customers can *enhance* or *detract from* customer satisfaction and perceptions of quality.[5]

Some of the ways fellow customers can negatively affect the service experience are by exhibiting disruptive behaviors, causing delays, excessively crowding, and manifesting incompatible needs. In restaurants, hotels, airplanes, and other environments in which customers are cheek to jowl as they receive the service, crying babies, smoking patrons, and loud, unruly groups can be disruptive and detract from the experiences of their fellow customers. In college classrooms and other types of education and training environments, customers often complain when fellow customers interrupt and/or detract from the experience of others by using their laptops or texting on their phones in distracting ways. In other cases, overly demanding customers (even customers with

TABLE 12.1 Levels, Characteristics, and Examples of Customer Participation across Different Services

Source: Adapted from A. R. Hubbert, "Customer Co-Creation of Service Outcomes: Effects of Locus of Causality Attributions," doctoral dissertation, Arizona State University, Tempe, Arizona, 1995.

Low: Consumer Presence Required during Service Delivery	Moderate: Consumer Inputs Required for Service Creation	High: Customer Cocreates the Service
Service is standardized.	Client inputs (information, materials) help customize a standard service.	Active client participation guides the customized service.
Service is provided regardless of any individual purchase.	Provision of service requires customer purchase.	Service cannot be created apart from the customer's purchase and active participation.
Payment may be the only required customer input.	Customer inputs are necessary for an adequate outcome, but the service firm provides the service.	Customer inputs, choices, and actions cocreate the outcome.
Consumer Examples		
Airline travel	Haircut	Marriage counseling
Motel stay	Annual physical exam	Personal training
Fast-food restaurant	Full-service restaurant	Weight reduction program
Business-to-Business Customer Examples		
Uniform cleaning service	Agency-created advertising campaign	Management consulting
Pest control	Payroll service	Executive management seminar
Interior greenery maintenance service	Freight transportation	Installation of computer network

legitimate problems) can cause a delay for others while their needs are met. This occurrence is common in banks, post offices, and customer service counters in retail stores. Excessive crowding or overuse of a service can also affect the nature of the customer's experience. Visiting Sea World in San Diego on a U.S. national holiday such as the Fourth of July is a very different experience from visiting the same park midweek in February.

Finally, customers who are being served simultaneously but who have incompatible needs can negatively affect each other. This situation can occur in restaurants, college classrooms, hospitals, and any service establishment in which multiple segments are served simultaneously. In a study of critical service encounters in tourist attractions across central Florida, researchers found that customers negatively affected each other when they failed to follow either explicit or implicit "rules of conduct." Customers reported such negative behaviors as pushing, shoving, smoking, drinking alcohol, being verbally abusive, and cutting in line. Other times, dissatisfaction resulted when other customers were impersonal, rude, unfriendly, or even spiteful.[6]

There are just as many examples of customers enhancing satisfaction and quality for their fellow customers as detracting from them. Sometimes the mere presence of other customers enhances the experience, for example, at sporting events, in movie theaters, and in other entertainment venues. In other situations, fellow customers provide a positive social dimension to the service experience, as suggested in the photo on page 351. In some situations, customers may help each other achieve service goals and outcomes.

The success of the Weight Watchers organization, for example, depends significantly on the camaraderie and support that group members provide each other. And health providers have long recognized the importance of family members (often viewed as customers in this context) in aiding hospital patients in their care and full recovery. Some hospitals have even started encouraging family members to stay and assist with their loved ones who are being cared for in intensive care units (ICUs), turning family members into active members of the health care team.[7]

Academic research also supports the power of other customers to influence service outcomes. In a study done with a franchise of Gold's Gym, it was found that customers who received support from other members of the gym were more likely to participate in positive ways like keeping the gym clean, cooperating with personnel, showing empathy toward other members, and encourageing others to join the gym.[8] The study of central Florida tourist attractions mentioned earlier found that customers increased the satisfaction of others by having friendly conversations while waiting in line, by taking photos, by assisting with children, and by returning dropped or lost items.[9] And an ethnographic study that observed hundreds of hours of customer interactions among travelers on the U.K. rail system found that customers often helped each other by (1) providing important service-related information (e.g., schedules, interesting features en route) that can reduce trip-related anxiety; (2) engaging in enjoyable conversation, thus making the trip more pleasant; and (3) serving as someone to complain to when mishaps and service failures occurred.[10]

The influence of fellow customers in helping others is even more apparent in some online service environments such as Facebook, LinkedIn, eBay, Amazon.com, and Craigslist, where customers literally cocreate services together. Customers helping each other is not limited to consumer services, as illustrated by networking giant Cisco. By giving business customers open access to its information and systems through its online self-service, Cisco enables customers to engage in a dialogue with each other, helping themselves and other customers who may be experiencing similar challenges. The Technology Spotlight in Chapter 7 discusses in greater detail how Cisco uses these online customer services in the context of self-service recovery.

CUSTOMERS' ROLES

The following sections examine in more detail three major roles played by customers in service cocreation and delivery: customers as productive resources, customers as contributors to service quality and satisfaction, and customers as competitors.

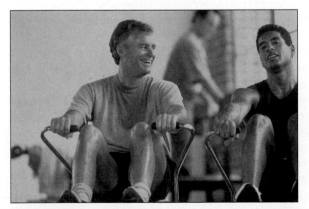
Social interactions with others can influence health club members' satisfaction with the service.

Customers as Productive Resources

Service customers have been referred to as "partial employees" of the organization—human resources who contribute to the organization's productive capacity.[11] Some management experts have suggested that the organization's boundaries be expanded to consider the customer as part of the service system. In other words, if customers contribute effort, time, or other resources to the service production process, they should be considered as part of the organization.

Customer inputs can affect the organization's productivity through both the quality of what they

Exhibit 12.1 Client Coproduction in Business-to-Business Services

What do firms like IBM, McKinsey, Accenture, and neoIT have in common? All can be described as knowledge-intensive business services (KIBS), whose value-added activities provide their business clients with highly customized services (e.g., technical engineering, consulting, software development, business process outsourcing). To develop and deliver optimal service solutions, KIBS rely on inputs and cooperation from their clients as integral coproducers of the services. The KIBS provider needs accurate and detailed information from the client, access to people and resources, and cooperation in terms of the deadlines and contingencies that inevitably arise.

Depth interviews and research conducted with clients of employees of an IT services provider ("TechCo") identified a number of *client* characteristics that can enhance the quality of the client's participation and the ultimate service outcome in these types of KIBS relationships. The characteristics are listed here with an illustrative quote from or about one of TechCo's clients, using disguised names. The researchers used disguised names in order to protect the identities of the actual companies. Clients who display these types of coproduction behaviors contribute to the success of their projects and are likely to get better outcomes and be more satisfied.

- **Communication openness.** The client is forthcoming and honest in sharing pertinent information for project success.

   PharmCo actually did the up-front work to understand what it is we have to do, when we have to do it, and how it fits into our overall scheme of things . . . We [spent] the first days doing nothing but teaching them about what we're trying to accomplish.
   —*TechCo, about PharmCo Client*

- **Shared problem solving.** The client takes individual initiative and shared responsibility for developing solutions to problems that arise in the relationship.

   I think, as a customer, I have a responsibility to bring some critical thinking to what they've brought to the table. Not just to accept it . . . [You need to be able to say,] "I don't know if that's going to work for our environment" or technically, "Why did you do that?" So a lot of it's just asking questions and saying, "Why are we doing it that way? Is that the best way to do it?"—GovCo Client

- **Tolerance.** The client responds in an understanding and patient manner in the face of minor project encumbrances.

   That certainly was our goal—not to have roadblocks, not to have problems . . . And even at that, it took us longer than we had hoped. Again, not anybody's fault, it's just one of those things. It's a process, and sometimes those processes take a little longer than you initially had planned for.—EduCo Client

- **Accommodation.** The client demonstrates a willingness to accommodate the desires, approaches, and expert judgment of the service provider.

   [If we saw something that didn't fit with our goals,] we'd call them and ask them . . . If they could do it, they would simply say, "Oh, you bet, no problem" . . . If it was something that we really couldn't monkey with too much, they'd come out and say, "No, you probably don't want to change that because of this

contribute and the resulting quality and quantity of output generated. In a business-to-business service context (see Exhibit 12.1), the contributions of the client can enhance the overall productivity of the firm in both quality and quantity of service.[12] In the hospital ICU example given previously, family members participate in caring for their loved ones in the ICU, thus increasing the quality of care and health care outcomes but also resulting in increased productivity as family members participate as "partial employees" of the hospital.[13]

Customer participation in service production raises a number of issues for organizations. Because customers can influence both the quality and the quantity of production, some experts believe the delivery system should be isolated as much as possible from customer inputs to reduce the uncertainty they can bring into the production process. This view sees customers as a major source of uncertainty—in the timing of their demands and the uncontrollability of their attitudes and actions. The logical conclusion is that any service activities that do not require customer contact or involvement should be performed away from customers: the less direct contact there is between the customer and the service production system, the greater the potential for the system to *reason and that reason" and we'd say, "Okay, that's fine" and we'd go on to the next one.—EduCo Client*

- **Advocacy.** The client firm provides a vocal advocate and salesperson for the project.

  [The scope of the project] was cumbersome. Had we not had involvement and not had a group of people who had ownership, who really wanted to succeed, we might have been inclined to say . . . "I don't really care how this turns out because the boss told me I need to do it. I don't care if it's ugly because I'm never going to use it." So, I think it was a combination of things. One is having people who have a vested interest in making sure it worked and knew why they were doing it and [second] continuous involvement.—AgCo Client

- **Involvement in project governance.** The client takes an active role in monitoring project progress toward the stated goal.

  We would have our meetings and we'd set these action items. We would say when they're supposed to be done, and we would set the next meeting before we ended that meeting so everybody knew what their expectations were.—DonorCo Client

- **Personal dedication.** The client demonstrates a sense of personal obligation for project success by performing individual responsibilities in a conscientious manner.

  I think that was one of the things that I probably did right—was staying that involved. But it was hard, from my perspective, because it took time away from other things that I had to do. But I think I brought some things to the project that, if I hadn't been as involved, I don't know that we would have had as successful an implementation of the three systems as I think we did.—GovCo Client

The challenge for KIBS firms is to develop processes, systems, and practices that will ensure that clients engage in these ways. The research suggests that these positive coproduction behaviors will be most likely when KIBS provider firms engage in (1) *client selectivity* (carefully screening clients in advance to ensure a good fit between provider and client); (2) *client training, education, and socialization* (making clients feel that they are part of the team by kicking off the relationship with a cooperative spirit, perhaps including events and expectations-setting workshops); and (3) *project leadership and client performance evaluation* (selecting the right project leaders on both sides and evaluating both on their relationship management skills as well as technical capabilities).

This research illustrates the importance of business clients as coproducers of the service and the value to both provider and client that can result from quality coproduction behaviors and associated business practices.

Source: L. A. Bettencourt, A. L. Ostrom, S. W. Brown, and R. I. Roundtree, "Client Co-Production in Knowledge-Intensive Business Services," *California Management Review* 44 (Summer 2002), 100–128; Copyright © 2002, by The Regents of the University of California. Reprinted from the California Management Review, Vol. 44, No. 4. by permission of The Regents.

operate at peak efficiency.[14] Other experts believe that services can be delivered most efficiently if customers are truly viewed as partial employees and their coproduction roles are designed to maximize their contributions to the service creation process. The logic behind this view is that organizational productivity can be increased if customers are educated to perform service-related activities they currently are not doing or to perform more effectively the tasks they are doing.[15]

For example, when self-service gasoline stations first came into being, customers were asked to pump their own gas. With customers performing this task, fewer employees were needed and the overall productivity of gas stations improved. Now most gas stations in the United States offer customers the option of paying for their gas at the pump by popping their credit cards into a slot on the pump or using a wireless device to complete their transactions with no human contact. Similarly, the introduction of many automated airline services such as baggage check-in and self-ticketing is intended to speed up the process for customers while freeing employees for other tasks.[16] Organizational productivity is increased by using customers as a resource to perform tasks previously completed by employees.

There are many examples of organizations seeking to increase productivity through transferring tasks to customers. Although organizations derive obvious cost benefits by involving them as coproducers, customers do not always like or accept their new roles, especially when they perceive the purpose to be bottom-line cost savings for the company. If customers see no clear benefit to being involved in coproduction (e.g., lower prices, quicker access, or a better-quality outcome), then they are likely to resent and resist their coproduction roles, particularly if they feel their own productivity or efficiency is suffering to benefit the company.[17] Similarly, employees can sometimes be frustrated by customer participation, as was discovered in research conducted in a professional banking context that explored the effects of customer participation on both customers and employees. While the research found that customer participation in general enhanced the experience and value for the customer, it created stress for employees, presumably due to disruptions in the employees' standard work procedures.[18]

Customers as Contributors to Service Quality and Satisfaction

Another role customers can play in service cocreation and delivery is that of contributor to their own satisfaction and the ultimate quality of the services they receive. Customers may care little that they have increased the productivity of the organization through their participation, but they likely care a great deal about whether their needs are fulfilled. Effective customer participation can increase the likelihood that needs are met and that the benefits the customer seeks are actually attained, especially for services such as health care, education, personal fitness, and weight loss, in which the service outcome is highly dependent on customer participation.

Research in education has shown that active participation by students—as opposed to passive listening—increases learning (a desired service outcome) significantly.[19] The same is true in health care; patient compliance, in terms of taking prescribed medications or changing diet or other habits, can be critical to whether patients regain their health (the desired service outcome).[20] Other research in financial and medical service settings has shown that effective coproduction by customers leads to greater loyalty to the service provider.[21] In a business-to-business context, companies in the trucking and shipping industries have found that in many situations customers cause their own *dissatisfaction* with the service by failing to pack shipments appropriately, resulting in breakage or delays while items are repacked. Thus, ineffective coproduction can result in negative outcomes and dissatisfaction.

Research suggests that customers who believe they have done their part to be effective in service interactions are more satisfied with the service. In a study of the banking industry, bank customers were asked to rate themselves on questions related to their contributions to service delivery in terms of what they did (e.g., cooperated with the bank employee and gave proper information) and how they did it (e.g., being friendly and courteous to the bank employee). Results of the study indicated that those customers who responded more positively to the questions about their own participation were also more satisfied with the bank.[22] Research in another context showed that customers' perceptions of service quality increased with greater levels of participation. Specifically, members of a YMCA who participated more in the club gave the club higher ratings on aspects of service quality than did those who participated less.[23]

Customers contribute to quality service delivery when they ask questions, take responsibility for their own satisfaction, and complain when there is a service failure. Consider the service scenarios shown in Exhibit 12.2.[24] The four scenarios illustrate the wide variations in customer participation that can result in equally wide variations

Exhibit 12.2   Which Customer (A or B) Will Be Most Satisfied?

For each scenario, ask, "Which customer (A or B) will be most satisfied and receive the greatest quality and value, and why?"

SCENARIO 1: A MAJOR INTERNATIONAL HOTEL

Guest A called the desk right after check-in to report that his TV was not working and that the light over the bed was burned out; both problems were fixed immediately. The hotel staff exchanged his TV for one that worked and fixed the lightbulb. Later they took him a fruit plate to make up for the inconvenience. Guest B did not communicate to management until checkout time that his TV did not work and he could not read in bed. His complaints were overheard by guests checking in, who wondered whether they had chosen the right place to stay.

SCENARIO 2: OFFICE OF A PROFESSIONAL TAX PREPARER

Client A has organized into categories the information necessary to do her taxes and has provided all documents requested by the accountant. Client B has a box full of papers and receipts, many of which are not relevant to her taxes but which she brought along "just in case."

SCENARIO 3: AN AIRLINE FLIGHT FROM LONDON TO NEW YORK

Passenger A arrives for the flight with a DVD player and reading material and wearing several layers of clothing; passenger A also ordered a special meal in advance. Passenger B, who arrives empty-handed, becomes annoyed when the crew runs out of blankets, complains about the magazine selection and the meal, and starts fidgeting after the inflight movie.

SCENARIO 4: ARCHITECTURAL CONSULTATION FOR REMODELING AN OFFICE BUILDING

Client A has invited the architects to meet with its remodeling and design committee made up of managers, staff, and customers to lay the groundwork for a major remodeling job that will affect everyone who works in the building, as well as customers. The committee has already formulated initial ideas and surveyed staff and customers for input. Client B has invited architects in following a decision the previous week to remodel the building; the design committee is two managers who are preoccupied with other, more immediate tasks and have little idea what they need or what customers and staff would prefer in terms of a redesign of the office space.

in service quality and customer satisfaction. Customers who take responsibility and providers who encourage their customers to become their partners in identifying and satisfying their own needs together produce higher levels of service quality. Our Global Feature shows how Sweden's IKEA, the world's largest retailer of home furnishings, has creatively engaged its customers in a new role: "IKEA wants its customers to understand that their role is not to *consume* value but to *create* it."[25]

In addition to contributing to their own satisfaction by improving the quality of service delivered to them, some customers simply enjoy participating in service delivery. These customers find the act of participating to be intrinsically attractive.[26] They enjoy using the Internet to attain airline tickets, doing all their banking via ATMs and online, pumping their own gas, or shopping at IKEA. Often customers who like self-service in one setting are predisposed to serving themselves in other settings as well.

Interestingly, because service customers must participate in service delivery, they frequently blame themselves (at least partially) when things go wrong. Why did it take so long to reach an accurate diagnosis of my health problem? Why was the service contract for our company's cafeteria food full of errors? Why was the room we reserved for our meeting unavailable when we arrived? If customers believe they are partially (or totally) to blame when failures such as these occur they may be less dissatisfied with the service provider than when they believe the provider is responsible.[27] A series of studies suggests the existence of this "self-serving bias." That is, when services go better than expected, customers who have participated tend to take credit for the outcome and are less satisfied with the firm than are those customers who have not participated. However, when the outcome is worse than expected, customers who have chosen to participate in service production are less dissatisfied with the service than are those who choose not to participate—presumably because the participating customers have taken on some of the blame.[28]

Customers as Competitors

The third role played by service customers is that of potential competitor. If self-service customers can be viewed as resources of the firm, or as "partial employees," they can also partially or entirely perform the service for themselves and not need the provider at all. Thus, customers in a sense are competitors of the companies that supply the service. Whether to produce a service for themselves (*internal exchange*)—for example, child care, home maintenance, or car repair—or have someone else provide the service for them (*external exchange*) is a common dilemma for consumers.[29] Similar internal versus external exchange decisions are made by organizations. Firms frequently choose to outsource service activities such as payroll, data processing, research, accounting, maintenance, and facilities management. They find it advantageous to focus on their core businesses and leave these support services to others with greater expertise. Alternatively, a firm may decide to stop purchasing services externally and bring the service production process in-house.

Whether a household or a firm chooses to produce a particular service for itself or contract externally for the service depends on a variety of factors. A proposed model of internal/external exchange suggests that such decisions depend on the following:[30]

- *Expertise capacity.* The likelihood of producing the service internally is increased if the household or firm possesses the specific skills and knowledge needed to produce it. Having the expertise will not necessarily result in internal service production, however, because other factors (available resources and time) will also influence the decision. (For firms, making the decision to outsource is often based on recognizing that, although they may have the expertise, someone else can do it better.)

- *Resource capacity.* To decide to produce a service internally, the household or firm must have the needed resources, including people, space, money, equipment, and materials. If the resources are not available internally, external exchange is more likely.

- *Time capacity.* Time is a critical factor in internal/external exchange decisions. Households and firms with adequate time capacity are more likely to produce services internally than are groups with time constraints.

- *Economic rewards.* The economic advantages or disadvantages of a particular exchange decision will be influential in choosing between internal and external options. The actual monetary costs of the two options will sway the decision.

- *Psychic rewards.* Rewards of a noneconomic nature have a potentially strong influence on exchange decisions. Psychic rewards include the degree of satisfaction, enjoyment, gratification, or happiness associated with the external or internal exchange.

- *Trust.* In this context, *trust* means the degree of confidence or certainty the household or firm has in the various exchange options. The decision will depend to some extent on the level of self-trust in producing the service versus trust of others.

- *Control.* The household or firm's desire for control over the process and outcome of the exchange will also influence the internal/external choice. Entities that desire and can implement a high degree of control over the task are more likely to engage in internal exchange.

IKEA of Sweden has managed to transform itself from a small, mail-order furniture company in the 1950s into the world's largest retailer of home furnishings. In 2011 more than 300 stores in more than 40 countries generated more than 23 billion euros in sales. The company sells simple, functional, yet well-designed furnishings, charging significantly less than its competitors.

THE "DO-IT-YOURSELF" (DIY) CONCEPT

A key to IKEA's success is the company's relationship with its customers. IKEA has drawn the customer into its production system: "if customers agree to take on certain key tasks traditionally done by manufacturers and retailers—the assembly of products and their delivery to customers' homes—then IKEA promises to deliver well-designed products at substantially lower prices." In effect, IKEA's customers become essential contributors to value—they create value for themselves through participating in the selection, transportation, and assembly processes.

IKEA has made being part of the value creation process an easy, fun, and pleasant experience for customers. The company's stores are a pleasure to shop in. The stores are set up with "inspirational displays," including realistic room settings and real-life homes that allow customers to get comfortable with the furnishings, try them out, and visualize the possibilities in their own homes. To make shopping easy, free strollers and supervised child care are provided, as are wheelchairs for those who need them.

When customers enter the store they are given catalogs, tape measures, pens, and notepaper to use as they shop, allowing them to perform functions commonly done by sales and service staff. After payment, customers take their purchases to their cars on carts; if necessary, they can rent or buy a roof rack to transport larger purchases. Thus, customers also provide furniture loading and delivery services for themselves. At home, IKEA customers take on the role of manufacturer in assembling the new furnishings following carefully written, simple, and direct instructions.

GLOBAL ADAPTATIONS

IKEA prints catalogs and provides detailed websites in many languages, making its products and instructions for their use accessible worldwide. In addition to tailoring its catalogs and websites, another key to IKEA's successful global expansion has been the company's policy of allowing each store to tailor its mix according to the local market needs and budgets. For example, Chinese customers save a high percentage of their income and are extremely price sensitive, so the prices there were initially the lowest in the world to lure the Chinese customers into the stores; $1 placemats and 12¢ ice cream cones are examples. And some furniture items were 50 to 60 percent less than similar items in the United States. The response has been extremely positive, with 9 IKEA stores now open in China and plans to open 12 more. The Beijing store that opened in 2006 is the largest IKEA store in the world outside of the flagship store in Sweden.

In addition to price variations, the store layout in Chinese stores was also adapted to reflect the design of many Chinese apartments. Because many of the apartments have balconies, the stores have a selection of balcony furnishings and displays. And because Chinese kitchens are generally small, relatively few kitchen items and furnishings are shown. Even IKEA's famous DIY assembly concept has been adapted to some extent in China. Because fewer people have cars and therefore use public transportation, IKEA has more extensive delivery service in China than in most countries. And because labor is cheaper in China, many customers choose to have their furniture assembled for them rather than doing it themselves. Another interesting adaptation to Chinese culture is IKEA's acceptance of extensive browsing by customers, in some cases even allowing customers and their children to nap in the display bed areas.

IKEA'S SUCCESS

IKEA's success is attributable in part to recognizing that customers can be part of the business system, performing roles they have not performed before. The company's flexible implementation of this idea through clearly defining customers' new roles and making it fun to perform these roles is the genius of its strategy. Through the process, customers around the globe cocreate their own experiences and contribute to their own satisfaction. And IKEA continues to experience financial success and acceptance globally with its strategy. In 2010, sales increased by 7.7 percent to 23.1 billion euros, and net income increased 6.1 percent to 2.7 billion euros.

Sources: http://www.ikea.com, August, 2011; B. Edvardsson and B. Enquist, "The IKEA Saga: How Service Culture Drives Service Strategy," *The Service Industries Journal* 22 (October 2002), pp. 153–186; P. M. Miller, "IKEA with Chinese Characteristics," *The China Business Review* (July/August 2004), pp. 36–38; M. Fong, "IKEA Hits Home in China," *The Wall Street Journal*, March 3, 2006, pp. B1; M. Wei, "In IKEA's China Stores, Loitering is Encouraged," *Bloomberg Businessweek*, October 28, 2010; Anonymous, "Business: The Secret of IKEA's Success," *The Economist*, February 26, 2011, pp. 67–68.

The important thing to remember from this section is that, in many service scenarios, customers can and often do choose to fully or partially produce the service themselves. Thus, in addition to recognizing that customers can be productive resources and cocreators of quality and value, organizations also need to recognize the customer's role as a potential competitor.

SELF-SERVICE TECHNOLOGIES—THE ULTIMATE IN CUSTOMER PARTICIPATION

Self-service technologies (SSTs) are services produced entirely by the customer without any direct involvement or interaction with the firm's employees. As such, SSTs represent the ultimate form of customer participation along a continuum from services produced entirely by the firm to those produced entirely by the customer. This continuum is depicted in Figure 12.1, using the example of retail gasoline service to illustrate the various ways the same service could be delivered along all points on the continuum. At the far right end of the continuum, the gas station attendant does everything from pumping the gas to taking payment. On the other end of the spectrum, the customer does everything; in between are various forms and levels of customer participation. Many service delivery options, across industries, could be laid out on this type of continuum from total customer production through total firm production.

A Proliferation of New SSTs

Advances in technology, particularly the Internet, have allowed the introduction of a wide range of self-service technologies that occupy the far left end of the customer participation continuum in Figure 12.1. These technologies have proliferated as companies see the potential cost savings and efficiencies that can be achieved, potential sales growth, increased customer satisfaction, and competitive advantage. The following is a partial list of some of the self-service technologies available to consumers.

- ATMs.
- Pay at the pump.
- Airline check-in.
- Hotel check-in and checkout.
- Automated car rental.
- Automated filing of legal claims.
- Online driver's license testing.
- Automated betting machines.
- Electronic blood pressure machines.
- Various vending services.
- Tax preparation software.
- Self-scanning at retail stores.
- Online banking.
- Vehicle registration online.
- Online auctions.
- Home and car buying online.
- Automated investment transactions.
- Insurance online.
- Package tracking.
- Internet shopping.
- Interactive voice response phone systems.
- Online training and education.

Not true "Switching costs"

The proliferation of SSTs has occurred for several reasons.[31] Many times firms are tempted by the cost savings that they anticipate by shifting customers to technology-based, automated systems and away from expensive personal service. If cost savings are the only reason for introducing an SST and if customers see no apparent benefits, the SST is likely to fail. Customers quickly see through this strategy and are not likely to adopt the SST if they have alternative options for service. Other times, firms introduce SSTs based on customer demand. For example, customers expect to find information,

FIGURE 12.1
Service Production Continuum

Source: Adapted from M. L. Meuter and M. J. Bitner, "Self-Service Technologies: Extending Service Frameworks and Identifying Issues for Research," in *Marketing Theory and Applications,* ed. D. Grewal and C. Pechmann (American Marketing Association Winter Educators' Conference, 1998), pp. 12–19. Reprinted by permission of the American Marketing Association.

Customer production		Joint production			Firm production
1	2	3	4	5	6

Gas station illustration
1. Customer pumps gas and pays at the pump with automation.
2. Customer pumps gas and goes inside to pay attendant.
3. Customer pumps gas and attendant takes payment at the pump.
4. Attendant pumps gas and customer pays at the pump with automation.
5. Attendant pumps gas and customer goes inside to pay attendant.
6. Attendant pumps gas and takes payment from customer at the pump.

services, and delivery options online. When they do not find what they want from a particular firm online, they are likely to choose a competitor. Thus, customer demand in some industries is forcing firms to develop and offer their services via technology. Other companies are developing SSTs to open up geographic, socioeconomic, and lifestyle markets that were not available through traditional channels.

Customer Usage of SSTs

Some of the SSTs listed earlier—ATMs, online ordering, and airline check-in—have been very successful, embraced by customers for the benefits they provide in terms of convenience, accessibility, and ease of use.[32] Benefits to firms, including cost savings and revenue growth, can also result for SSTs that succeed. Others—airline ticketing kiosks, grocery self-scanning—have been less quickly embraced by customers. With grocery self-scanning systems (as illustrated in the accompanying photo) the early reluctance of customers to adopt them reflected many factors, including fear of the technology, looking incompetent in front of other customers, desire for human interaction, and a sense that "scanning and bagging groceries is the store's job, not mine."

Customers help produce the service for themselves through scanning their own groceries.

SST failures result when customers see little personal benefit in the new technology or when they do not have the ability to use it or know what they are supposed to do. Often, adopting a new SST requires customers to change their traditional behaviors significantly, and many are reluctant to make those changes. For example, when the upscale auctioneer Christie's International ventured into live online auctions, the response from bidders was slow.[33] The company credited the slow response to clients' needing time to become familiar and grow comfortable with the technology and the new way of bidding, as well as to see more clearly how the online approach could benefit them. Christie's initial slow results were consistent with research on SSTs in other contexts. Research looking at customer adoption of SSTs found that "customer readiness" is a major factor in determining whether customers

ORGANIZATIONAL READINESS

Time opportunity cost? [handwritten annotation]

will even try a new self-service option.[34] Customer readiness results from a combination of personal motivation (What is in it for me?), ability (Do I have the ability to use this SST?), and role clarity (Do I understand what I am supposed to do?). In other cases, customers see no value in using the technology when compared to the alternative interpersonal mode of delivery, or the SSTs may be so poorly designed that customers may prefer not to use them.[35] Research shows that customers also react negatively when they are forced to use an SST, with no alternative service channel offered. Any choice at all will improve customer perceptions, and having an employee available to assist or provide backup support can help.[36]

Success with SSTs

Throughout the text we have highlighted some of the most successful self-service technologies in the marketplace: Cisco Systems (Chapter 7), Amazon.com (Chapter 4), and iPrint (the opening vignette in this chapter). These companies have been successful because they offer clear benefits to customers, the benefits are well understood and appreciated compared to the alternative delivery modes, and the technology is user-friendly and reliable. In addition, customers understand their roles and have the capability to use the technology.

From a strategic perspective, research suggests that, as firms move into SSTs as a mode of delivery, these questions are important to ask:[37]

- What is our strategy? What do we hope to achieve through the SST (cost savings, revenue growth, competitive advantage)?
- What are the benefits to customers of producing the service on their own through the SST? Do they know and understand these benefits?
- How can customers be motivated to try the SST? Do they understand their role? Do they have the capability to perform this role?
- How "technology ready" are our customers?[38] Are some segments of customers more ready to use the technology than others?
- How can customers be involved in the design of the service technology system and processes, so that they will be more likely to adopt and use the SST?
- What forms of customer education will be needed to encourage adoption? Will other incentives be needed?
- How will inevitable SST failures be handled to regain customer confidence?

STRATEGIES FOR ENHANCING CUSTOMER PARTICIPATION

The level and the nature of customer participation in the service process are strategic decisions that can impact an organization's productivity, its positioning relative to competitors, its service quality, and its customers' satisfaction. In the following sections we will examine the strategies captured in Figure 12.2 for involving customers effectively into the service delivery and cocreation process. The overall goals of a customer participation strategy will typically be to increase organizational productivity and customer satisfaction while decreasing uncertainty due to unpredictable customer actions

Define Customers' Roles

In developing strategies for addressing customer involvement in service cocreation and delivery, the organization first determines what type of participation is desirable from customers and how the customer wishes to participate. Identifying the current level of customer participation can serve as a starting point. Customers' roles may be partially

FIGURE 12.2
Strategies for Enhancing Customer Participation

Source: Adapted from M. L. Meuter and M. J. Bitner, "Self Service Technologies: Extending Service Frameworks and Identifying Issues for Research," in *Marketing Theory and Applications,* ed. D. Grewal and C. Pechmann (American Marketing Association Winter Educators' Conference, 1998), pp. 12–19. Reprinted by permission of the American Marketing Association.

Define Customers' Roles
• Clarify level of participation
• Identify specific jobs and tasks
• Understand implications for productivity, quality, and satisfaction

Recruit, Educate, and Reward Customers
• Identify and recruit appropriate segment(s)
• Educate customers for their roles
• Provide reasons to participate
• Reward customer performance

Manage the Customer Mix
• Assess compatibility of segments
• Isolate incompatible segments
• Enhance segment compatibility

Effective Customer Participation

predetermined by the nature of the service, as suggested in Table 12.1. The service may require only the customer's presence (a concert, airline travel), or it may require moderate levels of input from the customer in the form of effort or information (a haircut, tax preparation), or it may require the customer to cocreate the service outcome (fitness training, consulting, self-service offerings). In some cases, the service may be dependent on customers cocreating the service with and for each other, as in the case of eBay, Facebook, and many of the other social networking services available online.

The organization may decide that it is satisfied with the existing level of participation it requires from customers but wants to make the participation more effective. For example, Charles Schwab has always positioned itself as a company whose customers are highly involved in their personal investment decisions and it has communicated this role clearly to customers. The company's positioning around high customer involvement and self-service has been consistent over time, yet the actual role of the customer has changed. Technological advances, for example, have greatly facilitated the self-service role of Charles Schwab customers.

Alternatively, the organization may choose to increase the level of customer participation, which may reposition the service in the customers' eyes. Experts have suggested that higher levels of customer participation are strategically advisable when service production and delivery are inseparable; marketing benefits (cross-selling, building loyalty) can be enhanced by on-site contact with the customer; and customers can substitute for the labor and information provided by employees.[39] Higher levels of customer participation may also be advisable when increased participation is desired by customers and when it can enhance their satisfaction and service outcomes. For example, in health care, researchers and providers are working on ways to gain more active customer participation in treatment decisions. The Internet and other technological advances have

Technology Spotlight   Technology Facilitates Customer Participation in Health Care

Customer participation is facilitated by technology in many industries. For example, in education, technology allows students to interact with each other and their professors via e-mail, discussion boards, group chat sessions, and course materials provided online. In real estate, technology allows buyers to preview homes and develop lists of places they would like to visit without having to rely totally on a real estate agent to find all available properties. And in high-technology industries, business customers often interact with each other on the Web, helping each other solve problems, answering each other's questions, and so forth. All these examples show how technology—particularly the Internet—has facilitated customer participation and increased customer satisfaction.

Increased participation is particularly apparent in health care. There is probably no greater, higher-participation service context than health care, where the customer must participate and where the provider and customer clearly cocreate the service. Patient participation is required at multiple levels. To achieve optimal health outcomes, patients must

- Provide accurate information about symptoms and health background.
- Answer detailed questions.
- Help decide on a course of treatment.
- Carry out the prescribed regimen leading to recovery and/or prevention.

Technology is clearly influencing how customers perform these roles and shifting in some senses the power of information into the hands of consumers. Annual studies by the Pew Internet and American Life Project, funded by the Pew Charitable Trusts, illuminate the trends in online health care. This research showed that, as of 2011, 80 percent of U.S. Internet users, or approximately 59 percent of all adults in the United States, had gone online in search of health information. These percentages are similar to the number of users who are paying bills online, reading blogs, or using the Internet to look up an address or a phone number on any given day. They seek information about specific diseases, mental health, nutrition and fitness, drugs and drug interactions, and specific doctors and hospitals. More than 36 percent seek information for themselves and their own medical conditions, and 48 percent seek information on behalf of a friend or family member. People like getting health information this way because of the convenience, the wealth of information that is available, and the fact that research can be done anonymously. In the United States, people are even beginning to use their cell phones to look up health information. In 2011, 17 percent of cell phone owners used their phones in this way.

Thousands of Internet sites provide some type of health-related information. Some belong to health care providers like Mayo Clinic (www.mayo.edu) or pharmacy benefits providers like CVSCaremark (www.caremark.com). Others are operated totally online—like WebMD (www.webmdhealth.com) or Drugstore.com (www.drugstore.com)—without affiliation to a specific health care provider. Some respected sites are sponsored by governmental entities such as the U.S. Department of Health and Human Services (www.healthfinder.gov) and the National Library of Medicine and National Institutes of Health (www.medlineplus.gov). Yet other sites provide information for specific health conditions such as AIDS, depression, diabetes, and breast cancer. Still others such as Hospital Compare (www.hospitalcompare.hhs.gov) can help patients determine

helped propel customers into this role in taking responsibility for their own health and well-being, as illustrated in our Technology Spotlight.

Finally, the organization may decide it wants to reduce customer participation due to all the uncertainties it causes. For example, in 2011 a large number of Albertsons supermarkets, a prominent grocery chain in the United States, removed all of their self-service checkout equipment due to the uncertainties that resulted for customers and the company, as well as equipment failures and other issues. In extreme situations the strategy may be to isolate all but the essential tasks, keeping customers away from the best hospitals to go to based on various quality and health outcome criteria.

All this readily available medical information is changing the role of the health care consumer to one of active participant in diagnosing illnesses, assessing treatment options, and determining overall well-being. Armed with information, patients gain confidence in asking questions and seeking appropriate diagnoses. In some cases they can e-mail questions to their doctors or other providers or find support in chat groups, bulletin boards, and e-mail lists on the Internet. They are also comforted by what they find online and often make decisions or change their overall approach to maintaining their health based on what they find. Still, it is important to note that, while they play a growing role, online sources are still supplemental to health professionals, family, and friends as sources of health information.

Sources: S. Fox, "The Social Life of Health Information, 2011," The Pew Internet and American Life Project, May 2011, www.pewinternet.org.

the service facility and employees as much as possible.[40] Mail order is an example of this form of service. Customers are in contact with the organization via telephone or the Internet, never see the organization's facility, and have limited employee interactions. The customer's role is thus extremely limited and can interfere very little with the service delivery process.

Once the desired level of participation (from both the customer and firm perspectives) is clear, the organization can define more specifically what the customer's role and tasks entail. The range of possible roles and tasks are described next.

Helping Oneself

In many cases the organization may decide to increase the level of customer involvement in service delivery through active participation. In such situations, the customer becomes a productive resource, performing aspects of the service previously performed by employees or others. Many of the examples presented in this chapter are illustrations of customers "helping themselves" (IKEA of Sweden, Charles Schwab, and those in the Technology Spotlight). The result may be increased productivity for the firm and/or increased value, quality, and satisfaction for the customer.

Helping Others

Sometimes the customer is called on to help others who are experiencing the service. A child at a day care center might be appointed "buddy of the day" to help a new child acclimate to the environment. Long-time residents of retirement communities often assume comparable roles to welcome new residents. Many universities have established mentoring programs in which experienced students with similar backgrounds help newcomers adjust to and learn the system. Many membership organizations (like health clubs, churches, and social organizations) also rely heavily, although often informally, on current members to help orient new members and make them feel welcome. In a different context, social media and online game sites rely on customers to help each other and enhance each other's experiences. In engaging in these types of roles, customers are performing productive functions for the organization, increasing customer satisfaction and retention. Acting as a mentor or facilitator can have very positive effects on the person performing the role and is likely to increase his or her loyalty.

Promoting the Company

In some cases the customer's job includes a sales or promotional element. Service customers rely heavily on word-of-mouth endorsements in deciding which providers to try. They are more comfortable getting a recommendation from someone who has experienced the service than from advertising or other forms of nonpersonal communication. A positive recommendation from a friend, relative, colleague, or even an acquaintance can pave the way for a positive service experience. Many service organizations are imaginative in getting their current customers to work as promoters or salespeople. For example, a dental practice encourages referrals by sending flowers, candy, or tickets to a local sports event to its patients whose names appear frequently in its "who referred you?" database. Another example is a nightclub that holds regular drawings (using business cards left by its patrons). Those whose names are drawn get a free party (no entry charge) for as many of their friends as they want to invite.

Individual Differences: Not Everyone Wants to Participate

In defining customers' roles it is important to remember that not everyone will want to participate.[41] Some customers enjoy self-service, whereas others prefer to have the service performed entirely for them. Companies that provide education and training services to organizations know that some customers want to be involved in designing the training and perhaps in delivering it to their employees. Other companies want to hand over the entire training design and delivery to the consulting organization, staying at arms length with little of their own time and energy invested in the service. In health care, it is clear that some patients want lots of information and want to be involved in their own diagnosis and treatment decisions. Others simply want the doctor to tell them what to do. Despite all the customer service and purchase options now available via the Internet, many customers still prefer human, high-contact service

Exhibit 12.3 Working Together, U.S. Utility Companies and Customers Conserve Energy

New technologies are allowing utility companies to communicate directly with customers and provide them with innovative tools and information that are shaping energy consumption behavior. The result should benefit all parties by cutting greenhouse emissions from power plants, slowing down rising electricity costs, and saving customers money as well. Surveys suggest that U.S. consumers are becoming increasingly open and willing to make the adjustments needed to reduce energy consumption overall and to begin addressing climate change predictions and fears. The new energy saving tools include such things as online calculators, high-tech meters in homes, visible in-home displays that show energy consumption at different times of day, remote control devices, prepaid electricity, and innovative pricing.

Utilities across the United States are experimenting with different approaches. For example, in northern California, Pacific Gas & Electric has an online tool that shows customers how their personal energy consumption is tied to greenhouse gas emissions. This tool can help individual customers see how changes in their behavior can have significant energy and pollution-reducing results. Progress Energy in the Carolinas has many programs to double its energy conservation over just a few years. One example is a wireless device that measures the energy usage of individual appliances and allows customers to immediately see the reduction in dollar costs and kilowatt-hour savings when they turn off an appliance. In southern California, customers are volunteering to be part of a plan that allows the utility to turn their air-conditioning units off at predetermined times to save peak demand. One company, Southern California Edison, has a program called "Save Power Days," whereby residents are notified in advance when there is a "save power day." If those enrolled in the program reduce their energy consumption on those 12 to 15 days per year, they can save up to $100. And Florida Power & Light has a program for small-business owners that calculates how much energy different pieces of equipment use and when energy usage is most costly.

Another new technology is a "home electricity monitor," which helps customers determine their energy usage and what it is costing them in real time. The device, which connects to a customer's electronic breaker box, can transmit information to a display unit, which tells the customer what various power-using devices are costing. One early adopter of the technology discovered that her energy consumption rose significantly when she turned on her electric oven to heat up a pizza. By purchasing a toaster oven and using it and her microwave oven more often, she was able to reduce her energy consumption and her power bill.

All of these innovative programs depend on customer acceptance, participation, and significant changes in behavior. To be successful, these innovative programs require investments in consumer education and incentives that will encourage them to change their behavior. Through this process, utility customers become "partial employees" of the utility companies by monitoring their own energy consumption and taking actions to reduce it. The result is reduced costs for the energy company, reduced prices for customers, less energy consumption overall, and better air quality in the short and long term.

Sources: R. Smith, "Letting the Power Company Control Your AC," *The Wall Street Journal,* July 10, 2007, p. D1+; R. Smith, "New Ways to Monitor Your Energy Use," *The Wall Street Journal,* July 19, 2007, p. D1+; R. Gold, "The Power of Knowledge: With New Monitors, Homeowners Can Keep Track of Their Electricity Use In Real Time," *The Wall Street Journal,* February 28, 2011, p. R7; www.sce.com, 2011.

delivery rather than self-service.[42] Research has shown, for example, that customers with a high "need for human interaction" are less likely to try new self-service options offered via the Internet and automated phone systems.[43] Because of these differences in preferences, most companies find they need to provide service delivery choices for different market segments. For example, banks typically customize their services by offering both automated self-service options and high-touch, human delivery options.

Recruit, Educate, and Reward Customers

Once the customer's role is clearly defined, the organization can think in terms of facilitating that role. In a sense, the customer becomes a partial employee of the organization, and strategies for managing customer behavior in service production and delivery can mimic to some degree the efforts aimed at service employees discussed in Chapter 11. As with employees, customer participation in service production and delivery will be facilitated when (1) customers understand their roles and how they are expected to perform, (2) customers are able to perform as expected, and (3) customers receive valued rewards for performing as expected.[44] Through these means, the organization will also reduce the inherent uncertainty associated with the unpredictable quality and timing of customer participation. Exhibit 12.3 illustrates how the utility industry is innovating new services that engage customers as partial employees while rewarding them for their efforts. These initiatives also serve the larger common good by protecting the environment and preserving natural resources.

Recruit the Right Customers

Before the company begins the process of educating and socializing customers for their roles, it must attract the right customers to fill those roles. The expected roles and responsibilities of customers should be clearly communicated in advertising, personal selling, and other company messages. By previewing their roles and what is required of them in the service process, customers can self-select into (or out of) the relationship. Self-selection should result in enhanced perceptions of service quality from the customer's point of view and reduced uncertainty for the organization.

To illustrate, a child care center that requires parent participation on the site at least one-half day per week needs to communicate that expectation before it enrolls any child in its program. For some families, this level of participation will not be possible or desirable, thus precluding them from enrolling in the center. The expected level of participation needs to be communicated clearly to attract customers who are ready and willing to perform their roles. In a sense this situation is similar to a manufacturing firm's exercising control over the quality of inputs into the production process.[45]

Educate and Train Customers to Perform Effectively

Customers need to be educated, or in essence "socialized," so that they can perform their roles effectively. Through the socialization process, service customers gain an appreciation of specific organizational values, develop the abilities necessary to function within a specific context, understand what is expected of them, and acquire the skills and knowledge to interact with employees and other customers.[46] Customer education programs can take the form of formal orientation programs, written literature provided to customers, directional cues and signage in the service environment, and information obtained from employees and other customers.

Many services offer "customer orientation" programs to assist customers in understanding their roles and what to expect from the process before experiencing it. When customers begin the Weight Watchers program, for example, the company website and their first group meeting include a thorough orientation to the program and their responsibilities, as described in Exhibit 12.4.

Customer education can also be partially accomplished through written literature, online resources, and customer "handbooks." Many hospitals have developed patient materials, very similar in appearance to employee handbooks, to describe what the patient should do in preparation for arrival at the hospital, what will happen when he or she arrives, and policies regarding visiting hours and billing procedures. The information may even describe the roles and responsibilities of family members. For particularly complex health care situations (for example, cancer diagnosis, treatment, and recovery), patients may even need what is called a "nurse navigator" to provide one-on-one education, to guide them through the system, and to help them make decisions.[47]

Exhibit 12.4 Weight Watchers Educates and Orients New Members

When new members first join Weight Watchers, one of the largest and most successful commercial weight loss organizations in the world, they are thoroughly educated regarding the program and their responsibilities. For example, when a new member attends her first meeting at a local chapter of Weight Watchers, she receives an orientation to the program as well as step-by-step instructions, including a "Getting Started" packet; food-tracking journals; activity calculators; and weekly guides for cooking, eating out, and more. Prior to attending the meeting, a new member can find a great deal of orientation information online that describes the weekly meetings, what happens at the meeting, and what is expected of the customer. Through the orientation, the booklets, and the food and activity forms, the organization clearly defines the member's responsibilities and makes the plan as easy as possible to follow.

Although formal training and written information are usually provided in advance of the service experience, other strategies can continue customer socialization during the experience itself. On-site, customers require two kinds of orientation: *place orientation* (Where am I? How do I get from here to there?) and *function orientation* (How does this organization work? What am I supposed to do?).[48] Signage, the layout of the service facility, and other orientation aids can help customers answer these questions, allowing them to perform their roles more effectively. Orientation aids can also take the form of rules that define customer behavior for safety (airlines, health clubs), appropriate dress (restaurants, entertainment venues), and noise levels (hotels, classrooms, theaters). Customers may also be socialized to their expected roles through information provided by employees and by observing other customers. It has been said that, when McDonald's first went to England, the British customers were not accustomed to busing their own trays. They quickly learned, however, by observing the customers that McDonald's had hired to "demonstrate" appropriate busing behavior. These customers were paid to sit in the restaurants and, at predictable intervals, carry a dirty tray to the trash can and dispose of it.

If customers are not effectively socialized and educated, the organization runs the risk that inappropriate customer behaviors will result in negative outcomes for customers, employees, and the organization itself.[49]

Reward Customers for Their Contributions

Customers are more likely to perform their roles effectively, or to participate actively, if they are rewarded for doing so. Rewards are likely to come in the form of increased control over the delivery process, time savings, monetary savings, and psychological or physical benefits. For instance, some CPA firms require clients to complete extensive forms before they meet with their accountants. If the forms are completed, the CPAs will have less work to do and the clients will be rewarded with fewer billable hours. Those clients who choose not to perform the requested role will pay a higher price for the service. Online banking customers who perform services for themselves are also rewarded through greater access to the bank, in terms of both locations and times. In health care contexts, patients who perform their roles effectively are likely to be rewarded with better health or quicker recovery. For a long time airlines have offered price discounts and "web specials" for passengers who order tickets online, providing a monetary incentive for customer participation.

Customers may not recognize the benefits or rewards of effective participation unless the organization makes the benefits apparent to them. In other words, the organization needs to clarify the performance-contingent benefits that can accrue to customers, just as it defines performance-contingent benefits to employees. The organization also should recognize that not all customers are motivated by the same types of rewards. Some may value the increased access and time savings they can gain by performing their service roles effectively. Others may value the monetary savings. Still others may be looking for greater personal control over the service outcome.

Manage the Customer Mix

Because customers frequently interact with each other in the process of service delivery and consumption, another important strategic objective is the effective management of the mix of customers who simultaneously experience the service. If a restaurant chooses to serve two segments during the dinner hour that are incompatible with each other—for example, single college students who want to party and families with small children who want quiet—it may find that the two groups do not merge well. Of course, it is possible to manage these segments so that they do not interact with each other by seating them in separate sections or by attracting the two segments at different times of day. Serving incompatible customer segments is also an issue at professional sporting events where families with children may be sitting next to loud (and sometimes drunk and obnoxious) fans. Each of these groups has differing, and incompatible, goals for the experience. Similarly, many university golf courses must cater to both student customers (who are not knowledgeable of the rules of the game, lack proper equipment and clothing, and may be loud and inconsiderate of others) and older customers who know and follow the rules, generally have the proper equipment and clothing, and are respectful and serious when playing. Again, the two groups have different goals for the experience and different levels of understanding of the sometimes unstated rules.

The process of managing multiple and sometimes conflicting segments is known as *compatibility management,* broadly defined as "a process of first attracting [where possible] homogeneous consumers to the service environment, then actively managing both the physical environment and customer-to-customer encounters in such a way as to enhance satisfying encounters and minimize dissatisfying encounters."[50] Compatibility management is critical for some businesses (such as health clubs, public transportation, and hospitals) but less important for others. Table 12.2 lists seven interrelated characteristics that increase the importance of compatibility management for service businesses.

To manage multiple (and sometimes conflicting) segments, organizations rely on a variety of strategies. Attracting maximally homogeneous groups of customers through careful positioning and segmentation strategies is one approach. This strategy is used by the Ritz-Carlton Hotel, for which upscale travelers are the primary target segment. The Ritz-Carlton is positioned to communicate that message to the marketplace, and customers self-select into the hotel. However, even in that context there are potential conflicts—for example, when the hotel is simultaneously hosting a business convention, an NBA basketball team, and individual leisure travelers. Another strategy is often used in such cases. Compatible custers are grouped together physically, so that the segments are less likely to interact directly with each other. The Ritz-Carlton keeps meetings and large-group events separated from the areas of the hotel used by individual businesspeople. Many amusement parks (such as CedarPoint, Kings Island) that face similar issues offer a special fee for those who

TABLE 12.2 **Characteristics of Service That Increase the Importance of Compatible Segments**

Source: Adapted from C. I. Martin and C. A. Pranter, "Compatibility Management: Customer-to-Customer Relationships in Service Environments," *Journal of Services Marketing* 3, no. 3 (Summer 1989), pp. 5–15. Reprinted with the permission of MCB University Press.

Characteristic	Explanation	Examples
Customers are in close physical proximity to each other.	Customers will more often notice each other and be influenced by each other's behavior when they are in close physical proximity.	Airplane flights Entertainment events Sports events
Verbal interaction takes place among customers.	Conversation (or lack thereof) can be a component of both satisfying and dissatisfying encounters with fellow patrons.	Full-service restaurants Cocktail lounges Educational settings
Customers are engaged in numerous and varied activities.	When a service facility supports varied activities all going on at the same time, the activities themselves may not be compatible.	Universities Health clubs Resort hotels
The service environment attracts a heterogeneous customer mix.	Many service environments, particularly those open to the public, will attract a variety of customer segments.	Public parks Public transportation Open-enrollment colleges
The core service is compatibility.	The core service is to arrange and nurture compatible relationships between customers.	Big Brothers/Big Sisters Weight loss group programs Mental health support groups
Customers must occasionally wait for the service.	Waiting in line for service can be monotonous or anxiety producing. The boredom or stress can be magnified or lessened by other customers, depending on their compatibility.	Medical clinics Tourist attractions Restaurants
Customers are expected to share time, space, or service utensils with each other.	The need to share space, time, and other service factors is common in many services but may become a problem if segments are not comfortable with sharing with each other or if the need to share is intensified because of capacity constraints.	Golf courses Hospitals Retirement communities Airplanes

attend after 6:00 p.m. Their target for this special fee is typically price-sensitive teenagers and/or college students. Families with small children tend to go at the beginning of the day and are likely to have exited the park by early evening; thus, the pricing strategy keeps these incompatible segments separated in time.

Other strategies for enhancing customer compatibility include customer "codes of conduct," such as the regulation of smoking behavior and dress codes. Clearly such codes of conduct vary from one service establishment to another. Finally, training employees to observe customer-to-customer interactions and to be sensitive to potential conflicts is another strategy for increasing compatibility among segments. Employees can also be trained to recognize opportunities to foster positive encounters among customers in certain types of service environments.

Summary

This chapter focused on the role of customers in service cocreation and delivery. The customer receiving the service and fellow customers in the service environment can all cause a widening of gap 3 if they fail to perform their roles effectively. Customers may widen the service performance gap for a number of reasons: customers lack understanding of their roles, customers are unwilling or unable to perform their roles, customers are not rewarded for good performance, other customers interfere, or market segments are incompatible.

Managing customers in the process of service delivery is a critical challenge for service firms. Whereas manufacturers are not concerned with customer participation in the manufacturing process, service managers constantly face this issue because their customers are often present and active partners in service production and cocreation. As participants in service creation, production, and delivery, customers can perform three primary roles: *productive resources* for the organization, *contributors* to service quality and satisfaction, and *competitors* in performing the service for themselves.

Through understanding the importance of customers in service performance and identifying the roles played by the customer in a particular context, managers can develop strategies to enhance customer participation. Strategies include defining the customers' roles and jobs, recruiting customers who match the customer profile in terms of desired level of participation, educating customers so they can perform their roles effectively, rewarding customers for their contributions, and managing the customer mix to enhance the experiences of all segments. By implementing these strategies, organizations should see a reduction in the service performance gap due to effective, efficient customer contributions to service delivery.

Discussion Questions

1. Using your own personal examples, discuss the general importance of customers in the successful creation and delivery of service experiences.
2. Why might customer actions and attitudes cause the service performance gap to occur? Use your own examples to illustrate your understanding.
3. Using Table 12.1, think of specific services you have experienced that fall within each of the three levels of customer participation: low, medium, and high. Describe specifically what you did as a customer in each case. How did your involvement vary across the three types of service situations?

4. Describe a time when your satisfaction in a particular situation was *increased* because of something another customer did. Could (or does) the organization do anything to ensure that this experience happens routinely? What does it do? Should it try to make this situation a routine occurrence?

5. Describe a time when your satisfaction in a particular situation was *decreased* because of something another customer did. Could the organization have done anything to manage this situation more effectively? What could it have done?

6. Discuss the customer's role as a *productive resource* for the firm. Describe a time when you played this role. What did you do and how did you feel? Did the firm help you perform your role effectively? If so, how?

7. Discuss the customer's role as a *contributor to service quality and satisfaction.* Describe a time when you played this role. What did you do and how did you feel? Did the firm help you perform your role effectively? If so, how?

8. Discuss the customer's role as a potential *competitor.* Describe a time when you chose to provide a service for yourself rather than pay someone to provide the service for you. Why did you decide to perform the service yourself? What could have changed your mind, causing you to contract with someone else to provide the service?

Exercises

1. Visit a service establishment where customers can influence each other (such as a theme park, an entertainment establishment, a resort, a shopping mall, a restaurant, an airline, a school, or a hospital). Observe (or interview) customers and record cases of positive and negative customer influence. Discuss how you would manage the situation to increase overall customer satisfaction.

2. Interview someone regarding his or her decision to outsource a service—for example, legal services, payroll, or maintenance in a company or cleaning, child care, or pet care in a household. Use the criteria for internal versus external exchange described in the text to analyze the decision to outsource.

3. Think of a service in which a high level of customer participation is necessary for the service to be successful (health club, weight loss, educational setting, health care, golf lessons, online social media, or the like). Interview a service provider in such an organization to find out what strategies the provider uses to encourage effective customer participation.

4. Visit a service setting in which multiple types of customer segments use the service at the same time (such as a theater, golf course, resort, or theme park). Observe (or interview the manager about) the organization's strategies to manage these segments effectively. Would you do anything differently if you were in charge?

5. Visit iPrint's website (www.iPrint.com). Compare its printing service process to similar onsite services offered by FedEx Kinko's. Compare and contrast the customer's role in each situation.

Notes

1. P. B. Seybold, *Customers.com: How to Create a Profitable Business Strategy for the Internet and Beyond* (New York: Random House, 1998), pp. 235–244; www.iPrint.com, 2011.

2. See B. Schneider and D. E. Bowen, *Winning the Service Game* (Boston: Harvard Business School Press, 1995), chap. 4; L. A. Bettencourt, "Customer Voluntary Performance: Customers as Partners in Service Delivery, *Journal of Retailing*

73 (Fall 1997), pp. 383–406; P. K. Mills and J. H. Morris, "Clients as 'Partial' Employees: Role Development in Client Participation," *Academy of Management Review* 11, no. 4 (1986), pp. 726–735; C. H. Lovelock and R. F. Young, "Look to Customers to Increase Productivity," *Harvard Business Review* 57 (Summer 1979), pp. 9–20; A. R. Rodie and S. S. Kleine, "Customer Participation in Services Production and Delivery," in *Handbook of Services Marketing and Management,* ed. T. A. Swartz and D. Iacobucci (Thousand Oaks, CA: Sage, 2000), pp. 111–126; C. K. Prahalad and V. Ramaswamy, "Co-opting Customer Competence," *Harvard Business Review* 78 (January–February 2000), p. 7; and N. Bendapudi and R. P. Leone, "Psychological Implications of Customer Participation in Co-Production," *Journal of Marketing* 67 (January 2003), pp. 14–28.

3. S. L. Vargo, and R. F. Lusch, "Evolving to a New Dominant Logic for Marketing," *Journal of Marketing* 68 (January 2004), pp. 1–17; R. F. Lusch, S. L. Vargo, and M O'Brien, "Competing through Service: Insights from Service-Dominant Logic," *Journal of Retailing* 83, no. 1 (2007), pp. 5–18.

4. L. A. Bettencourt, S. W. Brown, A. L. Ostrom, and R. I. Roundtree, "Client Co-Production in Knowledge-Intensive Business Services," *California Management Review* 44 (Summer 2002), pp. 100–128.

5. See S. J. Grove and R. P. Fisk, "The Impact of Other Customers on Service Experiences: A Critical Incident Examination of 'Getting Along,' " *Journal of Retailing* 73 (Spring 1997), pp. 63–85; C. I. Martin and C. A. Pranter, "Compatibility Management: Customer-to-Customer Relationships in Service Environments," *Journal of Services Marketing* 3 (Summer 1989), pp. 5–15; and R. Nicholls, "New Directions for Customer-to-Customer Interaction Research," *Journal of Services Marketing* 24, no. 1 (2010), pp. 87–97.

6. Grove and Fisk, "The Impact of Other Customers on Service Experiences."

7. L. Landro, "ICUs' New Message: Welcome, Families," *The Wall Street Journal,* July 12, 2007, pp. Al+.

8. M. S. Rosenbaum and C. A. Massiah, "When Customers Receive Support from Other Customers," *Journal of Service Research* 9 (February 2007), pp. 257–270.

9. Grove and Fisk, "The Impact of Other Customers on Service Experiences."

10. K. Harris and S. Baron, "Consumer-to-Consumer Conversations in Service Settings," *Journal of Service Research* 6 (February 2004), pp. 287–303.

11. See P. K. Mills, R. B. Chase, and N. Margulies, "Motivating the Client/Employee System as a Service Production Strategy," *Academy of Management Review* 8, no. 2 (1983), pp. 301–310; D. E. Bowen, "Managing Customers as Human Resources in Service Organizations," *Human Resource Management* 25, no. 3 (1986), pp. 371–383; and Mills and Morris, "Clients as 'Partial' Employees."

12. Bettencourt et al., "Client Co-Production in Knowledge-Intensive Business Services."

13. Landro, "ICUs' New Message."

14. R. B. Chase, "Where Does the Customer Fit in a Service Operation?" *Harvard Business Review* 56 (November–December 1978), pp. 137–142.

15. Mills et al., "Motivating the Client/Employee System."

16. Marilyn Adams, "Tech Takes Bigger Role in Air Services," *USA Today,* July 18, 2001, p. 1.

17. See M. Xue and P. T. Harker, "Customer Efficiency: Concept and Its Impact on E-Business Management," *Journal of Service Research* 4 (May 2002), pp. 253–267;

and B. Kiviat, "The End of Customer Service," in "What's Next 2008," *Time Magazine*, March 13, 2008.

18. K. W. Chan, C. K. Yim, and S. S. K. Lam, "Is Customer Participation in Value Creation a Double-Edged Sword? Evidence from Professional Financial Services across Cultures," *Journal of Marketing* 74 (May 2010), pp. 48–64.

19. See D. W. Johnson, R. T. Johnson, and K. A. Smith, *Active Learning: Cooperation in the College Classroom* (Edina, MN: Interaction Book Company, 1991).

20. S. Dellande, M. C. Gilly, and J. L. Graham, "Gaining Compliance and Losing Weight: The Role of the Service Provider in Health Care Services," *Journal of Marketing* 68 (July 2004), pp. 78–91.

21. S. Auh, S. J. Bell, C. S. McLeod, and E. Shih, "Co-Production and Customer Loyalty in Financial Services," *Journal of Retailing* 83, no. 3 (2007), pp. 359–370.

22. S. W. Kelley, S. J. Skinner, and J. H. Donnelly Jr., "Organizational Socialization of Service Customers," *Journal of Business Research* 25 (1992), pp. 197–214.

23. C. Claycomb, C. A. Lengnick-Hall, and L. W. Inks, "The Customer as a Productive Resource: A Pilot Study and Strategic Implications," *Journal of Business Strategies* 18 (Spring 2001), pp. 47–69.

24. Several of the scenarios are adapted from C. Goodwin, "'I Can Do It Myself': Training the Service Consumer to Contribute to Service Productivity," *Journal of Services Marketing* 2 (Fall 1988), pp. 71–78.

25. R. Normann and R. Ramirez, "From Value Chain to Value Constellation: Designing Interactive Strategy," *Harvard Business Review* 71 (July–August 1993), pp. 65–77; www.ikea.com, 2011.

26. J. E. G. Bateson, "The Self-Service Customer—Empirical Findings," in *Emerging Perspectives in Services Marketing,* ed. L. L. Berry, G. L. Shostack, and G. D. Upah (Chicago: American Marketing Association, 1983), pp. 50–53.

27. V. S. Folkes, "Recent Attribution Research in Consumer Behavior: A Review and New Directions," *Journal of Consumer Research* 14 (March 1988), pp. 548–565; M. J. Bitner, "Evaluating Service Encounters: The Effects of Physical Surroundings and Employee Responses," *Journal of Marketing* 54 (April 1990), pp. 69–82.

28. Bendapudi and Leone, "Psychological Implications of Customer Participation in Co-Production."

29. R. F. Lusch, S. W. Brown, and G. J. Brunswick, "A General Framework for Explaining Internal vs. External Exchange," *Journal of the Academy of Marketing Science* 10 (Spring 1992), pp. 119–134.

30. Ibid.

31. See M. J. Bitner, A. L. Ostrom, and M. L. Meuter, "Implementing Successful Self-Service Technologies," *Academy of Management Executive* 16 (November 2002), pp. 96–109.

32. See P. Dabholkar, "Consumer Evaluations of New Technology-Based Self-Service Options: An Investigation of Alternative Models of Service Quality," *International Journal of Research in Marketing* 13, no. 1 (1996), pp. 29–51; F. Davis, "User Acceptance of Information Technology: System Characteristics, User Perceptions and Behavioral Impact," *International Journal of Man-Machine Studies* 38 (1993), pp. 475–487; L. M. Bobbitt and P. A. Dabholkar, "Integrating Attitudinal Theories to Understand and Predict Use of Technology-Based Self-Service," *International Journal of Service Industry Management* 12, no. 5 (2001), pp. 423–450;

J. M. Curran, M. L. Meuter, and C. F. Surprenant, "Intentions to Use Self-Service Technologies: A Confluence of Multiple Attitudes," *Journal of Service Research* 5 (February 2003), pp. 209–224; and S. Al-Natour and I. Benbasat, "The Adoption and Use of IT Artifacts: A New Interaction-Centric Model for the Study of User-Artifact Relationships," *Journal of the Association for Information Systems* 10, no. 9 (2009), pp. 661–685.

33. K. Crow, "Online Bids, Christie's Fine-Arts Patrons Are Slow to Click," *The Wall Street Journal,* July 12, 2007, pp. B1+.

34. M. L. Meuter, M. J. Bitner, A. L. Ostrom, and S. W. Brown, "Choosing among Alternative Service Delivery Modes: An Investigation of Customer Trial of Self-Service Technologies," *Journal of Marketing* 69 (April 2005), pp. 61–83.

35. M. L. Meuter, A. L. Ostrom, R. I. Roundtree, and M. J. Bitner, "Self-Service Technologies: Understanding Customer Satisfaction with Technology-Based Service Encounters," *Journal of Marketing* 64 (July 2000), pp. 50–64.

36. M. J. Reinders, P. A. Dabholkar, and R. T. Frambach, "Consequences of Forcing Consumers to Use Technology-Based Self-Service," *Journal of Service Research* 11 (November 2008), pp. 107–123.

37. Meuter, Bitner, et al., "Choosing among Alternative Service Delivery Modes"; see also Y. Moon and F. X. Frei, "Exploding the Self-Service Myth," *Harvard Business Review* 78 (May–June 2000), pp. 26–27; and M. J. Bitner et al., "Implementing Successful Self-Service Technologies."

38. A. Parasuraman and C. L. Colby, *Techno-Ready Marketing: How and Why Your Customers Adopt Technology* (New York: The Free Press, 2001).

39. Bowen, "Managing Customers as Human Resources."

40. Chase, "Where Does the Customer Fit in a Service Operation?"

41. Bateson, "The Self-Service Customer."

42. J. Light, "With Customer Service, Real Person Trumps Text," *The Wall Street Journal*, April 25, 2011, p. B7.

43. Meuter, Bitner, et al., "Choosing among Alternative Service Delivery Modes."

44. Bowen, "Managing Customers as Human Resources"; Schneider and Bowen, *Winning the Service Game,* chap. 4; Meuter, Bitner, et al., "Choosing among Alternative Service Delivery Modes"; Dellande et al., "Gaining Compliance and Losing Weight."

45. C. Goodwin and R. Radford, "Models of Service Delivery: An Integrative Perspective," in *Advances in Services Marketing and Management,* ed. T. A. Swartz, D. E. Bowen, and S. W. Brown, (Stamford, CT: JAI Press), pp. 231–252.

46. S. W. Kelley, J. H. Donnelly Jr., and S. J. Skinner, "Customer Participation in Service Production and Delivery," *Journal of Retailing* 66 (Fall 1990), pp. 315–335; Schneider and Bowen, *Winning the Service Game,* chap. 4.

47. L. Landro, "When a Doctor Isn't Enough," *The Wall Street Journal*, August 16, 2011, p. D1.

48. Bowen, "Managing Customers as Human Resources."

49. Ibid; see also L. C. Harris and K. L. Reynolds, "The Consequences of Dysfunctional Customer Behavior," *Journal of Service Research* 6 (November 2003), pp. 144–161.

50. Martin and Pranter, "Compatibility Management."

Chapter **Thirteen**

Managing Demand and Capacity

This chapter's objectives are to

1. Explain the underlying issue for capacity-constrained services: lack of inventory capability.

2. Present the implications of time, labor, equipment, and facilities constraints combined with variations in demand patterns.

3. Lay out strategies for matching supply and demand through (a) shifting demand to match capacity or (b) adjusting capacity to meet demand.

4. Demonstrate the benefits and risks of yield management strategies in forging a balance among capacity utilization, pricing, market segmentation, and financial return.

5. Provide strategies for managing waiting lines for times when capacity and demand cannot be aligned.

How to Fill 281 Rooms 365 Days of the Year

The Ritz-Carlton Hotel in Phoenix, Arizona, is an upscale hotel in the center of a metropolitan area of approximately 4 million people, the fifth largest metropolitan area in the United States. The hotel is frequently cited for its service and has been named the number one business hotel in Arizona by *Travel and Leisure* magazine several times in the past decade.[1] It has 281 luxury rooms, two restaurants, beautiful pools, and spacious meeting and conference facilities. These restaurants and meeting facilities are available to guests 365 days and nights of the year. Yet natural demand for them varies tremendously. During the tourist season from November through mid-April, demand for rooms is high, often exceeding available space. From mid-May through September, however, when temperatures regularly exceed 100 degrees Fahrenheit, the demand for rooms drops considerably. Because the hotel caters to business travelers and business meetings, demand has a weekly cycle in addition to the seasonal fluctuations. Business travelers do not stay over weekends. Thus, demand for rooms from the hotel's primary market segment drops on Friday and Saturday nights.

To smooth the peaks and valleys of demand for its facilities, the Phoenix Ritz-Carlton has employed a number of strategies. Group business (primarily business conferences) is pursued throughout the year to fill the lower demand periods. A variety of special event, sports, wedding, and getaway packages are offered year-round to increase weekend demand for rooms. During the hot summer months, the hotel encourages local Phoenix and nearby Tucson residents to experience the luxury of the hotel. One creative package used in the past included an attractively priced hotel stay combined with a "progressive dinner" at nearby restaurants. The progressive dinner started with a reception in the hotel, a walk to one restaurant for appetizers, followed by dinner at a second restaurant. The evening finished with champagne and dessert in the guests' rooms. By encouraging local people to use the hotel, the hotel increases its occupancy during slow demand times, while residents of the community get a chance to enjoy an experience they may not be able to afford during the high season.

Most downtown hotels in urban areas face the same weekly demand fluctuations that the Phoenix Ritz-Carlton deals with, and many have found a partial solution by catering to families and children on the weekends. For many dual-career couples, weekend getaways are a primary form of relaxation and vacation. The downtown hotels cater to these couples and families by offering discounted room rates, child-oriented activities and amenities, and an environment in which families feel comfortable. For example, the New York Palace Hotel—the closest hotel to American Girl Place—attempts to increase weekend stays by offering an "American Girl Place Package" to families with young daughters. The package, targeted for nonbusiness customers, comes with a complimentary American Girl Futon bed for an American Girl doll that girls can take home with them and includes turndown service for their dolls.

For the Ritz-Carlton Hotel in Phoenix and many other hotels, managing demand and utilizing the hotel's fixed capacity of rooms, restaurants, and meeting facilities can be a seasonal, weekly, and even daily challenge. Although the hotel industry epitomizes the challenges of demand and capacity management, many service providers face similar problems. For example, tax accountants and air-conditioning maintenance services face seasonal demand fluctuations, whereas services such as commuter trains and restaurants face daily and even hourly variations in customer demand. For some businesses, demand is predictable, as for a tax accountant. For others, such as management or technology consultants, demand may be less predictable, fluctuating based on customer needs and business cycles. Sometimes firms experience too much demand for the existing capacity and sometimes capacity sits idle.

Overuse or underuse of a service can directly contribute to gap 3: failure to deliver what was designed and specified. For example, when demand for services exceeds maximum capacity, the quality of service may drop because staff and facilities are overtaxed. And some customers may be turned away, not receiving the service at all. During periods of slow demand it may be necessary to reduce prices or cut service amenities; however, when firms change the nature of the service and, perhaps, the makeup of the clientele, they run the risk of not delivering what customers expect. For example, older travelers or business groups who are in a hotel on a weekend may resent the invasion of families and children because it changes the nature of the service they expected. At the pool, for example, collisions can occur between adults trying to swim laps and children playing water games.

In this chapter we focus on the challenges of matching supply and demand in capacity-constrained services. The service performance gap can occur when organizations fail to smooth the peaks and valleys of demand, overuse their capacities, attract an inappropriate customer mix in their efforts to build demand, or rely too much on price in smoothing demand. The chapter gives you an understanding of these issues and strategies for addressing them. The effective use of capacity is frequently a key success factor for service organizations.

THE UNDERLYING ISSUE: LACK OF INVENTORY CAPABILITY

The fundamental issue underlying supply and demand management in services is the lack of inventory capability. Unlike manufacturing firms, service firms cannot build up inventories during periods of slow demand to use later when demand increases. This lack of inventory capability is due to the perishability of services and their simultaneous production and consumption. An airline seat not sold on a given flight cannot be left in inventory and resold the following day. The productive capacity of that seat on that flight has perished. Similarly, an hour of a lawyer's billable time cannot be saved from one day to the next. Services also cannot be transported from one place to another or transferred from person to person. Thus, the Phoenix Ritz-Carlton's services cannot be moved to an alternative location in the summer months—say, to the Pacific coast, where summers are ideal for tourists and demand for hotel rooms is high.

The lack of inventory capability combined with fluctuating demand leads to a variety of potential outcomes, as illustrated in Figure 13.1.[2] The horizontal lines in Figure 13.1 indicate service capacity, and the curved line indicates customer demand for the service. In many services, capacity is fixed; thus, capacity can be designated by a flat horizontal line over a certain time period. Demand for service frequently fluctuates, however, as indicated by the curved line. The topmost horizontal line in Figure 13.1 represents maximum capacity. For example, in our opening vignette, the

FIGURE 13.1 **Variations in Demand Relative to Capacity**

Source: Lovelock, Christopher H.; Wirtz, Jochen, *Services Marketing*, 7th Edition, (c) 2011, chap. 9, p. 230. Reprinted by permission of Pearson Education Inc., Upper Saddle River, NJ.

horizontal line would represent the Phoenix Ritz-Carlton's 281 rooms, or it could represent 70,000 seats in a large university football stadium. The rooms and the seats remain constant, but demand for them fluctuates. The band between the second and third horizontal lines represents optimal capacity—the best use of the capacity from the perspective of both customers and the company (the difference between optimal and maximum capacity utilization is discussed later in the chapter). The areas in the middle of Figure 13.1 are labeled to represent four basic scenarios that can result from different combinations of capacity and demand:

1. *Excess demand.* The level of demand exceeds maximum capacity. In this situation some customers will be turned away, resulting in lost business opportunities. For the customers who do receive the service, its quality may not match what was promised because of crowding or overtaxing of staff and facilities.

2. *Demand exceeds optimum capacity.* No one is being turned away, but the quality of service may still suffer because of overuse, crowding, or staff being pushed beyond their abilities to deliver consistent quality.

3. *Demand and supply are balanced at the level of optimal capacity.* Staff and facilities are occupied at an ideal level. No one is overworked, facilities can be maintained, and customers are receiving quality service without undesirable delays.

4. *Excess capacity.* Demand is below optimal capacity. Productive resources in the form of labor, equipment, and facilities are underutilized, resulting in low productivity and lower profits. Customers may receive excellent quality on an individual level because they have the full use of the facilities, no waiting, and complete attention from the staff. If, however, service quality depends on the presence of other customers, customers may be disappointed or may worry that they have chosen an inferior service provider.

Not all firms will be challenged equally in terms of managing supply and demand. The seriousness of the problem will depend on the *extent of demand fluctuations over time* and the *extent to which supply is constrained* (Table 13.1).[3] Organizations in some service industries will experience wide fluctuations in demand (hospitals,

TABLE 13.1
Demand and Capacity for Service Providers

Source: Adapted from C. H. Lovelock, "Classifying Services to Gain Strategic Marketing Insights," *Journal of Marketing* 47 (Summer 1983), p. 17. Reprinted by permission from the American Marketing Association.

Extent to Which Supply Is Constrained	Extent of Demand Fluctuations over Time	
	Wide	**Narrow**
	1	2
Peak demand can usually be met without a major delay.	Electricity Natural gas Police and fire emergencies Internet services	Insurance Legal services Banking Laundry and dry cleaning
	4	3
Peak demand regularly exceeds capacity.	Accounting and tax preparation Passenger transportation Hotels Restaurants Hospital emergency rooms	Services similar to those in cell 2 that have insufficient capacity for their base level of business

transportation, restaurants), whereas others will have narrower fluctuations (insurance, laundry, banking). For some, peak demand can usually be met even when demand fluctuates (electricity, natural gas, Internet services), but for others peak demand may frequently exceed capacity (hospital emergency rooms, restaurants near football stadiums, hotels next to universities). Those firms with wide variations in demand (cells 1 and 4 in Table 13.1), and particularly those with wide fluctuations in demand that regularly exceed capacity (cell 4), will find the issues and strategies in this chapter particularly important to their success. Those firms that find themselves in cell 3 may decide a "one-time-fix" (as discussed in Chapter 9) to expand their capacity to match regular patterns of excessive demand will sufficiently address the situation. The industries in Table 13.1 are provided to illustrate where *most* firms in those industries would likely be classified. In reality, an individual firm from any industry could find itself in any of the four cells, depending on its immediate circumstances.

To identify effective strategies for managing supply and demand fluctuations, an organization needs a clear understanding of the constraints on its capacity and the underlying demand patterns.

CAPACITY CONSTRAINTS

For many firms, service capacity is fixed. As indicated in Table 13.2, critical fixed-capacity factors can be—depending on the type of service—time, labor, equipment, facilities, or (in many cases) a combination of these.

TABLE 13.2
Constraints on Capacity

Nature of the Constraint	Type of Service*
Time	Legal
	Consulting
	Accounting
	Medical
Labor	Law firm
	Accounting firm
	Consulting firm
	Health clinic
Equipment	Delivery services
	Telecommunications
	Network services
	Utilities
	Health clubs
Facilities	Hotels
	Restaurants
	Hospitals
	Airlines
	Schools
	Theaters
	Churches

* The examples illustrate the most common capacity constraint for each type of service. In reality, any of the service organizations listed can be operating under multiple constraints. For example, a law firm may be operating under constrained labor capacity (too few attorneys) and facilities constraints (not enough office space) at the same time.

Time, Labor, Equipment, and Facilities

For some service businesses, the primary constraint on service production is *time*. For example, a lawyer, a consultant, a hairdresser, a plumber, and a psychological counselor all primarily sell their time. In such contexts, if the service worker is not available or if his or her time is not used productively, profits are lost. If there is excess demand at a specific time, additional time cannot be created to satisfy it. From the point of view of the service provider, time is the constraint.

From the point of view of a firm that employs a large number of service providers, *labor* or staffing levels can be the primary capacity constraint. A law firm, a university department, a consulting firm, a tax accounting firm, and a repair and maintenance contractor may all face the reality that at certain times demand for their organization's services cannot be met because the staff is already operating at peak capacity. However, it does not always make sense (nor may it be possible in a competitive labor market) to hire additional service providers if low demand is a reality a large percentage of the time.

In other cases, *equipment* may be the critical constraint. For trucking or air-freight delivery services, the trucks or airplanes needed to service demand may be the capacity limitation. During the Christmas holidays, UPS, FedEx, and other delivery service providers face this issue. Health clubs also deal with this limitation, particularly at certain times of the day (before work, during lunch hours, after work) and in certain months of the year. For network service providers, bandwidth, servers, and switches represent their capacity constraints.

Finally, many firms face restrictions brought about by their limited *facilities*. Hotels have only a certain number of rooms to sell, airlines are limited by the number of seats on their aircraft, educational institutions are constrained by the number of rooms and the number of seats in each classroom, and restaurant capacity is restricted to the number of tables and seats available.

Understanding the primary capacity constraint, or the combination of factors that restricts capacity, is a first step in designing strategies to deal with supply and demand issues.

Optimal versus Maximum Use of Capacity

To fully understand capacity issues, it is important to know the difference between *optimal* and *maximum* use of capacity. As suggested in Figure 13.1, optimal and maximum capacity may not be the same. Using capacity at an optimal level means that resources are fully employed but not overused and that customers are receiving quality service in a timely manner. Maximum capacity, on the other hand, represents the absolute limit of service availability. In the case of a sporting event, optimal and maximum capacity may be the same. The entertainment value of the game is enhanced for customers when every seat is filled, and obviously the profitability for the home team is greatest under these circumstances (see accompanying photo on the next page). On the other hand, in a university classroom it is usually not desirable for students or faculty to have every seat filled. In this case, optimal use of capacity is less than the maximum. In some cases, maximum use of capacity may result in excessive waiting by customers, as in a popular restaurant. From the perspective of customer satisfaction, optimal use of the restaurant's capacity will be less than maximum use.

In the case of equipment or facilities constraints, the maximum capacity at any given time is obvious. There are only a certain number of weight machines in the health club, a certain number of seats in the airplane, and a limited amount of space in a cargo carrier. In the case of a bottling plant, when maximum capacity on the assembly line is exceeded, bottles begin to break and the system shuts down. Thus, it is relatively easy to observe the effects of exceeding maximum equipment capacity in many manufacturing situations.

For sports and other entertainment venues, maximum and optimal capacity may be close to the same.

When the limitation is people's time or labor, maximum capacity is harder to specify because people are in a sense more flexible than facilities and equipment. When an individual service provider's maximum capacity has been exceeded, the result is likely to cause decreased service quality, customer dissatisfaction, and employee burnout and turnover, but these outcomes may not be immediately observable, even to the employee. While it is relatively easy for firms to identify the maximum capacity for physical constraints like space, it is much more difficult to know what the maximum capacity of a human being is. As a result, firms may be able to push employees beyond their optimal capacity for a while, but not learn of the maximum capacity of an employee until the person quits or encounters health problems. Indeed, it is often easy for a consulting firm to take on one more assignment, taxing its employees beyond their maximum capacity, or for an HMO clinic to schedule a few more appointments in a day, stretching its staff and physicians beyond their maximum capacity. Given the potential costs in terms of reduced quality and customer and employee dissatisfaction, it is critical for the firm to understand optimal and maximum human capacity limits.

DEMAND PATTERNS

To manage fluctuating demand in a service business, it is necessary to have a clear understanding of demand patterns, why they vary, and the market segments that constitute demand at different points in time.[4]

The Charting of Demand Patterns

To begin to understand demand patterns, the organization needs to chart the level of demand over relevant time periods. Organizations that have good customer information systems can track this information very accurately. Others may need to chart demand patterns more informally. Daily, weekly, and monthly demand levels should be tracked, and if seasonality is a suspected problem, graphing should be done for data from at least the past year. In some services, such as restaurants or health care, hourly fluctuations within a day may also be relevant. Sometimes demand patterns are intuitively obvious; in other cases, patterns may not reveal themselves until the data are tracked.

Predictable Cycles

As service providers consider customer demand levels, predictable cycles may be detected, including daily (variations occur by hour), weekly (variations occur by day), monthly (variations occur by day or week), and/or yearly (variations occur according to months or seasons). In some cases, predictable patterns occur at all periods. For example, in the restaurant industry, especially in seasonal tourist locations, demand can vary predictably by month, by week, by day, and by hour. Similarly, the demand for a bank's services can vary by hour (with lunch time and end of the day with the most demand), by day of the week (with the last day of the week and the first day of the week being the most popular), and by day of the month (with the day that Social Security checks arrive being among the highest in demand).

If a predictable cycle is detected, the underlying causes should be identified. The Ritz-Carlton in Phoenix knows that demand cycles are based on seasonal weather patterns and that weekly variations are based on the work week (business travelers do not stay at the hotel over the weekend). Tax accountants can predict demand based on when taxes are due, quarterly and annually. Services catering to children and families are affected by variations in school hours and vacations. Retail and telecommunications services have peak periods at certain holidays and times of the week and day. When predictable patterns exist, generally one or more causes can be determined.

Random Demand Fluctuations

Sometimes the patterns of demand appear to be random—there is no apparent predictable cycle. Yet even in this case, causes can often be identified. For example, day-to-day changes in the weather may affect the use of recreational, shopping, or entertainment facilities. Good weather generally increases the demand for the services provided by an amusement park, but it has the opposite effect on movie theaters—people would rather not be inside when the weather is nice. Auto service centers generally find extremely poor weather (either very hot or very cold) increases the demand for their services, whereas mild weather does not seem to have as much of an effect on vehicles. Although the weather cannot be predicted far in advance, it may be possible to anticipate demand a day or two ahead. Health-related events also cannot be predicted. Accidents, heart attacks, and births all increase demand for hospital services, but the level of demand cannot generally be determined in advance. Natural disasters such as floods, fires, and hurricanes can dramatically increase the need for such services as insurance, telecommunications, and health care. Acts of war and terrorism such as that experienced in the United States on September 11, 2001, generate instantaneous need for services that cannot be predicted.

Cox Communications was faced with a sudden increase in demand for services in Baton Rouge, Louisiana, immediately after Hurricane Katrina struck in late August 2005. The category 5 hurricane, centered in New Orleans, resulted in more than 1,800 deaths and caused more than $80 billion in damages. A disaster of this magnitude increased the demand for Cox's services. Cox's customers needed access to its network, phone services, the Internet, and e-mail to communicate with family members and friends regarding their safety and whereabouts, then to make arrangements to begin the rebuilding process. In the aftermath of Hurricane Katrina, Baton Rouge's population doubled as people were forced to leave New Orleans. Many of those who took refuge in the city remained, increasing demand for Cox's services in a way no one could have predicted.[5]

Organizations such as Disney that predict customer patterns can use that information to anticipate demand for their service.

Our Global Feature illustrates how one company with seemingly random and chaotic demand for its services was able to change its business to serve customers. The feature is also a good example of organizational learning across cultures.

Demand Patterns by Market Segment

An organization that has detailed records on customer transactions may be able to disaggregate demand by market segment, revealing patterns within patterns. Or the analysis may reveal that demand from one segment is predictable, whereas demand from another segment is relatively random. For example, for a bank, the visits from its commercial accounts may occur daily at a predictable time, whereas personal account holders may visit the bank at seemingly random intervals. Health clinics often notice that walk-in or "care needed today" patients tend to concentrate their arrivals on Monday, with fewer needing immediate attention on other days of the week. Many auto service centers experience a similar pattern, as more walk-in customers arrive on Monday morning for car servicing and repair than any other day of the week. Knowing that this pattern exists, many health clinics and auto service centers tend to schedule future appointments (which they can control) for later days of the week, leaving more of Monday available for same-day appointments and walk-ins.

STRATEGIES FOR MATCHING CAPACITY AND DEMAND

When an organization has a clear grasp of its capacity constraints and an understanding of demand patterns, it is in a good position to develop strategies for matching supply and demand. There are two general approaches for accomplishing this match. The first is to smooth the demand fluctuations themselves by shifting demand to match existing capacity. This approach implies that the peaks and valleys of the demand curve (Figure 13.1) will be flattened to match as closely as possible the horizontal optimal capacity line. The second general strategy is to adjust capacity to match fluctuations in demand. This implies moving the horizontal capacity lines shown in Figure 13.1 to match the ups and downs of the demand curve. Each of these two basic strategies is described next with specific examples.

Shifting Demand to Match Capacity

With this strategy an organization seeks to shift customers away from periods in which demand exceeds capacity, perhaps by convincing them to use the service during periods of slow demand. This change may be possible for some customers but not for others. For example, many business travelers are not able to shift their needs for airline, car rental, and hotel services; pleasure travelers, on the other hand, can often shift the timing of their trips. Customers who cannot shift their demand and cannot be accommodated because of insufficient capacity represent lost business for the firm.

During periods of slow demand, the organization seeks to attract more and/or different customers to increase demand and thus better utilize its productive capacity. A variety of approaches can be used to shift or increase demand to match capacity. Frequently a firm uses a combination of approaches. Ideas for how to shift demand during both slow and peak periods are shown in Figure 13.2 and described in the following paragraphs.

Imagine a business in which customers' orders are unpredictable, where more than half of all customer orders are changed, often repeatedly and at the last minute, and where the product being delivered is never more than 90 minutes from spoiling. Welcome to the concrete delivery business. Cemex, based in Monterrey, Mexico, and founded in 1906, is a highly successful global player in this industry. The company operates in 50 countries across five continents with more than 47,000 employees and annual net sales in excess of $15 billion.

Yet when two internal consultants examined the business several years ago, they were amazed at the chaos that ruled the industry. Wild weather, unpredictable traffic, spontaneous labor disruptions, and sporadic government inspections of construction sites all combined with ever-changing customer orders to create a sense of chaos and uncontrollability in the business. Add this chaos to 8,000 grades of concrete available through a half-dozen regional mixing plants, and you have an extremely complex system to manage.

Historically, Cemex had attempted to run the business through controlling its customers, requiring them to stick with their orders and imposing fines for changed orders. Efficiency—not customers—ruled in Cemex's effort to conquer the natural randomness of demand and customers' needs to change orders at the last minute.

The company began searching for new ways to do business. It turned to FedEx and to the 911 emergency dispatch center in Houston, Texas, for ideas. What it found were organizations that, instead of trying to control demand for their services, had developed people and technology that could be flexible in meeting customers' seemingly random demand patterns. Instead of penalizing customers for changing their orders, FedEx does not restrict its customers and, in fact, guarantees delivery at a certain time to any and all locations. This ability to serve customers is made possible by sophisticated information systems that track demand and schedule pickups and deliveries, customer-focused frontline employees, and a customer-centric corporate culture that supports it all. From the 911 center in Houston, Cemex learned that even seemingly random occurrences such as emergency health needs and accidents occur in sufficient number to allow patterns of demand to be discerned and planned for. In terms of Figure 13.1, what FedEx and the 911 emergency center did was adjust their capacity to meet the peaks and valleys of customer demand rather than insisting that the customers adjust their demand to fit the company's constrained capacity.

The observations of how both FedEx and the 911 dispatch center handled demand fluctuations were a revelation to Cemex's team. The company went back

to Mexico determined to embrace the complexity of its marketplace and to do business on the customer's terms. The company launched a project called Sincronizacion Dinamica de Operaciones: the dynamic synchronization of operations. It unleashed trucks from previous zone assignments, allowing them to roam the city. It outfitted the trucks with transmitters and receivers connected to a global positioning system (GPS), so that locations, direction, and speed of every vehicle could be tracked. It enrolled its drivers in secondary education classes over a period of two years, so they would be more service oriented and able to deal with customers.

Impressed with FedEx's guaranteed service, Cemex worked toward being able to offer "same-day service, with free, unlimited order changes." It instituted a policy for guaranteed delivery: if a load failed to arrive within 20 minutes of its scheduled delivery time, the buyer received back 20 pesos per cubic meter—"guarantia 20 × 20"—amounting to roughly 5 percent of the total cost.

Cemex embraced the chaos of its industry instead of trying to adjust and change it. By using technology, people, and systems, it was able to match its capacity constraints with its customers' wildly fluctuating demands. And the company came out a winner. Cemex could afford to offer its 20 × 20 guarantee because its reliability regularly exceeded 98 percent!

Today, the company's focus on the customer is clearly stated on "The Cemex Difference" page of its website: "we tailor our products and services to suit customers' specific needs."

Sources: T. Petzinger Jr., "This Promise Is Set in Concrete," *Fast Company,* April 1999, pp. 216–218; see also T. Petzinger Jr., *The New Pioneers* (New York: Simon & Schuster, 1999), pp. 91–93. Reprinted with the permission of Simon & Schuster, Inc. Copyright © 1999 by Thomas Petzinger Jr.; updated with company information from the Cemex website, www.cemex.com, 2010.

FIGURE 13.2   Strategies for Shifting Demand to Match Capacity

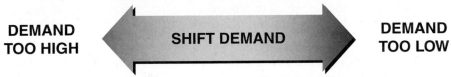

| DEMAND TOO HIGH | SHIFT DEMAND | DEMAND TOO LOW |

(Reduce Demand during Peak Times)

- Communicate busy days and times to customers.
- Modify timing and location of service delivery.
- Offer incentives for nonpeak usage.
- Set priorities by talking care of loyal or high-need customers first.
- Charge full price for the service—no discounts.

(Increase Demand to Match Capacity)

- Educate customers about peak times and benefits of nonpeak use.
- Vary how the facility is used.
- Vary the service offering.
- Differentiate on price.

Reduce Demand during Peak Times

One strategic approach to matching capacity and demand for a service provider focuses on *reducing demand* during times when customer demand is at its peak for the service.

Communicate with Customers   One approach for shifting demand is to communicate with customers, letting them know the times of peak demand to persuade them to use the service at alternative times and avoid crowding or delays. For example, signs in banks and post offices that let customers know their busiest hours and busiest days of the week can serve as a warning, encouraging customers to shift their demand to another time if possible. Forewarning customers about busy times and possible waits can have added benefits. Many customer service call centers provide a similar warning by informing waiting customers about approximately how long it will be until they are served. Those who do not want to wait may choose to call back later when the customer service department is less busy, leave a call back number, or visit the company's website for faster service.

Modify Timing and Location of Service Delivery   Some firms adjust their hours and days of service delivery to more directly reflect customer demand. Historically, U.S. banks were open only during "bankers' hours" from 10 a.m. to 3 p.m. every weekday—creating a heavy demand for their services during those hours. However, these hours did not necessarily match the times when most people preferred to do their personal banking. Now U.S. banks open early, stay open until 6 p.m. many days, and are open on Saturdays, better reflecting customer preferences and smoothing demand patterns. Many banks now have branches in hypermarkets such as Walmart and Meijer, and supermarkets such as Albertson's and Kroger, providing customers with multiple choices of both where and when to do their banking. Online banking has also shifted demand from branches to "anytime, anywhere" websites. Movie theaters often augment their primary viewing schedules by offering additional matinees on weekends and holidays to try to shift demand for their service.

Offer Incentives for Nonpeak Usage   In an attempt to shift demand away from peak times, some firms will offer incentives to encourage customers to shift their use of the service to other times. In northern Midwest states, swimming pool contractors offer additional amenities (e.g., free diving board, free heater, larger pool) to customers who are willing to postpone the purchase/use of their services until the end of the swimming season (say, September or October). Fitness centers that offer Pilates classes during times of lower demand often tout the advantages of smaller classes and increased instructor interaction with clients and frequently extend the class time by 25 percent or more.

Set Priorities   When demand for the service is high and there is limited capacity, service providers can prioritize who is served by taking care of loyal or high-need customers first. A tax firm might decide to serve its best customers rather than first-time walk-ins just prior to income tax due dates, and emergency medical centers move the most severe cases to the top of the priority list.

Charge Full Price   Firms generally charge full price for service during those periods of time that they know their services are historically in high demand; no discounts are allowed during such times. One of the busiest periods of the year for airlines are those days just before and just after the Thanksgiving holiday; for this reason, most airlines give priority for seating to those paying full fares and prohibit the use of frequent flyer miles for free seats on those days. Because demand is so high, customers looking for discounted or free tickets find that the days around this holiday have been "blacked out"; to travel on those days, they must purchase tickets at regular fares.

Increase Demand to Match Capacity

Other approaches service providers may consider in matching capacity and demand focus on *increasing demand* for service during times when the service is operating at less than full capacity.

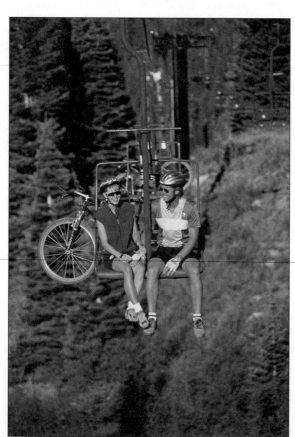

In summer months many ski resorts switch from targeting snow skiers to mountain bikers.

Educate Customers   Although a firm may know well and be able to anticipate times of increased demand, customers may not be aware of these times. Advertising and sales messages can be used to inform customers about times when demand is low. Electric utility companies often publicize periods of the day when demand for electricity is lower and urge customers to use washing machines or other equipment that consumes large amounts of energy during those times. Promotional campaigns can also emphasize different service benefits to customers during peak and slow periods. For example, air-conditioning firms often promote their preventive maintenance services in early spring, before temperatures get too high, encouraging customers to use their services before demand is high and pointing out the quick availability of their service people and the reduced anxiety from not waiting "until it is too late" by calling early.

Vary How the Facility Is Used   Another approach to increasing demand to change how the service facility is used, depending on the season of the year, day of the week, or time of day. For example, Whistler Mountain, a ski resort in Vancouver, Canada, offers its slopes to mountain bikers and its facilities for executive development and training programs during the summer, when snow skiing is not possible. A hospital in the Los Angeles area rents its facilities to film production crews who need realistic hospital settings for movies or television shows. Movie theaters are sometimes rented during weekdays by business groups and on Sunday mornings by church groups who have no building of their own. All of these are examples of how varying the use of the service facility can occur during a period of low demand.

Vary the Service Offering   A similar approach entails changing the nature of the service offering. Accounting firms, for example, focus on tax preparation late in the year and until April 15, when federal taxes are due in the United States. During other times of the year, they can focus on audits and general tax consulting activities. During professional basketball games, the demand for food at concession stands increases dramatically during the breaks between quarters—so much so that many customers decide not to make purchases for fear they will miss seeing the game because of long lines. In response to this situation, concessions at many arenas are now offered through menu orders taken by staff roaming through the aisles, and food is delivered right to customers' seats while the game is going on. In larger cities across the globe, McDonald's offers food delivery as a way to increase demand for its service.[6] In these examples, the service offering and associated benefits are changed to smooth customer demand for the organization's resources.

Care should be exercised in implementing strategies to change the service offering because such changes may imply and require alterations in other marketing mix variables—such as promotion, pricing, and staffing—to match the new offering. Unless these additional mix variables are altered effectively to support the offering, the strategy may not work. Even when done well, the downside of such changes can be confusion about the organization's image from the customers' perspective or a loss of strategic focus for the organization and its employees.

Differentiate on Price   A common response during periods of slow demand is to discount the price of the service. This strategy relies on basic economics of supply and demand. To be effective, however, a price differentiation strategy depends on solid understanding of customer price sensitivity and demand curves. For example, business travelers are far less price sensitive than are families traveling for pleasure. For the Ritz-Carlton in Phoenix (our opening vignette), lowering prices during the slow summer months is not likely to increase bookings from business travelers dramatically. However, the lower summer prices attract considerable numbers of families and local guests who want an opportunity to experience a luxury hotel but are not able to afford the rooms during peak season.

Heavy use of price differentiation to smooth demand can be a risky strategy. Customers may grow accustomed to the lower price and expect to get the same deal the next time they use the service. If communication with customers is unclear, customers may not understand the reasons for the discounts and will expect to pay the same during peak demand periods. Overuse or exclusive use of price as a strategy for smoothing demand is also risky because of the potential impact on the organization's image, the potential for attracting undesired market segments, and the possibility that those customers paying higher prices may feel they have been treated unfairly.

Adjusting Capacity to Meet Demand

A second strategic approach to matching supply and demand focuses on *adjusting capacity*. The fundamental idea here is to adjust, stretch, and align capacity to match customer demand (rather than working on shifting demand to match capacity, as just described). During periods of peak demand the organization seeks to stretch or expand its capacity as much as possible. During periods of slow demand it tries to shrink capacity so as not to waste resources. General strategies for adjusting the four primary service

FIGURE 13.3   **Strategies for Adjusting Capacity to Match Demand**

DEMAND TOO HIGH	ADJUST CAPACITY	DEMAND TOO LOW

(Increase Capacity Temporarily)

- Stretch people, facilities, and equipment temporarily.
- Use part-time employees.
- Cross-train employees.
- Outsource activities.
- Rent or share facilities and equipment.

(Adjust Use of Resources)

- Schedule downtime during periods of low demand.
- Perform maintenance and renovations.
- Schedule vacations and employee training strategically.
- Modify or move facilities and equipment.

resources (time, people, equipment, and facilities) are discussed throughout the rest of this section. In Figure 13.3, we summarize specific ideas for adjusting capacity during periods of peak and slow demand. Often, a number of different strategies are used simultaneously.

Increase Capacity Temporarily

Existing capacity can often be expanded temporarily to match demand. In such cases, no new resources are added; rather, the people, facilities, and equipment are asked to work harder and longer to meet demand.

Stretch People, Facilities, and Equipment Temporarily   It may be possible to extend the hours of service temporarily to accommodate demand. A health clinic might stay open longer during flu season, retailers are open longer hours during the holiday shopping season, and accountants have extended appointment hours (evenings and Saturdays) in the weeks just before tax deadlines. Indeed, in many service organizations, employees are asked to work longer and harder during periods of peak demand. For example, consulting organizations face extensive peaks and valleys with respect to demand for their services. During peak demand, associates are asked to take on additional projects and work longer hours. And frontline service personnel in banks, tourist attractions, restaurants, and telecommunications companies are asked to serve more customers per hour during busy times than during "normal" hours or days.

Facilities such as theaters, restaurants, meeting facilities, and classrooms can sometimes be expanded temporarily by the addition of tables, chairs, or other equipment needed by customers. Or, as in the case of a commuter train, a car that holds a fixed number of people seated comfortably can "expand" by accommodating standing passengers. Similarly, computers, power lines, tour buses, and maintenance equipment can often be stretched beyond what would be considered the maximum capacity for short periods to accommodate peak demand.

In using these types of "stretch" strategies, the organization needs to recognize the wear and tear on resources and the potential for inferior quality of service that may go with extended usage of such strategies. These strategies should thus be used for relatively short periods to allow for refreshment of the people who are asked to exceed their usual capacity and for maintenance of the facilities and equipment. Sometimes it is difficult to know in advance, particularly in the case of human resources, when capacity has been stretched too far.

Use Part-Time Employees In this situation the organization's labor resources are being aligned with demand. Retailers hire part-time employees during the holiday rush; tax accountants engage temporary help during tax season; tourist resorts bring in extra workers during peak season. To address the increased demand for package delivery at the end of the year, UPS has been known to hire more than 37,000 temporary employees to work between Thanksgiving and Christmas to handle the holiday rush.[7] Restaurants often ask employees to work split shifts (work the lunch shift, leave for a few hours, and come back for the dinner rush) during peak mealtime hours.

Cross-Train Employees If employees are cross-trained, they can shift among tasks, filling in where they are most needed. Cross-training increases the efficiency of the whole system and avoids underutilizing employees in some areas while others are being overtaxed. Many airlines cross-train their employees to move from ticketing to working the gate counter to assisting with baggage if needed. In some fast-food restaurants, employees specialize in one task (like making french fries) during busy hours, and the team of specialists may number 10 people. During slow hours the team may shrink to 3, with each of the remaining persons performing a variety of other functions. Grocery stores also use this strategy, with most employees able to move as needed from cashiering to stocking shelves to bagging groceries.

Outsource Activities Firms that find they have a temporary peak in demand for internal services may choose to outsource the service. For example, in recent years, many firms have found they do not have the capacity to fulfill their own needs for technology support, web design, and software-related services. Hospitals in Arizona often use health care staffing agencies to temporarily hire registered nurses for three months during the winter to handle the influx of winter visitors and the onset of the flu season. Rather than try to hire and train additional employees, these companies look to firms that specialize in outsourcing these types of functions as a temporary (or sometimes long-term) solution.

Rent or Share Facilities and Equipment For some organizations it is best to rent additional equipment or facilities during periods of peak demand. For example, express mail delivery services rent or lease trucks during the peak holiday delivery season. It would not make sense to buy trucks that would sit idle during the rest of the year. Sometimes organizations with complementary demand patterns can share facilities. An example is a church that shares its facilities during the week with a Montessori preschool. The school needs the facilities Monday through Friday during the day; the church needs the facilities in the evenings and on the weekend. Some businesses have been created to satisfy other businesses' fluctuating demand. For example, a firm may offer temporary office suites and clerical support to individuals who do not need such facilities and support on a continuous basis.

Adjust Use of Resources

This basic strategy is sometimes known as a "chase demand" strategy. By adjusting service resources creatively, organizations can, in effect, chase the demand curves to match capacity with customer demand patterns. People, facilities, and equipment are again the focus, this time with an eye toward adjusting the basic mix and use of these resources. Specific actions might include the following.[8]

Schedule Downtime during Periods of Low Demand If people, equipment, and facilities are being used at maximum capacity during peak periods, then it is imperative to schedule downtime during off-peak periods. Online banking services, for example, often schedule software upgrades on early Sunday morning (4:00 a.m. to 6:00 a.m.) to keep those affected by the disruption of their service to a minimum.

Strategy Insight Combining Demand (Marketing) and Capacity (Operations) Strategies to Increase Profits

In many situations, firms use multiple demand and capacity management strategies simultaneously to obtain optimal usage and maximize profits. Because each strategy involves costs as well as potential service quality, customer loyalty, and revenue outcomes, determining the appropriate mix can be a complex decision.

Research done for a ski resort illustrates how operations and marketing data can be combined into a sophisticated model to predict the right mix of strategies. The ski industry presents particularly interesting challenges for capacity management because the industry typically sees large fluctuations in demand based on seasonal, weekly, and even daily usage patterns; unpredictable weather and snowfall; a variety of skiing ability segments that use the resort in different ways; and demographic shifts over time. In addition, most resorts face constraints on their capacity due to environmental regulations that limit acreage and parking, as well as the large capital investment required for facility expansion and/or improvement. Furthermore, as ticket prices at ski resorts have continued to escalate, customer expectations have risen.

Powder Valley (PV, a disguised name), a ski resort in northern Utah, had consistently lost market share for five years to its rivals. Lack of facility improvements and increased marketing efforts by its competitors were cited as likely reasons for declining market share. To improve the situation, PV managers proposed several marketing strategies to increase demand on slow days and increase revenue per customer. Operations strategies that relied on acquisition of new terrain and new, faster ski lifts to improve the skiing experience and reduce waiting during peak demand periods were also proposed. Each of these strategies had its associated costs and less than totally predictable outcomes. Adding to

the complexity of the inherent trade-offs in the various strategies was the fact that the resort offered multiple activities (e.g., restaurants, skiing, shopping) for customers to choose.

The researchers working with PV proposed that the optimal profit strategy would require an integrated set of approaches representing both demand and capacity perspectives. Using data from the resort, they built a sophisticated simulation model to assess the impact on customer usage, waiting times, and profits of several strategies that were being considered, including:

- *Price variations.* Strategies aimed at leveling demand by charging lower prices for off-peak skiing.

- *Promotions of underutilized services.* Promotions to attract new customer segments or shift existing customers to underutilized services.

- *Information provision on waiting times.* Strategies that provide information about less crowded periods or shorter waiting times to move customers temporarily to underutilized services.

- *Capacity expansion.* Investments in additional fixed capacity for skiing such as adding new terrain or expanding the number of lifts.

- *Capacity upgrades.* Improving or replacing existing lifts to carry more skiers and/or run faster.

As input to their model, the researchers used historic data on daily demand, demand smoothing and capacity expansion options, service times for each lift, flow patterns across various lifts within the resort, travel time between lifts, customer perceptions, and customer choice data. By combining these marketing and operations data, the researchers showed that retaining the current customer mix, installing two new chairs, and providing waiting

Perform Maintenance and Renovations For almost all services, facilities and equipment need to be repaired and maintained periodically. Such scheduling should take place during periods of slow demand, as should renovations. Universities, for example, frequently arrange for the painting of classrooms or restriping of parking lots to be done when students are on a break.

Schedule Vacations and Employee Training Strategically To ensure that employees are available when most needed, employee vacations and training should take place during periods of slow demand. Some firms adjust capacity by laying employees off when they know demand will be low. Hotels in popular tourist destinations routinely lay time information would maximize profits for the resort. Adding new chair lifts with higher speeds and doubled seating capacity within the existing terrain was a more profitable approach than expanding to new terrain. The simulation model showed that, contrary to management predictions, smoothing demand across the day through differential pricing would actually decrease profits significantly. The model results were also useful in suggesting a priority order for the investments. The wait time signage investment was the least expensive and offered the largest single improvement for customers as well as the largest single profit impact. Upgrading at least one chair lift was the next priority.

Balancing demand and capacity can involve a complex set of decisions, and sometimes the outcomes are not obvious, especially when strategies seem to have contradictory objectives. For example in the PV simulation, a marketing objective of increased revenues through attracting more customers was contradicted by an operations objective of providing optimal wait times for lifts. As illustrated in the ski resort research, firms can combine marketing and operations data into one overall model and run simulated experiments to determine the best set of combined strategies. One company, ProModel, has developed simulations similar to the one described here that have been successfully used by such service providers as American Express, the American Red Cross, Disneyland, Chase Bank, Delta Air Lines, JetBlue, the Mayo Clinic, and UPS. The Salt Lake Organizing Committee for the 2002 Winter Olympics also used a similar simulation to evaluate and successfully optimize spectator flow, emergency planning, and transportation systems. Of course, the quality of the decisions based on simulation models is highly dependent on the accuracy of the assumptions in the model and the quality of the input data.

Managing demand and capacity in ski resorts can be very challenging.

Sources: M. E. Pullman and G. Thompson, "Strategies for Integrating Capacity with Demand in Service Networks," *Journal of Service Research* 5 (February 2003), pp. 169–183; ProModel Corporation (www.promodel.com).

employees off during the off season. In fact, some employees know this well in advance and look forward to working in ski resort hotels in the winter months and coastal resort hotels in the summer months. Throughout all of these strategies, such scheduling attempts to ensure that a provider's resources are in top condition and available when they are most needed.

Modify or Move Facilities and Equipment   Sometimes it is possible to adjust, move, or creatively modify existing capacity to meet demand fluctuations. Hotels utilize this strategy by reconfiguring rooms—two rooms with a locked door between can be rented to two different parties in high demand times or turned into a suite during slow demand.

The airline industry offers another example of this strategy. Using an approach known as "demand-driven dispatch," airlines often assign airplanes to flight schedules on the basis of fluctuating market needs.[9] The method depends on accurate knowledge of demand and the ability to quickly move airplanes with different seating capacities to flight assignments that match their capacity. The Boeing 777 aircraft is so flexible that it can be reconfigured within hours to vary the number of seats allocated to one, two, or three classes.[10] The plane can thus be quickly modified to match demand from different market segments, essentially molding capacity to fit demand. Another strategy may involve moving the service to a new location to meet customer demand or even bringing the service to customers. Mobile training facilities, pet grooming vans, and flu shot and blood donation facilities are examples of services that physically follow customers.

Combining Demand and Capacity Strategies

Many firms use multiple strategies, combining marketing-driven demand management approaches with operations-driven capacity management strategies. Figuring out which is the best set of strategies for maximizing capacity utilization, customer satisfaction, and profitability can be challenging, particularly when the service represents a constellation of offerings within one service setting. Examples of such services include theme parks with rides, restaurants, and shopping; hotel vacation villages with hotels, shopping, spas, pools, and restaurants; and ski resorts with ski slopes, spas, restaurants, and entertainment. Firms face complex problems in trying to balance demand across all the different offerings with an eye to quality and profitability. Our Strategy Insight describes a ski resort simulation that was created to use operations and marketing variables to determine the optimal combination of demand and capacity management strategies across the resort's various offerings and activities.

YIELD MANAGEMENT: BALANCING CAPACITY UTILIZATION, PRICING, MARKET SEGMENTATION, AND FINANCIAL RETURN

Yield management is a term that has become attached to a variety of methods, some very sophisticated, employed to match demand and supply in capacity-constrained services. Using yield management models, organizations find the best balance at a particular point in time among the prices charged, the segments sold to, and the capacity used. The goal of yield management is to produce the best possible financial return from a limited available capacity. Specifically, yield management—also referred to as *revenue management*—attempts to allocate the fixed capacity of a service provider (e.g., seats on a flight, rooms in a hotel, rental cars) to match the potential demand in various market segments (e.g., business traveler, tourist) so as to maximize revenue or yield.[11]

Although the implementation of yield management can involve complex mathematical models and computer programs, the underlying effectiveness measure is the ratio of actual revenue to potential revenue for a particular measurement period:

$$\text{Yield} = \frac{\text{Actual revenue}}{\text{Potential revenue}}$$

where

$$\text{Actual revenue} = \text{Actual capacity used} \times \text{Average actual price}$$

$$\text{Potential revenue} = \text{Total capacity} \times \text{Maximum price}$$

The equations indicate that yield is a function of price and capacity used. Recall that capacity constraints can be in the form of time, labor, equipment, or facilities. Yield is essentially a measure of the extent to which an organization's resources (or capacities)

Basic yield calculations can be done for any capacity-constrained service, assuming the actual capacity, average price charged for different market segments, and maximum price that could be charged are known. Ideally, yield will approach the number 1, or 100 percent, where

Yield = Actual revenue / Potential revenue

In this box we describe yield calculations for two simple examples—a 200-room hotel and a lawyer with a 40-hour work week—under different assumed pricing and usage situations. Although companies use much more complex mathematical models to determine yield, the underlying ideas are the same. The goal is to maximize the revenue-generating capability of the organization's capacity.

200-ROOM HOTEL WITH MAXIMUM ROOM RATE OF $200 PER ROOM PER NIGHT

Potential revenue = $200 × 200 rooms
= $40,000 per night

1. Assume: the hotel rents all its rooms at a discounted rate of $100 per night.

   Yield = ($100 × 200 rooms) / $40,000 = 50%

   At this rate, the hotel is maximizing capacity utilization but not getting a very good price.

2. Assume: the hotel charges its full rate but can only rent 40 percent of its rooms at that price, due to price sensitivity.

   Yield = ($200 × 80 rooms) / $40,000 = 40%

   In this situation the hotel has maximized the per-room price, but the yield is even lower than in the first situation because so few rooms are rented at that relatively high rate.

3. Assume: the hotel charges its full rate of $200 for 40 percent of its rooms and then gives a discount of $100 for the remaining 120 rooms.

Yield = [($200 × 80) + ($100 × 120)] / $40,000
= $28,000 / $40,000 = 70%

Clearly, the final alternative, which takes into account price sensitivity and charges different prices for different rooms or market segments, results in the highest yield among these three alternatives.

40 HOURS OF A LAWYER'S TIME ACROSS A TYPICAL WORK WEEK AT $200 PER HOUR MAXIMUM (PRIVATE CLIENT RATE)

Potential revenue = 40 hours × $200 per hour
= $8,000 per week

1. Assume: the lawyer is able to bill out 30 percent of her billable time at $200 per hour.

   Yield = ($200 × 12 hours) / $8,000 = 30%

   In this case the lawyer has maximized her hourly rate but has only enough work to occupy 12 billable hours.

2. Assume: the lawyer decides to charge $100 for nonprofit or government clients and is able to bill out all 40 hours at this rate for these types of clients.

   Yield = ($100 × 40 hours) / $8,000 = 50%

   In this case, although she has worked a full week, yield is still not very good, given the relatively low rate per hour.

3. Assume: the lawyer uses a combined strategy in which she works 12 hours for private clients and fills the rest of her time with nonprofit clients at $100 per hour.

   Yield = [($200 × 12) + ($100 × 28)] / $8,000
   = $5,200 / $8,000 = 65%

Again, catering to two different market segments with different price sensitivities is the best overall strategy in terms of maximizing revenue-generating capacity of the lawyer's time.

are achieving their full revenue-generating potential. Assuming that total capacity and maximum price cannot be changed, yield approaches a value of 1 as actual capacity utilization increases or when a higher actual price can be charged for a given capacity used. For example, in an airline context, a manager could focus on increasing yield by finding ways to bring in more passengers to fill the capacity or by finding higher-paying passengers to fill a more limited capacity. In reality, expert yield managers work on capacity and pricing issues simultaneously to maximize revenue across different customer segments. Exhibit 13.1 shows simple yield calculations and the inherent trade-offs for two types of services: hotel and legal.

Technology Spotlight Information and Technology Drive Yield Management Systems

Yield management is not a new concept. In fact, the basic idea behind yield management—achieving maximum profits through the most effective use of capacity—has been around forever. It is easy to find examples of capacity-constrained businesses using price to shift demand: theaters that charge different prices for matinees versus evening performances, intercity trains with different prices on weekdays than on weekends, ski resorts with cheaper prices for night skiing, and restaurants with "twilight" dinner specials. All these strategies illustrate attempts to smooth the peaks and valleys of demand using price as the primary motivator.

The difference in these basic pricing strategies and more sophisticated yield management approaches currently in use by airlines, car rental companies, hotels, shippers, and others is the reliance of these latter strategies on massive databases, sophisticated mathematical algorithms, and complex analyses. These forms of yield management consider not only price but also market segments, price sensitivity among segments, timing of demand, and potential profitability of customer segments—all simultaneously. What makes new forms of yield management possible are the technology and systems underlying them. Here are a few examples of what some companies and industries have done.

AMERICAN AIRLINES

American Airlines is the original pioneer and still the king of yield management. Beginning with Super Saver Fares in the mid-1970s, American has depended on systems developed by Sabre (the oldest and leading provider of technology for the travel industry) to support an exceedingly complex system of fares. Using a system of models containing algorithms that optimize prices, manage wait lists, and handle traffic management, American uses Sabre to allocate seats on every one of its flights. The number of seats sold on each of American's flights is continuously compared with a sales forecast for that flight. Blocks of seats are moved from higher to lower fares if sales are below projections. If sales are at or above the forecast, no changes are made. American's stated objective has historically been to "sell the right seats to the right customers at the right price."

AIR BERLIN

Air Berlin, Germany's second largest airline, provides relatively low-cost services to popular European holiday destinations, as well as to major cities in Europe, from more than 20 German airports and uses yield management in an effort to maximize passenger revenue. Its yield management process begins six to nine months prior to a flight's scheduled departure date. Air Berlin often

Implementing a Yield Management System

Our Technology Spotlight illustrates several examples of how information technology supports effective yield management applications. To implement a yield management system, an organization needs detailed data on past demand patterns by market segment as well as methods of projecting current market demand. The data can be combined through mathematical programming models, threshold analysis, or expert systems to project the best allocation of limited capacity at a particular point in time.[12] Allocations of capacity for specific market segments can then be communicated to sales representatives or reservations staff as targets for selling rooms, seats, time, or other limited resources. Sometimes the allocations, once determined, remain fixed. At other times allocations change weekly, or even daily or hourly, in response to new information.

sells initial blocks of seats at what it terms "headline prices" to price-sensitive customers and tour operators; any seats not initially sold are then managed through Air Berlin's yield management technology. Its yield management system requires massive amounts of data that take into account the season when the flight takes place, general popularity of the route, local holiday schedules and upcoming events, and exact time of departure. Similar to other airlines, Air Berlin adjusts its fares frequently, sometimes several times a day as the flight's departure date nears, to reflect customer demand and the time remaining until the departure date. However, because Air Berlin's focus is on relatively short routes, it offers only a single class of service on all of its flights and each flight is available on a one-way ticket basis. This practice means that each flight is subject to its own price management, enabling Air Berlin to charge passengers different fares on outbound flights and return flights. By developing profiles for each flight, Air Berlin's yield management technology helps it maximize passenger revenue by flight and by regions while maintaining high passenger load factors.

MARRIOTT HOTELS

The hotel industry has also embraced the concepts of yield management, and Marriott Hotels has been a leader. The systems at Marriott, for example, maximize

profits for a hotel across full weeks rather than by day. In its hotels that target business travelers, Marriott has peak days during the middle of the week. Rather than simply sell the hotel out on those nights on a first-come, first-served basis with no discounts, the revenue management system (which is reviewed and revised daily) projects guest demand both by price and by length of stay, providing discounts in some cases to guests who will stay longer, even on a peak demand night. One early test of the system was at the Munich Marriott during Oktoberfest. Typically, no discounts would be offered during this peak period. However, the yield management system recommended that the hotel offer some rooms at a discount, but only for those guests who stayed an extended period before or after the peak days. Although the average daily rate went down 11.7 percent for the period, occupancy went up more than 20 percent and overall revenues went up 12.3 percent. Using yield management practices, Marriott Hotels estimates it generates an additional $400 million per year in revenue.

Sources: The primary source for this Technology Spotlight is R. G. Cross, *Revenue Management* (New York: Broadway Books, 1997). Other sources include "Dynamic Pricing at American Airlines," *Business Quarterly* 61 (Autumn 1996), p. 45; Air Berlin's 2006 Company Prospectus and website (www.airberlin.com); and N. Templin, "Your Room Costs $250 . . . No! $200 . . . No," *The Wall Street Journal,* May 5, 1999, p. B1.

Research indicates that traditional yield management approaches are most appropriate for service firms when:

1. They have relatively fixed capacity.
2. They have perishable inventory.
3. They have different market segments or customers, who arrive or make their reservations at different times.
4. They have low marginal sales costs and high marginal capacity change costs.
5. The product is sold in advance.
6. There is fluctuating demand.
7. Customers who arrive or reserve early are more price sensitive than those who arrive or reserve late.[13]

When these conditions are present, yield management approaches can generally be employed to identify the best mix of service offerings to produce and sell in the period, and at what prices, to generate the highest expected revenue. These criteria exactly fit the situation for airlines, car rental agencies, and many hotels—industries that have effectively and extensively used yield management techniques to allocate capacity. In other services (entertainment, sports, fashion), those customers willing to pay the higher prices are the ones who buy early rather than late. People who really want to see a particular performance reserve their seats at the earliest possible moment. Discounting for early purchases would reduce profits. In these situations, the price generally starts out high and is reduced later to fill capacity if needed.

Interestingly, some airlines use both these strategies effectively. They start with discounted seats for customers who are willing to buy early, usually leisure and discretionary travelers. They charge a higher fare for those who want a seat at the last minute, typically the less-price-sensitive business travelers whose destinations and schedules are inflexible. However, in some cases a bargain fare can be found at the last minute as well, commonly via Internet sales, to fill seats that would otherwise go unoccupied. Online auctions and services offered by companies like Priceline.com or Expedia.com serve a purpose in filling capacity at the last minute, often charging much lower fares. (See the Technology Spotlight in Chapter 15 for examples of dynamic pricing via the Internet.)

Challenges and Risks in Using Yield Management

Yield management programs can significantly improve revenues. However, although yield management may appear to be an ideal solution to the problem of matching supply and demand, it is not without risks. By becoming focused on maximizing financial returns through differential capacity allocation and pricing, an organization may encounter these problems:[14]

- *Loss of competitive focus.* Yield management may cause a firm to overfocus on profit maximization and inadvertently neglect aspects of the service that provide long-term competitive success.

- *Customer alienation.* If customers learn that they are paying a higher price for service than someone else, they may perceive the pricing as unfair, particularly if they do not understand the reasons. However, a study done in the restaurant industry found that, when customers were informed of different prices being charged by time of day, week, or table location, they generally felt the practice was fair, particularly if the price difference was framed as a discount for less desirable times rather than a premium for peak times or table locations.[15] Customer education is thus essential in an effective yield management program.

- *Overbooking.* Customers can be further alienated if they fall victim (and are not compensated adequately) to the overbooking practices often necessary to make yield management systems work effectively. Research suggests that customers who experience negative consequences of revenue management (i.e., denied service or downgrades), particularly high-value customers, subsequently reduce their number of transactions with the firm.[16]

- *Incompatible incentive and reward systems.* Employees may resent yield management systems that do not match incentive structures. For example, many managers are rewarded on the basis of capacity utilization *or* average rate charged, whereas yield management balances the two factors.

- *Inappropriate organization of the yield management function.* To be most effective with yield management, an organization must have centralized reservations.

Although airlines and some large hotel chains and shipping companies do have such centralization, smaller organizations may have decentralized reservations systems and thus find it difficult to operate a yield management system effectively.

WAITING LINE STRATEGIES: WHEN DEMAND AND CAPACITY CANNOT BE MATCHED

Sometimes it is not possible to manage capacity to precisely match demand, or vice versa. It may be too costly—for example, most health clinics would not find it economically feasible to add facilities or physicians to handle peaks in demand during the winter flu season; patients usually simply have to wait to be seen. Or demand may be very unpredictable and the service capacity very inflexible (it cannot be easily stretched to match unpredictable peaks in demand). Sometimes waits occur when demand backs up because of the variability in length of time for service. For example, even though patients are scheduled by appointments in a physician's office, frequently there is a wait because some patients take longer to serve than the time allotted to them. The misalignment in capacity and demand is particularly troublesome in emergency health care, as is described in Exhibit 13.2.

For most service organizations, waiting customers are a fact of life at some point. Waiting can occur on the telephone (customers put on hold when they call in to ask for information, order something, or make a complaint) and in person (customers waiting in line at the bank, the post office, Disneyland, or a physician's office). Waiting can occur even with service transactions through the mail—delays in mail-order delivery—or backlogs of correspondence on a manager's desk.

In today's fast-paced society, waiting is not something most people tolerate well. As people work longer hours, as individuals have less leisure time, and as families have fewer hours together, the pressure on people's time is greater than ever. In this environment, customers are looking for efficient, quick service with no wait. Organizations that make customers wait may lose business or at the very least create dissatisfied customers.[17] Research suggests that waiting time satisfaction is nearly as important as service delivery satisfaction with respect to customer loyalty.[18] To deal effectively with the inevitability of waits, organizations can utilize a variety of strategies; four general strategies are described next.

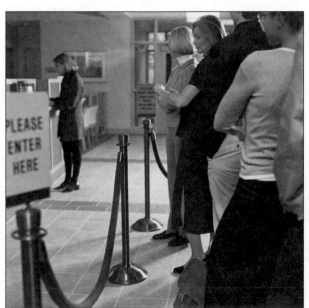
Customer satisfaction is heavily dependent on the amount of time customers spend waiting for a service.

Employ Operational Logic

If customer waits are common, a first step is to analyze the operational processes to remove any inefficiencies. It may be possible to redesign the system to move customers along more quickly. In introducing its express check-in, Marriott Hotels used an operations-based modification to eliminate much of the waiting previously experienced by its guests. Guests who use a credit card and preregister can avoid waiting in line at the hotel front desk altogether. The guest can make it from the curb outside the hotel to his or her room in as little as three

Nowhere is there a more vivid example of demand and capacity issues than in the nearly 5,000 emergency departments (EDs) in hospitals across the United States (*emergency department* is the preferred term within the medical community for what has traditionally been called the ER). In a typical ED, rooms are filled, the corridors may be clogged with waiting patients, wait time may be anywhere from 15 minutes to 8 or 10 hours, and ambulances are routinely turned away to seek other hospitals on what is called "reroute" or "diversion." Many experts have referred to these issues as a national crisis in health care. The emergency department is the front door of hospitals and is the treatment of last resort for many. Why has this overcrowding issue reached national proportions? Many factors come into play, including increased demand and severe capacity constraints.

INCREASED DEMAND FOR SERVICES

Emergency departments are to some extent victims of their own success. Decades of public health campaigns urging people to call 911 in case of medical emergency have been successful in educating people to do just that—and they end up in the ED. Many do indeed have life-threatening emergencies that belong in the ED. Others waiting in the ED are uninsured; as of 2010, more than 50 million people in the United States were uninsured. The ED is their only option, and legally the ED must care for them. But it is not only the uninsured and those with life-threatening emergencies who crowd the ED. It is also insured patients who cannot get appointments with their doctors in a timely manner or who learn that it may be their fastest entry into a hospital bed. Patients and their doctors are becoming aware that they can get sophisticated care in the ED relatively quickly. Thus, the demand for ED services has increased.

CAPACITY CONSTRAINTS

It is not just an increase in demand that is causing the overcrowding. It is also a shrinkage or unavailability of critical capacity at the same time. Doctors are overbooked in private practices, so patients who do not want to wait turn to the ED. Also, a shortage of specialists who

are willing to take patients on call from the ED results in increased waiting times because these patients waiting for specialized care occupy beds in the ED longer than necessary. Another very critical capacity constraint is the number of beds in hospitals. Over the years, many hospitals across the country have closed for financial reasons, reducing the number of beds available. So ED patients often cannot get beds right away even if they need one, increasing waiting time for themselves and others. There is a critical shortage of nurses as well, and a hospital bed requires a nurse to attend it before it can be occupied. In the 1990s enrollment in nursing programs slumped as people turned to more lucrative careers, and as of 2008 the average age of a registered nurse was 47. Many hospitals have 20 percent of their nursing slots empty. Staffing shortages in housekeeping also play a role. A bed may be empty, but until it is cleaned and remade, it is not available for a waiting patient. In some communities, patients may find that ED facilities are simply not available. Some hospitals have actually closed their emergency departments after determining that it is unprofitable to run them because of poor reimbursement rates. In other areas, population growth is outpacing hospital and ED construction.

minutes when escorted by a "guest service associate," who checks the guest into the hotel, picks up keys and paperwork from a rack in the lobby, and then escorts the guest directly to the room.[19] The U.S. Department of Transportation Security Administration (TSA) offers similar preferential treatment for selected frequent travelers through its "Registered Traveler Program."[20] Only U.S. citizens and permanent legal residents who meet certain flying criteria may apply. After registering with the system and

HOSPITALS' RESPONSES

To address this complex set of issues, a few changes have been made.

Technology

A partial solution has been to turn to technology to smooth the process of admitting patients into the ED and to track the availability of hospital beds. Some web-based systems are used to reroute ambulances to hospitals that have capacity. Other systems help EDs track the availability of rooms in their own hospitals in terms of knowing exactly when a bed is vacant and when it has been cleaned and is available—similar to what hotels have done for decades. Wireless systems for registering patients at bedside and "radar screens" that track everything going on in the ED are other partial solutions. These screens can track patients, staff, carts, and equipment, making the service delivery process more efficient and quicker.

Systems Improvements

Other hospitals have segmented their patients and have developed parallel "fast track" processes for dealing with minor emergency patients that can account for 30 to 50 percent of total visits. This process can be separated from the major-emergency situations that may require more time and special equipment. Quicker admitting processes are also being implemented. Kiosks have been installed in some hospitals to allow emergency patients to check themselves in and describe their symptoms to help speed up the admission process. Patients who are not experiencing true emergencies (true emergencies being gunshot victims or car accident victims with serious injuries) use touch screens to enter their name, age, and other personal information. Such kiosks display a list of ailments to choose from, like "pain" or "fever and/or chills," and a list of body parts to indicate where the discomfort is occurring. Once a patient's problem is entered into the system, it pops up on a screen accessible to nurses; those with chest pains, stroke symptoms, or other potentially serious issues take priority.

Yet another innovation is to have staff administer routine tests while the patient is waiting, so that the doctor who finally sees the patient has information at hand. This solution also satisfies the patient's need for "something to happen" during the waiting time. Giving patients pagers so they can do something else while waiting is another way that EDs are helping patients cope with the long waits.

Increasing Capacity

Another set of partial solutions relates directly to hospital and staff capacity issues. Some hospitals have added rooms and other facilities. More urgent care centers are being built to take some of the pressure off EDs. For patients who need to be admitted to the hospital, however, increasing capacity is not a total solution. The nursing shortage, one of the most critical problems, is very difficult to solve. Individual hospital systems have gotten creative in their efforts to steal nurses away from other hospitals, even recruiting heavily overseas. However, in the long term the solution rests more in making the occupation attractive in salaries and working conditions, thus increasing the number of people entering nursing programs.

It is obvious that this classic dilemma of matching supply and demand in a service context such as emergency care has multiple, deeply rooted causes. The solutions to the issues are also multifaceted—some can be undertaken by individual hospitals, whereas others need to be addressed by the entire health care industry.

Sources: L. Landro, "ERs Now Turn to Technology to Help Deal with Overcapacity," *The Wall Street Journal,* July 13, 2001, p. B1; J. Snyder, "Curing the ER," *The Arizona Republic,* December 9, 2001, pp. D1+; N. Shute and M. B. Marcus, CODE BLUE "Crisis in the ER," *US News & World Report,* September 10, 2001 pp. 54–61; U.S. Census Bureau; 2008 Nursing Shortage Fact Sheet, http://www.aacn.nche.edu/media/pdf/NrsgShortageFS.pdf, accessed December 27, 2010; J. Stengle, "ER Kiosks Let Patients Avoid Long Lines," *Associated Press,* September 13, 2007; R. Wolf, "Number of Uninsured Americans Rises to 50.7 Million," *USA* Today, September 17, 2010.

clearing an extensive background check, travelers who qualify for this program are allowed to bypass the usual security checkpoint in their designated airport and instead be screened through a security system that reads either their fingerprints or the irises in their eyes. They must still go through a metal detector and their bags are still passed through an X-ray scanner, but they get their own special line and are not randomly selected for additional screening.

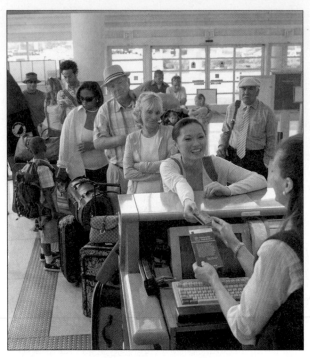

Waiting is common in many service industries.

When queues are inevitable, the organization faces the operational decision of what kind of queuing system to use or how to configure the queue. *Queue configuration* refers to the number of queues, their locations, their spatial requirement, and their effect on customer behavior.[21] Several possibilities exist, as shown in Figure 13.4. In the multiple-queue alternative, the customer arrives at the service facility and must decide which queue to join and whether to switch later if the wait appears to be shorter in another line. In the single-queue alternative, fairness of waiting time is ensured in that the first-come, first-served rule applies to everyone; the system can also reduce the average time customers spend waiting overall. However, customers may leave if they perceive that the line is too long or if they have no opportunity to select a particular service provider. The last option shown in Figure 13.4 is the take-a-number option, in which arriving customers take a number to indicate line position. Advantages are similar to the single-queue alternative with the additional benefit that customers are able to mill about, browse, and talk to each other. The disadvantage is that customers must be on the alert to hear their numbers when they are called. Research suggests that length of the queue and perceived cost of waiting are not the only influences on customers' likelihood of staying in line. In a series of experiments and field tests, researchers showed that, the larger the number of customers waiting in line *behind* a consumer, the more likely that consumer is to stay in line and wait for the service.[22]

Establish a Reservation Process

When waiting cannot be avoided, a reservation system can help to spread demand. Restaurants, transportation companies, theaters, physicians, and many other service

FIGURE 13.4
Waiting Line Configurations

Source: J. A. Fitzsimmons and M. J. Fitzsimmons, *Service Management,* 7th ed. (New York: Irwin/McGraw-Hill, 2011), chap. 12, p. 311. © 2011 by The McGraw-Hill Companies, Inc. Reprinted by permission of The McGraw-Hill Companies.

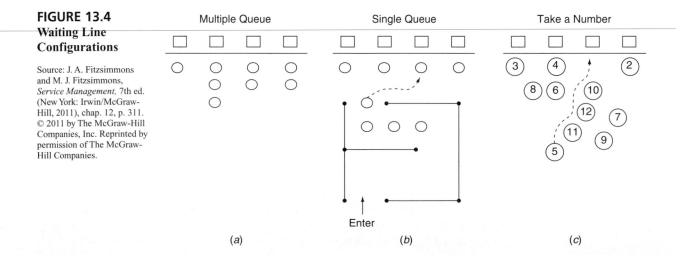

providers use reservation systems to alleviate long waits. The California Department of Motor Vehicles allows customers to make appointments via the Internet to help reduce the time they must spend waiting at its offices. The idea behind a reservation system is to guarantee the service will be available when the customer arrives. Beyond simply reducing waiting time, a reservation system has the added benefit of potentially shifting demand to less desirable time periods. A challenge inherent in reservation systems, however, is what to do about "no shows." Inevitably there will be customers who reserve a time but do not show up. Some organizations deal with this problem by overbooking their service capacity on the basis of past records of no-show percentages. If the predictions are accurate, overbooking is a good solution. When predictions are inaccurate, however, customers may still have to wait and sometimes may not be served at all, as when airlines overbook the number of seats available on a flight. Victims of overbooking may be compensated for their inconvenience in such cases. To minimize the no-show problem, some organizations (such as hotels, airlines, conferences/training programs, and theaters) charge customers who fail to show up or to cancel their reservations within a certain time frame.

Differentiate Waiting Customers

Not all customers need to wait the same length of time for service. On the basis of need or customer priority, some organizations differentiate among customers, allowing some to experience shorter waits for service than others. Known as "queue discipline," such differentiation reflects management policies regarding whom to select next for service.[23] The most popular discipline is first-come, first-served. However, other rules may apply. Differentiation can be based on factors such as these:[24]

- *Importance of the customer.* Frequent customers or customers who spend large amounts with the organization can be given priority in service by providing them with a special waiting area or segregated lines.
- *Urgency of the job.* Those customers with the most urgent need may be served first. This strategy is used in emergency health care. It is also used by maintenance services such as air-conditioning repair that give priority to customers whose air conditioning is not functioning over those who call for routine maintenance.
- *Duration of the service transaction.* In many situations, shorter service jobs get priority through "express lanes." At other times, when a service provider sees that a transaction is going to require extra time, the customer is referred to a designated provider who deals only with these special-needs customers.
- *Payment of a premium price.* Customers who pay extra (e.g., first class on an airline) are often given priority via separate check-in lines or express systems. At several Six Flags amusement parks, groups of up to six customers can purchase a Flashpass for about $45 per person (in addition to park entrance fees). Doing so allows them to use a palm-sized device, which is inserted at signs near the popular rides throughout the park, to keep their place in line virtually. The device sends a signal 10 minutes before it is time to come back and get on the ride (through a separate entrance), allowing customers to visit other attractions in the park without having to spend as much time in line. A "Gold" Flashpass can also be purchased, for about $35 more, to move customers up in a queue so that they experience very little or even no wait, and for $70 more a "Platinum" pass can be purchased that allows customers to ride a ride twice consecutively.[25] In recent years a variation of this service, Text-Q, developed by a company called Lo-Q, allows mobile phone users to reserve their place in

line by sending text messages. To use this service customers pay for a specified number of credits, which can then be used to avoid standing in a queue at amusement parks.[26]

Make Waiting More Pleasurable

Even when they have to wait, customers can still be satisfied, depending on how the wait is handled by the organization. Of course, the actual length of the wait will affect how customers feel about their service experience. But it is not just the actual time spent waiting that has an impact on customer satisfaction—it is how customers feel about the wait and their perceptions during it. The type of wait (e.g., a standard queue versus a wait due to a delay of service) can also influence how customers will react.[27] In a classic article entitled "The Psychology of Waiting Lines," David Maister proposes several principles about waiting, each of which has implications for how organizations can make waiting more pleasurable.[28]

Unoccupied Time Feels Longer Than Occupied Time

When customers are unoccupied they will likely be bored and will notice the passage of time more than when they have something to do. Providing something for waiting customers to do, particularly if the activity offers a benefit in and of itself or is related in some way to the service, can improve the customer's experience and may benefit the organization as well.[29] Examples include giving customers menus to look at while waiting in a restaurant, providing interesting information to read in a dentist's office, and playing entertaining programs over the phone while customers are on hold.

Preprocess Waits Feel Longer Than In-Process Waits

If wait time is occupied with activities that relate to the upcoming service, customers may perceive that the service has started and that they are no longer actually waiting. This in-process activity will make the length of the wait seem shorter and will benefit the service provider by making the customer better prepared when the service actually does begin. Filling out medical information while waiting to see the physician, reading a menu while waiting to be seated in a restaurant, and watching a videotape of the upcoming service event are all activities that can both educate the customer and reduce perceptions of waiting.

Research in a restaurant context has found that customers react more negatively to preprocess waits than to either in-process or postprocess waits; that is, preprocess waits are relatively more important in determining customers' overall satisfaction.[30] Other researchers have found that, if a wait is due to routine slowness of the process, then preprocess waits produce the most negative impact. However, if the wait is due to a service failure, then the in-process wait is viewed more negatively than the preprocess wait.[31] Thus, how customers perceive preprocess, in-process, and postprocess waits may depend to some extent on the cause of the wait.

Anxiety Makes Waits Seem Longer

When customers fear that they have been forgotten or do not know how long they will have to wait, they become anxious, and this anxiety can increase the negative impact of waiting. Anxiety also results when customers are forced to choose in a multiple-line situation and they discover they have chosen the "wrong" line. To combat waiting line anxiety, organizations can provide information on the length of the wait. At its theme parks, Disney uses signs at intervals along the line that let customers know how long the wait will be from that point on. Using a single line also alleviates customer anxiety over having chosen the wrong line. Explanations and reassurances that no one has forgotten them alleviate customer anxiety by taking away their cause for worry.

Uncertain Waits Are Longer Than Known, Finite Waits

Anxiety is intensified when customers do not know how long they will have to wait. Health care providers combat this problem by letting customers know when they check in how far behind the physician is that day. Some patients resolve this uncertainty themselves by calling ahead to ask. Maister provides an interesting example of the role of uncertainty, which he terms the "appointment syndrome."[32] Customers who arrive early for an appointment will wait patiently until the scheduled time, even if they arrive very early. However, once the expected appointment time has passed, customers grow increasingly anxious. Before the appointment time the wait time is known; after that, the length of the wait is not known.

Research in an airline context has suggested that, as uncertainty about a wait increases, customers become angrier, and their anger results in greater dissatisfaction.[33] Research also shows that giving customers information on the length of the anticipated wait and/or their relative position in the queue can result in more positive feelings and acceptance of the wait and ultimately more positive evaluation of the service.[34]

Unexplained Waits Are Longer Than Explained Waits

When people understand the causes for waiting, they frequently have greater patience and are less anxious, particularly when the wait is justifiable. An explanation can reduce customer uncertainty and may help customers estimate how long they will be delayed. One of us, when waiting once with our children to see a pediatrician, was told that the doctor was delayed because another child had arrived with possible life-threatening injuries and he chose to focus his attention on that child. As a parent who would want the same treatment for our children, the amount of extra wait time was acceptable—much more so than if there had been no explanation at all and we were left to think that perhaps the doctor had not yet arrived from his early morning trip to the golf course. Customers who do not know the reason for a wait begin to feel powerless and irritated.

Unfair Waits Are Longer Than Equitable Waits

When customers perceive that they are waiting while others who arrived after them have already been served, the apparent inequity will make the wait seem even longer. This situation can easily occur when there is no apparent order in the waiting area and many customers are trying to be served. Queuing systems that work on a first-come, first-served rule are best at combating perceived unfairness. However, other approaches may be required to determine who will be served next. For example, in an emergency medical care situation, the most seriously ill or injured patients would be seen first. When customers understand the priorities and the rules are clearly communicated and enforced, they will tend to see the wait as fair and the negative effects of having to wait will tend to be significantly dampened.[35]

The More Valuable the Service, the Longer the Customer Will Wait

Customers who have substantial purchases or who are waiting for a high-value service will be more tolerant of long wait times and may even expect to wait longer. For example, customers waiting to see a lawyer might consider a 15-minute wait to be acceptable, whereas the same wait at a convenience store might be considered completely unacceptable. In a supermarket, customers who have a full cart of groceries will generally wait longer than customers who have only a few items. And diners expect to wait longer for service in an expensive restaurant than they do when eating at a "greasy spoon."

Solo Waits Feel Longer Than Group Waits

People are more accepting of a longer wait when they are in a group than when they are alone because of the distractions provided by other members of the group. People also feel comfort in waiting with a group rather than alone.[36] In some group waiting situations, such as at Disneyland or when patrons are waiting in long lines to purchase concert tickets, customers who are strangers begin to talk to each other and the waiting experience can become a fun part of the total service experience.

Summary

Because service organizations lack the ability to inventory their products, the effective use of capacity can be critical to success. Idle capacity in the form of unused time, labor, facilities, or equipment represents a direct drain on bottom-line profitability. When the capacity represents a major investment (e.g., airplanes, expensive medical imaging equipment, or lawyers and physicians paid on a salary), the losses associated with underuse of capacity are even more accentuated. Overused capacity can also be a problem. People, facilities, and equipment can become worn out over time when used beyond optimal capacity. People can quit, facilities can become run down, and equipment can break. From the customer's perspective, service quality also deteriorates. Organizations focused on delivering quality service, therefore, have a natural drive to balance capacity utilization and demand at an optimal level in order to meet customer expectations.

Based on grounding in the fundamental issues, the chapter presented a variety of strategies for matching supply and demand. The basic strategies fall under two headings: *demand strategies* (shifting demand to match capacity) and *capacity strategies* (adjusting capacity to meet demand). Demand strategies seek to flatten the peaks and valleys of demand to match the flat capacity constraint, whereas capacity strategies seek to align, flex, or stretch capacity to match the peaks and valleys of demand. Organizations frequently employ several strategies simultaneously to solve the complex problem of balancing supply and demand.

Yield management is a sophisticated form of supply and demand management that balances capacity utilization, pricing, market segmentation, and financial return. This strategy is used by airline, hotel, shipping, car rental, and other capacity-constrained industries in which bookings are made in advance. Essentially, yield management allows organizations to decide on a monthly, weekly, daily, or even hourly basis to whom they want to sell their service capacity at what price.

In the last section of the chapter, we discussed situations in which it is not possible to align supply and demand. In these unresolved capacity utilization situations, the inevitable result is customer waiting. We described strategies for effectively managing waiting lines, such as employing operational logic, establishing a reservation process, differentiating waiting customers, and making waiting more pleasurable, or at least tolerable.

Discussion Questions

1. Why do service organizations lack the capability to inventory their services? Compare a car repair and maintenance service with an automobile manufacturer/dealer in terms of inventory capability.
2. Discuss the four scenarios illustrated in Figure 13.1 and presented in the text (excess demand, demand exceeds optimal capacity, demand and supply are balanced,

excess capacity) in the context of a professional basketball team selling seats for its games. What are the challenges for management under each scenario?

3. Discuss the four common types of constraints (time, labor, equipment, facilities) facing service businesses, and give an example of each (real or hypothetical).

4. How does optimal capacity utilization differ from maximum capacity utilization? Give an example of a situation in which the two might be the same and one in which they are different.

5. Choose a local restaurant or some other type of service with fluctuating demand. What is the likely underlying pattern of demand? What causes the pattern? Is it predictable or random?

6. Describe the two basic strategies for matching supply and demand, and give at least two specific examples of each.

7. What is yield management? Discuss the risks in adopting a yield management strategy.

8. How might yield management apply in the management of the following: a Broadway theater? a consulting firm? a commuter train?

9. Describe the four basic waiting line strategies, and give an example of each one, preferably based on your own experiences as a consumer.

Exercises

1. Choose a local service organization that is challenged by fixed capacity and fluctuating demand. Interview the marketing manager (or other knowledgeable person) to learn (a) in what ways capacity is constrained, (b) the basic patterns of demand, and (c) strategies the organization has used to align supply and demand. Write up the answers to these questions, and make your own recommendations regarding other strategies the organization might use.

2. Assume you manage a winter ski resort in Colorado or Banff, Canada. (a) Explain the underlying pattern of demand fluctuation likely to occur at your resort and the challenges it would present to you as a manager. Is the pattern of demand predictable or random? (b) Explain and give examples of how you might use both demand-oriented and capacity-oriented strategies to smooth the peaks and valleys of demand during peak and slow periods.

3. Choose a local organization in which people have to wait in line for service. Design a waiting line strategy for the organization.

4. Visit the website of Wells Fargo Bank (www.wellsfargo.com), a leader in online banking. What online services does the bank currently offer? How do these online services help Wells Fargo manage the peaks and valleys of customer demand? How do its strategies to use more ATMs, in-store bank branches, and other alternative delivery strategies complement the online strategies?

Notes

1. www.ritzcarlton.com, accessed January, 2011.
2. C. Lovelock, "Getting the Most Out of Your Productive Capacity," in *Product Plus* (New York: McGraw-Hill, 1994), chap. 16.
3. C. H. Lovelock, "Classifying Services to Gain Strategic Marketing Insights," *Journal of Marketing* 47 (Summer 1983), pp. 9–20.
4. Portions of this section are based on C. H. Lovelock, "Strategies for Managing Capacity-Constrained Service Organizations," in *Managing Services: Marketing,*

Operations, and Human Resources, 2nd ed. (Englewood Cliffs, NJ: Prentice Hall, 1992), pp. 154–168.

5. "Cable Company Provides Emergency Services Following Hurricane Katrina" case study on Cisco website, http://www.cisco.com/en/US/netsol/ns522/networking_solutions_customer_profile0900aecd8049247c.html, accessed October 2007.

6. M. Arndt, "Knock Knock, It's Your Big Mac," *BusinessWeek,* July 23, 2007, p. 36.

7. G. Bounds, "A Production with 37,500 Extras," *The Wall Street Journal,* December 22, 2010, pp. B1-B2

8. Lovelock, "Getting the Most Out of Your Productive Capacity."

9. J. M. Feldman, "Matching Planes to Demand," *Air Transport World* 39 (December 2002), pp. 31–33; J. M. Feldman, "IT Systems Start to Converge," *Air Transport World* 37 (September 2000), pp. 78–81.

10. Boeing website, http://www.boeing.com, accessed September 27, 2007.

11. See J. A. Fitzsimmons and M. J. Fitzsimmons, *Service Management: Operations, Strategy, and Information Technology,* 7th ed. (New York: McGraw-Hill, 2011), pp. 278–284; S. E. Kimes, "Yield Management: A Tool for Capacity-Constrained Service Firms," *Journal of Operations Management* 8 (October 1989), pp. 348–363; S. E. Kimes and R. B. Chase, "The Strategic Levers of Yield Management," *Journal of Service Research* 1 (November 1998), pp. 156–166; and S. E. Kimes, "Revenue Management: A Retrospective," *Cornell Hotel and Restaurant Administration Quarterly* 44, no. 5/6 (2003), pp. 131–138.

12. Kimes, "Yield Management."

13. R. Desiraji and S. M. Shugan, "Strategic Service Pricing and Yield Management," *Journal of Marketing* 63 (January 1999), pp. 44–56; Fitzsimmons and Fitzsimmons, *Service Management,* chap. 12, p. 311.

14. Kimes, "Yield Management."

15. S. E. Kimes and J. Wirtz, "Has Revenue Management Become Acceptable? Findings from an International Study on the Perceived Fairness of Rate Fences," *Journal of Service Research* 6 (November 2003), pp. 125–135.

16. F. v. Wangenheim and T. Bayón, "Behavioral Consequences of Overbooking Service Capacity," *Journal of Marketing* 71 (October 2007), pp. 36–47.

17. For research supporting the relationship between longer waits and decreased satisfaction, quality evaluations, and patronage intentions, see A. Pruyn and A. Smidts, "Customer Evaluation of Queues: Three Exploratory Studies," *European Advances in Consumer Research* 1 (1993), pp. 371–382; S. Taylor, "Waiting for Service: The Relationship between Delays and Evaluations of Service," *Journal of Marketing* 58 (April 1994), pp. 56–69; K. L. Katz, B. M. Larson, and R. C. Larson, "Prescription for the Waiting-in-Line Blues: Entertain, Enlighten, and Engage," *Sloan Management Review* 33 (Winter 1991), pp. 44–53; S. Taylor and J. D. Claxton, "Delays and the Dynamics of Service Evaluations," *Journal of the Academy of Marketing Science* 22 (Summer 1994), pp. 254–264; and D. Grewal, J. Baker, M. Levy, and G. B. Voss, "The Effects of Wait Expectations and Store Atmosphere on Patronage Intentions in Service-Intensive Retail Stores," *Journal of Retailing* 79 (Winter 2003), pp. 259–268.

18. F. Bielen and N. Demoulin, "Waiting Time Influence on the Satisfaction-Loyalty Relationship in Services," *Managing Service Quality* 17, no. 2 (2007), pp. 174–193.

19. R. Henkoff, "Finding, Training, and Keeping the Best Service Workers," *Fortune,* October 3, 1994, pp. 110–122.

20. E. Anderson, "Registered Traveler Land Opens Tomorrow at Airport," *Albany Times Union,* August 1, 2007, accessed via http://blog.timesunion.com/business/registered-traveler-lane-opens-tomorrow-at-airport/1870/ on December 27, 2010.

21. Fitzsimmons and Fitzsimmons, *Service Management,* chap. 12.

22. R. Zhou and D. Soman, "Looking Back: Exploring the Psychology of Queuing and the Effect of the Number of People Behind," *Journal of Consumer Research* 29 (March 2003), pp. 517–530.

23. Fitzsimmons and Fitzsimmons, *Service Management,* chap. 12.

24. Lovelock, "Getting the Most Out of Your Productive Capacity."

25. For example, see the Six Flags website, http://www.sixflags.com/greatadventure/tickets/flashpass.aspx, accessed December 27, 2010.

26. Lo-Q website, http://www.lo-q.com, accessed December 27, 2010.

27. For an excellent review of the literature on customer perceptions of and reactions to various aspects of waiting time, see S. Taylor and G. Fullerton, "Waiting for Services: Perceptions Management of the Wait Experience," in *Handbook of Services Marketing and Management,* ed. T. A. Swartz and D. Iacobucci (Thousand Oaks, CA: Sage, 2000), pp. 171–189.

28. D. A. Maister, "The Psychology of Waiting Lines," in *The Service Encounter,* ed. J. A. Czepiel, M. R. Solomon, and C. F. Surprenant (Lexington, MA: Lexington Books, 1985), pp. 113–123. For a recent study on the psychology of customer waiting, see K. A. McGuire, S. E. Kimes, M. Lynn, M. Pullman, and R. C. Lloyd, "A Framework for Evaluating the Customer Wait Experience," *Journal of Service Management* 21, no. 3 (2010), pp. 269–290.

29. S. Taylor, "The Effects of Filled Waiting Time and Service Provider Control over the Delay on Evaluations of Service," *Journal of the Academy of Marketing Science* 23 (Summer 1995), pp. 38–48.

30. R. L. Hensley and J. Sulek, "Customer Satisfaction with Waits in Multi-stage Services," *Managing Service Quality* 17, no. 2 (2007), pp. 152–173.

31. M. K. Hui, M. V. Thakor, and R. Gill, "The Effect of Delay Type and Service Stage on Consumers' Reactions to Waiting," *Journal of Consumer Research* 24 (March 1998), pp. 469–479.

32. Maister, "The Psychology of Waiting Lines."

33. Taylor and Fullerton, "Waiting for Services."

34. M. K. Hui and D. K. Tse, "What to Tell Consumers in Waits of Different Lengths: An Integrative Model of Service Evaluation," *Journal of Marketing* 60 (April 1996), pp. 81–90.

35. C. M. Voorhees, J. Baker, B. L. Bourdeau, E. D. Brocato, and J. J. Cronin Jr., "It Depends: Moderating the Relationships among Perceived Waiting Time, Anger, and Regret," *Journal of Service Research* 12 (November 2009), pp. 138-155.

36. J. Baker and M. Cameron, "The Effects of the Service Environment on Affect and Consumer Perception of Waiting Time: An Integrative Review and Research Propositions," *Journal of the Academy of Marketing Science* 24 (Fall 1996), pp. 338–349.

Part Six

Managing Service Promises

Chapter 14 Integrated Service Marketing Communications

Chapter 15 Pricing of Services

The fourth provider gap, shown in the accompanying figure, illustrates the difference between service delivery and the service provider's external communications. Promises made by a service company through its media advertising, sales force, and other communications may raise customer expectations that serve as the standard against which customers assess service quality. Broken promises can occur for many reasons: ineffective marketing communications, overpromising in advertising or personal selling, inadequate coordination between operations and marketing, and differences in policies and procedures across service outlets.

In service companies, a fit between communications about service and actual service delivery is necessary. Chapter 14 is devoted to the topic of integrated service

Provider Gap 4: The Communication Gap

marketing communications—careful integration and organization of all of a service marketing organization's external and interactive communications channels. The chapter describes why this communication is necessary and how companies can do it well. Successful company communications are the responsibility of both marketing and operations: marketing must accurately but beguilingly reflect what happens in actual service encounters, and operations must deliver what is promised in marketing communication. If communications set up unrealistic expectations for customers, the actual encounter will disappoint the customer.

Chapter 15 deals with another issue related to managing promises, the pricing of services. In packaged goods (and even in durable goods), many customers possess enough price knowledge before purchase to be able to judge whether a price is fair or in line with competition. With services, customers often have no internal reference point for prices before purchase and consumption. Techniques for developing prices for services are more complicated than those for pricing tangible goods, and all the approaches for setting prices must be adapted for the special characteristics of services.

In summary, external communications—whether from marketing communications or pricing—can create a larger customer gap by raising expectations about service delivery. In addition to improving service delivery, companies must also manage all communications to customers, so that inflated promises do not lead to higher expectations. Companies must also manage the messages conveyed by pricing, so that customer expectations are in line with what they perceive that they receive.

Chapter **Fourteen**

Integrated Service Marketing Communications

This chapter's objectives are to

1. Discuss the key service communication challenges.
2. Introduce the concept of integrated service marketing communications.
3. Discuss ways to integrate marketing communications in service organizations.
4. Present specific strategies for addressing service intangibility, managing promises, managing customer expectations, educating customers, and managing internal communications.

Coordinating Online and Offline Communication Channels at hotels.com

You have probably seen television commercials, print ads, online banners, or outdoor advertisements for hotels.com, an online travel site based in Dallas. These mass marketing channels are used to convince consumers to consider hotels.com when they are making vacation plans. If you are a customer of hotels.com, you also regularly receive e-mails and newsletters about their offerings. All of these communication vehicles are common to companies wanting to attract new users and increase usage from existing users. However, you may not know about the company's ingenious digital approach called Virtual Vacation, which builds on its offline communications to engage customers in a one-of-a-kind experience that is highly effective because of its integration with what it sells.

The Virtual Vacation campaign uses 3-D augmented reality technology to give users at a computer a live view of real-world environments of 10 major cities, complete with computer-generated sound or graphics. The tours integrate information about hotels.com throughout the in-depth tours, allowing users to purchase hotel rooms from the main site at any point. Because of this, the tours are not just entertaining but also rich in information. As Vic Walla, senior director of brand marketing, stated,

> We wanted to use digital to build a deeper experience for consumers. By [using] augmented reality tools, our customers were able not only to experience cities in 3-D, but they were also able to get more information about hotels.com. We used it as a vehicle to sell our brand.

If you go to www.virtualvacay.com, you will see the view shown in this chapter opener. It features the hotels.com. Claymation spokesman, named "Smart," who tells customers why they should use hotels.com. Because the Virtual Vacation is so strongly linked to the company's category and services, the sell is soft and seems natural. The company used its database of customers to reach customers through e-mail and newsletters, as well as online banners highly targeted to frequent travelers. One of the most difficult aspects of communicating about any offering is making sure that all sources of information convey the same message.

Hotels.com used a combination of media to tell consumers about the site. First, it used viral and social approaches, as well as public relations and traditional media. It also used print, TV, radio, and outdoor ad placements. At the bottom of all of the ads, it placed Facebook and Twitter page icons to get people to sign up on the social media sites. An interesting feature of the program is that the company recognized that it should use its online and offline channels differently. For direct marketing, it targeted depending on who the group was—for business travelers, it focused on the loyalty program; for families, it focused on family-friendly vacation destinations. Digital marketing ranked high in the approach because the company is a large player in search marketing.

The results of the integrated campaign were impressive. The company obtained more than 270 million impressions in public relations, as well as 236 articles from journalists and bloggers. Further, people spend, on average, five minutes on the site. Hotels.com captured e-mail addresses from those who visited the site and more addresses from others it sent the site to. It increased traffic, members of the loyalty program, and Google searches, as well as its market share, generating buzz in its key target audiences, which included travel enthusiasts and travel agents.

Sources: C. Birkner, "10 Minutes with Vic Walla, Senior Director of Brand Marketing at Hotels.com," *Marketing News*, March 15, 2011, pp. 22–23; "Augmented Reality Travel Strikes Again, Thanks to hotels.com"; Jaunted/Concierge.com, May 14, 2010.

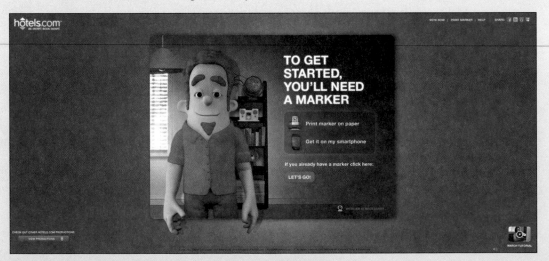

The hotels.com website showing its brand character "Smart."

A major cause of poorly perceived service is the difference between what a firm promises about a service and what it actually delivers. Customer expectations are shaped by both uncontrollable and company-controlled factors. Word-of-mouth communication, social media, publicity, customer-generated media, customer experiences with other service providers, and customer needs are key factors that influence customer expectations and are rarely controllable by the firm. Controllable factors such as company advertising, personal selling, and promises made by service personnel also influence customer expectations. In this chapter, we discuss both types of communication but focus more heavily on the controllable factors because these factors can be influenced by the company. Accurate, coordinated, and appropriate company communication—advertising, personal selling, and online and other messages that do not overpromise or misrepresent—is essential to delivering services that customers perceive as high in quality.

Because company communications about services promise what *people* do and because people's behavior cannot be standardized, as can physical goods produced by machines, the potential for a mismatch between what is communicated and perceptions of actual service delivery (provider gap 4, the communications gap) is high. By coordinating communication within and outside the organization, companies can minimize the size of this gap.

THE NEED FOR COORDINATION IN MARKETING COMMUNICATION

Marketing communication is more complex today than it used to be. In the past, customers received marketing information about goods and services from a limited number of sources, usually mass communication sources such as network television and newspapers. With a limited number of sources, marketers could easily convey a uniform brand image and coordinate promises. However, today's consumers of both goods and services receive communications from a far richer variety of marketing vehicles—websites, social media, mobile advertising, blogs, virtual communities, direct mail, movie theater advertising, e-mail solicitation, targeted magazines, and a host of sales promotions. Service consumers receive additional communication from servicescapes, customer service departments, and everyday service encounters with employees. These service interactions add to the variety, volume, and complexity of information that a customer receives. While a company cannot control outside sources, ensuring that messages from all company sources are consistent is a major challenge for service marketers.

Any company that disseminates information through multiple channels needs to be certain that customers receive unified messages and promises. These channels include not only marketing communication messages that flow directly from the company but also personal messages that employees send to customers. Figure 14.1 shows an enhanced version of the service marketing triangle that we presented in Chapter 11, emphasizing that the service customer is the target of two types of communication. First, external marketing communication includes traditional channels such as sales promotion, advertising, and public relations. Second, interactive marketing communication involves the messages that employees give to customers through such channels as personal selling, customer service interactions, service encounter interactions, social media, and servicescapes (discussed in Chapter 10). A service company must be sure that these interactive messages are consistent both among themselves and with those sent through external communications. To do so, the third side of the triangle, internal marketing communications, must be managed so that information from the company to employees is accurate, complete, and consistent with what customers are hearing or seeing.

FIGURE 14.1
**Communications
and the Service
Marketing Triangle**

Source: Adapted from
M. J. Bitner, "Building
Service Relationships: It's
All about Promises," *Journal
of the Academy of Marketing
Science* 23, no. 4 (1995);
and C. Gronroos, *Services
Management and Marketing*
(Lexington, MA: Lexington
Books, 1990).

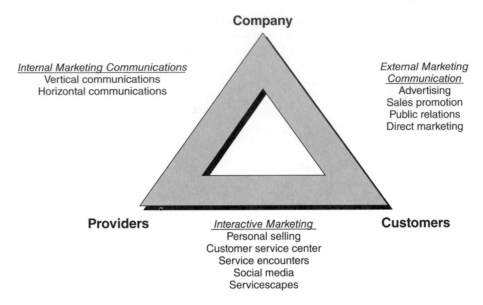

Company

Internal Marketing Communications
Vertical communications
Horizontal communications

*External Marketing
Communication*
Advertising
Sales promotion
Public relations
Direct marketing

Providers

Customers

Interactive Marketing
Personal selling
Customer service center
Service encounters
Social media
Servicescapes

The need for integrated marketing campaigns is evident in both business-to-business situations and business-to-consumer instances. In business-to-business situations, the problem often comes because multiple parts of a service organization deal with a client and do not communicate well internally. For example, consider a large business customer of IBM who buys hardware, software, and services. If the client deals with different employees in different parts of the organization, the company needs to—but may not—coordinate internally to ensure that it is sending the customer the same messages. Not only that, but each of these internal organizations may have its own promotional campaign with different promises and messages. An example from your own experience may illustrate what happens when service marketing communications are not integrated. Have you ever seen an advertisement for a service, such as a special sandwich from Subway, then gone to your local Subway and not found it available? Did the employee behind the counter offer a reason the sandwich was not available? Did he or she even realize that it was advertised and for sale elsewhere? One of us consulted for a bank on the West Coast in which both customers and employees constantly faced this situation. Bank marketing communication was changed frequently and quickly to meet competitive offerings, but the bank tellers' training in the new offerings did not keep pace with the changes in advertising. As a result, customers went in, expecting new accounts and rates to be available, and employees were embarrassed because they had not been informed.

This example demonstrates one of the main reasons integrated marketing communications have not been the norm in many companies. All too often, various parts of the company are responsible for different aspects of communication. The sales department develops and executes sales communication. The marketing department and the firm's advertising agency prepare and disseminate advertising. A public relations firm is responsible for publicity. Functional specialists handle sales promotions, direct marketing, and company websites. The human resource department trains frontline employees for service interactions, and still another area is responsible for the customer service department. Rarely is one person responsible for the overall communications strategy in a company, and all too often people responsible for the different communication components do not coordinate their efforts.

Today, however, more companies are adopting the concept of *integrated marketing communications (IMC),* where the company carefully integrates and organizes all of its external communications channels. As a marketing executive explained it,

> Integrated marketing communications build a strong brand identity in the marketplace by tying together and reinforcing all your images and messages. IMC means that all your corporate messages, positioning and images, and identity are coordinated across all venues. It means that your PR materials say the same things as your direct mail campaign, and your advertising has the same "look and feel" as your website.[1]

In this chapter we propose that a more complex type of integrated marketing communication is needed for services than for goods. External communications channels must be coordinated, as with physical goods, but both external communications and interactive communication channels must be integrated to create consistent service promises. To do that, internal marketing communications channels must be managed so that employees and the company are in agreement about what is communicated to the customer. We call this more complicated version of IMC *integrated service marketing communications (ISMC).* ISMC requires that everyone involved with communication clearly understand both the company's marketing strategy and its promises to consumers.

KEY SERVICE COMMUNICATION CHALLENGES

Discrepancies between what is communicated about a service and what a customer receives—or perceives that she receives—can powerfully affect consumer evaluations of service quality. The factors that contribute to these communication challenges include (1) service intangibility, (2) management of service promises, (3) management of customer expectations, (4) customer education, and (5) internal marketing communication. In this chapter, we first describe the challenges stemming from these factors and then detail strategies firms have found useful in dealing with them.

Service Intangibility

Because services are performances rather than objects, their essence and benefits are difficult to communicate to customers. Intangibility makes marketing communication for services more challenging for both marketers and consumers. The intangible nature of services creates problems for consumers both before and after purchase. Before buying services, consumers have difficulty understanding what they will be buying and evoking names and types of services to consider.[2] During purchase, consumers often cannot clearly see the differences among services. After purchase, consumers have trouble evaluating their service experiences.

Banwari Mittal described the difficulties associated with intangibility by dividing it into five properties, each of which has implications for service marketing communication. In his view, intangibility involves incorporeal existence, abstractness, generality, nonsearchability, and mental impalpability:[3]

- *Incorporeal existence.* The service product neither is made out of physical matter nor occupies physical space. Although the delivery mechanism (such as a Jiffy Lube outlet) may occupy space, the service itself (car servicing and oil change) does not. The implication is that showing the service is difficult, if not impossible.

- *Abstractness.* Service benefits such as financial security, fun, and health do not correspond directly with objects, making them difficult to visualize and understand. When businesses need consulting, for example, they often do not know where to begin because the concept is so vague that they do not understand the specific goals, processes, or deliverables they are seeking.
- *Generality.* *Generality* refers to a class of things, persons, events, or properties, whereas *specificity* refers to particular objects, people, or events. Many services and service promises are described in generalities (wonderful experience, superior education, completely satisfied customers), making them difficult to differentiate from those of competitors.
- *Nonsearchability.* Because service is a performance, it often cannot be previewed, or inspected in advance of purchase. If we are interested in finding a doctor, an air-conditioning repair firm, a personal trainer, or virtually any service, we cannot search with certainty the options as easily as we can search the shelves in a grocery store. Considerably more effort must be expended, and what we find may not be useful. For example, if a customer needs a plumber, the information contained in a source such as the Internet may not adequately discriminate among the choices.
- *Mental impalpability.* Services are often complex, multidimensional, and difficult to grasp mentally. When customers have not had prior exposure, familiarity, or knowledge, services are difficult to interpret. You may have experienced this when buying automobile insurance for the first time.

These five aspects of service intangibility make customers feel more uncertain about their purchases, and evidence indicates that, the greater the risk that customers perceive in purchasing services, the more actively they will seek and rely on word-of-mouth communications to guide their choices.[4] Word of mouth can be a very convincing source of information about services for consumers, but it is not under the control of the service provider.

Management of Service Promises

A serious problem occurs when companies fail to manage service marketing communications—the vows made by salespeople, advertising, and service personnel—and service falls short of what is promised. This sometimes occurs because the part of the company making the promise lacks the information necessary to make accurate statements. For example, business-to-business salespeople often sell services, particularly new business services, before their actual availability and without having an exact date of when they will be ready for market. Demand and supply variations make service provision possible at some times, improbable at others, and difficult to predict. The traditional functional structure in many companies (often called silos) also makes communication about promises and delivery difficult internally.

Management of Customer Expectations

Appropriate and accurate communication about services is the responsibility of both marketing and operations. Marketing must accurately (and compellingly) reflect what happens in actual service encounters; operations must deliver what is promised in communications. For example, when a management consulting firm introduces a new offering, the marketing and sales departments must make the offering appealing enough to be viewed as superior to competing service offerings. In promoting and differentiating the service, however, the company cannot afford to raise expectations above the level at which its consultants can consistently perform. If advertising, personal selling, or any other external communication sets up unrealistic expectations, actual encounters will disappoint customers.

Many product and service companies also find themselves in the position of having to actively manage customer expectations downward—to tell customers that service previously provided will be discontinued or available only at a higher price. Airlines cancel flights that are not full and charge for food. Credit card companies that offer multiple value-added services when interest rates are high withdraw these services when interest rates drop. Health care insurers cut back on service while raising prices, and hospital patients experience far shorter stays and fewer diagnostic procedures. In these situations—perhaps more than any others—the need to manage customer expectations is critical.

Customer Education

Service companies must educate their customers. If customers are unclear about how service will be provided, what their role in delivery involves, and how to evaluate services they have never used before, they will be disappointed. When disappointed, they will often hold the service company, not themselves, responsible. These errors or problems in service—even when they are "caused" by the customer—still lead customers to defect. For this reason the firm must assume responsibility for educating customers.

For services high in credence properties—expert services that are difficult for customers to evaluate even after they have received the services—many customers do not know the criteria by which they should judge the service. For high-involvement services, such as long-term medical treatment or purchase of a first home, customers are also unlikely to comprehend and anticipate the service process. First-time home buyers rarely understand the complex set of services (inspection, title services, insurance) and processes (securing a mortgage, offers and counteroffers, escrow) that will be involved in their purchases. Professionals and other providers of high-involvement services often forget that customers who are novices must be educated about each step in the process. They assume that an overview at the beginning of the service, or a manual or set of instructions, will equip the customer. Unfortunately, these steps are rarely sufficient, and customers defect because they can neither understand the process nor appreciate the value received from the service.

A final condition under which customer education can be beneficial involves services in which demand and supply are not synchronized, as discussed in Chapter 13. If the customer is not informed about peaks and valleys in demand, service overloads and failures, as well as underutilized capacity, are likely to result.

Internal Marketing Communication

Multiple functions in the organization, such as marketing and operations, must be coordinated to achieve the goal of quality service provision. Because service advertising and personal selling promise what *people* do, frequent and effective communication across functions—horizontal communication—is critical. If internal communication is poor, perceived service quality is at risk. If company marketing communication and other promises are developed without input from operations, contact personnel may not be able to deliver service that matches the image portrayed in marketing efforts.

Not all service organizations advertise, but all need coordination or integration across departments or functions to deliver quality service. All need internal communication between the sales force and service providers. Horizontal communication also must occur between the human resource and marketing departments. To deliver excellent customer service, firms must be certain to inform and motivate employees to deliver what their customers expect. If marketing and sales personnel who understand customer expectations do not communicate this information to contact employees, the lack of knowledge for these employees will affect the quality of service that they deliver.

A final form of internal coordination central to providing service excellence is consistency in policies and procedures across departments and branches. If a service organization operates many outlets under the same name, whether franchised or company owned, customers expect similar performance across those outlets. If managers of individual branches or outlets have significant autonomy in procedures and policies, customers may not receive the same level of service quality across the branches.

FIVE CATEGORIES OF STRATEGIES TO MATCH SERVICE PROMISES WITH DELIVERY

Figure 14.2 shows the major approaches to overcome the service communication challenges that we just described. The goal is to deliver service that is greater than or equal to promises made, and all three sides of the triangle must be addressed to do so.

Address Service Intangibility

Approaches to address service intangibility are (1) advertising and other communication strategies that clearly communicate service attributes and benefits to consumers and (2) strategies designed to encourage word-of-mouth communication.

If service companies recognize the challenges they face due to intangibility, they can use selected strategies to compensate. In one way or another, each of the individual strategies we discuss here focuses on ways to make the message dramatic and memorable.

Use Narrative to Demonstrate the Service Experience Many services are experiential, and a uniquely effective approach to communicating them involves story-based appeals. Showing consumers having realistic and positive experiences with services is generally more effective than describing service attributes, particularly because the

FIGURE 14.2
Five Major Approaches to Overcome Service Communication Channels

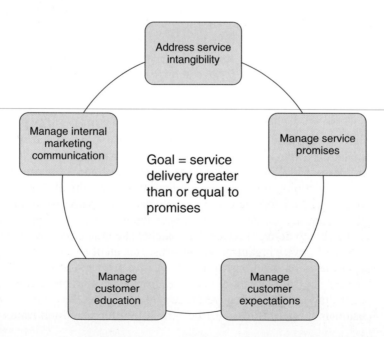

attributes themselves are often intangible. Research has concluded that consumers with relatively low familiarity with a service category prefer appeals based on stories to appeals based on lists of service attributes. An example of this is a State Farm campaign in which someone experiencing a situation in which a State Farm agent is needed simply calls out, "Like a good neighbor, State Farm is there," and an agent instantly appears to take care of the situation.

Present Vivid Information   Effective service marketing communication creates a strong or clear impression on the senses and produces a distinct mental picture. One way to use vivid information is to evoke a strong emotion such as fear. Using vivid information cues is particularly desirable when services are highly intangible and complex. A print example of vividness is shown in an ad for the United Negro College Fund. The abstract themes of "limitless potential" and "chance to achieve" are made vivid by a photograph of a mind filled with books.

Use Interactive Imagery   One type of vividness involves what is called *interactive imagery*.[5] Imagery (defined as a mental event that involves the visualization of a concept or relationship) can enhance recall of names and facts about service. Interactive imagery integrates two or more items in some mutual action, resulting in improved recall. Some service companies effectively integrate their logos or symbols with an expression of what they do, such as the Prudential rock—the rock symbolizes strength and stability. The accompanying photo shows an advertisement for The Travelers Companies Inc., a provider of property casualty insurance, that demonstrates interactive imagery. The umbrella symbolizes protection and reassurance, an appropriate symbol to identify an insurance company. An umbrella is believed to have first appeared in a Travelers ad in 1870 and the red umbrella became the official company trademark in 1959. The advertisement shown in the photo refers to the reacquisition in 2007 of the trademark from Citigroup, which also used the umbrella as part of its logo.

Focus on the Tangibles.   Another way that advertisers can increase the effectiveness of service communications is to feature the tangibles associated with the service, such as showing a bank's marble columns or gold credit card.[6] Showing the tangibles provides clues about the nature and quality of the service. The photo on page 424, which is an advertisement for the Sierra Club, features the tangible benefits of the club of protecting consumers, particularly babies, from the harm from mercury pollution.

Use Brand Icons to Make the Service Tangible   How does an advertiser of services gain in competitive differentiation and strong

Quick, name an insurance company.

The 33,000 people of Travelers proudly welcome back their classic icon. Complete with a brand-new stock symbol (TRV) and a new official name: The Travelers Companies, Inc.

TRAVELERS

©2008 The Travelers Companies, Inc. All rights reserved.

Interactive imagery is demonstrated by the Travelers umbrella.

brand awareness in a highly competitive market? In the fast-food and insurance industries, one answer is to create a recognizable brand icon that represents the company and generates brand visibility. One of the most enduring service brand icons is Ronald McDonald, the red-and-yellow clown that represents McDonald's and its children's charity, the Ronald McDonald House. McDonald's competitor Jack in the Box has its own mascot named Jack, a ball-shaped head with a pointed hat. In television advertising, he appears as the "founder" of the chain—part clown and part businessman in a suit with the head of the icon. He is always part fun and part serious. Advertising icons are even more critical in industries in which the service is complex and difficult to understand. Insurance is an example. American Family Life Insurance Company, or Aflac, a company that sells supplemental insurance on a voluntary basis in U.S. and Japanese worksites, faced a difficult challenge: getting potential customers to ask for its service by name. Enter the Aflac duck, an insistent and vocal character who screams, "Aflac!" in commercials in which actors are trying to solve their insurance problems. The duck, introduced in 2000, has generated such visibility that he has been featured on CNBC, *The Tonight Show with Jay Leno,* and *Saturday Night Live.* GEICO has TV ads such as the one shown in the image on this page, featuring the Cockney-speaking Gecko lizard. The GEICO Gecko reinforces the company's brand image with natural tenacity, constantly good cheer and an insatiable need to help people save money on car insurance. The GEICO Gecko has become a force to be reckoned with in the advertising world and was voted America's favorite advertising icon in 2005.[7]

Saving is easy.

Get a free car insurance quote today.

GEICO.
geico.com

The GEICO gecko is an advertising icon.

Use Association, Physical Representation, Documentation, and Visualization Leonard Berry and Terry Clark propose four strategies of tangibilization: association, physical representation, documentation, and visualization.[8] *Association* means linking the service to a tangible person, place, or object, such as "being in good hands with Allstate." *Physical representation* means showing tangibles that are directly or indirectly part of the service, such as employees, buildings, or equipment. *Documentation* means featuring objective data and factual information. *Visualization* is a vivid mental picture of a service's benefits or qualities, such as showing people on vacation having fun. Our Strategy Insight shows how marketing communication icons can be used as tangibles.

Feature Service Employees in Communication Customer contact personnel are tangible representations of the service and are an important second audience for service advertising.[9] Featuring actual employees doing their jobs or explaining their services in advertising is effective for both the primary audience (customers) and the secondary audience (employees) because it communicates to employees that they are important. Furthermore, when

Strategy Insight   Google's Strategy Dominates Web Advertising and Communication

Search engine Google is one of the most successful service marketing stories of the past two decades. Google's strategic vision is "to organize the world's information and make it universally accessible and useful." The company has achieved that vision, as you no doubt are aware, by becoming such a universally accessible and useful search engine that it draws nearly 60 percent of all consumer searches. You may not be aware, however, of how Google has built a toolbox of advertising approaches and in the process become the most important new advertising medium in the world. Advertisers spend more than 40 percent of online advertising revenue on search advertising, sponsored links, and Google content networks.

Search-based, or paid search, advertising is the most popular form of Internet advertising today. In this form of advertising, companies can either pay for small display ads to the right of listings or pay for listings themselves. The display ads, short messages to the right of the top-ranked searches that are relevant to the company, are called Google AdWords. When a consumer searches Google using one of those keywords, the advertiser's URL, along with its name and description, appears in a colored box beside the search results. The next time you call something up on Google, click on one or two of these boxes and you will see that they are advertisements. Companies can also pay for placement, which means that they buy rankings in the search results. When you call up a search on Google, some of the links in the column of search results have actually been purchased by advertisers. Google shades these paid listings to show consumers that these rankings are sponsored.

Google also provides business-to-business service by acting as a go-between for advertisers and websites through two other forms of advertising. In one, involving site-targeted ads, advertisers ask Google to find specific websites or website content (such as ice hockey or figure skating) that is relevant to what they offer. Advertisers choose their target audiences both by size and by interests, then give Google a list of keywords that describe the site. Google AdWords matches terms and creates a list of available content network sites where the company can advertise. Google AdSense is an advertising service targeted to website publishers. AdSense automatically crawls the content of a company's pages and delivers text or image ads that are relevant and high performing. Google then provides the ads to the sites for the companies. These two services actually work together—one is the source of advertisements and the other is the placement for the ads.

DoubleClick is a company that develops and provides the technology and services that place advertisements on websites, an approach called *ad serving*. Companies like DoubleClick provide software to websites and advertisers to place ads, count them, select the ads that will make the website or advertiser the most money, and track the progress of different advertising campaigns. For advertisers, DoubleClick chooses the websites with the best potential to sell products and services. For sites themselves, DoubleClick chooses advertisers offering products and services that best fit with the sites and brings in advertising revenues. For agencies, the company manages online inventory and reports and manages online activity. With the purchase of DoubleClick, Google gains a powerful advertising tool on its own but also will be able to offer advertisers the ability to create an integrated search-and-display campaign.

Upon purchasing YouTube, Google immediately began posting video images in Google's Video search index, so that users could be taken to YouTube.com to experience the videos. Google promises that, over time, Google Video will become even more comprehensive as it evolves into a service through which users can search for the world's online video content wherever it is hosted. A Google representative stated, "Ultimately, we envision most user-generated and premium video content being hosted on YouTube so that it can further enhance the YouTube experience. We also envision YouTube benefiting from future Google Video innovations—especially those involving video search, monetization and distribution."

Sources: G. Stricker, "A Look Ahead at Google Video and YouTube," www.google.com, January 25, 2007; A. Klaassen, "Sorry Yahoo, MSN. Google Just Got Bigger," *Advertising Age,* April 16, 2007, pp. 3+; R. D. Hof, "Is Google Too Powerful?" *BusinessWeek,* April 9, 2007, pp. 46–55; R. Farzad and B. Elgin, "Googling for Gold," *BusinessWeek,* December 5, 2005, pp. 60–70; www.google.com 2007; J. Graham, "Google Plans Ad 'Overlays' for Some YouTube Videos," *USA Today,* August 22, 2007, p. 2A; M. Helft, "Google Aims to Make YouTube Profitable with Ads," *New York Times,* August 22, 2007, p. C1.

Exhibit 14.1   Service Advertising Strategies Matched with Properties of Intangibility

Property of Intangibility	Advertising Strategy	Description
Incorporeal existence	Physical representation	Show physical components of service that are unique, indicate high quality, and create the right association.
Abstractness	Service consumption episode	Capture and display typical customers benefiting from the service, evoking particular incidents.
Generality	System documentation	Objectively document physical system capacity by showing facts and figures.
	Performance documentation	Document and cite past positive performance statistics.
	Service performance episode	Present a vivid story of an actual service delivery incident that relates to an important service attribute.
Nonsearchability	Performance documentation	Cite independently audited performance.
	Consumption documentation	Obtain and present customer testimonials.
Mental impalpability	Service process episode	Present a vivid documentary on the step-by-step service process.
	Case history episode	Present an actual case history of what the firm did for a specific client

Source: Adapted from B. Mittal, "The Advertising of Services: Meeting the Challenge of Intangibility," *Journal of Service Research* 2, no. 1 (August 1999), pp. 98–116.

employees who perform a service well are featured in marketing communication, they become standards for other employees' behaviors.

Earlier in this chapter, we discussed five aspects of intangibility that make service marketing communication challenging. In Exhibit 14.1, Mittal describes strategies that can be used in service advertising to overcome these properties. Through careful planning and execution, the abstract can be made concrete, the general can be made specific, the nonsearchable can be made searchable, and the mentally impalpable can be made palpable.

Recommendations and opinions from other customers are virtually always more credible than firm communications. In situations in which consumers have little information prior to purchase—something that occurs far more often in services than in goods because services are high in experience and credence properties—people turn to others for information rather than to traditional marketing channels. Service advertising and types of promotion can generate word-of-mouth communication that extends the investment in paid communication and improves the credibility of the messages.

Use Buzz, or Viral, Marketing   Buzz marketing, also called viral marketing, involves the use of real consumers to spread the word about products without (or without the appearance of) being paid by the company. Sometimes buzz marketing occurs simply because customers are avid fans of the service, and sometimes the company seeds customers with services or products. Chipotle Mexican Grill, a Denver-based company with nearly 600 outlets, avoids advertising and instead depends almost completely on the word-of-mouth communication its customers spread about its unique and tasty food. Chipotle's founder, M. Steven Ells, makes giving away samples of its food (as well as satisfying customers) the basis for its strategy. For example, when the chain opened a midtown Manhattan outlet in 2006, it gave burritos away to 6,000 people. Even though this cost the company $35,000, the strategy created 6,000 satisfied spokespeople.[10]

Leverage Social Media   Social media—interactive communication among customers on the Internet through such sites as Twitter, YouTube, and Facebook—are becoming avenues for consumers to exchange information. The growth of social media is affecting many aspects of consumer purchase behavior. In a comScore survey, almost 28 percent of consumers reported that social media influenced their decisions about holiday purchasing in 2009.[11] Another study showed that 61 percent of consumers rely on online ratings and reviews before making a purchase.[12] And 26 percent of consumers post online ratings and reviews.[13] According to a Nielsen study, a full 90 percent of consumers trust recommendations from other consumers versus 56 percent who trust brand advertising.[14] While social media are not controllable by the firm, the company can monitor the media and understand what consumers are saying and recommending. Formal methods and sophisticated technologies are being developed to track, monitor, and analyze online communication for brands. Nielsen BuzzMetrics, the innovator of this approach, gathers brand information online by trolling millions of lines of Internet communication to find out how customers feel about brands, how many are talking online, what issues they are discussing, how marketing is being viewed, and how efforts to affect word-of-mouth communications are being received. The service provides industry norms and benchmarks to the companies who buy their service as well as real-time alerts about issues.[15]

Aim Messages to Influencers   Improved technologies are now allowing companies to identify online influencers—those individuals with more connections than others and therefore more ability to influence others about services. Both researchers and research companies are developing technologies similar to the BuzzMetric approach described earlier that can identify those people in a viral community who are most critical to receive brand messages. When identified, these individuals can be "seeded"—given information about the service, invited to participate in special events, and otherwise encouraged to know and communicate about a service.

Create Advertising That Generates Talk Because It Is Humorous, Compelling, or Unique   A humorous commercial that generated talk and was highly popular first aired on the 2011 Super Bowl for CareerBuilder.com in which bad-driving monkeys squeeze a driver between them. Another humorous—and surprising—commercial was for GoDaddy and featured Joan Rivers as the new GoDaddy.com girl. The E-trade ads, always humorous, featured a talking baby being fitted for a new suit from a tailor named Enzo.

Feature Satisfied Customers in the Communication   Advertising testimonials featuring actual service customers simulate personal communications between people and are thereby a credible way to communicate the benefits of service. A successful advertising campaign for Blue Cross/Blue Shield of North Carolina features real customers whose family members suffered medical crises that were handled successfully by the health insurance company. The testimonials are powerful and believable are. The campaign helps restore faith in the health insurance and generates positive word of mouth.

In 2010, Xerox created a series of testimonial commercials with its business customers that were highly believable and successful. You can see them on YouTube by searching "Xerox commercials 2010."

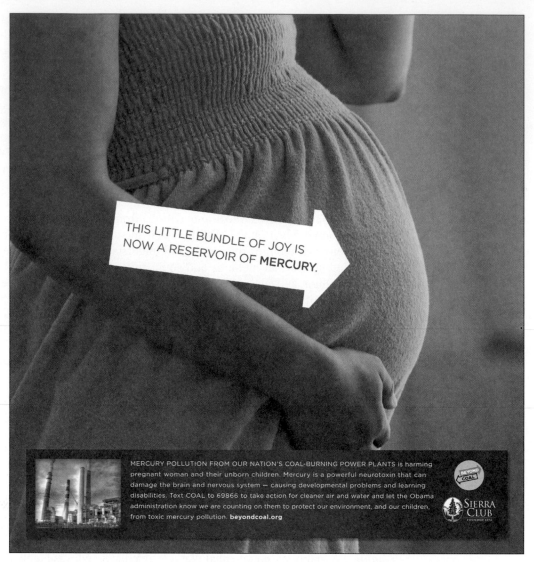

THIS LITTLE BUNDLE OF JOY IS NOW A RESERVOIR OF **MERCURY**.

MERCURY POLLUTION FROM OUR NATION'S COAL-BURNING POWER PLANTS is harming pregnant woman and their unborn children. Mercury is a powerful neurotoxin that can damage the brain and nervous system — causing developmental problems and learning disabilities. Text COAL to 69866 to take action for cleaner air and water and let the Obama administration know we are counting on them to protect our environment, and our children, from toxic mercury pollution. **beyondcoal.org**

This advertisement for the Sierra Club demonstrates in a tangible way the dangers of mercury pollution from coal-burning plants. Focusing on the unborn baby is a vivid way for the Sierra Club to communicate its message.

Generate Word of Mouth through Employee Relationships Research shows that customer satisfaction with a service experience alone is not sufficient to stimulate word-of-mouth activity. However, when customers gained trust in a specific employee, positive word of mouth would result. In this research, trust was shown to be a consequence of three aspects of the employee–customer relationship: a personal connection between employees and customers, care displayed by employees, and employee familiarity with customers.[16] Companies can strengthen the interpersonal bonds that lead to trust using strategies that focus on service design, support systems, employees, and customers.[17] Examples include designing the service environment so that opportunities for interactions between customers and employees are plentiful, using support systems (such as customer relationship management software) to help employees remember customer characteristics, and empowering employees to correct problems fully and quickly.

Manage Service Promises

In manufacturing physical goods, the departments that make promises and those that deliver them can operate independently. Goods can be fully designed and produced and then turned over to marketing for promotion and sale. In services, however, the sales and marketing departments make promises about what other employees in the organization will fulfill. Because what employees do cannot be standardized, greater coordination and management of promises are required. This coordination can be accomplished by creating a strong service brand and by coordinating all of the company's marketing communications.

Create a Strong Service Brand

Leonard Berry, an expert in *service branding,* emphasizes that branding plays a special role in service companies:

> Strong brands enable customers to better visualize and understand intangible products. They reduce customers' perceived monetary, social, or safety risk in buying services, which are difficult to evaluate prior to purchase. Strong brands are the surrogates when the company offers no fabric to touch, no trousers to try on, no watermelons or apples to scrutinize, no automobile to test drive.[18]

In contrast to branding in goods situations, where each product has its own brand, the primary brand in service is the company itself. The focus of brand creation is on awareness, meaning, and equity of the company. For example, companies like FedEx, Disney World, Starbucks, and Facebook all focus communication and information on their companies rather than individual services that the company offers. Therefore, the brand becomes the company's method of integrating marketing communication.

Figure 14.3 is a service branding model developed by Berry that shows the relationships among the main elements in creating a strong service brand.[19] The *presented brand* is the part of the brand image that the company controls and disseminates through all personal and impersonal channels. Advertising, the brand name itself, websites, employees, facilities, and all other types of information dissemination must be coordinated and controlled. These messages lead to *brand awareness,* the customer's recall and recognition of the brand. The higher and more positive the brand awareness, the stronger the brand image and the more differentiation—or *brand equity*—the service company has. *Customer experience with the company*—the actual interactions with company employees and other firm manifestations—is another element that shapes the brand and is likely to be more powerful than any marketing messages. No matter how effective and unified advertising is for a service, actual experiences disproportionately provide meaning to customers.

The Mayo Clinic, one of the strongest service brands in the world, carefully cultivates its brand through patient experience rather than media promotion, which it avoids. Strong core values, teamwork, physician responsibility, patient care, high-quality staff, and facilities all contribute to the Mayo Clinic Model of Care, which ensures that patient experience is strong enough to perpetuate the clinic's brand strength. Notably, the brand awareness of the Mayo Clinic is strong even though it

FIGURE 14.3
A Service Branding Model

Source: Leonard L. Berry, "Cultivating Service Brand Equity," *Journal of the Academy of Marketing Science* 28 (Winter 2000), pp. 128–137.

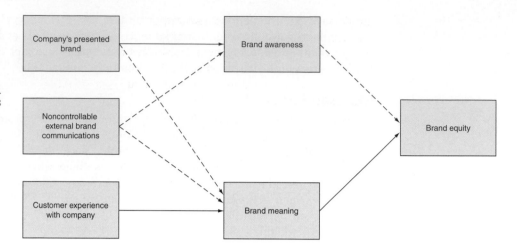

does not use media promotion. In a study in which primary decision makers in the United States were asked what health care institutions in the United States they would choose if they could go anywhere for a serious medical problem, almost 27 percent of respondents named Mayo Clinic, far more than the second choice, which was named about 9 percent of the time.[20] Other research indicates that 95 percent of Mayo clinic patients voluntarily say positive things about the clinic to others, a testament to the Mayo brand and to the positive experiences they have there.[21]

Figure 14.3 shows two other factors that shape the service brand. First, *noncontrollable external brand communications* involve information—such as word-of-mouth communication and publicity—that the company does not have in its power. These sources of communication are potent because they are perceived by customers to be credible and unbiased but can have either positive or negative effects on the service brand. In another section of this chapter, we describe ways to influence word-of-mouth communication in positive ways. Second, *brand meaning* is the collection of customers' associations with the brand. Brand meaning largely emanates from customer experience but is also shaped by the company's presented brand and external communications.

An example of a successful service brand based firmly in brand meaning is the Boston Red Sox baseball team. The team, which until 2004 had not won a World Series since 1918, has built a fan base with messianic loyalty through deliberate management and marketing strategies that have been highly successful.[22] Virtually all elements of the strategy involve giving fans a meaningful personal and community experience. First, owners created a community of fans around the team by deliberately building the stadium right in the middle of the city's neighborhoods and taverns. They knew that locating the field in the center of the city would encourage fans to come to multiple games. Second, rather than focus on superstar players, they emphasized Fenway Park itself, avoiding the loss of allegiance when star players left. As part of this approach, the builders created the "Green Monster," the unique left-field wall that became part of the Boston region's folklore. Third, owners and managers promised a competitive team but not a winning team, credibly managing fan expectations while delivering strong teams. Fourth, owners vowed to make the park "Friendly Fenway," partly by staging fun and entertaining events at games and partly by instilling in all vendors a strong fan-oriented culture. Finally, the team shows respect for its fans' desires for tradition: its uniforms, logo, and focus on the game itself have remained the same for more than half a century. The success of these strategies is evident every game. As of May 22, 2011, the Red Sox have sold out 657 consecutive games, an all time record for major league baseball and 200 games better than the next streak.

Coordinate External Communication

For any organization, one of the most important yet challenging aspects of managing brand image involves coordinating all the external communication vehicles that send information to customers. This task has become far more challenging in recent years because a notable trend is the proliferation of new media. Not only are traditional communication vehicles such as advertising, company websites, sales promotion, public relations, direct marketing, and personal selling proliferating, but many forms of new media are now available to marketers. Social media, digital signage, blogs, mobile advertising, many forms of Internet advertising, and increasing usage of product placement in movies and television all complicate the goal of coordinating messages. Our Global Feature shows an international campaign for Virgin Atlantic Airways that uses many elements of the *marketing communication mix.*

Advertising is any paid form of nonpersonal presentation and promotion of a company's offerings by an identified sponsor. Dominant advertising vehicles include television, radio, newspapers, magazines, outdoor signage, and the Internet. Because advertising is paid, marketers control the creative appeals, placement, and timing. Internet advertising has become a large portion of companies' advertising budgets (see the Technology Spotlight) and should be synchronized with traditional advertising vehicles. MasterCard's highly successful "Priceless" advertising campaign listed three or four tangible items and their prices followed by a key customer benefit that was "priceless." The campaign was an example of strong integration because it was flexible and carried a brand message that was relevant and also adapted well to different media, payment channels, and markets." The campaign, seen in 96 countries and 47 languages, generated strong brand recall and received the advertising industry's prestigious Gold Effie, Addy, and Cresta awards.[23]

Sales promotion includes short-term incentives such as coupons, premiums, discounts, and other activities that stimulate customer purchases and stretch media spending. The fast-food industry, including McDonald's, Burger King, and Wendy's, offers premiums such as action figures that link the chains' offerings to current movies and television shows. A particularly successful version of joint promotions between service advertisers and entertainment was created by CKE Restaurants' Carl's Jr. The restaurant incorporated footage of television season premieres, finales, and other television shows into the company's advertising, "[deliver] ing upwards of 30 percent of an increase in the impact of media spending."[24]

Public relations includes activities that build a favorable company image with a firm's publics through publicity, relations with the news media, and community events. Richard Branson, founder of Virgin Atlantic Airways (see the Global Feature) is a master at obtaining publicity for his airline. When launching the airline, he claimed, "I knew that the only way of competing with British Airways and the others was to get out there and use myself to promote it."[25] In the years since the airline's launch, his publicity-winning stunts included recording the fastest time across the Atlantic Ocean in a speedboat, flying a hot-air balloon across the Atlantic Ocean and from Japan to

A brand name that is known internationally for innovation, quality and a sense of fun—this is what we have always aspired to with Virgin. Richard Branson

Richard Branson, first known for Virgin Records, the legendary record label that signed the Rolling Stones, Janet Jackson, and The Human League, surprised the world in 1984 when he launched an upstart airline called Virgin Atlantic Airways. His vision was to create a high-quality, value-for-the-money airline to challenge the United Kingdom's market leader, British Airways. Over twenty-eight years later, Virgin Atlantic is the third-largest European carrier over the North Atlantic and includes destinations in the United States, the Caribbean, the Far East, India, China, Hong Kong, and Africa.

Parent company Virgin Group, with combined sales exceeding $20 billion, is known worldwide as an innovative global brand with megastore music retailing, book and software publishing, film and video editing facilities, clubs, mobile telecommunications, trains, and financial advising through more than 200 branded companies in 29 countries. Virgin Atlantic Airways' brand and marketing campaign epitomizes successful global communication, with universal marketing components that are integrated in theme and design across the world as well as individual advertisements that adapt to geographies.

Virgin Atlantic focuses on customer service and low cost while also being the first to offer up unique services. For example, Virgin Atlantic was the first airline to install in-flight entertainment systems and offer massages and beauty services in First Class. The red and white logo, in the shape of an airline tail fin, appears in all world wide marketing communication media including television, press, magazines, price promotions and outdoor posters. Another common image is the company's Flying Lady, a Vargas painting of a red-headed, scantily-dressed woman holding a scarf, but the eye is drawn to the Union Jack she is holding. Distinctive airplanes feature the Flying Lady on the fuselage and Union Jacks on their wings (which have recently undergone a facelift, and the red winglets now feature the "Virgin" in script). When the iridescent gleam combines with the plane's vibrant colors, the aircraft stirs up memories of the 1930s, when flying was glamorous and romantic.

As shown in the accompanying international advertisement, Virgin Atlantic Airways manages to translate its brand themes in culturally specific ways while retaining its global image. The Caribbean ad draws in readers with its bananas. Although the text and appeal change to suit the culture, all international advertisements contain the same Virgin Atlantic Airways logo and the same company colors.

Source: www.virgin-atlantic.com.

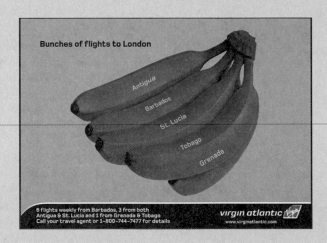

Canada, dressing up in everything from a stewardess's uniform to a bikini on Virgin flights, and being photographed in his bath.

Direct marketing includes the use of mail, telephone, fax, e-mail, and other tools to communicate directly with specific consumers to obtain a direct response. American Express is a service company that uses direct marketing extensively and ensures that it integrates well with all other messages, including interactive messages from employees. As the executive vice president of global advertising at American Express clearly states,

> Service brands are not created solely in advertising. In fact, much of a brand's equity stems from the direct consumer experiences with the brand. We partner with [a relationship marketing company] to help us manage consumer experiences with our brand across all products and services—Card, Travel, Financial Services, and Relationship Services—via all direct channels, including phone, Internet, and mail.[26]

Personal selling is face-to-face presentation by a representative from the firm to make sales and build customer relationships. One way that personal selling and advertising are integrated in business-to-business companies is through the development of advertising materials that salespeople distribute to customers. This approach not only creates an integrated message to customers but also keeps salespeople fully informed of the promises the company is making.

Manage Customer Expectations

Accurately promising when and how service will be delivered is one of the most important ways to close the communication gap. Among the most effective strategies to manage customer expectations are to make realistic promises; to offer service guarantees, options, and tiered-value offerings; and to communicate criteria customers can use to assess service.

Make Realistic Promises

The expectations that customers bring to the service affect their evaluations of its quality: the higher the expectation, the higher the delivered service must be to be perceived as high quality. Therefore, making promises about any aspect of service delivery is appropriate only when these aspects will actually be delivered. It is essential for a firm's marketing or sales department to understand accurately the levels of service delivery (percentage of times the service is provided correctly, or percentage and number of problems that arise) before making promises. To be appropriate and effective, communications about service quality must accurately reflect what customers will actually receive in service encounters.

Probably the simplest and most important point to remember is to promise what is possible.[27] Many companies hope to create the perception that they have high-quality service by claiming it in marketing communication, but this strategy can backfire when the actual service does not live up to the promises in advertising. In line with the strategies we discuss in the next section, all service communications should promise only what is possible and not attempt to make services more attractive than they actually are.

Offer Service Guarantees

As discussed in Chapter 7, service guarantees are formal promises made to customers about aspects of the service they will receive. Although many services carry implicit service satisfaction guarantees, the true benefits from explicit service guarantees—an increase in the likelihood of a customer's choosing or remaining with the company—come only when the customer knows that guarantees exist and trusts that the company will stand behind them.

Technology Spotlight   Grouping Customers Based on Online Activities

How do you use social media? Do you create content on blogs or other online media? Contribute reviews on websites like Amazon? Organize your online sources on a social bookmarking site? Are you a member of Facebook, Twitter, Foursquare, and other social websites? Or would you describe yourself as someone who reads what everyone else produces but does not participate in other, more active ways? These different ways that consumers interact with social media are the basis for the Social Technographics Profile Tool, which allows companies to understand their core audience's social tendencies. Based on the premise that consumers show differences in the way they use social media, Forrester Research Inc., one of the world's authorities on online activities, created this tool to help companies compare any two groups of people in their usage of social media. These technological behaviors are more useful than standard demographics or psychographics in understanding and targeting key customers.

To comprehend the Social Technographics Profile, refer to the ladder in this box. It demonstrates that customers can be classified into one or more of six groups based on the way they use social media. The higher on the ladder consumers are, the greater their influence. The following are the six groups:

- *Creators* (approximately 18 percent of online adults in the United States, 10 percent in Europe,

and 38 percent in Korea) are online customers who publish online regularly using blogs or sites like YouTube.

- *Critics* (25 percent of Americans, 20 percent of Europeans, and 36 percent of Japanese) respond to other people's content online but do not create their own.
- *Collectors* (10 percent of Americans and Europeans) save tags and URLs on social bookmarking sites, use RSS feeds, and otherwise aggregate information to organize it for themselves.
- *Joiners* (25 percent in the United States, 40 percent in Korea) participate in social networking sites such as Facebook, YouTube, and Twitter.
- *Spectators* (48 percent of Americans, 37 percent of Europeans, and 67 percent of Japanese) do not make any contributions themselves but read what everyone else produces, including online videos, blogs, reviews, and podcasts.
- *Inactives* are people who have computers but do not participate.

How does a company use the Social Technographics Ladder? Companies can study and compare different groups of consumers and then target their online strategy based on the composition that best suits these customers. For example, as you can see from the percentages listed, consumers in different countries have different profiles. Korea and Japan

Offer Choices

One way to reset expectations is to give customers options for aspects of service that are meaningful, such as time and cost. A clinical psychologist charging $100 per hour, for example, might offer clients the choice between a price increase of $10 per hour or a reduction in the number of minutes comprising the hour (such as 50 minutes). With the choice, clients can select the aspect of the trade-off (time or money) that is most meaningful to them. Making the choice solidifies the clients' expectations of service.

This strategy is effective in business-to-business situations, particularly in terms of speed versus quality. Customers who are time conscious often want reports, proposals, or other written documents quickly. When asked to provide a 10-page proposal for a project within three days, an architectural firm responded that it could provide either a 2-page proposal in three days or a 10-page proposal in a week. Its customer selected the latter option, recognizing that the deadline could be extended. In most business-to-business services, speed is often essential but threatens performance. If customers understand the trade-off and are asked to make a choice, they are likely to be more satisfied because their service expectations for each option become more realistic.

tend to have more consumers who are creators. Companies targeting young people in these geographies would want to engage them in activities and provide information to allow them to generate more content in social media. Identifying individuals in the creator group and giving them special attention or information would likely increase their positive influence on consumers in other categories. If a company were targeting a group in which few creators existed, its strategy could be to develop more reactive forms of content such as forums, reviews, and ratings.

Sources: C. Li and J. Bernoff, "The Social Technographics Profile: Grouping Customers Based on Online Activities," *Harvard Business Review,* 2008; C. Li and J. Bernoff, Groundswell: Winning in a world Transformed by Social Technologies Harvard Business Press, Boston, Massachusetts 2008); P. Levy, "Setting Social Strategy," *Marketing News,* March 15, 2011.

The Social Technographics ladder

Each step on the ladder represents a group of consumers more involved in the groundswell than the previous steps. To join the group on a step, a consumer need only participate in one of the listed activities at least monthly.

Creators

- Publish a blog
- Publish your own web pages
- Upload video you created
- Upload audio/music you created
- Write articles or stories and post them

Critics

- Post ratings/reviews of products or services
- Comment on someone else's blog
- Contribute to online forums
- Contribute to/edit articles on wiki

Collectors

- Use RSS feeds
- Add tags to web pages or photos
- "Vote" for websites online

Joiners

- Maintain profile on a social networking site
- Visit social networking sites

Spectators

- Read blogs
- Watch video from other users
- Listen to podcasts
- Read online forums
- Read customer ratings/reviews

Inactives

- None of these activities

Reprinted with Permission from C. Li and J. Bernoff, Groundswell: Winning in a World Transformed by Social Technologies, Harvard Business Press, 2008.

Create Tiered-Value Service Offerings

Product companies are accustomed to offering different versions of their products with prices commensurate with the value customers perceive. Automobiles with different configurations of features carry price tags that match not their cost but their perceived value to the customer. The same type of formal bundling and pricing can be accomplished in services, with the extra benefit of managing expectations.

Credit card companies offer tiered-value offerings. American Express has multiple levels of credit card services based on the type of service provided: the traditional green card offers basic service features, the gold card additional benefits, and the platinum card still more. Two advantages of tiered offerings are as follows:

1. The practice puts the burden of choosing the service level on the customer, thereby familiarizing the customer with specific service expectations.
2. The company can identify which customers are willing to pay higher prices for higher service levels.

The opportunity to set expectations accurately is present when the customer makes the decision at the time of purchase. Customers can be reminded of the terms of the agreement if they request support that is above the level in the contract.

Communicate the Criteria and Levels of Service Effectiveness

At times companies can establish the criteria by which customers assess service. Consider a business customer who is purchasing market research services for the first time. Because market research is an expert service, it is high in credence properties that are hard for customers to judge. Moreover, the effectiveness of this type of service differs depending on the objectives the client brings to the service. In this situation, a service provider can teach the customer the criteria by which to evaluate the service. The provider that teaches the customer in a credible manner will have an advantage in shaping the evaluation process.

As an example, consider research company A, which communicates the following criteria to the customer: (1) a low price signals low quality, (2) the reputation of the firm is critical, and (3) person-to-person interviews are the only type of customer feedback that will provide accurate information. A customer who accepts these criteria will evaluate all other suppliers using them. If research company B had talked to the customer first, consider these (very different!) criteria and their impact on the buyer: (1) market research companies with good reputations are charging for their reputation, not their skill; (2) telephone interviews have been found to work as well as person-to-person interviews; and (3) price does not indicate quality level.

The same approach can be used with service *levels* rather than evaluative criteria. If research company B provides four-day turnaround on the results of the data analysis, the company has just set the customer's expectation level for all other suppliers.

Manage Customer Education

As discussed in Chapter 12, customers must perform their roles properly for many services to be effective. If customers forget to perform their roles, or perform them improperly, disappointment may result. For this reason, communication to customers can take the form of customer education.

Prepare Customers for the Service Process

One of us, on a return trip from Singapore on Singapore Airlines, neglected to heed the airline's warning that return flights to the United States must be confirmed 24 hours in advance. Upon arrival at the airport to return home, the seat had been given to another customer who had conformed to the airline's request for confirmation. Depending on the perspective taken, you could argue that either the company or the customer was right in this situation. Whose responsibility is it to make sure that customers perform their roles properly?

Companies can avoid such situations by preparing customers for the service process. And companies may need to prepare the customer often, even every step of the way, for the subsequent actions the customer needs to take. A business-to-business example will help illustrate this strategy.

Customers of management consulting services purchase intangible benefits: marketing effectiveness, motivated workforces, and culture change. The very fact that companies purchase these services usually indicates that they do not know how to perform them alone. Many clients will also not know what to look for along the way to judge progress. In management consulting and other complex service situations, the effective provider prepares the customer for the service process and creates structure for the customer. At the beginning of the engagement, the management consulting firm establishes checkpoints throughout the process, at which times progress will be evaluated, and leads the customer to establish objectives for project completion. Because customers do not know what that progress will look like, the consulting firm takes the lead in setting goals or criteria to be examined at those times.

Confirm Performance to Standards and Expectations

Service providers sometimes provide service, even explicitly requested service, yet fail to communicate to the customer what has been accomplished. These providers stop short of getting credit for their actions when they do not reinforce actions with communication about their fulfillment of the request. This situation may happen under one or more of the following conditions:

- The customer cannot evaluate the effectiveness of a service.
- The decision maker in the service purchase is a person different from the users of the service.
- The service is performed out of sight of the customer.

When customers cannot evaluate service effectiveness, usually because they are inexperienced or the service is technical, the provider may fail to communicate specific actions that address client concerns because the actions seem too complex for the customer to comprehend. In this situation, the service provider can improve perceptions by translating the actions into customer-friendly terms. A personal injury lawyer who aids a client with the medical and financial implications of an accident needs to be able to tell the client in language the client can understand that the lawyer has performed the necessary actions.

When the decision maker in service purchases is different from the users of the service, a wide discrepancy in satisfaction may exist between decision makers and users. An example is in the purchase of information technology products and services in a company. The decision maker—the manager of information technology or someone in a similar position—makes the purchase decisions and understands the service promises. If users are not involved in the purchase process, they may not know what has been promised and may be dissatisfied.

Customers are not always aware of everything done behind the scenes to serve them well. Most services have invisible support processes. For instance, physicians frequently request diagnostic tests to rule out possible causes for illness. When these tests come back negative, doctors may neglect to inform patients. Many hairstyling firms have guarantees that ensure customer satisfaction with haircuts, permanents, and color treatments. However, only a few of them actively communicate these guarantees in marketing communication because they assume customers know about them. The firm that explicitly communicates the guarantee may be selected over others by a customer who is uncertain about the quality of the service. Making customers aware of standards or efforts to improve service that are not readily apparent can improve service quality perceptions.

Clarify Expectations after the Sale

When service involves a hand-off between sales and operations, clarifying expectations with customers helps the operations arm of the company align delivery with customer expectations. Salespeople are motivated and compensated to raise customer expectations—at least to the point of making the sale—rather than to communicate realistically what the company can provide. In these situations, service providers can avoid future disappointment by clarifying to customers what was promised as soon as the hand-off is made from sales to operations.

Manage Internal Marketing Communication

The fifth major category of strategies necessary to match service delivery with promises is managing internal marketing communications. Internal marketing communications can be both vertical and horizontal. *Vertical communications* are either downward, from management to employees, or upward, from employees to management. *Horizontal communications* are those across functional boundaries in an organization. A third strategy is *internal branding,* which consists of various strategies to sell the brand inside the company. Other strategies, discussed in the following paragraphs, include *creating effective upward communication, aligning back-office and support personnel with external customers*, and *creating cross-functional teams.*

Create Effective Vertical Communications

Companies that give customer-contact employees adequate information, tools, and skills allow them to perform successful interactive marketing. Some of these skills come through the training and other human resource efforts discussed in Chapter 11, but some are provided through *downward communications.* Among the most important forms of downward communications are company newsletters and magazines, corporate television networks, e-mail, briefings, videos and internal promotional campaigns, and recognition programs. One of the keys to successful downward communications is keeping employees informed of everything that is being conveyed to customers through external marketing. Employees should see company marketing communication before it is aired or published and should be familiar with the website, mailings, and direct-selling approaches used. If these vertical communications are not present, both customers and employees suffer—customers will not receive the same messages from employees that they hear in company external marketing, and employees will feel uninformed and not be aware of what their company is doing. Customers go to them, asking for services that have been marketed externally but not internally, making the employees feel uninformed, left out, and helpless.[28]

Create Effective Horizontal Communications

Horizontal Communications—communication across functional boundaries in an organization—facilitate coordinated efforts for service delivery. This task is difficult because functions typically differ in goals, philosophies, outlooks, and views of the customer—but the payoff is high. Coordination between marketing and operations can result in communication that accurately reflects service delivery, thus reducing the gap between customer expectations and actual service delivery. Integration of effort between marketing and human resources can improve the ability of each employee to become a better marketer. Coordination between finance and marketing can create prices that accurately reflect the customer's evaluation of a service. In service firms, all these functions need to be integrated to produce consistent messages and to narrow the service gaps.

One important strategy for effective horizontal communications is to open channels of communication between the marketing department and operations personnel. For example, when a company creates advertising that depicts the service encounter, it is essential that the advertising accurately reflect what customers will experience in actual service encounters. Puffery or exaggeration puts service quality perceptions at risk, especially when the firm is consistently unable to deliver to the level of service portrayed in the marketing communication. Coordination and communication between advertising and service providers are pivotal in delivering service that meets expectations.

Featuring actual employees doing their jobs or explaining the services they provide, a strategy mentioned earlier in this chapter, is one way to coordinate advertising portrayals and the reality of the service encounter. To create this type of advertising, the advertising department or agency interacts directly with service employees, facilitating horizontal communications. Similar benefits can be achieved if employees are included in the advertising process in other ways, such as by being shown advertising in its pretest forms.

Another important strategy for horizontal communications involves opening channels of communication between sales and operations. Mechanisms for achieving this goal can be formal or informal and can include annual planning meetings, retreats, team meetings, or workshops in which departments clarify service issues. In these sessions, the departments can interact to understand the goals, capabilities, and constraints of the other. Some companies hold "gap workshops" at which employees from both functions meet for a day or two to try to understand the difficulties in matching promises made through selling with delivery accomplished by operations personnel.[29]

Involving the operations staff in face-to-face meetings with external customers is also a strategy that allows operations personnel to more readily understand the salesperson's role and the needs and desires of customers. Rather than filtering customers' needs through the sales force, operations employees can witness firsthand the pressures and demands of customers. A frequent and desirable result is better service to the internal customer—the salesperson—from the operations staff as they become aware of their own roles in satisfying both external and internal customers.

Sell the Brand inside the Company

Having knowledge about what the company is doing in marketing communications is one aspect of internal marketing communication, but it is not enough. Consultant Colin Mitchell emphasizes, the importance of marketing the company's brand and brand message to employees, so that they can make powerful connections with customers.[30] He recommends three principles for bringing the brand alive: choosing the right moment to teach and inspire employees, linking internal and external marketing, and bringing the brand alive for employees. Choosing the right moment is essential because employees are not capable of or willing to accept too many change initiatives, and therefore the company has to be selective in identifying opportunities when it can create enthusiasm for the brand.

Linking internal and external marketing means that employees need to hear the same thing from management that customers hear. If customers hear that serving them is most important and employees are told that cost savings matter more, employees will be confused and unable to live the message. One of the best ways to link the two types of communication is to create advertising that targets both customers and employees. When IBM launched its highly successful e-business campaign, it took out a large advertisement in *The Wall Street Journal* to show its intent to both target audiences, then followed up with support for both audiences throughout the campaign.[31]

Bringing the brand alive to employees involves creating a strong emotional connection between employees and the company. Employees at Southwest Airlines are encouraged to live the Southwest brand by dressing informally (although still in uniform), ad-libbing when giving instructions both on the ground and in the plane, and decorating the check-in counters on holidays. Singapore Airlines, on the other hand, connects with its employees through the company's emphasis on grace, formal dress, quiet tone, and Asian food.

Create Effective Upward Communication

Upward Communications is also necessary in closing the gap between service promises and service delivery. Employees are at the front line of service, and they know—more than anyone else in the organization—what can and cannot be delivered. They know when service breakdowns are occurring and, very often, why they are happening. Having open communication channels from employees to management can prevent service problems before they occur and minimize them when they do take place.

Align Back-Office and Support Personnel with External Customers through Interaction or Measurement

As companies become increasingly customer focused, frontline personnel develop improved skills in discerning what customers require. As they become more knowledgeable about and empathetic toward external customers, they also experience intrinsic rewards for satisfying customers. Back-office and support personnel, who typically do not interact directly with external customers, miss out on this bonding and, as a consequence, fail to gain the skills and rewards associated with it.

Companies can create ways to facilitate the interaction between back-office and support personnel and external customers. Weyerhaeuser, for example, sends hourly employees to customers' plants to better understand their needs. When actual interaction is difficult or impossible, some companies videotape customers in their service facilities during the purchase and consumption process to vividly portray the needs and requirements of customers and to show personnel the support that frontline people need to deliver to those expectations.

When company measurement systems are established, employees are sometimes judged on the basis of how they perform for the next internal customer in the chain. Although this approach provides feedback in terms of how well the employees are serving the internal customer, it lacks the motivation and reward that come from seeing their efforts affect the end customer. FedEx has aligned internal personnel with the external customer using measurement. As we discussed in Chapter 9, FedEx's service quality indicator (SQI) computes daily the number of companywide service failures. To clearly communicate customer fail points to internal employees, the company created linking measures to trace the causes to each internal department. For example, the company's information technology department affects the SQI measurements and therefore has submeasures that provide feedback on how the department's work is affecting the SQI.

Create Cross-Functional Teams

Another approach to improving horizontal communications to better serve customers is to involve employees in cross-functional teams to align their jobs with end customer requirements. For example, if a team of telecommunications service representatives is working to improve interaction with customers, back-office people such as computer technicians or training personnel can become part of the team. The team then learns requirements and sets goals for achieving them together, an approach that directly creates communications across the functions.

The cross-functional team approach can best be explained by the examples of an advertising agency. The individual in an advertising agency who typically interacts directly with the client is the account executive (often called a "suit" by the creative staff). In the traditional agency, the account executive visits the client, elicits client expectations, and then interacts with the various departments in the agency (art, copywriting, production, traffic, and media buying) that will perform the work. All functions are specialized and, in extreme cases, get direction for their portion of the work right from the account executive. A cross-functional team approach has representatives from all the areas meet with the account executive, even the client, and collectively discuss the account and approaches to address client needs. Each team member brings his or her function's perspectives and opens communication. All members can then understand the constraints and schedules of the other groups.

Summary

Discrepancies between service delivery and external communications have a strong impact on customer perceptions of service quality. In this chapter we discussed the role of and need for integrated service marketing communications in minimizing these discrepancies. We described external and interactive communications using the service triangle and emphasized the need to coordinate all communication to deliver service that meets customer expectations. We emphasized the difficulties and possibilities associated with new media. We also discussed the factors that lead to challenges in service marketing communications, including service intangibility; management of service promises; and management of customer expectations, customer education, and internal marketing communication. We then examined strategies to address each of these service communications problems. To address service intangibility, we described specific strategies such as the use of vivid imagery and tangible icons in communications, as well as ways to maximize the use of word-of-mouth communication. To manage service promises, we delineated the need for a strong service brand, coordination of service promises, realistic promises, and service guarantees. To manage customer expectations, we suggested that allowing customers to choose among options, creating tiered-value options, communicating service effectiveness criteria, and negotiating unrealistic expectations can be effective. To improve customer education, we described the need to prepare customers for the service process, confirm performance to standards and expectations, clarify expectations after the sale, and teach customers to choose the best times to seek service. Finally, to manage internal communication, we discussed effective vertical communications, horizontal communications, and internal branding.

Discussion Questions

1. Think of another service company that provides integrated service marketing communications. Go to the service company's website and find the section where it posts its advertising and communication. Is the company's campaign as comprehensive and as integrated as Hotels.com's campaign, as described in the opening vignette? Why or why not? What should be added, changed, or deleted to improve the campaign?

2. Which of the key reasons for the communication gap (provider gap 4) discussed in the beginning of this chapter is the easiest to address in a company? Which is the hardest to address? Why?

3. Review the five general strategies for achieving integrated service marketing communications. Would all these strategies be relevant in goods firms? Which would be most critical in goods firms? Which would be most critical in service firms? Are there any differences between those most critical in goods firms and those most critical in service firms?

4. What are the most effective Internet advertisements you have seen? Why are they effective?

5. Using the section on managing customer expectations, put yourself in the position of your professor, who must reduce the amount of "service" provided to the students in your class. Give an example of each strategy in this context. Which of the strategies would work best with you (the student) in managing your expectations? Why?

6. Why are social marketing media like Facebook and YouTube so important in service firms? Are they important in product firms?

7. What other strategies can you suggest for leveraging consumer-generated media?

8. What other strategies can you add to the four offered in the section on customer education? What types of education do you expect from service firms? Give an example of a firm from which you have received adequate education. What firm has not provided you with adequate education?

Exercises

1. Go to the Google website and select the tab called "Business Solutions." This is the section of the site that describes the types of advertising that Google offers. Do the same thing for YouTube (you must go to "Company Information" and then to "Advertising"). Review these types of advertising, and describe the benefits and disadvantages of each. If you were an advertiser, which of these types of ads would you want to use? Why?

2. Find five effective service advertisements in newspapers and magazines. According to the criteria given in this chapter, identify why they are effective. Critique them using the list of criteria, and discuss ways they could be improved.

Notes

1. P. G. Lindell, "You Need Integrated Attitude to Develop IMC," *Marketing News,* May 26, 1997, p. 5.

2. D. Legg and J. Baker, "Advertising Strategies for Service Firms," in *Add Value to Your Service,* ed. C. Suprenant (Chicago: American Marketing Association, 1987), pp. 163–168.

3. B. Mittal, "The Advertising of Services: Meeting the Challenge of Intangibility," *Journal of Service Research* 2 (August 1999), pp. 98–116.

4. H. S. Bansal and P. A. Voyer, "Word-of-Mouth Processes within a Services Purchase Decision Context," *Journal of Service Research* 3 (November 2000), pp. 166–177.

5. K. L. Alesandri, "Strategies That Influence Memory for Advertising Communications," in *Information Processing Research in Advertising,* ed. R. J. Harris (Hillsdale, NJ: Erlbaum, 1983).

6. L. L. Berry and T. Clark, "Four Ways to Make Services More Tangible," *Business,* October–December 1986, pp. 53–54.

7. www.geico.com; www.Aflac.com; "Who's Your Favorite Advertising Icon?" advertising insert, *New York Times,* September 20, 2004, p. 6.

8. Berry and Clark, "Four Ways to Make Services More Tangible."

9. W. R. George and L. L. Berry, "Guidelines for the Advertising of Services," *Business Horizons,* May–June 1981, pp. 52–56.

10. M. Arndt, "Burrito Buzz—and So Few Ads," *BusinessWeek,* March 12, 2007, pp. 84–85.

11. G. Fulgoni, "No Time to Lose for Online Retailers," comScore Inc. blog, December 7, 2009.

12. M. Douglas, "Q&A," WOM Stats, www.womma.org, May 28, 2011.

13. "The 90/10 Split," www.emarketer.com, May 28, 2011.

14. Cited in S. Gupta, K. Armstrong and Z. Clayton, "Social Media," Harvard Business School, February 15, 2011, from a study by The Nielsen Company, "Trust, Value, and Engagement in Advertising," July 2009, http://blog.nielsen.com/nielsenwire/wp-content/uploads/2009/07/trustin advertising0709.pdf, accessed January 2010.

15. "VNU Brings Together BuzzMetrics, Intelliseek to Create Nielsen BuzzMetrics Service," www.prnewswire.com, September 25, 2006.

16. D. D. Gremler, K. P. Gwinner, and S. W. Brown, "Generating Positive Word-of-Mouth Communications through Customer-Employee Relationships," *International Journal of Service Industry Management* (January 2001), pp. 44–59.

17. Ibid, pp. 54–56.

18. Leonard L. Berry, "Cultivating Service Brand Equity," *Journal of the Academy of Marketing Science* 28 (Winter 2000), pp. 128–137.

19. The figure and definitions contained in this section are all from Berry, "Cultivating Service Brand Equity."

20. L. L. Berry and K. D. Seltman, " Building a Strong Brand: Lessons from Mayo Clinic," *Business Horizons* 50 (2007), pp.199–209.

21. Ibid., p. 201.

22. G. Rifkin, "How the Red Sox Touch All the Branding Bases," strategy + business .com, accessed April 2007.

23. www.mastercardinternational.com 2011.

24. Alice Z. Cuneo, "Sue Johenning," *Advertising Age,* September 27, 2004.

25. P. Denoyelle and J. Larreche, "Virgin Atlantic Airways—Ten Years Later," INSEAD Case, 1995.

26. D. E. Bell and D. M. Leavitt, "Bronner Slosberg Humphrey," *Harvard Business School Case 9-598-136,* 1998, p. 5.

27. Ibid.

28. L. L. Berry, V. A. Zeithaml, and A. Parasuraman, "Quality Counts in Services, Too," *Business Horizons,* May–June 1985, pp. 44–52.

29. V. A. Zeithaml, A. Parasuraman, and L. L. Berry, *Delivering Quality Service: Balancing Customer Perceptions and Expectations* (New York: The Free Press, 1990), p. 120.

30. C. Mitchell, "Selling the Brand Inside," *Harvard Business Review* 80 (January 2002), pp. 5–11.

31. Ibid., p. 9.

Chapter Fifteen

Pricing of Services

This chapter's objectives are to

1. Discuss three major ways that service prices are perceived differently from goods prices by customers.
2. Articulate the key ways that pricing of services differs from pricing of goods from a company's perspective.
3. Demonstrate what value means to customers and the role that price plays in value.
4. Describe strategies that companies use to price services.
5. Give examples of pricing strategy in action.

Airline Fees Baffle Consumers

In the good old days of traditional airline ticketing, customers could easily assess the cost of a ticket and compare the price of flights on competing airlines. A flight had a basic cost plus taxes, making the final price easy to determine. Not so today. With separate and different fees charged for such services as ticket changes, booking method (telephone, Web, or even kiosk), unaccompanied minors, pets, seat selection, premium seats, in-flight food and drinks, blankets/pillows, carry-on bags, checked bags, overweight bags, boarding order, and oversized bags, a potential passenger now finds it virtually impossible to know in advance what a flight will cost.

To make matters worse, few airlines charge extra fees for the same services—or charge an equal amount for the services that are the same—so comparisons across companies are difficult to make. For example, American Airlines and U.S. Airways offer and charge extra for regular seats at the front of the coach cabin. United, JetBlue, and Virgin America, on the other hand, offer and charge not for seat location but for seats configured with extra legroom. American, U.S. Airways, JetBlue, and Virgin America sell pillow and blanket sets rather than offering them for free. Allegiant sells blankets for $15, without pillows. And if you want to get on the plane before other passengers, United, American, Southwest, and AirTran airlines charge $10 or more to board right after First and Business Class.

The one airline that distinguishes itself because it *does not* charge for bags is Southwest Airlines, where the slogan is "Bags Fly Free." This price differentiator supports Southwest's low-cost airline positioning and generates goodwill from passengers. On the other hand, Spirit Airlines, also a low-fare carrier, negatively stands out because it is the first and only U.S. airline to charge passengers for bringing carry-on bags aboard. Spirit also charges passengers $5 for boarding passes printed by a Spirit check-in agent rather than printing their own passes online. The airline's newest fee is a $1 charge for printing a boarding pass at a Spirit airport kiosk.

Charging for individual services is a relatively new strategy for airlines in the United States, but it has been a common practice for Ryanair, Dublin's discount airline. The company, with an average fare ($53) that is almost half that of Southwest Airlines ($93), for prices charges premium its "extra" services such as baggage and online check-in. Depending on your perspective, it could be called penny-pinching (water costs almost as much as beer on U.S. flights) or pay-for-service (even making reservations online requires payment). While the fares are low, everything else costs. In fact, at one time the airline charged $34 for the use of a wheelchair! Customers aren't the only ones who have to pay: staff buy their own uniforms and provide their own pens. Michael O'Leary, CEO of Ryanair's holding company, clearly states his philosophy: "You want luxury? Go somewhere else."

Inspired by Southwest Airlines, O'Leary revolutionized the strategy for running a low-cost airline. He took Southwest's basic approach and built upon it. First, he cut costs in as many places as possible—selling virtually all tickets online, removing seatback pockets and window shades to save staff between-flight maintenance, and installing nonreclining seats to pack in more passengers. Second, he based his pricing strategy on fees for individual services, fees that were not directly comparable to other airlines, insulating the airline from head-to-head price competition. When larger airlines dropped fares, making them more competitive with Southwest and JetBlue, the discounters had to add amenities and/or eliminate cost-saving practices to compete. O'Leary kept fares low but charged for everything else to keep profits up. Kerry Capell of *BusinessWeek* likens this to strategies used with cell phones:

> He thinks like a retailer and charges for absolutely every little thing, except the seat itself. Imagine the seat as akin to a cell phone: It comes free, or nearly free, but its owner winds up spending on all sorts of services. Last year, Ryanair gave away 25% of its seats, a figure O'Leary thinks he can double within five years. In the not-too distant future, he wants all seats to go for free.

Among the other on-airplane money-making approaches O'Leary uses are advertising, sales of products such as cameras, and services such as bus and train tickets. The bus and train tickets are particularly useful to passengers, as the airline serves small, outlying airports, as does Southwest, that are not in major cities. Online, the company promotes and sells such services as hotels, rental cars, travel insurance, and gambling, from which it receives commissions. Planned in-flight mobile phone service will soon allow gaming on the planes themselves.

The pricing strategy is highly effective, making Ryanair Europe's most profitable airline. How interesting that Southwest, the most profitable airline in the United States, uses just the opposite strategy!

Sources: K. Capell, "Wal-Mart with Wings," *BusinessWeek,* November 16, 2006; www.ryanair.com, 2007; "Ultimate Guide to Airline Fees," compiled by Smarter Travel, www.smartertravel.com/blog/today-in-travel/airline-fees-the-ultimate-guide.html?id=2623262, July 2011; "Airlines Go Back to Boarding School to Move Fliers onto Planes Faster," *The Wall Street Journal,* July 21, 2011, p. D1.

According to one of the leading experts on pricing, most service organizations use a "naive and unsophisticated approach to pricing without regard to underlying shifts in demand, the rate that supply can be expanded, prices of available substitutes, consideration of the price–volume relationship, or the availability of future substitutes."[1] What makes the pricing of services more difficult than pricing of goods? What approaches work well in the context of services?

This chapter builds on three key differences between customer evaluation of pricing services and goods:

1. Customers often have inaccurate or limited reference prices for services.
2. Monetary price is not the only price relevant to service customers.
3. Price is a key signal of quality in services.

These three differences can have profound impact on the strategies companies use to set and administer prices for services.

The chapter also discusses common pricing structures, including (1) cost-based, (2) competition-based, and (3) demand-based pricing. One of the most important aspects of demand-based pricing is perceived value, which service providers must understand, so that they price in line with offerings and customer expectations. For that reason, we also describe how customers define value and discuss pricing strategies in the context of value.

THREE KEY WAYS THAT SERVICE PRICES ARE DIFFERENT FOR CUSTOMERS

What role does price play in customer decisions about services? How important is price to potential buyers compared with other factors and service features? Service companies must understand how pricing works, but first they must understand how customers perceive prices and price changes. The three sections that follow describe ways that customers perceive services, and each is central to effective pricing.

Customer Knowledge of Service Prices

To what extent do customers use price as a criterion in selecting services? How much do they know about the costs of services? Before you answer these questions, take the services pricing quiz in Exhibit 15.1. Were you able to fill in a price for each of the services listed? If you were able to answer the questions on the basis of memory, you have internal *reference prices* for the services. A reference price is *a price point in memory for a good or a service* and can consist of the price last paid, the price most frequently paid, or the average of all prices customers have paid for similar offerings.[2]

To see how accurate your reference prices for services are, you can compare them with the actual price of these services from the providers in your hometown. If you are like many consumers, you feel quite uncertain about your knowledge of the prices of services, and the reference prices you hold in memory for services are not generally as accurate as those you hold for goods. There are many reasons for this difference.

Service Variability Limits Knowledge

Because services are not created on a factory assembly line, service firms have great flexibility in the configurations of services they offer. Firms can conceivably offer an infinite variety of combinations and permutations, leading to complex and complicated pricing structures. As an example, consider how difficult it is to get comparable price quotes when buying life insurance. With the multitude of types (such as whole life

Exhibit 15.1   What Do You Know about the Prices of Services?

1. What do the following services cost in your hometown?

   Dental checkup _____

   General medical checkup _____

   Legal help with a DWI (driving while intoxicated) charge _____

   Dental braces _____

   Rental of a DVD for one night _____

   One hour of housecleaning _____

   Room at the Marriott _____

   Haircut _____

   Oil change and lube _____

2. Which of the following would you select if you needed a filling replaced in a tooth?

   a. Dentist A—cost is $75, located 15 miles from your home, wait is three weeks for an appointment and 1.5 hours in waiting room

   b. Dentist B—cost is $100, located 15 miles from your home, wait is one week for appointment and 0.5 hour in waiting room

   c. Dentist C—cost is $150, located 3 miles from your job, wait is one week for appointment and no time in waiting room

   d. Dentist D—cost is $225, located 3 miles from your job, wait is one week for appointment and no time in waiting room; nitrous oxide used, so no pain is involved

versus term), features (different deductibles), and variations associated with customers (age, health risk, smoking or nonsmoking), few insurance companies offer exactly the same features and the same prices. Only an expert customer, one who knows enough about insurance to completely specify the options across providers, is likely to find prices that are directly comparable.

How did you answer the questions about prices for a medical checkup? If you are like most consumers, you probably wanted more information before you offered a reference price. You probably wanted to know what type of checkup the physician is providing. Does it include X-rays and other diagnostic tests? What types of tests? How long does the checkup take? What is its purpose? If the checkup is undertaken simply to get a signature on a health form or a marriage certificate, the doctor may take a brief medical history, listen for a heartbeat, and measure blood pressure. If, however, the checkup is to monitor a chronic ailment such as diabetes or high blood pressure, the doctor may be more thorough. The point is that a high degree of variability exists across providers of services. Not every physician defines a checkup the same way.

Providers Are Unwilling to Estimate Prices

Another reason customers lack accurate reference prices for services is that many providers are unable or unwilling to estimate price in advance. For example, legal and medical service providers are rarely willing—or even able—to estimate a price in advance. The fundamental reason is that they do not know themselves what the services will involve until they have fully examined the patient or the client's situation or until the process of service delivery (such as an operation in a hospital or a trial) unfolds. Most hospitals contend that their fee schedules, called chargemasters, should not be made available to patients beforehand and have fought to keep them private.[3] In a business-to-business context, companies obtain bids or estimates for complex services such as consulting or construction, but this type of price estimation is typically not undertaken with end-consumers; therefore, they often buy without advance knowledge about the final price of the service.

Individual Customer Needs Vary

Another factor that results in the inaccuracy of reference prices is that individual customer needs vary. Some hairstylists' service prices vary across customers on the basis of length of hair, type of haircut, and whether a conditioning treatment and style are included. Therefore, if you ask a friend what a haircut costs from a particular stylist, chances are that your haircut from the same stylist will be a different price. In a similar vein, a service as simple as a hotel room will have prices that vary greatly: by size of room, time of year, type of room availability, and individual versus group rate. These two examples are for very simple services. Now consider a service purchase as idiosyncratic as braces from a dentist or help from a lawyer. In these and many other services, the fact that customers have different requirements will play a strong role in the price of the service.

Collection of Price Information Is Overwhelming in Services

Still another reason customers lack accurate reference prices for services is that customers feel overwhelmed with the information they need to gather. With most goods, retail stores display the products by category to allow customers to compare and contrast the prices of different brands and sizes. Rarely is there a similar display of services in a single outlet. If customers want to compare prices (such as for dry cleaning), they must drive to or call individual outlets or search on the Internet in situations where prices are available. This can be an overwhelming task for consumers, even for the most basic services, as illustrated in Exhibit 15.1.

When services are more specialized, finding out what they cost is even more difficult, See if you have reference prices for these providers: wedding adviser, pet chiropractor, baby-proofing expert, and executive coach. Your reference prices—if you can even come up with some—are probably even more uncertain and less accurate than for the services in the price quiz in Exhibit 15.1. Here are estimates from actual consultants: $5,500 for a wedding adviser's attention to all details, $70 to $140 a visit for chiropractic adjustment for pets, $300 to $450 to protect a house for and from a baby, and $1,300 for four hours of executive coaching.[4]

The fact that consumers often possess inaccurate reference prices for services has several important managerial implications. Promotional pricing (as in couponing or special pricing) may be less meaningful for services, for which price anchors typically do not exist. Perhaps that is why price is not featured in service advertising as much as it is featured in advertising for goods. Promotional pricing may also create problems if the promotional price (such as a $50 permanent wave special from a salon) is the only one customers see in advertising: it could become the customer's anchor price, making the regular price of $75 for a future purchase seem high by comparison.

The absence of accurate reference prices also suggests that advertising actual prices for services the customer is not used to purchasing may reduce uncertainty and overcome a customer's inflated price expectations for some services. For example, a marketing research firm's advertisements citing the price for a simple study (such as $10,000) would be informative to business customers who were not familiar with the costs of research studies and therefore would be guessing at the cost. By featuring price in advertising, the company overcomes the fear of high cost by giving readers a price anchor.

Prices Are Not Visible

One requirement for the existence of customer reference prices is *price visibility*—the price cannot be hidden or implicit. In many services, particularly financial services, most customers know about only the rate of return and not the costs they pay in the form of fund and insurance fees. In securities and term life insurance, customers are made aware of fees. However, price is invisible in certificates, whole-life insurance, and annuities (which have rear-load charges), and customers rarely know how they are charged or what they pay. Credit card fees are assessed on the basis of what consumers spend, and while customers may know their interest rates they are often shocked at what they are spending in fees to the financial institutions. Compounding and other financial practices—such as compressed periods to pay and dramatic increases in interest rates due to late payments—do not affect their costs until after they have made purchases.

For all the reasons discussed here, many customers do not see the price at all until *after* they receive certain services. Of course, in situations of urgency, such as in accident or illness, customers must make the decision to purchase without respect to cost. And if cost is not known to the customer before purchase, it cannot be used as a key criterion for purchase, as it often is for goods.

The Role of Nonmonetary Costs

Economists have long recognized that monetary price is not the only sacrifice consumers make to obtain products and services. Demand, therefore, is not just a function of monetary price but is influenced by other costs as well. Nonmonetary costs represent other sources of sacrifice perceived by consumers when buying and using a service. Time costs, search costs, and psychological costs often enter into the evaluation of whether to purchase or repurchase a service and may at times be more important concerns than monetary price. Customers will trade money for these other costs.

Time Costs

Most services require customers' direct participation and thus consume real time: time waiting as well as time when the customer interacts with the service provider. Consider the investment you make to exercise, see a physician, or get through the crowds to watch a concert or baseball game. Not only are you paying money to receive these services, but you are also expending time. Time becomes a sacrifice made to receive service in multiple ways. First, because service providers cannot completely control the number of customers or the length of time it will take for each customer to be served, customers are likely to expend time waiting to receive the service. The average waiting time in physicians'

Customers will trade money for time savings. Customers who purchase lawn care, housekeeping, and other services often do so because the value of their time is higher than the value of the money needed to purchase the service.

offices is 24 minutes, according to the American Medical Association.[5] Waiting time for a service is frequently longer and less predictable than waiting time to buy goods. Second, customers often wait for an available appointment from a service provider (in the price quiz, dentist A required a three-week wait, whereas dentist D required only one week). Virtually everyone has expended waiting time to receive services.

Search Costs

Search costs—the effort invested to identify and select from among services you desire—are often higher for services than for physical goods. Prices for services are rarely displayed on shelves of service establishments for customers to examine as they shop, so these prices are often known only when a customer has decided to experience the service. As an example, how well did you estimate the costs of an hour of housecleaning in the price quiz? As a student, it is unlikely that you regularly purchase housecleaning, and you probably have not seen the price of an hour of cleaning displayed in any retail store. Another factor that increases search costs is that each service establishment typically offers only one "brand" of a service (with the exception of brokers in insurance or financial services), so a customer must initiate contact with several companies to get information across sellers. Price comparisons for many services (e.g., travel and hotels) are now facilitated through the Internet, reducing search costs. Orbitz and Travelocity, for example, offer customers a search of most airlines (with the notable exception of Southwest, which does not participate in reservation services), many hotels, and rental car companies. However, as reflected in the chapter opener, the added fees that airlines now charge still make searching for the final costs of airline flights difficult.

Convenience Costs

There are also convenience (or, perhaps more accurately, inconvenience) costs of services. If customers have to travel to receive a service, they incur a cost, and the cost becomes greater when travel is difficult, as it is for elderly persons. Further, if a service provider's hours do not coincide with customers' available time, they must arrange their schedules to correspond to the company's schedule. And if consumers have to expend effort and time to prepare to receive a service (such as removing all food from kitchen cabinets in preparation for an exterminator's spraying), they make additional sacrifices.

Psychological Costs

Often the most painful nonmonetary costs are the psychological costs incurred in receiving some services. Fear of not understanding (insurance), fear of rejection (bank loans), and fear of outcomes (medical treatment or surgery) all constitute psychological costs that customers experience as sacrifices when purchasing and using services. New services, even those that create positive change, bring about psychological costs that consumers factor into the purchase of services. While many grocery stores now offer self-checkout that allows customers to bypass long lines, the number of customers who use them has not lived up to expectations. Many customers find the self-checkout lines confusing and frustrating to use, and others are embarrassed when they cannot move through them quickly.

Reducing Nonmonetary Costs

The managerial implications of these other sources of sacrifice are compelling. First, a firm may be able to increase monetary price by reducing time and other costs. For example, a service marketer can reduce the perceptions of time and convenience costs when use of the service is embedded in other activities (such as when a convenience store cashes checks, sells stamps, and serves coffee along with selling products). Second, customers may be willing to pay to avoid the other costs. Many customers willingly pay extra to have items delivered to their homes—including restaurant meals or bedroom furniture—rather than transporting the services and products themselves. Some customers also pay a premium for fast check-in and checkout (as in joining the Hertz #1 club), for reduced waiting time in a professional's office (as in so-called executive appointments where, for a premium price, a busy executive goes early in the morning and does not have to wait), and to avoid doing the work themselves (such as paying one and one-half times the price per gallon to avoid having to put gas in a rental car before returning it). If time or other costs are pivotal for a given service, the company's advertising can emphasize these savings rather than monetary savings.

Many other services save time, thus actually allowing the customer to "buy" time. Household cleaning services, lawn care, babysitting, personal shopper service, online banking, home delivery of groceries, house painting, and carpet cleaning—all these services represent net gains in the discretionary time of consumers and can be marketed that way. Services that allow the customer to buy time are likely to have monetary value for busy consumers.

Price as an Indicator of Service Quality

One of the intriguing aspects of pricing is that buyers are likely to use price as an indicator of both service costs and service quality—price is at once an attraction variable and a repellent.[6] Customers' use of price as an indicator of quality depends on several factors, one of which is the other information available to them. When service cues to quality are readily accessible, when brand names provide evidence of a company's reputation, or when the level of advertising communicates the company's belief in the brand, customers may prefer to use those cues instead of price. In other situations, however, such as when quality is hard to detect or when quality or price varies a great deal within a class of services, consumers may believe that price is the best indicator of quality. Many of these conditions typify situations that face consumers when purchasing services.[7] Another factor that increases the dependence on price as a quality indicator is the risk associated with the service purchase. In high-risk situations, many of which involve credence services such as medical treatment or management consulting, the customer will look to price as a surrogate for quality.

Because customers depend on price as a cue to quality and because price sets expectations of quality, service prices must be determined carefully. In addition to being chosen to cover costs or match competitors, prices must be selected to convey the appropriate quality signal. Pricing too low can lead to inaccurate inferences about the quality of the service. Pricing too high can set expectations that may be difficult to match in service delivery.

APPROACHES TO PRICING SERVICES

Rather than repeat what you learned about pricing in your marketing principles class, we want to emphasize in this chapter the way that service prices and pricing differ from both the customer's and the company's perspective. We discuss these differences in the context of the three pricing structures typically used to set prices: (1) cost-based, (2) competition-based, and (3) demand-based pricing. These categories, as shown in Figure 15.1, are the same bases on which goods prices are set, but adaptations must be made in services. The figure shows the three structures interrelating because companies need to consider each of the three to some extent in setting prices. In the following sections, we describe in general each basis for pricing and discuss challenges that occur when the approach is used in service pricing. Figure 15.1 summarizes those challenges.

FIGURE 15.1

Three Basic Marketing Price Structures and Challenges Associated with Their Use for Services

Challenges:
1. Small firms may charge too little to be viable.
2. Heterogeneity of services limits comparability.
3. Prices may not reflect customer value.

Challenges:
1. Costs are difficult to trace.
2. Labor is more difficult to price than materials.
3. Costs may not equal the value that customers perceive the services are worth.

Challenges:
1. Monetary price must be adjusted to reflect the value of nonmonetary costs.
2. Information on service costs is less available to customers; hence, price may not be a central factor.

Cost-Based Pricing

In cost-based pricing, a company determines expenses from raw materials and labor, adds amounts or percentages for overhead and profit, and thereby arrives at the price. This method is widely used by industries such as utilities, contracting, wholesaling, and advertising. The basic formula for cost-based pricing is

$$\text{Price} = \text{Direct costs} + \text{Overhead costs} + \text{Profit margin}$$

Direct costs involve the materials and labor associated with delivering the service, overhead costs are a share of fixed costs, and the profit margin is a percentage of full costs (Direct + Overhead).

Special Challenges in Cost-Based Pricing for Services

What is unique about services when using cost-based approaches to pricing? First, costs are difficult to trace or calculate in service businesses, particularly where multiple services are provided by the firm.[8] Consider how difficult it must be for a bank to allocate teller time accurately across its checking, savings, and money market accounts to decide what to charge for the services. Second, a major component of cost is employee time rather than materials, and the value of people's time, particularly nonprofessional time, is not easy to calculate or estimate. One of the major difficulties in cost-based pricing involves defining the units in which a service is purchased. Thus, the *price per unit*—a well-understood concept in the pricing of manufactured goods—is a vague entity. For this reason many services are sold in terms of input units rather than units of measured output. For example, most professional services (such as consulting, engineering, architecture, psychotherapy, and tutoring) are sold by the hour.

An added difficulty is that actual service costs may underrepresent the value of the service to the customer. A local tailor charges $10 for taking in a seam on a $350 ladies' suit jacket and an equal $10 for taking in a seam on a pair of $14 sweat shorts. The tailor's rationale is that both jobs require the same amount of time. What she neglects to see is that the customer would pay a higher price—and might even be happier about the alterations—for the expensive suit jacket and that $10 is too high a price for the sweat shorts.

Examples of Cost-Based Pricing Strategies Used in Services

Cost-plus pricing is a commonly used approach in which component costs are calculated and a markup added. In product pricing, this approach is quite simple; in service industries, however, it is complicated because the tracking and identification of costs are difficult. The approach is typically used in industries in which cost must be estimated in advance, such as construction, engineering, and advertising. In construction or engineering, bids are solicited by clients on the basis of the description of the service desired. Using their knowledge of the costs of the components of the service (including the raw materials such as masonry and lumber), labor (including both professional and unskilled), and margin, the company estimates and presents to the client a price for the finished service. A contingency amount—to cover the possibility that costs may be higher than estimated—is also stated because, in large projects, specifications can change as the service is provided.

Fee for service is the pricing strategy used by professionals; it represents the cost of the time involved in providing the service. Consultants, psychologists, accountants, and lawyers, among other professionals, charge for their services on an hourly basis. Virtually all psychologists and social workers have a set hourly rate they charge to their clients, and most structure their time in increments of an hour.

In the early 1900s, lawyers typically billed clients a certain fee for services rendered regardless of the amount of time they spent delivering them. Then in the 1970s, law firms began to bill on an hourly rate, in part because this approach offered accountability to clients and an internal budgeting system for the firm. One of the most difficult aspects of this approach is that recordkeeping is tedious for professionals. Lawyers and accountants must keep track of the time they spend for a given client, often down to 10-minute increments. For this reason the method has been criticized because it does not promote efficiency and sometimes ignores the expertise of the lawyers (those who are very experienced can accomplish much more than novices in a given time period, yet billings do not always reflect this). Clients also feared padding of their legal bills and began to audit them. Despite these concerns, the hourly bill dominates the industry, with the majority of revenues billed this way.[9]

Competition-Based Pricing

The competition-based pricing approach focuses on the prices charged by other firms in the same industry or market. Competition-based pricing does not always imply charging the identical rate others charge but rather using others' prices as an anchor for the firm's price. This approach is used predominantly in two situations: (1) when services are standard across providers, such as in the dry cleaning industry, and (2) in oligopolies with a few large service providers, such as in the rental car industry. Difficulties involved in provision of services sometimes make competition-based pricing less simple than it is in goods industries.

Special Challenges in Competition-Based Pricing for Services

Competition-based pricing, commonly practiced in goods firms, can be difficult for service firms. Small firms may find it difficult to charge the same prices that larger service firms charge and make margins high enough to remain in business. Many

Strategy Insight   "Congestion Pricing" as a Strategy to Change Driving Behavior in Big Cities

Congestion pricing is an approach designed to reduce traffic by increasing the cost of driving in the most popular and overcrowded areas in cities. Cities like London, Singapore, Stockholm, and Oslo—with dense central business districts—use pricing strategies to induce motorists to avoid driving into the city during peak times and to use alternative transportation. The purpose of congestion pricing is to signal to drivers the times when and locations where they should consider taking mass transit, reschedule their trips, or pay higher fees for driving.

LONDON'S SUCCESS

London's program began in 2003, when the city first charged drivers a premium to enter the city's grid-locked business district. While policymakers knew that the strategy would improve economic competitiveness and quality of life, they were less sure that drivers would respond. However, the results were dramatic: a 30 percent average drop in congestion, a 37 percent average increase in traffic speed to move motorists more quickly through the city, a 12 percent drop in particulate matter and nitrogen oxides in the air, a 20 percent decrease in fossil fuel consumption and carbon dioxide emissions, and a 20 percent increase in the use of public transportation. Besides reducing congestion, London raised hundreds of millions of dollars in new revenue, which it invested

in better transit. Perhaps even more encouraging is that 78 percent of the drivers who pay to enter the cordoned area are satisfied with the system.

STOCKHOLM'S TRIAL LEADS TO CUSTOMER ACCEPTANCE

Stockholm, Sweden, tried the pricing approach, which it called "cordon pricing," for the first half of 2006. The impact on public opinion was impressive. Before the trial, only 31 percent of residents were in favor of the strategy. After a 15 percent reduction in traffic and a 10 to 14 percent drop in carbon dioxide emissions, however, voters were far more favorable and passed a referendum to reinstate the charge. And a recent poll said that 67 percent of respondents now agree that it is good that the government introduced the system.

NEW YORK'S 'S UNSUCCESSFUL PLAN

In 2006, New York's mayor, Michael Bloomberg, proposed a congestion pricing plan in which the fees would be $8 for a car and $21 for a truck for each weekday trip into the "zone" (below 86th street) in Manhattan. These fees would not be imposed just to raise money, as most road and bridge tolls are, but to limit the number of cars that entered the city, with the purpose of reducing congestion. There would be no charge on weekends and no charge to drive in downtown areas outside the zone. Taxis, vehicles

mom-and-pop service establishments—dry cleaning, retail, and tax accounting, among others—cannot deliver services at the low prices charged by chain operations.

Further, the heterogeneity of services across and within providers makes this approach complicated. As an example, banks offer many types of accounts and services. To try to determine how a competitive bank prices for individual accounts and may differ in features and costs—and whether those prices give sufficient margins and profits—can be difficult. Only in very standardized services that a bank provides, such as ATM surcharges, can banks benefit from competitive prices. In 2007, Bank of America made headlines by raising ATM withdrawal charges for noncustomers to $3 per withdrawal. Other banks like Citi, Chase, Wachovia, and Wells Fargo did not immediately match the increase but did comment that they review what their competitors do in setting prices.[10]

Examples of Competition-Based Pricing in Service Industries

Price signaling occurs in markets with a high concentration of sellers. In this type of market, any price offered by one company will be matched by competitors to avoid giving a low-cost seller a distinct advantage. The airline industry exemplifies price with handicapped plates, buses, and emergency vehicles would not pay the fees. Bridge and tunnel tolls would be subtracted from the daily total. The federal government, which recently awarded the city a $350 million grant to help reduce traffic congestion, made the congestion pricing mechanism a condition of the grant. Proposed benefits of the plan include the same benefits realized by plans in other big cities—improving the health of New Yorkers due to reduced emissions, reducing street noise, increasing ridership on public transportation, and improving productivity.

The plan was strongly opposed by a broad array of politicians from Queens, Brooklyn, and New York's suburbs, who viewed the fee as overwhelmingly benefiting affluent Manhattanites.

SAN FRANCISCO'S PLAN

San Francisco has launched an experiment to eliminate congestion by changing the dynamics of parking. First, the plan changes the price of a parking space according to demand, thereby keeping spaces open on every block. Second, it uses sensors to lead drivers to open spaces, eliminating the congestion caused by circling drivers. San Francisco's congestion pricing spans a variety of approaches. One option includes increasing the toll on the Bay Bridge from $4 to $6 during rush hours; another is opening a toll lane where price increases as traffic

does on Interstate 680, a historically jammed stretch of highway. Other ideas are being considered: toll lanes for Highway 237 in the South Bay and for Interstate 580 in the East Bay, higher tolls during peak hours for other bridges, and charges for driving into downtown San Francisco.

The results of the experiment have been mixed. Traffic on the Bay Bridge has dropped 2.35 percent during the morning commute and 3.45 percent in the afternoon since the toll was raised in July 2010. This means that the time it takes to drive 5 miles from University Avenue in Berkeley to the Bay Bridge toll plaza has been reduced by 3 minutes to an average of 24 minutes during the morning rush. So far, the toll lane has not had much of an effect, mainly because the traffic congestion it was supposed to address has largely been tamed by the economic slump, according to a spokesman for the project.

Sources: "Congestion Pricing: A Smart Solution for Reducing Traffic in Urban Centers and Busy Corridors," www.environmentaldefense.org, 2007; Drum Major Institute for Public Policy, "Congestion Pricing: Good Policy for New York's Middle Class," *DMI Report 2007*, www.drummajorinstitute.org; "A Bonus for Congestion Pricing," *New York Times Digest*, August 15, 2007, p. 7; E. Thornton and M. Arndt, "Fees! Fees! Fees!" *BusinessWeek*, September 29, 2003; "Congestion Pricing, *The New York Times*, July 28, 2011; Zusha Elinson, "Want to Add to Congestion? Then It's Going to Cost You," *The New York Times*, May 5, 2011, p. A11.

signaling in services. When any competitor drops the price of routes, others match the lowered price almost immediately.

Going-rate pricing involves charging the most prevalent price in the market. Rental car pricing is an illustration of this technique (and an illustration of price signaling, because the rental car market is dominated by a small number of large companies). For years, the prices set by one company (Hertz) have been followed by the other companies. When Hertz instituted a new pricing plan that involved "no mileage charges, ever," other rental car companies imitated the policy. They then had to raise other factors such as base rates, size and type of car, daily or weekly rates, and drop-off charges to continue to make profits. Prices in different geographic markets, even cities, depend on the going rate in that location, and customers often pay different rates in contiguous cities in the same state. The Global Feature in this chapter illustrates some of the practices in pricing that differ across countries.

Demand-Based Pricing

The two approaches to pricing just described are based on the company and its competitors rather than on customers. Neither approach takes into consideration that

TIPPING

A Cornell University study revealed an interesting fact about tipping: the custom of tipping is more prevalent in countries where citizens value status and prestige than in countries where they do not. Michael Lynn found that the number of service professionals tipped is relatively small in countries where citizens value recognition and esteem less. "Tipping is really a form of conspicuous consumption. We tip more people in this country because we value status. Americans value recognition and esteem, and we receive that when we tip these service professionals."

One measure of the differences in tipping is the number of service professionals who are given tips in different countries. The United States leads the list with about 35 professions. Other countries that place a high value on recognition and esteem also tip a large number of professionals. These include Spain (29), Canada (25), India (25), and Italy (24). In contrast, in Denmark and Sweden, the number of tipped professionals is less than 10, reflecting the lower value placed on recognition and esteem in these countries. Tipping is not practiced at all in 11 countries: Brunei, Malaysia, Japan, Oman, New Zealand, Samoa, Singapore, South Korea, Thailand, United Arab Emirates, and Vietnam.

Magellan's, a company that sells travel supplies from two retail stores and a website, provides the following general regional tipping "tips" in a guide:

- In *Asia and the Pacific,* tipping could be considered insulting.
- In *Europe,* many hotels and restaurants add a service charge to the bill, making an additional tip unnecessary.
- In the *Middle East and Africa,* tips will not be seen as insulting but are unnecessary.
- In *Central and South America,* most restaurants and hotels add a service charge, making an additional tip unnecessary.

Magellan's guide details tipping standards for 70 countries, excerpts of which are presented here.

Country	Waiter/Waitress	Porter	Taxi Driver
Australia	10% in fine restaurants only	$1 to $2 per bag	Round up to next unit of local currency
Costa Rica	None	$1 per bag	10%
Denmark	None	$1 per bag	Round up
Greece	5 to 10% plus service charge	$1 per bag	Round up
Japan	None	None	None
Romania	Round up bill	$1 per bag	Round up
Venezuala		75¢ per bag	10%
Spain	7 to 10% plus service charge	$1 per bag	10%

customers may lack reference prices, may be sensitive to nonmonetary prices, and may judge quality on the basis of price. All these factors can be accounted for in a company's pricing decisions. The third major approach to pricing, *demand-based pricing,* involves setting prices consistent with customer perceptions of value: prices are based on what customers will pay for the services provided.

Special Challenges in Demand-Based Pricing for Services

One of the major ways that pricing of services differs from pricing of goods in demand-based pricing is that nonmonetary costs and benefits must be factored into the calculation of perceived value to the customer. When services require time, inconvenience, and psychological and search costs, the monetary price must be adjusted to compensate. And when services save time and search costs, the customer is willing to pay a higher monetary price. The challenge is to determine the value to customers of each of the nonmonetary aspects involved.

PRICELESS

Several restaurants in different parts of the world had an extraordinary approach to pricing, which might best be called voluntary pricing. These restaurants allow customers to pay whatever they think the meal is worth. A London restaurant called Just Around the Corner has found the policy to be extremely successful since it started in 1986, with most customers paying more for their meals than the restaurant would charge if it had set the prices. Customers averaged £25 ($41) for a three-course dinner, but some were especially careful to pay enough. "One night, four American government officials handed over nearly $1,000 for a meal worth less than $200. They asked if they had left enough." The owner, Michael Vasos, claimed, "I make more money from this restaurant than from any of my other [four] establishments." He believes his customers' generosity accounts for the success of the restaurant and its pricing policies, although others state that the fear of embarrassment common to the English prevents patrons from paying too little.

"Eat as you want, give as you feel," was the concept on which Annalaksmi, a group of restaurants in Singapore, Kuala Lumpur, Penang, Chennair, Coimbatore, and Perth was founded. "We believe in you, we trust you." The restaurant contends that its principal motive is service, . . . rather than profit, and it is run by volunteers who chose to cook, clean, serve, and wash dishes because they "[find] joy in the underlying philosophy of serve, love, and give." The restaurant asks customers to eat first, then pay whatever comes to mind. As they claim, "There is no right or wrong amount for the meal you had in Annalaksmi. We gratefully accept whatever it is."

PAY BY THE MINUTE IN TOKYO

Some restaurants in Japan are charging for dinner according to how quickly customers eat. At Dai-ichi Hotel Tokyo Seafort, diners punch a time clock when they start their meals, then pay 25 cents per minute until they clock out. Fast diners—like two young girls who gulped down platefuls of cake in 10 minutes and paid only $3—got bargain meals. Perhaps that was why the restaurant is popular among college students! Other franchise restaurants throughout Japan put time limits on their all-you-can-eat buffets. Prices ranged from $10 an hour to $100 for 90 minutes. During that time, diners consumed unlimited quantities of top-quality sushi or shabu shabu, a Japanese specialty consisting of thin slices of beef cooked in boiling broth. At one restaurant, Mo Mo Paradise in Tokyo, for example, diners pay $13.50 to eat for 90 minutes or $30 to eat as much as they wanted for as long as they wanted.

Sources: A. Sachs, "Eat All You Want; Pay by the Minute," *Washington Post,* September 26, 1999, p. H3; © 1999, *The Washington Post,* Reprinted with permission. "Study Examines Tipping," *Hotel and Motel Management,* March 17, 1997, p. 14; B. Ortega, "Priceless," *People,* February 15, 1999, p. 114; I. Wall, "It May Be a Dog-Eat-Dog World, but This Restaurant Won't Prove It," *The Wall Street Journal,* December 11, 1998, p. B1; www.londonrestaurantreview.com, July 23, 2007; G. Stoller, "Tipping Can Trip Up Any Globe Trotter," *USA Today,* September 11, 2007; www.Magellan.com., accessed September 2007; "Foreign Tipping Guide by Country and Region," *Flyer Talk,* www.flyertalk.com/forum/travelbuzz/738653-foreign-tipping-guide-country, accessed July 28, 2011.

Another way services and goods differ with respect to this form of pricing is that information on service costs may be less available to customers, making monetary price not as salient a factor in initial service selection as it is in goods purchasing.

Four Meanings of Perceived Value

One of the most appropriate ways that companies price their services is basing the price on the perceived value of the service to customers. Among the questions a service marketer needs to ask are the following: What do consumers mean by *value*? How can we quantify perceived value in dollars, so that we can set appropriate prices for our services? Is the meaning of value similar across consumers and services? How can value perceptions be influenced? To understand demand-based pricing approaches, we must fully understand what value means to customers.

This is not a simple task. When consumers discuss value, they use the term in many different ways and talk about myriad attributes or components. What constitutes value,

FIGURE 15.2
Four Customer
Definitions of Value

even in a single service category, appears to be highly personal and idiosyncratic. As depicted in Figure 15.2, customers define value in four ways:

1. Value is low price.
2. Value is whatever I want in a product or service.
3. Value is the quality I get for the price I pay.
4. Value is what I get for what I give.[11]

Let us take a look at each of these definitions more carefully.

Value Is Low Price Some consumers equate value with low price, indicating that what they have to give up in terms of money is most salient in their perceptions of value, as typified in these representative comments from customers:

For dry cleaning: "Value means the lowest price."

For carpet steam cleaning: "Value is price—which one is on sale."

For a fast-food restaurant: "When I can use coupons, I feel that the service is a value."

For airline travel: "Value is when airline tickets are discounted."[12]

Value Is Whatever I Want in a Product or Service Rather than focusing on the money given up, some consumers emphasize the benefits they receive from a service or product as the most important component of value. In this value definition, price is far less important than the quality or features that match what the consumer wants. In the telecommunications industry, for example, business customers strongly value the reliability of the systems and are willing to pay for the safety and confidentiality of the connections. Service customers describe this definition of value as follows:

For an MBA degree: "Value is the very best education I can get."

For medical services: "Value is high quality."

For a social club: "Value is what makes me look good to my friends and family."

For a rock or country music concert: "Value is the best performance."

For a hotel room for a honeymoon: "Value is a luxurious room with a hot tub."

Value Is the Quality I Get for the Price I Pay Other consumers see value as a trade-off between the money they give up and the quality they receive.

For a hotel for vacation: "Value is price first and quality second."

For a hotel for business travel: "Value is the lowest price for a quality brand."

For a computer services contract: "Value is the same as quality. No—value is affordable quality."

Value Is What I Get for What I Give   Finally, some consumers consider all the benefits they receive as well as all sacrifice components (money, time, effort) when describing value.

> *For a housekeeping service:* "Value is how many rooms I can get cleaned for what the price is."
> *For a hairstylist:* "Value is what I pay in cost and time for the look I get."
> *For executive education:* "Value is getting a good educational experience in the shortest time possible."

The four consumer expressions of value can be captured in one overall definition consistent with the concept of utility in economics: *perceived value is the consumer's overall assessment of the utility of a service based on perceptions of what is received and what is given.* Although what is received varies across consumers (some may want volume, others high quality, still others convenience), as does what is given (some are concerned only with money expended, others with time and effort), value represents a trade-off of the give-and-get components. Customers will make a purchase decision on the basis of perceived value, not solely to minimize the price paid. These definitions are the first step in identifying the elements that must be quantified in setting prices for services.

Incorporating Perceived Value into Service Pricing

The buyer's perception of total value prompts the willingness to pay a particular price for a service. To translate the customer's value perceptions into an appropriate price for a specific service offering, the marketer must answer a number of questions: What benefits does the service provide? How important is each of these benefits? How much is it worth to the customer to receive a particular benefit from a service? At what price will the service be economically acceptable to potential buyers? In what context is the customer purchasing the service?

The most important thing a company must do—and often a difficult thing—is to estimate the value to customers of the company's services.[13] Value may be perceived differently by consumers because of idiosyncratic tastes, knowledge about the service, buying power, and ability to pay. In this type of pricing, what the consumers value—not what they pay—forms the basis for pricing. Therefore, its effectiveness rests solely on accurately determining what the market perceives the service to be worth.

When the services are for the retail consumers, service providers can rarely afford to give each individual exactly the bundle of attributes valued. They will, however, attempt to find one or more bundles that address segments of the market. When individual customers are large (e.g., business-to-business customers or very large and profitable retail customers), the company may find it worthwhile to provide individual bundles to each customer. An interesting manifestation of demand-oriented pricing is shown in the Technology Spotlight.

One of the most complex and difficult tasks of service marketers is setting prices internationally. If service marketers price on the basis of perceived value and if perceived value and willingness to pay differ across countries (which they often do), then service firms may provide essentially the same service but charge different prices in different countries.

PRICING STRATEGIES THAT LINK TO THE FOUR VALUE DEFINITIONS

In this section we describe the approaches to service pricing that are particularly suited to each of the four value definitions. Exhibit 15.2 presents research approaches to setting prices.

Technology Spotlight   Dynamic Pricing on the Internet Allows Price Adjustments Based on Supply and Demand

When shopping for an airline ticket on the Internet, have you ever found a low-priced ticket that you did not purchase immediately, and then returned to the site four hours later to find the same ticket had increased $100 in price? This experience is *dynamic pricing* in action—the buying and selling of products in markets in which prices move quickly in response to supply and demand fluctuations. In the case of your airline ticket, chances are that other travelers had purchased tickets at the original low price, reducing the airlines' inventory and allowing the airline to gamble on getting customers to buy the remaining seats at higher prices.

Dynamic pricing is estimated to account for more than 45 percent of total online transactions. The approach—often incorporating auctions and other forms of online bidding—is typically used at the end of the supply chain to eliminate surplus inventory or perishable service capacity, as with airline seats. Dynamic pricing has allowed companies to generate significant revenue from excess supply or discontinued products, which they previously turned over to intermediaries. In the past, liquidators would receive unsold services, getting 5 cents on the dollar in liquidation fees in addition to whatever they could get from reselling the products. Not only did the firm not receive revenue from the sale of the services, but it would also have to pay for liquidation services.

AUCTIONS: EBAY AND 1,500 RIVALS

Online auctions represent dynamic pricing because customers pay what they are willing and they compete with each other on the goods they desire. eBay pioneered the Internet auction, but more than 3,000 websites now offer person-to-person online trading. Market leader eBay offers thousands of new items for auction each day. Whereas eBay focuses on consumer-to-consumer transactions, uBid.com acts as a consignment house for manufacturers selling directly to customers. uBid offers leading manufacturers' merchandise to consumers and businesses at prices lower than wholesale.

Most uBid auctions begin at $1 and allow market dynamics to set the price.

DUTCH AUCTIONS: KLIK-KLOK.COM, WRHAMBRECHT.COM

Dutch auctions, which originated in the Netherlands for selling services such as insurance and perishable items such as tulips, reverse the typical auction in that the prices go down as the auction progresses. Also unlike typical auctions, in which one of a particular type of product is sold at a given time, in Dutch auctions multiple—albeit limited—quantities of the same services are sold at the same time. The auction is very short, and the price drops rapidly over this time. At any given time (or price point), a bidder can stop the clock by bidding at the instantaneous price. The bid with time, price, and quantity is then recorded. This bidding continues until all bids have been received. At that point all winning bidders pay the same price, which is the lowest "successful" bid. The catch is that there is a limited supply of each product. As the clock progresses and the remaining available inventory decreases, the nonbidders (those waiting for the lowest selling price) risk not getting their desired quantities.

REVERSE AUCTIONS: HOTWIRE.COM AND PRICELINE.COM

Reverse auctions are used on the buy-side, allowing buyers to see the lowest bid, but they do not identify the buyer or the seller. The brand or identity of the seller is revealed only if the seller decides to accept the bid offered by the buyer. An advantage for buyers is that they do not need to guess at the price and can receive the same products and services offered elsewhere with static prices at significant discounts. A disadvantage is that, although buyers see a rating of the seller, they cannot be sure who the seller is and what the service outcome will be. The brand is eliminated as a signal of quality. Furthermore, the buyer has to sacrifice controls over some aspects of the service that is being consumed. For instance, on Priceline.com, the buyer does not have full control over time of the flights.

GROUP BUYING: ONLINECHOICE.COM

Group buying sites such as OnlineChoice.com aggregate demand for sellers. The sites offer group rates on long distance and cell phone service, automobile and term life insurance, and mortgages. The concept behind this form of dynamic pricing is that, the greater the number of people who want to buy products, the lower the price will be for everyone. Sellers generally bucket the prices of the product being sold based on the number of buyers. For example, for 0 to 10 buyers, the price for each buyer is $100; for 10 to 20 buyers, the price for each buyer is $95; and so on. Word of mouth is critical, because interested buyers are encouraged to enlist their friends and relatives to get a cheaper price for the whole group. Sellers motivate this action by placing an "Invite Your Friend" icon right next to the service or price information. Advantages of this form of dynamic pricing are that the price decreases as a greater number of people bid, and the exact service and its specifications are known to buyers when bidding.

FINDING THE LOWEST PRICE ACROSS INTERNET SITES: BUY.COM

Buy.com's slogan is "lowest prices on Earth." The Internet allows consumers to do quick price comparisons, and Buy.com wants to make sure its services and products end up being the lowest prices in everyone's search. To deliver on its promises, Buy.com uses software to monitor price changes for products on competing sites. When these price changes occur, the software then recommends price adjustments to Buy.com. The process is automated, but the decision to change prices is made by a manager, usually once a day rather than moment to moment. Buy.com relies on this strategy in highly competitive online categories such as computer software. The software makes recommendations throughout the day, and decisions are made the next morning. Prices tend to fall more often than they go up.

DINING WITH DYNAMIC PRICING

Flexible, or dynamic, pricing in the restaurant industry involves changing menu prices by hour or time of day to attract diners in nonpeak hours, such as afternoons between 2 p.m. and 6 p.m. or late evenings. Restaurants may use discounts, such as 15 to 30 percent off the total check, to build traffic during off-hours. Typically, the restaurants use a "dining aggregator," a site that collects and coordinates information about all restaurants in an area that want to offer dynamic pricing. For example, www.DinnerBroker.com, a novel dynamic-pricing website, represents 1,000 restaurants in more than 50 metropolitan areas that use off-peak discount programs to gain incremental business and new customers. DinnerBroker.com has an easy-to-use graphic matrix that allows users to see on one page all participating restaurants and the discounts they offer. The site also enables customers to make online reservations and offers access to prime-time tables. To participate in these services, DinnerBroker.com requires restaurants to pay a subscription of $49 a month and $1 for every off-hour reservation booked and fulfilled by the service.

Sources: M. Bazeley, "eBay has Strong Earnings in Quarter," *Knight Ridder Tribune Business News,* October 21, 2004, p. 1; G. Perakis, "Third Informs Revenue Management and Pricing Conference," *Journal of Revenue and Pricing Management,* January 2004, p. 388; V. Jayaraman and T. Baker, "The Internet as an Enabler for Dynamic Pricing of Goods," *IEEE Transactions on Engineering Management,* November 2003, p. 470; A. J. Liddle, "Using Web for Discounting Clicks with Digital Diners," *Nation's Restaurant News,* May 19, 2003, p. 172; C. T. Heun, "Dynamic Pricing Boosts Bottom Line," *Informationweek,* October 29, 2001; M. Vizard, "With So Very Few Internet Players, Is Dynamic Pricing Good for Our Economy?" *InfoWorld,* March 26, 2001; M. Vizard, E. Scannel, and D. Neel, "Suppliers Toy with Dynamic Pricing," *InfoWorld,* May 14, 2001; www.idine.com, 2007; www.klik-klok.com, 2011; www.wrhambrecht.com, 2011.

One of the reasons that pricing of services is more difficult than pricing of goods is that service units are more variable and difficult to identify than units of goods. Units of goods—automobiles, jeans, gallons of milk, and microwave ovens—are easy to define. Units of service are more difficult in part because they are sold by a variety of components. Information services, for example, are sold by the minute, the web page, the file (as in buying online music), or the search (as in finding and purchasing magazine articles). The services of your doctor are sold by the length and type of the visit, the test performed, the shot given, and the X-rays taken. Cable television is sold by the month (basic fees, premium charges for HBO and Showtime), by the type of equipment leased (digital video recorders, remote controls, digital cable boxes), and by the unit (pay-per-view movies). One approach to dealing with the complexity of pricing services is to develop modular service bundles.

As described in this chapter, pricing a service in line with what customers perceive it is worth is often difficult. Two approaches that have gained favor in recent years are modular service pricing and service tiering.

MODULAR SERVICE PRICING

Modular service pricing involves first identifying the basic and value-added services of a provider as components or building blocks for pricing. To create modules, the company first defines the full range of services that could meet customer needs and for which customers will pay. To create modular pricing, firms need the following:

1. Available prices for each different service.
2. The ability to combine prices and services using easy rules.
3. Minimum overlap among the service elements, so that customers do not pay twice for the same service.

One context in which modular pricing is being developed is publications (e.g., *The Wall Street Journal, Sports Illustrated, USA Today*) that are bundling their digital, print, and mobile subscriptions. As shown in the figure in this exhibit, publications are attempting to determine the customer-perceived value of digital, online, tablet, and mobile formats. The pricing models represent a major change from the past few years, when publications charged for print and gave away digital content. Publishers now recognize that today's consumer values digital content more than print, and they are pricing in line with this revised perception of value. The change illustrates a broader effort by publishers to change from print-only to print-plus-digital

combinations. However, media companies are still trying to maintain their print subscribers because advertisers pay much more for print ads than for digital ones.

Ideally, each component in a modular pricing framework has a price that is in line with customers' perceptions of the worth of that service, and customers can select the components individually and combine them in bundles. A difficulty in the current evolution to modular publication pricing is that each publication has a different approach, making choices confusing to customers. Some approaches are easier than others, as you can see if you try to make a choice for each publication in this exhibit.

SERVICE TIERING

Sometimes even good modular pricing can become too complex, and simpler ways to present the company's prices are needed. *Service tiering,* usually called versioning when applied to the pricing of goods, involves creating prices that correspond to the price points and value bundles of different customer segments. For example, Time Warner Cable offers service tiers that correspond to service components that are typically desired together. When customers buy the bundles, they receive discounts from what the services would cost individually.

In general, service tiers allow customers to quickly and simply match their desires and the price they are willing to pay with an offering from the company. The customer perceives a benefit in choosing one of the tiers because each tier provides a discount over individual services. The company enjoys a benefit because customers typically buy more services when they are sold in tiers than when they are offered individually. In the context of cable offerings, basic cable is an example of a low tier with a low price, whereas extended cable includes the addition of premium channels such as HBO, Showtime, and the Golf Channel for a higher price. The highest tier, for the highest price, might include all cable channels plus DVRs.

Modular pricing and service tiering allow the company to maximize sales from all parts of a service that the customer desires without having to create unique service bundles for each customer.

Sources: R. Docters, M. Reopel, J. Sun, and S. Tanny, "Capturing the Unique Value of Services: Why Pricing of Services Is Different," *Journal of Business Strategy* 25, no. 2 (2004), pp. 23–28; R. Adams, "Many Formats, One Price: More Publications Begin Bundling Their Digital, Print, and Mobile Subscriptions," *The Wall Street Journal*, May 16, 2011, p. B4.

PACKAGE DEALS IN MODULAR PUBLICATION PRICING
Package Deal

📖 **Print**	💻 **Online**	📱 **Tablet**	📲 **Mobile**

Package Deal	Price
The New Yorker Condé Cast 💻 📱 📖 💻 📱	$59/99/yr (on iTunes) $69.99 (through newyorker.com)
Sports Illustrated Time Inc. 💻 📱 📲 📖 💻 📱 📲	$3.99/mo $48.00/yr
Glamour Condé Cast 📱 📖 📱	$19.99/yr (on iTunes) $19.99/yr (through glamour.com)
The New York Times The New York Times Company 💻 📲 💻 📱 💻 📱 📲 📖 💻 📱 📲	$195.00/yr $260.00 $455.00 $254.80–$608.40
The Wall Street Journal Dow Jones & Company 💻 📲 💻 📱 📲 📖 💻 📱 📲	$155.00/yr $207.00 $455.00
The Economist (U.S. Edition) The New York Times Company 💻 📱 📲 📖 💻 📱 📲	$110.00/yr $126.99

Note: Magazine circulation data exclude single-copy sales and verified circulation
Sources: The Wall Street Journal, May 16, 2011, p. B4

Pricing Strategies When the Customer Means "Value Is Low Price"

When monetary price is the most important determinant of value to a customer, the company focuses mainly on price. This focus does not mean that the quality level and intrinsic attributes are always irrelevant, just that monetary price dominates in importance. To establish a service price in this definition of value, the marketer must understand to what extent customers know the objective prices of services in this category, how they interpret various prices, and how much is too much of a perceived sacrifice. These factors are best understood when the service provider also knows the relative dollar size of the purchase, the frequency of past price changes, and the range of acceptable prices for the service. Some of the specific pricing approaches appropriate when customers define value as low price include discounting, odd pricing, synchro-pricing, and penetration pricing (Figure 15.3).

Discounting

Service providers offer discounts to communicate to price-sensitive buyers that they are receiving value. Among the most prevalent discounting approaches are those from online companies such as Groupon, Living Social, Angie's List, and an ever-increasing number of competitors. These Web companies—of which Groupon was the first and remains the largest—offer daily discounts to consumers through e-mail, Facebook, and Twitter feeds. The discounts are all for local companies, most of which are services such as restaurants, cleaning services, massages, plumbing, home inspections, and hotels. Consumers request the deals and can bid for them until they are sold out. Online companies are paid sometimes as much as 50 percent of the revenue from purchased coupons.

Odd Pricing

Odd pricing is the practice of pricing services just below the exact dollar amount to make buyers perceive that they are getting a lower price. Dry cleaners charge $2.98 for a shirt rather than $3.00, health clubs have dues priced at $33.90 per month rather than $34, and haircuts are $9.50 rather than $10.00. Odd prices suggest discounting and bargains and are appealing to customers for whom value means low price.

Synchro-Pricing

Synchro-pricing is the use of price to manage demand for a service by capitalizing on customer sensitivity to prices. Certain services, such as tax preparation, passenger

FIGURE 15.3
Pricing Strategies When the Customer Defines Value as Low Price

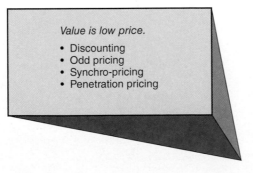

Value is low price.

- Discounting
- Odd pricing
- Synchro-pricing
- Penetration pricing

transportation, hotels, and theaters, have demand that fluctuates over time as well as constrained supply at peak times. For companies in these and other industries, setting a price that provides a profit over time can be difficult. Pricing can, however, play a role in smoothing demand and synchronizing demand and supply. Time, place, quantity, and incentive differentials have all been used effectively by service firms, as discussed in Chapter 13.

Place differentials are used for services in which customers have a sensitivity to location. The front row at concerts, the 50-yard line in football, center court in tennis or basketball, ocean-side rooms in resort hotels—all these represent place differentials that are meaningful to customers and that therefore command higher prices.

Time differentials involve price variations that depend on when the service is consumed. Telephone service after 11 p.m., hospital rooms on weekends, and health spas in the off-season are time differentials that reflect slow periods of service. By offering lower prices for underused time periods, a service company can smooth demand and gain incremental revenue.

Quantity differentials are usually price decreases given for volume purchasing. This pricing structure allows a service company to predict future demand for its services. Customers who buy a booklet of coupons for a tanning salon or facial, a quantity of tokens for public bridges, or packages of advertising spots on radio or television are all responding to price incentives achieved by committing to future services. Corporate discounts for airlines, hotels, and rental cars exemplify quantity discounts in the business context; by offering lower prices, the service provider locks in future business.

Differentials as incentives are lower prices for new or existing clients in the hope of encouraging them to be regular users or more frequent users. Some professionals—lawyers, dentists, electrologists, and even some physicians—offer free consultations at the front end, usually to overcome fear and uncertainty about high service prices. Other companies stimulate use by offering regular customers discounts or premiums during slow periods. Sports teams are now using differential prices as incentives to attract customers who would otherwise not be able to afford the high cost of attending sports events. The Phoenix Suns, in claiming that "you should have pricing for every pocketbook," revamped its ticket pricing by raising premium seats by 26 percent, decreasing arena seats by 31 percent, and adding 500 $10 tickets. The net result was a 6 percent increase in the average ticket price (paid for by the premium seat holders) but more attendance at the games because more fans in different segments could afford the seats.[14]

Penetration Pricing

Penetration pricing is a strategy in which new services are introduced at low prices to stimulate trial and widespread use. The strategy is appropriate when (1) sales volume of the service is very sensitive to price, even in the early stages of introduction; (2) it is possible to achieve economies in unit costs by operating at large volumes; (3) a service faces threats of strong potential competition very soon after introduction; and (4) there is no class of buyers willing to pay a higher price to obtain the service.[15] Penetration pricing can lead to problems when companies then select a "regular" increased price. Care must be taken not to penetrate with so low a price that customers feel the regular price is outside the range of acceptable prices.

FIGURE 15.4
**Pricing Strategies
When the Customer
Defines Value as
Everything Wanted
in a Service**

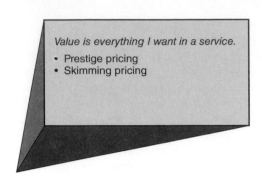

Value is everything I want in a service.
- Prestige pricing
- Skimming pricing

Pricing Strategies When the Customer Means "Value Is Everything I Want in a Service"

When the customer is concerned principally with the "get" components of a service, monetary price is not of primary concern. The more desirable intrinsic attributes a given service possesses, the more highly valued the service is likely to be and the higher the price the marketer can set. Figure 15.4 shows appropriate pricing strategies.

Prestige Pricing

Prestige pricing is a special form of demand-based pricing by service marketers who offer high-quality or status services. For certain services—restaurants, health clubs, airlines, and hotels—a higher price is charged for the luxury end of the business. For example, for hotel guests who crave pampering, many chains offer club floors that add high-end amenities into their offerings for large price increases. Some Ritz-Carltons offer free lunch foods such as sandwiches and salads with these high-priced rooms.[16] Some customers of service companies that use this approach may actually value the high price because it represents prestige or a quality image. Others prefer purchasing at the high end because they are given preference in seating or accommodations and are entitled to other special benefits. In prestige pricing, demand may actually increase as price increases because the costlier service has more value in reflecting quality or prestige.

Skimming Pricing

Skimming, a strategy in which new services are introduced at high prices, is an effective approach when services are major improvements over past services. In this situation, customers are more concerned about obtaining the service than about the cost of the service, allowing service providers to skim the customers most willing to pay the highest prices. Services related to anti-aging, such as Botox injections and laser liposuction, often are introduced at high prices, thereby attracting customers who are willing to pay more to obtain the services in the short term rather than wait until a later time, when the prices might be reduced.

Pricing Strategies When the Customer Means "Value Is the Quality I Get for the Price I Pay"

Some customers primarily consider both quality and monetary price. The task of the marketer is to understand what *quality* means to the customer (or segments of customers) and then to match quality level with price level. Specific strategies are shown in Figure 15.5.

FIGURE 15.5
**Pricing Strategies
When the Customer
Defines Value as
Quality for the
Price Paid**

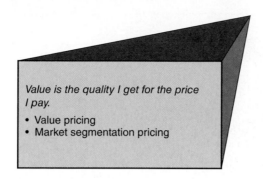

*Value is the quality I get for the price
I pay.*

• Value pricing
• Market segmentation pricing

Value Pricing

The widely used term *value pricing* has come to mean "giving more for less." In current usage, it involves assembling a bundle of services desirable to a wide group of customers and then pricing them lower than they would cost alone. Taco Bell pioneered value pricing with a $0.59 Value Menu. After sales at the chain rose 50 percent in two years to $2.4 billion, McDonald's and Burger King adopted the value pricing practice. The menu at Taco Bell has since been reconfigured to emphasize plain tacos and burritos (which are easier and faster for the chain to make) for less than a dollar. As mentioned in the chapter opener, Southwest Airlines also offers value pricing in its airline service: a low cost for a bundle of desirable service attributes such as frequent departures, friendly and funny employees, and on-time arrival. The airline offers consistently low fares with bare-bones service.

Market Segmentation Pricing

With *market segmentation pricing,* a service marketer charges different prices to groups of customers for what are perceived to be different quality levels of service, even though there may not be corresponding differences in the costs of providing the service to each of these groups. This form of pricing is based on the premise that segments show different price elasticities of demand and desire different quality levels.

Service marketers often price by *client category,* based on the recognition that some groups find it difficult to pay a recommended price. Health clubs located in college communities typically offer student memberships, recognizing that this segment of customers has limited ability to pay full price. In addition to the lower price, student memberships may also carry with them reduced hours of use, particularly in peak times. The same line of reasoning leads to memberships for "seniors," who are less able to pay full price but are willing to patronize the clubs during daytime hours, when most full-price members are working.

Companies also use market segmentation by *service version,* recognizing that not all segments want the basic level of service at the lowest price. When they can identify a bundle of attributes that are desirable enough for another segment of customers, they can charge a higher price for that bundle. Companies can configure service bundles that reflect price and service points appealing to different groups in the market. Hotels, for example, offer standard rooms at a basic rate but then combine amenities and tangibles related to the room to attract customers willing to pay more for the concierge level, jacuzzis, additional beds, and sitting areas.

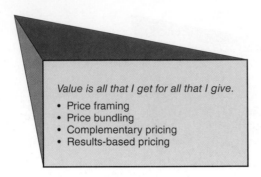

FIGURE 15.6
Pricing Strategies
When the Customer
Defines Value as All
That Is Received for
All That Is Given

Value is all that I get for all that I give.
- Price framing
- Price bundling
- Complementary pricing
- Results-based pricing

Pricing Strategies When the Customer Means "Value Is All That I Get for All That I Give"

Some customers define value as including not just the benefits they receive but also the time, money, and effort they put into a service. Figure 15.6 illustrates the pricing strategies described in this definition of value.

Price Framing

Because many customers do not possess accurate reference prices for services, service marketers are more likely than goods marketers to organize price information for customers so they know how to view it. Customers naturally look for price anchors as well as familiar services against which to judge focal services. If they accept the anchors, they view the price and service package favorably. Groupon, Living Social, and other online couponing sites let customers know the actual values of the offers being made as well as the discounted costs in the offer. As mentioned earlier in the chapter, customers often do not have a reference price for services—particularly household services such as plumbing, gutter cleaning, and pressure washing. Framing the offers by providing actual prices allows customers to recognize the value they will receive if they purchase the Groupon.

Price Bundling

Some services are consumed more effectively in conjunction with other services; other services accompany the products they support (such as extended service warranties, training, and expedited delivery). When customers find value in a package of interrelated services, price bundling is an appropriate strategy. Bundling, which means pricing and selling services as a group rather than individually, has benefits to both customers and service companies. Customers find that bundling simplifies their purchase and payment, and companies find that the approach stimulates demand for the firm's service line, thereby achieving cost economies for the operations as a whole while increasing net contributions.[17] Bundling also allows the customer to pay less than when purchasing each of the services individually, which contributes to perceptions of value.

The effectiveness of price bundling depends on how well the service firm understands the bundles of value that customers or segments perceive and on the complementarity of demand for these services. Effectiveness also depends on the right choice of services from the firm's point of view. Because the firm's objective is to increase overall sales, the services selected for bundling should be those with a relatively small sales volume without the bundling to minimize revenue loss from discounting a service that already has a high sales volume.

Complementary Pricing

Services that are highly interrelated can be leveraged by using *complementary pricing.* This pricing includes three related strategies—captive pricing, two-part pricing, and loss leadership.[18] In *captive pricing,* the firm offers a base service or product and then provides the supplies or peripheral services needed to continue using the service. In this situation the company could off-load some part of the price for the basic service to the peripherals. For example, cable services often drop the price for installation to a very low level, then compensate by charging enough for the peripheral services to make up for the loss in revenue. With service firms, this strategy is often called *two-part pricing* because the service price is broken into a fixed fee plus variable usage fees (also found in telephone services, health clubs, and commercial services such as rentals). *Loss leadership* is the term typically used in retail stores when providers place a familiar service on special largely to draw the customer to the store and then reveal other levels of service available at higher prices. Cleaners, for example, will offer a special low price to launder men's shirts to draw customers in to pay the higher regular prices for other items.

Results-Based Pricing

In service industries in which outcome is very important but uncertainty is high, the most relevant aspect of value is the *result* of the service. In personal injury lawsuits, for example, clients value the settlement they receive at the conclusion of the service. From tax accountants, clients value cost savings. From trade schools, students most value getting a job upon graduation. From Hollywood stars, production companies value high grosses. In these and other situations, an appropriate value-based pricing strategy is to price on the basis of results or outcome of the service.

The most commonly known form of results-based pricing is a practice called *contingency pricing,* used by lawyers. Contingency pricing is the major way that personal injury and certain consumer cases are billed. In this approach, lawyers do not receive fees or payment until the case is settled, when they are paid a percentage of the money that the client receives. Therefore, only an outcome in the client's favor is compensated. From the client's point of view, the pricing makes sense in part because most clients in these cases are unfamiliar with and possibly intimidated by law firms. Their biggest fears are high fees for a case that may take years to settle. By using contingency pricing, clients are ensured that they pay no fees until they receive a settlement. In these and other instances of contingency pricing, the economic value of the service is hard to determine before the service, and providers develop a price that allows them to share the risks and rewards of delivering value to the buyer.

Results-based pricing is demonstrated clearly in the online "pay-per-click" advertising industry. Rather than buying media with estimated audiences, companies that buy advertisements on Google and Yahoo! pay only for users who actually respond to their ads. Some public relations firms are also moving from charging fixed fees for obtaining media exposure for their clients to a results-based approach. Pay PerClip, for example, a division of a traditional public relations firm, bases its fees on very specific results—$750, for example, for a mention in a small-market newspaper.

The commission approach to service pricing is compelling in that agents are compensated most when they find the highest rates and fares. It would seem that agents have an underlying motivation to avoid the lowest fares and rates for their clients.

FIGURE 17.7
Summary of Service Pricing Strategies for Four Customer Definitions of Value

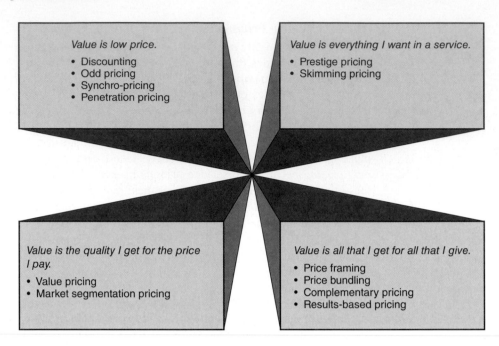

Value is low price.
- Discounting
- Odd pricing
- Synchro-pricing
- Penetration pricing

Value is everything I want in a service.
- Prestige pricing
- Skimming pricing

Value is the quality I get for the price I pay.
- Value pricing
- Market segmentation pricing

Value is all that I get for all that I give.
- Price framing
- Price bundling
- Complementary pricing
- Results-based pricing

Summary

This chapter began with three key differences between customer evaluation of pricing for services and goods: (1) customers often have inaccurate or limited reference prices for services, (2) price is a key signal of quality in services, and (3) monetary price is not the only relevant price to service customers. These three differences can have profound effects on the strategies that companies use to set and administer prices for services. The chapter next discussed common pricing structures, including (1) cost-based, (2) competition-based, and (3) demand-based pricing. Central to the discussion were the specific challenges in each of these structures and the service pricing techniques that have emerged in practice.

Finally, the chapter defined customer perceptions of value and suggested appropriate pricing strategies that match each customer definition. Figure 15.7 summarizes these definitions and strategies. The four value definitions include (1) value is low price, (2) value is everything I want in a service, (3) value is the quality I get for the price I pay, and (4) value is all that I get for all that I give.

Discussion Questions

1. Which approach to pricing (cost-based, competition-based, or demand-based) is the most fair to customers? Why?
2. Is it possible to use all three approaches simultaneously when pricing services? If you answer yes, describe a service that is priced this way.
3. For what consumer services do you have reference prices? What makes these services different from others for which you lack reference prices?
4. Name three services you purchase in which price is a signal to quality. Do you believe that there are true differences across services that are priced high and those that are priced low? Why or why not?

5. Describe the nonmonetary costs involved in the following services: getting an automobile loan, belonging to a health club, having allergies diagnosed and treated, attending an executive education class, and getting braces.

6. Consider the specific pricing strategies for each of the four customer value definitions. Which of these strategies could be adapted and used with another value definition?

Exercises

1. List five services for which you have no reference price. Now put yourself in the role of the service providers for two of those services and develop pricing strategies. Be sure to include in your description which of the value definitions you believe customers will possess and what types of strategies would be appropriate, given those definitions.

2. In the next week, find three price lists for services (such as from a restaurant, dry cleaner, or hairstylist). Identify the pricing base and the strategy used in each of them. How effective is each?

3. Consider that you are the owner of a new private college and can prepare a value/price package that is appealing to students. Describe your approach. How does it differ from existing offerings?

4. Go to the Priceline.com Internet site and become familiar with the way it works. Next, go to Orbitz and Travelocity and compare the way they operate. What are the benefits and trade-offs in using Priceline over Orbitz and Travelocity?

Notes

1. K. Monroe, "The Pricing of Services," *Handbook of Services Marketing,* ed. C. A. Congram and M. L. Friedman (New York: AMACOM, 1989), pp. 20–31.

2. Ibid.

3. W. Woellert, "How Much Is That Brain Scan?" *BusinessWeek,* November 8, 2004, p. 94.

4. V. M. Mallozzi and J. Gettleman, "Taming the Runaway Wedding Planner," *New York Times,* June 24, 2007; Pet Body Builders, www.petbodybuilders .com/services.html, accessed August 30, 2007; Child Safety Specialists, www. safe4mychild.com/about-us.html, accessed August 28, 2007.

5. E. Cohen, "Would Your Doctor Pay for Wasted Time?" www.cnn.com, accessed August 13, 2011.

6. Monroe, "The Pricing of Services."

7. V. A. Zeithaml, "The Acquisition, Meaning, and Use of Price Information by Consumers of Professional Services," in *Marketing Theory: Philosophy of Science Perspectives,* ed. R. Bush and S. Hunt (Chicago: American Marketing Association, 1982), pp. 237–241.

8. C. H. Lovelock, "Understanding Costs and Developing Pricing Strategies," *Services Marketing* (New York: Prentice Hall, 1991), pp. 236–246.

9. A. Stevens, "Firms Try More Lucrative Ways of Charging for Legal Services," *The Wall Street Journal,* November 25, 1994, pp. B1ff.

10. K. Chu, "Bank of America Raises ATM Surcharge," *USA Today* September 13, 2007, p. 2A.

11. V. A. Zeithaml, "Consumer Perceptions of Price, Quality, and Value: A Means-End Model and Synthesis of Evidence," *Journal of Marketing* 52 (July 1988), pp. 2–22.

12. All comments from these four sections are based on those from Zeithaml, "Consumer Perceptions," pp. 13–14.

13. B. Donan, "Set Price Metrics Parallel to Value Proposition," *Marketing News,* April 1, 2007, p. 6.

14. G. Boeck, "Teams Woo Fans with Cheaper Seats," *USA Today,* August 31, 2004, p. 3C.

15. Monroe, "The Pricing of Services."

16. B. DeLollis, "Hotels Take Pampering to Next Level on Club Floors," *USA Today,* June 19, 2007, p. 3B.

17. Monroe, "The Pricing of Services."

18. G. J. Tellis, "Beyond the Many Faces of Price: An Integration of Pricing Strategies," *Journal of Marketing* 50 (October 1986), pp. 146–160.

Part **Seven**

Service and the Bottom Line

Chapter 16: The Financial and Economic Impact of Service

In this final part of the text, we discuss one of the most important questions about service that managers have been debating over the past 25 years: is excellent service profitable to an organization? We pull together research and company experience to answer this question. We present our own model of how the relationship works and offer examples of the relationship in companies. Our model shows how service quality has offensive effects (gaining new customers) and defensive effects (retaining customers).

We also discuss several important performance models in this chapter. Return on service quality (ROSQ) is a modeling approach that allows a company to gauge the return on investments in different service activities. Customer equity is an extension of the ROSQ approach that compares investments in service with expenditures on other marketing activities. The balanced performance scorecard is an approach that includes multiple company factors, including financial, customer, operational, and innovative measures. The balanced performance scorecard allows a company to measure performance from the customer's perspective (Chapters 4 and 9), from the employee's perspective (Chapter 11), and from an innovation and new service perspective (Chapter 8). Thus, in Chapter 16, we synthesize the measurement issues that underlie the provision of service and offer a way for companies to demonstrate that service is accountable financially. These models help companies understand more accurately their benefits from investments in service excellence.

The Financial and Economic Impact of Service

This chapter's objectives are to

1. Examine the direct effects of service on profits.
2. Consider the effect of service in getting new customers.
3. Evaluate the role of service in keeping customers.
4. Discuss what is known about the key service drivers of overall service quality, customer retention, and profitability.
5. Discuss the balanced performance scorecard that allows for strategic focus on measurements other than financials.

What return can I expect on service quality improvements?

—A typical CEO

All authors of this text work with companies to improve their service quality and better meet their customers' expectations. The two most frequent questions asked by executives of these companies are

"How do I know that service quality improvements will be a good investment?"
"Where in the company do I invest money to achieve the highest return?"

For example, a restaurant chain, after conducting consumer research, found that service quality perceptions averaged 85 percent across the chain. The specific items receiving the lowest scores on the survey were friendliness of the wait staff (70 percent), wait time for service (78 percent), and limited menu (76 percent). The company's CEO wanted to know, first of all, whether making improvements in overall service quality or in any of the specific areas would result in revenues that exceeded their costs. Moreover, he wanted guidance as to which of the service aspects to tackle. He could determine how much each of the initiatives would cost to change, but that was as far as his financial estimates would take him. Clearly, the friendliness of the wait staff was most in need of change because it was rated lowest; but estimates indicated that it would also be by far the most expensive to change. What could he expect in return for improvements in each service area? Would adjustments in the other two factors be better investments? Which of the three service initiatives would generate noticeable improvements to raise the overall customer perceptions of the restaurant?

Ten years ago, these questions had to be answered on the basis of executive intuition. Today, more analytical and rigorous approaches exist to help managers make these decisions about service quality investments. The best known and most widely respected approach is called return on service quality (ROSQ) and was developed by Roland Rust, Anthony Zahorik, and Tim Keiningham, a team of researchers and consultants. The ROSQ approach is based on the following assumptions:

1. Service quality is an investment.
2. Service quality efforts must be financially accountable.
3. It is possible to spend too much on service quality.
4. Not all service quality expenditures are equally valid.

Their approach looks at investments in services as a chain of effects of the following form:

1. A service improvement effort will produce an increased level of customer satisfaction at the process or attribute level. For example, spending money to train the wait staff will likely increase customers' satisfaction level from the current low rating of 70 percent.
2. Increased customer satisfaction at the process or attribute level will lead to increased overall customer satisfaction. If satisfaction with the increased friendliness of the wait staff goes from 70 to 80 percent, overall service quality ratings may increase from 85 to 90 percent. (Both these percentage changes could be accurately measured the next time surveys are conducted and could even be projected in advance using the ROSQ model.)
3. Higher overall service quality or customer satisfaction will lead to increased behavioral intentions, such as greater repurchase intention and intention to increase usage. Customers who have not yet eaten at the restaurant will be drawn to do so, and many who currently eat there once a month will consider increasing their patronage.
4. Increased behavioral intentions will lead to behavioral impact, including repurchase or customer retention, positive word of mouth, and increased usage. Intentions about patronizing the restaurant will become reality, resulting in higher revenues and more positive word-of-mouth communications.
5. Behavioral effects will then lead to improved profitability and other financial outcomes. Higher revenues will lead to higher profits for the restaurant, assuming that the original investment in refurbishing the exterior is covered.

The ROSQ methodology can help distinguish among all the company strategies, processes, approaches, and tactics that can be altered. The ROSQ approach is informative because it can be applied in companies to direct their individual strategies. Software has been developed to accompany the approach, and consulting firms work with companies to apply it. No longer do firms like the restaurant discussed here have to depend on intuition alone to guide them in their service quality investments.

Sources: R. T. Rust, A. J. Zahorik, and T. L. Keiningham, *Return on Quality* (Chicago: Probus, 1994); R. T. Rust, C. Moorman, and P. R. Dickson, "Getting Return on Quality: Revenue Expansion, Cost Reduction, or Both," *Journal of Marketing* 66 (October 2002), pp. 7–24; R. T. Rust and T. S. Chung, "Marketing Models of Service and Relationships," *Marketing Science* 25 (November–December 2006), pp. 560–580.

Virtually all companies hunger for evidence and tools to ascertain and monitor the payoff and payback of new investments in service. Many managers still see service and service quality as costs rather than as contributors to profits, partly because of the difficulty involved in tracing the link between service and financial returns. Determining the financial impact of service parallels the age-old search for the connection between advertising and sales. Service quality's results—like advertising's results—are cumulative, and therefore evidence of the link may not come immediately or even quickly after investments. And like advertising, service quality is one of many variables—among them pricing, advertising, efficiency, and image—that simultaneously influence profits. Furthermore, spending on service per se does not guarantee results because strategy and execution must both be considered.

In recent years, however, researchers and company executives have sought to understand the relationship between service and profits and have found strong evidence to support the relationship. For example, one study examined the comparative benefits of revenue expansion and cost reduction on return on quality. The research addressed a common strategic dilemma faced by executives: whether to reduce costs through the use of quality programs, such as Six Sigma, that focus on efficiencies and cost cutting or to build revenues through improvements to customer service, customer satisfaction, and customer retention.[1] Using managers' reports as well as secondary data on firm profitability and stock returns, the study investigated whether the highest return on quality was generated from cost cutting, revenue expansion, or a combination of the two approaches. The results suggest that firms that adopt primarily a revenue expansion emphasis perform better and have higher return on quality than firms that emphasize either cost reduction or both revenue expansion and cost reduction together.[2]

Executives are also realizing that the link between service and profits is neither straightforward nor simple. Service quality affects many economic factors in a company, some of them leading to profits through variables not traditionally in the domain of marketing. For example, the traditional total quality management approach expresses the financial impact of service quality in lowered costs or increased productivity. These relationships involve operational issues that concern marketing only in the sense that marketing research is used to identify service improvements that customers notice and value.

More recently, other types of evidence have become available with which to examine the relationship between service and profitability. The overall goal of this chapter is to synthesize that evidence and to identify relationships between service and profits. In each section we assess the evidence and identify what is currently known about the topics. The chapter is organized using a conceptual framework linking all the variables in these topics.

SERVICE AND PROFITABILITY: THE DIRECT RELATIONSHIP

Figure 16.1 shows the underlying question at the heart of this chapter: how does service affect profits? Managers were first interested in this question in the late 1980s, when service quality emerged as a pivotal competitive strategy. The executives of leading service companies such as FedEx and Disney were willing to trust their intuition that better service would lead to improved financial success. Without formal documentation of the financial payoff, they committed resources to improving service and were

FIGURE 16.1
The Direct
Relationship
between Service
and Profits

richly rewarded for their leaps of faith. In the 1990s, the strategy of using service for competitive advantage and profits was embraced by forward-thinking manufacturing and information technology companies such as General Electric and IBM. However, executives in other companies withheld judgment about investing in service, waiting for solid evidence of its financial soundness.

Early evidence came from the U.S. General Accounting Office (GAO), which sought grounds for belief in the financial impact of quality in companies that had been finalists or winners of the Malcolm Baldrige National Quality Award. The GAO found that these elite quality firms had benefited in terms of market share, sales per employee, return on sales, and return on assets. Based on responses from 22 companies that won or were finalists, the GAO found that 34 of 40 financial variables showed positive performance improvements, while only 6 measurements were negative or neutral.[3] In subsequent years, evidence from more rigorous quantitative research showed the positive impact of service. One study showed the favorable financial impact of complaint recovery systems.[4] Another found a significant and positive relationship between patient satisfaction and hospital profitability.[5] Extending the definition of financial performance to include stock returns, another study found a significant positive link between changes in customer quality perceptions and stock return while holding constant the effects of advertising expenditures and return on investment. Many more studies have shown links between customer satisfaction and financial returns. Exhibit 16.1 reviews the studies that have examined links among customer satisfaction, service quality, and financial performance. This information is enlightening, for it validates that improving customer satisfaction and service quality generates financial returns.

While general questions such as the overall relationships among service quality, customer satisfaction, and company performance are relevant at a broad level, individual companies and researchers also have more focused questions about particular elements of the relationship. For example, what role does service quality have in getting customers? How does service quality contribute to keeping the customers a firm already has?

OFFENSIVE MARKETING EFFECTS OF SERVICE: ATTRACTING MORE AND BETTER CUSTOMERS

Service quality can help companies attract more and better customers to the business through *offensive marketing.*[6] Offensive effects (shown in Figure 16.2) involve market share, reputation, and price premiums. When service is good, a company gains a positive reputation and through that reputation a higher market share and the ability to charge more than its competitors for services. These benefits were documented in a classic multiyear, multicompany study called PIMS (profit impact of marketing strategy). The PIMS research shows that companies offering superior

Exhibit 16.1 Customer Satisfaction, Service Quality, and Firm Performance

A review of two decades of studies examining the links among customer satisfaction, service quality, and firm performance resulted in several important recurring findings across studies. Some studies explicitly consider the impact of service quality on financial performance, while others subsume service quality as a driver of customer satisfaction and therefore focus on the impact of overall customer satisfaction on financial performance. As discussed in Chapter 4, customer satisfaction is a broader concept than service quality, but service quality is almost always an important driver of customer satisfaction across all types of industries. Therefore, the results of the review of both concepts are relevant in this chapter. Because so many studies were examined in the review, only a subset is mentioned in this exhibit, but the complete list of sources can be found in the published review listed as the first reference in this exhibit.

Studies that were reviewed used a variety of metrics for financial performance: profit, stock price, Tobin's q (ratio of market value of a firm to the replacement cost of its tangible assets), return on assets (ROA), return on investment (ROI), abnormal earnings, and cash flows. The following is what the authors concluded.

Generalization 1: Improvements in customer satisfaction have a significant and positive impact on firms' financial performance.

Many studies have shown a strong link between customer satisfaction and firm profitability. For example, one comprehensive study by Anderson, Fornell, and Mazvancheryl using 200 of the *Fortune* 500 firms across 40 industries showed that a 1 percent change in ACSI (as measured by the American Customer Satisfaction Index on a 0–100 scale) is associated with 1.016 percent change in shareholder value as measured by Tobin's q. This implies that a 1 percent improvement in satisfaction for these firms will lead to an increase in the firm's value of approximately $275 million. Supporting this finding, a similar study by Gruca and Rego found that a 1-point increase in ACSI results in an increase of $55 million in a firm's net operational cash flow next year and a decrease of 4 percent in cash flow variability.

In a service-industry study using data from almost 8,000 customers of a national hotel chain, researchers found that return on investment in service quality (e.g., cleanliness) was almost 45 percent. Another study showed that a 1-point improvement in satisfaction (on a 7-point scale) increased ROA by 0.59 percent. With data from 106 firms in 68 industries during the period 1981–1991, still another study found that news reports about increases in customer service led to average cumulative abnormal earnings of about 0.46 percent, or $17 million in market value.

Collectively, these studies show a strong and positive impact of customer satisfaction on firm performance. They further provide a rough benchmark about the size of the impact: a 1 percent change in ACSI can lead to a $240 to $275 million improvement in firm value. In sum, these results provide a strong guideline to firms about how much they should spend on improving customer satisfaction.

Generalization 2: The link between satisfaction and firm performance is asymmetric.

An *asymmetric relationship* means that increases in customer satisfaction do not always have the same impact on firm performance as decreases in customer satisfaction. For example, a study by Anderson and Mittal found that a 1 percent increase in satisfaction led to a 2.37 percent increase in ROI, whereas a 1 percent drop in satisfaction reduced ROI by 5.08 percent (see the accompanying figure). Another study by Nayyar found that positive news about customer service led to an increase in compounded annualized rate (CAR) of about 0.46 percent, whereas reports of reductions in customer service were met with declines in CAR of about 0.22 percent. Still another study by Anderson and Mittal found that a drop in satisfaction produced twice the impact on ROI than an increase in satisfaction. In contrast, the Nayyar study found negative news of customer service had only half the impact on CAR than the positive news.

Generalization 3: The strength of the satisfaction–profitability link varies across industries as well as across firms within an industry.

The strength of the relationships among customer satisfaction, service quality, and profitability are not consistent across industries. In a study by Ittner and Larcker, the impact was found to be stronger in service industries than in durable and nondurable manufacturing firms. In that study, the ACSI had a positive but insignificant impact on market value of durable and nondurable

service achieve higher-than-normal market share growth and that service quality influences profits through increased market share and premium prices, as well as lowered costs and less rework.[7] The study found that businesses rated in the top fifth of competitors on relative service quality average an 8 percent price premium over their competitors.[8]

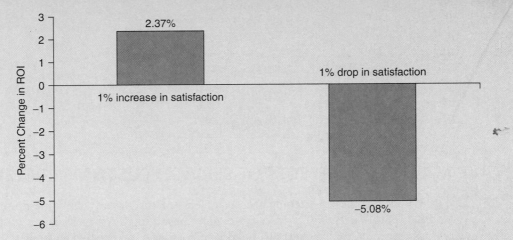

The Asymmetric Relationship between Satisfaction and ROI (Based on 125 Swedish Firms)

Source: E. Anderson and V. Mittal, "Strengthening the Satisfaction-Profit Chain," *Journal of Service Research* 3 (2000), pp. 107–120.

manufacturing firms and a positive and significant impact on the market value of transportation, utility, and communication firms. The effect was strongly negative for retailers. Another study by Anderson found that trade-offs between customer satisfaction and productivity (e.g., labor productivity) were more likely for services than for goods. Specifically, a simultaneous 1 percent increase in both customer satisfaction and productivity is likely to increase ROI by 0.365 percent for goods, but only 0.22 percent for services.

In addition to the differences found in the studies cited, Anderson et al.'s study found that, while a 1 percent change in satisfaction had an *average* impact of 1.016 percent on shareholder value (Tobin's q), the impact ranged from 2.8 percent for department stores to −0.3 percent for discount stores. Anderson and Mittal's study found that industry characteristics explain 35 percent of the variance in cash flow growth and 54 percent of the variance in cash flow variability. They also found that the influence of customer satisfaction on cash flow growth is greatest for low-involvement, routinized, and frequently purchased products (e.g., beer and fast food).

While this summary represents a considerable improvement over what we knew in the past, companies are very eager to learn more. This general information about the relationships among customer satisfaction, service quality, and financial performance will help them understand that investing in customer satisfaction and service quality is beneficial. Thus, indications are that the investments are worthwhile and that not investing can be harmful to firms. Later in the chapter, we will describe other, more specific information that firms want to understand about these relationships.

Sources: S. Gupta and V. Zeithaml, "Customer Metrics and Their Impact on Financial Performance," *Marketing Science* 25 (November–December 2006), pp. 718–739; E. Anderson, C. Fornell, and S. Mazvancheryl, "Customer Satisfaction and Shareholder Value," *Journal of Marketing* 68 (2004), pp. 172–185; C. Ittner and D. Larcker, "Are Non-Financial Measures Leading Indicators of Financial Performance? An Analysis of Customer Satisfaction," *Journal of Accounting Research,* 36, no. 3, (1998), pp. 1–35; R. Rust, A. Zahorik, and T. Keiningham, "Return on Quality (ROQ): Making Service Quality Financially Accountable," *Journal of Marketing* 59 (1995) pp. 58–70; T. S. Gruca and L. L. Rego, "Customer Satisfaction, Cash Flow and Shareholder Value," *Journal of Marketing* 69 (2005), pp. 115–130; E. Anderson and V. Mittal, "Strengthening the Satisfaction-Profit Chain," *Journal of Service Research* 3 (2000), pp. 107–120; P. Nayyar, "Stock Market Reactions to Customer Service Changes," *Strategic Management Journal* 16, no. 1 (1995), pp. 39–53.

To document the impact of service on market share, a group of researchers described their version of the path between quality and market share, claiming that satisfied customers spread positive word of mouth, which leads to the attraction of new customers and then to higher market share. They claim that advertising service excellence without sufficient quality to back up the communications will not increase market share.[9]

FIGURE 16.2
Offensive Marketing
Effects of Service on
Profits

DEFENSIVE MARKETING EFFECTS OF SERVICE: CUSTOMER RETENTION

When it comes to keeping the customers a firm already has—an approach called *defensive marketing*[10]—researchers and consulting firms have in the past 20 years documented and quantified the financial impact of existing customers. Customer defection is costly to companies because new customers must replace lost customers, and replacement comes at a high cost. Getting new customers is expensive; it involves advertising, promotion, and sales costs, as well as start-up operating expenses. New customers are often unprofitable for a period of time after acquisition. In the insurance industry, for example, the insurer does not typically recover selling costs until the third or fourth year of the relationship. Capturing customers from other companies is also an expensive proposition.

In general, the longer a customer remains with a company, the more profitable the relationship is for the organization:

> Served correctly, customers generate increasingly more profits each year they stay with a company. Across a wide range of businesses, the pattern is the same: the longer a company keeps a customer, the more money it stands to make.[11]

The money a company makes from retention comes from four sources (shown in Figure 16.3): costs, volume of purchases, price premium, and word-of-mouth communication. This section provides research evidence for many of the sources.

Lower Costs

Attracting a new customer is five times as costly as retaining an existing one. Consultants who have focused on these relationships assert that customer defections have a stronger effect on a company's profits than market share, scale, unit costs, and many other factors usually associated with competitive advantage.[12] They also claim that, depending on the industry, companies can increase profits from 25 to 85 percent by retaining just 5 percent more of their customers. The GAO study of semifinalists in the Malcolm Baldrige competition (described earlier in this chapter) found that quality reduced costs: order-processing time decreased on average by 12 percent per year, errors and defects fell by 10 percent per year, and cost of quality declined by 9 percent per year.

Consider the following facts about the role of service quality in lowering costs:

- "Our highest quality day was our lowest cost of operations day" (Fred Smith, founder and chairman of FedEx).
- "Our costs of not doing things right the first time were from 25 to 30 percent of our revenue" (David F. Colicchio, Hewlett-Packard Company).[13]

FIGURE 16.3
Defensive Marketing
Effects of Service on
Profits

- Bain and Company, a consulting organization specializing in retention research, estimates that, in the life insurance business, a 5 percent annual increase in customer retention lowers a company's costs per policy by 18 percent.

Volume of Purchases

Customers who are satisfied with a company's services are likely to increase the amount of money they spend with that company or the types of services offered. A customer satisfied with a broker's services, for example, will likely invest more money when it becomes available. Similarly, a customer satisfied with a bank's checking services is likely to open a savings account with the same bank and to use the bank's loan services.

Price Premium

Most of the service quality leaders in industry command higher prices than their competitors: FedEx collects more for overnight delivery than the U.S. Postal Service, Hertz rental cars cost more than Avis cars, and staying at the Ritz-Carlton is a more expensive undertaking than staying at the Hyatt. Therefore, offering high service quality often pays for itself in price increases.

Word-of-Mouth Communication

Because word-of-mouth communication is considered more credible than other sources of information, the best type of promotion for a service may come from other customers who advocate the services provided by the company. Word-of-mouth communication brings new customers to the firm, and the financial value of this form of advocacy can be calibrated by the company in terms of the promotional costs it saves as well as the streams of revenue from new customers. In fact, researchers have developed models of customer lifetime value, in which they can quantify the monetary worth of word-of-mouth communications, called *referral values,* for different segments of consumers.[14] As discussed in Exhibit 16.2, many companies are now using the extent of word of mouth as their main measure of customer loyalty.

Word-of-mouth communications are especially important for services high in experience qualities (where the customer must experience the service to determine its quality) and credence qualities (where the customer may not be able to determine the quality of the service even after it is delivered).[15]

Many questions remain about defensive marketing, among them the ones shown in Exhibit 16.3. Although research has come a long way, researchers and companies must continue working on these questions for a more complete understanding of the impact of service on defensive marketing.

Many different methods of customer measurement—customer satisfaction, service quality, loyalty, and retention, for example—have been used to predict a firm's financial performance. One metric that has become popular yet controversial in recent years is called the *Net Promoter Score (NPS)*. The score, developed by loyalty expert Frederick Reichheld, is based on the idea that word-of-mouth communication, rather than any of the other metrics, is the best predictor of growth and therefore financial performance.

The score itself is based on just one survey question: Would you recommend us to a friend or colleague? To get the NPS, a company asks consumers about the likelihood (out of 10) that they would recommend the company, then subtracts the proportion of "detractors" (who rate the company lower than 6) from the proportion of "promoters" (who rate the company at 9 or 10).

Executives of many of the world's most prestigious firms agree with Frederick Reichheld that the NPS is the "single most reliable indicator of a company's ability to grow." General Electric, American Express, Microsoft, Intuit, and The Progressive Corporation are but a few companies that have adopted the approach. The popularity of the Net Promoter Score comes in part because the approach is simple. To top management, long confused by the growing complexity of customer measurement and how to apply it, the idea of having just one number on which to focus is very appealing. And the measure is intuitive—if customers like the firm or its service enough to talk about them to others, that signals a stronger bond than merely being satisfied. The Net Promoter Score has becoe, in essence, a "magic number" for companies.

HOW DO COMPANIES MEASURE UP ON THE NET PROMOTER SCORE?

In many firms, promoters barely outnumber detractors, giving them NPS scores of only 5 to 10 percent.

NPS® Stars by Industry

Sources: Satmetrix 2010 Net Promoter Benchmark Study of US Consumers

Industry	Company	NPS
Airlines	Jet Blue	64%
Auto Insurance	USAA	78%
Banking	USAA	81%
Brokerage & Invesments	Charles Schwab	46%
Cable & Satellite TV	DIRECTV	27%
Cellular Phone Service	Verizon	41%
Computer Hardware	Apple	78%
Consumer Software	Adobe Systems	37%
Credit Cards	American Express	27%
Department, Wholesale & Speciality Stores	Costco	66%
Grocery & Supermarkets	Trader Joe's	69%
Health Insurance	BlueCross BlueShield of Illionois	5%
Homeowners Insurance	USSA	69%
Internet Service	Road Runner / Time Warner	21%
Life Insurance	State Farm	34%
Online Search & Information	Facebook	65%
Online Shopping	Amazon.com	71%

CUSTOMER PERCEPTIONS OF SERVICE QUALITY AND PURCHASE INTENTIONS

In Chapter 4 we highlighted the links among customer satisfaction, service quality, and increased purchases. Here we provide more research and empirical evidence supporting these relationships. For example, researchers at Xerox offered a compelling insight into the relationship between satisfaction and purchase intentions during the company's early years of customer satisfaction research. Initially, the company focused on satisfied customers, which they identified as those checking either a "4" or a "5"

Worse yet, many firms and industries have negative Net Promoter Scores, which means that they are constantly creating detractors. Some firms shine, however, and the previous chart indicates some of the stars.

CONTROVERSY: IS THE NET PROMOTER INDEX SUPERIOR, APPROPRIATE OR COMPLETE?

While executives are embracing the Net Promoter Score, researchers and loyalty experts other than Reichheld question the superiority, appropriateness, and completeness of the metric. For example, one researcher questioned whether word of mouth would be a better driver of growth than other factors, such as reducing customer loss or increasing current customers' volume through cross-sales and share of category purchase. More dramatically, would actions driven to increase word of mouth create stronger growth than actions to acquire profitable new customers?

Another key concern is the extent to which word of mouth is a relevant goal for all services in all contexts. Consumers feel strongly about some services, and these feelings drive word of mouth. Services (such as restaurants, vacations, and entertainment) are referral-worthy. However, the majority of services are unlikely to be interesting enough for customers to talk about them. From a practical standpoint, while using a single number provides a sign of health, as a thermometer does in signaling body temperature, it neither diagnoses firm problems nor describes how to treat them. For it to be actionable, companies must follow up with metrics that also contain other questions (such as those in Chapter 5 of this textbook) to identify what customers expect from and perceive about the company. In the drive to simplicity in using the Net Promoter Score, some companies do not follow up on the NPS with other metrics, research, or programs.

Reichheld's findings have been put to the test by other researchers. One team of loyalty experts matched the way that NPS was calculated using two to three years' worth of data from 21 companies and 15,500 interviews. While they expected that the findings would replicate what Reichheld had found, they did not. Furthermore, when comparing the results to the American Customer Satisfaction Index (ACSI), this team also found that the Net Promoter Score had no clear superiority to other measures. Another study on the subject does confirm a strong correlation between word of mouth and growth, but cannot confirm causality.

THE BOTTOM LINE

Loyalty expert Timothy Keiningham dismisses the quest for one magical number to measure loyalty, including NPS:

> Even the best ideas aren't universal. If they were, everybody would do them and they would already be known. You need to know what is the number one demonstration of loyalty from your customers, then model back from that—what causes that to happen and what causes that to break? And once you start thinking about it that way, you realize there isn't going to be a magic number because this is driven by different things depending on what industry you are in.

Sources: F. Reichheld and R. Markey, *The Ultimate Question 2.0: How Net Promoter Companies Thrive in a Customer Driven World* Boston, Messachusetts Harvard Business School Press, 2011); D. Grisaffe, "Guru Misses the Mark with 'One Number' Fallacy"; www.netpromter.com, July 15, accessed 2011; www.creatingloyalty.com/story.cfm?article_id=656, accessed September 2007; T. Keiningham, B. Cooil, T. Andreassen, and L. Aksoy, "A Longitudinal Examination of Net Promoter and Firm Revenue Growth," *Journal of Marketing* (July 2007), pp. 39–51.

on a 5-point satisfaction scale. Careful analysis of the data showed that customers giving Xerox 5s were six times more likely to indicate that they would-repurchase Xerox equipment than those giving 4s. This relationship encouraged the company to focus on increasing the 5s rather than the 4s *and* 5s because of the strong sales and profitability implications.[16] A recent and more encompassing update of the importance of scoring in the "top box" of customer satisfaction is shown in Figure 16.4. TARP Worldwide Inc. found similar results across 10 studies incorporating 8,000 customers worldwide. A full 96 percent of customers who report being "very satisfied" (i.e., they are in the *top box* in satisfaction) say they will "definitely repurchase" from the same company. When

Managers are only beginning to understand the topics discussed in this chapter. For each of the sections on the service quality/profitability relationship in this chapter, Exhibit 16.4 lists an inventory of questions that managers and researchers most want to know. To give you an idea of the specific questions that managers are asking, we elaborate here on the topic of defensive marketing.

1. *What is a loyal customer?* Customer loyalty can be viewed as the way customers feel or as the way they act. A simple definition is possible with some products and services: customers are loyal as long as they continue to use a good or service. For washing machines or long-distance telephone service, customers are deemed loyal if they continue to use the machine or telephone service. Defining customer loyalty for other products and services is more problematic. What is the definition of loyalty to a restaurant: always eat there, eat there more times than at other restaurants, or eat there at least once during a given period? These questions highlight the growing popularity of the concept of "share of wallet" that company managers are very interested in. *Share of wallet* refers to the percentage of spending in a particular category given to a particular service provider. The other way to define loyalty is in terms of the customer's sense of belonging or commitment to the product. Some companies have been noted for their "apostles," customers who care so much about the company that they stay in contact to provide suggestions for improvement and constantly preach to others the benefits of the company. Is this the best way to define loyalty?

2. *What is the role of service in defensive marketing?* Quality products at appropriate prices are important elements in the retention equation, but both these marketing variables can be imitated. Service plays a critical role—if not *the* critical role—in retaining customers. Providing consistently good service is not as easy to duplicate and therefore is likely to be the cementing force in customer relationships. Exactly how important is service in defensive marketing? How does service compare in effectiveness with other retention strategies such as price? To date, no studies have incorporated all or most factors to examine their relative importance in keeping customers.

3. *What levels of service provision are needed to retain customers?* How much spending on service quality is enough to retain customers? Initial investigations into this question have been argued but have not been confirmed. One consultant, for example, proposed that, when satisfaction rose above a certain threshold, repurchase loyalty would climb rapidly. When satisfaction fell below a different threshold, customer loyalty would decline equally rapidly. Between these thresholds, he believed that loyalty was relatively flat. The material discussed in Chapter 3 offered a different prediction. The zone of tolerance discussed in that chapter captured the range within which a company is meeting expectations. This framework suggests that firms operating within the zone of tolerance should continue to improve service, even to the point of reaching the desired service level. This hypothesis implies an upward-sloping (rather than flat) relationship between the zone of tolerance and retaining customers.

4. *What specific aspects of service are most important for customer retention?* Most companies realize that service is multifaceted and want to identify the specific aspects of service provision that will lead to keeping customers.

5. *How can defection-prone customers be identified?* Companies find it difficult to create and execute strategies responsive enough to detect customer defections. Systems must be developed to isolate potential defecting customers, evaluate them, and retain them if it is in the best interest of the company. One author and consultant advises that companies focus on three groups of customers who may be candidates for defection: (a) customers who close their accounts and shift business to a competitor, (b) customers who shift some of their business to another firm, and (c) customers who actually buy more but whose purchases represent a smaller share of their total expenditures. The first of these groups is easiest to identify, and the third group is the most difficult. Among the other customers who would be vulnerable are any customer with a negative service experience, new customers, and customers of companies in very competitive markets. Developing early warning systems of such customers is a pivotal requirement for companies.

Source: V. A. Zeithaml, "Service Quality, Profitability and the Economic Worth of Customers," *Journal of the Academy of Marketing Science,* January 2000, © 2000 by the Academy of Marketing Science.

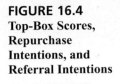

FIGURE 16.4
Top-Box Scores,
Repurchase
Intentions, and
Referral Intentions

Source: Information Courtesy
of TARP Worldwide, 2007.

they are only "somewhat satisfied," the number drops to only 52 percent, and only 7 percent of customers who are "neutral or very dissatisfied" will definitely repurchase.[17]

Evidence also shows that customer satisfaction and service quality perceptions affect consumer intentions to behave in many positive ways—praising the firm, preferring the company over others, increasing volume of purchases, or agreeably paying a price premium. Figure 16.5 shows these other relationships. Most of the early evidence looked only at overall benefits in terms of repurchase intention rather than extending past that relationship and examining specific types of behavioral intentions. Another, using information from a Swedish customer satisfaction barometer, found that stated repurchase intention is strongly related to stated satisfaction across virtually all product categories.[18]

Studies have found relationships between service quality and more specific behavioral intentions. One study involving university students found strong links between service quality and other behavioral intentions of strategic importance to a university, including behavior such as saying positive things about the school, planning to contribute money upon graduation, and planning to recommend the school to employers as a place from which to recruit.[19] Another comprehensive study examined a battery comprised of 13 specific behavioral intentions (such as saying positive things about

FIGURE 16.5
The Effects
of Service on
Behavioral
Intentions
and Behavior

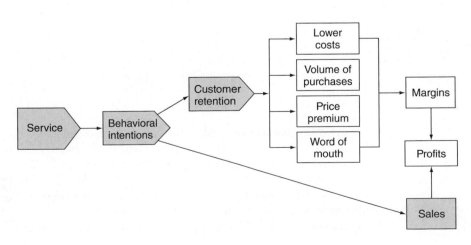

Exhibit 16.4 Service Quality and the Economic Worth of Customers: Businesses Still Need to Know More

Topic	Key Questions
Service quality and profitability: the direct relationship	1. What methodologies need to be developed to allow companies to capture the effect of service quality on profit within individual companies? 2. What measures are necessary to examine the relationship in a consistent, valid, and reliable manner? 3. How and why does the relationship between service quality and profitability vary by industry, country, category of business, or other variable? What does this imply for investment in service quality? 4. What are the moderating factors of the relationship between service quality and profitability? 5. What is the optimal spending level on service in order to affect profitability?
Offensive effects of service quality	1. What is the optimal amount of spending on service quality to obtain offensive effects? 2. To obtain offensive effects, are expenditures on advertising or service quality itself more effective? 3. In what ways can companies signal high service quality to customers to obtain offensive effects?
Defensive effects of service quality	1. What is a loyal customer? 2. What is the role of service in defensive marketing? 3. How does service compare in effectiveness to other retention strategies such as price? 4. What levels of service provision are needed to retain customers? 5. How can the effects of word-of-mouth communication from retained customers be quantified? 6. What aspects of service are most important for customer retention? 7. How can defection-prone customers be identified and then retained?
Perceptions of service quality	1. What is the relationship between customer purchase intentions and initial purchase behavior in services? 2. What is the relationship between behavioral intentions and repurchase in services? 3. Does the degree of association between service quality and behavior change at different quality levels?
Identifying the key drivers of service quality, customer retention, and profits	1. Which service encounters are most responsible for perceptions of service quality? 2. What are the key drivers of service quality, customer retention, and profits in each service encounter? 3. Where should investments be made to affect service quality, purchase, retention, and profits? 4. Are key drivers of service quality the same as key drivers of behavioral intentions, customer retention, and profits?

the company, remaining loyal to the company, and spending more with the company) likely to result from perceived service quality. The overall measure was significantly correlated with customer perceptions of service quality.[20] Individual companies have also monitored the impact of service quality on selected behavioral intentions. Toyota found that intent to repurchase a Toyota automobile increased from a base of 37 to 45 percent with a positive sales experience, from 37 to 79 percent with a positive service experience, and from 37 to 91 percent with both positive sales and service experiences.[21]

THE KEY DRIVERS OF SERVICE QUALITY, CUSTOMER RETENTION, AND PROFITS

Understanding the relationship between overall service quality and profitability is important, but it is perhaps more useful to managers to identify specific drivers of service quality that most relate to profitability (shown in Figure 16.6). Doing so will help firms understand what aspects of service quality to change to influence the relationship and, therefore, where to invest resources.

Most evidence for this issue has come from examining the effects of specific aspects of service (e.g., responsiveness, reliability, assurance, and tangibles) on overall service quality, customer satisfaction, and purchase intentions rather than on financial outcomes such as retention or profitability. As you have discovered in this text, service is multifaceted, consisting of a wide variety of customer-perceived dimensions and resulting from innumerable company strategies such as technology and process improvement. In research exploring the relative importance of service dimensions on overall service quality or customer satisfaction, the bulk of the support confirms that reliability is most critical; but other research has demonstrated the importance of customization and other factors. Because the dimensions and attributes are delivered in many cases with totally different internal strategies, resources must be allocated where they are most needed.[22]

Some companies and researchers have viewed the effect of specific service encounters on overall service quality or customer satisfaction and the effect of specific behaviors within service encounters. Marriott Hotels conducted extensive customer research to determine what service elements contribute most to customer loyalty. They found that four of the top five factors came into play in the first 10 minutes of the guest's stay—those that involved the early encounters of arriving, checking in, and entering the hotel rooms. Other companies have found that mistakes or problems that occur in early service encounters are particularly critical, because a failure at early points results in greater risk for dissatisfaction in each ensuing encounter. IBM found that the sales encounter was the most critical of all, in large part because interactions with salespeople establish customer expectations for the remaining service encounters.

Another way of looking at the problem, based largely in the operations and management literature, involves investigating the effect of service programs and managerial approaches within an organization on financial measures such as profitability. A customer-focused approach to metrics is described in the Strategy Insight.

FIGURE 16.6
The Key Drivers of Service Quality, Customer Retention, and Profits

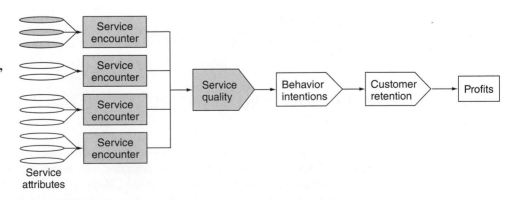

Strategy Insight Customer Equity and Return on Marketing: Metrics to Match a Strategic Customer-Centered View of the Firm

Although the marketing concept has articulated a customer-centered viewpoint since the 1960s, marketing theory and practice have become incrementally customer-centered. For example, marketing has only recently decreased its emphasis on short-term transactions and increased its focus on long-term customer relationships. Much of this refocus stems from the changing nature of the world's leading economies, which have undergone a century-long shift from the goods sector to the service sector.

Because service tends to be more relationship based, this structural shift in the economy has resulted in more attention to relationships and therefore more attention to customers. This customer-centered viewpoint is now reflected in the concepts and metrics that drive marketing management, including such metrics as customer value and voice of the customer. For example, the concept of brand equity, a fundamentally product-centered concept, is now being challenged by the customer-centered concept of *customer equity,* defined as the total of the discounted lifetime values summed over all the firm's customers.

In other words, customer equity is obtained by summing up the customer lifetime values of the firm's customers. In fast-moving industries that involve customer relationships, products come and go but customers remain. Customers and customer equity may be more central to many firms than brands and brand equity, although current management practices and metrics do not yet fully reflect this shift. The shift from product-centered thinking to customer-centered thinking implies the need for an accompanying shift from product-based metrics to customer-based metrics.

USING CUSTOMER EQUITY IN A STRATEGIC FRAMEWORK

Consider the issues facing a typical marketing manager or marketing-oriented CEO: How do I manage my brand? How will my customers react to changes in service and service quality? Should I raise prices? What is the best way to enhance the relationships with my current customers? Where should I focus my efforts? Determining customer lifetime value, or customer equity, is the first step, but the more important step is to evaluate and test ideas and strategies using lifetime value as the measuring stick. At a very basic level, strategies for building customer relationships can affect five basic factors: retention rate, referrals, sales, direct costs, and marketing costs.

Researchers Roland Rust, Valarie Zeithaml, and Kay Lemon have developed an approach based on customer equity that can help business executives answer their questions. The model that represents this approach is shown in the accompanying figure. In this context, customer equity is an approach to marketing and corporate strategy that finally puts the customer—and, more importantly, strategies that grow the value of the customer—at the heart of the organization. The researchers identify the drivers of customer equity—value equity, brand equity, and relationship equity—and explain how these drivers work, independently and together, to grow customer equity. Service strategies are prominent in both value equity and relationship equity. Within each of these drivers are specific actions ("levers") that the firm can take to enhance the firm's overall customer equity.

WHY IS CUSTOMER EQUITY IMPORTANT?

For most firms, customer equity—the total of the discounted lifetime values of all the firm's customers—is certain to be the most important determinant of the long-term value of the firm. Although customer equity will not be responsible for the entire value of the firm (e.g., physical assets, intellectual property, research and development competencies), the firm's current customers provide the most reliable source

COMPANY PERFORMANCE MEASUREMENT: THE BALANCED PERFORMANCE SCORECARD

Traditionally, organizations have measured their performance almost completely on the basis of financial indicators such as profit, sales, and return on investment. This short-term approach leads companies to emphasize financials to the exclusion of other performance indicators. Today's corporate strategists recognize the limitations of evaluating

The Customer Equity Model

of future revenues and profits—and provide a focal point for marketing strategy.

Although it may seem obvious that customer equity is key to long-term success, understanding how to grow and manage customer equity is much more complex. Growing customer equity is of utmost importance, and doing it well can lead to significant competitive advantage.

CALCULATING RETURN ON MARKETING USING CUSTOMER EQUITY

At the beginning of this chapter, we told you about an approach called return on quality that was developed to help companies understand where they could get the greatest impact from quality investments. A more general form of that approach is called *return on marketing,* which enables companies to look at all competing marketing strategy options and trade them off on the basis of projected financial return. This approach allows companies to not just

examine the impact of service on financial return but also compare the impact of service with the impact of branding, price changes, and all other marketing strategies. Using the customer equity model, firms can analyze the drivers that have the greatest impact, compare the drivers' performance with that of competitors' drivers, and project return on investment from improvements in the drivers. The framework enables what-if evaluation of marketing return on investment, which can include such criteria as return on quality, return on advertising, return on loyalty programs, and even return on corporate citizenship, given a particular shift in customer perceptions. This approach enables firms to focus marketing efforts on strategic initiatives that generate the greatest return.

Sources: R. Rust, K. Lemon, and V. Zeithaml, "Return on Marketing: Using Customer Equity to Focus Marketing Strategy," *Journal of Marketing* 68 (January 2004), pp. 109; R. Rust, V. Zeithaml, and K. Lemon, *Driving Customer Equity* (New York: The Free Press, 2000).

corporate performance on financials alone, contending that these income-based financial figures measure yesterday's decisions rather than indicate future performance. This recognition came when many companies' strong financial records deteriorated because of unnoticed declines in operational processes, quality, or customer satisfaction.[23] In the words of one observer of corporate strategy:

Financial measures emphasize profitability of inert assets over any other mission of the company. They do not recognize the emerging leverage of the soft stuff—skilled people and employment of information—as the new keys to high performance and near-perfect customer satisfaction. . . . If the only mission a measurement system conveys is financial discipline, an organization is directionless.[24]

For this reason, companies began to recognize that *balanced performance scorecards*—strategic measurement systems that captured other areas of performance—were needed. The developers of balanced performance scorecards defined them as follows:

> . . . a set of measures that gives top managers a fast but comprehensive view of the business . . . [that] complements the financial measures with operational measures of customer satisfaction, internal processes, and the organization's innovation and improvement activities—operational measures that are the drivers of future financial performance.[25]

Having a firm handle on what had been viewed as "soft" measures became the way to help organizations identify customer problems, improve processes, and achieve company objectives.

As shown in Figure 16.7, the balanced performance scorecard captures three perspectives in addition to the financial perspective: customer, operational, and learning. The balanced scorecard brings together, in a single management report, many of the previously separated elements of a company's competitive agenda and forces senior managers to consider all the important measures together. The scorecard has been facilitated by developments in enterprise-wide software that allow companies to create, automate, and integrate measurements from all parts of the company.

Methods for measuring financial performance are the most developed and established in corporations, having been created more than 400 years ago. In contrast,

FIGURE 16.7   **Sample Measurements for the Balanced Scorecard.**

Source: Adapted and reprinted by permission of *Harvard Business Review* an excerpt from R. S. Kaplan and D. P. Norton, "The Balanced Scorecard-Measures That Drive Performance," *Harvard Business Review* 70 (January–February 1992). Copyright © 1992 by the Harvard Business School Publishing Corporation; all rights reserved.

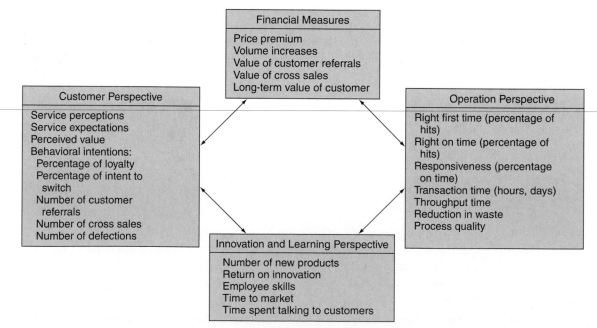

Technology Spotlight   Cost-Effective Service Excellence through Technology

In addition to affecting the top line by increasing revenues, companies across the globe are taking a hard look at what they can to do make bottom-line improvements by enhancing productivity, making processes more efficient, and innovating systems. Among the approaches that are effective in bottom-line improvement are reducing waste in the service system, standardizing service behaviors and actions, shifting the service boundary by having customers perform more of the service, and substituting technology for personal contact and human effort. We have discussed technology throughout this textbook, and in this spotlight we feature several ways that technology has been used to make service more efficient and therefore more profitable.

REDBOX

As the use of streaming videos is becoming popular and video stores are rapidly becoming obsolete, Redbox—the omnipresent movie-distributing kiosk—has become a profitable approach to video rental. The company's research demonstrated that two-thirds of all movies are selected between 4 p.m. and 9 p.m., leading the company to place its large red boxes in places like grocery stores and gas stations, where consumers typically are at that time. The company has nearly 28,000 kiosk locations and has rented 1.5 billion movies and 4 million video games. Sixty-eight percent of the U.S. population lives within a 5-minute drive of a Redbox kiosk. Even though the charge for customers is only $1 per DVD, the kiosks are very profitable: each Redbox becomes cash flow positive in four months. Blockbuster has entered the kiosk market with its own blue version called Blockbuster Express, but its 10,000 locations lag behind Redbox's sites.

LOUISE THE TECHNOLOGY NURSE

One of the highest costs in hospitals comes from preventable 30-day re-admissions, which can be as high as 4.4 million per year. Re-admissions are largely due to patient noncompliance with hospital instructions about medication and home care. The highest rates are for heart attacks (19.9 percent), heart failure

(24.7 percent), pneumonia (18.3 percent), and circulatory system disorders (10.4 percent). One of the newest strategies to assure that patients understand posthospital instructions is a virtual nurse—patient advocate"—named Louise. Developed by Boston University Medical Center, Louise is an animated character that explains medical instructions to patients on a computer screen, thereby carefully and fully communicating home care. On a laptop, Louise is wheeled to the patient's bedside and reviews the discharge packet while also looking at a paper copy. Patients can ask and re-ask questions using a touchscreen. Louise helped cut re-admissions by 30 percent in a 2008 study. Further, the virtual discharge system automates 30 minutes of time, for a savings in time for human nurses.

Sources: www.redbox.com, accessed August 2011; www.blockbusterexpress.com, accessed August 2011; L. Landro, "Don't Come Back, Hospitals Say," *The Wall Street Journal*, June 7, 2011; Agency for Healthcare Research and Quality 2011, hospitalcompare.gov, accessed August 2011.

The American Customer Satisfaction Index (ACSI) was created in 1994 by researchers at the University of Michigan along with the American Society for Quality in Milwaukee, Wisconsin, and CFI Group in Ann Arbor, Michigan. The ACSI model was derived from a model originally implemented in 1989 in Sweden called the Swedish Customer Satisfaction Barometer (SCSB). Claes Fornell, the chair of ACSI LLC and CFI Group, developed the model and methodology for both the Swedish and American versions.

The methodology from the American Customer Satisfaction Index is rapidly being adopted around the world. Developers include research groups, quality associations, and universities that participate in ACSI's international licensing program, called Global CSI[SM]. Thirteen countries throughout Europe (using what is called the Extended Performance Satisfaction Index), as well as Asia, South America, and the Middle East, have created customer satisfaction indexes for their own national economies by using Global CSI[SM].

According to the website of the ACSI, Indonesia is the newest licensee in Asia and released its first set of measures in the fall of 2011. The Dominican Republic launched INSAC, the country's first national customer satisfaction index in 2010, and plans are underway to add several more industries to it over the next few years. Great Britain's NCSI-UK (National Customer Satisfaction Index of the UK), which started in 2007, measures 16 industries representing a broad spectrum of the economy serving UK households.

Other countries that have adopted ACSI include Turkey, Mexico, South Korea, Sweden, Colombia, Barbados, and Singapore. The Customer Satisfaction Index of Singapore (CSISG) was launched in 2008. According to Caroline Lim, director of The Institute of Service Excellence, Singapore Management University, just as "ACSI has been the de facto standardized measure of customer satisfaction in the United States economy since 1994," CSISG was developed using the same proven and respected methodology to "complement the other traditional forms of measure of the quantity of economic

Reprinted with permission of the American Customer Satisfaction Index website.

output such as GDP to provide a more holistic picture of the Singapore economy."

Other countries are evaluating the implementation of ACSI-based models. If this trend continues, it may be possible to create an international system of customer satisfaction measurement using a common methodology to allow cross-national satisfaction and comparisons. While reaching firm conclusions is still premature because most economies do not yet measure customer satisfaction using this general approach, a recent study reveals interesting cross-national determinants of satisfaction:

- Consumers in self-expressive societies have higher levels of customer satisfaction than those in societies with survival values.
- Literacy rate, trade freedom, and business freedom have a positive effect on customer satisfaction.
- Per capita gross domestic product has a negative effect on customer satisfaction.

Sources: www.theacsi.org/index.php?option=com_content &view=article&id=219&Item=278; F. V. Morgeson III, S. Mithas, T. L. Keiningham, and L. Aksoy, "An Investigation of the Cross-National Determinants of Customer Satisfaction," *Journal of the Academy of Marketing Science* 39 (April 2011), pp. 198–215.

efforts to measure market share, quality, innovation, human resources, and customer satisfaction have only recently been created. Companies can improve their performance by developing this discipline in their measurement of all four categories.

Changes to Financial Measurement

One way that service leaders are changing financial measurement is to calibrate the defensive effect of retaining and losing customers. The monetary value of retaining customers can be projected through the use of average revenues over the lifetimes of customers. The number of customer defections can then be translated into lost revenue to the firm and become a critical company performance standard:

> Ultimately, defections should be a key performance measure for senior management and a fundamental component of incentive systems. Managers should know the company's defection rate, what happens to profits when the rate moves up or down and why defections occur.[26]

Companies can also measure actual increases or decreases in revenue from retention or defection of customers by capturing the value of a loyal customer, including expected cash flows over a customer's lifetime or lifetime customer value (as described in Chapter 6). Other possible financial measures (as shown in Figure 16.7) include the value of price premiums, volume increases, customer referrals, and cross-sales.

Customer Perceptual Measures

Customer perceptual measures are leading indicators of financial performance. As we discussed in this chapter, customers who are not happy with the company will defect and will tell others about their dissatisfaction. As we also discussed, perceptual measures reflect customer beliefs and feelings about the company and its products and services and can predict how the customer will behave in the future. Overall forms of the measurements we discussed in Chapters 4 and 5 (shown in the customer perspective box of Figure 16.7) are measures that can be included in this category. Among the measures that are valuable to track are overall service perceptions and expectations, customer satisfaction, perceptual measures of value, and behavioral intention measures such as loyalty and intent to switch. A company that notices a decline in these numbers should be concerned that the decline will translate into lost dollars for the company.

Operational Measures

Operational measures involve the translation of customer perceptual measures into the standards or actions that must be set internally to meet customers' expectations. Although virtually all companies count or calculate operational measures in some form, the balanced scorecard requires that these measures stem from the business processes that have the greatest effect on customer satisfaction. In other words, these measures are not independent of customer perceptual measures but instead are intricately linked with them. In Chapter 9 we called these customer-linked operational measures *customer-defined standards*—operational standards determined through customer expectations and calibrated the way the customer views and expresses them.

Innovation and Learning

The final area of measurement involves a company's ability to innovate, improve, and learn—by launching new products, creating more value for customers, and improving operating efficiencies. This measurement area is most difficult to capture quantitatively but can be accomplished using performance-to-goal percentages. For example, a company can set a goal of launching 10 new products a year, then measure what percentage of that goal it achieves in a year. If four new products are launched, its percentage for the year is 40 percent, which can then be compared with subsequent years.

Effective Nonfinancial Performance Measurements

According to field research conducted in 60 companies and survey responses from 297 senior executives, many companies do not identify and act on the correct non-financial measures.[27] One example involves a bank that only surveyed the satisfaction of customers who physically entered the branches (rather than all customers, including those who banked by phone or ATM), a policy that caused some branch managers to offer free food and drinks in order to increase their scores. According to the authors of the study, companies make four major mistakes:

1. *Not linking measures to strategy.* Companies can easily identify hundreds of nonfinancial measures to track, but they also need to use analysis that identifies the most important drivers of their strategy. Successful organizations use value driver maps, tools that lay out the cause-and-effect relationships between drivers and strategic success. Figure 16.8 shows the causal model developed by a successful fast-food

FIGURE 16.8
The Measures That Matter Most: A causal model for a fast-food company shows the critical drivers of performance and the concepts that lead to shareholder value.

Source: Christopher D. Ittner and David F. Larcker, "Coming Up Short on Nonfinancial Performance Measurement," *Harvard Business Review* 81 (November 2003), pp. 88–95.

chain to understand the key drivers of shareholder value. The factors on the right were identified as most important in leading to the concepts on the left, and the sequence of concepts from top to bottom shows the relationships among company strategies (such as selection and staffing) and intermediate results (such as employee and customer satisfaction) that result in financial results (such as sustained profitability and shareholder value). The study found that fewer than 30 percent of the firms surveyed used this causal modeling approach.

2. *Not validating the links.* Only 21 percent of companies in the study verify that the nonfinancial measures lead to financial performance. Instead, many firms decide what they are going to measure in each category and never link the categories. Many managers believed that the relationships were self-evident instead of conducting analysis to validate the linkages. This chapter's Strategy Insight showed one way that companies can create this type of linkage. In general, it is critical that companies pull together all their data and examine the relationships among the categories.

3. *Not setting the right performance targets.* Companies sometimes aim too high in setting improvement targets. Trying to make all customers 100 percent satisfied might seem to be a desirable goal, but many companies expend far too many resources to gain too little improvement in satisfaction. The study's authors found that a telecommunications company aiming for customers who were completely satisfied was wasting resources because these customers spent no more money than those who were 80 percent satisfied.[28]

4. *Measuring incorrectly.* Companies need to use metrics with statistical validity and reliability. Organizations cannot measure complex phenomenon with one or two simple measures, nor can they use inconsistent methodologies to measure the same concept, such as customer satisfaction. Another problem that companies may encounter is trying to use quantitative metrics to capture qualitative results for important factors such as leadership and innovation.

Creating a balanced scorecard in and of itself does not improve performance. Companies will not reap the benefits of techniques such as the balanced scorecard unless they address these four issues.

Summary

This chapter is divided into five sections, each of which assesses the evidence and identifies what is currently known about the relationship between service and profitability. The chapter used a conceptual framework to link all the variables in these topics: (1) the direct relationship between service and profits; (2) offensive effects of service quality, the ability to obtain new customers; (3) defensive effects of service quality, the ability to retain existing customers; (4) the relationship between service quality and purchase intentions; and (5) key drivers of service quality, customer retention, and profits. Considerable progress has been made in the investigation of service quality, profitability, and the economic worth of customers, but managers are still lacking many of the answers that would help them make informed decisions about service quality investments. The chapter also discussed approaches to measuring loyalty, including the popular Net Promoter Score, and to measuring return on marketing using the customer equity model. The chapter concluded with a discussion of the balanced performance scorecard approach to measuring corporate performance, which offers a strategic approach for measuring all aspects of a company's performance.

Discussion Questions

1. Why has it been difficult for executives to understand the relationship between service improvements and profitability in their companies?

2. What is the ROSQ model, and what is its significance to corporate America?

3. To this day, many companies believe that service is a cost rather than a revenue producer. Why might they hold this view? How would you argue the opposite view?

4. What is the difference between offensive and defensive marketing? How does service affect each of these?

5. What are the main sources of profit in defensive marketing?

6. What are the main sources of profit in offensive marketing?

7. How would the balanced performance scorecard help us understand and document the information presented in this chapter? Which of the five sections that discuss different aspects of the relationship between service quality and profits can it illuminate?

Exercises

1. Using the Internet, find the official site for the Net Promoter Score. Use the links in the site to locate other researchers' opinions of the measure, and make a list of the benefits and disadvantages discussed in those articles. If you were a CEO, would you use this measure as the "only number you need" to predict growth? Why or why not?

2. Interview a local firm and see what it knows about its key drivers of financial performance. What are the key service drivers of the firm? Does the company know whether these service drivers relate to profit?

3. Select a service industry (such as fast food) or a company (such as McDonald's) that you are familiar with, either as a customer or an employee, and create a balanced scorecard. Describe the operational, customer, financial, and learning measures that could be used to capture performance.

Notes

1. R. T. Rust, C. Moorman, and P. R. Dickson, "Getting Return on Quality: Revenue Expansion, Cost Reduction, or Both?" *Journal of Marketing* 66 (October 2002), pp. 7–24.

2. Ibid.

3. *Management Practice, U.S. Companies Improve Performance through Quality Efforts,* Report No. GAO/NSIAD-91-190 (Washington, DC: U.S. General Accounting Office, 1992).

4. R. Rust, B. Subramanian, and M. Wells, "Making Complaints a Management Tool," *Marketing Management* 3 (1993), pp. 40–45. R. Rust, Roland, C. Moorman, and G. Bhalla, "Rethinking Marketing," *Harvard Business Review*, January-February 2010; R. Rust, V. Zeithaml, and K. Lemon, "Customer-Centered Brand Management," *Harvard Business Review*, September 2004; S. Gupta and D. Lehmann, *Managing Customers as Investments*, Wharton School Publishing, 2005.

5. E. Nelson, R. T. Rust, A. Zahorik, R. L. Rose, P. Batalden, and B. Siemanski, "Do Patient Perceptions of Quality Relate to Hospital Financial Performance?" *Journal of Healthcare Marketing* 12 (December 1992), pp. 1–13.

6. C. Fornell and B. Wernerfelt, "Defensive Marketing Strategy by Customer Complaint Management: A Theoretical Analysis," *Journal of Marketing Research* 24 (November 1987), pp. 337–346; see also C. Fornell and B. Wernerfelt, "A Model for Customer Complaint Management," *Marketing Science* 7 (Summer 1988), pp. 271–286.

7. B. Gale, "Monitoring Customer Satisfaction and Market-Perceived Quality," *American Marketing Association Worth Repeating Series,* no. 922CS01 (Chicago: American Marketing Association, 1992).

8. Ibid.

9. R. E. Kordupleski, R. T. Rust, and A. J. Zahorik, "Why Improving Quality Doesn't Improve Quality (or Whatever Happened to Marketing?)," *California Management Review* 35 (Spring 1993), pp. 82–95.

10. Fornell and Wernerfelt, "Defensive Marketing Strategy by Customer Complaint Management"; Fornell and Wernerfelt, "A Model for Customer Complaint Management."

11. F. Reichheld and E. Sasser, "Zero Defections: Quality Comes to Services," *Harvard Business Review* 68 (September–October 1990), p. 106.

12. Ibid., p. 105.

13. D. F. Colicchio, regional quality manager, Hewlett-Packard Company, personal communication.

14. V. Kumar, J. A. Petersen, and R. P. Leone, "How Valuable Is Word of Mouth?" *Harvard Business Review* 85 (October 2007), pp. 139–146.

15. R. Hallowell, "Word-of-Mouth Referral," *Harvard Business School Module Note,* 2002.

16. J. L. Heskett, W. E. Sasser Jr., and L. A. Schlesinger, *The Service Profit Chain* (New York: The Free Press, 1997).

17. Information provided by TARP Worldwide Inc., August 2007.

18. E. W. Anderson and M. Sullivan, "The Antecedents and Consequences of Customer Satisfaction for Firms," *Marketing Science* 12 (Spring 1992), pp. 125–143.

19. W. Boulding, R. Staelin, A. Kalra, and V. A. Zeithaml, "Conceptualizing and Testing a Dynamic Process Model of Service Quality," report no. 92–121, Marketing Science Institute, 1992.

20. V. A. Zeithaml, L. L. Berry, and A. Parasuraman, "The Behavioral Consequences of Service Quality," *Journal of Marketing* 60 (April 1996), pp. 31–46.

21. J. P. McLaughlin, "Ensuring Customer Satisfaction Is a Strategic Issue, Not Just an Operational One," presentation at the AIC Customer Satisfaction Measurement Conference, Chicago, December 6–7, 1993.

22. Paul, Michael, Thorsten Hennig-Thurau, Dwayne D. Gremler, Kevin P. Gwinner, and Caroline Wiertz (2009), "Toward a Theory of Repeated Purchase Drivers for Consumer Services," *Journal of the Academy of Marketing Science*, 37 (2), 215-237.

23. R. S. Kaplan and D. P. Norton, "The Balanced Scorecard—Measures That Drive Performance," *Harvard Business Review* 70 (January–February 1992), pp. 71–79.

24. Ibid.

25. S. Silk, "Automating the Balance Scorecard," *Management Accounting,* May 1998, pp. 38–42.

26. Reichheld and Sasser, "Zero Defections," p. 111.

27. The material in this section comes from C. D. Ittner and D. F. Larcker, "Coming Up Short on Nonfinancial Performance Measurement," *Harvard Business Review* 81 (November 2003), pp. 88–95.

28. Ibid., p. 92.

Case 1

Zappos.com 2009: Clothing, Customer Service, and Company Culture

Frances X. Frei

Robin J. Ely

Laura Winig

On July 17, 2009, Zappos.com—a privately held online retailer of shoes, clothing, handbags, and accessories—learned that Amazon.com, Inc.—a $19 billion multinational online retailer of books, electronics, toys, and other merchandise—had won its board of directors' approval to offer to merge the two companies. (See **Exhibits 1, 2, 3,** and **4** for selected financials for both companies.)

Amazon had been courting Zappos since 2005, hoping a merger would enable Amazon to expand and strengthen its market share in soft-line retail categories such as shoes and apparel—categories the company considered strategically important to its business growth.[1] While Amazon's interest intrigued Zappos' CEO, Tony Hsieh, and chairman, COO, and CFO, Alfred Lin, the two senior executives had not felt the time was right until now. Amazon's offer—10 million shares of stock (valued at $807 million),[a] $40 million in cash and restricted stock units for Zappos' employees, and a promise that Zappos could operate as an independent subsidiary—was on the table. Zappos' financial adviser, Morgan Stanley, estimated the future equity value of an initial public offering to be between $650 million and $905 million; this estimate skewed the Amazon offer—at least in financial terms—toward the high end of Zappos' estimated market value. (See **Exhibit 5** for market values of comparable online and footwear retailers.) Hsieh and Lin knew that much of Zappos' growth, and hence its value, had been due to the company's strong culture and obsessive emphasis on customer service. In 2009, they were focusing on their three Cs—clothing, customer service, and company culture—the keys to the company's continued growth. Hsieh and Lin had only a few days to consider whether to recommend the merger to Zappos' board at their July 21 meeting.

ZAPPOS AND THE RISE OF ONLINE FOOTWEAR RETAILING

In late 1998, Nick Swinmurn, a 26-year-old marketing manager for an online car-buying service, went to a San Francisco–area shopping mall to purchase a pair of Airwalk shoes but could not find any in the color, style, and size he wanted. Swinmurn turned to the Internet but was frustrated by the lack of online footwear-only retailers: "[There were] a bunch of little sites but nothing that jumped out at you," he said.[2]

[a]Stock value based on the average closing price of Amazon shares for the 45 trading days ending July 17, 2009.

Professors Frances X. Frei and Robin J. Ely and Senior Researcher Laura Winig, Global Research Group, prepared this case. HBS cases are developed solely as the basis for class discussion. Cases are not intended to serve as endorsements, sources of primary data, or illustrations of effective or ineffective management.

EXHIBIT 1   Zappos Income Statement, 2007 to 2009 ($ thousands)

Source: Amazon.com Inc. S-4, filed July 27, 2009; and Amazon.com Inc. S-4/A, Pre-Effective Amendment to S-4, filed September 25, 2009.

	2007	2008		2009		
	12 months ended Dec 31	3 months ended June 30	6 months ended June 30	12 months ended Dec 31	3 months ended June 30	6 months ended June 30
Net revenues	526,829	152,613	285,323	635,011	165,236	309,099
Cost of revenues	333,884	97,158	181,406	411,650	106,555	201,092
Gross profit	192,945	55,455	103,917	223,361	58,681	108,007
Operating expenses:						
Sales, marketing and fulfillment	123,260	37,862	70,792	153,285	36,870	71,688
General and administrative	18,962	5,870	11,997	23,041	5,788	10,989
Product development	18,224	6,154	12,443	25,262	5,767	11,514
Total operating expenses	160,446	49,886	95,232	201,588	48,425	94,191
Income from operations	32,499	5,569	8,685	21,773	10,256	13,816
Interest and other income, net	731	133	325	559	101	173
Interest benefit (expense) associated with pre-ferred stock warrant	(10,825)	(5.771)	(5,746)	9,670	(12,441)	(13,721)
Other interest expense	(6,930)	(1,067)	(2,814)	(5,825)	(826)	(1,775)
Other financing charges	(335)	(121)	(280)	(832)	(102)	(226)
Income (loss) before provi-sion for income taxes	15,140	(1,257)	170	23,345	(3,012)	(1,733)
Provision for income taxes	(10,288)	(1,562)	(1,550)	(5,208)	(3,343)	(4,356)
Net income(loss) from continuing operations	4,852	(2,819)	(1.380)	20,137	(6,355)	(6,089)
Discontinued operations, net of tax	(3.084)	(679)	(1,525)	(9,365)	30	(14)
Net income (loss)	1.768	(3,498)	(2,905)	10,772	(6,325)	(6,103)

His experience inspired him to create an online footwear retail site, and in June 1999, Swinmurn launched ShoeSite.com. "We are taking a more dynamic approach to what has been a poorly presented category online," said Swinmurn, who soon renamed the site Zappos.com because, he explained, it was easy to remember and there was a "recognizable relation" to *zapatos*, the Spanish word for shoes.[3]

Zappos initially secured inventory through independent shoe stores, but by October 1999, the company had begun creating direct relationships with footwear manufacturers. By the end of 2000, Zappos offered more than 100 brands, including Bostonian, Sperry, Dexter, G.H. Bass, and Tommy Bahama.[4] The manufacturers agreed to ship orders directly to Zappos' customers so that the company could avoid carrying inventory.

EXHIBIT 2 **Zappos Balance Sheet, 2007 to 2009 ($ thousands)**

Source: Amazon.com Inc. S-4/A, Pre-Effective Amendment to S-4, filed September 25, 2009.

	As of December 31		As of June 30
	2007	**2008**	**2009**
Assets			
Current assets:			
Cash and cash equivalents	6,761	8,590	4,470
Restricted cash	1,687	2,245	2,176
Accounts receivable, net	8,461	6,772	5,039
Inventory, net	161,988	168,131	176,918
Deferred income taxes	12,267	15,890	15,890
Prepaid exp and other assets	2,496	3,253	3,328
Total current assets	193,760	204,881	207,821
Property and equipment, net	44,286	48,962	49,069
Deferred income taxes	3,098	708	708
Intangible assets, net	4,405	8,646	8,296
Other assets, net	705	2,075	1,860
Total assets	246,254	265,272	267,754
Liabilities and stockholder's equity			
Current liabilities:			
Accounts payable	76,055	69,792	61,823
Accrued and other liabilities	28,467	51,409	76,464
Deferred income taxes	527	559	559
Accrued sales returns	16,762	18,637	13,988
Current portion of loan obligations	2,747	4,863	18,722
Current portion of capital lease obligations	1,051	1,490	3,046
Revolving line of credit	29,000	26,006	35,000
Total current liabilities	154,609	172,756	209,602
Deferred rent	1,883	1,514	1,467
Deferred income taxes	3,418	2,870	2,870
Other long term liabilities	28,868	19,935	3,748
Loan obligations, noncurrent	20,188	15,777	0
Capital lease obligations, noncurrent	1,809	1,702	3,734
Total liabilities	210,775	214,554	221,421
Stockholders' equity:			
Convertible preferred stock	61,465	61,465	61,465
Common stock	16	16	16
Additional paid-in capital	2,092	6,557	8,275
Accumulated deficit	(28,092)	(17,320)	(23,423)
Total stockholders' equity	35,479	50,718	46,333
Total liabilities and stockholder's equity	246,254	265,272	267,754

EXHIBIT 3   Zappos Cash Flow Statement, 2007 to 2008 ($ thousands)

Source: Amazon.com Inc. S-4, filed July 27, 2009.

	As of December 31,	
	2007	2008
Operating activities		
Net income	1,768	10,772
Amortization of deferred financing costs	288	309
Depreciation and amortization	9,682	11,481
Impairment of fixed assets	2,133	638
Asset retirement obligation	62	59
Reserves on returns	3,813	1,875
Provision for bad and doubtful debt	63	145
Provision for excess and obsolete inventory	2,985	2,223
Stock-based compensation	1,997	2,884
Deferred income taxes	(2,980)	(927)
Cumulative effect of the adoption of FIN 48	(500)	n/a
Loss on disposal of property and equipment	350	6
Chg in carrying value of preferred stock warrants	10,825	(9,670)
Changes in operating assets and liabilities:		
Credit card and other receivables	(3,506)	1,545
Merchandise inventory	(20,681)	(8,366)
Prepaid expenses and other assets	(1,083)	(2,354)
Accounts payable	16,937	(7,443)
Accrued and other liabilities	11,494	22,415
Net cash provided by operating activities	33,647	25,592
Investing activities		
Purchase of property and equipment	(11,108)	(13,471)
Purchase of intangible assets	n/a	(4,850)
Purchase of 6pm.com intangible assets and inventory	(4,000)	n/a
Decrease in restricted cash	5,714	404
Net cash used in investing activities	(9,394)	(17,917)
Financing Activities		
Proceeds from exercise of employee stock options	204	282
Repurchase and retirement of stock	(3,000)	n/a
Excess tax benefit on stock awards	443	1,301
Increase in restricted cash	(404)	(962)
Borrowings under revolving line of credit	549,184	666,333
Repmt of borrowings under revolving line of credit	(564,965)	(669,327)
Borrowings under loans	3,501	271
Repayment of loan and construction payables	(2,595)	(2,566)
Payment of capital leases	(1,152)	(1,178)
Net cash used in financing activities	(18,784)	(5,846)
Change in cash and cash equivalents	5,469	1,829
Cash and cash equivalents at beginning of year	1,292	6,761
Cash and cash equivalents at end of year	6,761	8,590

EXHIBIT 4
Amazon.com
Inc., Income
Statement, Cash
Flow Statement, and
Balance Sheet, 2007
to 2008 ($ millions)

Source: Amazon.com, 2008
Annual Report, http://phx.
corporateir.net/External. File
?item=UGFyZW50SUQ9Mj
AyN3xDaGlsZElEPS0xfFR5
cGU9Mw= =&t=1, accessed
September 22, 2009.

	As of December 31, 2007	As of December 31, 2008
Income Statement		
Net sales	14,835	19,166
Income from operations	655	842
Net income	476	645
Basic earnings per share	$ 1.15	$1.52
Diluted earnings per share	$ 1.12	$1.49
Cash Flow Statement		
Net cash provided by operating activities	1,405	1,697
Purchases of fixed assets, including internal-use software and website development	(224)	(333)
Free cash flow	1,181	1,364
Balance Sheet		
Total assets	6,485	8,314
Long-term debt	1,282	409

EXHIBIT 5
Market Value of
Selected Online and
Footwear Retailers,
July 22, 2009
($ millions)

Source: Thomson One
Banker, accessed August
2009.

	Market Value
Amazon	38,148.44
Gap	11,260.58
Sears	7,856.02
Macy's	5,328.68
Nordstrom	5,248.89
Footlocker	1,669.01
Payless Shoesource	958.13
Genesco	439.45
Brown Shoe Company	299.85
DSW Shoe Warehouse	201.68
Shoe Carnival	156.04
Footstar	21.58
Bakers Footwear Group	5.68
Shoe Pavilion	0.02

In 1999, there were more than 1,500 retailing sites on the Internet with footwear offerings—though most were apparel retailers stocking a handful of complementary shoe styles.[5] U.S. online shoe sales were just under $48 million—less than one-tenth of 1 percent of the $37 billion U.S. footwear market. By contrast, mail-order catalog sales were 6.4 percent of U.S. footwear sales.[6]

The online footwear industry gained a higher profile after Nordstrom joined its ranks. The high-end retailer had launched its own apparel website in 1998 and learned that shoes sold disproportionately well online (30 percent of sales), compared to retail store sales (20 percent).[7] As a result, Nordstrom launched its own dedicated shoe site in the summer of 1999 with a $17 million advertising campaign.[8]

By the end of 1999, Zappos had begun to institute services such as free shipping, which fueled growth.[9] Indeed, from its inception, Zappos focused on delivering outstanding customer service to make the online shopping experience as easy and as close to a visit to a retail store as possible. For example, visitors could print a shoe sizing template or initiate live online chat sessions with product experts.[10] In addition, each shoe was photographed from nine different angles by Zappos photographers. Zappos employees wrote product descriptions for each shoe that included far more details about style, fit, and materials than those prepared by the shoes' manufacturers.

Early 2000s

By 2000, Zappos had 150 brands and 400,000 pairs of shoes in stock and was billing itself as the world's largest shoe store. The company had begun to switch from having manufacturers ship directly to its customers to carrying inventory.

In January 2000, Zappos secured $1.1 million in venture capital funding from Venture Frogs, an investment and incubation firm that Hsieh and Lin had formed two years earlier. Venture Frogs specialized in early-stage Internet, e-commerce, information, and telecommunications technology companies that were entering a "phase of unusual growth."[11] Hsieh and Lin knew something about such companies, having started—at the ages of 24 and 25, respectively—LinkExchange, an advertising network that they sold to Microsoft for $265 million in November 1998.[12] Hsieh and Lin met in college when Hsieh was running a pizza business (he rented his dorm's kitchen at night to make pizzas for students), and Lin, who bought whole pizzas and resold them by the slice in his dorm, was his best customer. When they encountered Zappos, said Lin at the time, they were "thoroughly impressed" with what it had accomplished over the previous seven months. "With our investment," they conjectured, "Zappos.com can continue to hold their position as the world's largest shoe store."[13]

When *PC Data Online* released its annual ranking of the top 10,000 e-commerce websites (segmented by category) in 2000, Zappos was honored as the highest-ranking "pure-play" online footwear retailer.[14] Zappos offered a larger selection of footwear than any other shoe store, online or offline. Zappos sales were outpacing online sales of retailers such as Lands' End, J. Crew, and Abercrombie & Fitch.[15] The site's overall ranking (1,134) indicated a 0.9 percent reach, which meant that almost 1 percent of all Internet users visited Zappos' site during June 2000.[16]

The investment community, however, was growing disenchanted with online footwear retailers. Some analysts claimed that the online footwear industry was little more than a high-tech catalog, serving to supplement sales for established brick-and-mortar chains or as a means for customers to research future in-store purchases. "The footwear market is not a hotbed of activity," said one analyst in 2001. "We view [it] as relatively laggard versus other categories of online retail. This is a market filled with more browsers than buyers, and dot-coms that don't have an offline presence are going to have a relatively inefficient business."[17]

Hsieh joined Zappos as co-CEO (with Swinmurn) in May 2001, noting that Zappos was "the most fun and the most promising" of all the companies he had encountered as a venture capitalist and would probably generate the greatest return for Venture Frogs. His instincts were good. By year's end, Zappos had grown to $8.6 million in gross merchandise sales. "We're still not at the point where we're trying to maximize our profit, because we still think there are a lot of growth opportunities," Hsieh said at the time.[18] In 2002, he announced a financial goal for Zappos: to grow to $1 billion in gross sales by 2010.[19] In 2003, Hsieh became sole CEO and Swinmurn became chairman.

2005 to 2008

By 2005, Zappos had outgrown its San Francisco headquarters. The company employed 100 call center staff and was in search of a less expensive base of operations. Las Vegas, Nevada, emerged as the best option because wages were lower and workers plentiful. In addition, the city was considered a good fit for the Zappos lifestyle. "Las Vegas is a 24-hour town and we have a 24-hour call center," said Donavon Roberson, Zappos' business development account manager. After receiving $35 million in investment capital from Sequoia Capital in 2005, Zappos moved its headquarters to Las Vegas.

Swinmurn, however, did not fully enjoy the move and the growth. "[Zappos] had become about processes and lawyers and getting a bunch of people to sign off before you could do anything," he said. "I prefer . . . being able to jump in and change things."[20] Shortly before Swinmurn left to pursue other interests, Lin joined as CFO, later taking up the roles of chairman and COO as well.

In the meantime, the online footwear retailing industry had grown to $2.9 billion in 2006, compared with just $954 million in 2002, and was projected to reach $5.2 billion by 2010.[21] Zappos, a $597 million company in 2006, faced new competition from mega-retailers: Gap Inc.–backed Piperlime.com and Amazon.com, which owned Endless.com, both launched footwear sites in early 2007.[22]

By 2008, Zappos had become a $1 billion retailer and reported net income of $10.8 million on 2008 net revenue of $635 million.[23] (See **Exhibit 6** for gross sales by year.) The company employed 700 "team members," as employees were called, in its Nevada office: 300 in its call center, 200 in merchandising, and the balance in supporting departments ranging from legal to accounting.

THE FIRST C: COMPANY CULTURE

Zappos' leadership viewed the company culture as the differentiator that afforded the company a competitive advantage. "Our belief is that if you get the culture right, then most of the other stuff—like great customer service or building a long-lasting, enduring brand—will happen naturally," Hsieh said. Lin agreed:

> I attended a conference where someone in the audience asked Starbucks chairman/CEO Howard Schultz why everyone at Starbucks smiled, and he said, "We only hire people that smile." We try to do the same thing at Zappos. We only hire happy people and we try to keep them happy. Our philosophy is you can't have happy customers without having happy employees, and you can't have happy employees without having a company where people are inspired by the culture. We view this as a strategic asset. We may have 1,200 to 1,500 brand relationships and a good head start against the competition, but that can be copied. Our websites, policies—all can be copied, but not our special culture.

EXHIBIT 6
Zappos Gross Sales by Year, 2000 to 2008 ($ millions)

Source: Company documents.

Year	Gross Sales
2000	1.6
2001	8.6
2002	32.0
2003	70.0
2004	184.0
2005	370.0
2006	597.0
2007	841.0
2008	1,014.0

In 2005, just after moving its company headquarters, Zappos had debuted its list of core values—developed as a means to ensure that everyone in the company played a role in building and supporting the culture. To create what would become the company's 10 core values, Hsieh solicited feedback from employees on what those values should be and, from that feedback, compiled an initial list of 37 potential core values and sent it to everyone in the company. A yearlong evaluation process pared the list down to 10. (See **Exhibit 7** for Zappos' core values.) "We now have a set of committable core values, meaning we are willing to hire and fire based on whether people are living up to those core values, independent of whether they're doing their specific job function well enough," said Hsieh. "Most organizations don't care about culture, at least not at the senior level. But if you truly care and manage for it, it is like managing anything else in the business. It is not hard; you just have to fundamentally support it."

Many of Zappos' 10 core values were grounded in research on factors such as worker efficiency and productivity. For example, Hsieh cited a study that found that people were happier and more engaged in their work if they made friends on the job. As a result, Zappos developed core value 7—build a positive team and family spirit—and encouraged managers to spend 10 percent to 20 percent of their time socializing with team members outside of work. "There's not so much separation between work and life here as there is at most companies," said Hsieh. "Zappos is like a lifestyle."

Zappos' culture soon caught on, attracting interest from other companies, the media, and academics interested in learning about the company. Zappos welcomed any and all visitors by offering guided tours of its Las Vegas headquarters. Visitors encountered a three-ring-circus ambience. In the lobby stood a three-seat shoeshine stand (like those traditionally found in railway stations) populated with full-sized costumed skeletons. A freshly stocked carnival-style popcorn machine sat next to the reception desk, and opposite that stood a Dance Dance Revolution arcade game. (See **Exhibit 8** for photographs of the Zappos headquarters.) The decor was testament to Zappos employees' drive to "create fun and a little weirdness."

Zappos hosted 8 to 10 tour groups per day in 2009. Roberson, who occasionally served as tour guide, led visiting academics down a corridor past the legal department to "Monkey Row," a group of cubicles positioned underneath a canopy of dense plastic vines, where senior managers, including Hsieh and Lin, sat. As the group passed the call center, merchandising, and accounting departments, Zappos employees greeted them with waves, hoots, cheers, and even, literally, bells and whistles. Roberson noted that the tour roughly followed the company's unofficial parade route: departments often sponsored themed parades—sometimes costumed—through the headquarters' halls.

EXHIBIT 7
Zappos' 10 Core Values

Source: Company documents.

1. Deliver WOW through service
2. Embrace and drive change
3. Create fun and a little weirdness
4. Be adventurous, creative, and open-minded
5. Pursue growth and learning
6. Build open and honest relationships with communication
7. Build a positive team and family spirit
8. Do more with less
9. Be passionate and determined
10. Be humble

EXHIBIT 8
Photographs
of Zappos
Headquarters

Source: Company documents
and casewriter.

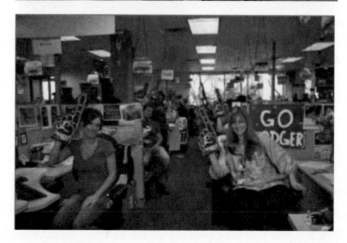

Just across the hall was Dr. David Vik's office: "For when you need a checkup from the neck up," explained Roberson, who noted that Vik was a retired chiropractor turned full-time employee performance coach. Next to Dr. Vik's office was a wall-mounted "confession bell," which employees rang for acts of public contrition (e.g., when they hit "reply all" on an e-mail). "They then make the walk of shame up to the bell to announce their transgression," explained Roberson.

In January 2008, Hsieh sent an e-mail to all Zappos employees asking them to write a few sentences describing what the Zappos culture meant to them. "We asked them to tell us what is different about it compared to other company cultures and what they like about the Zappos culture," explained Roberson. The resulting responses were compiled and published—unedited—in a 450-page book.

Hiring for Cultural Fit

Zappos screened job applicants to ensure they would fit within the Zappos culture. The evaluation began with the initial application—which featured a crossword puzzle on its cover and cartoon characters posing off-beat questions. (See **Exhibit 9** for a sample page from the Zappos employment application.) Applicants were asked to name their personal theme song, to rate themselves on a "weirdness" scale, and to assess how lucky they considered themselves to be. "If someone rates herself as being on the high end of the lucky scale, then she is probably going to be the type of person that we're looking for, who will be creative, adventurous, and can think outside of the box," said Christa Foley, recruiting manager.

All candidates underwent two interviews: a traditional skills-based interview conducted by the hiring manager and a "culture" interview conducted by recruiters in the human resources department. "The hiring manager will look for fit with team, relevant experience, and technical ability. The recruiting department is interviewing purely for culture fit. Candidates have to pass both interviews to be hired. We have actually passed on hiring a lot of really talented people that we know could make an immediate impact on the top or bottom line, but if they're not a culture fit, we won't hire them," said Hsieh.

"We ask 10 to 15 behavioral-based interview questions for each of our core values," Foley explained. "A successful candidate may not necessarily score high on each core value, but they cannot oppose any core value." That said, there *were* some deal-breaker questions. For example, if a candidate scored at either the very top or very bottom on the weirdness question, he or she would not be considered a good fit for the company. Coming up short on humility, another of the company's core values, could also disqualify a candidate, particularly for hires at the senior management level. "If someone is egotistical," Hsieh explained, "there's not even a discussion; we know we're not going to hire them."

Orientation and Initial Training

All new hires were expected to complete four weeks of paid training, which focused largely on call center training, regardless of the position of the new hire. "If you don't pass your four weeks of training, no matter what department you're in, you won't keep your job at Zappos," said Foley. In addition, the company weeded out uncommitted new hires by offering them $2,000 to leave the company; the offer was made during the first week of training. "The offer started at $100, but we slowly raised it because we want more people to take it," explained Rob Siefker, customer loyalty team (CLT) manager, though he noted that very few accepted the offer.

Pipeline

In 2008, Zappos' training communications and process developer, Roger Dana, and his team formalized a pipeline: a process used to develop employees from entry level to "the highest level of management." The pipeline required that all employees undertake 225 hours of "core level" training; this included 160 hours of initial new hire/customer loyalty training as well as additional courses on communicating effectively, coaching others, overcoming conflict, and managing stress. The newest class was entitled "Science of Happiness." "I'll admit, we went back to our desks and giggled a little bit when Tony asked us to develop a class on happiness," said Dana, but he explained that

EXHIBIT 9 **Zappos Employment Application Sample Page**

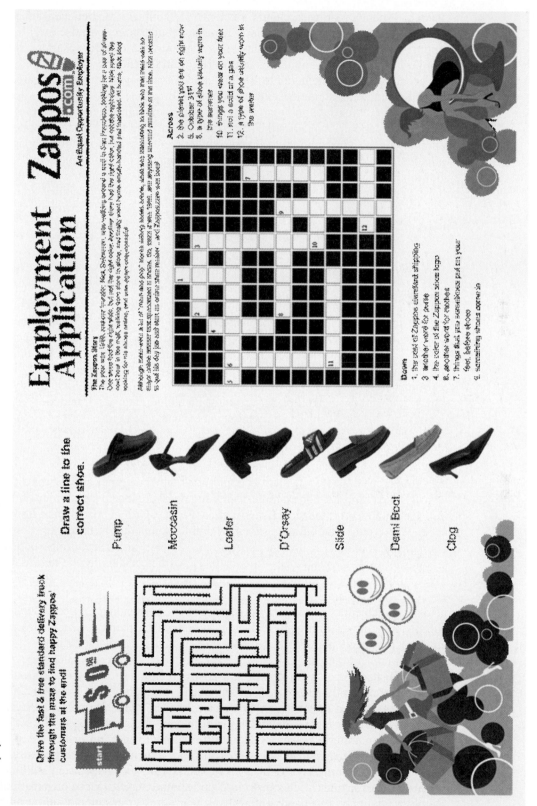

Source: Company documents.

Hsieh had spent a year researching the science of happiness and believed a class on the subject—which Hsieh defined as finding meaning and a larger purpose for life—would support the corporate culture. "Zappos' larger purpose should be about spreading happiness—delivering happiness to the world," said Hsieh.

Through the implementation of the pipeline, Zappos was highly transparent about the skills and courses employees were required to master in order to progress within the company. "We're a nonhierarchical company," explained Foley. "Everyone's role is important, and everyone has the same foundation," she said. Dana elaborated: "The pipeline sets the expectation that anyone could potentially rise to senior management." Indeed, after completing management training, managers could opt to undertake an additional 39 hours of leadership training, which included courses entitled "Inspiring Great Teams," "Leadership Zappos Style," and "Cultivating Culture." In addition, aspiring leaders were expected to teach either a pipeline or department course and deliver a presentation to Zappos employees, visitors, or a local school.

THE SECOND C: CUSTOMER SERVICE

Hsieh and Lin believed that a significant part of the company's rapid growth was due to its customers' loyalty (75 percent of Zappos orders were from repeat customers), which they attributed to their obsessive focus on delivering superior customer service. For the 96 percent of sales placed via the Zappos website, customer service took the form of fast, free shipping (in both directions); a wide selection of more than 1,200 brands (2.9 million products in inventory); the availability of special sizes; and a highly intuitive, consumer-friendly interface. Customers could simultaneously search by style, size, width, color, and gender and expect to find tens if not hundreds of matches—certain to be in stock (the site displayed only those shoes that were in inventory.)

While the vast majority of customers placed their orders directly through Zappos' website, an average of 5,100 calls per 24-hour day were handled by CLT members (call/contact center representatives). The CLT members were considered problem-solvers, since often customers who called had questions they could not answer for themselves using Zappos' website. For example, a CLT member might help a customer find a brand Zappos did not carry; indeed, in such a circumstance, CLT members were instructed to use the Internet to search for the shoes at multiple competitor websites.

In many traditional call centers, workers were given a time limit—perhaps 180 seconds or less—to finish a customer call. "Here, there's nothing like that," said Dana. "We want customers to think, 'Wow, I didn't feel rushed.' Our vision is that they'll tell 10 of their closest friends and they'll become customers." Zappos CLT members were held accountable for "wowing" customers with their outstanding service. "Quality assurance team members listen to the calls to ensure that CLT members establish a personal, emotional connection—we call it PEC—with customers," explained Lin.

CLT members were authorized—even encouraged—to take as much time as necessary to assist customers with their orders, answer their questions, and troubleshoot their problems. On July 5, 2009, one CLT member set a record with a 5-hour, 20-minute call from a woman interested in MBT "anti- shoes," which simulated the effect of walking on soft, uneven ground; the previous record was just over 4 hours, set by a call with a woman suffering from a condition that dulled sensation in her feet.[24] In both cases—and as often happened when CLT members engaged with Zappos customers— the conversations turned personal. "We started talking about her sister," said one CLT member. "She told me childhood stories," said another.[25] After such conversations, CLT members routinely sent handwritten thank-you notes to customers—thousands each month—and were quick to send bouquets of flowers or boxes of candy in sympathy or celebration. One CLT manager recalled that Hsieh had once remarked that service could always be improved. "If we didn't have to think about cost, the reps would personally get on a plane today and deliver that box."[26] Some of the highest costs were in staffing (more than 25 percent of the company's employees were CLT members earning an average of $14 to $15 per hour), and shipping costs, which were 17 percent of sales. This figure for shipping was higher than for comparable retailers since Zappos paid for upgraded shipping and return shipping; 35 percent of all sales were returned.

CLT members were not evaluated using traditional call center metrics such as average call handle time or cost per contact. Though Zappos did keep track of call-related statistics (average speed to answer the telephone was 17 seconds and the average call length was 5 minutes, for example), it did not use those statistics as performance metrics. Instead, Zappos relied on customer feedback to evaluate its CLT members. Customers wrote letters, blogged about their experience with Zappos, and even created and uploaded video testimonials onto Zappos' website. (See **Exhibit 10** for a sample of customers' e-mailed testimonials.)

Jane Judd, CLT senior manager, noted that call center turnover in 2009 was 7 percent (the industry standard was 150 percent). Some turnover could be ascribed to the transient nature of the Las Vegas community, and a portion was due to performance-based firings.

Fulfillment Operations

Zappos maintained its fulfillment center just outside Louisville, Kentucky, in two warehouses totaling 1 million square feet.

EXHIBIT 10
Selection of Customer Testimonials

Source: Company documents.

Hello, This is just a quick note to say thank you for outstanding customer service and shipment time. Every time I place an order with Zappos, I receive my goods 2 days later. I don't know how you do it, but you are doing something right. I don't mind paying more for my shoes on Zappos, because I know I can trust your quality. I've already received my order and I'm very pleased. Thanks and keep up the great work. I am telling all my friends about your wonderful website! Dina R.

Dear Zappos: Just a quick note to tell you that every time I call your company, the people I deal with are so nice. They are patient and helpful. Perhaps they should help the airline industry, in teaching good customer service, and manners. Your employees are the best. Thank you. Heidi

I just placed my order last night. I expected my order to arrive sometime between Sat. and Mon. or Tues. I was very surprised when I received an email telling me my order priority had been moved up just because you appreciated my business. Well, I have to say the very same to you. I received my order today. It was a pair of shoes for my son. He was so excited when he saw the UPS truck outside of our house. Again thank you all so very much! Keep up the excellent service! Renee W.

I just wanted to thank you for being so wonderful. Last week I ordered a pair of shoes but when I got them home the color didn't match so I needed to return them. What I didn't realize was that when I shipped them back to you, my cell phone charger was also in the box. The last couple of days I have been going crazy looking for it. But to my surprise it showed up today. My UPS driver just dropped off a tiny Zappos box. As I opened the box knowing that I hadn't ordered anything, I was amazed and grateful to find the charger in there. This little gesture just proves how much your company goes above and beyond for their customers and I for one truly, truly appreciate it. When you say "We are always here for you" you really mean it! I love your company, site, and all you stand for and do for your customers. I can't thank you enough for making my day! I hope you have a wonderful weekend! Lisa H.

Our jaws dropped that the birthday sneakers I ordered after 9 pm eastern time Monday with your free shipping, were sitting in my grandson's Arizona kitchen when he got home from school yesterday (Tuesday)!!! Zappos is the best! Thank you. Dianne W.

Receiving New merchandise and returned goods were accepted through separate warehouse receiving bays. The company's fulfillment centers were in a foreign trade zone,[b] which meant that its vendors could ship to Zappos directly, bypassing customs. Goods were received directly from airports' shipping docks in locked trailers that were not opened until they arrived at Zappos. It was a federal crime to take anything out of the Zappos building; the company had to account for all goods bought and sold, and had to keep whatever was not yet sold within the building.

Received goods were moved via conveyor belts from the receiving bays to the receiving platforms, where team members used foot pedals to move the boxes. "When workers de-case products, they only need to push them onto the conveyor belt, because if you have to pick up 5,000 shoe boxes a day, it becomes difficult for the workers," said Craig Adkins, vice president of services and operations.

There were 20 receiving stations on the receiving platform, and the department processed 40,000 items, on average, in a 24-hour shift. "Our goal in receiving is to process incoming merchandise within 24 hours of the time it comes off the truck," said Mary Johnson, a receiving team member. All products—shoes, clothing, accessories—were received and processed in the same area, with the exception of high-risk items (those deemed highly fragile or valuable).

A license plate number (LPN) label was assigned and affixed to each product that entered the warehouse. A receiving worker scanned each product's universal product code (UPC) and then linked the UPC to an LPN—a process that associated the product type, size, color, style, and other attributes with the LPN. Adkins explained:

> The LPN reveals the entire life history of an item: I know who received it, who put it away, who picked it, who shipped it, which customer had it, when they returned it—everything. And the benefit of this knowledge is quality. If something falls out of a bin, for example, I know exactly where it came from and can do an instantaneous inventory adjustment. We borrow against our inventory, so banks come in and do audits periodically. As long as I have worked here, we have never had a discrepancy on an audit—not by one single unit.

Once labeled, the product was pushed onto a conveyor belt and passed up through a sorter that directed the product to one of three storage areas: static racks, carousels, or the Kiva robot system. Shoes were housed primarily in the static shelves and carousels, while clothing, accessories, electronics, and other items were mainly stored in the Kiva system.

Put-away racks—static racks Static racks (also called put-away racks) were free-standing shelving units located near the middle of the warehouse. There were four sections on each of four floors, divided by five conveyor belts (three bringing in merchandise from receiving and two carrying picked merchandise to packing/shipping), with 101 shelves per section that together could hold 2.6 million items. Though shoes (and some apparel items) were assigned by section to the static racks, the precise shelf location was assigned by the put-away person. Johnson explained:

> If a team member is working the put-away area, they select an incoming product from the conveyor, scan the LPN, then select any available space in the static racks to store the product. They scan a location sticker on the shelf (which applied to an area measuring 18 inches wide by 20 inches high by 15 inches deep, roughly the size of 15 shoe boxes), and the system married the product to its shelf location. Team members can put away well over 100 items per hour.

[b]Foreign trade zones provided special customs procedures to U.S. companies that imported international goods for sale. Duty payments were deferred on goods until they were sold into the U.S. market and left the foreign trade zone.

Using this process, different brands, sizes, and types of shoes were shelved together. Although the result was a disheveled-looking warehouse, Johnson asked, "Can you imagine if you're trying to find an LPN on a whole rack of nothing but identical boxes? It would be very hard to do. So when the boxes are mixed up like this, it's very easy to find [the] product [you are looking for]."

Put-away team members worked side by side with pickers—those team members who retrieved products from the static shelves once an order was received. Pickers were given scanner guns that digitally displayed their picking assignments. Johnson explained:

> A "wave" of items (containing items from several orders) is sent, via scanner, to a picker. The wave displays items one at a time, only moving on to a new item once the first has been scanned as picked. Picked items are then dropped into oversized shopping carts that are then wheeled alongside the conveyor belts where each wave was loaded. Although items within a single wave are limited to one floor of the building, pickers might have to walk across several rows.

Johnson noted that a team member picked an average of 86 items per hour.

Carousels Zappos' carousel system held 1.5 million items and was the largest horizontal merchandise carousel in the United States. The company operated 30 carousels on each of four floors. Each carousel had 200 bays, and each bay contained four shelves, housing 12 to 15 boxes of shoes. Johnson explained how the carousels operated: "There are floor mats positioned in front of each carousel. When the carousel stops, that means that an order has been received and there's an item there, ready to be picked. Or, if someone is putting away, they can program the carousel to stop at the next available put-away shelf." As with the static shelves, there were conveyors moving merchandise in and out of the carousel area.

Though workers could pick merchandise from the carousels at nearly twice the rate (180 picks per hour) as the static racks, software crashes and mechanical breakdowns lowered the carousel utilization rate to 70 percent, compared with 100 percent for the static shelves. Both systems were installed in 2006 when the new warehouse opened, but the original plan called for 300 carousels and no static shelving. When Adkins joined the company just after the plan was approved, he expressed concern about the high capital expenditure of the carousels, predicting that the system's complexity and breakdowns would cost the company productivity. "At the time, I favored a low-tech approach," said Adkins, who recommended a mix of carousels and static shelves. "Our volume did not justify tens of millions of capital spending. We considered other methods, such as a tray system, but they do not offer sufficient return on investment until you're processing hundreds of thousands of units per day."

Pack/Ship The pack/ship area, which was used to box static shelf and carousel orders, had two packing lines: one for single-item orders and another for multiple-item orders, or multis. Single items were easiest to process. After a single item entered the packing area via conveyor (en route from the static racks or carousels), a team member scanned its LPN and printed out a packing slip, which contained a sticker with a bar code that was then applied to the outside of the shipping box. The packing slip was put into the shipping box along with the item, and the unsealed box was then conveyed to the "tape-and-apply" area.

For multis, each item in the order was picked and delivered to the packing area individually, so the items had to be gathered before they could be packed into shipping boxes. When the first item in an order arrived in the multis area, its LPN was scanned and identified to the team member as the first item in a multiple order. The team member then assigned that item to a bin and scanned the bin bar code, which married the item (and the order) to the bin. The next item in the order would automatically tell the team member which bin the first item had been assigned to; and if that next item was the last item in the order, the scanner would indicate that the order was complete. As in the single-product area, once the last item was scanned, a packing slip was printed out and the items were collected from the bin, boxed, and conveyed to the tape-and-apply area. Team members packed approximately 102 items an hour in the singles area and 125 in multis.

The elapsed time from when an order was received to when the box was loaded on a truck averaged 45 minutes for single-item orders and 3 hours for multis. "Most companies measure in hours, some in days. *Nobody* measures in minutes. And almost nobody believes our data when we tell them these numbers," said Adkins. "We have customers who place an order and then call and say, 'I just placed an order an hour ago and want to make a change,' and we tell them it has already shipped." Orders that were loaded onto a truck by 1:00 a.m. were usually delivered to customers the next day because of Zappos' proximity to its primary shipping company, UPS. "We try to push our volume into the evening because it will sit at the airport until 2:00 a.m. anyway," added Adkins.

Kiva In July 2008, Zappos purchased the Kiva Mobile Fulfillment System (Kiva MFS) because the company had exceeded its capacity for storage and processing. The Kiva MFS was an automated storage and retrieval system that used sophisticated software to control footstool-sized robots that moved inventory around the warehouse.[c] Products were stored in inventory pods (3,000 five-shelf storage units) in the center of the warehouse while team members stood at fulfillment stations at the front of the warehouse. When an order was received, one of Zappos' 75 robots retrieved the pod (or pods, in the case of multiple items within an order) where the ordered item was stored and brought the pod to a team member, who picked out the appropriate item and placed it in a shipping box. The team member then "released" the pod, and the robot carried it away to an open location on the warehouse floor.

The system could simultaneously pick orders and replenish inventory; on one side of the floor, goods were received into the system while, on the other, inventory pods were moved to team members for picking and packing. Although the put-away goal for the Kiva system was 150 items per hour, one worker noted that she worked at nearly twice that rate; the picking rate was 200 items per hour.[d]

Adkins noted that the Kiva MFS was twice as efficient as the static shelves and carousels in part because the receiving and put-away functions were done simultaneously. "We have 75 robots, but they are not all in use at the same time. If one fails, we have more off to the side so we can continue operations seamlessly," said Adkins.

In 2009, the Kiva MFS held about 15 percent of the company's inventory, but Adkins believed that Zappos would eventually increase its investment in the system.

---

[c]Adkins explained the value of the Kiva MFS software:
In the past, technology has been developed primarily for companies that operate distribution warehouses—in other words, they are designed to route boxes of products to retail stores. Accuracy was not necessarily a key metric. If the orders are only 90% accurate, what's the difference? Every Walmart uses the same 55,000 SKUs [stock-keeping units]—if they receive too much of one product in error, they'll still be able to sell it. Most of the existing software was adapted from this type of fulfillment, but Kiva is the first technology designed specifically for direct-to-customer fulfillment.

[d]Adkins explained why the system was so fast:
Kiva effectively eliminates bin dwell time—the amount of time one item sits awaiting the arrival of another in an order—because it retrieves products simultaneously. Robots retrieving different items for an order are coordinated to travel at the same time. For example, a customer orders sunglasses and body lotion. The sunglasses are stored in a pod located five minutes away, and body lotion is in a pod located three minutes away. When the order is received, the sunglasses pod begin to move toward the fulfillment station and, when it is three minutes away, the second pod begins to move so they both arrive at the pick station at the same time.

"The system's capital expenditure was the same as static shelves (and lower than the carousels), and it had lower installation and operational costs than either of our other two systems," he said. In addition, Kiva was quickly and easily scalable; Zappos could add capacity by merely adding inventory pods and additional robots.

Working in the Warehouse

The Kentucky warehouse ran shifts from 6:00 a.m. to 11:00 p.m. (though often the pack/ship department ran as late as 4:00 a.m.) and employed between 500 and 600 workers. Though Zappos' starting pay of $8.25 for a warehouse worker was average for the Louisville area, the benefits (free lunch, for example) added several dollars to the hourly rate, which, in addition to the traditional Zappos perks, aided with recruitment and retention. Johnson explained:

> There are computers set up for our Internet café and you can karaoke during your lunch break. We have Wii Guitar Hero and Rock Band video games—we get lots of perks. All the vending is free and they serve us soup, sandwiches, and salad three days a week; two days a week they even cater in. So that alone saves me a lot of money. It is a hot, boring job, and we may not get paid top dollar, but with our benefits and free food, it really makes a difference.

Team members were trained by department "qualifiers"—staffers responsible for awarding job qualification requirements (JQR) certification. "If you have a JQR, it means you are trained and qualified to do a particular job, such as receiving," explained Johnson, who noted that team members could earn as many as 10 JQRs for jobs throughout the warehouse.

Zappos rewarded its warehouse workers not for improving efficiency but for being flexible. "Pay increases are tied to JQRs, which allows us to flex to where labor is required. We had a snowstorm where we lost power for six hours. We didn't miss a truck, or miss any orders. We were able to shut receiving down and moved everybody to outbound because everyone was cross-trained. We made our orders for the day even though we were shut down for six hours," said Justin Williams, process manager.

Though many similar companies used pay-for-performance systems to boost worker productivity, Adkins believed Zappos workers were highly efficient due to the company's supportive culture. "I get calls all the time from efficiency consultants who say they can save me 20 percent if I use pay-for-performance. Then they come in and say, 'Your people seem to be working as fast as they can. You must have a pay-for-performance system already,' but we don't. Our workers work hard because we create an environment where they want to do well. We treat them with respect, treat them well, do extra for them, do whatever we can for them," said Adkins. Indeed, Adkins noted that Zappos' physical plant conditions were better than at other, comparable companies—cleaner and climate-controlled. "We installed chiller fans—32 feet in diameter—last year. That wasn't about efficiency, only about human comfort. The loss in labor efficiency [from overheated workers] could never pay for the cost of the chillers," he said.

Melissa Leary, fulfillment center recruiter, pointed out that although the Kentucky and Las Vegas operations shared core values, there was a noticeable difference between the cultures of the two sites. "We have the same values, and we're passionate [about them], but it is different because it has to be," she explained. "We're a production operation. In Las Vegas, 80 percent of their *job* is to be social [and interact with each other]. Here, we have to hit numbers. We have to make sure orders go out. We can't pull people from production to do parades; we use break time. That said, we encourage people to socialize with each other, but our proportions are more like 10 percent social and 90 percent production."

THE THIRD C: CLOTHING

In 2006, Zappos began to pursue several additional lines of business, including purchasing a discount footwear site, running e-commerce sites for other companies, offering private-label products, and providing online business advice. (See **Exhibit 11** for summaries of these lines of business.) Zappos had already begun testing sales of new product lines, including handbags, sunglasses, and accessories. "We always knew we wanted to be bigger than a shoe company, so we started into other categories where customers had expressed interest," explained Lin.

In the third quarter of 2006, Zappos tested offering athletic apparel—a natural vertical market since nearly 30 percent of the company's sales were for athletic shoes. The U.S. clothing market was four times as big as the shoe market, making it an attractive category for Zappos to pursue. "It is a large market and one we think we can address by creating a personal emotional connection with our customers. People love shoes, but they also establish an identity with the clothing they wear. Apparel seemed like a more powerful engine for growth and expansion than trying to grow internationally in just shoes and accessories," said Lin.

Within a year, Zappos had signed up 300 apparel brands. "We started with brands where we already had a relationship. Asics sells running shoes, so we started to sell running shorts and T-shirts. The North Face sells outdoor shoes, so we began to buy their clothing, too. Whenever we go into anything we start small and stay focused," said Lin. "It allows us to test." Lin noted that the margins and the return rates were the same for apparel as for shoes, though there were significant differences in the business model for the two categories. "In the shoe industry, there are only two seasons, but in clothing, there are four," he explained. "So trying to figure out what to buy and how quickly you need to sell it through is a new challenge." Zappos also learned that sizing was less standard for clothing than it was for shoes, and Lin believed that as the company grew the category, it would likely experience higher return rates as a result.

Zappos adjusted its warehouse operations to enable it to process clothing. "We knew that we needed more flexibility in terms of how clothing would be stored—hung and put away—so we ordered Kiva," said Lin.

In 2007, apparel was 5 percent of Zappos sales. The company was finding it challenging to get customers to think of Zappos as more than a shoe company. "Trying to sell cross-category takes more time than one might expect in terms of getting customers to think of us as a clothing company," said Lin. "The time it takes to educate the customers is taking a little longer. Maybe we're impatient, but shoes should be only 20 percent of our sales because apparel is four times the size of the footwear market. It is the inverse today, but perhaps we can change it over time."

The company sold $31 million in apparel in 2008 and set a goal of $66 million for 2009. Though the growth trajectory for clothing was improving, it still represented a very small portion of Zappos' business. Regardless of how big the company's apparel business grew, in the long term Hsieh and Lin wanted Zappos customers to associate the Zappos name with service, not with shoes—or even clothing. "We are a service company that happens to sell shoes. And clothing. And handbags. And accessories. And eventually anything and everything," was a popular Zappos saying.[27]

BEYOND 2009: CONTINUING TO GROW ZAPPOS

Zappos was affected by the 2008–2009 economic recession and laid off 8 percent of its workforce in November 2008. The company faced several financial challenges as it sought to reach its new growth goals. Although it anticipated generating sufficient

EXHIBIT 11
Zappos' Additional Lines of Business, Launched between 2006 and 2009

Source: Company interviews.

Powered by Zappos

In 2006, Zappos introduced Powered by Zappos (PBZ), a service whereby Zappos ran and maintained websites for other companies. Zappos warehoused the sites' inventory, shipped their products, and operated their call centers. In 2009, Zappos maintained PBZ sites for footwear and non-footwear manufacturers ranging from Clarks to Stuart Weitzman.

6pm.com

In July 2007, Zappos announced it would acquire 6pm.com from eBags.com. As Zappos' "value" site, 6pm.com offered merchandise at a 40 percent to 70 percent discount, but customers paid for shipping, and customer service was conducted largely via e-mail. 6pm. com provided lower quality service than Zappos. "They [customer service representatives] get the same training as Zappos.com team members, but use different terms and policies (e.g., returns were limited to 30 days, shipping charges applied, and the call center was open Sunday to Friday, from 9:00 a.m. to 5:00 p.m. rather than 24 hours a day, 7 days per week). The culture, however, is the same. There is a price sensitive customer and we want to service them," said Jeneen Minter, director of financial planning and analysis.

Hsieh believed that a pure discount model was not sustainable in the long term. "Most items on Zappos.com are not priced lower than brick-and-mortar stores—some might even be more expensive," he said. "Whether online or brick-and-mortar, anyone who competes on price alone is not going to have loyalty for long if they aren't always the lowest," said Hsieh.[28] Nevertheless, 6pm.com gave Zappos a site through which it could sell discontinued and past-season merchandise—a move that allowed the company to close all but one of the retail outlet stores it had begun to open starting in the early 2000s.

"This wasn't about adding new brands," said Hsieh, who noted that nearly 90 percent of 6pm.com's brands were already available through Zappos.com. "It was about appealing to new customers."[29]

Private Label

Zappos marketed 10 private-label footwear brands that in 2009 comprised just over 5 percent of the business. Labels included Gabriella, Rocha, type Z, Fitzwell, and RSVP. Hsieh explained the rationale for the growing business:

> Our philosophy toward private label is similar to our philosophy as a retailer. We're a full-margin retailer, and we don't want to compete on price. . . . Our strategy is to build a product that will be higher quality than a customer can typically get in that price range.[30]

Zappos Insights

Zappos Insights was a subscription-based online resource that Zappos developed in 2009. The site provided video interviews with Zappos senior management, articles, and other resources to share Zappos' learning and the story of its growth. Zappos described the product on its website:

> We are constantly asked for input and ideas to help many companies (or divisions within companies) get to the next level. Over time, we've found that many business leaders have the same (or very similar questions). We figured this could be a great way to share our learnings, and also allow your peer network to learn from questions others may have. With so many management consulting firms charging such high rates, we wanted to come up with something that's available to all businesses. To ensure that this information is available to as many individuals and businesses as possible, the membership is only $39.95 per month. Subscribing now guarantees that you'll immediately receive access to all the content on the site to help you take your business to the next level.[31]

free cash flow to pay off its inventory costs, capital loans, and equipment leases by the end of 2009, the company relied on several banks to provide it with a $100 million line of credit.

In 2009, the company focused on reducing capital expenditures and debt to improve cash flow. This meant that Zappos might need to defer growing its Kiva MFS. "The static shelves and carousel systems were built to last 15 to 20 years, and ours are only 3 years old. We have millions of dollars of underappreciated capital, so we really can't rip them out yet," said Adkins, who nevertheless hoped to be able to expand the Kiva MFS by 2012.

Hsieh and Lin considered the Amazon offer in light of Zappos' needs and opportunities. Lin summed up the situation:

> Amazon's technology and infrastructure are at a much higher scale than Zappos. Their website gets more hits, they have more R&D resources, they have much more targeted e-mail technology and a recommendation engine that they have built. We don't have the time or resources to build some of these tools. On the infrastructure side, they are operating at a much larger scale, and they know how to operate more efficiently. They have $4 billion on their balance sheet so that helps with our desire to grow faster. We do want some growth capital. We've been young and scrappy, managing business very tightly. With more people as well as capital, we can grow much faster.

In the meantime, Zappos needed to fund inventory for new lines and businesses. "Our inventory needs only grow," said financial analyst Chris Marlin. "Until now, 6pm.com, a new site which sold discontinued and past-season merchandise at a discount, has been using old Zappos inventory, but now it is beginning to buy its own." Lin pointed out that Zappos was quickly expanding its apparel offerings and expected the business to rival its footwear sales. "We should be able to accelerate our growth rate by being in apparel. Between 2009 and 2014, we want apparel to have the same growth rate as we had for the first five years of our footwear business," said Lin. "We want to outfit a person head to toe," he added.

Hsieh focused on inspiring Zappos employees. "Why don't all companies try to build strong cultures? I believe we accomplish more through inspiration than motivation," said Hsieh. "Inspire employees with a vision that's bigger than themselves, that goes beyond money, profits, and the size of the market share. It is about raising the bar for everyone," he said.

ENDNOTES

1. Amazon.com Inc., July 27, 2009, S-4 (Seattle: Amazon.com Inc., 2009), http://phx.corporate-ir.net/phoenix.zhtml?c=97664&p=IROLsecToc&TOC=aHR0c-DovL2NjYm4uMTBrd2l6YXJkLmNvbS94bWwvY29udGVudHMueG1sP2lwY WdlPTY0MzI5OTAmcmVwbz10ZW5rJnNNYQlJMPTE%3d&ListAll=1, accessed September 22, 2009.

2. Calmetta Y. Coleman, "Cyberspace resounds with clicks of shoe shoppers—people will buy footwear online because sizes are stable, feet don't fluctuate," *Wall Street Journal*, October 28, 1999, ABI/ProQuest, accessed May 5, 2009.

3. "Zappos.com: The Online Shoe Store Debuts New Site, New Features and Big Name Partners," PR Newswire, October 29, 1999, ABI/ProQuest, accessed May 5, 2009.

4. Ibid.

5. Coleman, "Cyberspace resounds."

6. Ibid.

7. Ibid.

8. Ibid.

9. "Zappos.com, World's Largest Shoe Store, Receives $1.1 Million in Financing," PR Newswire, January 19, 2000, ABI/ProQuest, accessed May 5, 2009.

10. "Zappos.com: The Online Shoe Store Debuts New Site."

11. "Zappos.com, World's Largest Shoe Store."

12. Ibid.

13. Ibid.

14. "Zappos.com Ranked #8 Clothing Web Site by PC Data Online: Highest-Ranking Footwear E-tail Site," PR Newswire, July 24, 2000, ABI/ProQuest, accessed May 5, 2009.

15. Ibid.

16. Ibid.

17. Susan Breitkopf, "Tangled Web: Now That the Dust Is Settling around the Internet Crash, Is There a Future in Footwear E-tailing?" *Footwear News*, July 30, 2001, ABI/ProQuest, accessed May 5, 2009.

18. Natalie Zmuda, "Surfing for Sales: Zappos Execs Aim to Hit $1 Billion," *Footwear News*, August 21, 2006, ABI/ProQuest, accessed May 15, 2009.

19. Ibid.

20. Meghan Cass, "Zappos Milestone: Q&A with Nick Swinmurn," *Footwear News*, May 4, 2009, http://about.zappos.com/press-center/zappos-milestone-qa-nick-swinmurn, accessed July 2009.

21. Wayne Niemi, "Internet Invasion; online sales continue to soar, and execs from top sites believe there's even more potential for growth. But as more newcomers enter the fray, competition is heating up," *Footwear News*, April 16, 2007, ABI/ProQuest, accessed May 15, 2009.

22. Ibid.

23. Claire Cain Miller, "Amazon's Long Courtship of Zappos," *New York Times* blog, July 28, 2009, http://bits.blogs.nytimes.com/2009/07/28/behind-the-scenes-of-the-amazon-zappos-deal, accessed September 16, 2009.

24. Alexandra Jacobs, "Happy Feet," *The New Yorker*, September 14, 2009, http://www.newyorker.com/reporting/2009/09/14/090914fa_fact_jacobs, accessed September 18, 2009.

25. Ibid.

26. Ibid.

27. Zappos.com, 2008 Culture Book, p. ii.

28. Niemi, "Internet Invasion."

29. Lindsay E. Sammon, "Zappos buy could spur online mergers," *Footwear News*, July 16, 2007, available ABI/ProQuest, accessed May 15, 2009.

30. Zmuda, "Surfing for Sales."

31. Zappos.com, "Why Join Zappos Insights?" Zappos website, http://www.zapposinsights.com/public/10.cfm, accessed July 24, 2009.

Case 2
Merrill Lynch: *Supernova*

Rogelio Oliva
Roger Hallowell
Gabriel R. Bitran

> There's a good chance that Supernova is the right thing at the right time. But I need to be sure before I recommend total adoption. Even if I do decide to back it, how do we roll it out? How can we get this organization, top, middle, and front-line, to buy into it—and change their behavior accordingly? Does everyone need to buy in, or will it be enough to have a "critical mass?" What would a critical mass look like?
>
> — *Jim Walker, managing director and chief administrative officer,*
> *Merrill Lynch Client Relationship Group*

Founded in 1907, Merrill Lynch grew rapidly under its founders' strategy to "Bring Wall Street to Main Street." In the 1970s, the firm became a powerful force in investment banking in addition to retail brokerage. By 2000, Merrill described itself as "the preeminent financial management and advisory company—serving governments, institutions, and investors throughout the world." In 2003, Merrill Lynch was one of the leading financial-services firms in the world, and was the largest of the "broker dealer" firms on Wall Street, employing more financial advisors (individuals who managed relationships with retail clients) than any of its competitors (see **Exhibit 1**).

Professor Rogelio Oliva, Roger Hallowell (MBA '89, DBA '97) of the Center for Executive Development, and MIT Sloan Nippon Telephone and Telegraph Professor of Management Science. It is based, in part, on research conducted by Bassim Halaby, Qunmei Li, Hugo Barra, Luca Donà, Geyza Salgado, Muhammad Farid, and Mary Schaefer of MIT Sloan. HBS cases are developed solely as the basis for class discussion. Cases are not intended to serve as endorsements, sources of primary data, or illustrations of effective or ineffective management.

EXHIBIT 1   **Stockbrokerages and Stockbrokers/Financial Advisors**

Source: Adapted from *Securities Industry Yearbook,* Securities Industry Association, Inc.: Washington, D.C., 2002.

Firm	Stockbrokers/FAs (Registered reps)	Rank
Merrill Lynch & Co., Inc.	15,753	1
Salomon Smith Barney Holdings, Inc.	13,826	2
Morgan Stanley	13,690	3
UBS PaineWebber Inc.	8,801	4
Edward Jones	8,595	5

EXHIBIT 2
**Market Share
for Traditional
(full-line) Brokers
and Discounters**

Source: Created using data
from Securities Industries
Association DATABANK.

Market Share of NYSE Commissions

Note: Post-1997, this chart may not reflect all full-line broker revenues as many full-line brokerages began to encourage their brokers/FAs to convert their accounts from commission generating (traditional) to fee-based (annuitized).

Jim Walker was a member of Merrill's Client Relationship Group, part of Merrill's Private Client Group, which was responsible for financial-advisory services for individuals (retail brokerage). The retail-brokerage environment had begun to change in the 1970s with the partial deregulation of stock brokering. Under deregulation, new firms entered the market with different service offerings. For example, Charles Schwab offered discounted trading directed by the investor, in contrast to the traditional brokerage model in which investors received advice from their stockbroker, and or placed orders through him or her. **Exhibit 2** illustrates market share of traditional brokers and discounters. Mutual-fund distribution was also deregulated in the 1970s, enabling firms such as Fidelity Investments to compete with stock brokerages indirectly by selling shares in their mutual funds to the public directly.[1]

FINANCIAL ADVISORS

Retail brokerages such as Merrill Lynch delivered their services to individual clients through stockbrokers, or "financial advisors" (FAs) as they were called at Merrill. Typically, an FA would bring clients to the firm through his or her relationships, networking, professional alliances, industry affiliations, and by "cold calling"[2] individuals thought to be good prospects.

Once an account was opened, the experience of an individual client varied considerably depending on his or her financial advisor. Some FAs routinely contacted clients to check on the client, offer advice on existing investments with the firm, and solicit additional business. Others rarely contacted their clients except to offer them new investment products the firm wanted to sell. For these FAs, contact with clients more often occurred when the client called to initiate a trade, or report a problem. According to a senior Merrill manager, "Unfortunately, a lot of our FAs fall into this category. The problem is, we've always charged for good service, and everyone has wanted to deliver it, but some of our people haven't followed through."

FA compensation, like that of most stockbrokers, was purely variable, based on the quantity of business they brought to the firm. Compensation was a combination of:

1. A percentage of the revenue generated from commission for buying and selling financial products in a client's account ("trades"). For example, if a client were charged $120 to trade 1,000 shares of stock, the FA might keep 40 percent.

[1]Prior to the 1970s, mutual-fund shares had to be sold through financial intermediaries such as stockbrokers. In 2003 Fidelity Investments was the largest mutual-fund company in the world.
[2]"Cold calling" meant contacting potential clients with no prior introduction, often by telephone or direct mail.

2. A percentage of the revenue generated from "annuitized," or fee-based accounts, in which a client did not pay to trade securities, but was annually charged a small percentage of assets, varying with the size of the account. For example, a customer with $1 million with the firm might pay 1 percent of assets.[3] The FA would keep a portion of that 1 percent. Increasing the portion of total assets in annuitized accounts was considered a priority by most Wall Street brokerages.

Stockbrokers in general, and Merrill Lynch FAs in particular, were well paid. Industry observers noted that Merrill FAs were particularly successful because the firm had been adept at hiring strong performers and weeding out the less successful. Some also believed that Merrill had done a better job than many of its competitors of ensuring a level of quality in the delivery of its service. Established brokers typically earned several hundred thousand dollars annually, with the most successful earning more than a million dollars each year.

FAs enjoyed the autonomy their jobs provided. According to one: "What *I* bring in, is *mine*. I work for Merrill Lynch, but I have my own clients. As long as I keep within the letter of the law I can serve them as I like and sell them any of Merrill's products. I'm in competition with every other FA in this office. If Merrill wants me to be a "we" person, they can pay me a salary—they don't."

Good FAs, like all good stockbrokers, were in demand among the various retail-brokerage firms, and could earn additional income by changing firms, when the acquiring firm would pay a substantial bonus to the new broker based on his or her "production" or historical revenue volume. The bonus was designed to compensate the stockbroker for the portion of clients who remained with the old firm rather than moving with the broker. However, the bonus more than compensated for the loss. In fact, many firms viewed the "signing bonus" as a way to acquire both brokers and clients. Historically, the relationship between the stockbroker and the client was considered to be stronger than the relationship between the client and the firm, or the firm and the stockbroker. Some brokers changed firms frequently.

Stockbroker acquisition was the job of the head of a local office. These individuals were often highly talented brokers who split their time between their own clients and managing the other brokers in the office. Many found the acquisition of new brokers a thrill, not unlike the acquisition of new clients.

FAs, like all stockbrokers, came from a variety of backgrounds. They typically had college educations, and all U.S. brokers were required to pass examinations such as the National Association of Securities Dealers' Series 7. All successful stockbrokers were gifted salespeople. Many used sporting terms to describe the acquisition of new clients, an activity (when successful) they uniformly enjoyed.

The acquisition of new clients resulted in what many brokers called their "book." This was a broker's list of clients having an account at the firm. Many firms, including Merrill Lynch, had encouraged their brokers to increase the size of their books, paying them incentives to open new accounts. According to one Merrill FA, "In the 1990s, Merrill ran what it called 'The Masters' program—you got a trip to Hawaii if you opened enough new accounts. Everyone was opening any account they could. Service, customer retention, and profitability didn't matter—it was all about new accounts." As a result, the size of their book came to be important to many FAs. Another noted: "I know I'm going to be OK, even in a downturn, if I've got a big book. All those names really make you feel secure, and that's important in a business

[3]The percentage varied considerably based on whether or not the client used third-party investment advice.

EXHIBIT 3
Merrill Lynch
Private Client
Group Field
Organization
Structure

Source: Merrill Lynch.

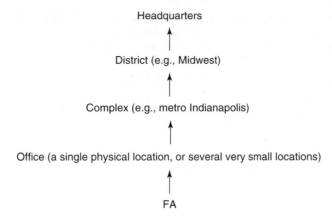

Headquarters

↑

District (e.g., Midwest)

↑

Complex (e.g., metro Indianapolis)

↑

Office (a single physical location, or several very small locations)

↑

FA

like this where you can only rely on yourself and you have to keep producing if you want to eat."

Merrill Lynch's FAs were thought to be among the best on Wall Street. The firm enjoyed a reputation for being an attractive place to work, based on (1) the support provided for brokers in the form of a strong brand and good financial products, and (2) the freedom brokers were given to effectively run their own businesses as long as they generated enough business, used Merrill Lynch financial products, and met basic ethical standards. An executive of another brokerage commented on Merrill Lynch and its FAs: "They're the best—they do what we do, what everyone does, but they do it better. How they 'out execute' us I'm not exactly sure, but they do it—again and again."

SUPERNOVA

Supernova was the name given to a new way to manage client relationships that originated in one of Merrill Lynch's Indianapolis offices (**Exhibit 3** illustrates Merrill's field organization structure). Unlike a strategic initiative from headquarters, it came up through the ranks as a strategy for implementation, in response to conceptual strategy set at the top.

The "father" of Supernova was Rob Knapp, who ran Merrill Lynch's Midwest district. In 1995, Knapp had had a good year in revenue terms, but was concerned about future revenues because his district ranked last in client satisfaction among the 32 districts in the country. Eighteen months later, following the implementation of a Supernova predecessor, Knapp's office ranked fourth.

Client Service before Supernova

Merrill's research led management to believe that three aspects of a relationship were critical to client satisfaction:

1. The frequency and quality of contact
2. Rapid response to problems
3. Attention to details

An FA commented on the ability to deliver these prior to Supernova:

> Most of us didn't pay any attention to frequency of contact—if a client called, we spoke to them. We didn't have time to make calls to clients because we were busy dealing with clients calling us—wanting us to fix problems they were having, hold their hands when

the markets declined, or do trades. Extra time was spent prospecting—and we had to do a lot of that given the number of clients who quit.

It was hard to respond to problems quickly. We used to get overwhelmed—my assistant was spending most of her time answering the phones—she didn't have time to deal with problems, which meant I had to deal with them, except I was supposed to be dealing with clients.

Attention to detail means things like being aware of life events for a client—an impending birth, retirement, the desire to refinance a mortgage. These are really important because they represent opportunities to meet a client's needs by selling them something they need and want. But we didn't have time to listen for these kinds of details—we were just trying to keep our heads above water.

According to Knapp: "The objective of Supernova is to create the 'ultimate' client experience. We asked ourselves, 'What would the ultimate client experience look like?' That was when we came up with 12-4-2."

12-4-2

12-4-2 was the Supernova description of what clients' minimum annual contact with their financial advisor should be: 12 monthly contacts (to stay in touch and ask for updates on financial goals or changes in needs), of which 4 were portfolio reviews, and 2 were face-to-face meetings. Some clients needed more contact, but 12-4-2 was the minimum.

12-4-2 was based on studies conducted within and outside of Merrill on client desires. According to one FA, 12-4-2 enforced discipline: "I'm just not that organized—I'm a people person. 12-4-2 forces me to make the contacts I know I should make, but I've always found excuses not to."

12-4-2 was predicated upon the completion of a financial plan for the client at the beginning of the relationship. Although Merrill had been encouraging all of its FAs to develop financial plans for their clients, according to several FAs, "More often than not, it wasn't happening."

While 12-4-2 was a breakthrough from the clients' perspective, it posed a dilemma for the FAs who wanted to implement it: there were too few hours in the day to deliver even a fraction of 12-4-2 because the average Merrill FA had 550 clients. As a result, the way FAs planning to adopt 12-4-2 conducted their business had to change. The changes ultimately becoming a part of Supernova, in addition to 12-4-2 and financial planning, were described as *segmentation, organization,* and *acquisition.*

Segmentation

Knapp used an analogy to suits to discuss the principle of client segmentation:

Let's say you really like the process of buying suits. Over the years, you develop a really big collection of suits. The problem is, you don't have the space to keep them all in good condition. Your closet's only big enough for 20. So you clean out your closet, and you send all but your 20 best suits to a relative. During the next year, you buy a few more suits—good ones. Remember, you *like* buying suits. At the end of the year, you clean out your closet again—and you force yourself to keep only the 20 best suits. Now, you have 20 really beautiful suits. You're happy, the suits have enough space in the closet, and you always look great.

It's no different with clients. The typical FA has 550. She can't give them all good service—there's not enough room in the closet. Most of them aren't capable of being very profitable—most aren't really good suits. Only by segmenting clients and only keeping the best can an FA have time to give them the service they need—that will make them loyal.

EXHIBIT 4   12-4-2 and the Need to Segment

Source: Merrill Lynch.

4A. Number of Primary Clients: 550		
12-4-2 Contacts per Week: 22 semi-annual, 22 quarterly, and 88 monthly calls		
	Assumptions	**Minutes Consumed**
Weeks per Year =	50	
Minutes Required for:		
Face-to-Face Meeting	90	1,980
Quarterly Phone Review	45	990
Monthly Phone Contact	15	1,320
Minutes Consumed per Week (in hours)		72
Time Available for Acquisition and Administration		0
4B. Number of Primary Clients: 200		
12-4-2 Contacts per Week: 8 semi-annual, 8 quarterly and 32 monthly calls		
	Assumptions	**Minutes Consumed**
Weeks per Year =	50	
Minutes Required for:		
Face-to-Face Meeting	90	720
Quarterly Phone Review	45	360
Monthly Phone Contact	15	480
Minutes Consumed per Week (in hours)		26
Time Available for Acquisition and Administration (in hours)		14

Note: Excludes nonprimary clients.

Knapp believed that the appropriate number of clients was 200 based on an analysis he conducted, which is illustrated in **Exhibits 4 (A)** and **(B)**. One Merrill office in which every FA adopted Supernova set a goal per FA of 200 clients, each having at least $1 million in annuitized assets at Merrill, or $10,000 in annual production (fees from trading).

The decision to keep or forgo a client was complex. Fortunately, an FA developed a spreadsheet model to help other FAs in the process. Developing the model took 11 months, however, once the model was completed an FA could conduct the analysis in approximately 30 minutes.

The FA who developed the model recognized that in order to deliver the high level of service he wanted all of his clients to receive he would have to reduce their number. He initially decided to keep only his top 100 clients. While that decision was easy, determining which clients made up his top 100 proved difficult.

Initially, he ranked his clients by revenue generation. Then, he ranked them by assets. He discovered that the two rankings were very different. Third, he ranked his clients by those he and his assistant liked doing business with. Again, the ranking was different from the earlier two. In all, he produced 11 rankings based on different criteria for keeping clients. He then decided to see which clients were on all 11 lists. Thirty-three clients appeared on every list. Those 33 generated 89 percent of his income during the previous year. In addition, his assistant noted that only 3 of the 53 clients she had helped with problems over the past five weeks were among the 33. Ultimately, the FA kept only those 33 clients, stating, "With those 33 I had 89 percent of my income and a lot fewer hassles—I've been able to spend my time giving them *really* great service and acquiring more *really* good clients. My income—and my life—has never been so good."

Most Supernova FAs decided to reduce their book to (1) 200 primary clients, (2) important family or business associates of those clients (whom FAs kept to avoid endangering the primary client relationship), and (3) those clients described as "necessary to keep if you want to get into heaven." The ratio of primary clients to important family or business associates was targeted at 3:1.

Clients whom an FA decided not to keep were given to another FA or were sent to the Financial Advisory Center, Merrill's centralized facility for smaller accounts, if their assets with Merrill totaled less than $100,000 and were unlikely to increase in the foreseeable future. The center served these accounts through a toll-free telephone number and proactively called them at least four times a year to ensure that their needs were being met. Many clients did not object to this new style of service; the center's client-retention rate was actually higher than that of the average FA's. FAs received payments from corporate for those clients sent to the center. Several FAs noted that once transferred, their clients increased the business they did with Merrill, and as a result, they earned considerably more on them than they had previously. FAs noted, however, that rumors about corporate ending the payments were rampant. Clients given to another FA were generally given away with no remuneration. According to one FA, "This way you're totally focused on the clients you're keeping—there's no looking over your shoulder."

Organization

Historically, each FA organized his or her practice in whatever way he or she thought best. Supernova did not require an FA to adopt a particular organization scheme, but it did provide tools that many Supernova FAs found useful. Merrill studies of FA desires indicated that what they wanted most was "more administrative support," followed closely by "help getting organized."

One of the biggest organizational problems FAs encountered involved using their time effectively. Day-to-day, this meant delegating routine, administrative tasks to their administrative assistants, called client associates. An FA using Supernova commented:

> In the past, clients wanted to speak with their FA whenever they had a problem or needed something. I can't blame them, otherwise they rarely spoke to their FA. Under Supernova, clients know they'll speak to their FA at least monthly, in fact, they know exactly when the conversation is scheduled for. As a result, if they have a problem or need a small, administrative change, the client associate can usually handle it.

Another FA added: "Clients used to feel it was OK to call and interrupt me whenever. Now, I'm more of a professional to them. Think about it—would you call your dentist and expect to speak with him immediately?"

In effect, under Supernova client associates "triaged" client telephone calls, only involving the FA when necessary.[4] Supernova client associates also prepared FAs' daily "folders." Each folder contained a client's most recent financial plan, amendments to it, and information on the client's family and business that the FA believed was germane to the relationship. This included mortgage and tax rates, real estate, insurance policies, hobbies, immediate family and important relatives/associates, and

---

[4]Note that for legal reasons, transactions involving buying or selling were conducted by FAs or registered client associates.

financial holdings not at Merrill. According to one Supernova FA: "I never want to be speaking with a client and not have the information I need to do my job—which is to take care of that client's total financial-service needs."

The folder supported the "folder system," which enforced discipline on the FA in the following way: client associates set up telephone or in-person meetings between the FA and clients, consistent with 12-4-2. These meetings were placed on the FA's calendar, with FA's dedicating between six and eight hours each day to these meetings (the time dedicated to meetings corresponded to the number of clients an FA could have under Supernova). Each morning, the FA would be given the folders for clients with whom he or she was meeting that day. These practices accomplished four things:

First, they forced the FA to make good on 12-4-2 without increasing his or her administrative burden.

Second, they ensured that he or she would have the most up-to-date information available for the meeting.

Third, they induced "folder guilt." If an FA didn't contact all the clients on the list for that day, her client associate would have wasted time preparing the folders. Because FAs tended to work closely with their client associates, folder guilt was often strong enough to get the FA to meet her contact obligations, something numerous "contact systems" had failed to do.

Finally, the folder system helped to ensure that the financial plan the client and the FA agreed to was implemented, an occasional failure in the past according to several FAs.

Client associates generally preferred to work under Supernova. According to one Supernova FA:

> The first three months on Supernova are hell for a client associate because the transition isn't easy—they're doing both the traditional work and the Supernova work. But once everyone settles into the Supernova routine, it's great. The client associate's day is much more predictable—prepare folders for the next day, set up meetings, and deal with a few problems. Because there are fewer clients—and happier clients—there are fewer problems, and everyone is happier.

Some FAs experimented with offering bonuses to their client associates to help them through the transition. At one office, client associates getting their FAs fully segmented and organized under Supernova received $1,000 directly from the FAs.

The Supernova Service Promise

Commitment to developing a financial plan for every client and 12-4-2, coupled with (1) segmentation and (2) organization, enabled Supernova FAs to make the following service promise to their clients:

You are guaranteed three things.

1. You will have a multi-generation financial plan in place.
2. You will be contacted by your FA at least 12 times every year.
3. You will receive rapid response to any problem you may have, hearing from us within 1 hour, and having resolution within 24.

Acquisition

The final part of Supernova was called "acquisition." As suggested by Knapp's suit analogy, each year a Supernova FA would acquire some new, high-quality clients, handing the least promising clients displaced by the new clients to another FA, or the Financial Advisory Center.

The time dedicated to 12-4-2 left between two and four hours each day for client acquisition, which the FAs found more than adequate. As one commented:

> At first, I was skeptical that this would be enough time. What I've found is that it's more than enough, for two reasons. First, since I segmented my book, gave up all but my top 200, and committed to 12-4-2, my client turnover has decreased dramatically. It used to be that I had to do a lot of selling just to stay even. In fact, for every new client I got, I usually lost a client—I had to run just to stay in place.
>
> Second, I've found that the best way to get new clients is through my existing clients. I've got a lot of clients who have been so impressed with the way I handle them, they've recommended me to their friends and relatives. I'm pretty obvious about wanting referrals, so they know I'm hungry for new business. But it doesn't seem to bother them, as long as I'm delivering on the service promise.

Many FAs found that referrals were their best source of new business. A number used their spare time to specialize in financial products of interest to their clients and potential clients. In one case, an FA lived in an area where many people with company retirement assets were about to retire. She developed expertise in individual retirement accounts (IRAs), becoming a local expert. Another FA had a prominent anesthesiologist as a client. In order to understand him better, he subscribed to anesthesiology journals and attended professional association meetings. As a result, he received four referrals that led to four new relationships, each of which brought in more than $1 million.

Supernova FAs found that their greatest problem was to force themselves to become actively involved in client acquisition once the initial disruption caused by converting to Supernova was over. According to one: "Under the Supernova way of doing things, you aren't constantly putting out fires or worrying about the fact that you're losing so many clients—because there aren't so many fires and your clients don't leave. To be honest, you have to light a fire under yourself to get more business instead of just taking it easy. I call this the 'golf problem'."

Some senior managers believed that the "golf problem" was serious because while FAs adopting Supernova very effectively experienced an immediate increase in compensation, the average new Supernova adopter saw an initial small reduction in pay. The senior managers attributed this loss to local management's failure to coach the average new adopters to begin their acquiring as early as possible in the transition process.

Transaction and Annuitized FAs

FAs adopting Supernova were both transactional FAs, who were paid by charging fees per trade, and annuitized FAs. Some were a combination of the two. According to one fully annuitized FA: "The soft underbelly of annuitized business is that unless you commit to providing a certain level of service, once you're being paid whether or not you do anything, there is less incentive to contact your client. Supernova solves that problem."

A transactional FA added: Once you call your client a few times having no intention of selling anything, it's a lot easier to sell the next time you call. Supernova also helps because it increases my knowledge of the client—when you know someone better, you can figure out what their needs are— and sell them what they want."

THE PROCESS OF ADOPTING SUPERNOVA

Supernova had been spread though road-show presentations made by users who were enthusiastic about what the program had done for them, their client associates, and their clients. Knapp often used a two-part pitch to "sell" Supernova to potential adopters. First, he described how good it felt to be delivering, "The Ultimate Client Experience." Second, he described Supernova as "Plan, Process, and Discipline," noting, "You're going from chaos to plan, process, and discipline— that gives you control of your time. Once you really move from chaos to control, you can't go back."

A Supernova office head noted:

> All of my FAs use Supernova—they have no choice. When I'm hiring, I look for people who are service-oriented, as opposed to transaction-oriented. Lots of people can sell a mother diapers. But can you make her feel good about them when they're dirty?
>
> I didn't force my experienced FAs to adopt the program. My immediate team adopted it, and the others liked what they saw: the phone doesn't ring very often; we meet with the people who pay us, and get rid of the rest; we do very little cold calling—we get new clients almost exclusively through referrals. Every FA in the office chose to join.

Support for FAs Adopting Supernova

The first step in Supernova adoption was called, "FA buy-in." Road shows alone did not ensure buy-in. Skeptical FAs, or those who did not attend road shows, could only be persuaded by a manager sitting down with them and making a compelling argument in favor of the program. Some managers asked the FA how much he or she would like to be earning in a few years. Inevitably, given that FA's current business, there was no way the number could be reached. Once the FA realized the implications of the current situation, the manager could illustrate how the income goal could be reached by adopting Supernova.

The second step in Supernova adoption was segmentation. After that was accomplished, financial planning, 12-4-2, organization, and acquisition were introduced. However, segmentation was often the most difficult to implement. According to an early Supernova adopter:

> Initially, most FAs don't cut their books deep enough, maybe to 300. It's really hard to cut—for years we've been told to get more names. After all, who knows if someone will win the lottery—and some of those clients have been with you for years. The problem is, you just can't give 12-4-2 service to 300 clients—you'll kill yourself trying. If the leadership isn't on top of it, these FAs usually fall off the wagon. A lot of the leadership is made up of the best transactional people we have—it's hardest for them to adopt a relationship perspective. Hunter-gatherers just don't turn into farmers overnight.

Adoption ranged from what one manager described as "They say their doing Supernova, but they haven't even segmented their book" to "Supernova evangelists."

Merrill Lynch assigned one employee to devote herself exclusively to the program. She spent her time organizing and participating in road-show presentations on Supernova and developing new segmentation and organization software to support the program. She stated:

> There's so much more I'd like to be doing. I need to be helping the FAs over hurdles. With Supernova, FAs have to fundamentally change. In some locations, the office head provides a lot of coaching and personal support. But in other offices, there's no one there to help. After we conduct our two-day kickoff road-show meeting, we try to find an FA in the office who's admired by his peers and is ahead of the pack on Supernova. We make that person the local resource for the other FAs. But they don't get anything for doing it, and they may or may not succeed at Supernova themselves.
>
> There's a lot we could be doing, like how to run the segmentation software, and how to set up a folder system. These things aren't brain surgery, but when you haven't done it before it's tough. We review these at the road shows, but people tend to forget over time. Most of it can be done over the phone—the average office only needs two hours a week of in-person assistance during those critical three months after a group of FAs decide to adopt Supernova. They usually need help segmenting, transitioning clients they are giving up, getting organized, and changing their day-to-day behaviors.

KNOWN CHALLENGES TO IMPLEMENTATION

Jim Walker had to decide whether or not to recommend the national roll out of Supernova. As part of his decision making, he reviewed data on Supernova results to date and projections for the future (see **Exhibit 5**). In addition, he identified the challenges he would encounter if he decided to go forward. Among Walker's concerns were the following:

Economic Backdrop

In 2003, times were not good for retail brokerages; stock prices were down, and trading volumes were depressed (see **Exhibit 6**). These conditions made people in the industry tense and directed the attention of Merrill's top managers to immediate issues such as meeting earnings projections. Conversely, some believed that a downturn was the best time to drive change through a brokerage firm since firms tended to poach each other's brokers less often while production was down.

Politics and Recognition

Supernova was seen as the child of its founders. Those in the firm who liked its founders tended to like it. Those with mixed feelings about its founders tended to be less positive. Professional jealousy may also have played a role in negative reactions. Recognition of, and or rewards for Supernova's founders might exacerbate this situation.

EXHIBIT 5   Selected Supernova Results and Projections

Source: Merrill Lynch.

Results
Merrill Lynch's Management Science Group studied a sample of 75 Supernova FAs and arrived at the following conclusions:

    Average number of clients: 208 with average assets of $333,000.

    Upon joining Supernova transferred 14 clients to another FA (average assets $153,000), and 67 clients to the centralized facility (average assets $30,000).

    Supernova FA production (revenue) increased 1 percent while production from a control group of non-Supernova FAs designed to mirror the demographics of the Supernova group decreased 6 percent. Total FA population production declined 12 percent (the markets were down during the period of the study).

    Market errors (mistakes in processing transactions due to FA or client associate errors Merrill was responsible for) declined 54 percent.

    The following client satisfaction measures improved:

- Satisfaction with client associate service
- Percentage of clients feeling they need more FA contact (declined)
- Percentage of clients feeling their FA exceeds in "looking out for their best interests"
- Satisfaction with FA (however, not by a statistically significant amount)

Projections

    Based on the above study, Merrill Lynch's Management Science group made the following projections, assuming Supernova were adopted by 200 FAs per district (approximately 20 percent of FAs):

- $130 million annual increase in FA production (with 90 percent confidence)
- $6.6 million annual reduction in market errors (with 90 percent confidence)
- Total: $58 million in annual pre-tax profit, requiring "some investment" to develop a supporting infrastructure (note that this projection may exclude most benefits from customer retention and word-of-mouth referral)

EXHIBIT 6   Merrill Lynch Financial Statements

Source: Merrill Lynch.

	Year Ended Last Friday in December		
	2002	**2001**	**2000**
Net Revenues			
Commissions	$ 4,657	$ 5,266	$ 6,977
Principal transactions	2,340	3,930	5,964
Investment banking			
Underwriting	1,710	2,438	2,699
Strategic advisory	703	1,101	1,381
Asset management and portfolio service fees	4,914	5,351	5,688
Other	751	528	967
	15,075	18,614	23,676
Interest and dividend revenues	13,178	20,143	21,176
Less interest expenses	9,645	16,877	18,086
Net interest profit	3,533	3,266	3,090
Total Net Revenues	18,608	21,880	26,766
Non-Interest Expenses			
Compensation and benefits	9,426	11,269	13,730
Communications and technology	1,741	2,232	2,320
Occupancy and related depreciation	909	1,077	1,006
Brokerage, clearing, and exchange fees	727	895	893
Advertising and market development	540	703	939
Professional fees	552	545	637
Office supplies and postage	258	349	404
Goodwill amortization	—	207	217
Other	611	902	903
Research and other settlement-related expenses	291	—	
(Recoveries)/expenses related to September 11	(212)	131	—
Restructuring and other charges	8	2,193	—
Total Non-Interest Expenses	14,851	20,503	21,049
Earnings Before Income Taxes and Dividends on Preferred Securities Issued by Subsidiaries	3,757	1,377	5,717
Income Tax Expense	1,053	609	1,738
Dividends on Preferred Securities Issued by Subsidiaries	191	195	195
Net Earnings	$ 2,513	$ 573	$ 3,784
Net Earnings Applicable to Common Stockholders	$ 2,475	$ 535	$ 3,745
Earnings Per Common Share			
Basic	$ 2.87	$ 0.64	$ 4.69
Diluted	$ 2.63	$ 0.57	$ 4.11

(Continued)

Organizational Leverage Points

Achieving change in any Merrill Lynch office required buy-in from the head of that office. That person could be thought of as an "organizational leverage point." However, according to one FA, "A lot of office managers were trained that you manage by hoping things will get better, and when they don't, by yelling at people, firing them, and hiring new ones." A Supernova office head continued: "Remember that lots of office heads are both managers and FAs. As a result, they're competing with the people they're supposed

EXHIBIT 6 Merrill Lynch Financial Statements continued

Consolidated Balance Sheets (dollars in millions, except per share amounts)		
	December 27, 2002	December 28, 2001
Assets		
Cash and cash equivalents	$ 10,211	$ 11,070
Cash and securities segregated for regulatory purposes or deposited with clearing organizations	7,375	4,467
Securities financing transactions		
Receivables under resale agreements	75,292	69,707
Receivables under securities borrowed transactions	45,543	54,930
	120,835	124,637
Trading assets, at fair value *(includes securities pledged as collateral of $11,344 in 2002 and $12,084 in 2001)*		
Contractual agreements	38,728	31,040
Corporate debt and preferred stock	18,569	19,147
Mortgages, mortgage-backed, and asset-backed securities	14,987	11,526
Equities and convertible debentures	13,530	18,487
U.S. Government and agencies	10,116	12,999
Non-U.S. governments and agencies	10,095	6,207
Municipals and money markets	5,535	5,561
	111,560	104,967
Investment securities	81,787	87,672
Other receivables	2,020	3,234
Customers *(net of allowance for doubtful accounts of $79 in 2002 and $81 in 2001)*	35,317	39,856
Brokers and dealers	8,485	6,868
Interest and other	10,581	8,221
	54,383	54,945
Loans, notes, and mortgages *(net of allowance for loan losses of $265 in 2002 and $201 in 2001)*	34,735	19,313
Separate account assets	13,042	15,965
Equipment and Facilities *(net of accumulated depreciation and amortization of $4,671 in 2002 and $4,910 in 2001)*	3,080	2,873
Goodwill *(net of accumulated amortization of $984 in 2002 and $924 in 2001)*	4,446	4,071
Other assets	4,454	2,478
Total Assets	**$ 447,928**	**$ 435,692**

to be managing—competing for space and resources in the office, and to a lesser degree, for clients. Every time I walk into an FA's office I know he's asking, 'Is what my manager's saying best for me—or for him?"

Heads of offices who had adopted Supernova and encouraged their FAs to do the same believed that Merrill's FAs could be broken down into three groups. Twenty percent would buy into Supernova quickly and adopt it with few problems. Another

EXHIBIT 6   Merrill Lynch Financial Statements   concluded

Consolidated Balance Sheets (dollars in millions, except per share amounts)		
	December 27, 2002	**December 28, 2001**
Liabilities		
Securities financing transactions		
Payables under repurchase agreements	$ 85,378	$ 74,903
Payables under securities loaned transactions	7,640	12,291
	93,018	87,194
Commercial paper and other short-term borrowings	5,353	5,141
Deposits	81,842	85,819
Trading liabilities, at fair value		
Contractual agreements	45,202	36,679
U.S. Government and agencies	14,678	18,674
Non-U.S. governments and agencies	7,952	5,857
Corporate debt, municipals and preferred stock	6,500	4,796
Equities and convertible debentures	4,864	9,911
	79,196	75,917
Obligation to return securities received as collateral	2,020	3,234
Other payables		
Customers	28,569	28,704
Brokers and dealers	16,541	11,932
Interest and other	20,724	18,773
	65,834	59,409
Liabilities of insurance subsidiaries	3,566	3,738
Separate accounts liabilities	13,042	15,965
Long-term borrowings	78,524	76,572
Total Liabilities	422,395	412,989
Preferred Securities Issued by Subsidiaries	2,658	2,695
Stockholders' Equity		
Preferred Stockholders' Equity *(42,500 shares issued and outstanding, liquidation preference $10,000 per share)*	425	425
Common Stockholders' Equity		
Shares exchangeable into common stock	58	62
Common stock *(par value $1.33 1/3 per share; authorized: 3,000,000,000 shares; issued: 2002—983,502,078 shares and 2001— 962,533,498 shares)*	1,311	1,283
Paid-in capital	5,315	4,209
Accumulated other comprehensive loss *(net for tax)*	(570)	(368)
Retained earnings	18,072	16,150
	24,186	21,336
Less: Treasury stock, at cost *(2002—116,211,158 shares; 2001—119,059,651 shares)*	961	977
Unamortized employee stock grants	775	776
Total Common Stockholders' Equity	22,450	19,583
Total Stockholders' Equity	22,875	20,008
Total Liabilities, Preferred Securities Issued by Subsidiaries, and Stockholders' Equity	**$ 447,928**	**$ 435,692**

20 percent were unlikely to ever buy into it. The remaining 60 percent would need 60 hours of coaching over two years. Coaching often involved asking questions such as:

1. What's your financial planning process?
2. What's your investment process?
3. What's your service delivery process?
4. What's your new business—your marketing—process?

Follow Up/Support

To date, Supernova had been spread through road shows and other presentations. While many FAs attended those road shows, only 2,000 had completely adopted Supernova. Another 4,000 had partially adopted Supernova. These FAs posed several risks. First, they jeopardized the Supernova "brand" in that their clients would not be as satisfied as those of complete adopters. Second, Supernova advocates agreed that a failure to fully adopt the program meant that its benefits for FAs, such as improved compensation and quality of work life, would not be enjoyed.

Client Expectations

Many Supernova FAs believed that after clients became accustomed to Supernova, their expectations for service rose dramatically. In the words of one, "We designed Supernova to spoil them—and it does." This situation created a problem in measuring customer satisfaction when comparing non-Supernova clients with Supernova clients. It also created a problem when service promises were made to clients by FAs who intended to fully adopt Supernova, but never completely implemented the program.

Changing Role of Some FAs

Historically, the individual FA often made recommendations on what investments a client should make. However, many FAs in general, and most Supernova FAs, saw their role as asset gathering and allocation, leaving asset management to professional asset advisors. Supernova FAs noted that they preferred this new role because it enabled them to provide consultative service, examining risk relative to reward, as opposed to selling a product. Many traditional FAs, who wanted to continue recommending investments, associated the new approach (gathering and allocation) with Supernova.

Misinterpretation

Walker often received calls from FAs interested in Supernova in which they asked him for the "Supernova software," believing that if they loaded it on their computers they would be "Supernova compliant." Walker felt that these FAs saw Supernova as an exercise in implementing technology. He noted, "We've got great new CRM software, the best out there. It will make good Supernova FAs even better. But it's only one piece of a complex solution."

Metrics

Both Supernova FAs and managers believed there was a problem with metrics, one noting: "We don't get paid as well for a lot of the new things we're selling under Supernova, like mortgages and insurance, despite their better profitability for the firm."

FA Nature

FAs valued their independence. According to a senior manager, "They don't want to walk in lock step. They like autonomy. Anything that looks like a requirement from a centralized authority is usually rejected out of hand, or at least fought vigorously."

Inclusion of Client Associates

Even though client associates were essential to Supernova's working effectively, most FAs made the decision to adopt it, or not, without involving their administrative assistants.

Exhibit 7 presents excerpts from an FA's presentation on Supernova. Exhibit 8 illustrates portions of the contents of a folder.

CONCLUSION

A Supernova FA commented: "Historically, when we sold a *product* to a client, Merrill Lynch made money and the FA made money. Supernova helps to solve the dilemma that created. Supernova enables us to earn our money for handholding, and to do it really well. It provides a business process—not a product. We've never had that before."

EXHIBIT 7   Excerpts from FA's Presentation on Supernova

Source: Company documents.

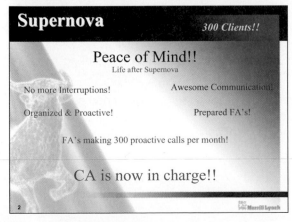

EXHIBIT 8 **Portions of a Folder's Contents**

Source: Company documents.

PROJECT SUPERNOVA
(12-4-2 The Ultimate Client Experience)

1.) 8 Outgoing Calls:

JG	___ ___ ___ ___ ___ ___ ___	Outgoing call to client was placed.
JG	___ ___ ___ ___ ___ ___ ___	Action Plan Proposal Report was reviewed and updated.
JG	___ ___ ___ ___ ___ ___ ___	Client portfolio was checked and reviewed.
JG	___ ___ ___ ___ ___ ___ ___	Client Performance was checked and reviewed.

2.) 2 Quarterly Phone Reviews:

___	___	Quarterly review call was placed.
___	___	Action Plan Proposal Report was reviewed and updated.
___	___	Market overview given to client.
___	___	Client Portfolio was checked and reviewed.
___	___	Client Performance was checked and reviewed.

3.) 2 Face to Face Reviews:

JG	___	Financial Foundation & IFF completed and updated.
JG	___	Reconfirm Financial goals and risk tolerance.
JG	___	Review Client performance vs. Goals.
JG	___	Review client portfolio for necessary adjustments.
JG	___	Introduce client to services they do not have.
JG	___	Smart Market (ASK FOR ADVICE.)
JG	___	Complete service questionnaire & schedule next appointment.

EXHIBIT 8   Portions of a Folder's Contents   continued

CLIENT ACTION PLAN

Client Name: _____

Performance Need: _____	**Risk Tolerance:** _____	**Time Horizon:** _____
Performance Want: _____	**Profile Score:** _____	**Allocation Type:** _____

BOSAR

<u>**Investment Assets:**</u>

Cash Flow Control:	**Discussed**	**Who**	**Done**
CMA Account	_____	____	_____
Visa Signature Card	_____	____	_____
Merrill Lynch Online	_____	____	_____
MLUA	_____	____	_____

Stocks/Equities:	**Discussed**	**Who**	**Done**
Consults	_____	____	_____
Strategy Power	_____	____	_____
MFA	_____	____	_____
Annuities	_____	____	_____

Bonds/Fixed Income:	**Discussed**	**Who**	**Done**
Municipal Bonds	_____	____	_____
Taxable Bonds	_____	____	_____
CD's	_____	____	_____

Asset Allocation:	**Discussed**	**Who**	**Done**
Reviewed Asset Allocation	_____	____	_____
Portfolio Re-balanced	_____	____	_____

<u>**Retirement:**</u> | _____ | ____ | _____ |

IRA's:	**Discussed**	**Who**	**Done**
Client #1 IRA Contribution	_____	____	_____
Client #2 IRA Contribution	_____	____	_____

(Continued)

EXHIBIT 8 **Portions of a Folder's Contents** **continued**

401K's:			**Discussed**	**Who**	**Done**
Client #1 Contribution Reviewed			_____	_____	_____
Client #1 Portfolio Allocation Reviewed			_____	_____	_____
Client #2 Contribution Reviewed			_____	_____	_____
Client #2 Portfolio Allocation Reviewed			_____	_____	_____
Rollover from Job Transition			_____	_____	_____

Net Worth:

Liability Management:	**Client Rate**	**Our Rate**	**Discussed**	**Who**	**Done**
Omega	_____	_____	_____	_____	_____
Mortgage	_____	_____	_____	_____	_____
Home Equity	_____	_____	_____	_____	_____
Commercial Loan	_____	_____	_____	_____	_____
Consumer Debt	_____	_____	_____	_____	_____

Tax Planning:

Tax Reduction Strategies:	**Client Tax Rate**	**Discussed**	**Who**	**Done**
Client Tax Information	_____	_____	_____	_____
Taxable Equivalent Yield	_____ = _____	_____	_____	_____
Year End Tax Wash Selling		_____	_____	_____

Education Planning:

Education Planning Strategies:			**Discussed**	**Who**	**Done**
UGMA/UTMA Accounts			_____	_____	_____
529 Account Funding			_____	_____	_____

EXHIBIT 8   Portions of a Folder's Contents   continued

Survivor Protection:

Life Insurance Established: **Discussed**   **Who**   **Done**

Client #1 Insured vs. Needs
Client #2 Insured vs. Needs

Income & Asset Protection:

Income Protection:

Client #1 Disability Insurance in Place
Client #2 Disability Insurance in Place

Asset Protection:

Long Term Care Insurance
Personal Excess Liability Insurance in Place
Home Owners Insurance Reviewed

Estate Planning:

Estate Planning issues:

Wills Updated and Reviewed
Living Trust Established
Assets and Accounts Re-titled for Trust
Beneficiaries Reviewed
Transfer On Death Completed

Providing for each Other:

Appoint Guardian for Minor Children
Durable Power of Attorney Appointed
Health Care Provider Appointed
Business Buy-Sell Agreement in Place

Wealth Replacement:

Wealth Replacement Trust
Wealth Replacement Insurance

(Continued)

EXHIBIT 8   Portions of a Folder's Contents   concluded

BE HUMAN!

I.) Client 1's Career:

Client 2's Career:

II. Client 1's Hobbies:

Cliennt 2's Hobbies:

III. Client 1's Passions:

Client 2's Passions:

Case 3
United Breaks Guitars

John Deighton
Leora Kornfeld

On July 8, 2009, United Airlines offered professional musician Dave Carroll $1,200 in cash and $1,200 in flight vouchers to 'make right' a situation in which his guitar had been damaged at Chicago's O'Hare airport during transfer from one airplane to another, in full view of passengers seated in the plane.

Carroll had spent 15 months seeking compensation, but the effort appeared to have reached an impasse when a United Airlines customer service representative told him that the airline had concluded that the damage was Carroll's responsibility and that she considered the matter closed. He replied that in that case he would be composing three songs about his experience and posting them to the video-sharing site YouTube. The first song was posted on July 6, 2009. At the same time, he wrote a blog entry detailing the ordeal and posted the link to the YouTube video on his Twitter account. Within a week the video had been viewed three million times, and United Airlines had reached out to Carroll to offer the compensation.

Online and offline media helped propagate the story. On July 22, 2009, *The Times of London* wrote that "the gathering thunderclouds of bad PR caused United Airlines' stock price to suffer a mid-flight stall, and it plunged by 10 percent, costing shareholders $180 million."[1] Hundreds of news reports repeated the story of how a single poorly handled customer complaint had, thanks to the power of social media, cost the company $180 million. News channel CNN urged viewers, "Anyone who's ever been frustrated with an airline needs to see this video."[2] The first song, "United Breaks Guitars," began to be referred to as the complaint anthem of airline travelers, and Carroll was called the Accidental Chief Marketing Officer of United Airlines. His catchy melody stuck in people's minds.

Carroll observed, "It's been said that in the old days (maybe only a decade ago) that people who had a positive customer service experience would share that with 3 people. If they had a bad experience, they would tell 14. . . . [A]s of today I have reached more than 6 million people on YouTube with my story and, according to some estimates, some 100 million people if you total all media references."[3]

By October 2009, the video seemed to have receded from the public mind. Worldwide viewings had slowed to 5,000 a day, and traffic to the websites of Dave Carroll and his band, Sons of Maxwell, had declined from 150,000 unique visitors a month in July 2009 to 2,000 in October. And yet evidence suggested that Carroll's song had had a more persistent influence on perceptions of the United Airlines brand. British blogger Peter Cochrane recounted an incident that took place in October 2009 on a shuttle bus from

Professor John Deighton and Research Associate Leora Kornfeld prepared this case. HBS cases are developed solely as the basis for class discussion. Cases are not intended to serve as endorsements, sources of primary data, or illustrations of effective or ineffective management.

his hotel to New York's JFK airport. "Barely awake," wrote Cochrane, "I heard the driver call for airlines and terminals. Someone piped up 'United' and the immediate rejoinder from the rest of the passengers was a chorus of the song 'United Breaks Guitars.'"[4]

Just what was the significance of this incident to a brand like United Airlines? Could its scale have been anticipated or influenced? How, when, and how much could the brand have reacted? And looking forward, what contingency planning would be appropriate? Was this kind of incident the responsibility of brand management, customer service management, or media and public relations, or did responsibility lie elsewhere in the organization?

UNITED AIRLINES

With close to 50,000 employees and more than 3,300 flights per day, United Airlines was one of the largest international airlines based in the U.S.[5] Since deregulation of the industry in 1978, airlines had been unconstrained by pricing and scheduling mandates. Deregulation initially yielded profits for the airlines, but profitability soon gave way to cycles of losses.

In common with all major airlines, United Airlines struggled with competitive fare slashing and high fuel costs. In December 2002, United filed for Chapter 11 bankruptcy protection. Its losses for the year totaled $3.21 billion. In 2003, it took further measures to trim operational costs, including a workforce reduction of 20 percent, renegotiation of salaries, and outsourcing of maintenance services, and its yearly loss decreased to $2.81 billion.[6] The layoffs and cuts continued, with flight attendants and in-flight services bearing the brunt of the reduction. In 2006, United laid off 11 percent of its salaried workers,[7] and in 2008 the airline announced it would no longer be handing out complimentary pretzels and biscuits to economy class passengers in North America.[8] Shortly thereafter, the American Customer Satisfaction Index Airline Rankings for 1996–2009 were released. United's score was the lowest, with the largest percentage drop in the 13 years of the survey (see **Exhibit 1**; United Airlines' stock price is shown in **Exhibit 2**).

THE INCIDENT

For more than 20 years, Dave Carroll had been making a modest living as a musician, performing his brand of pop-folk music with his band, Sons of Maxwell. Carroll's life as a working musician took him back and forth across Canada most years, into several U.S. cities, and sometimes to international destinations for music festivals. On March 31, 2008, Carroll and members of the band were flying from their hometown of Halifax, Canada, for a week of shows in Omaha, Nebraska. During a connection in Chicago, other passengers aboard the flight noticed some very rough handling of cargo, and Carroll's bandmates watched helplessly as Dave's $3,500 Taylor guitar was mishandled by United's baggage handlers. Carroll shared his concerns with a flight attendant. He was told, "Don't talk to me. Talk to the lead agent outside."[9] Carroll complied and was informed by the employee at the gate that he should take the issue up with the ground crew in Omaha. But the flight was delayed, and Carroll saw no ground crew when he arrived in Omaha after midnight.

On his return to the airport in Omaha, he spoke with a United agent, who advised him that he would need to start a claim at the originating airport, in Halifax. Once he was back in Halifax, Carroll was given a phone number that he called a few times, eventually being rerouted to a call center in India. Several calls later, Carroll was directed to United's baggage offices in Chicago, where he was told that he would need to bring the guitar to Chicago for inspection. When Carroll explained that he was over 1,200 miles away from Chicago, the agent told him to go through United's

EXHIBIT 1   **American Customer Satisfaction Index Airline Rankings, 1996–2009**

Source: American Customer Satisfaction Index, http://www.theacsi.org/index.php?option=com_content&task=view&id=147&Itemid=155&i=Airlines, accessed November 2009.

	Base-line	96	97	98	99	00	01	02	03	04	05	06	07	08	09	Previous Year % Change	First Year % Change
Southwest Airlines	78	76	76	74	72	70	70	74	75	73	74	74	76	79	81	2.5	3.8
All Others	NM[a]	74	70	62	67	63	64	72	74	73	74	74	75	75	77	2.7	4.1
Continental Airlines	67	66	64	66	64	62	67	68	68	67	70	67	69	62	68	9.7	1.5
Average Airline	**72**	**69**	**67**	**65**	**63**	**63**	**61**	**66**	**67**	**66**	**66**	**65**	**63**	**62**	**64**	**3.2**	**−11.1**
Delta Air Lines	77	67	69	65	68	66	61	66	67	67	65	64	59	60	64	6.7	−16.9
American Airlines	70	71	62	67	64	63	62	63	67	66	64	62	60	62	60	−3.2	−14.3
US Airways	72	66	68	65	61	62	60	63	64	62	57	62	61	54	59	9.3	−18.1
Northwest Airlines	69	67	64	63	53	62	56	65	64	64	64	61	61	57	57	0	−17.4
United Airlines	71	70	68	65	62	62	59	64	63	64	61	63	56	56	56	0	−21.1

[a] Not measured.

central baggage center in New York, which eventually led Carroll back to the call center in India.

To Carroll's delight, the customer service manager in India promised to get in touch with a United representative in Chicago. He did so, and the representative reviewed Carroll's file and made direct e-mail contact with him. It was now seven months since the process began, but Carroll felt that at last the matter was being addressed. When the e-mail arrived, however, the representative said she was sorry about what had happened to the guitar, but that standard airline policy held that claims be made within 24 hours of damage (a precaution against fraudulent claims). She told him that his claim was going to be denied. Carroll asked to speak with a supervisor, but was refused. His final request was for $1,200 worth of United flight vouchers, the amount he had paid to repair his guitar. The representative told him no, United considered the case closed, and there would be no further communication on the matter. "At that moment," wrote Carroll in his blog, "it occurred to me that I had been fighting a losing battle. . . . The system is designed to frustrate affected customers into giving up their claims and United is very good at it." In his final exchange with the representative, he told her that he would be writing three songs with video about United Airlines and sharing them on YouTube. His goal, he said, was to get one million hits in one year.[10]

Carroll wrote the first song, and with his friends at Curve Productions in Halifax, produced a biting video to accompany it. The budget for the video was $150, with people donating time, props, and locations for the shoot.[11] The location that stood in for the O'Hare airport tarmac was the fire station in Waverly, Nova Scotia, where Dave Carroll worked as a volunteer firefighter. On July 6, 2009, the video was posted to YouTube.

EXHIBIT 2 United Airlines Stock Price, 2009

Source: *Wall Street Journal* Market Data Center, http://online.wsj.com/mdc/public/page/marketsdata.html, accessed January 2010.

United Airlines Stock Price Compared with S&P Index, February to December 2009

Source: *Wall Street Journal* Market Data Center, http://online.wsj.com/mdc/public/page/marketsdata.html, accessed January 2010.

THE VIDEO TAKES OFF

Carroll's friend, Ryan Moore, posted the video to YouTube at about 10 p.m. on Monday, July 6. Throughout the night and the following day, a small team of friends used Twitter to introduce their followers to the video. They also tweeted to those on Twitter who had themselves tweeted about bad experiences with United Airlines, and to members of the media including Jay Leno, Jimmy Fallon, and Perez Hilton. They posted the story to Digg and other social news sites to which people could submit stories and vote them up and down.

At 1:49 p.m. on Tuesday, July 7, the video was picked up by Consumerist.com, a website affiliated with Consumers Union, America's leading not-for-profit consumer advocacy organization and the publisher of *Consumer Reports* magazine. That evening at 7:02 p.m., the story made its first mainstream news appearance in the travel section of the website of the *Los Angeles Times*. The reporter had seen the video when it was e-mailed to a colleague by a friend. The story reported that by that time the video had received 24,000 views and 461 comments, most of them maligning United Airlines.

On Wednesday, July 8, HuffingtonPost.com and NBCChicago.com relayed the story to their followers, and on that day there were 190,000 views on YouTube (see **Exhibit 3**). Mainstream media such as CNN, the CBS Morning Show, and Associated Press began calling Carroll for interviews, and on July 9 and 10 mainstream media mentions peaked at 150 and 155, respectively.

EXHIBIT 3

Media Activity

Source: Compiled by casewriters.

	YouTube Views per Day	Blogs per Day	Tweets per Day	Mainstream Media Mentions
6-Jul	0	0	20	0
7-Jul	25,000	50	50	0
8-Jul	190,000	180	200	40
9-Jul	500,000	420	860	150
10-Jul	910,000	140	900	155
11-Jul	650,000	80	500	50
12-Jul	240,000	90	250	20
13-Jul	210,000	140	300	30
14-Jul	190,000	45	280	60
15-Jul	180,000	45	560	10
16-Jul	120,000	0	220	15
17-Jul	90,000	10	230	5
18-Jul	80,000	20	80	5
19-Jul	60,000	20	80	0
20-Jul	70,000	40	60	5
21-Jul	95,000	10	20	0
22-Jul	50,000	0	30	40
23-Jul	180,000	30	350	40
24-Jul	190,000	60	200	30
25-Jul	120,000	40	150	5
26-Jul	100,000	45	140	5
27-Jul	80,000	50	160	0
28-Jul	90,000	45	140	0
29-Jul	70,000	60	100	0
30-Jul	70,000	80	110	5
31-Jul	50,000	50	80	0

EXHIBIT 3
(continued)

Source: Adapted from Media Miser website, http://www.mediamiser.com/resources/archive/090821_united.html, accessed October 2009.

New and Traditional Media Activity per Day, July 2009

Legend:
— YouTube (views per day)
—·— Tweets per day
---- Blogs per day
– – Mainstream media mentions

By Friday, July 10, YouTube views per day crested, with cumulative views reaching nearly 1.6 million. By this time "United Breaks Guitars" was YouTube's number one rated music video of all time, and number three in any category of video.[12] Beginning on July 23, a second surge in YouTube traffic arose when the British news media picked up the story. By the end of July, the video had been viewed 4.6 million times.

The popularity of "United Breaks Guitars" on YouTube spilled over to other online media. Traffic to Dave Carroll's website, www.davecarrollmusic.com, on which he sold his CDs, surged from a few hundred unique visitors per week to more than 20,000 per week (see **Exhibit 4**). Song sales on iTunes increased from one or two per day to hundreds per day. "United Breaks Guitars" became a Top 20 iTunes download in Canada and the number-one country music download in the United Kingdom for July 2009.[13] "My mother handles our mail-order," said Carroll. "I went round there on Saturday and her couch was piled high with CDs ready to be mailed out. It was the third 'couch full'. . . . We might have to hire someone to help her, or at least buy her a bigger sofa."[14]

On July 10, Bob Taylor of Taylor Guitars, the California-based manufacturer of high end guitars, posted a two-minute video on YouTube to express his support for Carroll and to offer advice on transporting guitars on planes. Taylor guitars were used by some of the top names in the music industry, among them Prince, Taylor Swift, and Aerosmith. In the description section of his YouTube video, Bob Taylor wrote, "Taylor has had an artist relationship with Dave for several years now. In 2006, our

EXHIBIT 4   **Website Traffic at www.davecarrollmusic.com, May–August 2009**

Source: Compete website, http://www.compete.com, accessed November 2009.

owners' magazine, *Wood & Steel,* reviewed Dave's CD, "Sunday Morning." As we've had an ongoing relationship, we have made the offer to replace and/or further repair his damaged 710ce . . . we've offered Dave [as a Taylor artist] our support, a choice of a new guitar, and to re-repair the damaged 710ce. Dave and his bandmate Julian made the trip to the Taylor factory in July and have met many of our staff. We'll also be running a story on Dave's experiences in the fall issue of *Wood & Steel*." In the video, Bob Taylor expressed his concern for Dave Carroll's situation and went on to say, "If your guitar is broken and you had it in a hard shell case, there was clearly some negligence and abuse there, because the case can protect the guitar from all kinds of damage."[15]

UNITED AIRLINES' RESPONSE

United Airlines had its own presence in both online and social media. Its website, like that of most commercial airlines, gave customers the ability to browse fares and schedules, make bookings, check their flyer miles balance, interact with customer service, file damaged baggage complaints, and view the latest news from the airline (see **Exhibit 5** for more information on united.com). In July 2009, United maintained a presence on Twitter that had approximately 18,000 followers. United Airlines used Twitter actively, tweeting two or three times a day with information useful to travelers, such as Twitter-only airfare deals and system disruptions. All United employees were encouraged to monitor social media for mentions of United Airlines. All they needed to do to monitor tweets involving United Airlines was to subscribe to the service and search for mentions.

At noon on July 7, before any blogger or mainstream news medium had reported the story, and with cumulative views of Carroll's video under 20,000, a United Airlines staff member read the following tweet from one of Carroll's friends: "psssst . . . @UnitedAirlines breaks guitars! And they don't even care!" Minutes later, Robin Urbanski of United Airlines' media relations team in Chicago called Rob Bradford, managing director of customer solutions at United, and told him, "We need to call Carroll." The call was made, but Carroll was not available to return the call until the next morning. Urbanski then sent out United's first tweet: "This has struck a chord w/us and we've contacted him directly to make it right."

United Airlines tracked the Twitter conversation throughout the day and onward, joining the conversation many times and frequently tweeting the sentence, "This has struck a chord with us," as new people joined the conversation. United would often have to state that it had reached out to Dave Carroll, as in this interchange:

- At 1:02 p.m., from a member of the public: "Check the @unitedairlines account. They've apologized and accepted responsibility. Cool stuff."

EXHIBIT 5   **United Airlines Website Traffic, 2007–2009**

Source: Compete website, http://www.compete.com, accessed November 2009.

- At 2:28 p.m., from one of Carroll's team: "word has it @UnitedAirlines isn't trying to make it right, they are just tweeting is that way."
- At 2:31 p.m., from United Airlines: "The word you hear is wrong. We have called him and the person who answered his phone scheduled a call for tomorrow morning."

United's Rob Bradford reached out to Carroll on July 8 to apologize for the situation and to ask if United could use the video internally to help change its culture.[16] He offered him $1,200 in cash, the amount Carroll had spent on repairing his guitar, plus $1,200 in flight vouchers. Carroll declined the offer and suggested that United give it to a customer of its choosing who had been affected in a similar way. The airline chose instead to donate $3,000 to a music school.

Meanwhile, the tweeting continued. United did not respond to taunting from Carroll's friends:

- At 1:46 p.m., on July 7: "Why'd you guys have to go and break his guitar? http://bit.ly/rI2ef Stop being a bully and fess up!"
- At 3:40 p.m., on July 7: "Learn from the United Breaks Guitars song that its NOT ok to treat any customer bad."
- At 9:50 p.m., on July 7: "You can say creatively that this has struck a chord with you but lets be real how do you plan on changing?"
- At 9:53 p.m., on July 7: "You realize that Dave Carroll is one of many people burned by your 'Airline' ~ how'd you plan to make things right 4them?" http://twitter.com/jononomoe
- At 9:55 p.m., on July 7: "And since I'm on a roll, shame on you for taking over a year to bother . . . too much truth in your bad PR?" http://twitter.com/?status=@jononomoe%20&in_reply_to_status_id=2525183920&in_reply_to=jononomoe

On more than one occasion, however, United Airlines used Twitter to try to defuse the situation:

- At 3:00 p.m., on July 8, from Ryan Moore: "i posted a video for a client of mine monday night and it's like the biggest vid on youtube canada now. http://bit.ly."
- At 3:39 p.m., on July 8, United Airlines replied: "Love your client's video. Not all r as honest as he. That is why policy asks for claims w/in 24 hours. No excuse; we're sorry."
- At 4:56 p.m., on July 8, from a Twitter member: "I love this song about @unitedAirlines Check it out! http://bit.ly/8RDMI"

- At 5:02 p.m., on July 8, from United Airlines: "It is excellent and that is why we would like to use it for training purposes so everyone receives better service from us."

United Airlines continued to monitor references to the video and react to them:

- At 6:00 p.m., on July 9, from a musician in Cleveland: "Funny how @ UnitedAirlines denies someone's claim until it's made public #UnitedBreaks-Guitars—You COULD have made it right a year ago."
- At 7:59 p.m., on July 9, United Airlines replied: "Absolutely right, and 4 that (among other things), we are v. sorry and are making it right. Plan 2 use video in training."

Occasionally, United made comments about the incident that were not reactions to other Twitter members' tweets:

- At 6:44 p.m., on July 10: "Wud like Dave 2 sing a happy tune—as asked we gave 3K to Thelonius Monk Institute of Jazz 4 music education 4 kids."
- At 6:46 p.m., on July 10: "Can't wait 2 make music w/Dave 2 improve service 4 all."

For the rest of the week, the Twitter feed served as the channel by which United responded:

- At 9:34 a.m., on July 10, a Florida resident wrote: "United Breaks Guitars! LOL this is a funny vid! I hope you guys buy him another."
- At 10:13 a.m., on July 10, United Airlines replied: "As Dave asked we donated 3K to charity and selected the Thelonius Monk Institute of Jazz 4 music education 4 kids."
- At 7:31 p.m., on July 13, a Twitter member commented: "The sad thing is, I still don't think @unitedairlines really gets what they did wrong."
- At 3:56 p.m., on July 13, another member commented: "It should have been fixed sooner & not have happened in the 1st place."
- At 11:24 a.m., on July 14, the airline replied: "Should it regretfully happen to anyone, pls file a claim w/in 24 hrs at airport, online or phone."
- At 6:45 p.m., on July 14, United Airlines continued: "That was a mistake that we made, have apologized for, have fixed, and most importantly, learned from too."

United Airlines was selective in the media it used to discuss the incident. It responded to inquiries from journalists about the incident, but did not address it on its website or its YouTube channel. It posted a comment to Carroll's band's YouTube channel, but the message was deleted. By August 2009, United was responding to tweets with direct messages (private communications through the Twitter medium) inviting a longer e-mail communication.

These e-mails came from Robin Urbanski in United's media relations group and read:

Yes, these videos have struck a chord with all of us here.

In recent statements on YouTube, Mr. Carroll described our baggage service representative as a "great employee who acted in the best interests of the company," and I could not agree more with that.

He has made his point, I have since been in contact with him to fix, and I am now his BFF.[*]

---

[*]Popular Internet abbreviation for 'best friend forever'.

> The second video is suggesting we do something that we've already done — and that is to provide our agents with a better way to escalate and respond to special situations.
>
> While his anecdotal experience is unfortunate, the fact is that 99.95 percent of our customers' bags are delivered on time and without incident, including instruments that belong to many Grammy award–winning musicians.
>
> As you know, in our business, how we conduct ourselves is important, and we do understand that treating each other and our customers in a courteous and respectful manner is a vital part of running a good airline.[17]

People who communicated with United Airlines' customer relations department received the following written response:

> Thank you for contacting United Airlines Customer Relations. I appreciate the opportunity to respond to your inquiry.
>
> At United, we continually work to ensure the proper handling of your items when you fly with us, and we transport thousands of checked bags each day without incident.
>
> We have had discussions with our customer to make what happened right, and at his request, we donated the money that would have gone toward a new guitar to the Thelonius Monk Institute of Jazz that provides music education for kids with potential. The video provides us with a unique learning opportunity that we plan to use for training purposes to ensure all customers receive better service from us.
>
> Your business is important to us, and I hope you will give us an opportunity to serve you in the future.

On September 14, Dave Carroll met with two senior vice presidents and a vice president as he was passing through O'Hare airport in Chicago. They gave him a tour of O'Hare's baggage-handling facilities and explained the challenges of shaping internal culture in an organization where many customer-facing employees spent most of their time traveling. They acknowledged that Carroll's claim should not have been denied and told him that customer service representatives were now being trained to use discretion in applying rules like the one requiring notification of damage to baggage within 24 hours.

THE AFTERMATH

The path of Carroll's life had been upended by the success of his song. As the media began to call, he and his wife reached out to his wife's father, Brent Sansom, an international management consultant: "Dad, I think we need your help." Sansom responded by relocating from Moncton, New Brunswick, to Halifax, Nova Scotia, and set about handling the hundreds of e-mails and phone calls that arrived every day from around the globe. "For the past four months we've been getting three to four hours of sleep a night," Sansom said. "We are being offered new audiences and distribution opportunities for Dave's music. There are new business relationships with manufacturers like Taylor Guitars and Calton Cases, and service providers such as Mariner Partners and RightNow Technologies, which offered customer experience software. There are speaking and live performance invitations, and companies want to commission songs and video recordings. Dave has done over 200 media interviews with everyone from the *Wall Street Journal* to Oprah Radio, *Rolling Stone* to the *Reader's Digest*. The story is resonating with many people."

FlyersRights.org, a large nonprofit airline consumer organization, organized what it called a stakeholder hearing on September 22 in the Rayburn House Office Building in Washington, D.C., on airline passenger rights, where Senator Barbara Boxer of California spoke and Carroll performed an acoustic version of "United Breaks Guitars." For a group of Canadian broadcasters lobbying against a proposed increase in cable fees, Carroll wrote "The Cable Song," which was broadcast after the local evening news across Canada for a week.

In October, Carroll traveled to Colorado to give the keynote address at the Right-Now Technologies User Summit. He took a United Airlines flight operated by a regional carrier, SkyWest, whose baggage was being handled under contract to Air Canada. One of Carroll's two items of luggage was lost, providing him with fresh material for his speech. Reporting on the story, the *New York Times* labeled him "the Everyman symbol of the aggrieved traveler."[18]

Advertising Age columnist David Klein reflected on the meaning of the "United Breaks Guitars" incident for marketing and branding in the age of social media, "To really incite the full range of customer reaction to a brand, and by full range I mean everything from bitter rage at the low end to fantastic appreciation at the high end, traditional advertising is not the way to do it. In these postmodern times where every interaction with the customer is a marketing event, the real crunch point comes when the customer meets your customer-service department. Seriously, who didn't enjoy watching musician Dave Carroll's takedown of United Airlines for not only breaking his guitar but then refusing to make things right by reimbursing him?"[19]

ENDNOTES

1. Chris Ayres, "Revenge is best served cold—on YouTube," *The Times* (U.K.), July 22, 2009, via Factiva.

2. CNN, *The Situation Room,* July 8, 2009, http://transcripts.cnn.com/TRAN-SCRIPTS/0907/08/sitroom. 03.html, accessed November 2, 2009.

3. Dave Carroll, "Statistical Insignificance," *AdWeek,* November 25, 2009, http://www.adweek.com/aw/ content_display/community/columns/other-columns/ e3ia7f0e1dcab3176840f88bf567f95ce7d, accessed December 5, 2009.

4. Peter Cochrane's Blog: "United breaks guitars?," October 14, 2009, http://networks. silicon.com/webwatch/0,39024667,39574741,00.htm, accessed October 23, 2009.

5. United Airlines website, http://www.united.com/pressreleases/0,7057,1,00.html, accessed October 22, 2009.

6. CBC News, "World airline woes: Carriers hit financial turbulence," January 29, 2004, http://www.cbc.ca/news/background/aircanada/airlinewoes.html#a6, accessed October 26, 2009.

7. "United Airlines Plans to Lay Off 11% of Its Salaried Workers," *New York Times,* June 15, 2006, http://www.nytimes.com/2006/06/15/business/15air.html, accessed October 27, 2009.

8. George Raine, "United Airlines to drop free snacks," *San Francisco Chronicle,* August 20, 2008, http://www.sfgate.com/cgi-bin/article.cgi?f=/c/a/2008/08/20/ BUC812E8DR.DTL#ixzz0VAYnTkI8, accessed October 26, 2009.

9. Dave Carroll blog posting, July 7, 2009, http://www.davecarrollmusic.com/story/ united-breaks-guitars, accessed October 23, 2009.

10. Ibid.

11. Linda Laban, "Dave Carroll Smashes YouTube Records with 'United Breaks Guitars,'" July 14, 2009, http://www.spinner.com/2009/07/14/dave-carroll-breaks-youtube-records-with-united-breaks-guitars/#, accessed October 26, 2009.

12. Ibid.

13. MktgCliks website, http://mktgcliks.blogspot.com/2009/07/united-breaks-guitars-united-airlines.html, accessed October 28, 2009.

14. Laban, 2009.

15. "Taylor Guitars Responds to United Breaks Guitars," YouTube video, http://www.youtube.com/watch?v=n12WFZq2__0, accessed October 25, 2009.

16. Dave Carroll, interviewed by Beverly Thomspon, "Online broken guitar video gets airline's attention," July 9, 2009, Canada AM, CTV, transcript via Factiva.

17. Brett Snyder, "United Aggressively Responds to 'United Breaks Guitars Part 2,'" BNET Travel website, http://industry.bnet.com/travel/10003236/united-aggressively-responds-to-united-breaks-guitars-part-2/, accessed December 8, 2009.

18. Christine Neggroni, "With video, a traveler fights back," *New York Times,* October 29, 2009, via Factiva, accessed November 4, 2009.

19. David Klein, "Your most crucial moment comes when the customer calls," *Advertising Age,* July 27, 2009, via Factiva, accessed November 2, 2009.

Case 4
Michelin Fleet Solutions: From Selling Tires to Selling Kilometers

CASE ABSTRACT

Michelin, a worldwide leader in the tire industry, launched in 2000 a comprehensive tire-management solution offer for large European transportation companies, called Michelin Fleet Solutions (MFS). With this new business model, the company ventured into selling kilometers – instead of selling tires. This decision moves the strongly product-driven firm into the new world of services and solutions. The shift is intuitively appealing, and it provides Michelin with an opportunity to differentiate itself in the tire business. After three years, however, expansion is far below expectations and profitability is terrible – despite the outside help of a strategy consulting firm. The case presents the decision point in 2003, whereby MFS's future has to be decided. Should Michelin seek to further develop this solution offer, and try to repackage the offer yet another time? Or was it just a passing fad that should be abandoned?

This case investigates the difficulties that industrial groups face when they transition from selling products to providing service. It enables participants to reflect on the following issues: What is the rationale for industrial groups moving towards solutions? What kind of business model reconfiguration does it imply? How does moving to solutions raise multiple challenges throughout the organization (e.g. in terms of sales force management, risk management, channel relationships etc.)?

CASE STUDY

On this gloomy day of January 2003, Jonas Pills hurried to take a cab in Clermont-Ferrand airport to reach Michelin's headquarters, in downtown Clermont. While in the cab, he reflected upon his forthcoming meeting at the French tire manufacturer's offices. After five years as a regional sales manager, Jonas had been appointed a year ago as Manager in Germany for the deployment of Michelin Fleet Solutions (MFS). Today would undoubtedly be decisive for MFS's future. Would Michelin pursue or abandon its solution business?

This seemed such a good idea to begin with. With MFS, Michelin had moved from its traditional business of manufacturing and selling tires toward the new world of service, i.e. offering transportation companies comprehensive tire fleet management solutions. This radical move was initiated in 2000 with promising growth prospects. The new offering was targeted at large European transportation companies such as Schenker, TNT, Geodis, or Norbert Dentressangle. However, three years later, the picture had become much darker: despite substantial investments, geographic expansion was still poor and MFS remained unprofitable. The situation had deteriorated to a

This case study was written by **Chloé Renault**, HEC 2006 and PhD Student at HEC, under the supervision of **Frédéric Dalsace**, Danone Chair of Social Business/Firm & Poverty and Associate Professor HEC Paris and **Wolfgang Ulaga**, Professor of Marketing IMD, Switzerland. The case was written as a basis for class discussion rather than to illustrate either effective or ineffective handling of an administrative situation. We would like to thank Stéphane Mamelle at Michelin for his assistance and support. Some data have been modified for reasons of confidentiality. Printed with permission from the author and www.ecch.com.

point where International Strategy Consulting (ISC – name disguised), a well-known consulting firm, had been appointed a few months earlier to help fix the problem. Clearly, drastic steps were required to keep MFS alive.

As he entered the building, Jonas met Pierre Dupuis, Michelin Fleet Solutions Director in Europe. They immediately discussed the most recent German sales figures. MFS's future critically depended upon its ability to succeed in this key market. They met Jean Baudriard, who was the European Director of the Truck and Buses (TB) Division. Typical of Michelin career paths, Jean had joined the company right after graduating as an engineer and had been working with Michelin for the past 30 years in various functions, including R&D, manufacturing, and sales. After a quick handshake, he immediately jumped to his main concern: "The Board members have added MFS on their next meeting's agenda. It's an explosive topic, and we must come up with clear recommendations. Should the company keep on developing this solution business? Should the MFS offer be repackaged? Or should it simply be abandoned? These are the questions we have to discuss today!"

UNDERSTANDING THE BUSINESS ENVIRONMENT

The Transportation Industry and Its Challenges

Jean Baudriard, TB Division Director, started the meeting by sharing insights from the latest market research on the transportation industry. "Road transportation has still the lion's share in the European market: 44 percent of European goods are transported by trucks, and this should not decrease as road transportation companies provide unequalled flexibility and competitive price. We expect 3 percent growth a year for road freight transport. The importance of door-to-door and just-in-time services further reinforces this competitive advantage. But keep in mind that transportation companies suffer from a negative image, as they are seen as a main source of CO_2 emissions. This really is under much political attention, and the idea of developing a carbon footprint responsibility for transportation companies is making its way."

Pierre, MFS Director, observed "There is an impressive consolidation process in this industry. Within only a few decades, truly European players have emerged, and this is unlikely to stop considering that 80 percent of European transportation companies still operate with less than 5 trucks. Small players are ideal targets for external growth. Take Geodis or Norbert Dentressangle, for instance: they have embarked on a substantial acquisition program to increase their network, and they are seriously seeking to challenge Schenker and DHL as market leaders." There were about 1,500 of such large European fleets, rapidly growing, and evolving in a hyper-competitive market.

"It is not only about consolidation, they have also changed their business model. Large transportation companies have now become genuine logistics service providers, with a dedicated logistics division offering a wide array of services from transportation outsourcing, supply chain management to one-stop shopping solutions," added Jonas Pills. A great number of retailers, consumer goods manufacturers, or automotive companies indeed increasingly relied on so-called "third party logistics" for their non-strategic processes (e.g. product delivery, inventory management, etc…), thus targeting higher returns on assets and increased flexibility in their supply chain.

The Truck and Buses Tire Industry

Truck and bus tires (TB tires) represent 27 percent of the tires sold in the world, and are the second tire market after passenger cars (60 percent). All tire makers have a broad and deep TB tire mix, as these tires must to be adapted to various road and usage conditions (e.g., highway, off-road, city, trailers…). Europe, a relatively mature market, accounts for 29 percent of the world's TB tire business, with 24.5 million tires sold in 2002.

The Truck and Buses tire market is relatively consolidated with Michelin, Bridgestone and Goodyear accounting for almost 18 percent of the market each. However, low-cost Asian firms are increasingly gaining traction. Considering that a tire is a labor-intensive product, competition from China and/or Korea is indeed a real threat. For example, in the same category, a Michelin TB tire (400 €/unit) and a Bridgestone tire (350 €/unit) are relatively close in terms of pricing, at least relative to the Chinese equivalent, aggressively priced below (at 250 €/unit). In this industry, price is a powerful selling argument, as some customers typically view tires as highly commoditized "dirty black things."

Truck and Buses Tires Within the Michelin Group

Michelin's mission is to "contribute to the mobility of goods and people" and the tire business accounts for 99 percent of the group's revenues. With global revenues of 15.6 billion Euros for 2002, the Michelin group is one of the three dominant players in the consolidated tire industry (Michelin 19.6 percent; Bridgestone 18.6 percent, Goodyear 18.2 percent market shares). It employs more than 125,000 people worldwide, has 70 industrial sites in 18 countries and a sales presence in more than 170 countries. Michelin strongly focuses on research and development and is acknowledged as the industry's leader in technology, offering premium tires and driving the market. The Truck and Buses division accounts for 25 percent of overall sales in 2002 and 40 percent of the group operating result.

Though usually considered as a simple commodity, TB tires are highly sophisticated and complex products (**Exhibits 1** and **2**). The TB tire market consists of two distinct but interdependent market segments: the "Original Equipment" market (OE) for truck manufacturers and the "Replacement" market (RT) for transportation companies.

Original Equipment is the original tire fitting on brand-new vehicles. Michelin's OE market share is around 65 percent in Europe. The main clients are truck manufacturers such as Mercedes, Man, Iveco or Renault. On this segment, transportation companies play an important prescriptive role as they decide what tire brands should be installed on their trucks. Michelin's sales people actively encourage these customers to request that their new vehicles be equipped with Michelin tires.

Replacement is the other avenue for the TB tire market. Tires wear out faster than the vehicle itself; as such, several replacements are necessary, making this market the most important with 80 percent of TB tires sales. On this RT market, price plays a critical role, and Michelin's market share in Europe is 21 percent.

Truck and Buses Tires in the Eyes of Distributors

Michelin addresses the replacement market almost exclusively through professional tire distributors. These distributors usually sell tires for different vehicles (trucks and cars) and from different brands. TB tires are service-intensive: they require constant monitoring, regular maintenance and repair, tasks which are time-consuming and require professional expertise (**Exhibit 2**). As a consequence, distributors often have a complementary service business, performing some tire maintenance activities.

Distributors are independent local or regional entrepreneurs or bigger networks. Among those distribution networks is Euromaster, Michelin's own distribution network created in 1994. It acts as an autonomous entity inside the group, selling both Michelin and competitors' brands. Euromaster has 1,700 centers in 10 European countries and employs 11,800 people.

EXHIBIT 1   Tire Basics

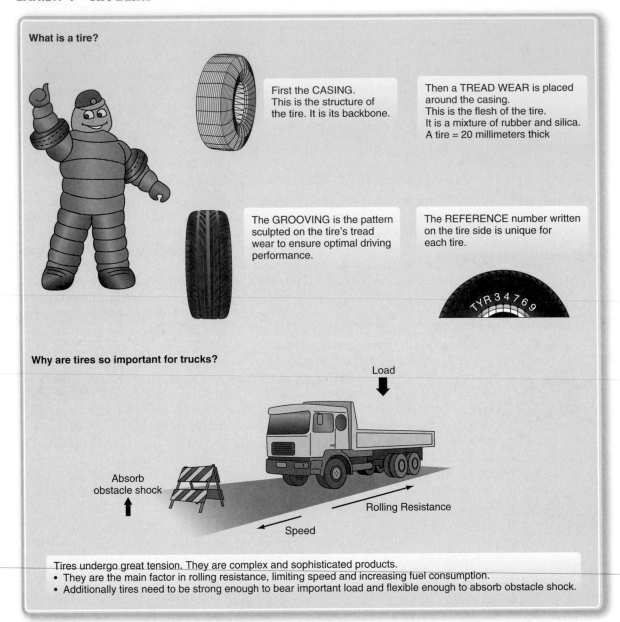

Truck and Buses Tires in the Eyes of End Users

Though they only account for 5 percent of a truck's running cost, TB tires play an important role for road transportation companies for two main reasons. First, tire-related breakdowns (e.g., punctured tires) have become the most frequent reason for a truck to stop, as engines' reliability dramatically increased. Second, tires have a strong impact on fuel consumption, the second most important cost factor after personnel. Twenty percent to 40 percent of a truck's consumption is directly linked to tires. "Tires are the easiest and most effective way to decrease a truck's environmental impact. If legal requirements call for carbon footprint reduction, they will become even more critical," observed Jean.

EXHIBIT 2   TB Tire, a Service-Intensive Product

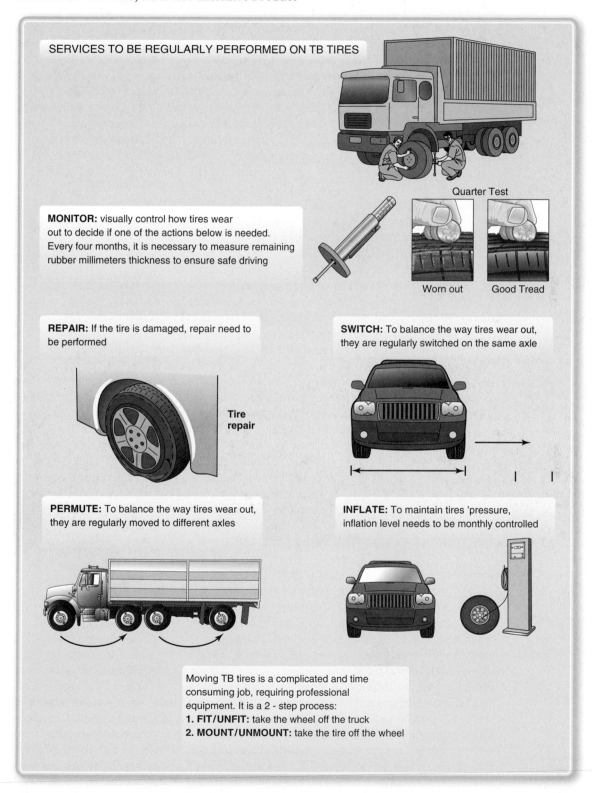

SERVICES TO BE REGULARLY PERFORMED ON TB TIRES

MONITOR: visually control how tires wear out to decide if one of the actions below is needed. Every four months, it is necessary to measure remaining rubber millimeters thickness to ensure safe driving

Quarter Test

Worn out   Good Tread

REPAIR: If the tire is damaged, repair need to be performed

Tire repair

SWITCH: To balance the way tires wear out, they are regularly switched on the same axle

PERMUTE: To balance the way tires wear out, they are regularly moved to different axles

INFLATE: To maintain tires 'pressure, inflation level needs to be monthly controlled

Moving TB tires is a complicated and time consuming job, requiring professional equipment. It is a 2 - step process:
1. **FIT/UNFIT:** take the wheel off the truck
2. **MOUNT/UNMOUNT:** take the tire off the wheel

In buying TB tires, most transportation companies adopt a multiple-sourcing strategy, buying different brands of tires for their vehicles and sourcing them from different distribution networks. With market consolidation, purchasing is becoming more professional, moving from an exclusive focus on price to a logic emphasizing "total costs of ownership" (TCO). In addition, international customers increasingly aim at consolidating tire-related processes across units and countries.

"With the most expensive tire on the market, we constantly need to justify our price premium to our clients," explained Jean. "Historically, we have always emphasized the longevity of our tires as our key selling point. Despite the progress made by our competitors we still have an edge here, as we estimate that our tires last an average of 200,000 kms, vs. 160,000 kms for competition. However, this advantage only materializes when our tires are properly taken care of. This is where we have a problem. Whenever service jobs are poorly performed, transportation companies don't get the most out of our tires. As a consequence, they are reluctant to pay a price premium."

Michelin designed long ago an ideal roadmap entitled '4-lives program' designed to maximize tire performance through optimal maintenance activities. Michelin's tire casings are specifically designed to allow both regrooving and retreading (**Exhibit 3**). "Regrooving means redesigning the tread pattern. It costs on average 50€ and extends the tire life by 25 percent. Retreading means that an entirely new tread wear is applied to the casing; this can be done only once, and is possible only because our casings are very robust. Retreading has a dramatic effect; while it costs around 150€, the end product is a tire that looks like new, lasts as long as a new tire and can later be regrooved again. When this program is correctly implemented, our tires last 2.5 times more than the average tire lifecycle and are no longer the most expensive on the market!", boasted Jean Baudriard.

While conceptually appealing, mastering the process in real operations is however much more difficult. Due to poor maintenance, the tires' full potential was indeed only rarely achieved. For instance, determining when exactly a tire needs retreading requires expertise and strong logistical command. "Trucks are the transportation firms' key assets, but by design these assets keep moving throughout Europe. This makes the tire maintenance quite difficult to organize" said Jean Baudriard. Indeed, transportation companies usually struggle with implementation, and the observed retreading rate is typically poor (50 percent vs a potential of 70 percent). As a consequence, customers were reluctant to pay a price premium.

STARTING TO SELL KILOMETERS

Michelin's Initial Presence in Services

As early as in the 20's, Michelin had experienced an alternative way to selling tires. In France, Michelin's R&D engineers' offered to take charge of selected customers' tire management as a way to perform tire testing under 'real conditions'. At about the same time, in the UK, the company had been offering tire management to coach fleets as a way to cope with a shortage of supply in that country. This agreement was still in place 70 years later. Both initiatives, though not strategically developed, generated more than 90 million euros in revenues in 2000.

The initial experience gained in both countries raised much attention and was soon seen as a unique opportunity for growth. As Michelin's R&D department frequently stated "Our tires last longer than any other but only if they are well managed. If we take charge of tire management, we will make sure that our clients can experience our unique value." Pierre Dupuis, MFS Director had a complementary view: "As our tires last longer, revenues coming from tire-related services will also last longer. We may end up making more money from tire-related services than from our traditional business."

EXHIBIT 3   The 4-Lives Program

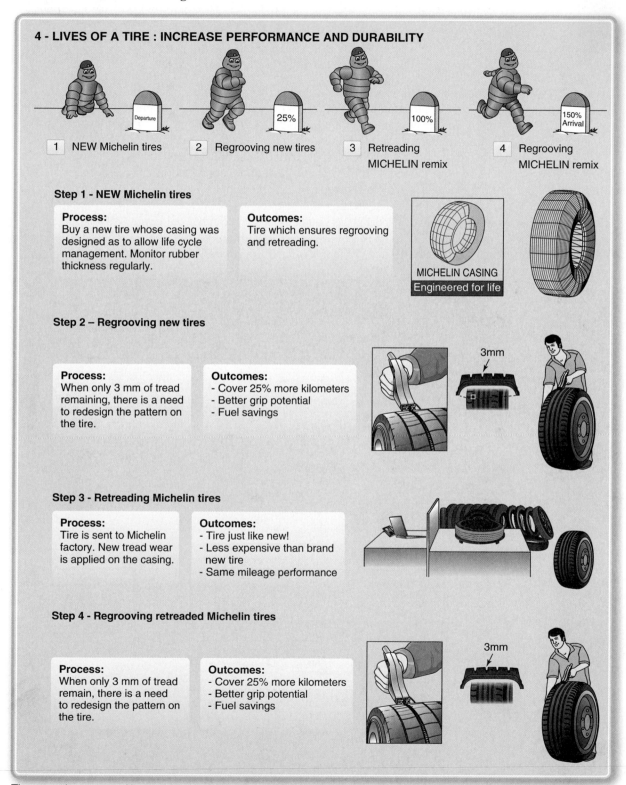

4 - LIVES OF A TIRE : INCREASE PERFORMANCE AND DURABILITY

| 1 NEW Michelin tires | 2 Regrooving new tires | 3 Retreading MICHELIN remix | 4 Regrooving MICHELIN remix |

Departure — 25% — 100% — 150% Arrival

Step 1 - NEW Michelin tires

Process:
Buy a new tire whose casing was designed as to allow life cycle management. Monitor rubber thickness regularly.

Outcomes:
Tire which ensures regrooving and retreading.

MICHELIN CASING
Engineered for life

Step 2 – Regrooving new tires

Process:
When only 3 mm of tread remaining, there is a need to redesign the pattern on the tire.

Outcomes:
- Cover 25% more kilometers
- Better grip potential
- Fuel savings

3mm

Step 3 - Retreading Michelin tires

Process:
Tire is sent to Michelin factory. New tread wear is applied on the casing.

Outcomes:
- Tire just like new!
- Less expensive than brand new tire
- Same mileage performance

Step 4 - Regrooving retreaded Michelin tires

Process:
When only 3 mm of tread remain, there is a need to redesign the pattern on the tire.

Outcomes:
- Cover 25% more kilometers
- Better grip potential
- Fuel savings

3mm

Tires must be regrooved by a professional according to Michelin recommendations. Retreading tires also requires to take them off the truck and send them to Michelin retreading lab. Mastering such a life cycle is complex.

Michelin Fleet Solution Offer

Considering the great potential ahead, Michelin Fleet Solutions was created in 2000 as a new division under the supervision of a European Sales Director (**Exhibit 4**). The objective was to promote a new business model across Europe: no longer focusing on selling a product – i.e. tires – but providing customers with a service, that is, the ability to drive.

MFS offered large European fleets (initially fleets with more than 200 vehicles) the complete management of their tire assets during a three to five year-period. A customer could decide to contract only a part of its fleet with MFS, thus granting Michelin exclusivity for the equipment of these vehicles. By outsourcing tire management, transportation companies could expect to gain peace of mind, achieve better cost control (less breakdowns, lower fuel expenses, better operations management, less administrative burdens) and benefit from Michelin's continuous innovation. Furthermore, customers could rely on Michelin's image and reputation in case of major emergencies (i.e. road accidents). For Michelin, this was a great way to develop long-lasting relationships with growing transport players and ensure that clients would eventually experience the full value of Michelin tires. Last, offering solutions was a way to escape the commodity trap by differentiating Michelin's offer from competition.

EXHIBIT 4   Organizational Chart

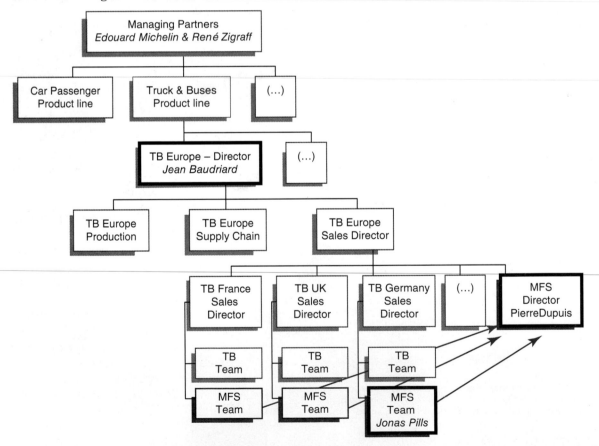

Bold boxes display protagonists in this case study.
Grey boxes represent MFS team members.

MFS charged its clients a monthly fee, which directly depended on the number of kilometers driven per vehicle. This allowed clients to turn all tire-related costs into a variable cost directly linked to the vehicle use. Vehicle fare per driven kilometer was contractually agreed upon and annually revised. Michelin's profitability depended on its ability to optimize tire management activities (such as the '4-lives program') and to control costs. "This is very different from our competitors, who charge customers for 'time and material'. For a 'time and material' customer, a truck breakdown represents an unforeseen cost factor, whereas with MFS, Michelin assumes the industrial risk in exchange for a predictable monthly fee. That's the reason why we call MFS a 'solutions offer.' Customers gain in flexibility and productivity, and we assume the industrial risk," observed Pierre Dupuis, MFS Director.

2000 Deployment

To expand this new promising model throughout Europe, Michelin added dedicated MFS sales teams to the existing traditional product sales force. To facilitate geographical expansion, the company adopted a new approach to service operations: Instead of managing fleets with its own employees placed within the transportation companies,' Michelin decided to rely on service provider networks to deliver the service to customers (**Exhibit 5**). In the meanwhile, an ambitious information system project was launched to support fleet management operations.

Disappointing Results

Within three years, 50 contracts were signed in 10 different countries, generating 70 million euros in annual revenue. These results were however disappointing. The sales force dedicated to MFS had a hard time selling the new solution offer. As one MFS sales man noted "This is a new job, and my tire expertise can hardly help me. Our product edge is no longer at the heart of the offer... I find it difficult to show the clients the value of this solution offer. We also face real problems in pricing: clients don't immediately see why they should pay more for tire management solutions than they used to pay when they only bought tires! They do not see the value brought by the extra activities we perform and the scope is so large that I find it difficult to list all these benefits. This solution offer is really very complex to sell!"

Difficulties went well beyond the contracting phase. Many fleets under contract were chronically unprofitable, and it was not uncommon to hear MFS Managers complain "We are losing our shirt here! We underestimated by far the costs involved. Whatever our ability to optimize costs, it will never be profitable with such low fees!" Correctly assessing the fee in the contractual phase was indeed very complex and the long-term implications of contractual agreements were often underestimated.

Conflict with the traditional product sales force was another big concern. "There is fierce competition between us. Product sales people can't stand us chasing after their biggest clients. I remember a meeting with a prospect client about six months ago to promote tire solutions. The customer had just met a week before with a Michelin product salesman openly criticizing our offer. We are both from the same company. This is just crazy."

In Germany, results for 2002 were disappointing with only 5,000 vehicles under contract out of an overall potential of 250,000 vehicles. Because this market accounted for 21 percent of sales in Europe, it was very important to succeed there. Conversely, failing on this market was simply threatening the mere existence of MFS. Jonas, MFS Manager in Germany, explained "The clients we approach understand what we offer but they do not see the extra value we bring. Additionally they see different downsides in this offer such as higher upfront cost, increased dependence, or high switching costs. To be honest, we don't do a good job in explaining to our customers the value they gain from working with us!" So far, competition was still quite scarce: only a few local actors were considering offering tire management solutions. However, it was acknowledged that Goodyear and Bridgestone would soon enter the market with competitive offers. It was high time to secure a substantial first mover advantage!

Consultants Come In

To solve these issues, ISC, a well-known international strategy consultancy firm was assigned in spring 2002 to investigate the reasons for MFS's poor performance. The consulting firm identified four important marketing issues regarding segmentation practices, selling, contracting and managing the relationships with third parties.

Client Segmentation

To meet profitability targets, ISC encouraged MFS to capture more value from customers by implementing a needs-based segmentation scheme. The underlying idea was that transportation companies had different priorities depending on the type of goods they transported such as bulk material, time pressured goods, or highly dangerous chemicals. MFS, the consultants said, had to design customized bundles to address these specific customer needs. ISC stressed that willingness to pay greatly varied according to the segments.

Sales Force Support

Michelin's sales force had a very hard time selling Fleet Solutions. Due to the nature of such contracts, selling MFS was a more complex process leading to longer sales cycles. As one sales manager recalled: "MFS is radically different from selling tires. I used to interact with local tire buyers, now I deal with the national Purchasing Director of large European transportation companies! These guys talk another language, and we need to roll out other arguments."

The consultancy firm conducted a massive training campaign, providing the sales force with new tools such as consistent contracting process and a new client-focused logic, shifting away from a historically strong product orientation. "Talk about the client, not about the tire!" became a guideline.

Contracting Process

ISC further encouraged Michelin to clarify its contract structure. The consultancy had found more than 72 different contract versions, each greatly varying in content. This increased confusion and complexity. The consultant advised MFS to streamline its contract structure around a small set of simple and comprehensive standards, with fee estimates, which could be complemented by additional options. This would facilitate sales people's job and increase the profitability of the contracts signed.

Turn Distributors into Close Service Providers

ISC also recommended fostering strong relationships with distributors to motivate them to cooperate with MFS as true service providers. Distributors were at first pretty unhappy to see Michelin entering the service domain. They feared the company would take away their clients, leading to massive revenue decrease. Only in a second phase, did they start to see the possible advantages of the MFS offer. As Jonas Pills explained, "It is a good opportunity for them. We bring new business at no cost. They also recognize they don't have the critical size to serve such big European accounts. Instead of performing services under their name, they now perform it under Michelin's name and altogether they get higher revenues!" Service providers, as the consultancy firm clearly stressed, played a critical role in MFS European roll-out model, as they now prescribed and delivered services to clients in the name of Michelin (**Exhibit 5**).

TIME FOR DISCUSSION AND DECISION

A few months after the consultancy work, the situation was still below expectations. Business expansion was anemic; profitability was terrible, giving voice to internal opponents who openly criticized MFS's long-term viability. Additionally, several Board members started to ask some hard questions about when MFS was to gain traction. It was in this context, that Jonas Pills, Pierre Dupuis and Jean Baudriard had to review the situation and decide upon MFS future.

Sales Force Progress

Pierre Dupuis, MFS Director, started by pointing at the significant progress made by Michelin's sales force: "Training programs have brought their first results, and we now

EXHIBIT 5   European Roll-Out Models

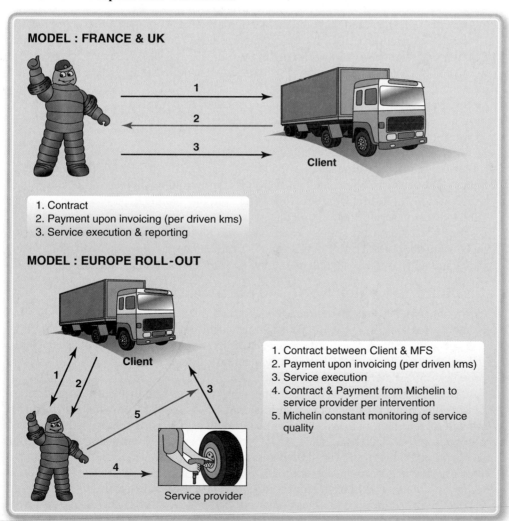

perform much better. Recent contracts should be profitable. Our efforts of educating customers show results. They now understand much better the benefits of outsourcing tire-management".

Jean Baudriard, Director of TB Europe, underlined the conflicting relationship between traditional product sales teams and MFS teams. "We still have a big issue here: Sales Directors complain to me very often. They fear that the development of managed fleets will lead to sales decline in the replacement market. Some of them are still very angry that their top performing sales people were moved to MFS three years ago. In the future, we really need to find ways to better coordinate actions and objectives". Tensions mostly came from conflicting interests: while the traditional product sales force's objective was to place as many tires as possible and to increase tire-related sales, MFS in turn, by its very nature, aimed at getting the most out of existing tires, thus potentially harming the sales of new tires. This was a thorn in the eye of Michelin's traditional sales force, which was compensated on the basis of the number of tires sold. The fact that MFS allowed Michelin to gain new customers and secure existing accounts did little to appease product sales people.

Operational Excellence

It was generally accepted that both sales and marketing were the key leverage to MFS success as advocated by ISC. Pierre Dupuis was however not at ease with such a quick conclusion. "Out of the 700 MFS employees, only 25 are Key Account Managers. It is not just about sales!" Having a professional background in the service industry, he was convinced that service execution was at the heart of turning MFS into a success. "In a solution business, signing a contract is not enough. It is just like getting married: it is only once you have signed that the real life starts. Therefore, I am not sure we should focus so much on the sales stage only."

"I think our success will depend upon operational excellence. If you investigate our past success, Michelin employees in the field play a critical role. They bring an incredible value that the clients immediately perceive. If transportation companies outsource their tire management to Michelin, it is to benefit from this unique expertise. That's why we need to excel in service delivery. In this respect, capitalizing so much on service providers may be dangerous: they become the ones who inspect the vehicles, prescribe the job, and, eventually, execute it. But, this is an incredible responsibility on their shoulders! If they don't deliver, it backfires on us. And if they do, they become a competitor."

Distributors in Their New Role of Service Providers

Tire management solutions in France and England were mostly performed by Michelin's own 450 front-line employees. "The European roll-out model is completely different: it is about entrusting some third parties with delivering Michelin's promise," concluded Pierre Dupuis. Even if Michelin had been working for a long time with service providers, never had the company relied on third-party providers to such an extent.

"From a strategic perspective, developing very close relationships with service providers could bring far-reaching strategic advantage. As we start bringing them business, we will increase our bargaining power by building a partnering relationship, where we both depend on each other. Service providers will perceive the value of working with Michelin, and not only for the solution business," thought Jean Baudriard.

Jonas provided some insight from his operational experience: "I have some clients telling me that our solution's biggest weakness is our own distribution network. This is because distributors sometimes do not fully comply with contract settings. It is true that I cannot fully guarantee the consistency of the service we provide throughout the country. It would require massive investments in quality control, reporting tools, and training of service providers. To be honest, we have underestimated these aspects, thinking that most of the job was done once we signed a contract. This is actually only the emerging part of the iceberg."

"It might however be feasible in the future," added Jonas Pills. "We have already adopted the policy of paying their performed service a little more than market value to encourage quality standards and compensate for the possible decrease of business due to a drop in replacement tires sales." Pierre Dupuis reacted: "It is a good start… but this may not be sufficient. We do not only entrust them with service execution, but also with an important part of our cost structure."

Managing Costs

As Pierre further explained, "Since we rely on service providers to optimize tires, it also means that we rely on them to optimize our cost structure. For instance, we lose money whenever the '4-lives program' is not managed properly, for example if tires are not regrooved at the right time, or if casings disappear. . . We have service providers with only 45 percent retread rate instead of the 70 percent target. We need to change the key performance indicators (KPI): it is no longer about tire sales but about the retread rate! If we can't control these issues, we are bound to be unprofitable. Furthermore, if we consider that the average millimeter (mm) of rubber potential per new tire is 15 mm to 20 mm, don't forget that anytime we are missing to exploit one single mm of rubber means adding 5 percent to 7 percent on our costs. Jonas and Jean were bewildered at the financial implication of such a figure.

Another unexpected phenomenon further deteriorated MFS margins: signing a contract had a tendency to change drivers' behavior: "There is a temptation that truck drivers behave less carefully, once they know that tires are handled by us. This can make quite a difference, as one can leave a lot of millimeters of rubber on the road."

Organizational Issue

"If we talk about cost structure, this activity brings a lot of turmoil within our legal and administrative organization", remarked Jean, "Our legal department doesn't feel comfortable with the idea of committing to multi-year contracts. What is more, I'll need to talk to our Administrative Director. She's mad at you. Our administrative people are overwhelmed with MFS invoices coming from the service providers. She says that one invoice out of three comes from your teams while you represent only 5 percent of the company business! It is incredible."

Feeling the criticism, Pierre tried to better explain why so many invoices needed processing. "That's quite unfortunate, but there is not much we can do about this. Every time a service provider performs any act on a vehicle under contract, he addresses us an invoice. Just imagine the amount of invoices coming in." Jonas discretely smiled. Relationships between MFS teams and service support were always complicated because of their specific needs. Jean had not even mentioned the specific key performance indicators MFS people kept asking for. The geographical expansion would for sure only further add to existing frictions. In addition, Michelin's legal experts would have to help assess and hedge the legal risks involved.

Information System

"I guess, it is also time to bring up the difficulties we have in running our information system," Jean added. "Do we now have a functioning tool?" "Not yet," moaned Pierre. "So far, we really failed; we do not have a thorough enough command of the process and therefore do not fully understand what the information system should provide us with. We will have to reconfigure everything, and this will take time. Part of our challenge is that it is no longer about selling tires. It is about managing complex selling and delivery processes."

MFS, Lipstick on a Pig?

"Precisely, Jean snapped. "Let me set some things straight. "This company was not designed to manage invoices or conduct never-ending IT development projects. We have been manufacturing and selling great tires successfully for decades. Our new 'Energy' tire line has unmatched fuel saving performance. I don't understand what this is all about. MFS gives us all a headache, and hurts the profit of our division. I'm not sure our Board members want to hear that story any longer." He leaned back in his chair and added: "Even if these solution offers were working properly, don't you think this is far beyond our core business? Michelin is a tire manufacturer. Full stop!""

Pierre knew that this argument would be brought up at some point. Jean had not even insisted on quoting MFS's terrible financial results in detail. After substantial investments, MFS had never been profitable once in three-years time! People legitimately started questioning the reason of supporting the program any longer… He had overheard recently some of his colleagues talking of the "MFS abyss," which was only due to the big boss having a crush on the project. Some of his MFS team members had also reported they felt looked down upon by colleagues. Even worse, one of the Board members officially referred to MFS as putting "lipstick on a pig." Pierre felt unsure: he, too, had considered the possibility of getting out, but he still believed that MFS had a great potential ahead.

TIME FOR DECISION

Jean, Pierre and Jonas were expected to provide clear recommendations on Michelin's Board meeting next month. After three years of continuous investments, struggling with implementation issues, and painful lessons learned in the process, results achieved still remained below expectations. What was to be done?

Was Michelin's strategic move to enter solutions business with Michelin Fleet Solutions the right decision? Should the company pursue this painful path? Should it repackage its existing "solution offer" and charge for "time and material" in the very same way its main competitors were doing? Or even go back to its traditional business model, i.e. manufacturing and selling tires?

If they recommended pursuing the MFS Program, how could the current turmoil be overcome? Was it mostly, as advocated by ISC, a marketing issue or were larger issues at stake?

These were some of the questions the three men had to decide upon in the coming hours, which promised to be tense and intense.

Case 5

ISS ICELAND

The Island

Iceland, an island nation in the North Atlantic located between Scotland and Greenland, had a 2009 population of 313,000 people. Citizens could trace their lineage back to the Viking adventurers who settled the island in the first millennium. Until the Second World War, Iceland was part of Denmark, and most of its customs and ideology followed the Scandinavian model. The labor market was considered flexible and liberal, and typical for Scandinavia, labor was expensive. Immigration was modest, estimated at 10,000 to 15,000 individuals.

Iceland's economy was traditionally dependent upon fisheries and had long been dominated by periods of boom and bust. Following an extended boom during which it grew extraordinarily rapidly (unemployment was 0.8 percent for most of 2008), the late 2008 financial crisis resulted in a troubled economy in 2009: all six of Iceland's major banks were nationalized, the Icelandic Kronor (ISK) lost much of its value against the Euro, and unemployment began to climb (see **Exhibit 1** for data on exchange rates and **Exhibit 2** for unemployment data). Despite these challenges, Iceland's standard of living was among the highest in the world and its infrastructure was among the most developed. Other sectors of the economy included fishing, some manufacturing, diversified services, as well as extensive use of the island's hydroelectric, and geothermal power sources.

ISS

ISS had 2008 revenues of 68,829 million DKK,[1] making it the seventh largest outsourcing company in the world. In 2009, ISS defined itself as being in "Facility Services," with numerous offerings such as cleaning (54 percent of revenues), catering, security, property services and office support. ISS was in the process of transitioning itself and its clients to what it called "Integrated Facilities Management."[2]

ISS had grown through a combination of acquisition and organic growth. The ISS business model was highly decentralized, each country acting like a separate principality, with financial reporting administered from headquarters in Copenhagen.

Despite its size, ISS was a niche player in the cleaning world. Most of its competitors were small companies that may, or may not, have adhered to local labor requirements, and benefited from having ownership in close proximity, sometimes actively supervising employees. In contrast, ISS policy required adherence to local laws and guidelines. While country management often had powerful financial incentives designed to encourage them to act like owners, actual ownership was in the hands of ISS's private equity investors, Goldman Sachs and EQT, an investment vehicle of

---

[1] 7.4 DKK = 1 Euro, 5.7 DKK = 1 US$.

[2] Integrated Facilities Management enabled a customer to outsource most aspects of managing its facilities to a third party such as ISS, which provided the services as a bundle. Adherents of the strategy believed it would help to de-commoditize the service offering by delivering a differentiated solution, as well as present opportunities for employees to grow in their jobs through cross training and advancement.

Roger Hallowell wrote this case on behalf of the Scandinavian International Management Institute (SIMI). Copyright 2009 SIMI. The case was written for class discussion rather than to illustrate either effective or ineffective handling of an administrative situation.

EXHIBIT 1
Exchange Rates

Source: www.exchange-rates.org

April 2008	1 € = 117 Icelandic Kronor
	1 $ = 80 Icelandic Kronor
April 2009	1 € = 168 Icelandic Kronor
	1 $ = 127 Icelandic Kronor

EXHIBIT 2
Icelandic Unemployment

Source: www.icenews.is

2008 (most of year):	0.8%
October 2008:	1.9%
April 2009:	8.2% (9.4% men, 6.6% women)

Sweden's Wallenberg family. As a result, ISS was rarely the price leader in a market, instead tailoring its value proposition to those customers who cared about quality and were willing to pay for it.

ISS ICELAND

Before

The Iceland operation was acquired by ISS in 2000. At the time it was approximately twice as large as its nearest competitor. Guðmundur Guðmundsson[3] worked for the company before the acquisition, being made CEO in 2000, a position he still held in 2009. He commented:

Before the acquisition we were a traditional command and control organization. We had rigid job descriptions and job rules, including processes for accomplishing work. Supervisors' jobs were to inspect quality and ensure productivity. We believed it wasn't fair for a cleaner to have 200 bosses (remember that everyone believes they are an expert on cleaning), so we insisted that all requests and comments from customers go through the ISS supervisor assigned to the account, or the ISS office. This resulted in time lags and loss of information.

We also had a detailed process for dealing with complaints, but it wasn't focused on either customer or employee satisfaction. The number of complaints received was a key metric, and we used it to "send a signal" to a supervisor. As a result, supervisors spent their time focused on conducting inspections and communicating problems. I typically got two or three calls each day in which a customer was yelling at me. Once a week I was told, "This is your last chance." There was a lot of fire fighting—in many ways we were managing to the complaints. It was not a learning process; we fixed the complaint, but not the underlying problem.

Our supervisors worked set hours, generally 13:00 (1:00 PM) until 20:00 (8:00 PM). They were required to be at their desks at our headquarters from 13:00 until 15:00 for what we called "phone time." After that they went into the field to conduct inspections with the goal of finding what was wrong, in order to prevent complaints.

Our system was based on control and inspection; it was complex and the results were insufficient.

---

[3]The Icelandic ð was pronounced like the letter "d" in English.

A New Value Proposition

Following the acquisition in 2000, ISS Iceland adopted a new value proposition. According to Guðmundsson:

> The new value proposition has two dimensions: the first is that of the classic outsourcer, enabling our customers to focus on what they do best, leaving non-core tasks, for example cleaning, to us. The second has to do with defining "What business are we in?" or rather, "What is the feeling we want to create in our customers?" We express it by saying, "We are creating wellbeing for our customers." This posed a problem for us. We knew that too often our employees didn't feel good about their jobs, and we knew that if you don't feel good about your job, it's hard to feel good about yourself. As a result, we had to ask, "Can employees who aren't feeling good about themselves, or their job, create wellbeing in customers?" The answer had to be no, at least on a long-term basis.
>
> There were two other related issues: first, I believe that people who don't feel good about themselves are not as productive or quality-minded. Second, given the transition the company was making from night work (cleaning only), toward integrated facilities management, where more and more of our employees work alongside our customers in the day, how employees appear—which reflects how they feel about their jobs—matters. We concluded from all of these issues that we had to do something about employee wellbeing.

Enhancing Employee Wellbeing to Increase Customer Satisfaction

Before 2000, sources of complaints were not tracked. In 2000, Guðmundsson began to track the reasons behind complaints, and learned that 50 percent were due to lack of information among users. For example, if a customer went from five-day-per-week cleaning to three-day-per-week cleaning, but didn't inform their end users, complaints would be filed when no one came in Tuesday and Thursday. A more thorough analysis of complaints led Guðmundsson to believe that approximately 95 percent of work was being done to contract standards and that 95 percent of ISS employees came to work intending to do their best, but that communication was failing. He therefore set out to fix communication.

In 2000, communication was centered on what was wrong, specifically the 5 percent of work that wasn't in-compliance. Because complaints were the basis of communication, management was focused on the negative, resulting in what executives called "less-than-satisfied" employees.

Guðmundsson discussed the working environment:

> Keep in mind that cleaners get to work when others go home. They largely work alone. No one is interested in their job or contribution, but everyone has an opinion if something is missed. It is like working in a "vacuum;" you don't communicate and you don't get positive feedback.

Communication also focused customers on the negative. According to an executive, "When all conversations focus on what's wrong, even when those problems are only minor, the customer is left with the feeling that something really is wrong." He continued, "It also sends customers the signal that service quality is binary (either right or wrong), which excludes the possibility of customers receiving more value than they expect and being "delighted."

Reversing this negative spiral required a change in philosophy. According to Guðmundsson:

> Even with all of our supervisors, the average ISS worker will often go a week or two without contact from the office. We require supervisors to see employees at least once a month, but that isn't often. The first question we had to answer was "Can we trust our

people?" Some managers argued, "Sure—but control is better." My argument was "If we can't trust these people, we can't have them working for us." Fortunately, we came to the conclusion that we can trust them—and we found out that by trusting people, we made our lives so much easier. But we quickly learned that if we were going to trust them, we needed to manage them differently.

Managing workers differently started with creating a customized value proposition for each employee. This began by understanding their needs as individuals. A supervisor provided an example, "I had a hippie lady who was a great cleaner, but was miserable in her job. Once I figured out that she was a 'night person' who had been given a day shift, I was able to change her hours and she came alive."

Managing differently included giving responsibility to employees. Instead of management dictating how to get the work done, employees were given the tools and training that they needed and allowed to decide who did what job and when, including setting their schedules based on their needs and the customer's.

Other dimensions of managing differently included (1) cross training whenever possible in order to increase independence and make work more interesting, and (2) motivating employees to communicate with customers.

Guðmundsson recognized that these changes would not be successful unless he could change the basis of communication between both (a) the customers and the company, and (b) the supervisors and workers. At the time, that basis was complaints, and was thus overwhelmingly negative. He commented:

I knew we had a problem, but I didn't have the solution. I wanted to change our focus from focusing on the 5 percent that was wrong to focusing on the 95 percent that was right, while still fixing the 5 percent. I looked around for best practices, and found a company in Finland called SOL. It had a simple philosophy: "trust people, give them freedom, praise them." We had already decided to trust people and to give them freedom, but we were missing the praise.

Giving and Getting "a Praise"

We wanted the context for communication with customers to be appropriate. Given that 95 percent of our interactions with customers were positive, we felt that most communication should be in a positive context. The question was, how to make that happen—especially after we had trained our customers to communicate with us in a negative, complaint context. A praise solved this for us.

COO Jón Trausti

"A praise" was the expression used to refer to the first question on ISS Iceland's customer satisfaction survey, specifically, "Is there something you can praise the cleaner or the service for?" (See **Exhibit 3**.) An employee got "a praise" when he or she was mentioned in response to the question. Managers believed that while the question surprised some customers, the vast majority liked it. According to a manager, "It created the opportunity for a more constructive and professional dialogue with customers, placing the interaction in a positive context—this changed the mindset of the customers, leaving them with the feeling that most of what we did was good." As customers became accustomed to providing praise, they began to do so without being asked, as in **Exhibit 4**. Any praise resulted in recognition for the employee and general celebration.

An employee spoke about getting a praise:

You get a praise and you want more. You also become more open—I feel more free to receive praise, and I am less defensive—it makes moving forward so much easier.

EXHIBIT 3   ISS Iceland Customer Satisfaction Survey

1) Is there something you can praise the cleaner or the service for?

2) How have we done in meeting your expectations?

3) How responsive is ISS when you have a problem or need something extra?

4) How could we improve the service we deliver to you?

Responses could be both quantitative (a scale was provided) and qualitative.

EXHIBIT 4   ISS Iceland Unsolicited Customer Praise: Three Customer E-Mails

Subject:	Praise about the food
Message:	I am very satisfied with the meals. The salad has a lot of variety and the meals have been very good for a long time. The fish is always excellent. Best thanks and keep going.
Subject:	Classroom cleaning
Message:	I am a teacher who is very satisfied with the cleaning in the classroom. It is very well done. In the morning the chalkboard is always very clean, and sometimes the cleaner has also cleared up the desk. I want to praise the cleaners and send them my appreciation.
Subject:	The positive presence of a cleaner
Message:	We recently changed to a daytime cleaning from night time. I have to admit I was in doubt, or almost prejudiced. How wrong I was. The cleaner is so positive and cheerful, polite and somehow manages to organize her job around the office, without us almost noticing. The best thing is that rather than letting small things annoy me, I can ask her to fix them, and she does it with a smile.

NB: These e-mails sound somewhat awkward as they are translated from the Icelandic with minimal interpretation.

Two employees described how they felt about their jobs and receiving praise:

You have to make your work plan because you will be working alone. You are the general manager, the worker, and the quality inspector. If you do well, you hear it, and that makes you feel good. . . The supervisor knows you're doing a good job, and you know you're doing a good job, but you don't get ignored because things are good.

Over the ten years I was in my previous job I was never given a pat on the back and told, "well done." When I started here I could feel the positive attitude and the trust. . . It's more like family work here.

It was the supervisors' duty to bring "a praise" earned by an employee to him or her, and, importantly, to use it as a learning process to enable the employee to do even better in the future.

Role of the Supervisor

According to an executive, "Supervisors were crucial in bridging the gap between the employee in the field and the company." By 2001 it was clear that the traditional role of the supervisor was no longer optimal in the new model. The supervisors' role changed from "prevent complaints" to "enable praises." Pragmatically, this meant that their visits to employees changed from "inspections" to "support." To enable that change, job conditions and (often) the type of person in the job needed to change.

Supervisors' hours became totally flexible, their results being measured in customer satisfaction and worker efficiency, as opposed to hours worked. Supervisors were no

EXHIBIT 5
Operations
Organization
Structure

CEO
⋮
COO
⋮
3 Service Managers
⋮
26 Supervisors
⋮
900 Workers (800 in Reykjavik region)

longer asked to be at their desks in the office at specific times. Instead, they were given a mobile phone, and a car. If they chose to come into the office, they had access to a workstation and support from managers (see the organization chart in **Exhibit 5**). Workstations required less space than individual desks, enabling ISS to remain at the same headquarters location despite growth.

Some supervisors relished this new flexibility; others found it difficult to manage. A former supervisor commented:

> There is stress. You're "on" 24/7. You have to make everyone happy, customer first, employee second, company third. Everyone wants a little piece of you, and you want to do well for everyone.

Many supervisors successfully embraced the challenge of work/life balance, in part through a program ISS established creating teams of supervisors that enabled calls to be funneled to an "on-call" individual.[4] Others came to resent the new model, largely due to their inability to "shut off" work during parts of the day. Most of those chose to leave the position. Overall, the company was regarded as a leader in work/life balance, being recognized with a first place award in enabling work/life balance through flexibility based on a study of Icelandic companies conducted by the city of Reykjavik in conjunction with the European Union and the Gallop Research Organization.

The source of supervisors changed from former cleaners and other cleaning organizations' supervisory staff to teachers and other professionals who enjoyed "helping people." These new supervisors had strong opinions about their employees. According to one:

> I'm sure that you need to spend more time hiring and training to be sure you're getting the right person with the right attitudes, and to ensure that person has the right skills. Cleaning can be a lonely job—working after everyone else has gone home. For some people it's wonderful, but it's not for everyone.

Change could also be seen in what supervisors chose to do, and not to do. According to a senior manager, "Supervisors used to jump in and do the cleaning themselves. They don't do that anymore—supervisors have 20–30 customers and up to 50 employees, so they can't."

Trausti, COO since 1999, commented on the changes in supervisors:

> Before 2000 the supervisors weren't allowed to make any decisions. Now, we say, "The customers are *your* customers. You hire and fire employees, and brief us once a month."

---

[4]Supervisors formed teams by choosing a colleague who knew enough about their customer and employee portfolios to back them up during hours when they were off duty and not able to be reached.

Of course, the service managers review customer and employee data, and we have monthly meetings with the supervisors to discuss issues and review documentation.

It isn't always easy for the supervisors. We tell them they may not focus on the negative. They have to start a meeting with an employee by talking about what's going well. And it has to be sincere. After that they can share what needs to improve. I spend four hours with every small group of new supervisors giving training on how to provide praise. It's not easy for us in Iceland—we are so focused on sincerity that praise has to be grounded in facts.

A supervisor commented on receiving praise herself:

Supervisors have to be reminded to praise, and we need to get praise regularly. Sometimes you have to go fishing for a praise—that's not good, except that it reminds you to go out and give your cleaners some praise.

Supervisors earned 370,000 ISK per month (including car and phone). Salaries were fixed with bonuses insignificant. In contrast, a teacher with 35 years experience earned 265,000 ISK per month. Cleaners earned 170,000 ISK. A supervisor described her feelings about motivation:

In Iceland most people don't do things for a bonus. We like to cooperate, we like to be trusted, and we like flexibility. At ISS there is an attitude I would describe as, "I trust you, but you have to show me the results." People who are willing to deliver the results feel well in their work here because of the trust, the freedom, and the positive thinking.

RESULTS

Complaints had declined dramatically since 2000. According to Trausti:

When I started as COO in 1999 I got several calls from unsatisfied customers every day. Now, I get 2–3 a year. Why? Because we have fewer problems, and those we have are dealt with by the employees and supervisors quickly.

Customer satisfaction data was unavailable due to the fact that ISS Iceland's database provider had gone bankrupt in 2008, making historical data inaccessible.

Employee turnover declined steadily from a high of 131 percent in 1999 to 69 percent in 2007 (unemployment never rose above 3.4 percent during that period).

Cross sell was believed to have benefited from higher levels of customer satisfaction occurring since 2000. One example was ISS's entering the catering business, described by a senior manager, "We started catering in 2006. We're now the third largest caterer in Iceland. Forty percent of the catering customers are new to ISS. Sixty percent used us for another service. Now we're working on cross selling catering-only customers our cleaning services."

Guðmundsson discussed customer retention, "We haven't lost a major customer in years. We've come close, but we've been able to save the relationships—we recently had an incident where we saved a relationship due to the particular worker we had on site. Of course, retention may change with the recession." **Exhibit 6** shows annual revenue lost as a percent of sales.

Revenue growth averaged 17.6 percent during the 2000–2007 period, the majority of which was organic.

EXHIBIT 6 ISS Iceland Contract Losses as a Percent of Sales

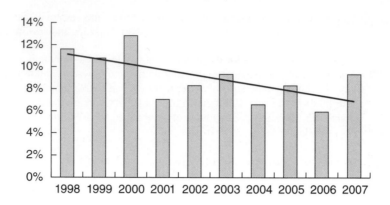

CONCLUSION

By 2009 ISS Iceland was six times larger than its largest competitor.[5] Services provided included daily office cleaning, hospital cleaning, food hygiene, catering, and industrial cleaning. Executives noted that the changes they had initiated had improved employee and customer wellbeing, but that the programs were getting old and needed to have, in their words, "new life breathed into them." While the economic climate had dramatically changed, recruiting employees remained a challenge. Guðmundsson had seen different companies outside of financial services take different approaches to the recession. Some cut all non-essential expenses and focused entirely on getting basic work done. Others were exploiting the downturn, cutting costs where possible, but also investing in those areas they believed would contribute to their differentiation to enhance growth once the economy recovered.

In this context, Guðmundsson pondered:

> Praise has become second nature at ISS Iceland. But we aren't over doing it—people aren't getting a praise for just doing their job, and they shouldn't. Still, how do I keep people talking about the importance of praise? Our database provider went bankrupt a year ago, and since then we haven't sent out a customer survey asking for a praise. What should we do to not only keep this topic alive, but to take it to the next level?

In Copenhagen, ISS Executives were also asking questions in a somewhat similar context. They had the task of ensuring that ISS was exploiting potential synergies, while navigating the company though the worldwide recession. While ISS was what could be described as a "responsible" private equity holding, it did have considerable debt (see **Exhibit 7**). Should headquarters executives be spreading the ideas about praise developed in Iceland throughout the ISS world?[6] Or, was this the time to retrench the company and allow local managers to operate as they thought best without interference from headquarters?

[5] 2008 results for ISS Iceland showed revenue of 134 million DKK that placed it 40th out of the 50 countries for which ISS reported results. 2008 Operating margin was 7.6 percent, placing ISS Iceland as the 7th most profitable (as a percent of sales) country at ISS. In 2007, ISS Iceland reported 173 million DKK in revenue (ranking 31st) with a 7.7 percent profit margin (10th most profitable in 2007).

[6] Executives recognized that "praise" was a culturally sensitive topic and that any program involving praise would need to be tailored for local cultural issues. Even in the relatively homogeneous Icelandic environment, cultural sensitivity was in issue as Icelandic women felt that, for example, men from Poland found receiving praise from a woman to be awkward, and praise to men or women from Asia had to be given extremely carefully.

EXHIBIT 7   ISS Consolidated Financials (abridged)

Source: www.ISSWorld.com

Amounts in DKK millions (unless otherwise stated)	2008	2007	2006	2005[1]
Revenue	68,829	63,922	55,772	31,741
Operating profit before other items	4,061	3,635	3,234	1,932
Operating margin before other items, %[2]	5.9	6.0	5.8	6.1
EBITDA [2]	4,622	4,484	3,764	1,979
Adjusted EBITDA[2]	4,930	4,680	3,979	2,383
Operating profit[2]	3,753	3,639	3,019	1,528
Net finance costs	(2,731)	(3,017)	(2,351)	(1,721)
Profit before goodwill impairment/amortisation of brands and customer contracts	494	376	226	(410)
Net profit/(loss) for the year[2]	(631)	(442)	(809)	(945)
Additions to property, plant and equipment, gross	964	938	907	576
Cash flow from operating activities	4,334	3,713	3,195	2,109
Investments in intangible assets, property, plant and equipment, net	(718)	(715)	(843)	(372)
Total assets	53,605	55,348	52,253	46,456
Goodwill	27,259	27,593	26,178	22,995
Carrying amount of net debt[2]	29,385	29,245	26,271	22,741
Total equity	3,533	5,518	5,980	6,774
Financial ratios[2]				
Interest coverage	1.8	1.6	1.7	1.4
Cash conversion, %[2]	103	99	102	145
Employees on full-time, %	69	68	66	61
Number of employees	472,800	438,100	391,400	310,800
Growth				
Organic growth, %	5.3	6.0	5.5	-
Acquisitions, net, %	6	9	15	-
Currency adjustments, %	(3)	(0)	0	-
Total revenue, %	8	15	20	-

[1] The 2005 figures for ISS Holding do not represent full year figures as the company was founded on 11 March 2005, while ISS A/S was acquired on 9 May 2005.
[2] See key figures and definitions in the Annual Report 2007.

Case 6
People, Service, and Profit at Jyske Bank

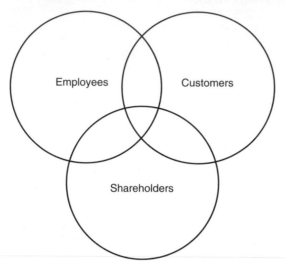

The Jyske Bank Group is managed and operated as a business. At the same time, we attach great importance to treating our three groups of stakeholders—shareholders, customers and employees—with equal respect. This is illustrated by three equally big overlapping circles which must remain in perfect balance. If the balance shifts in favor of one or two of the groups, this will be to the long-term detriment of all the groups.

—*Jyske Bank Management Philosophy*

In 2003, Jyske Bank Group's primary operations consisted of Jyske Bank, which was the third largest bank in Denmark after Den Danske Bank and Nordea's Danish operations (see **Exhibit 1**). Jyske Bank was created in 1967 through the merger of four Danish banks having their operations in Jutland, Jyske being Danish for "Jutland-ish." Jutland was the large portion of Denmark attached to the European mainland to the north of Germany. Until the late 1990s, Jyske Bank was characterized as a typical Danish bank: prudent, conservative, well-managed, generally unremarkable, and largely undifferentiated.

Beginning in the mid-1990s, Jyske Bank embarked on a change process that led to its no longer being characterized as either unremarkable or undifferentiated. By 2003 its unique "flavor" of service made it a leader in customer satisfaction among Danish banks (see **Exhibit 2**). At the heart of these changes was the bank's determination to be, in the words of one executive, "the most customer-oriented bank in Denmark." The bank achieved its goal by focusing on what it called *Jyske Forskelle,* or Jyske Differences.

This case was written by Roger Hallowell, CBS-SIMI Executive. It is intended to be used as a basis for class discussion rather than to illustrate either effective or ineffective handling of an administrative situation. The case was made possible by the cooperation of Jyske Bank.
© 2003 CBS-SIMI Executive. Printed with permission from the author and ecch.com.

EXHIBIT 1
Danish Banks
Shareholders' Equity
at January 1, 2002

Source: Jyske Bank.

	Bank	Shareholders' Equity
1.	DDB	57.091
2.*	Jyske Bank	6.174
3.	Sydbank	3.435
4.	Nykredit Bank	2.708
5.	Spar Nord	1.692
6.	Arbejdernes Landsbank	1.518
7.	Amtssparekassen Fyn	994
8.	Amargerbanken	956
9.	Sparbank Vest	841
10.	Sparekassen, Kornjylland	816
11.	Ringkøbing Landbobank	794
12.	Alm. Brand Bank	749
13.	Forstædernes Bank	706
14.	Loskilde Bank	698
15.	Lån Lan& Spar Bank	589
16.	Nørresundby Bank	583
17.	Sparekassen Sjælland	582
18.	Sparekassen Lolland	559
19.	Nordvestbank	545

*Note: Nordea is not shown as it was a Swedish bank with operations in Denmark, having acquired Unibank.

DENMARK

At the onset of the twenty-first century Denmark had a population of approximately five million. A member of the European Union retaining its own currency (the Danish Kronor, DKK[1]), Denmark was the southernmost of the Scandinavian countries. Denmark had been a wealthy country for hundreds of years. This was originally due to its strategic location in the Baltic Sea (see **Exhibit 3**) enabling it to extract tolls from merchants who were forced to sail within cannon range of its shores. More recently, much of Denmark's wealth came from high-value-added goods such as agricultural products, pharmaceuticals, machinery, instruments, and medical equipment, in addition to a highly-developed service sector including shipping.

Following the Second World War, Denmark adopted a social welfare system its government described as follows:

> The basic principle of the Danish welfare system, often referred to as the Scandinavian welfare model, is that all citizens have equal rights to social security. Within the Danish welfare system, a number of services are available to citizens, free of charge. . . . The Danish welfare model is subsidized by the state, and as a result Denmark has one of the highest taxation levels in the world.[2]

JUTLAND

Jutland was physically separated from Denmark's capital, Copenhagen (see **Exhibit 3** for a map). Copenhagen, with a population comprising almost one-quarter of all Danes, was located on the island of Zealand (*Sjaelland*). Jutland's isolation from the capital prior to modern transportation led to its people being characterized differently

[1] Euro bought approximately DKK 7.4 and U.S. $1 bought approximately DKK 6.3 as of June 10, 2003.
[2] See www.denmark.dk.

EXHIBIT 2 Danish Banks' Quality of Service Metrics

Source: survey of 1,750 small companies conducted by the Danish newspaper *Erhvervs Bladet,* 22 March 2002, p. 2.

Part I: Analysis of Bank Image						
						Chose This Bank If We Want to Change Banks
	Total Image	Willingness to Take Risk	Management	They Are a Strategic Coach for Me	Service and Customer Treatment	Expert in Advice and Competence	
Jyske Bank	1	1	1	1	1	1	1
Sydbank	2	2	3	2	2	2	2
Spar Nord Bank	3	4	4	3	3	5	5
Midtbank/ Handeslbank	4	6	7	4	6	4	7
Amagerbanken	5	3	5	6	4	8	6
Amtssparekassen Fyn	6	5	6	5	5	7	8
Nordea	7	7	8	8	7	6	3
Danske Bank	8	8	2	7	8	3	4
BG Bank	9	9	9	9	9	9	9

Part II: (A) Consumer Satisfaction Survey; Very Satisfied

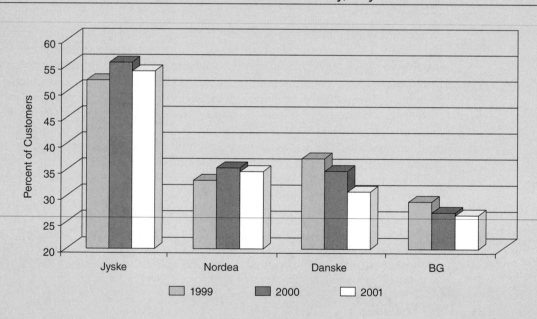

continued

EXHIBIT 2   Danish Banks' Quality of Service Metrics—continued

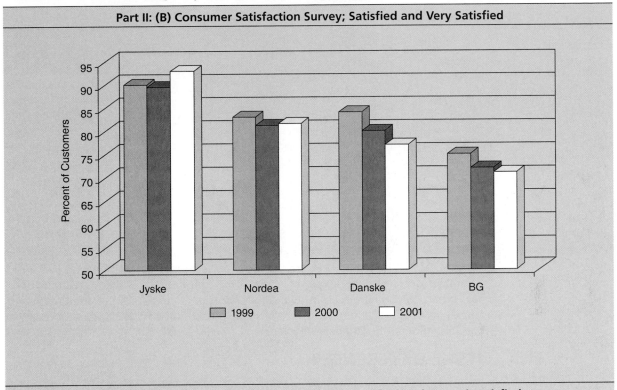

Part II: (B) Consumer Satisfaction Survey; Satisfied and Very Satisfied

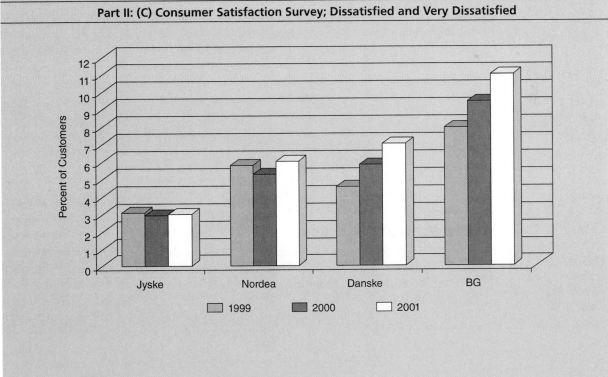

Part II: (C) Consumer Satisfaction Survey; Dissatisfied and Very Dissatisfied

EXHIBIT 3
Denmark

Source: CIA World Factbook.

from their Zealander neighbors: Jutlanders were supposed to be honest, unpretentious, egalitarian, open and direct in their communication style (candid), commonsensical, frugal, sober-minded, and relatively unsophisticated, at least in contrast to those, as one Jutlander put it, "slippery people from Copenhagen."

JYSKE DIFFERENCES

Jyske Differences stemmed from Jyske Bank's core values. These stood as central tenets, guiding virtually all aspects of the organization's life. As one manager pointed out, the values were consistent with the bank's Jyske heritage: "Really, when we started talking about our core values, and their Jyskeness, we just became overt about values we had long held." Jyske Bank's core values, published for employees, customers, and shareholders, were that the bank should (1) have common sense; (2) be open and honest; (3) be different and unpretentious; (4) have genuine interest and equal respect for people; and (5) be efficient and persevering. See **Exhibit 4** for a more detailed description.

The core values led management to reevaluate how the bank did business with its customers. Managers determined that if the bank were to be true to its values, it would have to deliver service differently from both how it had in the past, and how other banks delivered service. Jyske Differences were thus operationalized as specific practices that distinguished Jyske Bank.

Competitive Positioning

Managers looked to Jyske values and differences for the bank's competitive positioning. This process was aided by a Dutch consultant, whose market research indicated that Jyske bank's core target market of Danish families and small-to-medium sized Danish companies (earnings were 40 percent commercial, 60 percent retail) generally liked the idea of a bank that was Jyske. Additional research suggested that what managers described as the "hard factors" of price, product, and location had become *sine qua non* in the eyes of customers. In contrast, "soft factors" relating to an individual customer's relationship with her service providers served as the basis for differentiation, specifically, "being nice," "making time for the customer," and "caring about the customer and his family."

Managers felt that the "genuine interest" component of the bank's values dictated a shift from traditional product focused selling to a customer-solution approach. They characterized the new approach by contrasting the statement, "Let me tell you about our demand-deposit account," with the question, "What do you need?"

Although the bank's core financial products remained essentially similar to those of other Danish banks,[3] the way they were delivered changed. This required significant changes in the branches, both tangible and intangible, and how they were supported. Tools were developed to support solution-based service delivery. For example, new IT systems helped employees take customers through processes to determine their needs and find appropriate solutions. In one, the customer and her banker filled out an online investor profile to determine what style of investment products were most appropriate for her based on risk aversion, time frame, and return goals, among other factors. A manager commented that, "The tools themselves aren't proprietary. We've seen other financial services with similar programs—it's how our people use them that makes the difference." Another stated, "Our tools are designed either to enhance our ability to deliver solutions, or to reduce administrative tasks and increase the amount of time our people can spend with customers—delivering solutions."

Finally, being overtly Jyske meant that the bank would no longer be a good place for any customer meeting its demographic criteria for two reasons. First, delivering this type of service was expensive. As a result, the bank charged a slight premium, and targeted only those customers who were less likely to represent a credit risk. Second, the bank would have a personality. According to one manager, "The danger in having a personality is, someone, inevitably, won't like you." Senior management considered this the price of being candid, and welcomed the effect it had on some customers. For example, Jyske Bank's cash/debit card had a picture of a black grouse on it, black grouses being found in Jutland's rural countryside. When a few customers complained that the bird didn't seem very business-like, or wasn't hip (one was "embarrassed to pull it out at the disco") managers were happy to invite them to open accounts at competitor institutions. A manager noted:

> Actually, if no one reacts to our materials, they're not strong enough. Some people should dislike us. After all, we're only about 6 percent of the market. I don't want everyone to like us—we're not for everyone and don't want to be.

Tangible Differences

Account Teams

Delivering on the bank's competitive positioning required a number of tangible changes in its service delivery system. These began with assigning each customer a branch employee to serve as primary point of contact. Over time, managers discovered that this created problems, because customers often arrived at a branch when their service provider was busy with other customers or otherwise unavailable. Nevertheless, managers were committed to providing individualized service. According to one, "How can we be honest in saying we care about customers as individuals if we don't get to know them as individuals? And without knowing them, we can't identify and solve their problems." The solution was found in account teams: each customer was assigned to a small team of branch bankers. These employees worked together to know and serve their customers, sitting in close physical proximity within the branch.

---

[3]Typical core financial products included house, car, and personal loans as well as cash management and investment services for individuals, as well as loans, cash management, and investment services for small-to-medium sized companies. Jyske Bank did not offer credit cards.

EXHIBIT 4   Jyske Bank's Core Values

Common Sense

>>*With both feet placed firmly on the ground, we think before we act*<<

That means that we:

- consider common sense our best guide
- apply common sense when solving problems and meeting daily challenges
- allow common sense to override awkward customs and routines
- take action whenever we encounter examples of bureaucratic procedures
- observe existing rules and regulations
- accept that control measures are necessary to a certain degree
- generate satisfactory short- and long-term financial results by pursuing sound business practices
- apply common sense whenever we incur group expenses

Open and Honest

>>*We are open and honest in both word and action*<<

That means that we:

- keep each other up-to-date on relevant matters, and do not misuse information obtained in the course of our work
- restrict the degree of openness only by business considerations or by consideration for other stakeholders
- respect agreements entered into and do not betray the Bank's confidence
- strive towards making important decisions concerning individual employees on the basis of a constructive dialogue
- communicate openly about the mistakes we make and the problems we encounter
- accept that mistakes are made, that they are corrected, and that focus is then on learning from the process
- listen openly to new ideas and constructive criticism

Different and Unpretentious

>>*We think and act differently and are generally unpretentious*<<

That means that we:

- encourage creativity and initiative by being untraditional
- are full of initiative, and are committed and proactive
- encourage relaxed and straightforward communication—both internally and externally

Branch Design

Jyske Bank planned to spend approximately DKK 750 million to physically redesign its branches (most of this had been spent by 2003). Danish observers described the new branches as looking "like an advertising agency" or "a smart hotel." These effects were accomplished through the use of modern, upscale materials such as light wood, warm colors, and original art. Branch redesign also included changes in the way customers interacted with their bankers, made possible by architectural and design changes. For example, customers waiting for their banker could help themselves to fresh coffee in a small part of the branch resembling a café. A customer commented on the café, "It means more than you initially think—it makes you feel welcome, it says they're really interested in me." Fruit juice was available for children, who could amuse themselves with toys in the play center. Bankers' desks were now round tables, signifying equality. A team of three or four bankers sat at a single large round table, with customers making themselves comfortable between the bankers' work stations. Customers

Genuine Interest and Equal Respect

>>*We demonstrate insight and respect for other people*<<

That means that we:

- recognize that no two people are alike
- seek lasting relations with shareholders, customers, and employees
- offer qualified advice matching the financial needs and requirements of each customer
- have job security based on mutual obligations and that we pay attention to individual and personal needs
- allow the highest possible degree of personal influence on assignments, working hours, and place of work

Efficient and Persevering

>>*We work consistently and with determination to reach our goals*<<

That means that we:

- use JB 2005 (the bank's core values) as a guide in our daily work
- are not blown off course because of external circumstances—but take a bearing and plot a new course when this is deemed appropriate
- adopt an organization which promotes efficiency
- consider security important to efficiency
- are convinced that efficiency increases with the level of personal responsibility
- allow employees to assume personal responsibility for day-to-day decisions—even when the basis for decision making may not be 100% perfect
- acquire the level of skills required through personal and professional development
- act on the basis of competence rather than organizational charge
- support our decisions by well-founded arguments

could see bankers' computer screens, reinforcing openness. Customers' ability to view the screens also facilitated the use of IT programs designed to structure interactions between account team members and customers. As equals, bankers and customers sat in the same type of chairs, and bankers no longer sat on a raised dais, the origins of which went back to feudal times when the heads of certain people were supposed to be higher than those of others. If a conversation required more discretion, specially designed meeting rooms giving the feeling of "home" were available. **Exhibit 5** contains pictures of a remodeled branch.

Details

Jyskeness was infused into the bank wherever possible, a formal policy requiring Jyske differences to be considered in all product and IT development. No detail was too small: for example, although employees' business cards had their pictures on them, as one manager put it, "They were bad pictures, really gray. They weren't warm—the

EXHIBIT 5 **Pictures of a Remodeled Branch**

Source: Jyske Bank

(A)

(B)

(C)

(D)

people in them looked stiff and uncaring." To make them more Jyske, the bank hired a professional photographer who worked with each employee to "get the genuine interest in that employee's eye to come to life." Each picture was then tinted slightly yellow to make it resemble "an old family photo."

Intangible Differences

Delivering the bank's new competitive positioning also required numerous intangible changes and other changes not immediately visible to the customer. Managers stated that the most important of these involved training and empowering those employees closest to the customer to serve the customer.

Training

Before a branch was remodeled, all staff took part in special training sessions. These included teambuilding and customer service, drawing on best practices from the "traditional" retail sector.

Empowering the Branches

Jyske Bank leadership examined its organizational structure, asking, "Where is value created?" and "Where should decisions be made in order to create the most value?" The answer to both questions was "in the branches."

Previously, almost all lending decisions of any consequence required approval at the branch, regional, and headquarters levels. Specifically, a customer would approach an employee for a loan. The request would be communicated to the branch manager. The branch manager would then make out the formal application, which if the loan was for more than DKK 3 million, was sent to a regional office with the branch manager's comments. The regional office would then comment on the application, and if the loan were for more than DKK 15 million, send it to headquarters for approval, where additional comments were added to the application. Loans of more than DKK 30 million also required approval from the head of credit for the bank as a whole. In examining this process, managers discovered that most of the debate and communication were among individuals in the middle, rather than between the employee closest to the customer (who presumably had the most information about the customer) and the ultimate decision maker.

After reviewing the situation, the bank's leadership stated, "If we are to be true to our value of using common sense, we shouldn't need so many people, and so many layers, reviewing loans." First, the process was changed so that the employee receiving the request for the loan completed the formal application. This empowered that employee by giving him ownership of the loan, which he was trained in how to handle. He was also put in charge of pricing the loan, as long as his suggested pricing was within a set range of where the final approval authority felt it should be. Most loans received final approval from the branch manager, who was either selected in part based on her credit skills or given additional training in credit. A few loans required approval at the regional level because of their size. In these instances, the employee completing the application sent it directly to the regional head of credit. Ninety-eight percent of loans were handled at the branch or regional levels, where loans of up to DKK 90 million were approved. The credit department at headquarters was disbanded, leaving only the bank's head of credit who reviewed loans of more than DKK 90 million. This additional review was retained for loans of this size because exposure to the customer would be so great that default could significantly affect the bank's capital.

The changes implemented were originally designed to affect internal processes. However, they also improved customers' experiences. For example, managers believed that because the employee in direct contact with the customer made the application, the quality of information in applications increased; as a result, more borrowers worthy of credit received it, and the quality of loans in the bank's portfolio improved. In addition, the time to reach a decision for the largest loans declined from a maximum of three weeks to ten days. Smaller loans able to be approved within the branch could be made almost instantly. Finally, customers' expectations regarding price and terms were more often included in the application. This helped the approving authority to see whether the loan, in a form acceptable to the bank, was likely to be accepted by the customer, saving time and effort when customers' expectations were inconsistent with the bank's requirements.

The streamlined approval process did not pose a credit risk, according to managers, because of the combination of: (1) improved branch credit skills, (2) lack of incentive to make poor loans (branch managers had no incentives immediately related to loan volume or quality), and (3) a robust internal auditing function that monitored credit quality.

At the same time that the credit process was redesigned, the bank consolidated from five regions to three, and increased spans of control so that between 35 and 45 branches reported to each business unit director, who had a staff of marketing, credit, human resources, and control professionals at the regional level (many of whom had previously been at headquarters).

A senior manager commented on the roles of headquarters, the regions, and the branches:

> Headquarters is where we transform our values and strategy into products, processes, and information technology. The three regions are where we make sure that what comes from headquarters is translated for the local marketplace, and where we ensure that Jyske Differences are being acted upon—that customers experience them. The 119 branches are where we serve customers and thus where value is really created. Twenty percent of what we do is development at headquarters, and 80 percent is implementation in the field, supported by the regions. Given the small size of our branches we need the regional level to ensure that implementation is done right.

Empowerment Throughout the Bank

Empowerment was not limited to the branches. Throughout the bank, employees were encouraged to make decisions of all sorts if they felt comfortable doing so. In general, employees were encouraged to ask themselves, "Does it make sense to ask for help or permission? Is there a business reason for asking? Is this something you've never done before? Is this a 'big' decision (big being relative)? Is it debatable, or is it a new principle?" In general, employees were told, "When in doubt, ask. However, if there is no doubt, go ahead." Managers were expected to set an example.

Examples of this policy in action included working hours and vacation time. One employee noted, "If your job makes it possible, you set your hours, you just have to agree with your colleagues, you don't need approval from your boss. You do the same with holidays." A manager noted, "The union[4] at headquarters didn't have a problem with this, but the union in Copenhagen worried that employees might misuse the flexibility."

---

[4]As was typical in Scandinavia, most employees and managers were members of a union.

Another example involved the amount employees were able to spend on meals and entertainment while traveling or entertaining customers. Previously, there had been a set amount, DKK 125, and bills consistently came to DKK 125. Consistent with its value of common sense, the bank changed the policy to be (paraphrased) "Spend what you need to spend." This resulted in what an executive stated was a "substantial decline in travel and entertainment expenses." When asked, "How do you get a system like this to work?" he replied:

> First, you tell people what's expected.
>
> Second, you check on their behavior. If they are buying expensive wine, you ask, "Why?" You explain what makes sense, and why. You do it in a way that tells them you honestly want to help them improve.
>
> Third, if there are continued problems, this person may not be right for the bank.
>
> The real challenge is when we hire someone from another bank. We expect them to be up to speed quickly because of their background, but they aren't used to making these kinds of decisions—they have to be taught how.

Management Style

A senior manager commented:

> You can train and educate all day long, but unless your managers and employees are committed to Jyske Differences, they just won't happen. Getting them committed required a great deal of my effort.
>
> When we started this process there were times when it was hard—really hard. The branch managers didn't think strategically—they sat in their offices and focused on their day-to- day work. I wanted the branch manager to get up on a hill and look around, to get a bigger picture. To get them to change I asked them questions: What's the market? Where—and who—are your competitors? What are your strengths and weaknesses, how do they tie to Jyske Differences? Now, contrast what you need with what you have. Are the teams in your branch living up to the demands? What do you need to do to ensure that that they will? There will be resistance; understand where it is coming from. One way to deal with it is to make agreements with individuals on how they will develop new skills. If there is a complete mismatch you may need new team members, but for the most part, you can coach your people through this kind of change—you can lead them.

According to another executive:

> The branch managers have to be able to motivate employees to work a little harder, and differently. The most successful give their employees a lot of latitude for decision making. They do a lot of training, 80 percent of which is on the job. When it isn't, it's mostly role playing. There aren't any high-powered incentives to offer, but there are really good tools coming out of IT. It's more *how the branch managers do it* than *what they do.* They constantly link the tools, training, and behaviors to our Jyske values. They get their employees to share the values and act on them.

A third noted:

> When I have a difficult situation I look for what I call a "culture carrier." I try to put that person into the middle of it, because they live our values. What I usually see is that the other employees who are on the fence about the values start to come over—they see the example and they like what they see. This leaves the few people who really don't want to be Jyske on the outside, and they tend not to last long. Most people are willing to change, but they've got to be supported in the process.

Human Resources

Legal aspects of human resources, record keeping, and training were centralized at headquarters. In contrast, advice on how to deal with human issues was provided by human resource professionals located in the field (at the regional level). They delivered this advice to general managers in the field such as branch managers. The branches had to pay for this service, and they could choose to either buy the service or do without if they preferred.

Selection An executive discussed employee selection at the bank:

> It's very important. For most of the jobs, we're not only looking for banking skills, we're looking for social abilities—service mindedness and compatibility with our Jyske values: openness, genuine interest in other people. You can smell it when you speak with someone. We don't have a systematic approach to this, although when we're hiring someone from another bank we ask why they want to work for us and listen for answers consistent with Jyske values. We can train most banking skills, but we can't train these attitudes. Maybe our biggest challenge is hiring people with them, and getting a few of our established employees to adopt them.

Some departments of the bank asked potential hires to write about themselves. A manager noted, "We're looking to see whether they're engaged in what they do, or if they're promoting themselves."

Training A manager in human resources commented:

> We have told every employee that his or her development is his or her responsibility. We believe development is incredibly important. While my peers at other Danish banks are cutting staff and saving every way possible, our goal is to get employees and managers to invest in more development. But it's up to the individual to decide what to invest in. We're outsourcing a lot of development activities, but we keep anything related to Jyske values in house.

Incentives Managers pointed out that the bank had few monetary incentives. The few in place consisted of three types, stock, one-time payments, and annual raises.

> Stock incentives: if the bank's annual performance was above the average of the top ten Danish banks', a stock option grant valued at DKK 8.000 was made available to all employees and managers. In addition, any employee could use up to DKK 13.200 to buy company stock annually at a 20 percent discount. If the bank's annual performance was among the top three Danish banks', the discount rose to 40 percent.
>
> One-time payments: for truly exceptional work, employees could be awarded one-time payments. Fewer than 1 percent of individuals at the bank received this type of payment.
>
> Raise incentives: employees and managers received annual salary increases based on their manager's evaluation of their work. The highest raise practicably possible was 10 percent, although an employee or manager in the top 15 percent of performers (the highest level) typically received a raise of approximately 7 percent. Salary raises were eventually limited as total salary had to remain within the bands established for a particular position. Once an increase was granted it became a permanent part of the employee's salary.

Commitment An employee commented on what it was like to work for Jyske Bank: "I'm not restricted. I don't have to leave my head at home—I can take it with me to work and I'm supposed to." Another commented:

> You're treated as a human being here. At other banks you have to be really careful what you say. Here, you can be open and honest—I can approach anyone—even the CEO.

Jyske Bank is a way of life. You come in at 8:00 and you leave when you collect your pension. I pay a premium for this, I could earn more at another bank, but it's worth it for me. At some banks, bankers have prostituted themselves for higher pay, stuffing products down the throats of customers those customers may not need. We don't.

Anders Dam, Jyske Bank's CEO, stated:

If you can create an environment in which people aren't talking about money, but where they gain value in their relationships with their colleagues and their customers, where the bank will take care of those who work hard even if they get sick, then people will be committed to the bank.

Metrics and Financial Results

Bank managers frequently referred to the importance of measuring performance, in both quantitative and qualitative ways, and at a variety of locations in the bank. Traditional financial measures were considered important, but not all-important. In addition to traditional measures, Jyske Bank implemented an information technology system to measure account profitability on a risk-adjusted basis (risk adjusted return on capital, or RAROC). This had been a considerable effort and was just coming on-line in 2003.

Customer and employee measures were also considered important. Managers reported that employee satisfaction was higher at Jyske Bank than at any of its major competitors based on data collected by independent third parties. Several sources of data indicated that Jyske Bank customer satisfaction was also the highest among the bank's major competitors (see **Exhibit 2**). Customer satisfaction could be tracked to the regional level. Plans were in place to be able to measure and report it at the branch, and eventually the individual customer, levels.

Financial and selected operating results are presented in **Exhibit 6**. Jyske Bank took a conservative approach to earnings, writing off its entire investment in remodeling branches, building a new headquarters, and new information technology systems in the years in which spending occurred. This amounted to DKK 302 million in 2002, DKK 253 million in 2001, DKK 194 million in 2000, and DKK 212 million in 1999. Results for 2002 also reflected an extraordinary tax payment of DKK 222 million, which was described as "a potential liability in light of discussions with the Danish tax authorities."[5]

Jyske Bank's statement of core values and principles included the following:

. . . the aim is for Jyske Bank every year to be one of the top performing Danish banks . . . Jyske Bank is thus an excellent choice for shareholders who want to make a long-term investment and who do not attach great importance to decisions which generate only short-term price increases.

Communication

Management believed that most employees liked working for the bank and appreciated Jyske Differences as they affected their jobs. Sustaining Jyske Differences required the bank to remain independent, not an easy task in the Scandinavian banking market, which had consolidated considerably during the 1990s and early twenty-first century. Executives believed that they had taken the right steps to remain independent by investing in employees, systems, and infrastructure that would enable the bank to deliver superior value to its targeted customers, and thus achieve superior financial returns. This economic model was built on the bank's value chain (see **Exhibit 7**).

---

[5]According to an executive, "If we are right [and we eventually reverse the charge] we have an upside. If we are wrong it won't impact future results. All in all the tax issue is not related to the 2002 result and it would be more correct to judge the result before tax."

EXHIBIT 6   Jyske Bank Group Financial and Selected Operating Results

Source: Jyske Bank

Five-Year Summary of Financial Results					
Summary of Profit and Loss Account (DKKm)	**2002**	**2001**	**2000**	**1999**	**1998**
Net interest income	**2,826**	2,623	2,350	2,078	2,133
Dividend on capital holdings	**64**	98	69	52	34
Net fee and commission income	**758**	668	759	646	594
Net interest and fee income	**3,648**	3,389	3,178	2,776	2,761
Revaluations	**386**	129	379	631	−361
Other ordinary income	**203**	213	162	175	219
Operating expenses and depreciation	**2,598**	2,443	2,142	2,014	1,764
Losses and provisions for bad debts	**408**	286	318	248	197
Revaluation of capital interests	**−148**	−112	−4	−44	52
Profit/loss on ordinary activities before tax	**1,083**	890	1,255	1,276	710
Tax	**572**	267	172	379	199
Profit/loss for the year	**511**	623	1,083	897	511
Summary of Balance Sheet (DKKm)	**2002**	**2001**	**2000**	**1999**	**1998**
Advances	**95,302**	82,537	75,362	49,790	39,762
Deposits	**58,963**	54,393	52,267	49,813	43,816
Issued bonds	**43,362**	36,964	26,902	192	623
Total assets	**153,169**	133,156	127,359	92,557	76,938
Shareholders' funds	**6,658**	6,174	5,887	5,391	5,108
Supplementary capital	**2,000**	2,663	2,110	1,395	434
Key Figures	**2002**	**2001**	**2000**	**1999**	**1998**
Per Jyske Bank share					
Core earnings	**23.17**	25.39	22.07	14.68	19.89
Profit/loss on ordinary activities before tax	**29.32**	24.11	31.86	29.58	15.77
Net profit/loss for the year	**13.84**	16.77	27.51	20.83	11.22
Dividend	**0.00**	0.00	0.00	3.20	2.80
Price at year-end	**192**	177	161	149	123
Book value	**178**	170	157	131	114
Price/book value	**1.08**	1.04	1.03	1.14	1.08
Price/earnings	**13.8**	10.5	5.9	7.2	10.9
The Jyske Bank Group					
Solvency ratio	**11.3**	11.4	11.0	10.5	10.4
Core capital ratio	**8.2**	7.9	8.0	8.2	9.5
Income on every krone of expenditure	**1.36**	1.33	1.51	1.56	1.36
Total provisions as % of total loans	**1.8**	1.9	2.0	2.7	3.0
Losses and provisions for the year as % of total loans	**0.4**	0.3	0.4	0.4	0.4

continued

EXHIBIT 6   **Jyske Bank Group Financial and Selected Operating Results—continued**

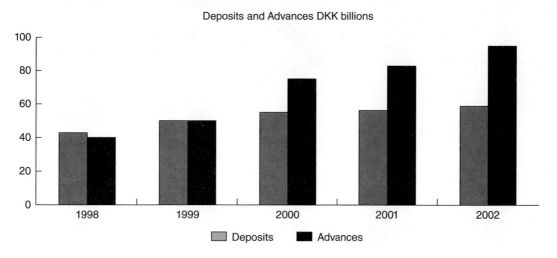

Deposits and Advances DKK billions

Customers

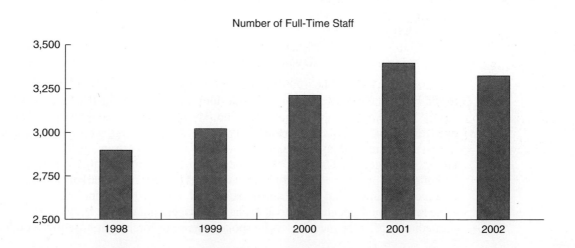

Number of Full-Time Staff

EXHIBIT 7
The Jyske Bank
Value Chain

Source: Jyske Bank's
adaptation of Heskett, Sasser,
and Schlesinger's Service
Profit Chain, see Heskett
et al., 1997.

Internal Service Quality

Staff Retention

Staff Satisfaction

Staff Efficiency

External Quality

Client Satisfaction

Client Loyalty

Rising Business
Volume and
Profitability

Delivering that value required considerable change. One manager stated a point that several alluded to:

> If you want employees to behave differently, you have to be sure they know what that means—how they should behave going forward, and why they should change. We can't ask people to change without communicating this kind of information to them—it's not fair.

Bank leadership believed that communication should be, in the words of an executive, "a car wash, not a waterfall—communication must come from all directions at once, not just cascade down from above." In that spirit, in 1997 communication reinforced Jyske values and differences when the bank produced a video tape on Jyske Differences made available to all employees. This was designed to look like a television talk show. The host was a prominent Danish television personality and the guests were Anders Dam and Danish experts on business. Each was interviewed and they discussed what Jyske Differences were, how they were being implemented, and what they meant to employees and customers, supported by video clips of employees and customers in the branches.

Communication efforts continued in 1999, executives planning a surprise for the bank's strategic meeting, to which all employees were invited every third year.

The Battle at Vejle   The 1999 strategic meeting took place in Vejle, the closest city to the bank's headquarters with an auditorium large enough for the 82 percent of the bank's 3,107 employees who chose to attend. The meeting opened with a panel of senior executives, some of whom were from Jyske Bank, and others who were strangers. A grim-faced Anders Dam got up, and introduced one of the strangers as "the CEO of a large, very large, Swedish bank." Dam then continued, explaining that the Swedish bank had offered to buy Jyske Bank for almost twice its current stock market valuation, a premium of 2.3 times what other Danish banks had recently been acquired for. A fax was to be sent to the Copenhagen stock exchange, suspending trading in Jyske Bank shares immediately after the meeting. As he spoke, a sense of foreboding rose in the audience.

Non-Scandinavians should note that despite the currently cozy relationship between Swedes and Danes, they fought against one another for many centuries, Southern Sweden once having been a Danish possession.

The CEO of the Swedish bank took the podium and announced (in Swedish, which is very difficult for most Danes to understand) that his Danish was very poor, so that he would "speak Scandinavian, very slowly," after which he continued to deliver his address in Swedish.

He stated, among other things, that "You—Jyske Bank, you are good, very good. But are you good enough? For tomorrow? For the future? For a world without borders across the continent?" After his speech Anders Dam took the podium again and asked for an "immediate and honest response" from the employees. Over the course of several questions and responses it became clear that although the takeover was friendly, the integration would be anything but. In the words of the Swedish CEO, "A merger has certain administrative advantages, which will require an adjustment in staffing." Eventually, a manager got up and said, "Do something for the environment. Put the Swedes on the ferry and send them back!" His suggestion received wild applause.

After a pause, Anders Dam returned to the podium and, now smiling, explained that it had all been a joke, which he called "Jyske Fun." He added that he was "proud, proud as a peacock of your reaction to the joke," being delighted that the vast majority of the audience flatly rejected the idea of being acquired. One questioner put it bluntly, stating that (paraphrased) "Jyske Bank couldn't live Jyske Differences, couldn't do the things for employees and customers they had been working so hard on, if it were to be acquired." Dam finished his speech by pointing out that if Jyske Bank were to remain independent in the increasingly-competitive environment Danish banks now faced, everyone would have to contribute.

Part of that contribution was an effort to diversify the bank's type of shareholders and increase their number in order to ensure that they shared its long-term perspective on financial performance. Employees encouraged customers to consider purchasing Jyske Bank Group shares. Between the "Battle at Vejle" and 2003, the number of shareholders increased from 150,000 to more than 200,000.

Managers and employees agreed that the message of the "Battle at Vejle" was heard throughout the organization and that Jyske Fun was a good idea. Subsequent examples of it included the only national advertising campaign the bank had engaged in during the past decade, which was effectively a dog beauty contest with entry requiring a visit to a local branch. When asked why advertising was so limited, an executive replied:

> Two reasons. First, we rely on word of mouth, so we don't need to advertise that much—
> our advertising cost as a percentage of revenue is half what banks of similar size spend.
> Second, we have to be absolutely sure we can consistently deliver Jyske Differences
> before we advertise them.

Later in 1999, communication efforts continued when managers created a video tape illustrating Jyske Differences in an unusual way. The tape introduces Max Performa, an ex-KGB agent hired by a mysterious and beautiful senior manager of a competitor bank. Performa is assigned to find out if Jyske Differences are actually being delivered at Jyske Bank's branches. He checks off each Jyske Difference as he experiences it, pretending to be a Jutlandish farmer wanting a loan (speaking Danish with a thick Russian accent). In the course of applying for the loan he discovers that Jyske Differences are being delivered, among them that the employee opening his account has the authority necessary to meet his needs (*common sense*), that the bank will go to great lengths to show *genuine interest* in him (he and the branch manager drink an entire bottle of vodka one afternoon), and that Jyske Bank *is different* and isn't for everyone: when he complains about the black grouse on his debit card he is politely told he might be happier banking with a competitor. At the end of the tape the viewer learns that the mysterious senior manager who hired Performa actually works for Jyske Bank.

Executives believed that they needed to constantly reinforce the message that remaining independent required every employee to work a little harder, and to behave in a manner consistent with Jyske Differences. To deliver that constant reinforcement, they printed the bank's values and Jyske Differences in materials that managers were asked to discuss with their employees. On one occasion, branch employees were asked to come in on a Saturday, without pay, to discuss the values and differences and their implications for day to-day behavior. Eighty percent chose to come in.

In 2002, communication efforts included the bank's strategic employee meeting, called "Return to Vejle." The meeting, complete with live, high-energy music (a locally popular drum duo) and entertainment, celebrated the bank's accomplishments and served as a reminder of what still needed to be done.

Finally, in 2002 the bank introduced what it called a "tool box" for communicating value chain information to and from the branches. The tool box enabled each branch to select elements on the bank's value chain (see **Exhibit 7**) and measure the branch's performance against goals related to that element. The tool box delivered regularly updated information including guides such as green or red lights describing the branch's performance on the selected value chain elements. An executive described the tool box as "a way to operationalize the value chain so that everyone in the organization understands how they need to behave on a day-to-day basis in order to optimize it."

CONCLUSION

The bank's leadership believed that Jyske values and differences, and the bank's value chain, provided ways to achieve the balance they wanted among their three stakeholders: employees, customers, and shareholders. Several leaders commented that with the large capital investments behind them as of 2003, net income would increase considerably in the coming years, assuming the recession of 2001 and 2002 was over. Shareholders had received a 17.8 percent annual return on their investment for the ten years prior to year-end 2002. Anders Dam's 2002–2003 goal for shareholders was to increase the bank's stock multiple approximately 40 percent to the level of Danske Bank's, the largest and most richly-priced bank in Denmark. This was achieved in July 2003.[6] While the bank's leadership was pleased with the bank's success, they were more interested in determining how the bank would remain in a position of leadership while still keeping the interests of its key stakeholders in balance.

---

[6]Managers attributed the increase in the bank's stock price multiple to recognition among stock analysts that investments in Jyske Differences made in the previous five years and expensed immediately were bearing fruit.

Case 7

JetBlue: *High-Flying Airline Melts Down in Ice Storm*

Joe Brennan, Ph.D., University at Buffalo, The State University of New York
Felicia Morgan, Ph.D., University of West Florida

INTRODUCTION

On Wednesday, February 14, 2007, JetBlue Airways Corp. (NYSE:JBLU) suffered the most severe service disruption in its seven-year history. A winter storm snarled operations at the regional carrier's JFK International Airport in New York, its main East Coast hub, forcing the airline to cancel more than half of its flights. Ten planes sat unable to move on icy runways in New York, trapping passengers inside for up to 10 hours. JetBlue's ordeal continued for nearly a week. The airline had trouble resuming normal operations when additional storms struck, leaving planes and crews out of position. The carrier ultimately cancelled nearly 1,900 flights, affecting 130,000 travelers, before it was able to restore normal operations on February 20. The unprecedented service failure would force the airline to grant $26 million in passenger refunds and vouchers and to spend another $4 million on employee overtime and other storm-related costs.[1]

Although the massive Valentine's Day storm affected every airline flying East Coast routes, the news media focused their attention on JetBlue's problems. Commentators wondered if the company that had once promised to "bring humanity back to air travel" had abandoned its commitment to stellar customer service and become yet another uncaring airline. Stranded passengers wasted no time publicizing their complaints on blogs and in the media, and skittish investors began unloading JBLU stock. This was the worst crisis in the young company's history. JetBlue's management had to act quickly to regain customer loyalty, reverse a barrage of hostile press coverage, and reconfigure operations to prevent a similar disaster from recurring.

"MAKING FLYING HAPPIER AND EASIER FOR EVERYONE"

The airline was founded in 1998 by 38-year-old David Neeleman, who saw himself as "bringing humanity back to air travel and making the experience of flying happier and easier for everyone."[2]

A former Mormon missionary, Neeleman started his first company, a travel business, while a student at the University of Utah. He went on to establish a regional carrier, Morris Air, and in 1992 sold it to Southwest, where he became executive vice president. The entrepreneurial Neeleman lasted for six months at Southwest, where his fast-paced style did not suit the more cautious corporate culture. As one of his colleagues there later said, "He didn't understand the nuance of the organization. He needed to walk, not run."[3] Still in his 30s, Neeleman moved on to co-found WestJet, a Canadian regional airline, and after making it profitable, he helped develop Open Skies, an electronic ticketing system later acquired by Hewlett Packard.

NOTE: This case is based entirely on published sources and has been prepared for teaching purposes.

In 1998, Neeleman gathered a team of investors and seasoned airline industry executives and founded "New Air Corporation." The firm changed its name to JetBlue in July 1999, when it announced that it would offer low-cost, high-quality service to and from New York City, as "New York's hometown airline." At that time, the CEO promised that JetBlue would be a "new kind of low fare airline," offering the types of amenities reserved for pricier carriers, including wider seats, more legroom and storage space, and 24 channels of inflight television. The company's press release promised innovations like touch-screen check-in and "fares 65 percent less than other airlines on identical routes." JetBlue began flying in February 2000, offering non-stop service between New York and Fort Lauderdale, Florida.

The traveling public responded favorably to Neeleman's offer of excellent customer service, upscale amenities, and low fares. Thanks to its younger fleet and newer staff, the firm enjoyed lower maintenance and labor costs than its old-school competitors. It was also well-capitalized; the combination of lower costs and a strong balance sheet helped JetBlue avoid the major losses its competitors incurred after September 11, 2001, and positioned it to take market share away from them. Neeleman took the company public in April 2002. By the end of 2004, JetBlue was flying high. Its revenues had quadrupled—and the company had made a profit every year. It had climbed to 11th place in revenue passenger miles generated, and had done so with fewer planes than many of its bigger competitors.[4] **Exhibits 1**, **2**, **3**, and **4** provide data about the airline's growth and performance.

FLYING HIGH IN A TURBULENT INDUSTRY

By 2005, Neeleman was leading one of the few successful start-ups in the highly competitive U.S. airline business. More than 100 airlines had been launched since the industry was deregulated in 1978, but only a handful had survived the tremendous competitive pressures in this mature industry.[5] The events of September 11, 2001, had a significant impact on the U.S. economy in general and on the airlines in particular. In 2000, the industry generated total sales of $120 billion; over the next two years, revenues plummeted to $105 billion, and it would be five years before sales recovered (see **Exhibit 5** on page 596). The airlines also faced strongly rising fuel prices, heavy debt loads, and increasing pension liabilities related to their aging workforces.[6] By September, 2005, four major carriers (United, US Airways, Delta, and Northwest), representing 40 percent of the industry's total capacity, were operating under Chapter 11 protection.[7,8]

During this period, JetBlue had effectively established a powerful brand and carved out a distinct and profitable position as a low-cost airline offering a high level of service. The firm strove to provide every customer with "the JetBlue Experience," which combined value, service, and style. Passengers enjoyed free co-branded amenities, including brand name snacks, Dunkin Donuts coffee, XM satellite radio, DIRECTV satellite television, and Bliss Spa comfort kits. Passengers could watch live television, listen to satellite radio, purchase 20th Century Fox inflight movies, and sip wines chosen by "low fare sommelier" Josh Wesson of Best Cellars, a value-oriented chain of retail wine shops. The JetBlue Experience also included innovation. From its inception, all JetBlue travel had been ticketless, all fares one-way, and all seats assigned. It was the first airline to deploy the new Embraer 190 regional jet and the first to offer free live television; in 2002 it acquired inflight television provider Live TV and began marketing the service to other airlines.

EXHIBIT 1 Jet Blue Financial Data

Source: Standard & Poor's Net Advantage Company Profiles, 3/10/07

Revenues (Million $) for Fiscal Year Ending Dec.

	2006	2005	2004	2003	2002	2001
1Q	490	374.2	289	217.1	133.4	63.85
2Q	612	429.1	319.7	244.7	149.3	78.4
3Q	628	452.9	323.2	273.6	165.3	82.61
4Q	633	446	334	262.9	187.3	95.56
Year	2,363	1,701	1,266	998.4	635.2	320.4

Earnings Per Share ($) for Fiscal Year Ending Dec.

	2007	2006	2005	2004	2003	2002
1Q	E−0.15	−0.18	0.04	0.09	0.11	0.1
2Q	E0.22	0.08	0.08	0.13	0.24	0.1
3Q	E0.20	N/A	0.01	0.05	0.17	0.08
4Q	E0.16	0.1	−0.25	0.01	0.11	0.1
Year	E0.43	N/A	−0.13	0.29	0.65	0.37

Income Statement (Million $).

	2006	2005	2004	2003	2002	2001
Net Inc.	−1	−20	47.5	104	54.9	38.5
Depr.	154	117	77.4	50.4	26.9	10.4
Int. Exp.	146	91	44.6	23.7	15.7	6.1
Eff. Tax Rate	NM	NM	38%	41%	42%	8.10%
Pretax Inc.	9	−24	76.8	175	95	41.9
Oper. Inc.	281	165	190	219	132	37.2
Revs.	2,363	1,701	1,266	998	635	320

Other Financial Data (Million $).

	2006	2005	2004	2003	2002	2001
Cash	10	6	410	571	247	263
Curr. Liab.	854	676	486	370	270	0
LT Debt	2,626	2,103	1,396	1,012	639	291
% Ret. on Equity	NM	NM	6.7	19.1	25.6	
Total Cap.	3,714	3,130	2,275	1,782	1,093	615
Total Assets	4,843	3,892	2,799	2,186	1,379	820
% Net Inc.of Revs.	NM	NM	3.7	10.4	8.6	12
% LT Debt of Cap.	70.7	67.2	61.4	56.8	58.5	47.3
Curr. Assets	927	635	515	646	283	0
Curr. Ratio	1.1	0.9	1.1	1.7	1	0
Cash Flow	153	97	125	154	75.9	32
Cap. Exp.	996	941	617	573	544	0
% Ret. on Assets	NM	NM	1.9	5.8	5.3	0
Common Equity	952	911	756	671	415	324

Data as originally reported; before results of discontinued operations and/or specific items.
Per share data adjusted for stock dividends as of ex-dividend date.
E—Estimated. N/A—Not Available. NM—Not Meaningful.
JetBlue Airways Corp. Nasdaq:JBLU

EXHIBIT 2 **JetBlue's Growth**

Sources: Jet Blue 10K reports, Air Transport Association of America, Standard & Poor's.

	Revenue Passengers (000s)	Revenue Passenger Miles (millions)	Operating Revenues (million $)	Employees (full- and part-time)	Operating Aircraft	Destinations
2000	1,144	1,005	320.4	1,174	10	12
2001	3,117	3,282	320.4	2,361	21	18
2002	5,752	6,836	635.2	4,011	37	20
2003	9,012	11,527	998.4	5,433	53	21
2004	11,783	15,730	1,266	7,211	69	30
2005	14,729	20,200	1,701	9,021	93	33
2006	18,565	23,320	2,363	10,377	119	49

"Revenue passengers" represents the total number of paying passengers on all flight segments flown.
"Revenue passenger miles" represents the number of miles flown by revenue passengers.
Employee count does not include LiveTV employees.

SERVICE EXCELLENCE

JetBlue has sought to provide what it calls "the best customer service in the business," and has won dozens of top awards for its performance.[9] In 2007, it was named the number three most admired airline by *Fortune* and best in customer satisfaction by *Market Metrix.* In 2006, it was picked as the best domestic airline by both *Conde Nast Traveler* and *Travel + Leisure,* the best low cost/no frills airline by OAG, and the best U.S. airline in the annual quality ranking survey conducted by the University of Nebraska–Omaha and Wichita State University. In 2006, JetBlue enjoyed the second-lowest rate of customer complaints among the 10 largest U.S. airlines (see **Exhibit 6** on page 596).

Neeleman's vision of a new category of airline, one that would make flying more fun and more civilized, was as compelling for employees as it was for passengers. A former missionary to Brazil, Neeleman had an extraordinary ability to connect with people and to inspire them, like the pilot who told *Fast Company,* "I would walk through fire for him."[10] He traveled frequently on JetBlue flights, working alongside employees, talking with pilots in the cockpit, visiting with customers about their experiences, and asking how the airline could better serve them. Neeleman and his executive team placed a high value on involving employees in all aspects of the business

EXHIBIT 3
Passengers per Employee

Source: authors' calculations.

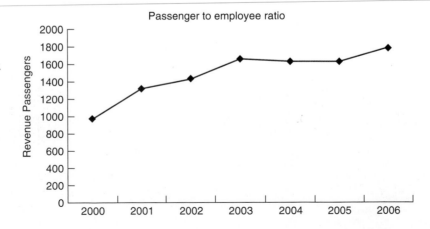

EXHIBIT 4   Top 25 U.S. Airlines, 2003

Source: Air Transport Association of America Annual Report, 2004.
Note: Airlines listed in **bold** are members of the Air Transport Association of America.

	Revenue Passengers Enplaned[1] (Thousands)		Revenue Passenger Miles[1] (Millions)		Cargo Revenue Ton Miles[2] (Millions)		Operating Revenues[2] (Millions)	
1	American	88,151	American	120,004	FedEx	9,487	American	$17,403
2	Delta	84,076	United	103,857	UPS	4,624	FedEx	16,807
3	Southwest	74,719	Delta	89,154	Atlas	3,006	Delta	14,203
4	United	66,018	Northwest	68,459	Northwest	2,184	United	13,398
5	Northwest	51,865	Continental	56,886	American	2,012	Northwest	9,184
6	US Airways	41,250	Southwest	47,940	United	1,888	Continental	7,333
7	Continental	38,474	US Airways	37,727	Delta	1,349	US Airways	6,762
8	America West	20,031	America West	21,266	Polar	1,115	Southwest	5,937
9	Alaska	15,046	Alaska	14,557	Continental	865	UPS	3,046
10	American Eagle	12,474	ATA	11,840	Gemini	732	America West	2,223
11	AirTran	11,651	JetBlue	10,442	ABX	700	Alaska	2,019
12	Continental Express	11,227	AirTran	7,159	Evergreen Int'l	677	ATA	1,398
13	Comair	10,935	Continental Express	5,769	Kalitta	660	Continental Express	1,311
14	Skywest	10,719	Hawaiian	5,560	US Airways	361	ABX	1,161
15	**ATA**	9,386	Comair	5,227	**ASTAR**	348	American Eagle	1,128
16	Atlantic Southeast	9,205	Frontier	4,666	World	301	Comair	1,032
17	**JetBlue**	8,949	Spirit	4,578	Air Transport Int'l	203	**JetBlue**	998
18	Atlantic Coast	8,390	Skywest	4,232	Florida West	197	AirTran	918
19	Air Wisconsin	5,865	American Eagle	4,135	Express.Net	165	Atlantic Coast	876
20	Mesaba	5,702	Atlantic Southeast	4,008	Tradewinds	164	Atlantic Southeast	837
21	**Hawaiian**	5,597	Atlantic Coast	3,320	**Southwest**	141	**Hawaiian**	706
22	Frontier	5,061	Continental Micronesia	2,286	Kitty Hawk	122	Frontier	590
23	Horizon	4,934	Air Wisconsin	2,212	Ryan Int'l	118	Air Wisconsin	527
24	**Aloha**	4,119	**Midwest**	1,969	Centurion	118	World	475
25	Spirit	4,105	Aloha	1,968	Southern	106	Horizon	464

[1] Scheduled service only   [2] All services   ■ ATA member

595

EXHIBIT 5
Total Revenues,
U.S. Airlines

Source: Datamonitor Industry
Profiles, 2005, 2006.

Year	$ billion	% Growth
2000	120.0	
2001	111.9	−6.8%
2002	105.0	−6.1%
2003	110.2	4.9%
2004	116.3	5.6%
2005	125.0	7.5%

and cultivating a sense of teamwork. All employees are called "crewmembers," and supervisors attend "Jet Blue University" for a course in the company's principles of leadership taught by Neeleman and chief operating officer Dave Barger. Al Spain, senior vice president of operations, said, "There is no 'they' here. It's 'we' and 'us.' We succeed together or we fail together."[11]

Even after the ice storm, employees defended the airline. On February 19, someone who identified him- or herself as a JetBlue employee posted a response to a blogger who had been critical of the company's handling of the situation:

> Had you booked a ticket on Delta or American, your flight would have been cancelled and you wouldn't have gotten a refund. You would have had to fly at another time, but you wouldn't have been compensated for your delay—at all . . . in no way. In fact, they wouldn't have apologized . . . at all . . . EVER!
>
> What happened to all of you (including my fellow pilots and flight attendants that were stuck right along with you—and just as miserable as you were) was awful, not cool, uncomfortable, a huge pain in the ass and a really, really, really bad day.
>
> That's about it though. See, when you travel it's like buying a lottery ticket: if you get to your destination hassle free—you win! If you have issues along the way . . . that's life! But if you get a refund for your troubles . . . that's amazing! . . .
>
> I'm sorry you went through what you went through on Valentine's Day, and I want you to come back to jetBlue so I can give you the jetBlue Experience you've grown accustomed to and we do our best to deliver every day.[12]

WARNING LIGHTS IN THE COCKPIT

In May 2004, *Fast Company* profiled the young CEO, praising his hands-on approach and warning that it would be increasingly hard to maintain as JetBlue got bigger:

> Much that's distinctive about this airline—from the enthusiasm of its employees to its relentless customer focus to its hip, slightly countercultural image—is precisely the

EXHIBIT 6
Customer
Complaint Rates for
the 10 Largest U.S.
Airlines (2006)

Source: U.S. Department of
Transportation Air Travel
Consumer Report, Feb. 2007;
Wall Street Journal,
March 27, 2007.

Airline	Complaints per 1 Million Passenger Emplanements
United Airlines	13.60
US Airways	13.59
American Airlines	10.87
Delta	10.35
Northwest Airlines	8.84
Continental Airlines	8.83
AirTran Airways	6.24
Alaska Airlines	5.24
JetBlue Airways	3.98
Southwest Airlines	1.82
Average of all airlines	**8.67**

sort of thing you can pull off when you're small, and that becomes far tougher the bigger you get. Can JetBlue maintain those qualities as it morphs from nimble start-up into the bureaucracy that's required to manage a vastly more complex operation?

It's a question that applies to many truly innovative companies these days. Call them postmodern corporations, perhaps. If they pull off this transition, they become big, but remain in important ways the antithesis of bigness-think Starbucks, Dell, and Amazon. Like JetBlue, they depend on flexibility, speed, and a sense of intimacy with employees and customers alike. Put another-way, the challenge JetBlue now faces is this: Is small scalable?[13]

Neeleman began flying into turbulence in 2005. At the same time as *Fast Company* was pondering his ability to save his company from the fate of People Express, a similar concept which failed in the 1980s, rivals Delta and United were launching Song and Ted, low-cost/high-frills offerings meant to directly compete with JetBlue. Labor and maintenance expenses began to creep up as JetBlue's people and planes got older and the company experienced problems with the introduction of a brand-new aircraft type, the Embraer 190. As is often the case when an airline brings a new type of aircraft into its fleet, JetBlue experienced unexpected glitches. Not only did the new Embraer 190s arrive behind schedule, installing the in-flight entertainment system so integral to the JetBlue passenger experience took longer than expected. Also, pilots and mechanics used to doing things a certain way on the existing fleet experienced significant learning curves in operating the new aircraft. On-time performance eroded and flights were canceled.[14] In addition, Florida and the Gulf Coast, important markets for JetBlue, were ravaged by Hurricanes Rita, Wilma, and Katrina in the summer of 2005. The demand for air travel to the affected regions fell, petroleum refineries were closed, and JetBlue's fuel costs soared 52 percent. At the end of 2005, the company reported its first-ever operating loss, $20 million.[15]

Neeleman and Barger discussed these challenges in the company's 2005 Annual Report and offered a plan for recovery. They planned to grow revenues by raising average fares, using capacity more efficiently and adding service to small and medium-sized cities where a relative lack of competition would allow JetBlue to command a price premium. They also reiterated the airline's commitment to reliable service, which meant "operating flights even with a delay rather than canceling the flight for the schedule's convenience." To manage costs, they promised to improve workforce productivity through better training, smarter business processes, and more extensive use of automation, and they said they would control the risk of rising fuel prices through financial hedging strategies. The executive team also refused bonuses, and Neeleman delayed the delivery of 36 new aircraft.[16]

By the end of 2006, Neeleman and Barger's plan to grow their way out of trouble seemed to be working. Revenues rose 39 percent in 2006, to $2.36 billion. The firm enjoyed three successive profitable quarters, ending the year just $1 million in the red. In January 2007, David Neeleman told investors, "I'm tremendously proud of the efforts our crewmembers have made in advancing our plan to institutionalize low-cost carrier spending habits and improve revenue overall." Dave Barger said that the airline's performance in 2006 "positions us well for 2007, a year in which we plan to grow capacity 11 to 14 percent, while continuing to enhance the JetBlue Experience." Investors appeared to share management's confidence. Towards the end of 2006, analysts began to upgrade their recommendations, and by mid-January, the stock price had soared to a new 52-week high. No one knew the turbulence that lay just ahead.

STORMY WEATHER

On its seventh anniversary, February 11, 2007, JetBlue was operating some 500 flights a day to 50 cities in the U.S., Mexico, and the Caribbean. David Neeleman had built one of the very few successful major new airlines since the industry was deregulated nearly 30 years before. The company's prospects seemed bright. And then, three days later, JetBlue was hit with the worst crisis in its history.

February 14 began as a normal day at JetBlue's Forest Hills, New York headquarters, near John F. Kennedy International Airport. The company had issued a routine news release shortly after 9 a.m., announcing that it had formed a partnership with Cape Air to offer service to four communities on Cape Cod. The day before, a front had moved into the New York City region from the west, dropping one-tenth of an inch of snow. Heavy snow was in the forecast for upstate, but it appeared that the city would be spared the brunt of the storm. At the airport's weather station, the barometer started falling at midnight. By dawn, what had been light snow in the early morning hours had become ice pellets and light freezing rain, with temperatures hovering in the upper 20s. No one seemed to know that by lunchtime, barometric pressure would drop nearly an inch and a full blown nor'easter would be raking the airport with winds gusting up to 40 miles per hour, coating planes and runways with ice. Early that morning, in keeping with the airline's desire to avoid cancellations, JetBlue gate agents loaded passengers onto six planes, in hopes that they could get out during a break in the weather. These planes remained stuck at the gate; while over the course of the morning, four more JetBlue aircraft arrived and remained on the tarmac, unable to reach the terminal because all gates were occupied, and ground equipment used to tow planes was frozen in place.

As the hours crept by for the passengers and crewmembers stuck onboard the 10 airliners, JetBlue's operations appeared to have become paralyzed. The problems at JFK, its East Coast hub, rippled throughout JetBlue's system. Its 800 number, staffed by home-based workers in Utah, was overwhelmed by the crush of calls from customers seeking information or trying to rebook delayed flights. Its New York-based 20-person crew services department, which handles the scheduling of crewmembers, was also overwhelmed.

The storm showed signs of relenting by early afternoon, as freezing snow changed into light snow, and JetBlue officials kept the loaded planes in place, apparently still hoping to salvage some of the flights. By 3 p.m., however, they had admitted defeat and asked the Port Authority of New York and New Jersey for help in rescuing stranded passengers. The last passengers entered the terminal after 7 p.m., having sat onboard for six to 10½ hours.

Television news crews were waiting for the passengers in the terminal. WABC-TV interviewed some of the 134 passengers on Flight 751, which had been bound for Cancun, Mexico. "There was no power and it was hot. There was no air. They kept having to open the actual plane doors so we could breathe," said one passenger.

"Nobody gave us any answers. They kept telling us we know as much as you do. And I said, I don't work here, you work here, give me answers," another passenger said.

"Everybody is incredibly tired and frustrated and we didn't expect to be in New York tonight, so it's ridiculous. Just sitting there and sitting there and them saying they were going to pull us into the gate and they never did. There was very little food. It was just a nightmare," a third passenger was quoted as saying.[17]

JetBlue's problems quickly became national headline news. Yossi Glieberman, a 41-year-old Brooklyn man who came in on a flight from Nashville that could not make it to the gate, told *Newsday* that the pilots provided frequent updates and flight attendants distributed snacks liberally, allowed passengers to recharge cell phones and let children help push the service carts.[18] "It could have been worse," he said of the nine-hour ordeal. Other fliers were less complimentary. An unnamed man told ABC World News, "My vacation is canceled. No flights out. I can't go anywhere. They can't get me out on vacation. My kids are home in four-degree weather when we're supposed to be on a beach with 90-degree weather."[19] Cheryl Chesner, a bride who had to cancel her honeymoon trip to Aruba, told the *San Francisco Chronicle,* "It was the worst. It was horrific."[20]

One customer, a New York resident who was angry about missing a much-anticipated Valentine's Day trip home to Los Angeles with her new boyfriend, started a blog called www.jetbluehostage.com.[21] Using the screen name "Gen Starchild," she wrote, "Nothing says 'I love you' like being held hostage on a frozen plane with the man you love, 99 strangers, 4 other people you happen to know, 4 screaming babies and 3 rambunctious kids running about, nothing but chips and soda for sustenance, faulty power, unreliable direct TV, and an overfilled sewage system for 11 hours."

The blog became well-known and led to an interview for Gen and her boyfriend on CNN. JetBlue's public relations department asked her to meet with David Neeleman. She recapped the March 5 meeting on her blog:

> It went a lot like this.
>
> Canned answer
> Canned answer
> *We're sorry*
> *It'll never happen again*
> *I don't have the answer, this is who you need to talk to.*
> *I'm sorry.*
> Etc.
>
> Then he hit a wall and I could actually see the change in him. From the beginning of the meeting, he was playing these passive aggressive "you're not important" games, by taking FOUR PHONE CALLS, on his mobile at that. Not from JetBlue employees concerned about the weather cancellations. Calls from his wife. Calls from his neighbor. I'm the queen of mind games, you can't pull that on me.

Gen Starchild and her fellow "hostages" were not the only travelers inconvenienced by the events of February 14, though they may have been the most visible. And JetBlue was not the only carrier grounded by the storm. Between February 13 and 15, American cancelled 914 flights, or 13.4 percent of its schedule; United grounded 865 flights (17.1 percent); US Airways 728 (19.6 percent); and Contintental 119 (3.7 percent). By comparison, JetBlue's 634 cancelled flights represented 39.6 percent of its schedule.[22]

In all, some 250 flights, nearly half of JetBlue's entire schedule, were cancelled on Valentine's Day. The following days were also plagued by problems, because the ice storm had left airplanes and crews out of position and additional winter weather created more headaches. Internal communications and coordination between airline staff seemed to be a problem. A woman who took a JetBlue flight from California to New York on February 17 posted this report on jetbluehostage.com: "JetBlue's system was completely overloaded. The staff at Burbank had no clue what was going on—the lack of pilots was a total shock to them—and there were so few staff actually at JFK that no passengers could get answers. A man with a bullhorn finally came out (because the baggage carousel board was completely inaccurate) to tell people which flights were coming out on which carousels."

In an effort to restore order, the airline cancelled some of its flights on February 15 and 16, but problems persisted, so managers took the unprecedented step of preemptively cancelling ("precancelling") 23 percent of all flights over the next two days in order to reposition planes and allow pilots and crews to rest. This action demonstrated a significant shift in thinking on the part of JetBlue managers, who had always tried to take a "wait-and-see approach" with the weather.[23] Announcing the move on February 17, spokeswoman Jenny Dervin told *The New York Times:* "Sometime in the afternoon, it just fell apart. The folks running the operation are just exhausted. We said, 'Let's stop the madness.'"[24] "We ran into an operational death spiral," Dervin told *Newsweek.*[25] The pre-cancellations, which fell over the President's Day long weekend, worked, and by Monday, February 20 JetBlue was back to normal.

JETBLUE WORKS TO REBUILD PUBLIC TRUST

As the airline's executives struggled to climb out of the operational death spiral, its public relations staff got busy trying to repair the firm's damaged image. On the evening of February 14, JetBlue issued a public apology and announced that it would give a full refund and a free roundtrip ticket to any passenger detained onboard for more than three hours; it would also give refunds to any passenger whose flight was cancelled. Over the next few days, the airline announced that it was relaxing its policies about rebooking so that customers who were affected by the storm would not be penalized for rebooking new flights. Throughout the ordeal, top executives practiced their commitment to "visible leadership." Dave Barger went to JFK on the 14th to oversee the operational response and speak with passengers and crewmembers. David Neeleman became the company's public face, granting dozens of media interviews, in which he accepted responsibility, expressed remorse, and pledged to prevent this kind of problem from happening again. In a front-page *New York Times* story on Sunday, February 19, Neeleman said he was "humiliated and mortified" and promised that JetBlue would pay penalties to customers if they were the victims of mistakes by the airline.[26]

One week after the Valentine's Day ice storm, the operations were finally back to normal. Neeleman had issued a personal apology, which appeared in his blog and in full-page ads in major newspapers (see **Exhibit 7**). The airline also published a Customer's Bill of Rights, specifying how and when it would compensate passengers for delays and other problems (see **Exhibit 8**). Reactions to Neeleman's apology and the Bill of Rights were generally positive. On February 21, *USA Today* published an editorial calling JetBlue's service failure "inexcusable" but praising its response. The paper contrasted JetBlue's handling of the Valentine's Day snafu to similar, smaller-scale strandings by American and United in December and wrote that it hoped this would touch off "a round of competition over customer-service guarantees, instead of the usual cost-cutting."[27]

The business press, however, was far less kind. In a stinging rebuke, *BusinessWeek* struck JetBlue from its list of "customer service champs." The magazine's March 5 cover (see **Exhibit 9**) was headlined "Our first-ever ranking of companies where the consumer is king. Here's the magnificent 25—and one extraordinary stumble." The cover graphic was a numbered list of the top four companies, with a squiggly blue line drawn through JetBlue's name. The editors said kicking the airline off the list was a "tough call." Despite Neeleman's candid, public apologies, "the road to recovery isn't paved with TV appearances," the magazine cautioned.

> What matters most is execution—doing the deep, hard organizational work to ensure the crisis never happens again. While JetBlue recognizes that fact, it still has plenty to prove . . . JetBlue has piled up service accolades faster than most airlines collect

EXHIBIT 7   **David Neeleman's Apology**

Dear JetBlue Customers,

We are sorry and embarrassed. But most of all, we are deeply sorry. Last week was the worst operational week in JetBlue's seven year history. Many of you were either stranded, delayed or had flights cancelled following the severe winter ice storm in the Northeast. The storm disrupted the movement of aircraft, and, more importantly, disrupted the movement of JetBlue's pilot and inflight crewmembers who were depending on those planes to get them to the airports where they were scheduled to serve you. With the busy President's Day weekend upon us, rebooking opportunities were scarce and hold times at 1-800-JETBLUE were unusually long or not even available, further hindering our recovery efforts.

Words cannot express how truly sorry we are for the anxiety, frustration and inconvenience that you, your family, friends and colleagues experienced. This is especially saddening because JetBlue was founded on the promise of bringing humanity back to air travel, and making the experience of flying happier and easier for everyone who chooses to fly with us. We know we failed to deliver on this promise last week.

We are committed to you, our valued customers, and are taking immediate corrective steps to regain your confidence in us. We have begun putting a comprehensive plan in place to provide better and more timely information to you, more tools and resources for our crewmembers and improved procedures for handling operational difficulties. Most importantly, we have published the JetBlue Airways Customer Bill of Rights—our official commitment to you of how we will handle operational interruptions going forward—including details of compensation. We invite you to learn more at jetblue.com/promise.

You deserved better—a lot better—from us last week and we let you down. Nothing is more important than regaining your trust and all of us here hope you will give us the opportunity to once again welcome you onboard and provide you the positive JetBlue Experience you have come to expect from us.

Sincerely,

David Neeleman
Founder and CEO

complaints . . . plus JetBlue's trumpeting of its own customer-friendly approach, means its passengers' expectations are inevitably higher. Other airlines, after all, had long waits at JFK . . . but interminable delays, cancellations and service snafus, says UNC Kenan-Flagler Business School professor Valarie Zeithaml, can be "more detrimental [to JetBlue] than to a larger airline. It runs totally counter to who they are coming out and saying they are and what they live."[28]

Other observers raised questions about Neeleman's leadership. On February 20, Larry Kudlow, host of CNBC's Kudlow and Co., said:

The guy's a great entrepreneur. He created and built and grew this company. OK, no question about it. But how many times in the past do we know that entrepreneurial CEOs are not necessarily the ones that take these companies to the next stage where management and administration are really the keys? He clearly struck out on management, information, communications, where's this equipment, where were the pilots, how to get in touch with one another, where are the flight attendants? And I know he's made a lot of mea culpas, and I appreciate his character in doing that, but the fact remains: Can he manage a large airline company?

Earlier that day, the embattled CEO held a news conference at which said he had no intention of stepping down from his post. "I'm the founder of the company, I'm the CEO, and I think I'm uniquely qualified to deal with these issues."[29]

The incident also spurred calls by passenger advocates for tougher oversight by the federal government. The Coalition for Airline Passengers' Bill of Rights, a newly formed group, used JetBlue's woes to again demand relief. The coalition was formed

EXHIBIT 8 JetBlue Customer Bill of Rights

JetBlue Airways Customer Bill of Rights

JetBlue Airways exists to provide superior service in every aspect of our customer's air travel experience. In order to reaffirm this commitment, we set forth this Bill of Rights for our customers. These Rights will always be subject to the highest level of safety and security for our customers and crewmembers.

INFORMATION

JetBlue will notify customers of the following:

- Delays prior to scheduled departure
- Cancellations and their cause
- Diversions and their cause

CANCELLATIONS

All customers whose flight is cancelled by JetBlue will, at the customer's option, receive a full refund or re-accommodation on a future JetBlue flight at no additional charge or fare. If JetBlue cancels a flight within 12 hours of scheduled departure and the cancellation is due to a Controllable Irregularity, JetBlue will also provide the customer with a Voucher valid for future travel on JetBlue in the amount paid to JetBlue for the customer's roundtrip.

DEPARTURE DELAYS

1. Customers whose flight is delayed prior to scheduled departure for 1-1:59 hours due to a Controllable Irregularity are entitled to a $25 Voucher good for future travel on JetBlue.
2. Customers whose flight is delayed prior to scheduled departure for 2-3:59 hours due to a Controllable Irregularity are entitled to a $50 Voucher good for future travel on JetBlue.
3. Customers whose flight is delayed prior to scheduled departure for 4-5:59 hours due to a Controllable Irregularity are entitled to a Voucher good for future travel on JetBlue in the amount paid by the customer for the oneway trip.
4. Customers whose flight is delayed prior to scheduled departure for 6 or more hours due to a Controllable Irregularity are entitled to a Voucher good for future travel on JetBlue in the amount paid by the customer for the roundtrip.

OVERBOOKINGS (As defined in JetBlue's Contract of Carriage)

Customers who are involuntarily denied boarding shall receive $1,000.

GROUND DELAYS

For customers who experience a Ground Delay for more than 5 hours, JetBlue will take necessary action so that customers may deplane. JetBlue will also provide customers experiencing a Ground Delay with food and drink, access to restrooms and, as necessary, medical treatment.

Arrivals:

1. Customers who experience a Ground Delay on Arrival for 30-59 minutes after scheduled arrival time are entitled to a $25 Voucher good for future travel on JetBlue.
2. Customers who experience a Ground Delay on Arrival for 1-1:59 hours after scheduled arrival time are entitled to a $100 Voucher good for future travel on JetBlue.
3. Customers who experience a Ground Delay on Arrival for 2-2:59 hours after scheduled arrival time are entitled to a Voucher good for future travel on JetBlue in the amount paid by the customer for the oneway trip.
4. Customers who experience a Ground Delay on Arrival for 3 or more hours after scheduled arrival time are entitled to a Voucher good for future travel on JetBlue in the amount paid by the customer for the roundtrip.

Departures:

1. Customers who experience a Ground Delay on Departure for 3-3:59 hours are entitled to a $100 Voucher good for future travel on JetBlue.
2. Customers who experience a Ground Delay on Departure for 4 or more hours are entitled to a Voucher good for future travel on JetBlue in the amount paid by the customer for the roundtrip.

JetBlue Airways
Forest Hills Support Center
118-29 Queens Blvd
Forest Hills, NY 11375

1-800-JETBLUE   1-800-538-2583   jetblue.com

*These Rights are subject to JetBlue's Contract of Carriage and, as applicable, the operational control of the flight crew.

This document is representative of what JetBlue intends to incorporate into its Contract of Carriage, the legal binding document between JetBlue and its customers.

EXHIBIT 9
Cover of
BusinessWeek,
March 5, 2005

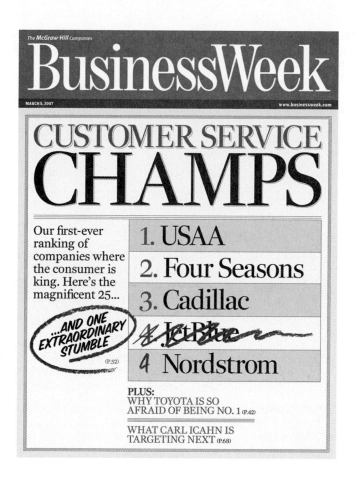

by Tim and Kate Hanni, a Napa, California couple who were trapped on the ground for nine hours in Austin, Texas by American Airlines in late December 2006. The Hannis described their experience in a February 4 letter to the *Mobile (Ala.) Press-Register.*[30] These angry, frustrated travelers demanded that Congress pass new laws to force airlines to refund 150 percent of the ticket price to passengers stranded more than three hours and inform passengers about what's going on within 10 minutes of a prolonged delay. They launched a website, strandedpassengers.blogspot.com, and within its first month reportedly collected 4,200 signatures on a petition.[31]

A similar incident in 1999, when Northwest Airlines detained passengers for seven hours on a snow-covered runway in Detroit, had sparked calls for action by Congress. The airline industry staved off new regulations then by promising to take care of the problem. Now, in the wake of the Hannis' experience and the JetBlue debacle, it appeared that federal lawmakers were ready to act. Over the President's Day weekend, before JetBlue issued its own Bill of Rights, U.S. Senators Barbara Boxer (D–Calif.) and Olympia Snow (R–Maine) proposed a new law to prevent airlines from holding passengers onboard for more than three hours and to require them to provide food, water, and clean toilets. Congressman Mike Thompson, a Democrat who represented the Hannis' district, promised to introduce a similar bill in the House. Sen. Boxer told National Public Radio:

> We have to protect the people of the United States of America. We have to protect their families. We have to protect our children. And now, post-9/11, it's very difficult for passengers to complain about anything because of the seriousness of what happened

on 9/11. Passengers who cause any trouble at all can get themselves in a lot of trouble. So when you're on an aircraft, you're pretty much—have to comply with everything. And here you're in a situation where you're in a lockdown, almost a hostage situation. It's just unacceptable. This is a very simple thing we're talking about. It's common sense. The airlines, I think, will benefit from it, and I hope we can get it done. I'm not naive about it. Every single time there's a regulation we propose, there's an outcry. The automobile industry didn't want to do seatbelts. They didn't want to do airbags. Now they take credit for it. So, you know, there is a role for the government, since we are really responsible for licensing these airlines.[32]

Aviation experts warned that the proposed new regulations could actually make things worse for passengers by depriving the airlines of flexibility. Daryl Jenkins, a consultant who teaches airline management, told *USA Today* that the proposal was "totally impractical . . . What if a plane is ordered after three hours to go back to the terminal when they are second in line to take off? That doesn't make sense." John Cox, a former airline pilot, said that it would reduce the reliability of the system because airlines need to keep flights ready to take off as soon as the weather permits. Returning them to the terminal could increase delays.[33]

WHAT LIES AHEAD FOR JETBLUE?

Three weeks after the crisis, Neeleman was still communicating with customers about the company's response. It appeared that some customers were confused by the conditions for when the company would and would not offer compensation for delays. Neeleman explained the differences between "controllable" and "uncontrollable" delays on his blog, "David's Flight Log."[34]

On March 8, the company announced that John Owen, executive vice president–supply chain and information technology, had resigned but would remain with the company as a "senior advisor" through the end of 2008, and that Russell Chew had been hired to serve as chief operating officer. Chew, a veteran of American Airlines and the Federal Aviation Agency, "brings a big-airline perspective to JetBlue . . . Russ will be in charge of making sure our operations run on time and as scheduled, so that you don't have to rely on our Bill of Rights for compensation," Neeleman told customers. "Because let's face it—getting a $25 voucher or more is nice, but it's better to arrive or depart on time." Chew will report to Dave Barger, who would remain with the company as "President and Founding Crew Member."

The press continued to raise questions about JetBlue's long term viability, however. On March 12, *BusinessWeek* cited unnamed "industry sources" as saying that, as part of its 2006 cost cutting moves, the company had sacrificed needed upgrades to its reservations, call center, and crew scheduling systems. It also warned that the market may be tapped out, quoting a consultant who said, "there aren't too many markets you can throw 150-seat airplanes into," and raised the specter of a unionization drive among pilots who have watched the value of their stock options fall.[35]

The market appeared to have lost confidence in the once high-flying company. By March 14, JetBlue's stock price had fallen to $11.75, 11 percent below its February 14 closing price of $13.23.

One month after the ice storm, JetBlue's management team was still digging out.

CHALLENGES

JetBlue was confronted with some serious issues as it continued to try to recover from its Valentine's Day meltdown. Although operations had returned to "normal," the company had spent millions of dollars on passenger refunds and vouchers, employee overtime, and other storm-related costs. JetBlue executives had spent countless hours practicing "visible leadership" and David Neeleman, the public face of the airline, had accepted responsibility, expressed remorse repeatedly, and promised that this type of problem would never happen again. But, could JetBlue depend on Neeleman to lead the company out of trouble? Did the executives at JetBlue learn enough from their service failure to fix what was wrong and prevent it from happening again? If not, what further action should be taken? What, if any, strategic and operational changes should be made to ensure the company's full recovery?

SOURCES

1. Wong, Grace. "JetBlue fiasco: $30M price tag: CEO Neeleman pledges reforms, vows to keep job after cancellation leaves passengers stranded; airline back to full schedule." CNNMoney.com, February 20, 2007.

2. Neeleman, David. "Dear JetBlue Customers." David's Flight Log, http://www.jetblue.com/about/ourcompany/flightlog/, February 22, 2007.

3. Salter, Chuck. "And Now the Hard Part." Fast Company 82, May 2004.

4. Air Transport Association. 2004 Economic Report. www.airlines.org, accessed March 10, 2007.

5. Salter, op. cit.

6. Weber, Harry R. and Joshua Freed. "Delta, Northwest file for Chapter 11 bankruptcy protection." Associated Press, September 14, 2005.

7. Ibid.

8. Carpenter, Dave. "Leaner United might be bankruptcy model for Delta, Northwest." Associated Press, September 18, 2005.

9. JetBlue Airways Corporation. http://www.jetblue.com/about/ourcompany/history/about_ourhistory.html.

10. Salter, op. cit.

11. Ibid.

12. JetBlue Hostage website. http://www.jetbluehostage.com.

13. Salter, op. cit.

14. Reed, Dan. "Loss Shifts JetBlue's Focus to Climbing Back Into Black." USA Today, February 21, 2006.

15. JetBlue Airways Corporation. Annual Report 2005. http://investor.jetblue.com/phoenix.zhtml?c=131045&p=irol-reportsAnnual

16. Foust, Dean. "Is JetBlue the Next People Express?" BusinessWeek, March 12, 2007.

17. Lipoff, Phil. "A Nightmare for JetBlue: Planes ran out of food and water as they sat for over 8 hours." WABC-TV, New York, February 14, 2007.

18. Strickler, Andrew. "Stormy Weather: Waiting til they're blue; Jet Blue passengers stranded on planes for hours amid icy snarl at JFK gates." Newsday, February 15, 2007.

19. Gibson, Charles. "JetBlue's Airline Meltdown." ABC World News Now, February 19, 2007.

20. Armstrong, David. "Beleaguered air passengers want new laws." San Francisco Chronicle, February 16, 2007.

21. JetBlue Hostage website, op. cit.

22. Carey, Susan and Andrew Pasztor. "Behind Travel Mess: New Rules for Sleet." The Wall Street Journal, March 23, 2007.

23. Lyons, Patrick. "A Snowshocked JetBlue Hits the Cancel Button." The Lede, March 16, 2007. http://theledeblogs.nytimes.com/2007/03/16/a-showshocked-jetblue-hits-the-cancel-button/

24. Bailey, Jeff. "JetBlue Cancels More Flights in Storm's Wake." The New York Times, February 18, 2007.

25. Sloan, Allan and Temma Ehrenfeld. "Skies Were Cloudy Before Jet Blew It." Newsweek 149:10, March 5, 2007.

26. Bailey, op. cit.

27. USA Today. "Crisis Management Says a Lot About an Airline." February 21, 2007.

28. McGregor, Jena. "An Extraordinary Stumble at JetBlue." BusinessWeek, March 5, 2007.

29. Wong, op. cit.

30. Hanni, Tim and Kate Hanni. "Family Endures 57-hour Journey from San Francisco to Mobile." Mobile Press-Register, February 4, 2007.

31. Martinez, Michael. "Boxer to Introduce Airline Passengers' Bill of Rights: Crusade picks up steam after this week's JetBlue delays." San Jose Mercury News, February 15, 2007.

32. Block, Melissa. "Air Passengers Rights Bill Introduced in Senate." National Public Radio, February 20, 2007.

33. Levin, Alan. "Bill of Rights for Fliers Questioned." USA Today, February 22, 2007.

34. Neeleman, David. David's Flight Log. http://www.jetblue.com/about/ourcompany/flightlog/

35. Foust, op. cit.

Case 8

Using Services Marketing to Develop and Deliver Integrated Solutions at Caterpillar in Latin America

Holger Pietzsch, Caterpillar, Inc.
Valarie A. Zeithaml, University of North Carolina

> 'Any industrial manufacturer that has not awakened to the fact that it must become a service business is in serious peril today.'[1]

Jose "Pepe" Brousset, Marketing and Operations Director of the Latin America Commercial Division (LACD) of Caterpillar, Inc., called the division's Dealer Advisory Panel to order in the spring of 2006 with the message that the company's five-year growth targets could not be met unless the organization moved from a product focus to an integrated customer focus. His plan was that LACD would pilot the development and deployment of a plan for services that could be sold with Caterpillar's heavy equipment in the form of customer service agreements (CSAs). The initiative was a direct consequence of Caterpillar's enterprise strategy known as Vision 2020. This strategy stipulated that growth of the distribution system of the company would be a critical success factor for the future: Specifically, Vision 2020 specified that "[Caterpillar's] distribution system will be the global benchmark in delivering *integrated business solutions* [our emphasis] to customers." A key performance metric of this strategy was the volume of service business generated through CSAs. CSAs had been offered by Caterpillar dealers in the past but the many difficulties encountered had led to doubts about the ability of the company to make money with CSAs. These difficulties included the lack of consistency across Latin American counties, inability to deliver, and inability to calculate costs and benefits of the CSAs.

Caterpillar, like many highly successful product companies, embraced what might best be termed a product focus. The company, dealers, and suppliers worked as a team to provide what they believe is the most extraordinary product support system in the world. Their formula for success can be stated briefly:

> Find out what products customers want. Design and build them. Keep 'em running.
> When they wear out, rebuild or recycle. Do it better than anybody else.

Services were a different story. Except for the company's very large mining customers, and other large users with whom dealers had strong relationships that involved many types of services that created integrated solutions, the company had not consistently adopted a customer focus with service.

Pepe Brousset's goal was to develop, deploy, and pilot a plan using the best practices in service to redefine the CSA value proposition and to grow customer service

---

[1] G. Allmendinger and R. Lombreglia, "Four Strategies for the Age of Smart Services," *Harvard Business Review,* October 2005.

This case was prepared under the auspices of the Latin American Commercial Division of Caterpillar, Inc. It was written by Holger Pietzsch and Valarie A. Zeithaml as a basis for class discussion rather than to illustrate either effective or ineffective handling of an administrative situation. Copyright 2008 by Holger Pietzsch of Caterpillar, Inc. and Valarie A. Zeithaml of the University of North Carolina at Chapel Hill.

agreements at an average 30 percent per year between 2006 and 2010. While service did not have to be limited to CSAs in achieving this goal, he strongly believed that learning how to deliver service through these agreements was the best approach to making both the company and its dealerships ready for the challenges involved in delivering service. His immediate goal was to convince the members of the Dealer Advisory Panel that this plan was also in their best interests.

CATERPILLAR: THE COMPANY

On November 24, 1904, Benjamin Holt tested the first track-type tractor. Shortly after, the first Caterpillar trademark was copyrighted. In April 1925, C.L. Best Tractor Co. and The Holt Manufacturing Company merged to form the Caterpillar Tractor Company. By the 1930's the East Peoria, Illinois, plant had become one of America's major industrial complexes and by 1951 the company opened its first overseas manufacturing facility in the United Kingdom.

Exhibit 1, shows the history of Caterpillar from that point on. Some of the highlights, as shown in the exhibit, include (1) the addition of Caterpillar to the Dow Jones Industrial Average, replacing Navistar, in 1991; (2) the naming of Caterpillar as one of Fortune Magazine's most admired companies in 1997; (3) and Caterpillar becoming the world's largest producer of diesel engines in 1999.

EXHIBIT 1   **The History of Caterpillar**

Year	Key Event	Sales (in millions)
1925	Holt and Best merge to form Caterpillar Tractor Company headquartered in Peoria, Illinois	13.8
1928	Acquisition of the Russel Motorgrader Company accelerating the entry into the rod construction	35.1
1931	Caterpillar starts to use Diesel engines, becoming the world's largest diesel manufacturer, decison made to change product color from grey to High-way Yellow	24.1
1939	First line of Marine engines and electric power generators	58.4
1946	Expansion program increases manufacturing facilities by 50%	128.4
1951	First overseas plant opens in the United Kingdom	394.3
1955	Australia subsidiary announced	533.0
1966	Sales in USSR resume after three decades of hiatus	1,524.0
1970	Sales outside the US exceed sales inside the US for the first time	2,127.8
1976	Piracicaba plant opens in Brazil	5,043.2
1981	Caterpillar Leasing company formed (predecessor of Caterpillar Financial Corporation)	9,160.0
1982	Company suffers loss of $180 Million, first loss since 1932. Employment reduced by 29%	6,472.0
1986	Name change from Caterpillar Tractor Company to Caterpillar Inc.	7,380.0
1987	Caterpillar Logistics Services Inc. formed	8,294.0
1988	New trademark (logo) introduced	10,435.0
1991	Caterpillar added to Dow Jones industrial average, replacing Navistar	10,182.0
1997	Fortune magazine names Caterpillar one of the most admired companies in the world	18,925.0
1999	Caterpillar becomes world's largest producer of diesel engines	19,702.0
2006	Total sales exceed 41 Billion dollars	41,517.0

By the year 2000 Caterpillar manufactured more than 300 different models including engines and turbines from five horsepower to over 22,000 horsepower in 88 manufacturing locations. Seventy five percent of products were made in the U.S., while 50 percent of sales were outside the U.S. In 2006, total sales of Caterpillar products exceeded 41 billion dollars.

Caterpillar Products

Caterpillar provides a wide range of products used in many different industries. The majority of machine applications address earth-moving needs including excavation, loading, and carrying of material. Skid steer loaders, backhoe loaders, wheeled excavators, and compact wheel loaders (see Exhibit 2) perform the work in urban and general construction. Articulated trucks, hydraulic excavators, scrapers, motor graders, and track-type tractors are used in larger earth-moving projects such as road, airport, or heavy construction tasks. Wheel dozers and material handlers operate in demolition and waste applications. Mining operations are more complicated and require a multitude of equipment including off-highway trucks and underground mining equipment. Wheel loaders are key machines in the material-handling process of quarries or industrial applications. Caterpillar diesel engines are used in highway trucks, boats, locomotives, or oil platforms. Finally, a large range of power generations sets provides electricity in a variety of applications.

EXHIBIT 2   **Examples of Caterpillar Products**

Motor Grader

Skid Steer Loader

Articulated Truck

Track Type Tractor

Wheel Loader

Off Highway Truck

Backhoe loader

Hydraulic Excavator

Caterpillar Services

Despite the fact that Caterpillar is largely a product firm, the company offers several services that complement its products. Largely, these services consist of services that refurbish used machine and engine components into "like-new" condition, financing and insurance services for equipment owners, equipment rental, and logistics services.

CATERPILLAR: THE DEALERS

Caterpillar prides itself on enduring and close relationship with its dealers. In 2006, over 180 independent dealers around the world represented the company's products, managed customer relationships, serviced the equipment, and provided parts throughout the lifetime of the equipment. Dealers invested millions of dollars in parts inventories, warehouses, service shops, tools, information technology, and rental fleets. Collectively, the dealerships employed more people than Caterpillar itself. Many dealers were family-owned businesses but some were much larger—with revenues exceeding a billion dollars. For example, one Caterpillar dealer, Finning International, operated in Canada, South America, and Europe and employed more than 12,000 employees.

Caterpillar dealers form a distribution channel unmatched in the industry, and the dealer network is one of Caterpillar's principal competitive advantages. No other heavy equipment manufacturer offers comparable coverage in terms of quantity and quality of customer contact points. Many dealerships have represented the Caterpillar brand for more than half a century and have established long lasting relationships with their customer bases—sometimes over generations.

COMPETITIVE LANDSCAPE

Besides the goal of increasing revenues, the most important reason for the Vision 2020 objective to move into services was that competition was heating up and the company saw the potential for competitors to capture the growth and profits that Caterpillar assumed it would achieve. Competition came from a number of different places. Third party service providers that allowed customers to outsource their entire fleet management for both Caterpillar and non-Caterpillar equipment were emerging. Compared to Caterpillar's nationally-organized dealer network, these service companies operated internationally, allowing customers to work on construction projects all over Latin America without having to engage with multiple Caterpillar and non-Caterpillar service providers. While their service offerings and competencies were generally less sophisticated than those of Caterpillar dealers, they were developing successful customer relationships within certain market segments. Fluor, a Fortune 500 company, through one of its subsidiaries—Ameco provided total service solutions, and had successfully grown its fleet management business in Latin America.

Other competitors, aftermarket suppliers and distributors, were commercializing "will-fit" parts that, though inferior in quality and durability, were sold at significantly lower price points. While offering no services, these companies held about 30 percent to 50 percent of the aftermarket in parts.

Thousands of small local workshops also offered repair services ranging from simple repairs to complex ones. Many of them had been established by former Caterpillar dealer mechanics and enjoyed high customer acceptance, but none had the financial reserves to invest in large outlets or market coverage. Many customers also had their own mechanics, which they used for both maintenance and repair activities. Small workshops and customer mechanics had difficulty keeping up with the increasingly sophisticated technology built into new machines, which required both specialized tools as well as expertise. Consequently many of them focused on servicing older machines.

Finally, competitive manufacturers like Komatsu, John Deere, and Volvo had established their own dealer networks in Latin America. While largely focusing on their own machines rather than Caterpillar equipment, they often had the same customers because owners had equipment from different manufacturers. Owners of mixed fleets carefully considered the performance of the product support organizations before purchasing new equipment, making service capability a key factor in new purchases.

THE CATERPILLAR–DEALER RELATIONSHIP

As a company, Caterpillar for a significant portion of its business interacts with end users through its independent dealers. They are responsible for initiating and supporting customer relationships and the types of services provided. Product and service offerings could vary significantly between dealers.

As a corporation, Caterpillar's headquarters and factories rely on regional marketing profit centers (MPCs) to work with the dealer network for product commercialization and distribution (see Exhibit 3). The main MPC for Latin America (LACD)

EXHIBIT 3
The Caterpillar–
Dealer Relationship

is situated in Miami, a regional hub to serve Mexico, the Caribbean, and Central and South America. Several smaller commercial teams in district offices are also located in the dealer's territories for ongoing support. LACD's marketing profit center has employees in both product divisions and product support divisions. These employees work as liaisons between headquarters and the dealers, offering the skills and knowledge of Caterpillar to their functional counterparts in the dealer organizations for strategic and operational issues. LACD's region includes over twenty different dealers (generally one per country) whose organizations themselves are usually divided into equipment sales, parts sales, and equipment service. Depending on customer needs, all three parts of the dealerships may interact individually with the customer. Figure 3 shows the relationship among Caterpillar, the MPCs, and the dealers.

This organizational division both in the MPCs and in the dealerships themselves fostered expertise and consistency within divisions, but over time had created functional silos that had different priorities and performance goals. For example, while the product support organization was responsible for increasing the sales of CSA, they were not the department responsible for machine sales, where the primary sales contract was set up. The machine sales people were not required to include CSAs in offers to customers and, in fact, were not inclined to do so because in many cases they were not fully informed about CSAs (including information about what the dealership was capable of promising) and were not awarded incentives for selling them.

Product support—including global and fast availability of spare parts, local dealer expertise, repair facilities, and skilled technicians—were key differentiators for Caterpillar. Both Caterpillar and its dealers prided themselves on their "built-to-last" philosophy and commitment to keep customers' equipment up and running at the lowest possible cost. Sophisticated processes, tools, software, and component replacement programs had made maintenance and repairs increasingly faster and more effective.

Performance measures in the dealer organizations were typically focused on cost, revenues, or operations to maximize the offering, but few on customer profitability or customer service quality perceptions. For example, both Caterpillar and dealers regularly measured parts turnover, work in progress, time utilization of mechanics, and repair profitability. These measures generated savings in cost and time, but were not linked to customer satisfaction or revenue increases.

Customers' most important service requirement is maximum up-time of their equipment. Idle equipment or equipment being repaired can be extremely costly for customers, due to the loss of production (e.g., for a gold mine), idle time of other pieces of machinery requiring the repaired equipment for operations (e.g., trucks in absence of a loading excavator), and potential penalties for late delivery of the project (e.g., for road construction companies).

Given these risks many larger customers (owning five machines or more) developed their own product support infrastructure including service shops, the hiring, employment and training of technicians, and the development of maintenance and repair procedures. Being a product company, Caterpillar segmented the marketplace simply in terms of products and industries. Sales and product organizations were set up by the type of products that customers owned (e.g., excavators, wheel loaders, power systems), and dedicated teams were developed for particular industries such as mining, general construction, or heavy construction.

On the product support side, customers could be classified into three segments which could be viewed in terms of the benefits they sought: (1) "do it myself," (2) "work with me," or (3) "do it for me." "Do it for me" customers were defined as owners that outsourced the majority of their product support activities to dealers. Many of them were large and loyal companies. "Do it with me" customers took care of their own day-to-day product support but used dealer services for more complex repair needs. Many medium-sized, traditional construction customers fell into this category. "Do it myself" customers generally used internal or competitive resources to satisfy their product support needs. Most small and/or general construction customers fell into this segment.

Identification of customers that fell into these segments was possible but complex and required multiple assumptions concerning the customer's total repair needs. Some customers could also fall into more than one segment, preferring dealer services for their newer machines but performing their own repairs on older equipment.

GENERAL CONSTRUCTION CUSTOMERS

Because Caterpillar's product line was so diverse, its customers varied greatly in size and requirements. For its very largest customers—typically those who purchased mining and construction equipment—dealers provided customized and full service. The most important considerations for these customers included productivity and up-time—having equipment in working condition 100 percent of the time. Customers paid for CSA and repair services to achieve these goals and were typically very satisfied.

This group of customers, however, was not the segment from which further growth of market share was expected in the future. For this reason, the LACD division chose to focus on the general construction customer.

General and urban construction companies and subcontractors of major construction projects used Caterpillar type of equipment for its versatility rather than its productivity. These smaller customers also had to manage short-term affordability and cash flow limitations, contributing to a situation where they postponed preventive and small repairs as long as possible. Lack of emphasis in these areas sometimes resulted in costly repairs and these unplanned downtimes were disruptive to customer operations. However, because these customers considered machine up-time as less important for their business, they were less willing to pay for premium parts and parts availability, and often migrated to a patchwork of internal or external lower-priced suppliers for product repair and support needs.

CUSTOMER SUPPORT AGREEMENTS (CSAs)

Over the years, Caterpillar dealers had packaged services into customer service agreements (CSAs)—flexible contracts that could include virtually any services that customers wanted and that dealers could provide. These customer services agreements could be highly customized in content, length, and cost—many involving total maintenance and repair contracts where customers outsourced the entire machine product support of all of their equipment. The agreements were sold separately from the machines at purchase and were delivered through the dealer product support organizations. CSA for larger customers had demonstrated significant benefits regarding the risks and costs of unplanned machine downtime and resulted in high levels of customer loyalty. The current degree of customization and complexity, however, limited the CSA marketability and the dealer's operational efficiency to serve the growing number of customers in the general construction market.

The smaller and simple contracts, called preventive maintenance agreements (PM CSAs), were purchased by many small customers. Preventive maintenance contracts basically involved the provision of superior Caterpillar oils and filters at predetermined service intervals and were delivered through a dealer field technician who traveled to customer sites. Some technician activities, such as visual machine inspection, monitoring of the condition of the machine, and feedback discussions with the customer, were not built explicitly into the contracts. They were extra services but were not neceserally offered and executed consistently. Many of these extra services, and the preventive maintenance intervals themselves, went unnoticed by business owners because field technicians interacted with operators and machines and did not always come into contact with those who purchased the contracts. Consequently, many decision makers and purchasers of the equipment did not recognize the benefits of the agreements and did not renew the CSAs once expired. Some dealers, however, had turned PM CSA contracts into a dedicated business. They had dedicated PM technicians, specialized PM service trucks, and proactive processes that provided regular feedback to customers on the condition of their machine, potential issues, and recommended solutions.

CSAs were typically sold by either the machine or product support sales reps and delivered by the service organization. Given unprecedented construction growth in the mid 2000s, the industry was suffering from technician shortage resulting in capacity bottlenecks in fulfilling CSA promises. Facing this situation, the sales organizations were sometimes reluctant to sell CSAs if they were concerned that the service organization would not deliver on the promise. In addition to these concerns, the dealer sales force was generally more comfortable selling solutions based upon tangible product differentiation than advocating intangible services that are harder to explain, sell, and differentiate.

CSA customers generally demonstrated higher loyalty and repeat business than non-CSA customers. A key driver of their loyalty seemed to be the quality of service provided in the field by technicians (e.g., accessing the machine at regular intervals for preventive maintenance tasks such as changing oil and filters as well as some diagnostic services called "condition monitoring"). Dealers had different philosophies regarding the degree to which field technicians were trained and empowered to act upon recommended repairs that they identified as a result of their preventive maintenance work. Most dealers used entry-level technicians for the basic work on preventive maintenance contracts; they were then responsible to relay the machine condition information to the product support sales organization for follow-up and quoting on additional work that could be done to improve the condition of the machine. Other dealers had decided to empower their technicians for a larger portion of the process. Generally customers appreciated both the speed of service as well as the quality of the resulting machine condition advice.

THE SERVICES MARKETING INTERVENTION

The recent and consistent growth of the Latin American economies had attracted an increasing number of competitive equipment distributors—all of them selling at lower price points than Caterpillar. Most of them had a limited product support infrastructure at their disposal. As a consequence the LACD management team decided to leverage Caterpillar's product support strength as a differentiator in all customer decisions—before, during, and after the machine purchase. Recognizing that Caterpillar excelled in making products but had limited experience in designing and delivering solution services, Pepe Brousset in 2006 invited an expert in the services marketing field to attend the dealer advisory panel. He had taken a services marketing course in his graduate program and recognized that many different concepts and tools were available that could help the company and believed that having an expert spend a day describing what services industries know about services marketing and service quality would open their eyes.

Especially useful to the group was the *gaps model of service quality*.[2] The model explains the nature and impact of each gap on the customer experience, brand

[2]The Gaps model of service quality and most other elements of Services Marketing mentioned in this paper have been developed or described by Valarie Zeithaml, Professor at UNC Chapel Hill. She is also the Co–author of *Services Marketing,* McGraw-Hill; the most extensive work that the team has found on the topic.

EXHIBIT 4
The Customer Gap

Zeithaml, Parasuraman, and Berry, *Delivering Quality Service: Balancing Customer Perceptions and Expectations.*

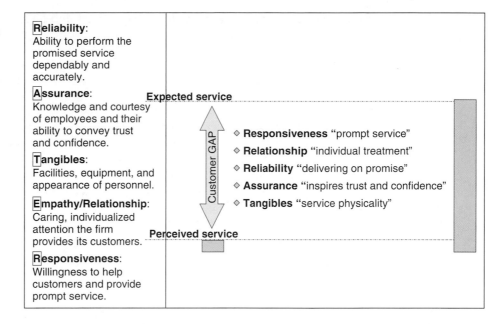

Reliability:
Ability to perform the promised service dependably and accurately.

Assurance:
Knowledge and courtesy of employees and their ability to convey trust and confidence.

Tangibles:
Facilities, equipment, and appearance of personnel.

Empathy/Relationship:
Caring, individualized attention the firm provides its customers.

Responsiveness:
Willingness to help customers and provide prompt service.

Expected service

Customer GAP

◇ **Responsiveness** "prompt service"
◇ **Relationship** "individual treatment"
◇ **Reliability** "delivering on promise"
◇ **Assurance** "inspires trust and confidence"
◇ **Tangibles** "service physicality"

Perceived service

positioning, and service differentiation. Services marketing comprises a collection of tools and methodologies to assess and address the critical service capabilities required to close those gaps. Other concepts covered were service blueprinting, customer-defined service standards, and integrated services marketing communication.

The dealer advisory panel embraced the concept of services marketing, and decided to adapt the concepts to Caterpillar to grow its services business. Exhibits 4 and 5 show the gaps model concepts.

EXHIBIT 5
The Service Quality Gaps Model

Zeithaml, Parasuraman, and Berry, *Delivering Quality Service: Balancing Customer Perceptions and Expectations.*

Expected service

Customer GAP

Gap 4
External communications to customers
- Lack of integrated service mkt communications
- Inefficient management of customer expectations
- Over promising
- Inadequate horizontal communications

Gap 3
Actual service delivery
- Deficiencies in human resource policies
- Failure to match supply and demand
- Customer not fulfilling roles
- Problems with intermediaries/channels

Gap 2
Customer driven service designs and standards
- Poor service design
- Absence of customer defined standards
- Inappropriate physical evidence and servicescape

Gap 1
Company's understanding of customer expectations
- Inadequate research
- Lack of upward communication
- Insufficient relationship focus
- Inadequate service recovery

Perceived service

THE SERVICE QUALITY PROJECT IN LACD

Caterpillar and the dealer advisory panel decided to conduct a pilot program for CSAs by working through the gaps model at three dealers in Latin America. These dealers were chosen because they were responsible for key countries or territories in LACD and had shown promising customer and services focus in previous initiatives. Their combined sales exceeded 1 billion dollars and their strategic plans had identified CSAs as a key success factor for future growth.

A core team was formed consisting of members from Caterpillar LACD, corporate staffers from Peoria, and the pilot dealerships. Each pilot dealer assigned project leaders from their dealerships that served as members of the core project team. Initial training on services marketing and its elements were held at LACD headquarters in Miami on the key steps and processes and then follow-up occurred within the dealerships with district support from Caterpillar. Caterpillar LACD core team members were responsible for action items in the individual functions they represented such as product support, marketing, and communication. LACD also assumed the overall coordination of the implementation plan and managed the relationship with the consultant and strategic advisor.

GAPS ASSESSMENT WITH THREE PILOT DEALERSHIPS

After learning about the gaps model, members of the core team conducted a general assessment of each service gap based on feedback from the dealer advisory panel and other sources such as marketing research conducted both by Caterpillar itself and the dealers. They identified the following key issues in each of the four provider gaps.

The Listening Gap (Gap 1)

Using existing surveys conducted by Caterpillar called "customer value surveys," the team grouped survey items by the service quality dimension shown in Exhibit 6. Each dimension was then mapped on an importance/performance matrix shown in Figure 6.

EXHIBIT 6
The Importance/Performance Matrix

The research provided several key findings:

- **Responsiveness** was the most influential factor on customer loyalty and underperformed as compared to other factors. This dimension required urgent attention.
- **Empathy (Relationship), Reliability,** and **Assurance** tracked above average in perception and importance. They provided competitive differentiation but none of them were positioned as a dominant element of the value proposition. All of them show significant potential for improvement.
- Customer performance perception of **tangibles** was high but had relatively low impact on the overall customer loyalty.

To address these issues, the team concluded that (1) service reliability, responsiveness, and relationship needed improvement; (2) product differentiation and quality could not offset these issues; and (3) dealer product support operations and marketing capabilities played an equally important role in addressing these critical customer requirements. The team also recognized that customer surveys were sporadically performed and only partially designed for the purpose of service quality feedback. In support of Caterpillar's services strategy, the LACD service operation manager recognized that the customer value survey measures were inadequate for capturing and addressing customer satisfaction with individual interactions. The customer value surveys fell into the category of "relationship surveys" and were conducted annually. Post-interaction customer surveys, which captured customer reactions immediately after service calls, were thought to be necessary to prioritize operational improvement projects in the areas that were truly valued by the customer. Also, dealers and Caterpillar employees in the regions lacked the tools to interpret the results of surveys and to translate them into specific strategies.

Segmentation was also a key issue. The team estimated that accelerated growth could be best achieved by developing and communicating attractive service packages to small customers. Analysis of various factors identified characteristics of certain groups of small customers that were good targets. Overall satisfaction and loyalty indicators of some customers were significantly better and CSA renewal rates were notably higher. At the same time, these dealers had a higher share of wallet with these CSA customers, and the continuous experience and constant customer contact allowed dealers to identify, quote, and win many repeat repair opportunities. These customers would be ideal to focus on as the pilot project unfolded.

The Service Designs and Standards Gap (Gap 2)

The project identified a number of important issues in the standards and measures gap. First, very few CSAs were created, branded, positioned, and marketed based upon the timing, piece of mind, risk reduction, relationship, or convenience they provided to customers. CSAs were created in an ad hoc manner; they varied across dealerships and often across customers within dealerships. With this variability, it was never quite clear what had been promised to customers and expectations often were not met. Second, while machine salespeople felt very comfortable selling the attributes and benefits of the heavy equipment, they were unsure about what to offer and promise in the CSAs, largely because salespeople were not the employees who delivered on the CSAs. Further, CSA selling materials did not exist for them to understand what was possible and what options could be offered. Third, performance standards were typically operationally focused and not customer driven.

Dealers had different opinions on what customers expected and measurement to standards was not captured except on an ad-hoc basis. One difficulty in making promises involved the fact that customers were often located far from dealers, meaning that travel time complicated the process of setting standards. Among other things, the absence of standards and measures made it difficult to know what to promise customers when problems occurred. Dealerships were organized in silos—sales, product support, parts—and interacted inconsistently with each other and rarely planned together. Finally, each of the Latin American countries was different in structure, cultures, and laws, making the sharing of practices less than ideal.

Provider Gap 3: The Service Performance Gap

There were a number of major issues identified in Gap 3. First, there was an inadequate supply of qualified mechanics and few sources to find new ones. Technicians were also selected, trained, and rewarded for their technical performance. Attention was not given to their interaction or communication skills, which could become very important in describing issues to customers and in suggesting additional work that should be done on machines.

The lack of teamwork and communication among parts, service, and sales departments made the provision of service difficult. Formal ways to communicate about what should be done, what had been accomplished, and how well it had been performed did not exist. Dealers did not have a reliable system for keeping track of which customer machines had reached their service intervals, the contractual time for service. The scheduling process for field technicians was complex and based on cumbersome systems, which further complicated timely and responsive technician appointments.

Customers contributed to the difficulties in this gap. When they called for service, they often did not tell the dealers where their machines were physically located on the customer's property. Many customers actually forgot to inform the dealer that their machines had reached the service interval and were due for service.

Supply and demand often did not match, as most customers wanted machines maintained and inspected with little advance notice or after business hours. During peak construction season (e.g., in spring and early summer) the industry frequently suffered from technician shortages. Equally of concern were slow times when few customers needed or wanted repairs.

Finally the actual inspection and recommendation reports provided as part of the CSAs (and eagerly consulted and stored by customers) were functional but unattractively presented.

Provider Gap 4: The Communication Gap

Caterpillar promotion material almost exclusively focused on product features and benefits. At the time the project began, there were no brochures or advertisements describing CSAs, which limited the ability to sell CSAs both externally and internally. Externally, customers could not be certain that Caterpillar could deliver something for which there were no tangible representations or written descriptions. Customers could not compare different options or packages and evaluate those against alternative services. Different types of CSAs were named and described the same way and carried no specific slogans or descriptions that easily explained the difference in value.

Internally, these materials would have helped employees understand what the service offerings were and how they differed. The absence of clearly defined service features occasionally led to over-customization or over-promising. The lack of written communication also confused the verbal communication. The sales force had no consistent selling process or message that explained and differentiated the individual CSA offerings. This created an unclear competitive positioning.

DECISIONS AND IMPLEMENTATION AS THE PILOT BEGAN IN 2007

Now that the team had learned the basics about service quality delivery and assessed the state of each service quality gap for the three pilot dealers, they were ready to develop a plan for developing, designing, and delivering CSAs in the three dealerships. They knew that they had a great deal of ground to cover and that they faced many challenges. They also knew that LACD's successful development and deployment of CSAs was essential. As they met to plan their next steps, they laid out some of the issues most on their minds.

What else did they need to learn in Gap 1 about customer needs and expectations? They had general information from the customer value surveys, but this information did not tell them what features customers expected in the CSAs. What were they and how could they find out? In particular, how could they find out what they needed to know to established standards in Gap 2?

Should they offer different CSAs to the different segments of general construction? What would that imply for research, standards, and implementation?

What standards and measures should be set in Gap 2 to deliver to customer expectations? How formal should they be? How should they create and design the new CSAs? How should they get everyone in the dealerships to learn about them and get on board to deliver them?

How should the dealerships overcome all the Gap 3 issues that they faced to insure consistent delivery?

What internal and external materials were necessary to communicate the CSAs to salespeople and customers? What else would be needed?

Photo Credits

Page 284, © Mario Tama/Getty.

Page 292, © Holland American Line, Inc.

Page 293, © Cheers Boston.

Page 299, © Mayo Clinic.

Page 301, © Michael Lassman/Bloomberg via Getty.

Chapter 11
Page 312, © John A. Rizzo/Getty RF.

Page 328 (top & bottom), © Google.

Chapter 12
Page 348, © Deere & Company, European Office.

Page 351, © David Madison/Stone/Getty.

Page 359, Courtesy NCR FastLane ™ Self Checkout from NCR Corporation.

Chapter 13
Page 381, © Doug Pensinger/Getty.

Page 383, ©Ilene MacDonald/Alamy RF.

Page 384, © CEMEX.

Page 386, © Steve Bly/Getty.

Page 391, © Getty RF.

Page 397 & 398, © Ryan McVay/Getty RF.

Page 400, © Digital Vision/Getty RF.

Chapter 14
Page 412, © Hotels.com.

Page 419, Courtesy of Travelers and Fallon Worldwide.

Page 420, © GEICO.

Page 424, © Sierra Club.

Page 428 (top), © Virgin Atlantic Airways Ltd.

Page 428 (bottom), Courtesy Virgin Atlantic Airways; Red Advertising & Marketing/ Barbados WI.

Chapter 15
Page 445, © AP Photo/The Patriot-News, John C. Whitehead.

Chapter 16
Page 487, © The McGraw-Hill Companies, Inc., Mark A. Dierker, photographer.

Index